D1709775

FAMOUS FIGHTERS
of the Second World War

FAMOUS FIGHTERS
of the Second World War

William Green

SECOND EDITION REVISED

Illustrated by G. W. Heumann and
Peter Endsleigh Castle, A.R.Ae.S.

DOUBLEDAY & COMPANY, INC.
GARDEN CITY, NEW YORK

CONTENTS

FOREWORD

by

Group Captain J. E. "JOHNNIE" JOHNSON, D.S.O., D.F.C.

In this book the author has achieved the formidable and painstaking task of describing the development history, and more briefly the operational history, of most of the best-known fighter aeroplanes used during the Second World War.

From the outbreak of the war until the spring of 1941 our fighters were generally employed on *defensive* operations and we judged the quality of both our own and the *Luftwaffe's* aeroplanes on four main characteristics—speed, rate of climb, manœuvrability, and fire power. As a *defensive* fighter it was generally agreed, by fighter pilots of many nationalities, that the immortal Spitfire was superior to any other Allied or enemy fighter. There were occasions when the *Luftwaffe* possessed a decided advantage, and I am thinking especially of 1942 when the Focke-Wulf 190s gave our Spitfire Vs a very hard time. However, we redressed this disadvantage with the introduction of the best Spitfire of them all, the Spitfire IX, which was such a delight to fly. Again, in late 1944, the *Luftwaffe* caught us unawares with their jets; especially the Messerschmitt 262. In the *Luftwaffe* a storm of controversy arose over the role of the Messerschmitt 262 as to whether it should be developed as a fighter or a bomber. Fortunately, for the Allies, Hitler himself decreed that this fine aeroplane was to be a bomber and all this is well described by William Green. Had the correct types and quantities of this jet been produced by the German aircraft industry—and this was within their capabilities—then we might well have lost our hard-won air superiority over north-west Europe at a critical phase of the war.

When we began our long bout of *offensive* fighting in the summer of 1941 we soon realised that an important requirement of the *offensive*, or strategic, fighter is a reasonable radius of action. Various types of long-range tanks were hung on our Spitfires but we never attained a radius of action of more than three hundred miles; this carried us just within the borders of Germany from our bases in southern England. How we longed for a Spitfire which could fly to Berlin and back, so that we fighter pilots of the Royal Air Force could play our part in the great daylight battles of 1943 and 1944 fought over Germany between the *Luftwaffe* and the Eighth Air Force. But we had to be content with fighter sweeps and escorts to bombers over France and the Low Countries while the Mustang, with its radius of action of six hundred miles, fought the Messerschmitt 109s and Focke-Wulf 190s over the Reich and gained an ever-increasing dominance over the *Luftwaffe* from which it never recovered. I would say, therefore, that the Mustang was the best *offensive* fighter of this era.

So much for the aeroplanes. But we must not forget that the aeroplane, however perfect, is only a vehicle and it is transformed from an inanimate machine into a living, eager craft by the pilot:

"Oh! I have slipped the surly bonds of Earth
   And danced the skies on laughter-silvered wings;
Sunward I've climbed, and joined the tumbling mirth
   Of sun-split clouds,—and done a hundred things
You have not dreamed of—wheeled and soared and swung
   High in the sunlit silence."[1]

We should also remember that our basic rules of air fighting were handed down to my generation from our illustrious forbears of the First World War. All the lessons of surprise, the tactical use of sun and cloud, team fighting, straight shooting, and the importance of guarding the "blind spots" were recorded from the exploits of the great fighter pilots of that generation: the lion-hearted Ball, for whom air fighting was a gladiatorial combat; McCudden, the great tactician; and Mannock, the acknowledged top-scorer, who was both an individualist and a successful leader of fighter formations—to name but a few. We fighter pilots of the second great conflict owe a great deal to these men and we like to think that when our turn came we lived up to their code and their great traditions of chivalry in the air. We also like to think that we inherited some of their personal qualities so necessary for successful fighter pilots and leaders. For a leader of fighter formations must not only be a good individualistic pilot, he must possess determination, dash and aggression, but with the moral courage to break off an engagement when necessary. He must possess keen eyesight and the ability to shoot straight and have the patience to hold his fire until he is within range of his opponent. He must have quick reactions, a knowledge of his opponent's mentality and the hunter's instinct to anticipate his moves. Above all, he must always remember that success in modern air fighting is not in the scoring of a personal victory, but lies in the achievement of a decisive success with his formation.

I congratulate William Green on his excellent book. I hope that it will gain the success his efforts deserve and that it will be used as a reference and authoritative volume for many years to come. In my opinion it ranks high amongst the best of its type.

[1] From "High Flight" a poem in *Sunward I've Climbed* by John Gillespie Magee, edited by Hermann Hagedorn (The Macmillan Co., New York).

7

INTRODUCTION

Fame, according to the Oxford English Dictionary, is the condition of being much talked about, and the fighter aircraft whose stories are recounted in the following pages *were* much talked about during the Second World War. They have all found their places in the annals of aerial warfare and to varying degree typify their epoch. Each suffered its shortcomings which imposed limitations on the tactics employed by its pilots; each experienced both success and failure and each possessed its own distinctive personality which evoked strong affection or profound dislike in the pilot that flew it. It has been said that the Spitfire, the Messerschmitt Bf 109, the Thunderbolt and the Zero-Sen each evinced characteristics associated with the nation that conceived it. But whatever its nationality and whatever the roles that the exigencies of war demanded of it, it was to find a niche in aviation's metaphorical "hall of fame".

The fighters of the six nations—the principal antagonists of the Second World War—represented in the following pages were not *all* supremely successful yet they achieved fame, for success and fame do not necessarily go hand in hand and some highly successful warplanes saw little fame. To be truly successful, a combat aircraft had to enjoy the smiles of fortune, chance playing as vital a role as technical competence and design ingenuity. The fighter had to be flown in the right place at the right time by pilots whose élan could turn its attributes to best advantage and whose skill could overcome its shortcomings by evolving suitable combat tactics. If chance placed the fighter in the right place at the right time with the right pilot, and if its qualities transcended the good, then it was likely to be numbered among the élite few, the truly great.

Fewer than a dozen of the fighters to be found in this volume are numbered among this select gathering, but no amount of technical brilliance could *ensure* success in combat and a lack of operational success did not necessarily debar a fighter from achieving fame. A case in point is the Defiant, which, despite the considerable ingenuity displayed in its design, was born of an outmoded philosophy which precluded its chances of operational success. Nevertheless, it captured public imagination and received much favourable publicity when, during the evacuation from Dunkirk, one squadron equipped with this fighter claimed 57 'kills', and the fact that these claims were later found to be appreciably exaggerated could not nullify the fame that the Defiant enjoyed on the strength of its brief "hour of glory".

The fame of other fighters stemmed from their link with epic actions which stirred public imagination; the Wildcat and Wake Island, the Gladiator and Malta, to quote but two examples. Some gained spurious fame which owed more to the highly coloured imaginings of propagandists than to operational success, and there were those fighters, such as the Macchi-Castoldi series, whose fame was confined largely to the land of their origin owing to wartime distortion and misrepresentation of their abilities for purposes of propaganda. Some of the fighters described truly changed the course of the conflict, the Hurricane and Spitfire in the 'Battle of Britain' for example, and the Hellcat and Corsair in the Pacific; one, the Gladiator, marked the end of an era in fighter design, while others, such as the Polikarpov-designed I-16 and the Messerschmitt Me 262, signified the beginnings of new eras.

But whatever the nationality or relative success enjoyed by the fighters described, an attempt has been made to relate their stories objectively and place them in perspective against the background of fighter development of their time.

WILLIAM GREEN.

August 1975

The photograph above depicts the Bf 109 V4, the fourth prototype and the first machine to test the hub-firing 20-mm.
MG FF cannon. The V4 was, in fact, the first prototype for
the B-series fighter. The photo on the right shows the original
prototype, the Bf 109 V1, with Kestrel engine and the undercarriage braced in the "down" position for initial taxying
trials.

THE MESSERSCHMITT Bf 109

An important attribute of any successful combat aircraft is often said to be its suitability for development.
A capacity for modification or adaptation to take
larger and more powerful engines, heavier armament
and other operational equipment as such becomes
available, without necessitating an extensive re-design
of fundamental components and consequent major
retooling may well be of incalculable value. Germany's Messerschmitt Bf 109 single-seat fighter was
an excellent example of such development suitability.
In its final production models it differed radically from
its original prototype of 1935, but the changes were
introduced gradually, and thus the flow of new
machines to the squadrons was never stemmed.

It has been claimed that the Bf 109 served as a prototype for international fighter construction; it has been
referred to as the progenitor of the high-powered,

single-seat, low-wing monoplane fighter. In fact it
made its début but a few weeks before Britain's
Hawker Hurricane, and a mere six months before its
major wartime antagonist, the Supermarine Spitfire,
but it attained service status considerably earlier than
either one of its contemporaries, and it was subsequently to claim the distinction of being produced in
larger numbers than any other combat aircraft of the
Second World War. During its infancy it appeared
to lack the hallmark of the thoroughbred, but success
came with maturity for, despite several widely
publicised shortcomings, the Bf 109 was a highly
successful combat aeroplane.

The Bf 109 was conceived in the summer of 1934,
when the German Air Ministry issued a requirement
for a single-seat interceptor fighter monoplane with
which to replace the obsolescent Heinkel He 51 and

(Below, left) The first Jumo-powered prototype, the Bf 109 V2, and (right) the first production prototype, the Bf 109 V7.

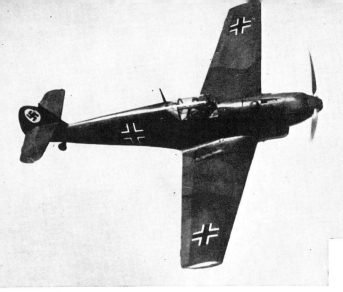

(*Left*) *The first production model, the Bf 109B, which was tested operationally in Spain, and, immediately below, the Bf 109B-1 in squadron service with the Luftwaffe. The Bf 109C-0 (below, centre), pre-production version of the second production model, carried the heavier armament of four MG 17 machine-guns. The Bf 109C was also service tested in Spain where, flown by Werner Mölders, it achieved considerable success. The Bf 109D (bottom) employed the 960 h.p. DB 600 engine and a similar but strengthened airframe to that of the initial production B-model. The Bf 109D only equipped one Luftwaffe Gruppe.*

Arado Ar 68 biplanes then serving the Luftwaffer's fighter elements. Four manufacturers were awarded prototype development contracts: the Arado Flugzeugwerke produced the Ar 80V1, the Bayerische Flugzeugwerke produced the Bf 109V1, the Ernst Heinkel A.G. produced the He 112V1, and the Focke-Wulf Flugzeugbau produced the Fw 159V1. Of these, the Focke-Wulf fighter employed the new and relatively untried Junkers Jumo 210A engine which delivered 610 h.p. for take-off, and the others used the most powerful and reliable foreign engine available at that time, the Rolls-Royce Kestrel V which provided 695 h.p. for take-off.

Trials with the four fighter prototypes, held at Travemünde during late October 1935, left no doubt as to the superiority of the Bayerische Flugzeugwerke and Ernst Heinkel products. Both machines were low-wing, all-metal aircraft with retractable undercarriages, and their performances were closely comparable. The He 112V1 possessed the more pleasing contours, and its better streamlined form compensated for its heavier structure. Its undercarriage had a wider track than that of the Bf 109V1, and it did not possess the latter's enclosed cockpit which was looked upon initially with considerable distrust. Some surprise was, therefore, evinced when the Bf 109 was selected as the winner of the contest, and an order for ten machines placed with the Bayerische Flugzeugwerke.

Professor Willy Messerschmitt had joined the Bayerische Flugzeugwerke in 1927, and at the end of 1933 was joined by Dipl. Eng. W. Rethel, formerly of Arado. Headed by Messerschmitt and aided by Rethel, the design team strove to achieve optimum performance by designing the smallest possible airframe that could accommodate the most powerful aero engines at that time under development in Germany. The angular lines of the fighter gave it an air of ruthless efficiency, perhaps in keeping with its German origin, and although the wing loading of the prototype was less than 24 lb./sq. ft., the design team anticipated the higher loadings to come, for among the new fighter's innovations were high-lift devices such as automatic leading-edge slots to give increased aileron control near the stall, large slotted flaps and slotted ailerons which depressed 10° when the flaps were fully lowered. The ground angle was steep in order to obtain the steepest practicable incidence and, therefore, the highest lift coefficient when landing.

Powered by the 695 h.p. Rolls-Royce Kestrel V engine, the first prototype of the new fighter, the Bf 109V1, bearing the factory number 758 and the civil registration D-IABI, was completed in the summer of 1935 and flown in September. In October, after the initial flight trials had been successfully concluded, the machine was flown to the Rechlin experimental establishment by test pilot Knoetsch. Unfortunately, the undercarriage collapsed during the landing at Rechlin, and the prototype suffered superficial damage. Nevertheless, repairs were effected in time for the machine to be flown to Travemünde later that month to participate in the fighter trials.

In the meantime work was progressing at Augsburg on further prototypes, and the Bf 109V2 (Werk

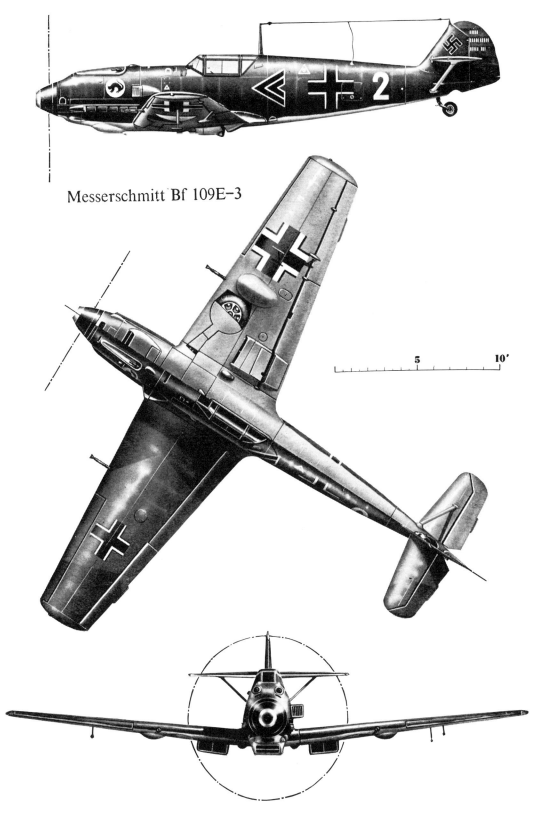

Messerschmitt Bf 109E-3

5   10'

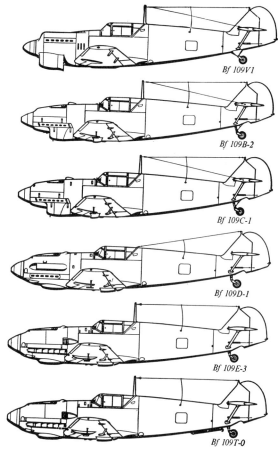

Bf 109V1

Bf 109B-2

Bf 109C-1

Bf 109D-1

Bf 109E-3

Bf 109T-0

The fourth prototype, the Bf 109V4, was initially fitted with the trio of MG 17 guns but later conducted the first air firing trials with the 20-mm. MG FF cannon. However, owing to cooling difficulties, the cannon seized after firing a few shells, and it also vibrated badly, so the Bf 109V5 and V6 were completed with the armament of three machine-guns, as was also the production prototype, the Bf 109V7, which flew early in 1937. By this time preparations for quantity production of the Bf 109B fighter had reached an advanced stage at Augsburg, and deliveries of the pre-production Bf 109B-0 for service evaluation were imminent.

Flight testing of the prototype had not progressed entirely smoothly. The steep landing attitude disconcerted service test pilots, and the fighter had a tendency to drop its port wing just before touch-down. Wing flutter and tail buffeting were experienced, the wing slots malfunctioned, the narrow-track under-carriage failed frequently owing to weak attachment points, and the aircraft tended to swing seriously during take-off and landing. Nevertheless, despite the inauspicious commencement of its career, Germany was determined to impress the world with the capabilities of the reviving German aircraft industry, and from the beginning of 1936 the press department of the German Air Ministry devoted much of its time to eulogizing Germany's "new wonder fighter".

The fighter had first been seen in public when Oberst Franke—the pilot who was later to be decorated for "sinking" the *Ark Royal* in 1939—demonstrated the Bf 109V1 in 1936, during the Olympic Games held in Berlin. But by 1937 the foreign technical press was becoming increasingly sceptical of the impressive claims made for this fighter which only a few privileged foreigners had seen. Sensing this, Germany decided that a practical demonstration of the fighter's capabilities would do much to raise German aviation prestige. Accordingly, it was decided to send a demonstration team equipped with Bf 109 fighters to the International Flying Meeting held at Zurich in July 1937.

The team comprised two Bf 109B-1s, a Bf 109B-2, and the Bf 109V13. Led by Major Seidemann, who was later to command the Fliegerkorps Afrika, the three Bf 109Bs won the contest for a circuit of the Alps by military aeroplanes, covering the distance of 228 miles in 57 minutes 7 seconds at an average speed of 233.5 m.p.h. Oberst Franke won the Alpenflug in the Bf 109B-2, covering a circuit of 31.4 miles four times at an average speed of 254.54 m.p.h. He also won the Alpine circuit contest for single military aeroplanes in the Bf 109V13 at an average speed of 241.3 m.p.h., and the dive-and-climb competition, in which he reached 9,840 feet and returned to 1,060 feet in 2 minutes 5.7 seconds. The Bf 109V13 was a standard B-series airframe adapted to take the 960 h.p. Daimler-Benz DB 600 engine; and to further the considerable prestige gained by the fighter at Zurich, a specially boosted DB 601 engine, delivering 1,650 h.p. for short periods, was fitted in this prototype and the aircraft used by Dr. Hermann Wurster to raise the

Nr.809), registered D-IUDE, was flown in January 1936, being transferred to Travemünde, via Rechlin, on the 21st of that month. This prototype was fitted with the new Junkers Jumo 210A engine of 610 h.p. which drove a two-blade, fixed-pitch wooden airscrew. Provision was made for the installation of two 7.9-mm. MG 17 machine-guns in the upper decking of the nose, this armament being proposed for the Bf 109A production model. The Bf 109V3 (Werke Nr.810), registered D-IHNY, which followed in June 1936, was generally similar to its predecessor, but it had meanwhile been decided by the German Air Ministry that the armament of two MG 17 guns would be totally inadequate in the light of intelligence reports on the unprecedented armament of eight machine-guns proposed for installation in the Hurricane and Spitfire, and the Bf 109A production model was abandoned in favour of the more heavily armed Bf 109B, no A-series machines being completed. It was proposed that the Bf 109B would initially carry three MG 17 machine-guns, two in the top cowling and synchronized to fire through the airscrew, and the other firing through the airscrew boss. The latter gun would eventually be supplanted by a 20-mm. MG FF (Oerlikon) cannon which would endow the fighter with a longer-ranging armament than that of either of its British contemporaries.

international speed record for landplanes to 379.39 m.p.h. on November 11, 1937.

Eighteen months later Germany was to adopt subterfuge in a successful attempt to gain further acclaim for what was by then Germany's standard fighter. On April 26, 1939, the world was informed that a "specially modified version of the Luftwaffe's single-seat fighter" had raised the world air speed record to 469.22 m.p.h. However, the so-called "Me 109R" record-breaking machine bore no relationship to the Bf 109 fighter other than a common design team, for it was in fact the first prototype of an entirely *new* design, built specifically for the record attempt and fitted with a special engine giving 2,300 h.p. for short bursts.

During the spring of 1937 the small pre-production batch of Bf 109B-0 fighters was issued to an experimental unit for service evaluation. This version was powered by the 610 h.p. Jumo 210B engine, but the first production model, the Bf 109B-1, which followed closely on the heels of the pre-production machines, received the 635 h.p. Jumo 210D, with which it was supplied to the newly formed Richthofen Jagdgeschwader. The Bf 109B-1 attained 292 m.p.h. at 13,100 feet, and attained an altitude of 19,685 feet in 9.8 minutes. Service ceiling was 26,575 feet, and empty and loaded weights were 3,483 lb. and 4,850 lb. respectively. The limitations of the fixed-pitch wooden airscrew necessitated its early replacement by a two-blade variable-pitch metal airscrew, and a licence to manufacture the Hamilton airscrew was acquired from the U.S.A. This new airscrew was fitted to the Bf 109B-2, the first production machines of this type having the Jumo 210E engine with two-stage supercharger, but the majority having the Jumo 210G of 670 h.p.

By now the civil war was raging in Spain, and the Polikarpov-designed I-15 (TsKB-3) and I-16 (TsKB-12) fighters supplied by Russia to the Republican forces outperformed and outgunned the elderly Heinkel He 51 biplanes used by the Condor Legion which was supporting General Franco and the Nationalists. In July 1937 the first and second Staffeln of the Jagd Gruppe J/88 fighting in Spain were re-equipped with some twenty-four Bf 109B fighters, the civil war presenting Germany with an admirable opportunity to test her new fighter under operational conditions. It was here that the ill-founded legend of structural weakness—a legend that was later fostered by Germany's enemies and was to cling to the fighter throughout its operational career—was first started; an isolated incident of a damaged Bf 109B losing its tail in a high-speed dive being exaggerated to such an extent that it was popularly believed that this fighter would fall apart under high-stress manœuvres.

Although the Bf 109B was still prone to wing flutter and tail buffeting, it proved highly successful. While largely used for bomber escort duties and for occasional fighter sweeps over Republican airfields, Oberstleutnant Harder built up a considerable score of "kills" in his Bf 109B, and the machine proved to be an effective weapon against the Russian fighters.

However, one major shortcoming was revealed, inadequate armament. The three 7.9-mm. MG 17 machine-guns provided insufficient range and weight of fire, and several B-model airframes were fitted with a 20-mm. MG FF cannon in place of the centrally-mounted MG 17. But this cannon was unreliable and still prone to seizing after only a few shots had been fired. This and severe vibration while firing prevented its widespread use. At Augsburg extensive armament tests were undertaken. The Bf 109V8 was fitted with two wing-mounted MG 17 machine-guns, in addition to the two mounted in the engine cowling, although these aggravated the flutter problem until the ailerons were balanced and the wing leading edge stiffened. The next prototype, the Bf 109V9, had two 20-mm. MG FF cannon installed in the wings. These machines served as prototypes for the production C-series

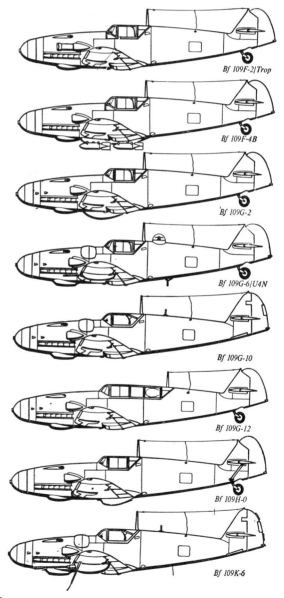

Bf 109F-2/Trop

Bf 109F-4B

Bf 109G-2

Bf 109G-6/U4N

Bf 109G-10

Bf 109G-12

Bf 109H-0

Bf 109K-6

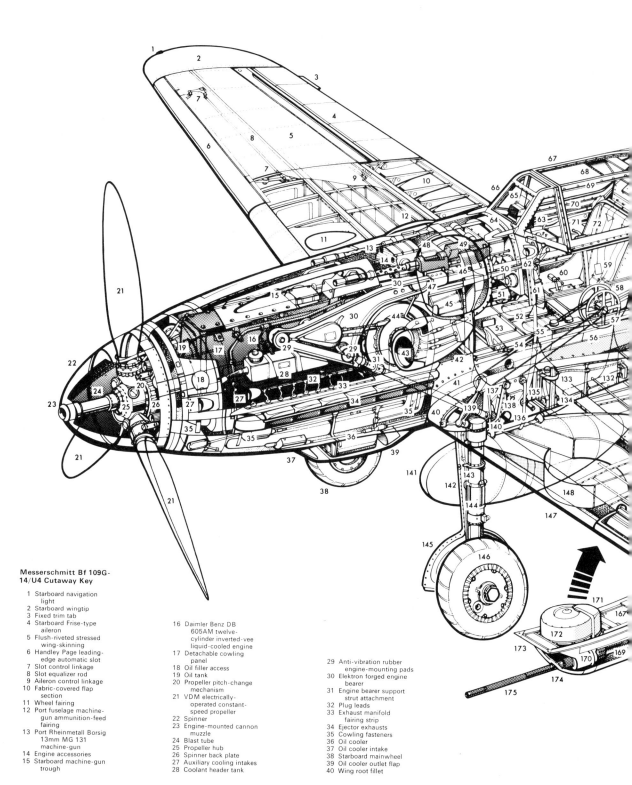

Messerschmitt Bf 109G-14/U4 Cutaway Key

1 Starboard navigation
   light
2 Starboard wingtip
3 Fixed trim tab
4 Starboard Frise-type
   aileron
5 Flush-riveted stressed
   wing-skinning
6 Handley Page leading-
   edge automatic slot
7 Slot control linkage
8 Slot equalizer rod
9 Aileron control linkage
10 Fabric-covered flap
   section
11 Wheel fairing
12 Port fuselage machine-
   gun ammunition-feed
   fairing
13 Port Rheinmetall Borsig
   13mm MG 131
   machine-gun
14 Engine accessories
15 Starboard machine-gun
   trough

16 Daimler Benz DB
   605AM twelve-
   cylinder inverted-vee
   liquid-cooled engine
17 Detachable cowling
   panel
18 Oil filler access
19 Oil tank
20 Propeller pitch-change
   mechanism
21 VDM electrically-
   operated constant-
   speed propeller
22 Spinner
23 Engine-mounted cannon
   muzzle
24 Blast tube
25 Propeller hub
26 Spinner back plate
27 Auxiliary cooling intakes
28 Coolant header tank

29 Anti-vibration rubber
   engine-mounting pads
30 Elektron forged engine
   bearer
31 Engine bearer support
   strut attachment
32 Plug leads
33 Exhaust manifold
   fairing strip
34 Ejector exhausts
35 Cowling fasteners
36 Oil cooler
37 Oil cooler intake
38 Starboard mainwheel
39 Oil cooler outlet flap
40 Wing root fillet

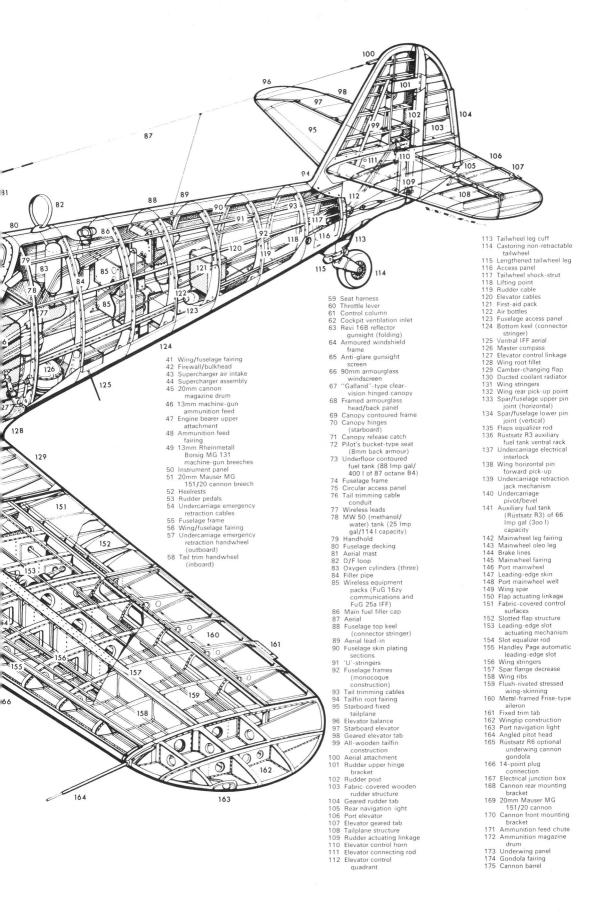

41 Wing/fuselage fairing
42 Firewall/bulkhead
43 Supercharger air intake
44 Supercharger assembly
45 20mm cannon magazine drum
46 13mm machine-gun ammunition feed
47 Engine bearer upper attachment
48 Ammunition feed fairing
49 13mm Rheinmetall Borsig MG 131 machine-gun breeches
50 Instrument panel
51 20mm Mauser MG 151/20 cannon breech
52 Heelrests
53 Rudder pedals
54 Undercarriage emergency retraction cables
55 Fuselage frame
56 Wing/fuselage fairing
57 Undercarriage emergency retraction handwheel (outboard)
58 Tail trim handwheel (inboard)

59 Seat harness
60 Throttle lever
61 Control column
62 Cockpit ventilation inlet
63 Revi 16B reflector gunsight (folding)
64 Armoured windshield frame
65 Anti-glare gunsight screen
66 90mm armourglass windscreen
67 "Galland"-type clear-vision hinged canopy
68 Framed armourglass head/back panel
69 Canopy contoured frame
70 Canopy hinges (starboard)
71 Canopy release catch
72 Pilot's bucket-type seat (8mm back armour)
73 Underfloor contoured fuel tank (88 Imp gal/ 400 l of 87 octane B4)
74 Fuselage frame
75 Circular access panel
76 Tail trimming cable conduit
77 Wireless leads
78 MW 50 (methanol/ water) tank (25 Imp gal/114 l capacity)
79 Handhold
80 Fuselage decking
81 Aerial mast
82 D/F loop
83 Oxygen cylinders (three)
84 Filler pipe
85 Wireless equipment packs (FuG 16zy communications and FuG 25a IFF)
86 Main fuel filler cap
87 Aerial
88 Fuselage top keel (connector stringer)
89 Aerial lead-in
90 Fuselage skin plating sections
91 'U'-stringers
92 Fuselage frames (monocoque construction)
93 Tail trimming cables
94 Tailfin root fairing
95 Starboard fixed tailplane
96 Elevator balance
97 Starboard elevator
98 Geared elevator tab
99 All-wooden tailfin construction
100 Aerial attachment
101 Rudder upper hinge bracket
102 Rudder post
103 Fabric-covered wooden rudder structure
104 Geared rudder tab
105 Rear navigation light
106 Port elevator
107 Elevator geared tab
108 Tailplane structure
109 Rudder actuating linkage
110 Elevator control horn
111 Elevator connecting rod
112 Elevator control quadrant

113 Tailwheel leg cuff
114 Castoring non-retractable tailwheel
115 Lengthened tailwheel leg
116 Access panel
117 Tailwheel shock-strut
118 Lifting point
119 Rudder cable
120 Elevator cables
121 First-aid pack
122 Air bottles
123 Fuselage access panel
124 Bottom keel (connector stringer)
125 Ventral IFF aerial
126 Master compass
127 Elevator control linkage
128 Wing root fillet
129 Camber-changing flap
130 Ducted coolant radiator
131 Wing stringers
132 Wing rear pick-up point
133 Spar/fuselage upper pin joint (horizontal)
134 Spar/fuselage lower pin joint (vertical)
135 Flaps equalizer rod
136 Rüstsatz R3 auxiliary fuel tank ventral rack
137 Undercarriage electrical interlock
138 Wing horizontal pin forward pick-up
139 Undercarriage retraction jack mechanism
140 Undercarriage pivot/bevel
141 Auxiliary fuel tank (Rüstsatz R3) of 66 Imp gal (3oo l) capacity
142 Mainwheel leg fairing
143 Mainwheel oleo leg
144 Brake lines
145 Mainwheel fairing
146 Port mainwheel
147 Leading-edge skin
148 Port mainwheel well
149 Wing spar
150 Flap actuating linkage
151 Fabric-covered control surfaces
152 Slotted flap structure
153 Leading-edge slot actuating mechanism
154 Slot equalizer rod
155 Handley Page automatic leading-edge slot
156 Wing stringers
157 Spar flange decrease
158 Wing ribs
159 Flush-riveted stressed wing-skinning
160 Metal-framed Frise-type aileron
161 Fixed trim tab
162 Wingtip construction
163 Port navigation light
164 Angled pitot head
165 Rüstsatz R6 optional underwing cannon gondola
166 14-point plug connection
167 Electrical junction box
168 Cannon rear mounting bracket
169 20mm Mauser MG 151/20 cannon
170 Cannon front mounting bracket
171 Ammunition feed chute
172 Ammunition magazine drum
173 Underwing panel
174 Gondola fairing
175 Cannon barrel

which were essentially similar to the B-model apart from their armament.

The pre-production Bf 109C-0 and the initial production Bf 109C-1 both carried four MG 17 machine-guns, and the Bf 109C-2 sub-type had a further MG 17 firing through the airscrew hub. The experimental Bf 109C-4 had four MG 17 guns and a single 20-mm. MG FF cannon, but this version was not placed in service. In August 1938 twelve Bf 109C-1 fighters arrived in Spain to re-equip the third Staffel of J/88 which was subsequently commanded by Werner Mölders, who became the top-scoring German fighter pilot in Spain.

While work was progressing on the improvement of the fighter's armament, parallel experiments were being conducted with a view to improving performance. An early 960 h.p. Daimler-Benz DB 600 engine was installed in a standard B-series airframe to form the Bf 109V10. Two further prototypes, the V11 and V12, were fitted with the production type DB 600A, resulting in a substantial improvement in performance, a maximum speed of 323 m.p.h. being attained, and service ceiling being boosted to 31,170 feet. With this engine a new sub-type, the Bf 109D, entered production late in 1937, the pre-production Bf 109D-0 fighters employing converted B-model airframes and carrying an MG 17 machine-gun in each wing as first introduced on the Bf 109C. In addition, a single engine-mounted MG FF cannon

was carried. A small production batch of Bf 109D-1 fighters followed to equip one Gruppe, but the availability of the redesigned DB 601 engine, incorporating direct fuel injection and improved supercharging capacity, had led to the abandonment of further production of the DB 600 and, in consequence, the Bf 109D in favour of the Bf 109E with the later engine, and ten of the Bf 109Ds were sold to Switzerland and three to Hungary.

The Bf 109E was the first true mass-production model of the basic design, and by the end of 1939 it had replaced all previous models in first-line service with the Luftwaffe, and thirteen Gruppen, each of forty aircraft, were operating with this type when the Second World War commenced. This fighter was referred to throughout the war years as the "*Me* 109", but the contraction "Bf" for Bayerische Flugzeugwerke was the prefix used for all versions of the 109 by official German handbooks and documents, including those produced after the company was reconstituted as the Messerschmitt A.G.

The first true prototype for the E-series was the Bf 109V14 which was powered by the 1,100 h.p. DB 601A

(Left) The Bf 109V14, prototype for E-series, and (right) the Bf 109E-1 in (top) 1940 finish and (bottom) 1939 finish.

(Right) The Bf 109F-3, which was placed in production early in 1942, was the first F-model to employ the DB 601E engine. The Bf 109F-4 (below) differed in having the hub-firing 15-mm. MG 151 cannon replaced by a 20-mm. MG 151. The F-4/B and F-4/Trop were fighter-bomber and tropicalized variants respectively. The F-4/R1 could employ GM-1 power boost.

engine and was flown during the early summer of 1938. This carried an armament of two wing-mounted MG FF cannon and two MG 17 machine-guns in the engine cowling. The Bf 109V15 differed in having an engine-mounted MG FF cannon and no wing guns. The pre-production Bf 109E-0 fighters appeared late in 1938, and both these and the initial Bf 109E-1 fighters carried an armament of four MG 17 machine-guns as the MG FF cannon was still considered to be inadequately developed for operational use. The Bf 109E-1 and E-1/B fighter-bomber, the latter carrying four 50-kg. bombs or one 250-kg. bomb, were standard equipment with the Luftwaffe by the time Germany went to war, and by the end of 1939 production had been transferred from the Augsburg factory to the new Regensburg plants (Regensburg-Prüfening and Regensburg-Obertraubling). The Erla plant at Leipzig-Mockau, the Ago factory at Oschersleben, the Fieseler plant at Kassel, the Arado factory at Warnemünde, and the W.N.F. factories at Delitzsch and Wiener-Neustadt were being integrated in the mass-production programme for this fighter, and a total of 1,540 machines had been produced.

By standards appertaining at that time, the Bf 109E was a very good fighter. It handled well and possessed excellent low-speed control response and "feel", although above 300 m.p.h. the controls became extremely heavy, and the ailerons in particular became almost immovable at around 400 m.p.h., making rolling virtually impossible. It lacked the manœuvrability of the Spitfire, nor did it possess the British fighter's turning circle, but its angle of climb was extremely good, being developed at low airspeeds. The Spitfire enjoyed a slight margin in speed, but both the climb rate and ceiling of the Bf 109E were superior, and the German fighter was definitely the better above 20,000 feet. In a vertical dive the Spitfire could not stay with the Bf 109E; but light though the rudder was at low and medium speeds, the absence of a cockpit-operated rudder trim was a serious fault because the rudder became very heavy in a dive, and then reversed trim, resulting in considerable pilot fatigue.

The direct injection pumps of the DB 601 engine had an advantage over the carburetters of the Merlin, and the engine did not cut out or splutter under negative "g". The stall was gentle with no tendency to spin, ample warning of its approach being given through aileron vibration and tail buffeting.

With the slotted flaps lowered to 20°, the take-off run was remarkably short and, the mainwheels being positioned well forward of the centre of gravity, fierce braking was permitted immediately on touchdown, resulting in a short landing run and fast taxying. However, the tendency to swing on take-off and landing, that had first manifested itself during tests with the early prototypes, continued to plague the Bf 109E and contributed substantially to the Luftwaffe's high accident rate, some 1,500 Bf 109 fighters being lost between the beginning of the war and the autumn of 1941 in accidents caused by unintentional swings. Only after the tailwheel had been fitted with a locking device which operated when the throttle was fully opened did the tendency to swing lessen.

The Bf 109E airframe (Werke Nr.5604) employed to test features for the F-model. This was first flown on July 10, 1940.

The Bf 109E-1 carried two 7.9-mm. MG 17 machine-guns in the engine cowling and one MG 17 or 20-mm. MG FF cannon in each wing. With the latter guns installed the weight of fire was 290 lb./min. Empty and loaded weights were 4,360 lb. and 5,400 lb. respectively and, with a wing area of 174 sq. ft., the wing loading was 32.1 lb./sq. ft. Overall dimensions included a span of 32 ft. 4½ in., a length of 28 ft. 4 in., and a height of 7 ft. 5½ in. with tail down. Maximum speed was 354 m.p.h. at 12,300 feet, and at economical cruising speed (62.5 per cent rated power) and allowing for climbing at full throttle to operating altitude after taking-off, the range was 412 miles at 16,400 feet. Initial climb rate was 3,100 ft./min., service ceiling was 36,000 feet, and the absolute ceiling was 37,500 feet. The Bf 109E-1/B fighter-bomber utilized the "Revi" gun-sight as a bomb-sight, and the angle of dive for bombing was graphically shown by a red line painted on either side of the cockpit canopy at 45° to the horizon to enable the pilot to put the machine into the correct diving angle. For high-altitude bombing the diving speed was 403 m.p.h., and for bombing from a low altitude the recommended diving speed was 373 m.p.h. The maximum permissible diving speed was 446 m.p.h.

The main sub-type of the E-series, the Bf 109E-3, entered production late in 1939. This model differed from its production predecessor in having provision for one 20-mm. MG FF cannon firing through the

airscrew boss, in addition to the paired guns above the engine and in the wings. However, the engine-mounted cannon was still unreliable and was seldom used operationally. More Bf 109E-3 fighters were built than any other model of the E-series, and by the beginning of 1940 the production rate had attained some 150 machines per month, a total of 1,868 being completed during 1940. Of these, 304 machines were exported to foreign air forces, including Bulgaria (19), Japan (2), Hungary (40), Rumania (69), Slovakia (16), Switzerland (80), Russia (5), and Yugoslavia (73).

By the turn of the year the Bf 109E-4 had supplanted the E-3. This model reverted to the twin engine-mounted MG 17 guns and pair of MG FF cannon, but the latter were of an improved type. The E-4/B was a fighter-bomber variant. The year 1941 saw the introduction of numerous improvements: the Bf 109E-4/N was fitted with the 1,200 h.p. DB 601N engine which was chiefly distinguished for its petrol injection system and the automatically-controlled hydraulic coupling to the supercharger drive. This version was later employed primarily in North Africa; the Bf 109E-5 was a special short-range reconnaissance model with reduced armament (two MG 17) and a camera in place of the wireless, and the E-6 was similar but employed the DB 601N engine. The Bf 109E-7 was normally a fighter equipped to carry an external jettisonable tank, but some of this sub-series were later converted for low-flying attack roles in North Africa, extra armour being bolted beneath the engine and coolant radiators, and designated Bf 109E-7/U2, the suffix "U" indicating "modification". The Bf 109E-7/Z was fitted with a special bi-fuel "power boosting" system known as GM-1, the E-8 was a further fighter variant in which all the progressive improvements incorporated in earlier models became standard, and the final sub-type of the E-series, the Bf 109E-9, was a reconnaissance aircraft carrying an RB 50/30 camera and a 66 Imperial gallons drop-tank.

(Top, left) The Bf 109F-1, first delivered to operational units in January 1941. One example of this aircraft was captured intact within a few months of its service début. (Left) The Bf 109F-4/B fighter-bomber and, below, the Bf 109F-0 powered by the DB 601N engine and first evaluated by the Luftwaffe late in 1940.

In 1940, when work was progressing rapidly on Germany's first aircraft carrier, the *Graf Zeppelin*, a ship-board fighter variant of the Bf 109E-3 was produced by the Fieseler-Werke. Known as the Bf 109T (the "T" indicating "Träger" or "Carrier"), this fighter possessed increased wing area, and spoilers fitted on the wing upper surfaces at one-third chord to steepen the gliding angle and reduce the landing run. The outer wing panels were folded manually, and an arrester hook was fitted. Only ten fighters of this type were completed by Fieseler, and these were subsequently reconverted to standard Bf 109E-3 configuration.

(Above and below). The Bf 109G-0 which retained the DB 601E engine of the F-model as the DB 605A-1 was not ready for installation for initial trials.

More extensive aerodynamic improvements made necessary to take full advantage of the increased power available from later Daimler-Benz engines were initiated in the spring of 1940. A standard Bf 109E airframe (Werke Nr.5604) was fitted with a 1,200 h.p. DB 601E-1 engine housed in an entirely re-designed, symmetrical cowling. The supercharger air intake was re-designed and positioned further out from the engine cowling to increase the ram effect, the airscrew spinner was enlarged, and the diameter of the airscrew reduced by some six inches. Shallower underwing radiators were fitted, incorporating boundary layer by-passes, and the braced tailplane was replaced by a cantilever structure. This experimental machine was flown for the first time on July 10, 1940, at Augsburg-Haunstetten, and subsequently served as the first prototype for the F-series fighters.

The Bf 109F embodied all the modifications included on the experimental machine and also an extensively re-designed wing which was tested on two further E-airframes. The new wing featured rounded tips and slightly increased span. The slotted ailerons were replaced by Frise-type surfaces, and plain flaps of reduced area replaced the slotted flaps that had been standard on all previous models. In addition, a retractable tailwheel was fitted. The first pre-production Bf 109F-0 fighters were delivered to Luftwaffe test centres for evaluation late in 1940. These were powered by the DB 601N engine which also powered the majority of the Bf 109F-1 production batches, and an armament of two MG 17 machine-guns and one MG FF cannon was carried.

The first Bf 109F-1 fighters were delivered to operational units in January 1941, but in February three early production machines were lost in temporarily inexplicable circumstances. In each case the pilot announced over the R/T that his engine was vibrating violently, and immediately thereafter his aircraft dived out of control, the pilot having no time to bail out. A few weeks later a fourth accident occurred when the tail assembly of a Bf 109F-1 broke off in mid-air.

Upon examination it was discovered that all the screws on the tail assembly/fuselage joint had been torn out. This could only have been caused by tremendous vibrations for which the engine could not be held responsible as it was found to have suffered damage only in the crash. Suspicion then fell on the tail spar since the rivets between the ribs and the elevators were all loose, missing or broken. Prolonged investigations ascertained that when the bracing struts of the Bf 109E tail assembly were omitted on the Bf 109F and stronger but less ribbing used, the proportion of the rigidity to the strength of the member was altered. The result was that the tailplane had a frequency of oscillation which, at certain r.p.m., was overlapped by the engine, and the resultant sympathetic vibrations tore out the tail spars.

Within a few months of the service debut of the Bf 109F-1, in July 1941 a well-known German fighter pilot, Peter Pingel, was forced down over Britain, his Bf 109F-1 being virtually intact. This aircraft was subsequently repaired, enabling British test pilots to ascertain its handling characteristics and performance.

The Bf 109F-2 differed from the initial production model in having the engine-mounted MG FF replaced by a 15-mm. MG 151 which substantially increased fire power because of its higher velocity and better trajectory. However, there were conflicting opinions among the leading German fighter pilots concerning the armament of the Bf 109F. Adolf Galland considered the reduced number of guns to be a retrogressive step, while Werner Mölders favoured this light armament. Later, the Bf 109F-4/R1 was to appear with a 20-mm. MG 151 cannon mounted in a gondola under each wing; but while this improved the fighter's effectiveness as a bomber destroyer, it adversely affected the machine's powers of manœuvre and reduced its potency in fighter-versus-fighter combat.

(Right) The Bf 109G-2 was generally similar to the Bf 109G-1 but did not possess a pressure cabin. It was intended for medium-altitude roles. (Below) The Bf 109G-6/R2 carried two 21-cm. rocket projectile tubes in place of the underwing gun gondolas.

The Bf 109F-2/Z had GM-1 power-boosting equipment, and the F-2/Trop was a tropicalized version for use in North Africa. Both the F-1 and F-2 production models were intended to have the DB 601E engine of 1,300 h.p., but delivery delays had necessitated the installation of the DB 601N, and it was not until the Bf 109F-3 appeared on the production lines early in 1942 that the DB 601E was installed. With this engine the Bf 109F-3 could attain a maximum speed of 390 m.p.h. at 22,000 feet. Normal cruising range was 440 miles at 310 m.p.h. at 16,500 feet, and service ceiling was 37,000 feet. Empty and loaded weights were 4,330 lb. and 6,054 lb. respectively, and wing loading had risen to 34.8 lb./sq. ft. The Bf 109F-4 had the engine-mounted 15-mm. MG 151 cannon replaced by a 20-mm. MG 151, and the F-4/B and F-4/Trop were fighter-bomber and tropicalized versions respectively. The Bf 109F-4/R1 could have a GM-1 power boosting system in place of the additional 20-mm. cannon underwing, and it was intended to fit four RZ 65 air-to-air or air-to-ground rocket missiles on underwing racks, but this armament was never perfected for operational use. The Bf 109F-5 was used primarily for long-range reconnaissance duties, carrying a 66 Imperial gallon drop-tank, and the F-6 was another reconnaissance variant which, generally unarmed, had an RB 50/30, RB 20/30 or RB 75/30 camera in place of the radio.

Several F-series airframes were utilized for experimental purposes. One Bf 109F-1 was fitted with boundary layer fences for comparison purposes with the leading-edge slots; one was fitted with an elongated wing for high-altitude trials, another had a vee-type or "butterfly" tail assembly, two others had single and twin nosewheels, while yet another had the DB 601N engine replaced by a BMW 801 radial for comparison with the Fw 190. The latter experiment was unsuccessful as the slim fuselage married to the bulky engine resulted in extreme turbulence in the area of the tail assembly. One other interesting experiment

was the Bf 109Z, the marriage of two standard Bf 109F-1 fuselages and port and starboard wings with a new centre wing section and tailplane which joined the two fuselages to form "Siamese twins". This was built to test the possibilities of the proposed Me 609, but the prototype was never flown.

A total of 2,628 Bf 109E and F fighters was produced in 1941, and of this total some 60 per cent was produced by the Erla plant at Leipzig-Mockau (683) and the W.N.F. factories at Delitzsch and Wiener-Neustadt (836). During the spring and summer of 1942 the assembly lines began to switch to the production of the Bf 109G, deliveries of which commenced in the late summer of 1942 and which was appearing on all war fronts by the end of that year. With the phasing out of the F-series, the basic Bf 109 design might be considered to have passed the peak of its development, for with the introduction of the G-series the constant operational demands for increased fire power and additional equipment brought with them a serious deterioration in the fighter's flying characteristics. The Bf 109G could not be flown in a landing circuit with flaps and undercarriage down other than at full throttle, and experienced German operational pilots have described its landing characteristics as "malicious". Nevertheless, some 70 per cent of all the Bf 109 fighters produced during the war years were of the G-series.

The most important change denoted by the introduction of the Bf 109G was the installation of the more powerful DB 605A engine in which the cylinder block had been re-designed to obtain the maximum possible bore with the existing cylinder centres, the permissible r.p.m. increased, and numerous other changes made in comparison with the DB 601. These changes resulted in an output of 1,475 h.p. at 2,800 r.p.m. at sea-level, and 1,355 h.p. at 18,700 feet. However, this engine was not available for installation in the twelve pre-production Bf 109G-0 fighters which retained the DB 601E engine of the preceding production model. The Bf 109G-0 was fitted with a pressurized cockpit, a feature which was becoming increasingly necessary in view of the altitudes to which air combat had by that time risen, and this was also fitted in the first production model, the Bf 109G-1, which was powered by the DB 605A-1 engine with GM 1 power boost.

The Bf 109G-1 which was dubbed "Gustav" by its

20

pilots, carried a single engine-mounted 20-mm. MG 151 cannon and two MG 17 machine-guns mounted over the engine. The latter 7.9-mm. guns were replaced by 13-mm. MG 131 machine-guns in the tropicalized Bf 109G-1/Trop, the installation necessitating the provision of fairings over the gun breeches. The G-2 was generally similar but had no pressure cabin. It was used primarily in the fighter-reconnaissance role, and the service test group at Guyancourt, France, experimented with a ventral gun pack in which two rear-firing MG 17 machine-guns were fitted. The G-3 was similar to the G-1 but fitted with FuG 16Z radio in place of the earlier FuG 7A, while the G-4 was an unpressurized version of the G-3.

The Bf 109G-5 received the DB 605D engine which had a supercharger of increased diameter and a methanol/water injection system. The two agents were contained in a jettisonable tank under the fuselage and fed to the engine in times of emergency. When injected into the cylinders with the 100-octane fuel, the methanol and water increased the amount of combustible mixture per unit volume of the cylinder, the increase in thermal efficiency temporarily boosting power to 1,800 h.p. at sea-level. The G-5/R2 was fitted with a taller fin and rudder assembly and lengthened tailwheel leg in a fresh attempt to cure the swerve which still characterized take-off and landing. The new tail assembly was made of wood in an attempt to conserve light metals. The Bf 109G-6, which could be fitted with several alternative versions of the DB 605, carried a 30-mm. MK 108 cannon firing through the airscrew boss, two 13-mm. MG 131 machine-guns above the engine, and two 20-mm. MG 151 cannon in underwing gondolas. The MK 108 used explosive ammunition, and its muzzle velocity was only 1,760 ft./min., but it proved to be an effective anti-bomber weapon. In the G-6/U4 version the MG 151 cannon were replaced by two MK 108s.

The Bf 109G-6/U4N was an improvised night fighter to use "Wilde Sau" tactics. This variant was fitted with "Naxos Z" warning and homing receivers with a range of thirty miles. The rotating antenna was installed aft of the cockpit, but the radar scope merely indicated direction and not distance. Two Staffeln were equipped with this improvised night-fighter and operated briefly in the Cologne area, but the majority of these machines were destroyed in landing accidents owing to the inadequate night-flying experience of their pilots. The Bf 109G-6/R1 was a fighter-bomber conversion of the basic sub-type, and the G-6/R2 carried two WG 21 rocket tubes in place of the underwing gun gondolas. The WG 21 missiles were of 21-cm. calibre, and fighters so equipped were mostly used by the J.G.1. and J.G.26 "Schlageter" units, but the missiles reduced maximum speed by some 25 m.p.h. and disrupted the airflow over the elevators, and only limited success was attained.

The Bf 109G-7 was a proposed version in which all the successive modifications to the G-6 version became standard, but this type did not enter production. The G-8 reverted to the old tail assembly and was a fast reconnaissance model fitted with an RB 12.5/7 or RB 32/7 camera. The engine-mounted MK 108 was removed. The fastest sub-type of the G-series was the Bf 109G-10 which, powered by the DB 605D engine and aided by GM 1, attained 428 m.p.h. at 24,250 feet. Climb to 20,000 feet was effected in 6 minutes, and range was 350 miles. No wing guns were carried, and the engine-mounted MK 108 was optional. The Bf 109G-10/U4 carried two additional MK 108 cannon with eighty rounds per gun in a belly tray, but this was subsequently replaced by a non-jettisonable long-range tank known as the "Irmer-Behälter". The G-10/R2 and R6 received the new tail assembly, the elongated tailwheel leg, FuG 25a equipment for friend-foe identification, and a modified cockpit canopy known as the "Galland hood".

Several Bf 109G-1 airframes had an additional seat installed and were redesignated Bf 109G-12 operational trainers. The pupil and instructor were seated in tandem, and the side windows of the rear cockpit were bulged in order to improve the instructor's view. The last of all the G-series fighters to attain operational status was the Bf 109G-14. This model was generally similar to the G-6 and could be fitted with the DB 605A, AM, AS, ASB, ASM or D engine, and armament comprised two MG 131 machine-guns and one 20-mm. MG 151 in the fuselage, and provision was made for the fitting of two MG 151 cannon underwing. One 250-kg. bomb or two WG 21 rockets could be carried, and the "Galland hood" was standard. The G-14/Trop was a tropicalized version, and the G-14/R2 received the new wooden tail unit first fitted to the G-5/R2 but retained the short tailwheel leg. The final production G-series aircraft, the Bf 109G-16, did not reach operations. It was generally similar to the G-14 but retained the old-type cockpit hood, and was heavily armoured for the close-support role.

Despite the advent of the very much superior Focke-Wulf Fw 190 fighter, production of the now elderly Bf 109 was progressively increased. Total production for 1942 amounted to 2,664 machines. This total was not very much greater than that for the previous year, a fact accounted for by the phasing out of the Bf 109F in favour of the G-series, and the retooling of the Ago factory at Oschersleben, the Fieseler factory at Kassel, and the Arado factory at Warnemünde for other aircraft types, but in 1943 production rose to 6,418 aircraft. In that year the Industria Aeronautica Romana (I.A.R.) factory at Brasov, in Rumania, the Hungarian Waggonwerke D.F.A.G. at Budapest, and a Messerschmitt-controlled plant at Györ in Hungary had completed retooling and commenced deliveries of the Bf 109G. Although the various complexes of factories controlled by the Messerschmitt A.G. were increasingly heavily bombed in 1944, production figures still increased in leaps and bounds, the unprecedented total of 14,212 machines being delivered in that year. Of these, 6,318 were produced by Messerschmitt's Regensburg factories which reached their production peak in October 1944

Last of the service line, the Bf 109K-6

with the delivery of 755 aircraft. Small numbers of Bf 109G fighters were exported in 1943–44, this type being delivered to the air forces of Bulgaria (145), Finland (70), Japan (2), Rumania (70), Slovakia (15), Spain (25), and Hungary (59). Surprisingly, in the few months of 1945, before Germany's collapse, when communications had been disrupted and few factories above the surface of the ground were intact, the German aircraft industry still succeeded in producing 2,969 Bf 109 fighters, of which 1,074 were produced at Regensburg.

In 1943, development of a specialized high-altitude version of the basic Bf 109F/G series was commenced. A small number of pre-production aircraft, designated Bf 109H-0, were converted from standard Bf 109F airframes by the insertion of additional wing sections which increased span by 6 ft. 6 in. and the attachment of a new, long-span tailplane which was reinforced by stout struts. The Bf 109H-0 was powered by the DB 601E engine, but the production Bf 109H-1 had the DB 605A with GM-1 boost and was used in the summer of 1944 by the service test group at Guyan-court. Intended for fighter-reconnaissance duties, the Bf 109H-1 was able to reach an altitude of approximately 47,000 feet, and attained a maximum speed of 466 m.p.h. Armament comprised two 7.9-mm. MG 17 machine-guns and one 30-mm. MK 108, and it was proposed to install two 13-mm. MG 131 guns in the wings. However, the long-span wing fluttered severely in dives, and further development was abandoned in favour of the Focke-Wulf Ta 152H. At one time several developments of the basic type were proposed, including the Bf 109H-2 which was to have had a Jumo 213E "power egg" and pressure cabin, and the Bf 109H-5 with the DB 605L engine.

In the early autumn of 1944 the first aircraft of the K-series made their appearance with service test groups. The pre-production machines were designated Bf 109K-0 and were essentially similar to the Bf 109G but incorporated minor structural differences and standardized on the DB 605D engine with MW 50 power boost. Three sub-types were produced, the Bf 109K-4 and K-6, powered by the DB 605ASCM/DCM, and the K-14 powered by DB 605L. The Bf 109K-4 carried an armament of two 15-mm. MG 151 guns over the engine and one engine-mounted MK 108 or MK 103. A pressure cabin was fitted and the "Galland hood" was adopted as standard. Maximum speed at sea-level was 377 m.p.h., and at 19,685 feet was 452 m.p.h. Service ceiling was 41,000 feet, and

climb to 16,400 feet took 3 minutes, and to 32,800 feet took 6.7 minutes. Range at a loaded weight of 6,834 lb. was 356 miles, and maximum take-off weight was 7,400 lb. The Bf 109K-6 differed primarily in its armament which comprised two 13-mm. MG 131 guns over the engine, an engine-mounted 30-mm. MK 108 or MK 103, and two MK 103 cannon under-slung on the wing. Maximum take-off weight was 7,920 lb., and maximum speed was 440 m.p.h. at 19,700 feet. The Bf 109K-14 carried two MG 131 and one MK 108, and attained 455 m.p.h. at 37,750 feet. The two earlier versions were entering service at the end of the war, but the Bf 109K-14 had not attained operational status.

The Bf 109L was basically a G-series airframe in which the fuselage section had been increased to merge with a Junkers Jumo 213E "power egg". The wing span was increased to 43 ft. 9 in. and the area to 236 sq. ft. Theoretical maximum speed was 476 m.p.h. at 35,000 feet, but development was never completed. Another version under development at the end of the war was the Bf 109S. This development was being undertaken by Caudron-Renault in Paris, and a prototype, the Bf 109V24, was tested in the Chalais-Meudon wind tunnel. The Bf 109S was to have incorporated a system of air discharge over the wing to improve control at low forward speeds, and was nearing completion at the time of France's liberation.

The Messerschmitt Bf 109 was a standard Luftwaffe single-seat fighter for nearly a decade. No exact figures are available for the total number of fighters of this type produced, but it is believed that more than 33,000 were built between 1936 and the end of the Second World War, representing more than sixty per cent of all the single-engined fighters produced by Germany during that period. Manufacture of the Bf 109 continued in Czechoslovakia and Spain after World War II, endowing Professor Messerschmitt's fighter with a record for production longevity. Having fought on every front upon which the Luftwaffe was engaged, and having been produced in greater numbers than any other combat type, the Messerschmitt Bf 109 probably ranks second only to the Supermarine Spitfire as one of the true "immortals" of the Second World War.

Messerschmitt Bf 109K-4

Dimensions :	Span, 32 ft. 6½ in. ; length, 29 ft. 4 in. ; height (one airscrew blade vertical—tail down), 12 ft. ; wing area, 173 sq. ft.
Armament :	Two 15-mm. MG 151 cannon and one 30-mm. MK 103 or MK 108 cannon, the latter firing through the airscrew boss.
Power Plant :	One Daimler-Benz DB 605ASCM/DCM twelve-cylinder inverted-Vee liquid-cooled engine with MW 50 methanol/water injection providing 2,000 h.p. at 2,800 r.p.m. for take-off and 1,800 h.p. at 2,800 r.p.m. at 16,700 ft.
Weights :	Loaded, 7,438 lb. ; wing loading, 42.5 lb./sq. ft.
Performance :	Maximum speed, 377 m.p.h. at sea-level, 452 m.p.h. at 19,685 ft. ; range (at 6,834 lb.), 355 miles at 19,685 ft. ; initial climb rate, 4,823 ft./min. ; time to 16,400 ft., 3 min., to 32,800 ft. 6.7 min., to 39,370 ft., 10.2 min. ; service ceiling (at 7,438 lb.), 41,000 ft.

Above is illustrated one of the first of thirteen YP-38 Lightnings ordered for service evaluation, and (right) the original XP-38 Lightning prototype. The YP-38 was redesigned for production, and differed from the XP-38 primarily in having V-1710-27/29 engines with outwardly-rotating airscrews in place of the V-1710-11/15 engines with inwardly-rotating airscrews.

THE LOCKHEED LIGHTNING

"Der Gabelschwanz Teufel"—the fork-tailed Devil— was a sobriquet not lightly applied by the Luftwaffe to the Lockheed P-38 Lightning which gave considerable cause to be known to Japanese and German alike. Although quantitatively the Lightning was produced in smaller numbers than any other major U.S.A.A.F. combat fighter, with a total, to August 1945, of 9,923 delivered from the factories, it served on every battlefront in a wide variety of roles, ranging from fighter-bombing to casualty evacuation and smoke laying. If slightly slower and less manoeuvrable than the more widely used Mustang and Thunderbolt, the Lightning offered the advantage of twin-engine operation, with its additional safety factor, added to an excellent combat range.

The Lightning was particularly interesting for the number and variety of its innovations. Apart from being Lockheed's first venture into the military field, the Lightning was the first squadron fighter equipped with turbo-superchargers, the first aircraft of twin-boom configuration to be adopted by the U.S.A.A.F., and the first twin-engined single-seat fighter used by that air arm. Design work began in 1937 to meet an official specification for a high-altitude interceptor. The specification called for a maximum speed of at least 360 m.p.h. at 20,000 feet, and 290 m.p.h. at sea-level; an endurance at full throttle of one hour at 20,000 feet, and the ability to take off and land over a 50-foot obstacle within 2,200 feet.

The Lockheed design staff, headed by H. L. Hibbard, considered that no engine available at that time was capable of giving sufficient power to meet the required performance, and this, together with other factors, determined the twin-engined layout. The twelve-cylinder Allison engine of 1,710 cu. in. capacity, which had just completed a 150-hour type approval test at 1,000 b.h.p., was selected and, from six possible arrangements, the radical twin-boom configuration was finally selected. The booms provided convenient mountings for the turbo-super-chargers, as well as the engines, radiator baths, and main undercarriage wheels, while the twin fin-and-rudder tail assembly increased the effective aspect ratio of the tailplane by endplate effect, providing stability over a large C.G. range.

Another advantage of the twin-boom layout was the possibility it offered of installing the armament in the central nacelle, unhampered by synchronizing gear, and allowing sighting of the parallel streams of fire up to the maximum range of 1,000 yards. For its day, the design provided for the exceptionally heavy armament of one 23-mm. Madsen cannon with fifty rounds of ammunition, and four 0.5-in. Colt MG-53 machine-guns with 1,000 rounds per gun, compared with the standard U.S. fighter armament of one

23

THE LOCKHEED LIGHTNING

0.5-in. and 0.3-in. gun with about 300 rounds per gun. Electrically-heated, the machine-guns had a combined rate of fire of 3,200 r.p.m.

After detailed drawings had been submitted to Wright Field, an official contract for one prototype was issued in June 1937, and the Lockheed Model 322 became the XP-38. Construction of the prototype proceeded fairly rapidly despite the radical features that it embodied. At 14,800 lb. it weighed more than a bombed-up Blenheim I, then Britain's standard medium bomber, and its wing loading was almost twice that of contemporary fighters. A species of Fowler flap had therefore been developed, but during wind-tunnel tests a wing fitted with these flaps tended to turn over because of pressure reversal—a phenomenon which later occurred in production aircraft. Few difficulties were presented by the installation of the Allison V-1710-11/15 (C9) engines, which developed 960 b.h.p. at 12,000 feet and 1,090 b.h.p. at 13,200 feet. To combat torque, inwardly-rotating handed Curtiss electric airscrews were used, a special version of the Allison engine being produced with a left-hand rotating airscrew shaft. A novel feature

(*Above*) *One of the few RP-38s. These were modified from first production P-38s, an extra cockpit being installed in the port boom.* (*Below*) *A Lockheed L-322-61 Lightning I, the export model of the P-38 for the R.A.F. The machine illustrated below (AF105) and that at the bottom of the page (AF106) were two of the few which reached Britain for evaluation.*

of the supercharger installation was that the intercooler formed part of the outer wing leading-edge, and this typically Lockheed cleanliness of design was evident throughout the entire airframe.

In keeping with the very best Hollywood tradition, the completed XP-38 was taken from its hangar late at night on December 31, 1938, stripped down, covered with canvas, and loaded on to three trucks. With great secrecy, the cortège, escorted by mobile police, travelled by a lonely route to March Field, near Riverside, where the then Lieut. B. S. Kelsey was to begin flight tests. On its first ground run, however, the brakes failed and the XP-38 ended ignominiously in a ditch. Notwithstanding this accident and despite flap flutter, a successful first flight was made on January 27, 1939, and on February 11 the prototype made a notable cross-country flight from March Field, California, to Mitchell Field, New York, with two stops for fuel, in 7 hours 2 minutes. With the aid of a brisk tail wind the indicated cruising speed was at times as high as 420 m.p.h.

Unfortunately, the XP-38 undershot on the approach to Mitchell Field and was completely destroyed, but the impetus to all aircraft production plans given by the Presidential programme resulted in a Limited Procurement Order for thirteen YP-38s for service evaluation. The YP-38 was re-designed for production, and included the installation of Allison V-1710-27/29 (F2) engines of 1,150 b.h.p., with spur reduction gearing instead of the former epicyclic type. The airscrews became outwardly-rotating, and the thrust line was raised, the lip intake being replaced by two coolant segments.

Due in no small measure to the situation in Europe, a production order was placed for sixty-six P-38 fighters in September 1939 while the YP-38s were still under construction, and before the first service test aircraft had flown on September 16, 1940, with Marshall Headle at the controls, a second order for 607 P-38s had been placed. In March 1941 the Army received its first YP-38 for evaluation trials. This had an armament of one 37-mm. cannon and two 0.5-in. Colt MG-53 machine-guns plus two 0.3-in.

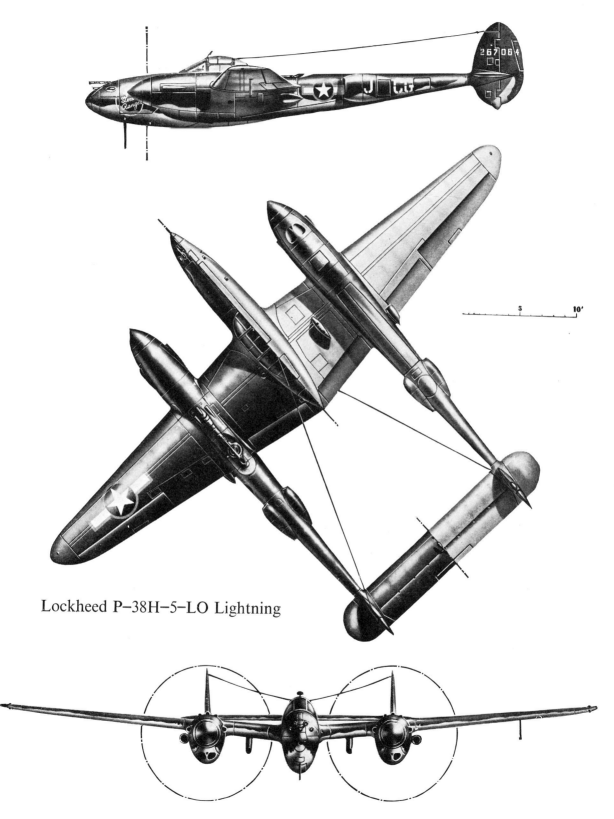

Lockheed P–38H–5–LO Lightning

THE LOCKHEED LIGHTNING

(Left) The first L-322-60 Lightning II (AF221) which was taken over by the U.S.A.A.F. (right) but retained the R.A.F. serial number. It is seen during smoke-laying experiments.

Colt MG-40 machine-guns. At 14,348 lb., the YP-38 was lighter than the overweight XP-38 due to structural re-design.

By now production was lagging seriously behind schedule, and all thirteen YP-38s had not been completed until June 1941, although the first batch of thirty production P-38s, with similar engines but reverting to four 0.50-in. machine-guns and having armour plate that had become an obvious necessity during air combat over Europe, was following closely on their heels. The production aircraft had a loaded weight of 15,340 lb. and a maximum speed of 395 m.p.h., but on the eve of Pearl Harbour the official inventory showed only sixty-nine on strength, including some of the later P-38Ds.

One early P-38 was fitted with a pressure cabin and redesignated XP-38A, but development was abandoned. The P-38B and P-38C were undeveloped projects, but the P-38D was the first really combat-worthy version. Embodying the requirements indicated by reports on air warfare over Europe, the P-38D, which was delivered to the U.S.A.A.F. in August 1941, was fitted with self-sealing fuel tanks, a retractable landing light, and provision for flares. From the old high-pressure oxygen supply system the P-38D changed to a low-pressure system, standard on all subsequent production models. A change in tail-plane incidence, together with a redistribution of elevator mass balances, increased the mechanical advantage of the elevator control, resulting in the elimination of buffeting and facilitating dive recovery. Originally named Atlanta, this and subsequent models of the P-38 were christened Lightning by the U.S.A.A.F.

Only thirty-six P-38Ds were built, the next version, the P-38E, having a major change of armament with the 37-mm. Oldsmobile cannon replaced by a gun of 20-mm. Hispano type. This model also featured a re-designed nose section with double the ammunition capacity of earlier machines, and revised hydraulic and electrical systems. SCR-274N radio was installed. In the middle of 1941 the Hamilton Standard Hydromatic airscrews with hollow steel blades were replaced on the production line by Curtiss Electric airscrews with dural blades. A total of 210 P-38Es was built.

Chronologically, the Lightning Mark I for the R.A.F. was the next model produced, deliveries commencing in December 1941. The contract for these aircraft was signed in March 1940 under the Lend-Lease scheme, but the U.S.A. was not anxious to have the turbo-superchargers exported to Europe at that stage of the war, and these, together with the opposite-rotating airscrews, were removed. As the higher-powered F2 Allison had not been released for export, the Model 322-61 Lightning I, or "castrated P-38" as it was christened at the factory, was fitted with two of the early C15 type engines, with the suffix "R" to indicate right-hand rotation of both airscrew shafts. The performance of this hybrid was poor, and the 143 Lightning Is built were mostly sent to a modification centre at Dallas, Texas, subsequently being employed as trainers and for various experimental roles. At about this time the P-38 made its first operational sortie and kill. Within minutes of the U.S. declaration of war against the Axis an Iceland-based Lightning shot down a Focke-Wulf Condor over the Atlantic.

In March 1942 the first deliveries of the F-4 were made. Otherwise similar to the P-38E from which it was converted, the F-4 had the nose armament supplanted by four K-17 cameras for reconnaissance duties. A drift sight and auto pilot were standard in the photographic Lightnings, which were painted a cerulean blue.

(Below, top) The first truly operational Lightning, the P-38F, photographed on Guadalcanal. (Below, bottom) A P-38F-13-LO tested with two torpedoes slung inboard of the engines.

The first truly operational Lightning was the P-38F of late 1942 which had 1,325 h.p. Allison V-1710-49/52 (F5) engines, and a loaded weight of 14,850 lb. Five hundred and twenty-seven machines of this sub-type were built, including several variants. The P-38F-1-LO had SCR-535 and SCR-522 radio, and was the first version of the Lightning to have racks under the inner wings for bombs or fuel tanks. With a normal capacity of 1,000 lb., each rack could also carry a Smoke Curtain Installation, a 22-in. torpedo, or long-range fuel tanks of either 165 or 310 U.S. gallons capacity. With the smaller tanks the total fuel capacity became 630 U.S. gallons and the maximum range 1,750 miles.

Lightnings of this type took part in their first large-scale combat operations during the North African campaign, in November 1942, where mixed success was encountered. Because of the tactics of the enemy aircraft the Lightnings were frequently forced to come down from their rated altitude and fight at heights in the vicinity of 15,000 feet, and against fighters it was not entirely successful. The twin engines restricted manœuvrability to some extent, and the Lightning was unique among fighters of World War II in employing a wheel control instead of the conventional stick, a feature which may also have resulted in reduced ease of manœuvre. Nevertheless, it proved an effective bomber destroyer and had a sensational zoom climb that could rarely be matched. It wreaked great execution among Rommel's air transport well out to sea, and it was in North Africa that the Germans first applied their appropriate nickname to the P-38.

To provide trainee fighter pilots with air experience of the P-38, in the U.S.A. several P-38Fs had their radio equipment removed and a crude seat installed on the main spar. These were dubbed "Piggy-back" Lightnings, the pupil sitting most uncomfortably with his head rammed against the cockpit roof. No dual control was fitted, but some idea of the combat tactics and aircraft handling could be gained from the back seat. The P-38F-5-LO introduced A-12 oxygen equipment, while the P-38F-13-LO had modified instruments meeting the British Approved Specification No. 2338. An important modification in the P-38-15-LO to improve manœuvrability was the introduction of a combat setting of 8° to the flaps for rapid extension to tighten turns by increasing the CL. The photo-reconnaissance version of the P-38F was designated F-4A, and twenty machines were modified to undertake this role.

Apart from the change to the 1,325 h.p. V-1710-51/55 (F10) engines with increased boost ratings but limited to 1,150 h.p. at 27,000 feet owing to inadequate cooling, and the installation of SCR-274N radio and A-9 oxygen equipment, the P-38G was similar to its predecessor. Superchargers of B-13 type were installed on the P-38G-3-LO, and the P-38G-5-LO also had revised supercharger equipment and resistance instruments. With a loaded weight some 200 lb. less than that of the P-38F, the P-38G was the most widely built of the early Lightnings, some 1,082 being manu-

factured during 1942, including 181 modified as F-5A photo-reconnaissance aircraft, and another 300, with intercoolers, as F-5Bs.

As a result of a new contract, work was started late in 1941 on a further version of the Lightning for the R.A.F., the Model 322-60, generally similar to the P-38G apart from British instruments and radio equipment. Designated Lightning II, the type again failed to reach squadron service in the R.A.F., and the batch of Lightning IIs was taken over by the U.S.A.A.F.

In the summer of 1942 the first P-38s had been allocated to the U.S. air forces in the United Kingdom, and because of the premium on transatlantic shipping space it was decided to take advantage of the Lightning's exceptional range and try flying it across. No fighters had previously flown this hazardous route, but the pilots of the 1st and 14th Fighter Groups successfully pioneered the way, and before the route had closed for the winter 179 out of a total of 186 Lightnings that had taken-off from the U.S.A.

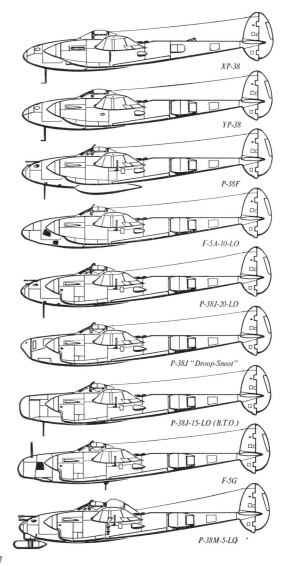

XP-38

YP-38

P-38F

F-5A-10-LO

P-38J-20-LO

P-38J "Droop-Snoot"

P-38J-15-LO (B.T.O.)

F-5G

P-38M-5-LO

(Top to bottom) An F-5A-10-LO, an F-5B-1-LO, and an F-5G.

(Above) A P-38J fitted with skis.

reached their destination, via Labrador, Greenland and Iceland, escorted by Boeing B-17 Fortresses for navigational direction. Early in 1943 about fifty P-38s flew the South Atlantic to North Africa, and soon the type was literally in world-wide service.

One of the most brilliant achievements of the Lightning was the interception of Admiral Yamamoto's Mitsubishi Ki.21 transport, in April 1943, by the 339th Fighter Squadron, some 550 miles from its base on Guadalcanal. A consignment of 165 and 310 U.S. gallon drop-tanks was flown out especially for the operation, which had been planned from an intercepted Japanese itinerary, and sixteen Lightnings assembled for the rendezvous with the Japanese transport. By brilliant flight-planning, the interception was made precisely on schedule and, despite an escort of Mitsubishi A6M fighters, Yamamoto's Ki.21 was shot down in flames by Lieut. Thomas G. Lanphier, later to become a Lockheed test pilot.

A change to the 1,425 h.p. V-1710-89/91 (F15) engines, M-2C cannon in place of the M-1, and an increase to 1,600-lb. bomb capacity for each under-

wing rack were characteristics of the P-38H-1-LO which went into service in May 1943. It also featured an attempt to overcome the persistent cooling trouble at maximum power by introducing automatically-operated oil radiator flaps. The F17 series engines of the P-38H-5-LO had B-33 type turbo-superchargers giving improved altitude performance. Incidentally, during oxygen tests a P-38 established an unofficial altitude record by climbing to 44,940 feet. The photographic reconnaissance version was designated F-5C, and 128 machines were modified for this role, plus a sole F-5D which had a "Piggy-back" seat for an additional crew member and V-1710-49/53 engines. Prior to the invasion of Italy, F-5 pilots of the 12th Photographic Reconnaissance Squadron of the 3rd Photographic Group mapped 80 per cent of the country in 300 sorties.

Throughout all modifications, the contours of the Lightning had remained virtually unchanged, and it was not until the appearance of the P-38J, which came into operational use in August 1943, and its equivalent photographic reconnaissance versions, the F-5E and F, which made their début one month later, that appreciable differences manifested themselves. Although having the same engines as the P-38H, the P-38J-1-LO and subsequent aircraft had a beard radiator under each drive shaft, resulting from the sandwiching of the inter-cooler air intake between the oil radiator intakes. From the P-38J-5-LO production batch, the leading-edge space formerly occupied by the intercooler was occupied by two 55 U.S. gallon fuel tanks, increasing total internal fuel capacity to 410 U.S. gallons, or 1,010 gallons with drop-tanks. The ferry range then became 2,260 miles and endurance 12 hours. The price paid for these modifications was a slight increase in drag; but with a maximum speed of more than 420 m.p.h. at altitude, the P-38J, as the fastest variant of the entire Lightning series, saw the re-introduction of the wing instability problems first experienced in the wind-tunnel tests of 1938.

Compressibility had dogged the Lightning during its early career when it affected the tailplane, but by careful filleting of the wing/fuselage junction this difficulty was eventually overcome. To counteract a strong nose-down pitching moment at high speed in later Lightnings, a small electrically-operated dive flap was introduced under each wing, starting with the P-38J-25-LO. In March 1944 Colonel Benjamin Kelsey reached an indicated speed of more than 750 m.p.h. in a dive in a P-38, but it was later discovered that compressibility error on the air-speed indicator at about 550 m.p.h. gave a greatly exaggerated reading. Nevertheless, the Lightning handled well at very high speeds, and its strong airframe withstood excessive aerodynamic loading.

To increase manœuvrability the ailerons of the P-38J-25-LO and succeeding variants were fitted with a power-boosting system which consisted of a hydraulically actuated bell-crank and push-pull rod. This boosting system was one of the first applications of powered controls to any fighter, and required only 17 per cent of the previous stick forces. The P-38J had a maximum weight of 17,500 lb., and a total of 2,970 machines was completed.

By the spring of 1944 there were thirteen P-38 Groups in overseas operational service with the U.S.A.A.F., fighting on every battlefront. In Europe, serving principally with the tactical Ninth Air Force, the Lightnings operated on long-range fighter escort and ground-attack duties, while in the Pacific their exceptional range put them in the forefront of the island-hopping campaign. The first bomber-escort missions to

(*Above*) *The P-38M two-seat night-fighter with raised second cockpit.*

Berlin were mounted by Lightnings, although they were outclassed by the more manœuvrable Fw 190 and the later Bf 109s. In the Pacific, however, Lightnings claimed more Japanese aircraft destroyed than did any other fighter, and the leading American fighter ace of World War II, the late Major Richard Bong, scored all forty of his victories while flying a P-38 in that theatre. He was closely followed by another Lightning pilot, MacGuire, with thirty-eight Japanese victories; while in Europe Jenkins and White scored sixteen and twenty-two victories respectively with their Lightnings.

An E.T.O. (European Theatre of Operations) modification to some P-38Js and subsequent types involved the replacement of the standard nose by an extra crew position with a transparent bomb-aiming nose and Norden bomb-sight. These so-called "droop-snoot" Lightnings were used to lead formations of P-38s each carrying two 2,000-lb. bombs which were released on instructions from the lead bombardier. Following the success of this development, other Lightnings had the visual bomb-aiming position replaced by "Mickey" type radar, or B.T.O., which enabled attacks to be delivered even when the target was obscured by cloud. Some of the aircraft so modified were P-38Ls, which, with 1,600 h.p. V-1710-111/113 (F30) engines, were the version of the Lightning built in largest quantities. The P-38K, with V-1710-75/77 (F17) engines and larger airscrews, had been built only in prototype form, but 3,810 P-38Ls were produced by Lockheed at Burbank, and a further 113 by Vultee at Nashville. An additional 1,887 machines were cancelled with the advent of V-J Day. Except for the war emergency rating of its engines, the P-38L was generally similar to the previous model, although the P-38L-5 saw the introduction of underwing rocket "trees" for ten 5-in. projectiles. The photo-reconnaissance model was designated F-5G.

The Lightning's load-carrying capabilities were put to some unusual uses at a late stage in the war when cargo and personnel pods were developed for attachment to the bomb pylons. Self-contained P-38 groups in the Pacific carried spares and ground crews in order to utilize newly captured airstrips without having to await the arrival of supporting transport. On other occasions, for swift casualty air evacuation, the

Lightning became an air ambulance. Modified droptanks, with transparent noses, were produced, each carrying two stretcher cases. Other unusual applications included the use of some P-38s as glider tugs, each having a maximum tow of three laden gliders, while one P-38 was successfully flown with skis.

Although one or two TP-38L-LO Lightnings were produced, with tandem seating for training purposes, the final production version, which saw operational service in the Pacific during the last few days of the war, was the P-38M. Completing the Lightning's versatility, the P-38M was a modified L-model with two seats and radar to suit it for the night-fighter role, all the normal armament load being carried. ASH-type radar was mounted under the nose, with presentation in a raised rear cockpit for the observer. The result of this improvisation was an effective night fighter with very little performance penalty over the standard single-seat Lightning.

It was appropriate that the Lightning should terminate a distinguished combat career by being the first U.S.A.A.F. aircraft type to land in Japan after V-J Day.

Lockheed P-38L Lightning

Dimensions :	Span, 52 ft. ; length, 37 ft. 10 in. ; height, 12 ft. 10 in. ; wing area, 328 sq. ft.
Armament :	One 20-mm. Hispano AN-M2C cannon with 150 rounds, and four 0.5-in. Browning machine-guns with 500 rounds per gun, all mounted in the fuselage nose with parallel fire. Ten 5-in. rocket projectiles on underwing zero-length mounts, or up to 4,000 lb. load of external stores.
Power Plants :	Two Allison V-1710-111/113 Vee-12 liquid-cooled engines each developing 1,425 h.p. at sea-level and 26,500 ft., and 1,600 h.p. under war emergency conditions at 26,500 ft., and driving three-blade Curtiss Electric fully-feathering airscrews. Fuel capacity (wings) : Two main tanks each containing 90 U.S. gal., two reserve tanks each containing 60 U.S. gal., two leading-edge tanks each containing 55 U.S. gal.—total, 410 U.S. gal. Two 75, 150, 165 or 300 U.S. gal. external drop-tanks could be carried.
Weights :	Empty, 14,100 lb., combat loaded, 17,500 lb. ; wing loading, 53.3 lb./sq. ft. at loaded weight.
Performance (at loaded weight) :	Maximum speed, 360 m.p.h. at 5,000 ft., 390 m.p.h. at 15,000 ft. ; service ceiling, 40,000 ft. ; maximum range at sea-level, 900 miles, at 30,000 ft., 2,260 miles ; ground run to clear 50-ft. obstacle : take-off, 2,400 ft. ; landing, 3,400 ft.

THE KAWASAKI HIEN

In the spring of 1945, B-29 Superfortress crews became aware of the existence of an extremely formidable interceptor fighter which was being met in formation strength at altitudes above 30,000 feet over the Japanese home islands. The new warplane was fast, highly manœuvrable and unidentifiable—it appeared in none of the aircraft recognition manuals. In fact it was a complete surprise to the Allied air forces. Paradoxically, it was almost as much a surprise to the Japanese themselves. With their backs literally against the wall, the Japanese Army Air Force had created a new fighter, not in years or months, but in weeks. Known as the Ki.100 or Type 5, service models were in operational use in March 1945 even though the prototype had flown but one month previously.

The Type 5 was probably the best fighter to reach operational status with the Army; and although it came into existence in record time, its history really dated back several years, for it was actually a re-engined version of the Ki.61 Hien—an improvisation, but a remarkably successful one.

The Kawasaki Kokuki Kogyo K.K. acquired the manufacturing rights in the powerful new Daimler-Benz liquid-cooled inline engine series in 1937. Three years were to pass before the Japanese Army were to take advantage of this purchase. The war in Europe had alerted the Army to the possible need for heavier fighters comparable with the latest European designs, and in February 1940 Kawasaki received development contracts for two new fighter designs under the Ki.60 and Ki.61 designations. Work began immediately on the Ki.60, and the German DB 601A engine was selected as the power plant. Samples of the DB 601A had been purchased and these were earmarked for use in the prototypes of the new fighter which were being built at the Kagamigahara factory adjacent to the Kagamigahara Military Airfield, near Gifu on Honshu.

The first prototype Ki.60 was a highly streamlined monoplane, obviously influenced by European practice, and in March 1941, some nine months before the first flight of the parallel Ki.61 the Ki.60 was flown. Its speed proved to be 350 m.p.h. at 16,400 feet, making it the fastest Army fighter built at that date; but perhaps it was too fast, for it was undoubtedly ahead of its time as far as the Japanese

Army was concerned. Although they viewed the project with interest they had made no serious plans to introduce a heavy fighter, and current J.A.A.F. requirements did not warrant the expense and loss of production facilities for an aircraft not urgently needed. As a result the Ki.60 was abandoned in favour of the lighter Ki.61, then reaching an advanced stage.

While construction of the Ki.60 and Ki.61 fighters had been proceeding, the experimental engine shops at Kawasaki's Akashi factory, near Kobe, had been actively engaged in development work on the new Ha.40 engine, a twelve-cylinder liquid-cooled power plant derived from the DB 601A and rated at 1,175 h.p. Lighter in weight than the DB 601A installed in the Ki.60, the Ha.40 was selected for installation in the Ki.61, the first prototype of which was completed in December 1941. Somewhat similar in appearance to the Ki.60, the new fighter was some two feet longer and had a five feet greater span. In its early tests the Ki.61 achieved a speed of 368 m.p.h., a performance never to be achieved by production models until the introduction of the higher-powered Ki.61-II in 1943. Twelve Ki.61 prototypes were constructed, differing from each other in minor details. All twelve prototypes were extensively tested in the spring and summer of 1942, and with the fall of the Philippines the Army had an opportunity to examine captured examples of the Curtiss P-40E and fly them in comparative tests with the Ki.61. Examples of the Messerschmitt Bf 109E also arrived in Japan in June 1942, and the prototypes of the Ki.61 proved superior to both American and German fighter types.

Production of the Ki.61 had already been initiated, the type being accepted by the Japanese Army as the Type 3 Fighter Model 1 (Ki.61-I) and named Hien (Flying Swallow). The Ha.40 engine had also entered production as the Type 2 (Ha.60/22) rated at 1,100 h.p., and the first production Hien was completed at the Kagamigahara factory in August 1942, being delivered to the J.A.A.F. in the same month. One of the Ki.61 prototypes was subsequently fitted with a surface evaporation cooling system and tested at the Akashi plant for four months in the summer of 1943, reaching a speed some 25 m.p.h. higher than the version fitted with an orthodox radiator. Production tempo increased rapidly and thirty-four Hien fighters were completed in 1942. Despite the production difficulties later encountered, the monthly output attained over 100 machines in November 1943 and reached its peak of 254 machines in July 1944. Production fell quickly after this as the Ki.61-I was phased out in favour of progressive developments of the Hien, but 2,654 had been built by the time the initial production model had been completely supplanted on the assembly lines.

The Kawasaki (Ki.61-Ia) Type 3 Fighter Model 1A Hien with wing-mounted German Mauser cannon.

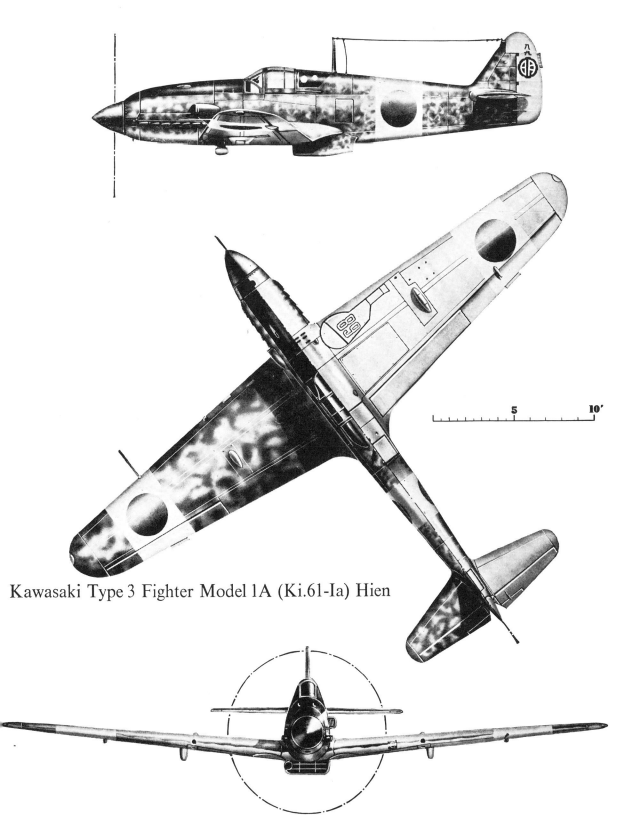

Kawasaki Type 3 Fighter Model 1A (Ki.61-Ia) Hien

5   10'

(Left) The experimental Ki.61-III. (Right) The Type 3 Fighter Model 2A (Ki.61-IIa).

The initial production model, the Type 3 Fighter Model 1, carried an armament of two 7.7-mm. machine-guns in the fuselage and two 12.7-mm. machine-guns in the wings. It embarked upon its operational career in April 1943 in New Guinea, where the code-name "Tony" was applied by the Allied forces. It was quickly discovered that the Ki.61-I Hien was under-armed and so the fighter was modified to carry two 20-mm. Mauser cannon in the wings in place of the 12.7-mm. guns, and production continued in August 1943 as the Model 1A (Ki.61-Ia). The Mauser and its ammunition were imported from Germany and production continued uninterruptedly while supplies lasted. However, as the tide of war turned against Germany the arms shipments to Japan were curtailed and the continuation of supply was extremely doubtful. Only 800 cannon reached Japan, and as a result only 400 Hien fighters received these guns. As an interim measure the Hien continued in production armed with four 12.7-mm. guns as the Model 1B (Ki.61-Ib).

While production continued with the interim Ki.61-Ib, the Hien was being extensively modified to improve control in combat, ease ground maintenance and mount two domestically produced Type Ho-5 cannon of 20-mm. calibre. The experimental model was completed in January 1944, and the aircraft entered production as the Model 1C (Ki.61-Ic). This new version of the Hien lacked several of the faults that had characterized its production predecessors and, in particular, field maintenance was simplified by the fitting of a removable rear fuselage. Final production model of the Model 1 version of the Hien was the Ki.61-Id, which had two 30-mm. cannon in place of the 20-mm. Ho-5 guns.

As the standard Japanese Army fighter of the 1943–44 period, the Hien was seen in every theatre of operations in which the J.A.A.F. participated. Following its introduction in New Guinea, the Hien appeared over Rabaul in New Britain, the Admiralty Islands, the mainland of China, and later in the defence of Manila and the Leyte peninsula in the Philippines late in 1944. As the air war advanced into the skies over the Japanese home islands the Hien again appeared, and it was also used on Army Taiatari (suicide) missions, being regarded as a good aircraft for ramming B-29 Superfortresses as its design enabled the pilot to jump clear just before the moment of impact. The Hien proved to be one of the finest all-round fighters of the J.A.A.F., and one respected by the Allied pilots opposing it. Its maximum speed of 348 m.p.h. at 16,400 feet was adequate to meet most demands made of it; and its diving characteristics

were far superior to other Japanese fighters, as is evidenced by the fact that it could hold its own in a dive against the heavier American fighters. Allied pilots reported that the defensive tactics employed by Hien pilots were difficult to counter as the aircraft seldom offered itself as a good target. When engaged at disadvantage it would either go into a half-roll and then dive or turn in and under the opposing aircraft in the event of a deflection shot set-up. Armour protection for both pilot and fuel was provided in later models primarily for psychological reasons, fostering the aggressive employment of the Hien by its pilots.

As the Hien's use was extended, defects in the Ha.40 became an ever-increasing source of trouble. The Ha.40 had proved to be an unreliable engine which varied greatly in rated power between individual models owing to a lack of quality control in production. Main-bearing failures and oil-system faults plagued maintenance personnel and pilots alike, and in December 1943 production was cut in order to re-evaluate the Ha.40 programme. Limited production continued, however; but no remedy had been found for the bearing failures, and by the spring of 1944 production of the Hein was dropping owing to lack of Ha.40 engines and stalled completely in the following summer owing to a severe shortage of cylinder blocks and crankcases. It was during this period that a new power plant was under development, the Ha.140 rated at 1,400 h.p.

Paralleling development of the Ha.140 engine were extensive changes to the Hien airframe, work having begun in September 1942 on a new variant known as the Type 3 Fighter Model 2 (Ki.61-II). The fuselage had been lengthened by the new engine and wing area had been increased 10 per cent from 216 sq. ft. to 237.6 sq. ft., and a re-designed cockpit hood had been added to improve pilot visibility. The first Ki.61-II was completed in August 1943, but production was immediately hampered by teething troubles with the new Ha.140 engine. The J.A.A.F. was demanding utmost speed, but only eight aircraft had been completed by January 1944. The Army was quickly disenchanted with the Ki.61-II, which did not meet expectations. Teething troubles in the engine and structural weaknesses in the airframe resulting from the additional power made a re-design of the entire project necessary. As Ha.140 development continued, the Kawasaki design staff began work on an entirely new version of the Hien, the Ki.61-II-Kai, which reverted to the original Model 1 wing, possessed a much stronger airframe, a revised cockpit canopy with improved vision, and a re-designed fin of greater area. The first Ki.61-II-Kai was completed in April

1944, and the type entered production at the Kagami-gahara factory as the Type 3 Fighter Model 2A (Ki.61-IIa) armed with two 12.7-mm. machine-guns in the fuselage and two 20-mm. cannon in the wings, and as the Model 2B (Ki.61-IIb) with four 20-mm. cannon.

War conditions were changing rapidly. The Japanese were aware of the existence of the B-29 Superfortress and it was only a matter of time before this American heavy bomber would be operating over Japan. The Army therefore assigned top priority to the production of the new fighter for bomber interception. Production began immediately and appeared to be well under way when suddenly it was completely stopped by a total lack of engines. Shortages of materials and mechanical failures had severely cut production schedules of the Ha.140, which was to continue in short supply until the end of the war. The few Ha.140 power plants that were completed were of such poor quality that they were almost useless, and as a result over 50 per cent of these engines were returned to the Akashi factory for reworking. Continued failures in the main bearings, superchargers, oil and coolant systems made the Ha.140 a most troublesome power plant in service use and, in consequence, the Ki.61-II-Kai a totally unreliable aircraft. Thirty Ki.61-II-Kai aircraft were produced in the spring of 1944 before production was stopped through a lack of engines. Production was resumed on a limited scale in August and continued at a slow pace.

Airframe manufacture had progressed at a moderate rate despite the fact that engine output could not keep pace. The result was a large number of Ki.61-II-Kai Hien airframes without engines. Of the 374 airframes produced up to the early part of 1945, power plants were available for but a small proportion of them. To add to the difficulties B-29s began to appear over the Kawasaki factories, and on January 19, 1945, the Akashi plant was hit with 155 tons of bombs. The raid damaged every important building and engine production was brought virtually to a standstill. Total Ha.140 production up to the time of this raid had been ninety-nine engines; and of the ninety-nine Ki.61-II-Kai fighters in which these had been installed, more than one-third had been destroyed in raids.

The sixty-odd Hien Model 2 fighters that were delivered to the J.A.A.F. were immediately assigned to duty as interceptors—a role for which, in theory, they were well suited. The increase in power provided the Hien Model 2 with a greatly increased maximum speed despite the fact that the variations in rated power due to the poor quality of workmanship in the Ha.140 engine kept the performance below anticipated results. In top condition the Ki.61-II-Kai Hien was rated at 379 m.p.h. at 19,680 feet, but few exceeded the 370 m.p.h. mark. However, this fighter had one point in its favour: it was able to maintain combat formation at altitudes as great as 33,000 feet. It also had a useful climb rate, attaining 16,400 feet in 6.5 minutes. The final development retaining the liquid-

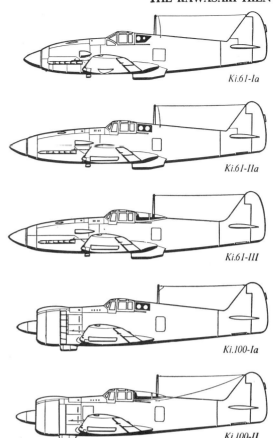

Ki.61-Ia

Ki.61-IIa

Ki.61-III

Ki.100-Ia

Ki.100-II

cooled engine was the Type 3 Model 3 (Ki.61-III) which was similar to the Model 2 but featured a cut-down rear fuselage and an all-round vision hood. Work on this development of the Hien was abandoned when production of the fighter was totally suspended, although the new cockpit enclosure was to reappear on late-production models of the Type 5 fighter.

Faced with the lack of power plants and a growing supply of airframes in open storage, the Government Munitions Ministry, an organization formed late in the war to co-ordinate all aircraft production, demanded immediate action to get these aircraft into the air. Radical methods were necessary if use was to be made of these idle airframes. With a total lack of Ha.140 engines, the only alternative was to modify the airframes to make use of another power plant. In November 1944 Kawasaki began design work on the adaptation of the Ki.61-II-Kai airframe to take the Mitsubishi Ha.112-II fourteen-cylinder twin-row air-cooled radial of 1,500 h.p. The project was designated Ki.100, and the Ha.112-II engine, designed by M. Fujiwara, was the most reliable power plant of known performance available. It had been in production for the Japanese Navy as the MK8K Kinsei 62 and, as the Type 4, production for the Army began in the summer of 1944.

One of the toughest problems facing the Kawasaki design staff was the mounting of a large-diameter radial engine in an airframe designed for a narrow

THE KAWASAKI HIEN

inline engine. The diameter of the Ha.112-II was some forty-eight inches as opposed to a thirty-three-inch fuselage width. To aid the design team an example of the Focke-Wulf Fw 190A, then used by the J.A.A.F. for comparison purposes, was delivered to the Kagamigahara factory, the engine being removed and studied as a reference for the new mounting. The Ki.61-II-Kai firewall was extended and the Ha.112-II mounted with the exhaust pipes arranged on both sides of the fuselage, clear of the airframe itself. Three prototypes of the Ki.100 were built, the first being test flown on February 1, 1945.

The results of flight testing were phenomenal. The improvisation had created a far better fighter than could possibly have been envisaged. It was immediately placed in quantity production. The first Type 5 fighters (Ki.100-Ia), were direct modifications of existing airframes, and 275 were produced from these stocks, thirty-six being delivered in March, eighty-nine in April and 131 in May, and immediately assigned to operational units. The last converted airframes were delivered in June, with further machines built from the outset as Ki.100-Ib fighters following on. The Ki.100-Ib differed from the converted Ki.100-Ia in having an all-round vision hood similar to that fitted to the Ki.61-III. Plans were prepared to increase production to 200 units per month, but a series of destructive air raids transformed the picture. The Kagamigahara plant was first seriously hit on the morning of June 22, 1945, when 116 tons of bombs were dropped on the factory by B-29s. A second and even more damaging raid came on June 26, when the plant was almost completely destroyed. The Ichinomiya plant, a former spinning mill converted for Ki.100 production as part of the Kawasaki dispersal programme, was also knocked out.

Following these attacks only another ninety-nine Ki.100 fighters were completed. Airframe assemblies were dispersed throughout the surrounding woods and in a shrine a half-mile away from the Kagamigahara factory. The dispersed units completed components and carried them piece by piece to the remains of the factory for final assembly. Production continued in this manner until the end of the war.

The Type 5 fighters that did attain service quickly proved themselves as formidable weapons. Although maximum speed was only 367 m.p.h. at 32,800 feet, which was slightly less than that of the Ki.61-II, manoeuvrability at altitude was infinitely better, as was also climb rate. Armament comprised two 12.7-mm. machine-guns and two 20-mm. cannon, but some operational units removed the machine-guns in order to increase high-altitude performance. Shackles were also fitted for two 550-lb. bombs. The manoeuvrability of the Ki.100 began to fall off above 26,000 feet, and because of the extremely high altitudes at which the B-29 Superfortresses approached their targets the fighters laboured under a serious disadvantage. Nevertheless they acquitted themselves well. At lower altitudes the Ki.100 was superlative, and one of the first squadrons to employ this fighter

destroyed fourteen Grumman F6F Hellcat fighters over Okinawa in one engagement without loss to themselves. However, the biggest test came in the summer of 1945 when P-51 Mustangs escorted the B-29 Superfortresses over Japan. The Ki.100 versus Mustang battles were ferocious and their outcome was usually determined by piloting skill and numerical advantage rather than any discrepancy between the relative standards of the fighter types involved.

One of the Ki.100's best features was its simplicity in both flight and maintenance. Even inexperienced pilots could be quickly checked out on this fighter and the Ha.112-II engine gave maintenance crews very little trouble. The Ki.100s served mainly on home-defence duties, operating from Chofu and Yokkaichi airfields on Honshu, and against Okinawa-based American aircraft from Kyushu.

In March 1945 work began on an improved version of the Type 5 fighter known as the Ki.100-II. This was an attempt to increase the service ceiling and altitude performance by fitting a Mitsubishi Ha.112-IIru engine with an Ru-102 turbo-supercharger. The power rating of the engine was the same as that installed in the Ki.100-Ib but output at altitude was greatly improved, and a methanol-water injection system was added to increase top speed for short bursts. The turbine was placed below the engine, and the supercharger installation was the same as that of the experimental Ki.102A twin-engined fighter. The space limitations did not permit the installation of an intercooler, and the air was ducted directly from the compressor to the carburettor. Although this reduced the efficiency of the unit, speed was still boosted by 30 m.p.h. at 30,000 feet. The first prototype Ki.100-II was completed in May 1945, only six weeks after design had commenced, and three further prototypes had been completed when the war ended.

Plans were in hand for large-scale production of the Ki.100-II as the Type 5 Fighter Model 2, production being scheduled to commence in September 1945. The production model was to have featured a plywood empennage structure which had been evolved by Kawasaki as part of a programme for substituting wood for more critical materials. At last the Army looked as though it would possess a fighter capable of meeting the Superfortress satisfactorily at the bomber's best operating altitudes, but the war ended and with it the hopes of the Japanese Army pilots.

Kawasaki Type 3 Fighter Model 1A (Ki.61-Ia)

Dimensions : Span, 39 ft. 4 in. ; length, 29 ft. 4 in. ; height, 12 ft. 1½ in. ; wing area, 215.278 sq. ft.

Power Plant : One Kawasaki Ha.40 Type 2 (Ha.60/22) twelve-cylinder liquid-cooled inverted-Vee engine rated at 1,160 h.p. at 2,500 r.p.m. for take-off and 1,100 h.p. at 12,600 ft.

Armament : Two 7.7-mm. Type 89 machine-guns in the upper decking of the forward fuselage and two 20-mm. Mauser MG 151 cannon in the wings.

Weights : Empty, 5,798 lb. ; loaded, 7,650 lb. ; wing loading, 35.535 lb./sq. ft.

Performance : Maximum speed, 348 m.p.h. at 16,404 ft.; 302 m.p.h. at sea-level ; climb to 16,400 ft., 7 min. ; service ceiling 32,800 ft. ; maximum range, 1,118 miles at 215 m.p.h. at 1,500 ft.

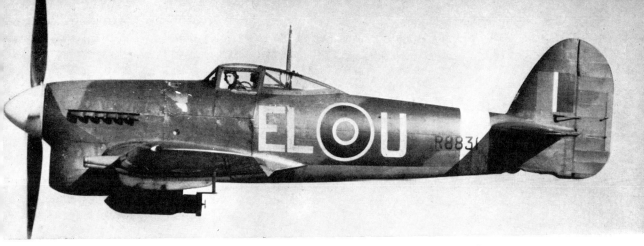

A Hawker Typhoon IB with underwing bomb load and early cockpit hood.

THE HAWKER TYPHOON AND TEMPEST

It is an accepted maxim for successful aircraft development that future requirements should always be the principal concern of the chief designer and his project design team. The company which allows itself to become wholly preoccupied with the development of an established design may produce, as a result, an outstanding aeroplane, but the policy is a short-sighted one if no new prototype is following to consolidate this success. Thus, the fact that Sydney Camm, Hawker Aircraft's chief designer, was at work on a new fighter as a potential replacement for the Hurricane as early as 1937, when the first production aircraft of that type had still to fly, reflected no lack of confidence in the Hurricane's potentialities but the natural desire to ensure that its service successor would be a product of the same stable.

This massive new fighter, the heaviest and most powerful single-seat single-engined warplane envisaged at the time of its design, was to suffer a long gestatory period. It was to be pressed into operational service before it was fully developed and, in consequence, acquire a worse reputation among its pilots than that of any fighter preceding it. It was fated to be rarely employed in the interceptor role for which it was originally conceived. Yet, despite its vicissitudes, it was to blossom into one of the most formidable weapons evolved during the Second World War; a close-support fighter that was to turn the scales in many land battles and upset many conceptions of land warfare.

In January 1938, barely two months after the début of the first production Hurricane, Hawker Aircraft received details of specification F.18/37, calling for a large single-seat fighter offering a performance at least 20 per cent higher than that of the Hurricane and achieving this with the aid of one of two 24-cylinder engines in the 2,000 h.p. class then under development —the Napier Sabre "H" type and the Rolls-Royce Vulture "X" type. Sydney Camm had commenced investigating the possibilities of just such a fighter in March 1937, and had already roughed out a design built around the Napier Sabre engine and housing twelve 0.303-in. Browning guns with 400 r.p.g. in its 40-foot wings. At the proposal of the Air Ministry, Camm also prepared studies for an alernative version of his fighter powered by the Rolls-Royce Vulture engine, and increased the ammunition capacity of both machines to 500 r.p.g.

Further discussions over military loads and equipment followed, and revised tenders were submitted to

(Top) The first Tornado prototype (P5219) with ventral radiator bath, and (immediately above) the second Tornado prototype (P5224). (Below) The first prototype Typhoon (P5212).

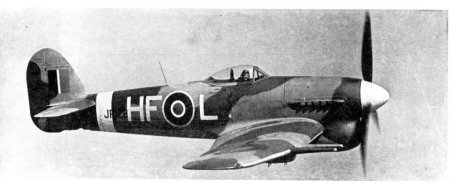

An early production Typhoon IA with solid rear cockpit fairing (above), and a late production Typhoon IB with "bubble" type canopy (below).

(Top) The Centaurus Tornado (HG641) in its original form, and (immediately above) after revision for high-speed flight testing. (Below) The sole production Tornado (R7936) fitted with de Havilland contraprops.

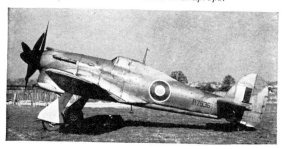

the Air Ministry at the beginning of 1938 for both the Type "N" and the Type "R", as the alternative Sabre- and Vulture-powered fighters had become known. These tenders were formally accepted on April 22, 1938, and four months later, on August 30, two prototypes of each fighter were ordered. Structurally both types were similar: the wings were all-metal, the front fuselage was of steel tubing, and the aft section consisted of a stressed-skin, flush-riveted monocoque—the first Hawker designs to employ this form of construction. Uniformity between the two fighters was, in fact, achieved to a remarkable degree, but the designs did differ in one important respect initially—the Vulture-powered fighter made use of a ventral radiator while the Sabre-driven machine had one of "chin" type.

Throughout 1938 construction of the two massive fighters proceeded in parallel, and work progressed simultaneously on the preparation of production drawings. As a result of the slightly more advanced development status of the Vulture engine which had been designed along more conventional lines than the Sabre, the Type "R" was the first of the two fighters into the air, flying in October 1939. Named appropriately enough Tornado, the initial flight trials of the prototype were promising, and a production order for 1,000 Tornados was placed at the beginning of November, it being proposed that the new fighter should be built both by Hawker and by A. V. Roe at Woodford. However, the flight test programme soon began to run into trouble. Compressibility effects, about which little was known at that time, began to manifest themselves, and it was decided that the ventral radiator bath was unsuitable for the speeds approaching 400 m.p.h. that were being achieved for the first time. The radiator was, therefore, moved forward to the nose, a position already selected for that of the Type "N", by now dubbed Typhoon; but the first prototype Tornado (P5219) only flew long enough to indicate the beneficial results of the change before it was totally destroyed.

Meanwhile, on December 30, 1939, the first Napier Sabre engine had been delivered to Hawker Aircraft, and the first prototype Typhoon (P5212) emerged from the experimental shop to fly on February 24, 1940. It too became the subject of a quantity production order which, it was planned, should become the responsibility of Gloster Aircraft, whose assembly lines were emptying of Gladiator biplanes and whose design office was already immersed in the development

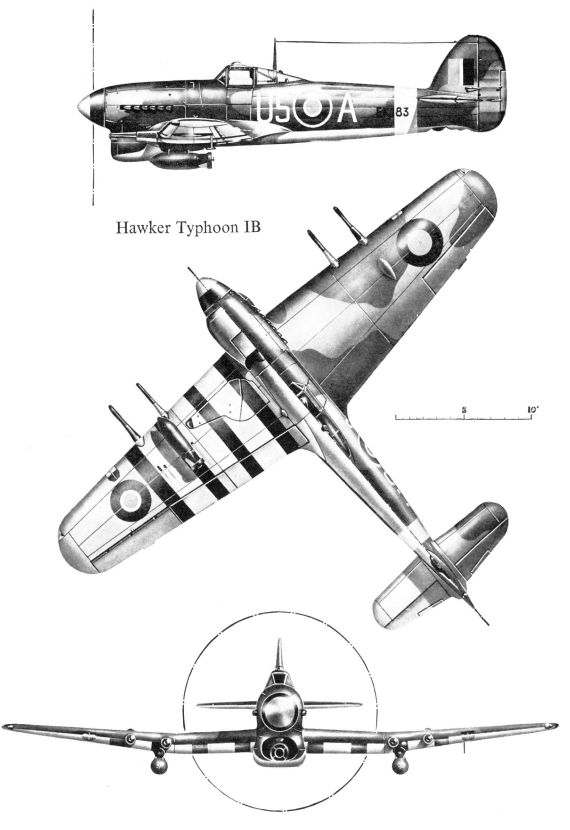

Hawker Typhoon IB

5   10'

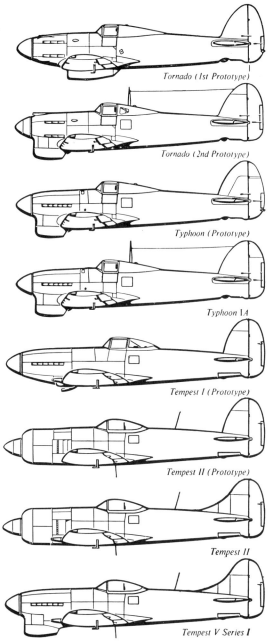

Tornado (1st Prototype)

Tornado (2nd Prototype)

Typhoon (Prototype)

Typhoon IA

Tempest I (Prototype)

Tempest II (Prototype)

Tempest II

Tempest V Series I

engine was fitted so close to the leading edge of the wing that severe vibration was experienced as the slipstream buffeted the thick wing roots. On an early test flight the stressed-skin covering began to tear away from its rivets, and the Typhoon's pilot, Philip G. Lucas, only just succeeded in bringing the prototype in to a landing.

Apart from structural teething troubles, the Sabre engine, although a compact and exquisite power plant, called for a considerable amount of development, and it was perhaps fortunate for the future of the Typhoon that, in May 1940, the grave war situation led to the cancellation of all priority for Typhoon and Tornado development in order to allow every effort to be put into the production of sorely needed Hurricanes. Design development was allowed to continue, however, and during 1940 three alternative engine installations were proposed for the Tornado— the Fairey Monarch, the Wright Duplex Cyclone, and the Bristol Centaurus—and experimental drawings for the Centaurus installation were completed. Development on the Typhoon included the design of a modified wing containing two 20-mm. Hispano cannon in place of the six 0.303-in. Brownings, the construction of an experimental set of wings containing a total of six cannon, and the initiation of a design study of a Typhoon variant with thinner wings of reduced area and lower profile drag. This latter study was later to arouse interest at the Air Ministry and eventually result in the Tempest. However, by October 1940 enthusiasm had been revived and production of the Tornado and Typhoon reinstated, production deliveries of both being scheduled for the following year.

The Tornado weighed 8,200 lb. empty and 10,580 lb. loaded. Its maximum speed was 425 m.p.h. at 23,000 feet. A. V. Roe had prepared a production line at Woodford, and the first production Tornado (R7936) was delivered early in 1941. But this was fated to be the *only* production Tornado, for difficulties with the Vulture resulted in the decision to remove this power plant from the aero-engine development programme, this decision also cancelling production of the Tornado. However, in February 1941, Hawker's received a contract to convert a Tornado to take a Bristol Centaurus radial engine. Among the modifications required were a new centre fuselage and engine mounting. The new prototype (HG641) was assembled from Tornado production components and flown for the first time on October 23, 1941. The first Centaurus installation had an exhaust collector ring forward of the engine from which a single external exhaust stack pipe led back under the root of the port wing. This arrangement soon proved unsatisfactory, so the oil-cooler duct was enlarged and led forward to the nose, while twin exhaust pipes led back from the front collector ring through this fairing to eject under the belly of the fuselage. A level speed of 421 m.p.h. was attained with the Centaurus-Tornado, and this was slightly higher than that attainable by the Sabre-powered Typhoon, but the Typhoon airframe

of the first British turbojet-driven aircraft. Although, like those of the Tornado, the first flights of the Typhoon prototype indicated a promising fighter, the machine proving relatively easy to fly at high speeds, its low speed qualities left much to be desired, and it had a marked tendency to swing to starboard during take-off. The "X" form of the Tornado's Vulture engine had not permitted installation above the front spar as was the Typhoon's Sabre and, in consequence, the overall length of the former was 32 ft. 6 in. as compared with the 31 ft. 10 in. of the latter. Owing to the size and weight of the Sabre and the need to preserve c.g. balance, the Typhoon's could not be adapted to take the radial engine. The second prototype Tornado (P5224) had, in the meantime, been completed, and the sole production Tornado (R7936) later played a useful role as a test-bed for de Havilland and Rotol contraprops.

The first production Typhoon IA (R7082) with the 2,200 h.p. Sabre IIA engine was completed by Gloster and flown on May 26, 1941. Production of this version, with its twelve Browning guns, was in limited quantity, and those built were used principally for the development of operational techniques. But the cannon-armed Typhoon IB was following closely on the heels of the Mark IA, and the Air Ministry was pressing for its rapid service introduction to counter the new Focke-Wulf Fw 190. Nos. 56 and 609 Squadrons based at Duxford began to receive their Typhoons in September 1941, before the fighter was fully developed, and these squadrons were forced to take on part of the onus of unearthing the new machine's numerous faults.

The decision to use the Typhoon before it was adequately developed for operational use was ultimately justified by the results, but the price of its premature introduction was high. In the first nine months of its service life far more Typhoons were lost through structural or engine troubles than were lost in combat, and between July and September 1942 it was estimated that at least one Typhoon failed to return from each sortie owing to one or other of its defects. Trouble was experienced in power dives—a structural failure in the tail assembly sometimes resulted in this component parting company with the rest of the airframe. In fact, during the Dieppe operations in August 1942, when the first official mention of the Typhoon was made, fighters of this type bounced a formation of Fw 190s south of Le Tréport, diving out of the sun and damaging three of the German fighters, but two of the Typhoons did not pull out of their dive owing to structural failures in their tail assemblies.

Despite this inauspicious start to its service career and the unenviable reputation that the Typhoon had gained, operations continued and the accident rate declined as the engine teething troubles were eradicated, although the tail failures took longer to solve, despite immediate strengthening and stiffening as soon as the trouble manifested itself. In November 1942 No. 609 Squadron, led by Wing-Commander Roland Beamont, was moved to Manston in an attempt to combat the near-daily tip-and-run raids which were being made by Fw 190s and could rarely be intercepted by Spitfires. The Typhoon enjoyed almost immediate success. The first two Messerschmitt Me 210 fighter-bombers to be destroyed over the British Isles fell to the guns of Typhoons, and during the last comparatively ambitious daylight raid by the Luftwaffe on London,

on January 20, 1943, five Fw 190s were destroyed by Typhoons.

On November 17, 1942, Wing-Commander Beamont had flown a Typhoon on its first night intrusion over Occupied France and, subsequently, the fighter was employed increasingly for offensive duties, strafing enemy airfields, ships and railway transport. The success of the Typhoon in the ground-attack role led to trials with two 250-lb. or two 500-lb. bombs which were carried on underwing racks. This load was later increased to two 1,000-lb. bombs, but the

(Top) The Tempest V prototype (HM595), and (immediately above) the Tempest V (SN354) experimentally fitted with 40-mm. cannon. (Below) The Tempest I prototype (HM599) with the Sabre IV engine.

A production Tempest V Series I (below) with the protruding Mk. II cannon.

(Top to bottom) A production Tempest II, the Typhoon (R8694) fitted with an annular radiator, and the Tempest (NV768) fitted with an annular radiator and a conventional spinner.

Typhoon was not to find its true element until it was adapted to carry airborne rocket projectiles—four under each wing. By D-Day, in June 1944, the R.A.F. had twenty-six operational squadrons of Typhoon IBs. Without its underwing load the Typhoon IB weighed 11,300 lb.; and with two 500-lb. bombs and the necessary racks, 12,400 lb. Maximum speed was 398 m.p.h. at 8,500 feet and 417 m.p.h. at 20,500 feet, and an altitude of 20,000 feet could be attained in 7.6 minutes. Between the prototype and production stages several design changes had been made. These included the re-design of the fin and rudder, the re-disposition of the wheel fairings and the introduction of a clear-view fairing behind the cockpit. On the first few Typhoon IAs the solid rear fairing was retained; later a transparent fairing was fitted, but this was abandoned in favour of the first sliding "bubble" hood to be used by an operational fighter.

The Typhoon IB, by now affectionately known as the "Tiffy", distinguished itself particularly in the Battle of Normandy, where it decimated a large concentration of armour ahead of Avranches, disposing of no fewer than 137 tanks, and opening the way for the liberation of France and Belgium. For use in the tactical reconnaissance role, the Typhoon F.R.IB was developed early in 1945. In this version the two inboard cannon were removed and three F.24 cameras were carried in their place. One Typhoon was also converted as a prototype night-fighter, with A.I. equipment, special night-flying cockpit and other modifications. Production of the Typhoon, which was entirely the responsibility of Gloster Aircraft, totalled 3,330 machines.

Work had been going on in the Hawker design office since 1940 on the development of a new thin wing section. It had already been established that the N.A.C.A.22-series wing section employed by the Typhoon was entirely satisfactory at speeds in the vicinity of 400 m.p.h. but encountered compressibility effects at higher speeds. In dives approaching 500 m.p.h a very sudden and sharp increase in drag was experienced, accompanied by a change in the aerodynamic characteristics of the fighter, which affected the pitching moment and rendered the machine nose-heavy. No actual design work on the new wing was begun until September 1941, and the wing section eventually adopted for development had its point of maximum thickness at 37.5% of the chord. The thickness/cord ratio was 14.5% at the root and 10% at the tip, giving a wing five inches thinner at the root than that of the Typhoon.

This thin wing could not contain a comparable quantity of fuel to that housed by the Typhoon's wing, so a large fuselage tank had to be adopted. This necessitated the introduction of an additional fuselage bay, increasing the overall length by twenty-one inches forward of the c.g. This added length found its inevitable compensation after initial prototype trials in a larger fin and tailplane. The wing area was also increased, and an elliptical planform was adopted, presenting a chord sufficient to permit the four 20-mm. Hispano cannon to be almost completely buried in the wing. All these modifications added up to a radically changed Typhoon, but it was as the Typhoon II that two prototypes were ordered in November 1941. However, in the middle of the following year the name Tempest was adopted. Alternative installations of the Sabre engine were designed for these prototypes; the first (HM595) had a Sabre II and a front radiator similar to that of the standard Typhoon, while the second (HM599) had a Sabre IV engine and wing leading-edge radiators.

Piloted by Philip Lucas, the first prototype Tempest was flown on September 2, 1942, but prior to this, in February 1942, a production order had been placed and the first production machine flew in June 1943 with Bill Humble at the controls. During flight trials the first Tempest prototype had exceeded 477 m.p.h. in level flight, and the first production model was essentially similar to the first prototype with the chin-type radiator. This was designated Tempest V, and the initial production batch, the Series I, had Mk. II cannon which projected slightly ahead of the wing leading edge, but the Series II had the short-barrelled Mk. V cannon which did not project, and also featured a detachable rear fuselage, small-diameter wheels and a rudder spring tab. Powered by a 2,420 h.p. Sabre IIB engine, the Tempest V attained a maximum speed of 435 m.p.h. at 17,000 feet. The

820-mile range of the Tempest V in clean condition was an appreciable improvement over that of the Typhoon, and was due not only to the small additional quantity of fuel carried but to the aerodynamic refinement of the later machine which permitted a higher cruising speed for the same power.

The first squadrons to be equipped with Tempest Vs were Nos. 3 and 486 at Newchurch, Dungeness, the first of these receiving its equipment early in 1944. By May five Tempest Vs had been lost due to engine failure, and this was discovered to be due to an over-speeding of the airscrew, resulting in an uncontrollable increase in engine revolutions, the failure of the bearings and the collapse of the oil system. In June modified airscrews were fitted which solved the problem, and two days after the invasion of the Continent, on June 8, 1944, the Tempests met enemy aircraft in combat for the first time, destroying three Bf 109G fighters without loss to themselves. On June 13 the first flying bombs were launched against England, and the Tempest, being the fastest low-medium altitude fighter in service with the R.A.F., became the mainstay of Britain's fighter defence against the pilotless missiles, destroying 638 of these weapons by the beginning of September. The Tempest V was also employed on the Continent for train-busting and ground-attack duties.

Meanwhile the second prototype (HM599), designated Tempest I, had proved sufficiently promising for production plans to be initiated. In the light of experience gained with the Centaurus-powered Tornado and the suitability of the Tempest fuselage for the radial engine, a Centaurus version of the Tempest was also initiated as the Mark II, and production drawings were prepared in parallel with those of the Mark I. In the event, the Tempest I was later abandoned while the Mark II was allowed to proceed to the production stage following the successful flight trials with the prototype, LA602, which commenced on June 28, 1943. The first production Tempest II flew fifteen months later, but the first unit, No. 54 Squadron, was not equipped with this fighter until November 1945, and was thus too late to participate in the war. The Tempest II was powered by the 2,500 h.p. Bristol Centaurus V or VI eighteen-cylinder, air-cooled, two-row radial, and attained a maximum speed of 440 m.p.h. at 15,900 feet and 406 m.p.h. at sea-level. Its range on internal fuel was 775 miles and initial climb rate was 4,520 ft./min.

Schemes for the utilization of the Griffon IIB and the Griffon 61 engines accounted respectively for the Tempest III and Tempest IV designations, neither passing the project stage. Nor did an alternative armament proposal based on the use of 0.5-in. machine-guns. The final Tempest variant was the Mark VI, which, appearing in 1945, was powered by the 2,700 h.p. Sabre VA engine and, except in having small intake ducts in the wing roots, was outwardly indistinguishable from the Tempest V. By and large, both the Typhoon and Tempest escaped the fate of so many aeroplanes of being used as test-beds for a variety of experiments. The Typhoon was designed in a naval fighter variant to meet the requirements of specification N.11/40, and one prototype was converted to this standard under the Hawker project designation P.1009. Another Typhoon modification, the P.1010, was to have had leading-edge radiators and a turbo-blower, but work on this was not proceeded with.

As part of their engine development programme, Napier's designed an annular cowling for the Sabre to replace the familiar chin-type radiator bath. The first such installation was on a Typhoon IB (R8694), but most of the development was undertaken with a Tempest V (NV768) which flew with several different types of annular radiator and hollow spinner. Another experimental Tempest V (SN354) had a 40-mm. gun under each wing in a long fairing.

As the Typhoon's immaturity faded it achieved widespread acclaim as a "rocketeer", being transformed from a fighter of dubious reliability into one of the Allies' most potent weapons. Likewise, its progressive development, the Tempest, gained for itself a place in the history of the air war for its part in reducing the depredations of the flying bombs against England.

Hawker Tempest F.Mk.V Series II

Dimensions :	Span, 41 ft. 0 in. ; length, 33 ft. 8 in. ; height, 16 ft. 1 in. ; wing area, 302 sq. ft.
Armament :	Four 20-mm. Hispano Mk. V cannon with 150 rounds per gun, and eight 60-lb. rocket projectiles or two 1,000-lb. bombs.
Power Plant :	One Napier Sabre IIB 24-cylinder, liquid-cooled, horizontal-H engine providing 2,420 h.p. at 3,850 r.p.m. at sea-level, and 2,045 h.p. at 13,750 ft.
Weights :	Empty, 9,250 lb. ; loaded, 11,400 lb. ; maximum, 13,500 lb.
Performance :	Maximum speed, 435 m.p.h. at 17,000 ft., 416 m.p.h. at 4,600 ft., 392 m.p.h. at sea-level ; maximum cruising speed, 391 m.p.h. at 18,800 ft. ; initial climb rate, 4,700 ft./min. ; time to 10,000 ft., 2.7 min. ; time to 20,000 ft., 6.1 min. ; service ceiling, 36,000 ft. ; range at 210 m.p.h. at 5,000 ft., (160 Imp. gal.) 820 miles, (250 Imp. gal.) 1,300 miles.

The final Tempest variant, the Mk VI, powered by a Napier Sabre VA.

The prototype Thunderbolt, the XP-47B, which was flown for the first time on May 6, 1941.

THE REPUBLIC THUNDERBOLT

When, in January 1943, the U.S.A.A.F.'s 56th Fighter Group arrived in the United Kingdom with its massive Republic P-47 Thunderbolts, R.A.F. fighter pilots banteringly suggested that their American colleagues would be able to take evasive action when attacked by undoing their harnesses and dodging about the fuselages of their huge mounts. The Thunderbolt was certainly big. In fact it was the largest and heaviest single-engined single-seat fighter ever built! But sheer size was not to prove detrimental to the Thunderbolt's subsequent operational career. It was to undertake 546,000 combat sorties between March 1943 and August 1945, and only 0.7 per cent of the fighters of this type despatched against the enemy were to be lost in combat.

The story of the Thunderbolt began in June 1940 when, realizing the deficiencies of U.S.A.A.F. fighter equipment, new requirements were formulated at a meeting at Wright Field. Among the companies consulted with regard to the new fighter specification was the young Republic Aviation Corporation, which possessed an invaluable background of fighter design experience inherited from its predecessor, the Seversky Aircraft Corporation. Republic's chief engineer, Alexander Kartveli, who, like his former chief, Major

Alexander P. Seversky, was of Russian extraction, had already supplied his stubby little P-35 to the U.S. Army, and his company held contracts for limited production of the P-43 Lancer, which, unlike other U.S. fighters, had an excellent high-altitude performance. However, the Lancer did not meet the new performance requirements, and neither did the Republic P-44 Rocket, a prototype of which was actually under construction at Republic's Farmingdale plant. Nevertheless the legacy of experience gained with these fighters was to provide an invaluable background for the evolution of a new machine that *did* fulfil the performance specified.

At that time Kartveli had a new fighter on the drawing-boards which had been designated XP-47. Conforming with the official policy prevailing at the time of its conception, the fighter was a relatively lightweight machine, designed around a 1,150 h.p. Allison V-1710-39 liquid-cooled Vee-twelve engine and carrying an armament of two 0.5-in. machine-guns. But the estimated performance of the fighter project fell far short of what was now considered to be essential in the U.S.A.A.F.'s future fighter. Kartveli therefore abandoned the Allison-engined fighter and also scrapped the semi-completed prototype of the P-44 in order to concentrate all resources on the development of a radically different fighter.

The most powerful engine available was the new 2,000 h.p. Pratt and Whitney Double Wasp eighteen-cylinder two-row radial, and without such power as this Kartveli could see no way of meeting the performance and load-carrying demands being made by the U.S.A.A.F. From an engineering standpoint, the requirements presented some enormous problems, but far more problems were presented by the engine. The first

A P-47B Thunderbolt (41-5931), the first production model which entered service with the 56th Fighter Group in November 1942.

The P-47D-11-RE Thunderbolt (42-75568) with belly shackles for a 500-lb. bomb or drop-tank.

of these was the need for an efficient super-charging duct system that would offer the least interrupted airflow. Kartveli therefore adopted the unorthodox method of designing this feature first and then building up the fuselage around it; the large turbo-supercharger was stowed internally in the rear fuselage, with the large intake for the air duct mounted under the engine, together with the oil coolers. Exhaust gases were piped back separately to the turbine and expelled through a waste gate in the bottom of the fuselage, and ducted air was fed to the centrifugal impeller and returned, via an intercooler, to the engine under pressure. Surprisingly, all this ducting of gases under temperature and pressure did not prove very vulnerable in combat, for the fighter was to become renowned for its ability to absorb battle damage and return home.

The conventional three-bladed airscrew could not efficiently utilize the power of the new engine and a four-bladed airscrew was adopted. Although this airscrew was an admirable solution to the power gearing of the engine, there remained the problem of providing sufficient ground clearance for its 12-foot diameter. If a conventional undercarriage were to be employed its suspension would have been too far outboard to permit the wing installation of the guns and ammunition requested by the U.S.A.A.F., and therefore Republic had to design a telescopic landing gear which was nine inches shorter when retracted than when extended. Numerous other problems were to be faced in absorbing the loads and stresses which would be imposed when a battery of eight 0.5-in. guns (a phenomenally heavy armament for that time) was fired simultaneously, and in providing the necessary tankage for the quantities of fuel stipulated to make the machine the first true single-engined strategic fighter. Thus, it was only to be expected that when the first prototype, the

XP-47B Thunderbolt, made its first flight, on May 6, 1941, it dwarfed not only its pilots but all previous fighters and, with a loaded weight of 12,086 lb., turned the scales at more than twice the weight of most of its contemporaries. Its 2,000 h.p. XR-2800-21 engine gave it a maximum speed of 412 m.p.h.

To increase the tempo of flight development of the XP-47B such leading test pilots as Colonel Ira C. Eaker were employed, and at one time it was hoped that the design could benefit from combat testing with the R.A.F. in the Middle East. Production difficulties caused General "Hap" Arnold to notify the British Air Ministry, in September 1941, that it was considered inadvisable to do this until various teething troubles were eradicated, and an optimistic estimate of May 1942 was established as a target date for the Thunderbolt to be combat ready. This was eventually to prove almost a year out. Numerous problems soon presented themselves as the XP-47B test programme advanced. At altitudes above 30,000 feet ailerons "snatched and froze", the cockpit canopy could not be opened and control loads became excessive. Blunt-nosed ailerons, a jettisonable canopy and all-metal control surfaces were eventually to be fitted to resolve these problems, and balanced trim tabs were adopted to reduce rudder pedal loads.

(Immediately below) A P-47C-2-RE (41-6245) with lengthened fuselage, and (bottom) a P-47D-1-RE (42-7922) with identification stripes.

THE REPUBLIC THUNDERBOLT

Production commenced in the spring of 1942 with the P-47B, the first being delivered some eight months after the prototype had made its début. The P-47B differed from the prototype only in having a sliding hood in place of the hinged canopy, a re-designed aerial and a production R-2800-21 engine, but the addition of internal operational equipment had increased the gross weight by 1,270 lb. to 13,356 lb., although maximum level speed had been raised to 429 m.p.h. One hundred and seventy-one P-47B Thunderbolts were built, and the first unit to receive this fighter, the 56th Fighter Group, was equipped in November 1942. In January 1943 this group of three squadrons, plus the 78th Fighter Group which had been similarly equipped, joined the U.S. Eighth Air Force in the United Kingdom, where two months were spent in working up to operational standard.

The first tasks of the Thunderbolt, which began on April 8, 1943, were high-altitude escort duties and fighter sweeps in which the new aircraft acquitted itself well, despite the inexperience of its pilots. It was soon discovered that the heavy Thunderbolt could outdive any Luftwaffe, or, for that matter, Allied, fighter, providing a decisive method of breaking off combat when necessary, but at low and medium altitudes it could not match the rate of climb or manœuvrability of German fighters. One shortcoming, which was even more marked in other Allied fighters, was that of insufficient range to permit deep penetration into Germany, but means were already being sought to add to the P-47B's 307 U.S. gallons of internal fuel. At the time of the Thunderbolt's European début radial-engined single-seat fighters were a rarity, the only other such fighter operational in Europe being the Fw 190A. To prevent confusion between the two fighters of the opposing sides the engine cowlings of the Thunderbolts were painted white, and white bands were painted around the vertical and horizontal tail surfaces—an appropriate comment on recognition standards appertaining at that time, as it would seem impossible to mistake the sleek and beautifully-contoured German fighter for the portly Thunderbolt.

Towards the end of 1941 the P-47C was introduced on to the Farmingdale production line. The "C" had a slightly lengthened forward fuselage (which increased overall length from 35 ft. to 36 ft. 1 in.) and a new engine mounting, but more important were its special shackles to enable a 200 U.S. gallon ventral drop-tank to be carried. This greatly extended the Thunderbolt's radius of action, although the take-off weight had risen to 14,925 lb. Eighth Air Force strength was greatly reinforced by many of the 602 P-47Cs that were built, and deep penetrations by drop-tank-carrying Thunderbolts began in July 1943.

Production really got into its stride with the P-47D, which, in its early series, was similar to the previous model, except for the standardization of water injection for more prolonged combat power on the R-2800-21 or -59 engine, and more extensive armour protection for the pilot. The injection of water into

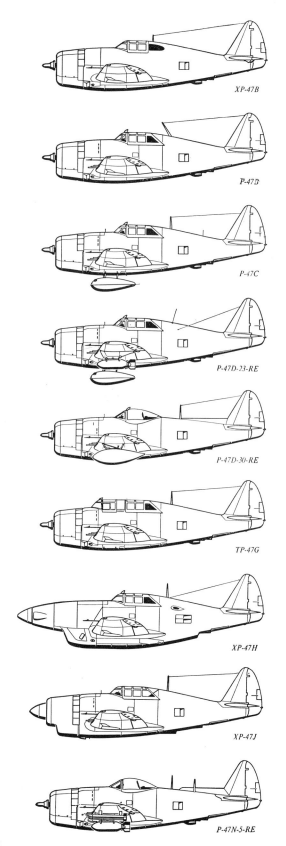

XP-47B

P-47B

P-47C

P-47D-23-RE

P-47D-30-RE

TP-47G

XP-47H

XP-47J

P-47N-5-RE

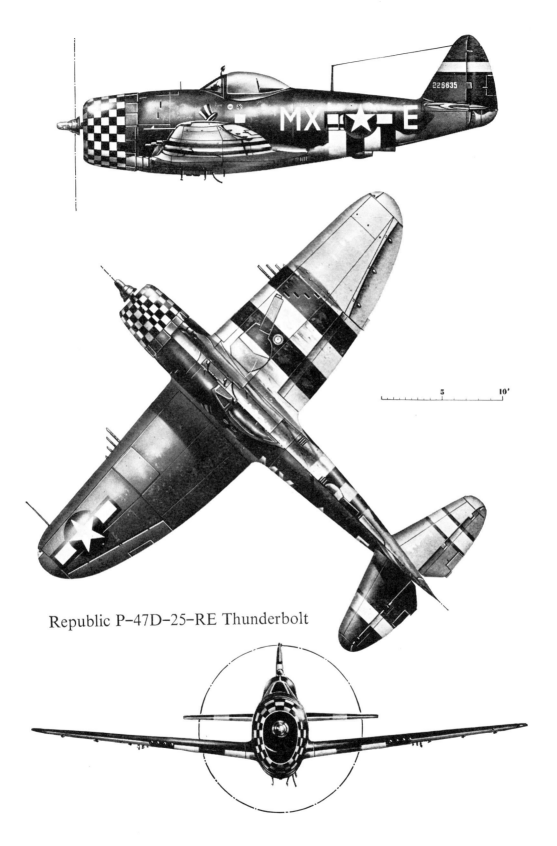

Republic P-47D-25-RE Thunderbolt

THE REPUBLIC THUNDERBOLT

(*Top to bottom*) *The pressurized XP-47E; a TP-47G converted from a P-47G-15-CU; the XP-47H modified from a P-47D-15-RE.*

the intake manifold enabled a war emergency rating of no less than 2,300 h.p. to be extracted from the Double Wasp engine at 27,000 feet, and the maximum speed was raised to 433 m.p.h. at 30,000 feet. Coupled with the formidable dive performance, this made the Thunderbolt ideal for top cover of the high-flying B-17 Fortress and B-24 Liberator formations, and an ascendancy of victories over opposing Luftwaffe fighters was soon established.

Several outstanding Thunderbolt pilots soon emerged in the European theatres of operations, of whom Lt.-Col. F. S. Gabreski was to become the highest scoring with thirty-one confirmed victories. Other Thunderbolt-mounted aces included Captain R. S. "Bob" Johnson with twenty-eight "kills", and

the well-known Colonel H. "Pop" Zemke with some twenty enemy aircraft to his credit. Perhaps the most outstanding tribute to this aircraft's ability to absorb punishment as well as hand it out is the fact that all ten of the leading Thunderbolt aces survived the war.

The P-47D was the first version of the Thunderbolt to serve with the U.S.A.A.F. in the Pacific, with the 348th Fighter Group, commencing with escort missions from Brisbane, Australia. Many strikes were made against long-distance targets in the area, for which the P-47D's additional fuel capacity provided by drop-tanks on underwing pylons proved invaluable. Such was the demand for the Thunderbolt at this stage of the war that in 1942 the Curtiss-Wright company, although heavily involved with P-40 production, was called in to build 354 P-47Ds, which were designated P-47G-1-CU to 15-CU. Two of these were subsequently modified as two-seat tandem trainers by the replacement of one fuselage fuel tank with an extra cockpit. The TP-47G, as the conversions were known, retained the full eight-gun armament of the standard single-seater.

Towards the end of 1943 the Eighth Air Force Thunderbolts began returning from escort missions "on the deck", strafing targets of opportunity with their unused ammunition, and their success led to the adaptation of the P-47 for what was to become perhaps its most successful role—that of a fighter-bomber. The P-47D-6-RE to -11-RE and P-47G-10-CU to -15-CU had only belly shackles which could accommodate one 500-lb. bomb, but later series with underwing pylons were able to carry either two 1,000-lb. bombs, with suitable wing stiffening, three 500-lb. bombs, or a combination of bombs and fuel tanks. With a full ordnance load the number of rounds of ammunition for each of either six or eight 0.5-in. Browning machine-guns was reduced from the maximum of 425 to 267, but the firepower of one Thunderbolt remained tremendous. At about this time a number of Thunderbolts suffered engine failure over the Continent. It was discovered that, due to the weight of the bombs and drop-tanks added to that of the aircraft, the Thunderbolt built up terrific speeds during bombing attacks, causing a surge or vapour lock in the fuel

(*Below*) *A P-47D-25-RE (42-26635), the first Thunderbolt variant to be fitted with a "bubble" canopy.*

lines, the fuel pump being unable to meet the "g" loads imposed by the dive starved the engine.

Of the 3,963 P-47D-1-RE to -22-RE Thunderbolts produced, many went as new equipment to the tactical Ninth and Fifteenth U.S. Air Forces in the United Kingdom and Italy, doing invaluable work against ground targets. Meanwhile Thunderbolts continued long-range escort duties in Europe and the Far East, eventually reaching as far as Berlin from bases in the U.K. With the introduction of the P-47D-20-RE, "universal" wing and fuselage mountings were fitted for various combinations of up to 2,500 lb. of bombs, two 150-gallon tanks and one 75-gallon tank and, later, rocket projectiles in a tube cluster. Paddle-bladed air-screws of increased diameter were fitted to absorb the full war emergency power of the R-2800-59 engine, increasing the high-altitude climb rate by 400 ft./min., and a longer tailwheel leg was fitted to increase ground clearance with a full bomb load. Three hundred and forty early series P-47Ds were supplied to the R.A.F. as Thunderbolt F.Is, serving with Nos. 5, 34, 113, 123 and 135 Squadrons, principally in the Far East.

From the extensive combat experience gained with the Thunderbolt emerged the fact that a 20° blind spot existed to the rear because of the fuselage decking. One P-47D was therefore modified by cutting down the top of the rear fuselage and fitting the "bubble" type cockpit hood of a Hawker Typhoon, which had been the first fighter so fitted. The modified aircraft was known as the XP-47K, and when the "bubble" hood was introduced on to the Thunderbolt assembly lines, by this time increased by an additional Republic plant at Evansville, the new series became the P-47D-25-RE. With the R-2800-59 or -63 engine, this series also had stronger belly shackles with a capacity for a 110-gallon tank which, with the 270-gallon main fuselage tank and two 150-gallon underwing tanks, brought the total fuel load to 780 U.S. gallons.

In all, no fewer than 12,602 P-47Ds of various series were built—almost undoubtedly the largest production quantity of one sub-type of any fighter. From the P-47D-27-RE onwards the loss of aft keel surface occasioned by the "bubble" canopy installation was rectified by the addition of a dorsal fin which success-

(Top to bottom) The XP-47J, the fastest Thunderbolt; the XP-47K modified from a P-47D to test "bubble" canopy; the second YP-47M, later converted as XP-47N.

fully restored stability. Underwing zero-length launching stubs for a total of ten 5-in. HVAR missiles and blunt-nosed ailerons were also fitted. The high diving speeds attained in combat by the Thunderbolt had run into the edge of compressibility, and the new ailerons, together with an electric dive recovery flap on the under surfaces of each wing, were short-term measures to improve control when shock-waves formed on ailerons and elevators.

During 1944 the Thunderbolt became operational in all active war theatres, excepting Alaska, and served with the Free French and Russian forces as well as with the U.S.A.A.F. and R.A.F. The P-47D was primarily employed on long-range ground-attack missions, bombing and strafing communications,

(Below) A P-47N-1-RE (44-88119), a version of the Thunderbolt intended specifically for Pacific operations.

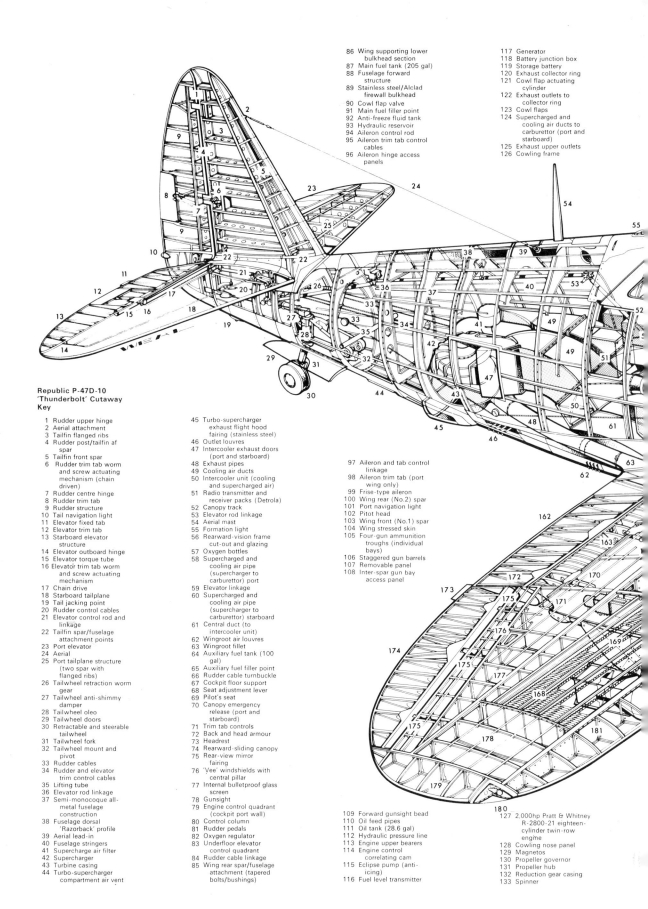

86 Wing supporting lower bulkhead section
87 Main fuel tank (205 gal)
88 Fuselage forward structure
89 Stainless steel/Alclad firewall bulkhead
90 Cowl flap valve
91 Main fuel filler point
92 Anti-freeze fluid tank
93 Hydraulic reservoir
94 Aileron control rod
95 Aileron trim tab control cables
96 Aileron hinge access panels

117 Generator
118 Battery junction box
119 Storage battery
120 Exhaust collector ring
121 Cowl flap actuating cylinder
122 Exhaust outlets to collector ring
123 Cowl flaps
124 Supercharged and cooling air ducts to carburettor (port and starboard)
125 Exhaust upper outlets
126 Cowling frame

Republic P-47D-10 'Thunderbolt' Cutaway Key

1 Rudder upper hinge
2 Aerial attachment
3 Tailfin flanged ribs
4 Rudder post/tailfin af spar
5 Tailfin front spar
6 Rudder trim tab worm and screw actuating mechanism (chain driven)
7 Rudder centre hinge
8 Rudder trim tab
9 Rudder structure
10 Tail navigation light
11 Elevator fixed tab
12 Elevator trim tab
13 Starboard elevator structure
14 Elevator outboard hinge
15 Elevator torque tube
16 Elevator trim tab worm and screw actuating mechanism
17 Chain drive
18 Starboard tailplane
19 Tail jacking point
20 Rudder control cables
21 Elevator control rod and linkage
22 Tailfin spar/fuselage attachment points
23 Port elevator
24 Aerial
25 Port tailplane structure (two spar with flanged ribs)
26 Tailwheel retraction worm gear
27 Tailwheel anti-shimmy damper
28 Tailwheel oleo
29 Tailwheel doors
30 Retractable and steerable tailwheel
31 Tailwheel fork
32 Tailwheel mount and pivot
33 Rudder cables
34 Rudder and elevator trim control cables
35 Lifting tube
36 Elevator rod linkage
37 Semi-monocoque all-metal fuselage construction
38 Fuselage dorsal 'Razorback' profile
39 Aerial lead-in
40 Fuselage stringers
41 Supercharge air filter
42 Supercharger
43 Turbine casing
44 Turbo-supercharger compartment air vent

45 Turbo-supercharger exhaust flight hood fairing (stainless steel)
46 Outlet louvres
47 Intercooler exhaust doors (port and starboard)
48 Exhaust pipes
49 Cooling air ducts
50 Intercooler unit (cooling and supercharged air)
51 Radio transmitter and receiver packs (Detrola)
52 Canopy track
53 Elevator rod linkage
54 Aerial mast
55 Formation light
56 Rearward-vision frame cut-out and glazing
57 Oxygen bottles
58 Supercharged and cooling air pipe (supercharger to carburettor) port
59 Elevator linkage
60 Supercharged and cooling air pipe (supercharger to carburettor) starboard
61 Central duct (to intercooler unit)
62 Wingroot air louvres
63 Wingroot fillet
64 Auxiliary fuel tank (100 gal)
65 Auxiliary fuel filler point
66 Rudder cable turnbuckle
67 Cockpit floor support
68 Seat adjustment lever
69 Pilot's seat
70 Canopy emergency release (port and starboard)
71 Trim tab controls
72 Back and head armour
73 Headrest
74 Rearward-sliding canopy
75 Rear-view mirror fairing
76 'Vee' windshields with central pillar
77 Internal bulletproof glass screen
78 Gunsight
79 Engine control quadrant (cockpit port wall)
80 Control column
81 Rudder pedals
82 Oxygen regulator
83 Underfloor elevator control quadrant
84 Rudder cable linkage
85 Wing rear spar/fuselage attachment (tapered bolts/bushings)

97 Aileron and tab control linkage
98 Aileron trim tab (port wing only)
99 Frise-type aileron
100 Wing rear (No.2) spar
101 Port navigation light
102 Pitot head
103 Wing front (No.1) spar
104 Wing stressed skin
105 Four-gun ammunition troughs (individual bays)
106 Staggered gun barrels
107 Removable panel
108 Inter-spar gun bay access panel

109 Forward gunsight bead
110 Oil feed pipes
111 Oil tank (28.6 gal)
112 Hydraulic pressure line
113 Engine upper bearers
114 Engine control correlating cam
115 Eclipse pump (anti-icing)
116 Fuel level transmitter

127 2,000hp Pratt & Whitney R-2800-21 eighteen-cylinder twin-row engme
128 Cowling nose panel
129 Magnetos
130 Propeller governor
131 Propeller hub
132 Reduction gear casing
133 Spinner

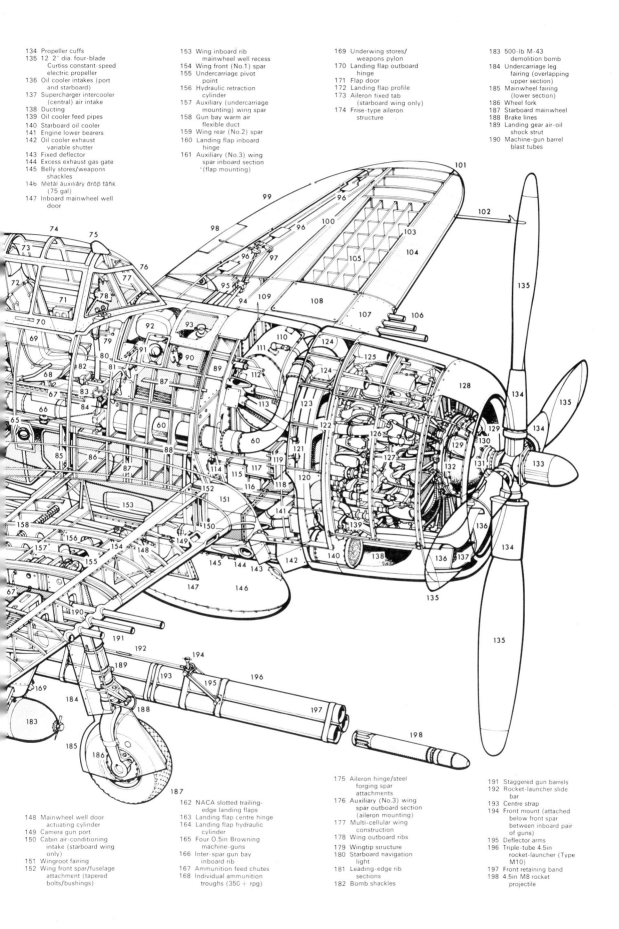

134 Propeller cuffs
135 12·2" dia. four-blade Curtiss constant-speed electric propeller
136 Oil cooler intakes (port and starboard)
137 Supercharger intercooler (central) air intake
138 Ducting
139 Oil cooler feed pipes
140 Starboard oil cooler
141 Engine lower bearers
142 Oil cooler exhaust variable shutter
143 Fixed deflector
144 Excess exhaust gas gate
145 Belly stores/weapons shackles
146 Metal auxiliary drop tank (75 gal)
147 Inboard mainwheel well door

153 Wing inboard rib mainwheel well recess
154 Wing front (No.1) spar
155 Undercarriage pivot point
156 Hydraulic retraction cylinder
157 Auxiliary (undercarriage mounting) wing spar
158 Gun bay warm air flexible duct
159 Wing rear (No.2) spar
160 Landing flap inboard hinge
161 Auxiliary (No.3) wing spar inboard section (flap mounting)

169 Underwing stores/weapons pylon
170 Landing flap outboard hinge
171 Flap door
172 Landing flap profile
173 Aileron fixed tab (starboard wing only)
174 Frise-type aileron structure

183 500-lb M-43 demolition bomb
184 Undercarriage leg fairing (overlapping upper section)
185 Mainwheel fairing (lower section)
186 Wheel fork
187 Starboard mainwheel
188 Brake lines
189 Landing gear air-oil shock strut
190 Machine-gun barrel blast tubes

148 Mainwheel well door actuating cylinder
149 Camera gun port
150 Cabin air-conditioning intake (starboard wing only)
151 Wingroot fairing
152 Wing front spar/fuselage attachment (tapered bolts/bushings)

162 NACA slotted trailing-edge landing flaps
163 Landing flap centre hinge
164 Landing flap hydraulic cylinder
165 Four 0.5in Browning machine-guns
166 Inter-spar gun bay inboard rib
167 Ammunition feed chutes
168 Individual ammunition troughs (350 + rpg)

175 Aileron hinge/steel forging spar attachments
176 Auxiliary (No.3) wing spar outboard section (aileron mounting)
177 Multi-cellular wing construction
178 Wing outboard ribs
179 Wingtip structure
180 Starboard navigation light
181 Leading-edge rib sections
182 Bomb shackles

191 Staggered gun barrels
192 Rocket-launcher slide bar
193 Centre strap
194 Front mount (attached below front spar between inboard pair of guns)
195 Deflector arms
196 Triple-tube 4.5in rocket-launcher (Type M10)
197 Front retaining band
198 4.5in M8 rocket projectile

airfields, bridges and troop concentrations. From the United Kingdom, Ninth Air Force Thunderbolts did much to soften up Hitler's much-vaunted Atlantic Wall prior to D-Day, while in Burma R.A.F. and Tenth Air Force P-47Ds operated side by side in the Arakan campaign. Five hundred and ninety P-47D-25 and later series Thunderbolts were supplied to the R.A.F., by whom they were designated Thunderbolt F.B.II and operated by Nos. 30, 42, 60, 79, 81, 113, 131, 258, 261 and 615 Squadrons, again almost entirely in the Far East. Production of the P-47D continued throughout 1944, but with the introduction of the P-51 Mustang into the E.T.O. the majority of the Eighth Air Force Thunderbolt groups began to be re-equipped with the lighter aircraft for bomber escort. Nevertheless, although supplanted in the high-altitude escort role, the Thunderbolt continued to knock up an impressive number of "kills" against the Luftwaffe while engaged on its destructive ground-strafing career.

This emphasis on low-level operations resulted in the abandoning of the XP-47E, which had been adapted from the 171st production P-47B by the installation of a pressurized cockpit, Another 1943 prototype development which supplied some useful aerodynamic information before it was destroyed in an accident was the XP-47F—a P-47B with a laminar-flow wing. Two P-47D-14-REs were modified as flying test-beds for the 2,500 h.p. Chrysler XIV-2220-1 sixteen-cylinder inverted-Vee liquid-cooled engine, being re-designated XP-47H. The Chrysler engine conferred a speed of more than 490 m.p.h. on the Thunderbolt, but the fastest variant was the XP-47J, which achieved 504 m.p.h. in August 1944. It retained the 2,100 h.p. R-2800-61 engine, but this was very closely cowled and fan-cooled, and there was a separate ventral intake for the CH-5 turbo-supercharger. Only six Browning machine-guns were fitted in this *lighter* (13,350 lb.) variant which did not see production. One P-47D-20-RE with an R-2800-59 engine was modified by the installation of a larger fuselage fuel tank, becoming the sole XP-47L.

With the advent of the V-1 flying bomb and turbo-jet- and rocket-propelled fighters, a "sprint" version of the P-47 was produced for extra speed, fitted with the R-2800-57(C) engine, and the larger CH-4 turbo-blower developing a war emergency power, with water injection, of 2,800 h.p. at 32,500 feet. This variant was designated YP-47M, and the three Thunderbolts of this type produced proved the effectiveness of the additional power, which, with the removal of underwing racks, enabled a maximum speed of 470 m.p.h. to be attained at 30,000 feet at a weight of 14,700 lb. One hundred and thirty P-47M Thunderbolts were subsequently built and were operated mostly in France after D-Day.

At this stage Thunderbolts were occasionally being used for medium-altitude level bombing on the formation principle, carrying, it may be remarked, over half the normal bomb load of a four-engined B-17 Fortress. Using M.R.C.P. ground radar, a formation of Thunderbolts would be directed to a target, possibly hidden by ten-tenths cloud, and would release their bombs on a radio signal, usually with remarkable accuracy. During the first five months of 1945 Thunderbolts flew an average of 1,677 hours and dropped 541 tons of bombs per day. From D-Day to V-E Day, Thunderbolt ground-attack operations were claimed to have accounted for 86,000 railway coaches, 9,000 locomotives, 68,000 motor vehicles and 6,000 armoured vehicles in Germany alone.

The final production version of the Thunderbolt was the P-47N, which was produced expressly for operations in the Pacific theatre where the principal requirement was range. Using the P-47M fuselage with its 270- and 100-gallon fuel tanks, and the same engine, the P-47N had re-designed and strengthened wings of eighteen inches greater span and twenty-two square feet extra area to cater for the record gross weight of 20,450 lb. The wings housed internal tanks (two of 93-gallon capacity) for the first time, and with external tanks the maximum fuel load attained a formidable 1,266 gallons giving an ultimate range of 2,350 miles. The new wing incorporated larger ailerons and square-cut tips which increased the roll rate, and the P-47N coupled increased manœuvrability with a maximum speed of 460 m.p.h. at 30,000 feet. A strengthened undercarriage was needed to cope with the gross weight of the production model which had risen by 750 lb. to 21,200 lb. A total of 1,667 P-47N-1-RE to -25-RE Thunderbolts was built, while the Evansville plant completed a further 149 out of an order for 5,934 by V-J Day. The R-2800-77 engine was used in late production batches of the P-47N, and this fighter gave excellent service in the Pacific, particularly in escorting B-29 Superfortresses, flying with them all the way from Saipan to Japan, and on many other long over-water trips.

The Thunderbolt dropped 132,000 tons of bombs, expended over 135 million rounds of ammunition, 60,000 rockets and several thousand gallons of Napalm. The official figures also credit the Thunderbolt with the destruction of 4.6 enemy aircraft for each Thunderbolt lost in aerial combat. This effort required 1,934,000 flying hours and 204,504,000 gallons of fuel. Two-thirds of all Thunderbolts produced reached overseas combat commands, and 54 per cent of these were lost to enemy action and other causes—an interesting and typical attrition rate for a wartime fighter.

Republic P-47D-25-RE Thunderbolt

Dimensions : Span, 40 ft. 9 in. ; length, 36 ft. 1 in. ; height, 14 ft. 2 in. ; wing area, 300 sq. ft.

Armament : Six or eight 0.5-in. wing-mounted Browning machine-guns with 267 or 425 rounds per gun and up to 2,500 lb. of bombs or ten 5-in. HVAR missiles.

Power Plant : One Pratt and Whitney R-2800-59 Double Wasp eighteen-cylinder two-row radial engine developing 2,000 h.p. for take-off and 2,300 h.p. at 31,000 ft. with turbo-supercharging.

Weights : Empty, 10,700 lb. ; combat, 14,600 lb. ; maximum loaded, 17,500 lb.

Performance : Maximum speed, 429 m.p.h. at 30,000 ft., 406 m.p.h. at 20,000 ft., 375 m.p.h. at 10,000 ft., 350 m.p.h. at sea-level ; initial climb rate, 2,780 ft./min., 1,575 ft./min. at 30,000 ft. ; service ceiling, 40,000 ft. ; range, 950 miles at 10,000 ft.

A production Beaufighter IF night-fighter (T4638) in early night finish.

THE BRISTOL BEAUFIGHTER

Before the advent of the Second World War the multi-engined two-seat fighter had received sporadic attention in most countries, but as the fighter was envisaged primarily as a day interceptor, a task which could be fulfilled most effectively by the less expensive single-seat single-engined machine, little real effort was placed behind the development of the longer-ranging, heavier combat aircraft, except in Germany where the long-range strategic fighter received close attention from the mid-'thirties, resulting in the Bf 110. Britain's lack of long-range heavy fighters when the war started was a source of acute embarrassment to the R.A.F. Single-engined interceptors such as the Hurricane and Spitfire lacked the endurance for effective standing patrols, and it was soon discovered that the heavy long-range fighter would be invaluable to perform a wide variety of tasks. The result was a piece of true British improvisation—the Bristol Beaufighter, which entered service a year after the outbreak of war, at a time when it was most sorely needed.

The fact that a heavy twin-engined fighter such as the Beaufighter was available as soon as the late autumn of 1940 was largely due to the foresight and enterprise of the Bristol Aeroplane Company in envisaging the probable need for a high-performance long-range fighter capable of undertaking duties of a more aggressive nature than those foreseen by official specifications. At the end of 1938 L. G. Frise and his design team began the design of what was virtually a fighter variant of the Beaufort general reconnaissance and torpedo-bomber. The initial proposal was framed, as far as possible, to meet the requirements of specification F.11/37, and envisaged an aeroplane using a large proportion of Beaufort components, including the wings, tail assembly and undercarriage, a pair of Hercules radial engines and carrying a battery of four 20-mm. Hispano cannon. The economy of the proposal was of obvious appeal to the government, struggling to meet the vast requirements of a major rearmament programme, and, as the Type 156, four prototypes were ordered.

Little more than eight months after the design had been initiated, the first prototype of what had by now been named Beaufighter was complete and successfully flew for the first time on July 17, 1939, with Captain Uwins at the controls—exactly two weeks after a production contract for 300 machines had been placed to specification F.17/39. The Beaufighter prototype (R2052) had two two-speed supercharged Bristol Hercules radials which were mounted well ahead of the wing leading edges to avoid vibration. This necessitated cutting down on other weight forward of the c.g. and resulted in the Beaufighter's characteristic abbreviated fuselage nose. The main fuselage and the engine mountings were, in fact, the only entirely new components. The outer wings, including the ailerons, flaps and tanks; the whole of the retractable landing gear and hydraulic systems; and the aft section of the fuselage, complete with tailplane, elevators, fin, rudder and tailwheel, were identical to those of the Beaufort, while the centre section, with tanks and flaps, was similar apart from certain fittings. Official trials commenced at an all-up weight of 16,000 lb. after the first prototype's delivery to the R.A.F. on April 2, 1940, and a maximum speed of 335 m.p.h. was attained at 16,800 feet.

A second prototype (R2053), with detail changes and production Hercules II engines rated at 1,300 h.p. at 2,800 r.p.m. for take-off, had also been delivered to the R.A.F. by the end of April, but with full equipment all-up weight had crept up to 18,531 lb. and performance was disappointing, while little benefit was expected to result from the installation of the

The first prototype Beaufighter (R2052).

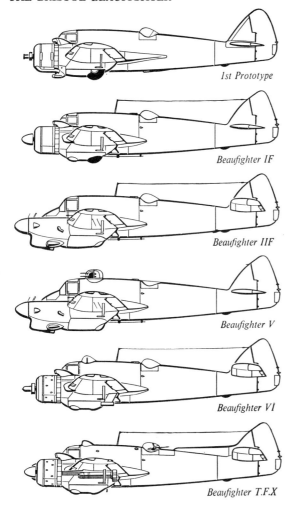

1st Prototype

Beaufighter IF

Beaufighter IIF

Beaufighter V

Beaufighter VI

Beaufighter T.F.X

Hercules III of 1,400 h.p. for take-off in production Beaufighters. However, greater advantages were anticipated from the installation of the Hercules VI, a version designed to take full advantage of 100-octane fuel, or the Rolls-Royce Griffon. Neither of these engines being immediately available for installation, the 1,500 h.p. Hercules XI—a modified III operating on 100-octane fuel—was selected to power the initial production Beaufighter Mk. I as an alternative to the Hercules III. In view of the demands being made on Hercules production by the Short Stirling bomber, an alternative Rolls-Royce Merlin-engined Beaufighter, the Mark II, was also ordered by the Air Ministry for production until the Hercules shadow factory achieved full output. Further attention was given in 1940 to the Type 158, a slim-fuselage version of the Beaufighter that had been first proposed in the closing weeks of 1938, and which was popularly referred to as the "sports model". Two versions of the Type 158 were proposed, the Beaufighter III with Hercules VI engines and the Beaufighter IV with Rolls-Royce Griffons, but neither version was in fact built.

With the Beaufighter I established in production at Filton, deliveries to the R.A.F. began on July 27,

1940, on which date five machines were handed over, another five following on August 3. The Beaufighter I carried an armament of four 20-mm. Hispano cannon mounted in the lower portion of the fuselage nose and six 0.303-in. Browning machine-guns in the wings and outboard of the oil-cooler ducts, two in the port wing and four in the starboard wing. The pilot was seated close up to the nose with an unrestricted forward view, although the view to either side was strictly limited by the bulk of the engine nacelles, and the observer was seated aft of the wings. The Beaufighter was the only aircraft in production for the R.A.F. which could carry the 1.5-metre A.I.Mk.IV radar without sacrificing duration or fire power and, consequently, the first Beaufighter Is had already been earmarked for the night-fighter role. Nos. 25 and 29 Squadrons each received a Beaufighter on September 2, 1940, and No. 29 Squadron became fully operational on Beaufighters on September 17, with No. 25 Squadron following on October 10. On November 11 the first Luftwaffe aircraft, a Junkers Ju 88A, fell to the guns of a Beaufighter.

The Beaufighter IF was soon bearing the brunt of the action against German night bombers. Weighing 20,800 lb. all-up, it attained a maximum speed of 323 m.p.h. at 15,000 feet, had a range of 1,500 miles at 194 m.p.h., an initial climb rate of 1,850 ft./min., and a service ceiling of 28,900 feet. Although the Beaufighter IF handled well it was tricky under certain conditions. There was a strong tendency to swing on take-off and the danger of flick rolling in the event of an engine cutting suddenly. On landing, the Beaufighter's large flap area pulled the aircraft up rapidly, but there was a tendency to veer from the straight which, if unchecked, resulted in a ground loop, the c.g. being so far aft. The first few Beaufighter Is were delivered without the wing-mounted machine-guns, and initially it was found that when the cannon were fired the recoil caused the nose to dip enough for the pilot to lose his target. The seriousness of this fault was such that thought was given to alternative armament and, with one pair of cannon and the wing-mounted machine-guns supplanted by a Boulton Paul turret containing four 0.303-in. guns and mounted just aft of the pilot's cockpit, the Beaufighter V was produced. Only two examples (R2274 and R2306) were completed, both being converted Merlin-engined Mark IIs, and these were used experimentally by No. 29 Squadron during the early months of 1942, but the installation of the turret drastically reduced performance, and the Beaufighter V was abandoned.

Three of the first production Beaufighters had been allocated to Rolls-Royce in 1939 when the Griffon had been considered as a prospective power plant, and these subsequently became the prototypes of the Beaufighter II. One, R2062, was destroyed before completion in an enemy raid on Hucknall on September 27, 1940, but the others, R2058 and R2061, were delivered with Merlin X engines, which provided 1,075 h.p. for take-off, in October and December 1940. These were followed on March 22, 1941, by the first

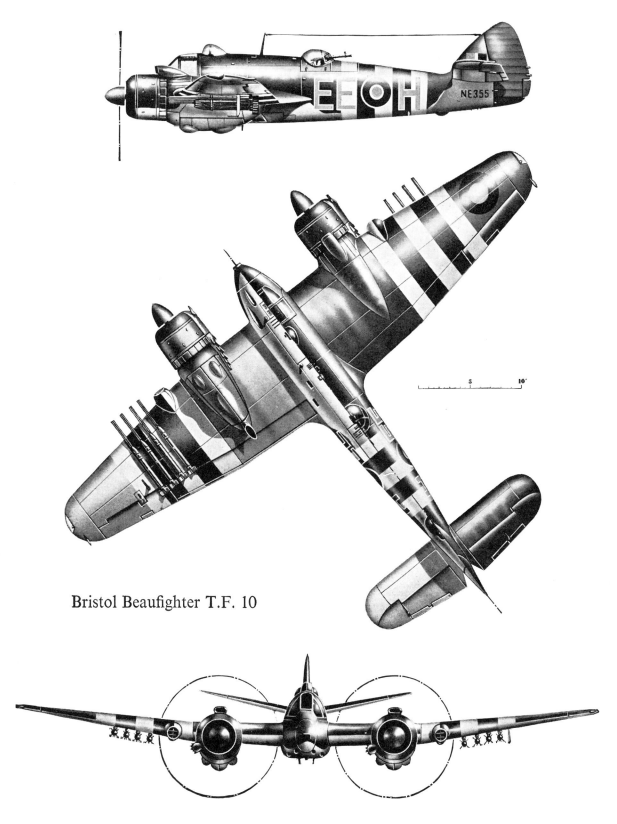

Bristol Beaufighter T.F. 10

(*Top, left*) *A Beaufighter IIF* (R2270) *with dihedral tailplane.* (*Top, right*) *A Beaufighter II* (T3032) *with dorsal-fin extension later adopted for the Mark X.* (*Below, left*) *A Beaufighter IIF* (R2402), *and* (*below, right*) *an experimental Beaufighter I* (R2268) *with twin fins and rudders.*

production Beaufighter II with 1,280 h.p. Merlin XX engines, 450 aircraft of this type being built. The reduction in drag resulting from the cleaner engine nacelles housing the Merlins improved performance slightly, but the reduced side area ahead of the c.g. made it rather unstable directionally. Some lack of stability had already been experienced on the early Beaufighter Is, and several modifications were made in attempts to overcome this fault. One Beaufighter I (R2268) was flown with a broad-chord tailplane and, later, twin fins and rudders. Eventually, however, the introduction of twelve degrees of dihedral on the tailplane was found to provide the answer, and this modification was adopted retrospectively and for all subsequent production aircraft.

To make possible a rapid build-up of Beaufighter production, arrangements were made for its manufacture at two factories in addition to Filton: a Bristol-operated shadow plant at Weston-super-Mare and the Fairey Aviation factory at Stockport. The first Beaufighter to be built by Fairey was flown on February 7, 1941, being followed by the first from Weston-super-Mare on the 20th of the same month. By this time production of the Hercules engine was also mounting rapidly, and Hercules VIs, which offered 1,615 h.p. for take-off, began to be available for Beaufighter installation. The Hercules VI was first tested in the Filton-built Beaufighter I (R2130) and in the third and fourth aircraft off the Weston-super-Mare production line, and with the new engines, and designated Beaufighter VI, the more powerful version supplanted the Marks I and II in production.

In the meantime numerous experiments were being made with Beaufighters. At Filton one was engaged on the flight development of the Youngmann-Fairey bellows-type dive brake which was operated by means of a venturi intake under each wing. Centimetric A.I.Mk.VII radar with its distinctive "thimble" nose was installed in Beaufighter I X7579, and the fourth prototype (R2055) was fitted with two 40-mm. cannon —a Vickers "S" to starboard and a Rolls-Royce

"BH" in the port side of the fuselage—being tested in this form at Dunfold during 1941. At the Rolls-Royce flight-test establishment at Hucknall the second Beaufighter II prototype (R2061) was fitted and flown with special cowlings designed for the Exe engine, and a production aircraft (T3177) was flown with Griffon IIB engines. Plans to improve the high-altitude performance of the Beaufighter by installing Griffon 61 or Hercules VIII engines did not materialize, however.

Simultaneously, new operational roles were being developed which were to lead to two distinct production varieties of each of the early Marks, depending on the equipment carried. The "F" suffix applied to Marks I, II and VI indicated the fighter role, while versions employed by Coastal Command for shipping strikes and the protection of coastal shipping bore the suffix "C". The Coastal Command variant was evolved during 1941 from experiments with two of the first production batch of Beaufighter Is. They were provided with special Coastal Command radio and navigation facilities, including a folding chart table in the cockpit above the cannon feeds. To exploit the Beaufighter's potentialities in more aggressive roles, No. 252 Squadron was formed in Coastal Command in the autumn of 1941. The first eighty Beaufighter ICs were produced at Filton for the use of Nos. 252 and 272 Squadrons, and subsequently the Stockport and Weston-super-Mare factories turned over completely to this variant. Adaptable for desert warfare, the first ICs had a 50 Imperial gallon Wellington tank on the fuselage floor, but the extra range needed was later gained by fitting new wing tanks as alternative installations to the machine-guns. Operating from the coasts of Norway to the Bay of Biscay, the Coastal Command Beaufighters became progressively more important, and, with desert equipment, they began to make their presence felt in the Western Desert.

By the beginning of 1942 the Beaufighter VI was beginning to supplant earlier Marks. Powered by the Hercules VI or XVI, this was the first type to be fitted with a 0.303-in. Vickers "K" gas-operated machine-

(Top, left) A Beaufighter VIC with experimental torpedo installation. (Top, right) A standard Beaufighter VIC. (Below, left) A Beaufighter VIF, and (below, right) one of the two Beaufighter Vs with dorsal turret.

gun in the observer's station. A 50-gallon fuel tank was fitted in the starboard wing gun bay and a 24-gallon tank in the port bay. Two 29-gallon tanks were also installed outboard of the engine nacelles. Various combinations of armament could be fitted to suit operational tactics, and two 500-lb. bombs could be slung underwing or, in lieu of the wing guns, eight rocket projectiles could be carried. Empty and loaded weights (the latter including a 500-lb. bomb load) were 14,875 lb. and 22,779 lb., maximum speed was 315 m.p.h. at 14,000 feet, range was 1,540 miles at 190 m.p.h., initial climb rate was 2,000 ft./min., and service ceiling was 26,000 feet. The Beaufighter VI was the first version of this aircraft to be used by the R.A.F. in India and Burma and the South-West Pacific, where, against the Japanese, it earned the grim nickname "Whispering Death". It was also the first Mark to equip U.S.A.A.F. night-fighter squadrons.

In March 1942 the Bristol Aeroplane Company proceeded with the detail design of a torpedo-carrying Beaufighter VIC, and in April the company gained official permission to produce a trial installation for the carriage of a 22.5-in. American or 18-in. British torpedo. This experimental machine (X8065) was flying by May 1942, and before it crashed, during torpedo-dropping trials at Gosport, the soundness of the scheme had been proven. Sixteen aircraft were therefore converted to equip a trial squadron which achieved its first operational success on April 4, 1943, when two enemy ships were sunk off Norway. The appearance of the fast torpedo-carrying Beau-fighter, which also combined the functions of reconnaissance and escort fighting, revolutionized air-sea warfare, and the success of the "Torbeau" resulted in the production of two new Marks for R.A.F. Coastal Command. These

were powered by a modified version of the Hercules VI engine having cropped impellers and the super-chargers locked in "M" ratio, with fully automatic car-burettors. These engines, designated Hercules XVII, gave 1,735 h.p. at 500 feet and were well suited to the low altitudes at which Coastal Command operated its Beaufighters. With these engines and equipped to carry a torpedo it was designated Beaufighter T.F.X, but without torpedo gear it was the Mark XIC.

The Beaufighter VII was the designation applied to an aircraft which was to be fitted with two Bristol Her-cules VIII engines with turbo-superchargers and driving four-blade airscrews, but this installation called for ex-tensive alterations to the standard production Beau-fighter and was abandoned while still on the drawing-board. Marks VIII and IX were numbers reserved for Beaufighters to be built in Australia but never allotted.

(Above) The Griffon-powered Beaufighter IIF, and (below) a Beaufighter I (X7579) with experimental "thimble" nose.

THE BRISTOL BEAUFIGHTER

The Beaufighter T.F.X was the final major production variant and passed through several important modification stages without any change in its Mark number. These included, in particular, the introduction of A.I.Mk.VIII radar in a "thimble" nose—this radar having been found suitable for ASV use—and a large dorsal fin (after a trial installation on a Beaufighter II, T3032) to give the required directional stability and linked with an increase in elevator area to improve longitudinal stability. Before deliveries of the Beaufighter X could begin, a batch of sixty Beaufighter VIs with Hercules XVI engines and provision for torpedo-carrying was built. These were designated Beaufighter VI (I.T.F.)—interim torpedo fighter—and were converted to Mark Xs when more Hercules XVII engines became available.

The last version of the Beaufighter to serve with R.A.F. Fighter Command was the Mark VIF. Many of these were fitted with A.I.Mk.VII or VIII in the "thimble" nose, the first such being used by Nos. 604 and 68 Squadrons. The Beaufighter VIF served in the Western Desert and Italy, as well as in the U.K.

During 1941–42 fifty-four Fairey-built Beaufighter ICs were supplied to the Royal Australian Air Force, and plans were prepared for the production of this aircraft in Australia. There was some initial indecision as to the type of engine to be used for Australian-built Beaufighters. The first proposal was for the use of Hercules XXVIs with Bendix carburettors. This version would have been otherwise similar to the Beaufighter VIC and designated Mark VII. As a safeguard against the possibility of delays in the delivery of adequate quantities of Hercules engines from Britain, one of the Fairey-built Beaufighter ICs (A.19-2) was fitted experimentally with two Wright Double-row Cyclone GR-2600-A5B engines. The larger diameter of the Cyclones necessitated the enlarging and lengthening of the nacelles, which were extended beyond the wing trailing edges. The Cyclone-Beaufighter was flown successfully, but by that time a final decision had been made in favour of the Hercules, and production commenced on a Beaufighter variant essentially similar to the T.F. Mark X. Designated Beaufighter 21, the Australian production model had four 0.5-in. guns in place of the six 0.303-in. guns in the wings. Provision was made for a Sperry auto-pilot, and Hercules XVIII engines were fitted—similar to the Hercules XVII but with both supercharger gears fully operational. The first Australian-built Beaufighter 21 was flown on May 26, 1944. The Beaufighter XX was similar but had Hercules XVII engines and was produced for R.N.Z.A.F. squadrons. A total of 364 machines had been built in Australia when Beaufighter production ceased there at the end of 1945. The R.A.A.F. squadrons flying Fairey-built Beaufighters were gradually re-equipped with Australian-built machines, and wreaked great havoc among the Japanese along the coast of New Guinea, in the Celebes and the Philippines.

A British-built version with Bendix carburettors and Hercules XXVII engines was planned as the Beaufighter XII. This was intended to have strengthened wings to carry a 1,000-lb. bomb outboard of each engine nacelle. This strengthened wing was, however, produced for the Beaufighter X. As the bomber version of the Beaufighter X was not ready in time, many existing Beaufighters were modified for fighter-bombing during the invasion of the European continent by Allied forces in 1944, carrying two 500-lb. bombs under the fuselage and a 250-lb. bomb beneath each wing.

When the last Beaufighter (SR919) left the Bristol Aeroplane Company's Weston-super-Mare works on September 21, 1945, a total of 5,562 aircraft of this type had been produced in the United Kingdom. Of these some 1,063 were Mark VIs and 2,231 were Mark Xs. During its operational career it had played a prime role in defeating the Luftwaffe's night "blitz" of 1940–41, and it had operated in every major campaign of the war, carrying out the last operational sortie of the European war, a strike against German shipping in the Skagerrak, and serving with distinction in the Pacific until the capitulation of Japan. The Beaufighter may have been the product of improvisation but it was a remarkably successful one.

Bristol Beaufighter T.F.X

Dimensions :	Span, 57 ft. 10 in. ; length, 41 ft. 4 in. ; height, 15 ft. 10 in. ; wing area, 451 sq. ft.
Power Plants :	Two Bristol Hercules XVII fourteen-cylinder two-row sleeve-valve radial engines rated at 1,725 h.p. at 2,900 r.p.m. for take-off and 1,395 h.p. at 2,400 r.p.m. at 1,500 ft.
Armament :	Four 20-mm. Hispano cannon in the fuselage nose and six 0.303-in. machine-guns in the wings and one 0.303-in. Vickers "K" or Browning gun in manually-operated dorsal position ; one 18-in. torpedo externally under fuselage. Eight rocket projectiles could be carried as alternative to the wing guns.
Weights :	Empty, 15,592 lb. ; disposable load, 9,808 lb. ; loaded, 25,400 lb.
Performance :	Maximum speed, 320 m.p.h. at 10,000 ft., 305 m.p.h. at sea-level ; initial climb rate (with torpedo), 1,600 ft./min. ; service ceiling (without torpedo), 19,000 ft. ; range (with torpedo and normal tankage), 1,400 miles, (with torpedo and long-range tanks), 1,750 miles.

(Left) A late production Beaufighter T.F.10, and (right) an Australian Beaufighter 21.

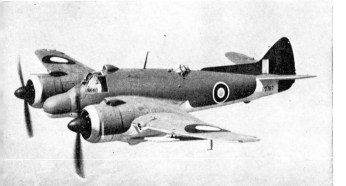

The photograph above depicts the Me 262V3 during the summer of 1942. This, the third prototype, was actually the first to fly solely on turbojet power. The photo on the right shows the second prototype, the Me 262V2. The first four prototypes carried the identification letters PC + UA, UB, UC and UD respectively.

THE MESSERSCHMITT ME 262

It is axiomatic that technical superiority can cancel out overwhelming numerical superiority, and the technical advances embodied by the Messerschmitt Me 262 were such that this one amazing aircraft could, late in the war, have regained for Germany something of the ascendancy in European skies enjoyed by the Luftwaffe during the war's earliest stages. Instead, the Me 262 became the symbol of the vacillation and irresolution with which Germany's leaders plagued their country's aircraft manufacturing programmes. Fear of risking political security by supporting the development of such a radical aircraft, a psychology engendered by the German system of rigid dictatorship, and belated recognition of this fighter's true potentialities resulted in the loss to Germany of a weapon that would undoubtedly have had a profound effect on the air war. Thus, the Me 262 is famed not for its operational exploits, although these were quite spectacular, but for the radical innovations that it first introduced to combat flying, for it was the first warplane employing the turbojet as the prime mover to achieve operational status.

The Me 262 was first envisaged in the autumn of 1938 when the German Air Ministry requested the Messerschmitt A.G. to design a suitable airframe to accommodate radically new powerplants, axial-flow turbojets which were in their preliminary development stages at the Junkers Flugzeug und Motorenwerke A.G. and the B.M.W. Flugmotorenbau G.m.b.H. Labelled "Projekt 1065", the preliminary design studies for the proposed aircraft were completed in June 1939, and the Messerschmitt A.G. was ordered to proceed with the construction of a mock-up. This mock-up was inspected by German Air Ministry officials, and on March 1, 1940, an order was placed for three prototype airframes which were to be powered by B.M.W. P.3302 turbojets—later to become known as the B.M.W. 109-003A—which were expected to be available for trial installations during the following summer. The first 109-003 turbojet was run in 1940, but the thrust obtained was only 570 pounds compared with a design figure of 1,500 pounds, and was obviously inadequate to meet the power requirements of the new fighter, which, in the meantime, had been allotted the type number Me 262. The alternative Junkers Jumo 109-004 turbojet offered no solution, for this unit did not commence bench running until November 1940 and had promptly encountered serious development troubles.

Messerschmitt proceeded with the construction of the three experimental airframes which were completed in April 1941. In the meantime the development of both the airframe and the turbojets with which they were to be powered had received very low priority ratings. General Ernst Udet considered the jet fighter to be superfluous to the Luftwaffe's requirements, believing that Germany would win the war with the conventional aircraft that she already had in production. These sentiments were echoed by Field-Marshal Milch, who openly questioned the value of even continuing experimental work. Nevertheless despite the very cool attitude towards the jet fighter evinced by both the Air Ministry and the Luftwaffe, the Messerschmitt design team retained their enthusiasm for the project and, as there was no likelihood of obtaining suitable turbojets for at least six months, the decision was made to adapt the first prototype airframe to take a 700 h.p. Junkers

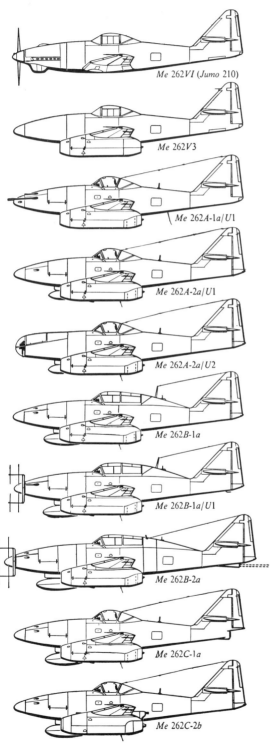

Me 262VI (Jumo 210)

Me 262V3

Me 262A-1a/U1

Me 262A-2a/U1

Me 262A-2a/U2

Me 262B-1a

Me 262B-1a/U1

Me 262B-2a

Me 262C-1a

Me 262C-2b

Jumo 210G piston engine in the fuselage nose in order to determine the flight characteristics of the airframe.

With the Jumo 210G engine installed, the first prototype, the Me 262V1, was flown for the first time on April 4, 1941 and, although seriously under-powered, a further six flights were made. On July 25 the Air Ministry decided to order a further five prototypes, but it was not until mid-November that the first turbojets were delivered to the Messerschmitt factory. These were two early B.M.W. 109-003 units each delivering 1,000 pounds of thrust. They were fitted to the Me 262V1 but, as a safety precaution, the nose-mounted piston engine was retained. The first flight test with these turbojets fitted was attempted on November 25, 1941, but the turbine blades, over-strained at take-off revolutions, broke off, and both turbojets failed. It was not until nearly eight months later that the first Jumo 109-004 turbojets arrived for installation. This engine was at that time giving some 1,850 pounds static thrust and had been success-fully flight tested beneath an Me 110. They were installed in the third prototype airframe, the Me 262V3, and the first flight was made on July 18, 1942, this being also the first flight of this fighter on jet power alone.

The obvious success of initial flight trials once the Jumo turbojets were installed increased the German Air Ministry's interest in the project, but after the chief test pilot of the Lufwaffe's experimental establishment at Rechlin had crashed, on August 11, 1942, while taking-off for his second flight test of the Me 262V3, official interest again cooled, and development of the fighter continued with no higher priority rating than that which had already prolonged its gestation. The indifference of the Air Ministry shocked Messerschmitt officials, for without the Ministry's active support it was impossible to establish an adequate production line or even undertake a sufficiently comprehensive research and development programme.

Despite official apathy and the Messerschmitt concern's already extensive commitments in the development and production of other aircraft types, a serious attempt was made on the part of the company to increase the development tempo of the fighter. The second prototype airframe, the Me 262V2, was now fitted with the Jumo turbojets and flown for the first time on October 2, 1942, and the Air Ministry relented to the extent that it placed an order for fifteen pre-production machines, this order being increased to thirty machines in October. At a conference in Berlin on December 2, 1942, the Air Ministry decided that a production rate of twenty machines per month should be attained in 1944. In vain Messerschmitt officials stressed the potentialities of the fighter and the inadequacy of this proposed production pro-gramme, but the Air Ministry remained adamant, stating that there was no real need for such an air-craft and that the numbers scheduled for production would suffice for operational trials.

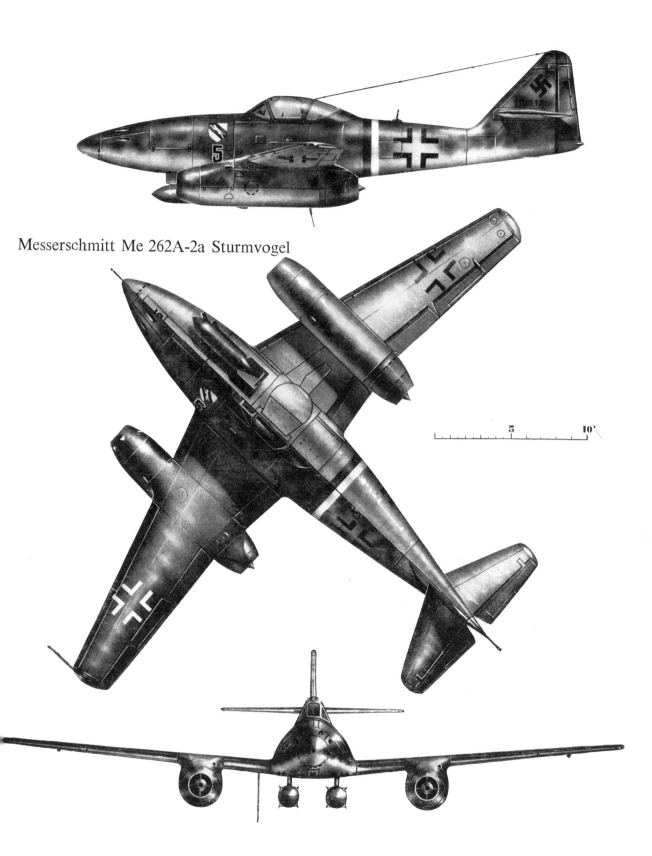

Messerschmitt Me 262A-2a Sturmvogel

5   10'

THE MESSERSCHMITT ME 262

The photograph above depicts the Me 262 V5 employed for the first (fixed) nosewheel tests in June 1943. Two Borsig take-off-assistance rockets may be discerned under the fuselage centre section. The photographs below show the initial production model, the Me 262 A-1a Schwalbe (Swallow), first production deliveries of which were made in May 1944.

On March 2, 1943, the first prototype airframe, the Me 262 V1, which had been rebuilt after the damage it had suffered when testing the B.M.W. engines and now fitted with the more powerful Jumo units, was flown at Messerschmitt's test centre at Lechfeld, where it was joined during the following month by a fourth prototype, the Me 262 V4. In May, Messerschmitt informed General Galland that tests with the radical new fighter were now progressing well, and on the 22nd of that month Galland visited Lechfeld and personally tested the Me 262 V4. He immediately realised that the aircraft opened up completely new tactical possibilities, and sent an enthusiastic report to Field-Marshal Milch. He was sure that, providing suitable tactics were evolved, the Me 262 could swing the balance of air superiority back in Germany's favour. He demanded immediate mass production of the new fighter, saying that one Me 262 would be worth three conventional fighters. His efforts brought some results, for by the end of May Milch had approved plans for the production of the Me 262. On July 23 the Me 262 V4 was demonstrated before Marshal Goering, who was equally enthusiastic and immediately reported on its performance to Adolf Hitler. Nevertheless, Hitler refused to increase the priority given to the jet fighter and expressly forbade any preparation for mass production.

The first four prototypes were generally similar, being powered by early Junkers Jumo 109-004A turbojets and having retractable tailwheel-type undercarriages. This type of undercarriage, originally adopted to avoid the complications that were expected to arise from the use of the then still relatively unorthodox nosewheel-type undercarriage, presented several serious problems. The long nose of the aircraft obstructed the pilot's forward view when the aircraft was in the taildown position, the downward-directed jet blast flung up large pieces of concrete and earth from the runways and, with the centre of gravity aft of the main wheels, it was only by applying the brakes at about 100 m.p.h. that it was possible to raise the tail for take-off. The Air Ministry had therefore ordered that pre-production and subsequent

machines should be fitted with a nosewheel undercarriage, and to test this feature the fifth prototype, the Me 262V5, was fitted with a fixed nosewheel. Flight tests with this commenced on June 26, 1943, and their success led to the installation of a completely retractable nosewheel on the Me 262V6 which flew in October. This prototype was the first machine to be fitted with the Jumo 109-004B turbojets of 1,980 lb. thrust which were scheduled for installation in production models.

An Me 262A-2a Sturmvogel (Stormbird) fighter-bomber with two 550-lb. bombs.

The Me 262V6 was demonstrated before Goering, Milch, Galland and others at Regensburg on November 2, and Goering promised the project his fullest backing but asked Professor Messerschmitt if his fighter could be adapted to carry bombs, saying that he wished to indicate to Messerschmitt the trend of Hitler's thoughts. A few weeks later, on November 26, the Me 262V6 was flown to Insterburg, in East Prussia, and demonstrated before Hitler, who immediately acclaimed the aircraft as a *bomber*!

Plans for the quantity production of the Me 262 were at last approved, although the backing of the Air Ministry remained unrealistic, for no proposals were made to terminate production of any other type in order to provide the necessary resources for Me 262 production. However, that the Luftwaffe at last recognised the worth of the fighter is indicated by its Programme No. 223 which called for a production rate of sixty machines per month from May 1944, with mass production commencing as soon as tooling, raw materials and labour became available.

Several more prototypes were completed; the Me 262V7 flown in November 1943 was fitted with a pressure cabin, the V8 had four 30-mm. MK 108 cannon for air-firing trials, the V9 flown in January 1944 was employed to test radio and other equipment, and the V10, first flown on May 1, 1944, was fitted with bomb pylons underwing and Borsig assisted-take-off rockets. The first thirteen pre-production Me 262A-0 fighters for service evaluation were completed and flown in March and April 1944, and subsequently production tempo increased rapidly.

The initial production model, the Me 262A-1a, was dubbed "Schwalbe" (Swallow) and carried an armament of four 30-mm. MK 108 cannon in the fuselage nose, the two upper cannon each having 100 rounds per gun and the two lower cannon having 80 rounds per gun. Two Jumo 004B-1, B-2 or B-3 turbojets were installed, and radio equipment included FuG 16ZY with ZVG and FuG 25a. The Me 262A-1a/U1 differed solely in the type of armament installed (two 20-mm. MG 151 with 146 rounds per gun, two 30-mm. MK 108 with 66 rounds per gun, and two 30-mm. MK 103 with 72 rounds per gun). The Me 262A-1a/U2 was a bad-weather fighter with additional radio equipment

(FuG 125), and the A-1a/U3 was an unarmed reconnaissance variant with the nose armament replaced by two vertically-mounted RB 50/30 cameras. The Me 262A-1b was a later modification of the A-1a with underwing racks for twenty-four 5-cm. R4M air-to-air rocket missiles. About forty machines were fitted with these racks during the closing weeks of the war.

Despite Hitler's desire to use the Me 262 Schwalbe as a bomber, the existing programme for the testing and production of the machine had gone relatively unchanged, apart from the development of the Me 262V10 bomber prototype. When, during a production conference in the summer of 1944, Hitler asked how many of the completed machines were able to carry bombs, he was told by Field-Marshal Milch that the Me 262 was being built exclusively for the fighter role. Hitler immediately ordered the modification of all existing machines as bombers and expressly forbade any further reference to the Me 262 as a fighter! This order was incomprehensible both to the manufacturers and to the Luftwaffe, but Hitler, who thought only in terms of retaliation, was adamant. The Me 262, which was highly unsuitable for the bombing role, lacking the necessary range, weight-lifting capacity and bomb sight, had to be employed as a *bomber*! The modifications necessitated by this order resulted in a four-month delay in the tactical employment of the Me 262, and when reconversion to the fighter role took place further delays resulted.

The conversion of the Schwalbe fighter for the bombing role resulted in the Me 262A-2a Sturmvogel (Stormbird). It was originally intended that the upper pair of 30-mm. cannon should be removed, but in actual fact the majority of the aircraft of this series retained their full complement of cannon. Two 1,100-lb. bombs or one 2,200-lb. bomb could be carried, although the externally-mounted bombs reduced the maximum speed of the Sturmvogel by as much as 120 m.p.h., bringing it within the speed range of Allied piston-engined interceptors until the bombs had been dropped. The Me 262A-2a/U1 was generally similar to the A-2a, but two of the MK 108 cannon were removed to provide space for the

THE MESSERSCHMITT ME 262

TSA bomb-aiming device. The A-2a/U2 featured a bulged wooden nose section which housed a second crew member in a prone position with a Lotfe 7H bomb sight in a glazed nose cone. Only one prototype of this version was completed. The Me 262A-3a was intended for the dual role of ground support and interception, having extensive armour protection around the cockpit and fuel tanks, and the A-5a was a reconnaissance-fighter with two 30-mm. MK 108 cannon, two RB 50/30 vertically-mounted cameras in the nose, and pylons for two 66-gall. or one 132-gall. long-range tanks under the fuselage.

The Me 262 was never a novice's aircraft. It was not that its flying characteristics were bad. On the contrary, they were excellent. They were such that they led pilots to mistakenly believe that no special training was required. The major problems stemmed from the turbojets, which, according to Junkers officials, were never really ready for operational service when they were frozen into assembly-line production. The throttles had to be handled with great care, and advanced very slowly, otherwise fire burned out the turbine section through fuel being admitted too rapidly, or the engine compressor stalled, particularly at high altitudes. When an engine stopped, and providing the turbine had not burned out, it could theoretically be restarted with the aid of a built-in Riedel starter motor. This was, however, of unsatisfactory design and rarely functioned correctly and, although the aircraft flew quite well on one engine, landings in this condition invariably led to trouble. The

resultant high accident rate rendered the development of a dual-control trainer version essential.

A tandem-seat model, designated Me 262B-la, was therefore produced. The installation of the second seat reduced internal fuel capacity and necessitated the attachment of pylons carrying either two 66-gall. auxiliary fuel tanks or one 132-gall. tank. The standard four 30-mm. MK 108 cannon armament was retained, but only some fifteen Me 262B-la dual-control trainers were delivered before Germany's defeat.

In February 1945, Oberleutnant Walter, a fighter pilot experienced in the employment of "Wilde Sau" tactics—a method of night fighting in which single-seat aircraft without radar equipment co-operate with searchlights and rely on visual contact—achieved several successes against Mosquitos with an Me 262 over Berlin at night. Proposals for night-fighting variants of the Me 262 had been made earlier, and an experimental single-seat Me 262 had been tested with an SN-2 "Lichtenstein" radar array in the nose. It was therefore decided to adapt the existing Me 262B-la two-seat trainer to serve as an interim night fighter under the designation Me 262B-la/U1. FuG 218 radar was installed, and radio and communications equipment included FuG 16ZY and ZVG, FuG 25a and FuG 125 and 120a. It was planned to tow a 198-gall. auxiliary tank, or "Deichselschlepp", to increase patrol endurance. The first of these conversions crashed, killing the test pilot, but successful trials were conducted with the remaining two conversions.

It was proposed that further examples of the Me 262B-la/U1 should be produced for use until the special night-fighter adaptation of the design, the Me 262B-2a, was available, but no further machines were completed before the war's end. The Me 262B-2a night fighter had a lengthened fuselage (two sections increasing overall length by 3 ft. $11\frac{1}{4}$ in. being inserted fore and aft of the cockpit), internal fuel capacity increased by 257 galls., a forward-firing armament of four 30-mm. MK 108 cannon supplemented by two remotely-controlled and obliquely-mounted MK 108 cannon in a "Schräge Musik" installation. Radar and radio equipment was generally similar to that of the Me 262B-la/U1 apart from the addition of FuG 350 ZC "Naxos", and one prototype of the Me 262B-2a was flight tested. A

(Above) Me 262A used for SN-2 radar tests. (Below) An Me 262B-1a/U1 with radar array removed from nose.

(Above) One of three machines used to test the 50-mm. MK 114 cannon.

further prototype was fitted with centimetric radar in a blunt-tipped nose, but Germany collapsed before test flights with this machine could be made.

As the defeat of Germany became more assured, highest priority was given to the development of interceptor variants of the Me 262, and particularly to the development of rocket boosted models. The first of these to be tested was the Me 262C-la which had a Walter HWK 109-509A bi-fuel rocket motor in the tail with T-stoff (198 galls.) and C-stoff (132 galls.) tanks installed in the fuselage. The Me 262C-la could attain 38,400 feet altitude from a standing start in 4·5 minutes, and the first test flight was made on February 27, 1945.

Another rocket-boosted version was the Me 262C-2b which was powered by two B.M.W. 003R units each of which comprised a standard 1,760 lb. thrust B.M.W. 003A turbojet and a B.M.W. 718 bi-fuel rocket motor which augmented thrust by 2,700 lb. for three minutes. The airframe and armament of the Me 262C-2b were similar to those of the A-la variant, but the B.M.W. 003R mixed power units proved to be too complex. It was necessary, according to the throttle setting and altitude, to make continuous adjustments to the fuel supply, and during bench-testing the B.M.W. 718 rocket blew up and burned fiercely at the least provocation. Only one flight test with the Me 262C-2b was made. The projected production version of the rocket-boosted fighter, the Me 262C-3, was to have had a jettisonable Walter rocket motor mounted externally under the fuselage centre section and fed via a flexible line from a jettisonable fuel tank mounted a few feet ahead of the rocket motor.

Conducted simultaneously with tests on rocket-boosted bomber interceptor versions of the Me 262 were experiments with different types of armament intended primarily for bomber destruction. The projected Me 262D was to have been fitted with the SG 500 "Jagdfaust" which comprised twelve rifled mortar barrels situated in the nose of the aircraft, pointing forward and upward. Each barrel contained a 50-mm. shell, these being fired simultaneously as soon as the Me 262D was lined up with the belly of the enemy bomber, recoil being counteracted by counterweights fired downward from the barrels. The Me 262E was a further projected version carrying forty-eight 5-cm. R4M missiles, twelve under each wing like the Me 262A-lb, and twenty-four in a nose container. Another version of the Me 262E was to have had a 50-mm. MK 114 cannon installed in the nose, but this project was abandoned after the limited success of trials with four experimental machines rebuilt from Me 262A-la airframes.

In the last few months of the war every emphasis was placed upon the mass production of the Me 262, and in March 1945 a letter from Hitler's headquarters gave the Me 262 production programme priority over all and any production in Germany. Control was taken out of the hands of Reichsminister Speer and placed under Obergruppenführer Kemmler of the S.S., who placed his officers in the factories, but by that time the production situation was hopeless. A total of 1,433 Me 262s was produced in Germany during the war years, and it has been estimated by Messerschmitt officials that a further 497 aircraft were lost due to bombing attacks and dispersal problems. A total of 568 Me 262s had been produced by January 1, 1945, and a further 865 were manufactured in the first four months of 1945. Nevertheless, hardly more than 100 participated in operations.

For those which did get into combat remarkable successes were claimed. The Me 262 first entered service in the bomber role with the K.G.51 bomber group during the Allied invasion of Europe, and K.G.6, K.G.27 and K.G.54 were also re-equipped with the type. The first Me 262 *fighter* unit was a special "Kommando" which operated from Achmer, near Osnabruck and, until his death, was commanded by Major Nowotny, one of the Luftwaffe's leading fighter aces. The pilots of this special unit later formed the nucleus of the first jet-fighter group, J.G.7, which was commanded by Colonel Steinhoff and took heavy toll of Allied bombers. The last operations with the Me 262 were undertaken by an élite fighter unit, J.V.44, led by General Galland. In April 1945, this unit, flying Me 262A-1b fighters each carrying twenty-four 5-cm. R4M missiles, engaged formations of Boeing Fortresses over Westphalia. The missiles were launched against formations outside the range of the defensive fire, and the unit scored numerous successes, a considerable number of Fortresses being destroyed or damaged.

Messerschmitt Me 262A-1a Schwalbe

Dimensions : Span, 40 ft. 11½ in., length, 34 ft. 9½ in., height, 12 ft. 7 in., wing area, 234 sq. ft.

Armament : Four 30-mm. MK 108 cannon aimed to converge at 400-500 yards.

Power Plant : Two Junkers Jumo 109-004B-1, B-2, or B-3 each rated at 1,980 lb. static thrust. Fuel capacity (J-2 diesel oil), 565 Imp. galls.

Weights : Empty, 9,741.5 lb., loaded, 14,101 lb., wing loading, 60.34 lb./sq. ft.

Performance : Maximum speed, 538 m.p.h. at 29,560 ft., 540 m.p.h. at 19,684 ft., 500 m.p.h. at sea level, initial climb rate, 3,937 ft./min., climb rate at 19,684 ft., 2,165 ft./min., climb rate at 29,560 ft., 1,082 ft./min. ; service ceiling, 37,565 ft.; range, 298 mls. at sea level, 526 mls. at 19,684 ft., 652 mls. at 29,560 ft. Take-off run to clear 50 ft. obstacle, 3,280 ft., landing speed, 108 m.p.h.

The A6M5 Model 52, the version of the Zero-Sen produced in largest numbers.

THE MITSUBISHI ZERO-SEN

To the Japanese the Zero-Sen was everything that the Spitfire was to the British nation. It symbolized Japan's conduct of the war, for as its fortune fared so fared the Japanese nation. The Zero fighter marked the beginning of a new epoch in naval aviation: it was the first shipboard fighter capable of besting its land-based opponents. It created a myth—the myth of Japanese invincibility in the air, and one to which the Japanese themselves fell victim as a result of the almost total destruction of Allied air power in the early days of the Pacific war. In its day the Zero was the world's foremost carrier-based fighter, and its appearance over Pearl Harbour came as a complete surprise to the American forces. Its successive appearance over every major battle area in the opening days of the war seemed to indicate that Japan possessed unlimited supplies of this remarkable fighter, and its almost mystical powers of manœuvre and ability to traverse vast stretches of water fostered the acceptance of the myth of its invincibility in Allied minds.

Unbeknown to the Allies was the fact that the Zero-Sen possessed many shortcomings which were only to be revealed six months later when a virtually intact specimen was obtained. Prior to this event, any captured part of a Zero-Sen was regarded as a prize. Piece by piece Allied intelligence teams endeavoured to rebuild an example of this fighter for evaluation, only to be met by failure. Then, on June 3, 1942,

Flight Petty Officer Tadayoshi Koga left the flight deck of the carrier *Ryujo* in his Mitsubishi A6M2 Model 21 fighter as part of a task force assigned to attack Dutch Harbour in the Aleutian Islands. His Zero, which had been built only the previous February, was on its first operational mission, a mission that was also to prove its last in the service of the Japanese Navy. On his way back to the *Ryujo*, Koga found that two bullets had punctured his fuel supply and he informed his flight commander that he intended to land on a small island designated as an emergency landing field for crippled planes. Five weeks later an American naval scouting party discovered the Japanese fighter upside down in a marsh on the island of Aktan, its pilot dead with a broken neck.

This single fighter was probably one of the greatest prizes of the Pacific war. Hardly damaged, it was shipped back to the U.S.A. where it was exhaustively tested. The tests revealed the fighter's faults and shattered the myth that surrounded it.

The Zero was originally conceived as a replacement for the Mitsubishi Type 96 (A5M) fighter, the first of the Japanese Navy's operational monoplanes. On October 5, 1937, the Japanese Navy furnished the Mitsubishi and Nakajima companies with its requirements for a new fighter with a maximum speed exceeding 310 m.p.h., the ability to climb to 9,840 feet in 3.5 minutes, manœuvrability and range exceeding any existing fighter and an armament of two cannon and two machine-guns. These demands were far in excess of any previously made of the Japanese aircraft industry and, viewing them as unrealistic, the Nakajima company withdrew from the project following a design meeting at Yokosuka on January 17, 1938. Mitsubishi alone accepted the task of meeting the requirements of the 12-Shi (twelfth year of the

An A6M2 Model 21. The Japanese word Hokokugo (meaning Patriotism) followed by the number "433" on the fuselage side indicates that this was the 433rd Zero-Sen presented to the Japanese Navy by public subscription.

The A6M3 Model 32, the "clipped" version of the Zero-Sen, was only partially successful and was succeeded in production by the A6M3 Model 22 which reverted to the full-span wing.

Showa reign) project as it was known, and design work began under the direction of Jiro Horikoshi, chief designer of Mitsubishi Jukogyo K.K.

The chosen power plant was the Mitsubishi MK2 Zuisei 13 (Auspicious Star), a fourteen-cylinder twin-row radial of 780 h.p., later known under the unified JNAF/JAAF designation system as the Ha.31/13. This engine was selected owing to its light weight and small diameter, and a two-blade constant-speed airscrew was fitted. Extreme care was given to structural weight as manœuvrability was directly related to wing loading, and extensive use was made of Extra-Super Duralumin (E.S.D.), a tough, lightweight alloy developed for aircraft use by the Sumitoma Metal Industry Company. Work on the prototype progressed rapidly, and changes requested after inspections of the 12-Shi mock-up on April 17 and July 11, 1938, were progressively incorporated.

On March 16, 1939, at Mitsubishi's Nagoya plant, the first prototype was completed. Engine tests were conducted on March 18, and the aircraft was transferred to the Navy's Kasumigaura airfield for flight testing. Here, on April 1, 1939, one of Mitsubishi's test pilots, Katsuzo Shima, flew the new fighter for the first time. The flight was an outstanding success, the only troubles manifesting themselves being in the wheel brakes, the oil system and a slight tendency to vibrate. Continued testing indicated that the vibration could be controlled by the use of a larger airscrew of three-bladed type. The prototype was accepted by the Navy on September 14, 1939, as the A6M1 Carrier Fighter, and, in the meantime, a second prototype had been completed, passing the manufacturer's flight tests on October 18, 1939, and being accepted by the Navy one week later. Both A6M1 prototypes carried two 20-mm. cannon in the wings and two 7.7-mm. guns in the fuselage upper decking.

While flight testing of the A6M1 was under way, a new power plant passed its Navy acceptance tests, the Nakajima NK1C Sakae 12 (Prosperity) of 925 h.p., which was only slightly larger and heavier than the Zuisei. The Sakae 12 (Ha.35/12) was also a fourteen-cylinder twin-row radial, and the Navy decided that this engine should be installed in the third prototype which would be known as the A6M2. Flight tests with the third machine began on January 18, 1940, and it was discovered that, with its new-found power, the fighter amply exceeded the original performance requirements which had been regarded as impossible a few months earlier. Even while the final acceptance of the A6M2 as a production fighter was in the balance, the Japanese Navy requested that a number of machines be delivered for operational use in China to meet growing aerial opposition. Fifteen A6M2s were accordingly delivered for service in China and, on July 21, 1940, left Japan for the Chinese mainland—almost eighteen months before the attack on Pearl Harbour. The new fighters were enthusiastically received in China, and at the end of July the A6M2 was officially adopted as the Type O Carrier Fighter, Model 11, popularly known in Japan as the Zero-Sen (Zero Fighter). At this time, production models of Navy aircraft were assigned type numbers based on the last number of the current Japanese year, and as 1940 was the year 2600 in the Japanese calendar, the A6M series was known as the Zero.

The A6M2-K Zero-Rensen Model 11 tandem two-seat conversion trainer which was produced in 1942. A similar conversion of the later A6M5 was also made in 1944 by the 21st Naval Air Arsenal at Omura.

(Above) An A6M2 Model 11 Zero-Sen captured in China, and (below) an A6M2 Model 21 similar to the type employed in the attack on Pearl Harbour.

The Type O Model 11 fighters first appeared over Chungking in August 1940. Approaching at an altitude of 27,000 feet, they shot down all the defending Chinese fighters literally before the defending aircraft knew what had hit them. They were used over many Chinese battle-areas throughout the following months, and in over a year of operational use not one Zero-Sen was captured or inspected by the Chinese or American observers. As a result of the new fighter's performance, General Chennault attempted to warn the U.S.A.A.F. of the Zero's capabilities, but his warning was ignored and the new fighter remained an enigma to the western nations.

Production tempo built up rapidly after acceptance by the Navy, the first assembly line being started at Mitsubishi's No. 3 airframe plant at Nagoya. Continued testing of the A6M1 and A6M2 prototypes resulted in the loss of the second A6M1 when a wing spar failed. This caused great concern, and the wing structure was re-designed and incorporated in the twenty-second Model 11. Sixty-four Type O Model 11 fighters had been completed when the Model 21 was introduced on the assembly line in November 1940. While the Model 11 had been making its

The A6M2-N floatplane fighter produced between April 1942 and September 1943 by Nakajima.

operational début in China, secret carrier acceptance trials were being conducted. Initially, the A6M2 failed to pass these tests, but after modifications all shipboard requirements were met. The wing was modified to permit twenty inches of each tip to fold upwards and, with this modification, the Zero became the Model 21. In February 1941, beginning with the 127th production Zero, the Model 21 was fitted with a new aileron tab balance which was linked to the undercarriage retraction mechanism and reduced the stick forces needed for high-speed control.

The A6M2 Model 21 was the version of the Zero employed at Pearl Harbour and throughout the Pacific during the early stages of the war. With its maximum speed of 317 m.p.h. at 16,400 feet and ability to climb to 19,680 feet in 7 minutes 27 seconds, it possessed an ascendancy over any other fighter type in the Pacific. Production of the Model 21 by Mitsubishi totalled 740 aircraft, and Nakajima also began to build this model in November 1941 at its Koizuma factory. When the war commenced on December 7, 1941, the Japanese Navy had well over four hundred Zero fighters, primarily Model 21s, available.

The initial success of the A6M2 Model 21 prompted the Navy's decision to adapt the machine as a floatplane fighter which was a new concept, intended to provide air cover for Japanese ground forces during amphibious operations prior to the capture of land bases. The project was assigned to Nakajima because of that company's floatplane experience, and the construction of a prototype known as the AS-1 began in February 1941. The design was accepted by the Navy under the designation A6M2-N (the suffix "N" indicating a floatplane adaptation of the A6M2) and entered production in April 1942 as the Type 2 Floatplane Fighter Model 11 (subsequently allocated the code-name "Rufe" by the Allies). A total of 327 A6M2-Ns was built at Nakajima's Koizuma factory, production being completed in September 1943. As a result of changes in the tactical situation, the A6M2-Ns were used either as defensive fighters or for reconnaissance. They were first encountered at Guadalcanal and were later assigned to the Fifth Fleet during the Aleutians campaign, being based at Kiska and Attu. The A6M2-N, despite its maximum speed of only 271 m.p.h., was also based at Shimushu in the defence of Paramushiro in northern Japan and later on Lake Biwa for the defence of the home island of Honshu.

With the coming of war and the greatly increased demand for pilots, it became Japanese Navy policy to contract for a two-seat conversion trainer variant of each new single-seat fighter. The A6M2 Model 21 was the first fighter to come under this new programme, and work commenced on its modification early in 1942 as the 17-Shi Fighter Trainer. A second seat was added for the instructor, an enlarged canopy was fitted (which did not, incidentally, enclose the pupil's seat), and small horizontal fins were added to the rear fuselage for stability. Armament was reduced to two 7.7-mm. machine-guns, and the maximum speed was 296 m.p.h. at 13,120 feet. After successful

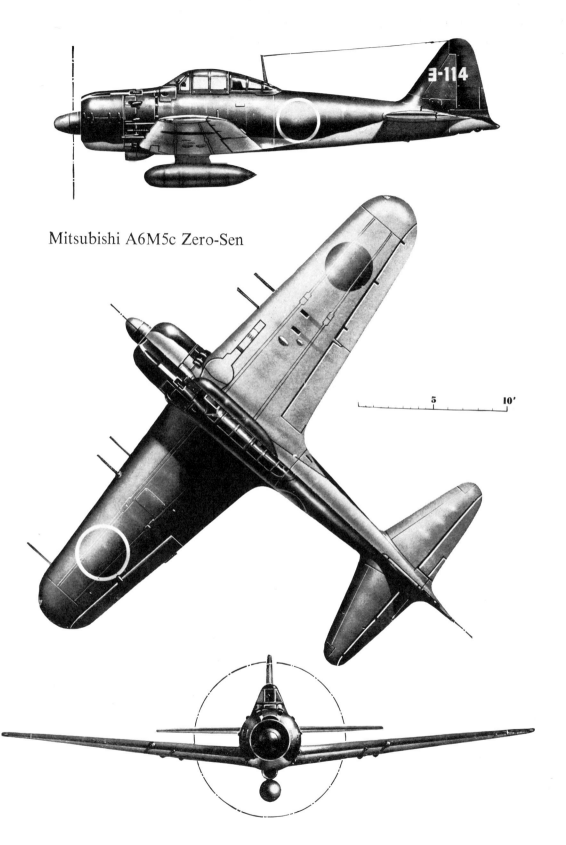

Mitsubishi A6M5c Zero-Sen

5   10'

Naval evaluation, it entered production as the A6M2-K Zero-Rensen (Zero Fighter Trainer), being constructed at the Sasebo 21st Naval Air Arsenal late in 1942 and at Hitachi's Chiba plant in May 1944. Sasebo built 236 Zero-Rensens and Hitachi 272.

In June 1941, flight testing of a new and more powerful version of the Zero began, the A6M3. Powered by the 1,130 h.p. Sakae 21 (Ha.35/21) fitted with two-speed supercharger, the A6M3 attained a

maximum speed of 341 m.p.h. at 20,500 feet and possessed increased range, but on all other counts it failed to measure up to the Japanese Navy's expectations. It was finally decided to remove the folding wingtips and the tab balances. The result was essentially a "clipped" Zero and, known as the A6M3 Model 32, it carried the same armament as the earlier A6M2. When the Allies first encountered the A6M3 in action over New Guinea in September 1942, they thought it to be a new type, and assigned to it the code name "Hap", later changed to "Hamp" to avoid embarrassing General "Hap" Arnold. This was again changed to "Zeke 32" when it was discovered that the *new* fighter was nothing more than a modified Zero. The clipped wings reduced manoeuvrability compared with the full-span version, but they did increase the maximum speed slightly as well as improve the diving speed and controllability. A total of 343 A6M3 Zero fighters was completed by Mitsubishi. Early in 1942, before its operational début, the A6M3 was modified by the installation of fuel tanks in the wings. The full wing span and folding tips were again used and, as the A6M3 Model 22, it became the prime carrier fighter of the A6M3 series, 560 being built by Mitsubishi.

By the advent of 1943 the war situation had taken a critical turn for Japan. Allied strength was slowly but surely increasing and had, with few exceptions, consistently beaten the Japanese after the Battle of Midway. Japanese naval air power in particular had suffered severely as the Zero-Sen became outclassed by more modern Allied fighters. This forced the Japanese Navy to press for the rapid development of improved variants of the Zero, as the Navy's new series of fighter aircraft had yet failed to materialise. The A6M5 Model 52 was the direct result of the Navy's new demands. It was essentially a compromise between performance and produceability. Based to a large degree upon the A6M3 Model 32, the new variant retained the wing of reduced span introduced on the earlier fighter but the tips were rounded. The engine was still the Sakae 21 but the exhaust stacks had been modified to give thrust augmentation. Speed was boosted to 358 m.p.h. at 22,000 feet.

The prototype A6M5 Model 52 was completed in August 1943 as the first of the A-Type fighters. The Japanese Navy's war had become a defensive one and it had separated its fighters into three classifications. The A-Type, or Ko-Sen, was a light fighter operating in either shipboard or land-based forms; the B-Type, or Otsu-Sen, was a heavier land-based fighter for interception duties, and the C-Type, or or Hei-Sen, was a night fighter. Although produced as A-Types, the Zero was later called upon to undertake the duties of both B- and C-Type fighters. More A6M5s were produced than any other model of the Zero-Sen, production being undertaken both by Mitsubishi and Nakajima. Plans were also prepared to produce the type at Hitachi, but Japan capitulated before any production aircraft had been delivered by this company. Mitsubishi alone completed 747 of the

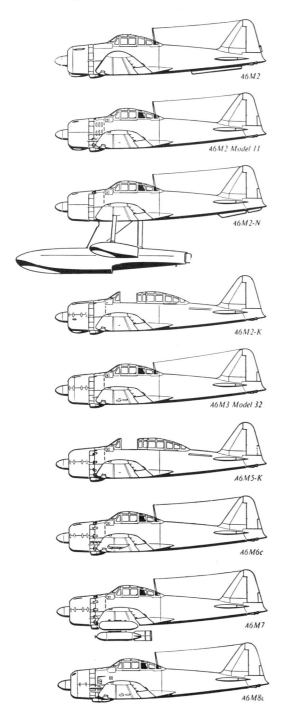

A6M2

46M2 Model 11

46M2-N

46M2-K

A6M3 Model 32

A6M5-K

A6M6c

A6M7

A6M8c

original A6M5 model, and over half of the Zero's total production comprised Model 52 series aircraft built between autumn 1943 and the end of the war.

The A6M5 was also selected for modification as a two-seat trainer under the A6M5-K designation, and work on the prototypes began at the Naval Air Arsenal at Omura in August 1944, the first model being completed in March 1945.

An A6M5 Model 52 converted for use as a dive bomber.

Production was assigned to Hitachi as the Zero-Rensen Model 22, but only seven pre-production machines were completed.

The A6M5 Model 52 was employed throughout the war zones and became numerically the most important Japanese fighter. As the war progressed combat experience dictated changes, and the Navy consistently demanded a complete revision of the basic design to raise it to Allied standards. However, Mitsubishi was preoccupied with development of the newer 17-Shi Reppu (Hurricane) with which it was planned to replace the Zero, as well as other more advanced fighter projects, and so the Navy's request went unheeded. The Japanese Navy was forced, therefore, to make do with adaptations of the basic A6M5. The first revised model was the A6M5a Model 52A with heavier fire-power. The wing was modified to incorporate a belt-feed system for the 20-mm. cannon, and the number of rounds was increased to 125 per belt, a gain of twenty-five shells per cannon over the Model 52. The strengthened wing also increased the permissible diving speed by 50 m.p.h., bringing it appreciably closer to Western standards. The prototype was completed late in 1943, and the delivery of production models commenced in March 1944. Mitsubishi built 391, and Nakajima also produced the type.

The A6M5b Model 52B was a Mitsubishi private venture modification coincidental with the Model 52A and intended to increase both fire power and pilot protection. One of the 7.7-mm. guns was replaced by a 12.7-mm. weapon, bullet-proof glass was added to the cockpit canopy, and automatic fire extinguishers were installed. Production began at Mitsubishi's 3rd airframe plant in April 1944, and 470 fighters of this type were built. First of the heavy fighters was the A6M5c Model 52C which catered for the Navy's requests for additional armament, armour, fuel tankage and bomb racks. Mitsubishi felt that the Sakae 21 engine would provide insufficient power for the appreciably heavier fighter if a radical drop in performance was not to be suffered, and suggested the installation of the more powerful Kinsei 62 engine. The Navy refused to accept this proposal and suggested instead the installation of an improved model of the Sakae with water-methanol injection. This improved engine was not available in time for installation in production A6M5c Zero fighters, the increased weight proved too much for the power plant installed and production was terminated after the

completion of only 93 aircraft. However, although the basic Model 52C was a failure, its armament pattern of two 13-mm. guns and two 20-mm. cannon in the wings plus a 13-mm. gun in the fuselage was followed on all subsequent versions of the Zero produced in any quantity.

Late in 1944 the improved Sakae did become available for use and was installed in the A6M6c Model 53C. Produced for the Navy as the Nakajima NK1P Sakae 31, the new engine had the same rated horse power as the Sakae 21 but had a water-methanol injection system for short bursts of speed. The A6M6c was similar to the A6M5c apart from the engine and the addition of self-sealing wing tanks. In addition to its normal armament, two launching rails for air-to-air rocket missiles were mounted under each wing. One prototype of the A6M6c was built by Mitsubishi late in 1944, and production was assigned to Nakajima by whom it was produced at Koizuma. Although better than its predecessor, the A6M6c proved a disappointment, as its Sakae 31 did not produce the expected boosted power and its injection system was troublesome and difficult to maintain.

At this time existing Japanese Navy dive bombers were too heavy to operate from light carriers and various Zero fighters were selected for modification to fulfil this role. The belly fuel tank was replaced by a 550-lb. bomb, and Zero dive bombers were assigned to several light carriers and also operated from bases in the Philippines. In combat the makeshift bomb-release mechanism frequently failed to function, forcing the aircraft to return to its base without having accomplished its mission. The weight of the bomb on the return flight severely reduced the anticipated range and many of these modified Zeros ran out of fuel before regaining their bases. This problem did not apply to suicide missions, as the return flight was obviously not a factor to be considered. Modified Zeros assigned to Air Group 201 in the Philippines became the first Japanese aircraft used on planned suicide missions against American surface vessels. Air Group 201, assisted by volunteer pilots from Air Group 601 and other Navy units in the area, became the first Kamikaze (Divine Wind) suicide squadron in the Japanese Naval Air Force. The outstanding successes gained by this form of attack led to the formation of other Kamikaze units, and the bomb-carrying Zeros became the prime suicide attack bombers of the Navy.

Normal Navy dive-bomber units equipped with

THE MITSUBISHI ZERO-SEN

An A6M6c Model 53C which employed water-methanol injection.

modified Zeros still suffered from the aircraft's limited range and unreliable bomb-release mechanism. Mitsubishi therefore produced a modification of the Model 52 as the A6M7, and production began in May 1945 as the Model 63. Power was again provided by the Sakae 21 and armament was similar to that of the A6M5c. The A6M7 Model 63 had a reinforced stabiliser, an almost fool-proof bomb-release mechanism and carried two underwing drop tanks. The type was hastily produced both by Mitsubishi and Nakajima and assigned to Navy dive-bomber units.

The last model of the Zero-Sen was a radical departure from its predecessors insofar as the engine was concerned, this being changed for the first time since the fighter had entered production in 1940. As a result of severe bomb damage to the Nakajima and Ishikawajima plants producing the Sakae, and the former company's concentration on the Homare engine for the Shiden and Ginga aircraft, the Sakae was soon in short supply. The Navy therefore agreed to Mitsubishi's proposal to use their MK8K Kinsei 62 (Ha.33/62), a fourteen-cylinder twin-row radial of 1,500 h.p. This proposal had been made consistently by Mitsubishi and equally consistently rejected by the Navy until the shortage of Sakae engines left no choice.

With the acceptance of the new power plant for the Zero-Sen in November 1944, work began on the A6M8c Model 54C. The forward half of the fuselage was completely redesigned and strengthened to absorb the increased power and larger diameter of the Kinsei. Additional fuel tankage and automatic fire extinguishers were added and the fuselage armament was removed, leaving two 13.2-mm. and two 20-mm. guns in the wings. The first prototype was completed in March 1945 after continued delays resulting from bombing attacks and shortages of materials. The initial flight-test programme began in April, indicating a number of faults in the fuel and oil systems, and the machine was returned to the factory for these to be eradicated. Following the changes, the fighter was accepted by the Navy on May 25, 1945, and a second prototype was accepted a month later, the two being extensively tested by the Yokosuka Experimental Air Corp's Proving Division throughout July, and accepted for production as the Type O Model 64.

The A6M8c Model 64 was the white hope of the

Japanese Navy as it was the first Zero-Sen to have its performance *improved* by modification in well over a year and would soon be available in quantity without the extended delays of developing an entirely new fighter type. Tests with the prototypes had revealed a maximum speed of 358 m.p.h. at 19,680 feet and the ability to climb to that altitude in 6 min. 50 secs. Its normal loaded weight was 6,940 lb., a substantial increase over the A6M5. Construction of the A6M8c was assigned to Mitsubishi's dispersed Suzuka, Shimonosho and Omi factories, as well as Nakajima's Wakaguri, Shizuna and Koizuma plants. The importance placed on this one fighter is indicated by the plans to produce 6,300 machines of this type during the 1946 fiscal year, but no production A6M8c was flown.

A number of Zeros were modified by the naval arsenals as well as by crews in the field, but these aircraft were not allocated separate numbers. One such modification was the adaptation of Model 52 fighters as B-29 Superfortress interceptors. The armament was changed to two 20-mm. cannon in each wing with a further 20-mm. cannon mounted in the rear fuselage behind the pilot and aimed obliquely to the left, firing upwards at an angle of some 30%.

More Zero-Sens were produced than any other wartime Japanese aircraft. Mitsubishi alone produced 3,879 aircraft of this type, Nakajima built 6,215 which, together with the 844 trainer and float-plane variants produced by Sasebo, Hitachi and Nakajima, brought the grand total of A6M series aircraft to 10,938. The Zero-Sen possessed complete mastery in the air over the Pacific until the Battle of Midway in June 1942, the actual turning point of the Pacific War although recognised by only a few at the time. The value of the fighter steadily declined and its lowest point was reached when it was selected to lead the Navy's Air Force in mass suicide—and the Japanese nation followed. The installation of the Kinsei engine brought Zero-Sen closer to Allied standards attained at that stage in the war, but the moment for decision had passed and, with it, victory for the Allies had become a foregone conclusion. The fighter that started the Pacific war was no longer able to fight it—nor was the nation that conceived it.

Mitsubishi A6M6c Model 53C Zero-Sen

Dimensions : Span, 36 ft. 1 in. ; length, 29 ft. 9 in. ; height, 9 ft. 2 in. ; wing area, 229.271 sq. ft.

Armament : Two Type 99 (Oerlikon) 20-mm. cannon and two 13.2-mm. machine-guns in wings and one 13.2-mm. machine-gun and one 7.7-mm. machine-gun in the upper decking of the engine cowling.

Power Plant : One Nakajima NK1P Sakae 31 fourteen-cylinder air-cooled two-row radial engine rated at 1,120 h.p. at 2,800 r.p.m. for take-off and 1,210 h.p. (war emergency rating) at 8,000 ft., 1,055 h.p. at 20,400 ft.

Weights : Empty, 3,920 lb. ; normal loaded, 6,026 lb. ; maximum, 6,508 lb.

Performance : Maximum speed, 346 m.p.h. at 19,680 ft., 289 m.p.h. at sea-level ; cruising speed (75% power), 201 m.p.h. ; maximum range (normal fuel), 1,130 miles at 152 m.p.h., 875 miles at 212 m.p.h. ; initial climb rate, 3,140 ft./min. ; time to 20,000 ft., 7.8 min. ; service ceiling, 35,100 ft.

70

M.C.200 Saetta fighters of the initial production series operated by the 371° Squadriglia of the 22° Gruppo "La Cucuracha". The hundredth and subsequent production Saetta fighters discarded the cockpit canopy which was disliked by Italian service pilots.

THE MACCHI-CASTOLDI SERIES

The development of the Macchi-Castoldi fighter presents an interesting parallel with that of the Supermarine Spitfire. Neither Italian or British fighter was the logical outcome of a line of fighting aircraft, both designers drawing heavily upon high-speed design experience gained with racing seaplanes. The Spitfire's pedigree stemmed from the Schneider Trophy floatplanes which eventually gained the Trophy outright for Britain, and the sires of the Macchi-Castoldi fighter were no less illustrious, including such superb high-speed seaplanes as the M.C.72 which gained for Italy the World Air Speed Record on several occasions. The same basic airframes were retained throughout the development lives of both fighters, these being adapted to take

progressively more powerful engines and heavier armament. Both were undeniably thoroughbreds but although the genealogical processes which brought the two fighters to the peak of their development resulted in warplanes comparable with the best extant, the Macchi-Castoldi design failed to achieve the fame of its British contemporary.

In times of war many facts are distorted or misrepresented for purposes of propaganda, and combatants invariably belittle the weapons of their opponents. The capabilities of Italian fighter aircraft and the qualities of their pilots were particularly vilified during the Second World War, yet Allied pilots who encountered them in combat accorded them the highest respect. Italy's fighters had their share of short-

The prototype M.C.200 Saetta (MM 336) which flew for the first time on December 24, 1937 with Giuseppe Burei at the controls.

D

(*Above and below*) *M.C.200 Saetta fighters of the initial production series with sliding cockpit canopies.*

(*Above*) *The first production M.C.200 Saetta (MM 4495) with Fiat-Hamilton constant-speed airscrew. This was replaced by a Piaggio P.1001 airscrew on the twenty-sixth and subsequent machines.*

time when prototypes of the Hurricane and Spitfire had just commenced flight trials, but Mario Castoldi did not share the fortune of Sydney Camm and Reginald Mitchell in having as superlative an engine as the Rolls-Royce Merlin around which to design his fighter. The lack of a low-drag, high-powered liquid-cooled engine placed Castoldi at a serious disadvantage. The only reliable engine suitable for fighter installation and readily available in Italy was the Fiat A.74 R.C.38. This was a magnificent power plant but, derived from Gnôme-Rhône designs, it was rated at only 870 h.p. and was a bulky, drag-producing air-cooled radial. Another stumbling block in the way of Castoldi's endeavours to attain extreme cleanliness of line was official insistence on the best possible field of view for the pilot. This necessitated seating the pilot high in the fuselage, producing a humped-back effect which, together with the radial engine, removed all trace of the fighter's ancestry.

Shortly after the completion of the Ethiopian Campaign, the Regia Aeronautica Staff had produced a specification for a fast, single-seat bomber interceptor monoplane as a part of Programme 'R' calling for three thousand new aircraft and including the re-equipment of three Stormi Caccia Terrestre with the new fighter monoplane. Initially, the specification demanded an aircraft possessing an endurance of one hour and an armament of one 12.7-mm. machine gun. However, both endurance and armament were doubled shortly after the specification was issued. A number of prototypes were built to compete, including the Caproni Vizzola F.5, the Aeronautica Umbra T.18, the I.M.A.M. Ro.51, the Reggiane Re.2000, and the Fiat G.50, and Macchi's entry in the contest, the M.C.200, flew for the first time on December 24, 1937 with Macchi's test pilot, Giuseppe Burei, at the controls.

comings, but they were, for the most part, competently-designed, singularly manoeuvrable machines with exceptionally well-harmonised controls and few vices. They were pilot's aeroplanes in every respect, and the pilots themselves lacked none of the élan of their opponents.

The best of Italy's wartime fighters were undoubtedly those designed by Ing. Mario Castoldi of Aeronautica Macchi, but whereas the Schneider Trophy seaplane experience of Reginald J. Mitchell was clearly discernible in the contours of the Spitfire, the influence of its floatplane ancestors was not so immediately apparent when the first Macchi-Castoldi fighter made its début. Work on the new fighter had begun at a

The prototype M.C.200 (MM 336) was an all-metal cantilever low-wing monoplane with an hydraulically-retractable undercarriage and fully-enclosed, all-round-vision cockpit canopy. Although lacking much of the elegance of such fighters as the Spitfire and Messerschmitt Bf 109, with their liquid-cooled engines, the M.C.200 proved to possess exceptional manoeuvrability for a monoplane. Stability was of a very high order, and handling was finger-light under all conditions. Climb rate was good but one of the outstanding characteristics of the Macchi-Castoldi fighter was its high dive rate, Burei attaining 500 m.p.h. in a terminal-velocity dive during official trials at Guidonia. Selected as the winner of the contest in 1938, the M.C.200 was awarded a production contract calling for ninety-nine machines (MM 4495 to MM 4593), deliveries beginning during the spring of 1939.

The first twenty-five production M.C.200s had a Fiat-Hamilton constant-speed airscrew, but this was supplanted by a Piaggio P.1001 airscrew also of constant-speed type on the twenty-sixth and subsequent machines. The Fiat A.74 R.C.38 fourteen-cylinder two-row geared and supercharged air-cooled radial engine offered 870 h.p. at 2,520 r.p.m. for take-off and was internationally rated at 840 h.p. at 2,400 r.p.m. at 12,500 ft. and 740 h.p. at sea level. All fuel was accommodated in the fuselage, a 52.3 Imp. gal. (62.8 U.S. gal.) tank being installed in front of the cockpit, beneath the gun breeches and ammunition containers, and one 16.5 Imp. gal. (19.8 U.S. gal.) tank being fitted beneath the pilot's seat, both tanks having some protection. Provision was made for a 33 Imp. gal. (39.6 U.S. gal.) ventral auxiliary tank. Two 12.7-mm. Breda-SAFAT machine guns were installed immediately ahead of the cockpit, the first thirteen production M.C.200s having provision for 310 rounds per gun but subsequent machines having ammunition capacity increased to 370 r.p.g., and an unusual feature was the installation of ammunition indicators in the cockpit which registered the number of rounds remaining per gun. A San Giorgio-type reflector sight was fitted, and radio equipment consisted of a simple ARC-1 receiver, although full R/T was later installed. The two-spar wings were built in three sections, the centre section being built integral with the fuselage, and the entire trailing edges were hinged, the outer sections acting as ailerons and the inner sections as landing flaps, these being interconnected so that the ailerons drooped at a slight angle when the flaps were lowered. The flaps were hydraulically operated as was also the undercarriage, and the main members initially carried the hinged inboard fairing doors on the main legs, these being transferred to the fuselage on later series. The tailwheel was also fully retractable on early production M.C.200s but was fixed on later machines. The fuselage was oval in section, and an anti-turnover pylon was mounted aft of the pilot. The tailplane was of variable incidence type ($+1°45'$ to $-5°30'$), and all movable tail surfaces were fabric-covered.

It was originally proposed to assign the first production M.C.200 fighters to the 4º Stormo (the

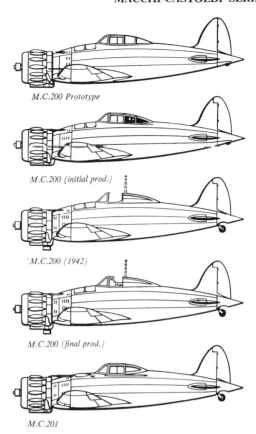

M.C.200 Prototype

M.C.200 (initial prod.)

M.C.200 (1942)

M.C.200 (final prod.)

M.C.201

Francesco Baracca Stormo) then equipped with the Fiat C.R.42 Falco biplane, but despite the extreme manoeuvrability of the Macchi-Castoldi fighter by monoplane standards, the 4º Stormo pilots were loath to exchange the greater manoeuvrability of their biplanes for the higher performance of the monoplane. Biased against the monoplane, they considered its spinning characteristics dangerous and disliked its enclosed cockpit which they felt restricted vision in combat and presented a hazard in the event of the pilot having to leave the plane quickly in an emergency. The pilots of the 1º Stormo were, on the contrary, most anxious to convert to the new high-speed monoplane. Pilots of this Stormo had formed the Gruppo "La Cucaracha" which had fought over Spain with Fiat C.R.32 biplanes. With the end of the Spanish Civil War and the return of the Italian pilots to Campoformido, the 1º Stormo began re-equipping with C.R.42 Falcos, but their experiences over Spain had convinced them that the day of the fighter biplane was drawing to a close, and they were delighted to exchange their C.R.42s for the M.C.200s of the 4º Stormo.

In service with the Regia Aeronautica, the M.C.200 was named Saetta which could be translated as both Lightning and Arrow (the weapons of Jupiter), but the fighter suffered a number of teething troubles, the most serious being a tendency to spin without warning under certain circumstances. This was eventually

M.C.200 Saetta fighter of the 81° Squadriglia of the 1° Stormo Caccia operating over Russia with the Corpo di Spedizione Italiano.

rectified by modifications to the wing, but the modifications delayed production deliveries, and only twenty-nine Saetta fighters had entered service by November 1, 1939, all but twelve of these being unserviceable. Although deliveries to the Regia Aeronautica were considered urgent, export orders for the Saetta were, nevertheless, solicited, and the Danish government was on the point of signing a contract for twelve of the Macchi-Castoldi fighters for its Naval Air Service when, on April 9 1940, Denmark was invaded by German forces. Two months later, when Italy entered the war, the Regia Aeronautica had taken delivery of 156 Saetta fighters and, in addition, orders had been placed for a further 572 machines. Macchi's Varese-Schiranna and Lonate Pozzolo plants were devoted solely to Saetta production, and the S.A.I. Ambrosini factory at Passignano and the Breda factory at Sesto S.Giovanni were in process of tooling up for the fighter.

The Saetta was serving principally with the 6° Gruppo Autonomo based at Catania, and the 152° and 153° Gruppi of the 54° Stormo based at Airasca, Turin, and Vergiate, Varese, but these units did not participate in the brief fighting with the French as the Macchi-Castoldi fighter had been grounded as the result of two temporarily inexplicable fatal crashes. There had been considerable delay in ascertaining the cause of these accidents, and at one time it seemed possible that manufacture of the fighter would have to be halted. Before this serious step could be taken, however, it was discovered that the accidents had resulted from an unpredictable high-speed stall which occurred under a rarely-encountered combination of circumstances. Once the cause of the trouble had been discovered it was quickly remedied by a simple modification to the aerofoil, and within two weeks of Italy entering the war the Saetta was fully operational.

The first Saetta fighters to see action were twenty-six machines forming part of the 6° Gruppo Autonomo of the 1° Divisione Caccia Terrestre based in Sicily. These participated in the air war over Malta

where they encountered the Hawker Hurricane for the first time, proving to be only slightly slower than the British fighter. The Saetta had, however, a considerably better climb rate and could outdive and outturn the Hurricane with ease. Its sturdy structure was found to be capable of absorbing considerable punishment, and it evinced no serious vices. It was very stable on the ground, and both take-off and landing runs were short. At the same time, the Saetta-equipped 370° Squadriglia of the 1° Stormo operating from Alghero, Sardinia, was performing in the escort role, accompanying S.M.79 and Ju 87B bombers on anti-shipping strikes in the Mediterranean, but it was not until 1941 that the Macchi-Castoldi fighter began to see extensive action.

On December 9, 1940, the Regia Aeronautica had the following home-based Saetta units: the 157° Gruppo with thirty-six machines at Caselle Torinese, the 22° Gruppo with thirty-seven machines at Ciampino for the defence of Rome, the 21° Gruppo with seventeen machines at Capodichino for the defence of Naples, and the 362° Squadriglia with twelve machines at Sarzana for the defence of La Spezia, the last three mentioned units also possessing a number of Fiat G.50s. In addition, the 1° Stormo had sixty-one Saettas plus some Fiat C.R.42s at Catania and Palermo. For operations over Greece, the 370° Squadriglia with nine Saettas was based at Foggia, the 372° Squadriglia with thirteen machines was based at Brindisi, and the 373° and the 374° squadriglie each with twelve machines were based at Bari and Grottaglie respectively.

Until the end of February 1941, Fiat C.R.42s and G.50s had borne the brunt of the aerial warfare over Greece and Albania, but the appearance of Hurricanes necessitated the re-equipment of the 150° Gruppo with the Saetta at Valona, and the transfer of the 22° Gruppo to Tirana. At about the same time, the first Saettas were sent to Libya where the 374° Squadriglia arrived in April 1941, operating from Castel Benito. It was joined in North Africa by the similarly-equipped

153º Gruppo on July 2, 1941, by which time the 4º Stormo's 10º Gruppo and the 54º Stormo had been sent to Sicily to operate Saettas against Malta. With the formation of the Corpo di Spedizione Italiano for operations against the Soviet Union, the 22º Gruppo with fifty-one Saettas was transferred to Russia on August 12, 1941, beginning operations from Krivoy Rog on the 27th with a close-support mission over Dnepropetrovsk during which eight confirmed "kills" and four "probables" were claimed by the Italian pilots. The Saettas successively operated from Krivoy Rog, Zaporozhye and Stalino, and for a period the 22º Gruppo was attached to the German *Stalino Nahkampffuehrer* which undertook fighter sweeps, close support duties, and acted as escort for Luftwaffe bomber and reconnaissance units. Subsequently, the 22º Gruppo took an active part in the assault on the Kerch Peninsula, receiving considerable praise from the German 17th Army for its close-support activities in the Slavjansk and Izyum sectors. During the spring of 1942, the Saettas of the 22º Gruppo were taken over by the 21º Gruppo, the strength of which was raised to four Squadriglie in June of that year, two of these operating from Tazinskaja as escorts for Luftwaffe Ju 87s. When finally repatriated to Italy in May 1943, the Italian fighters had claimed eighty-eight Russian aircraft in combat for the loss of fifteen Macchi-Castoldi fighters, and had undertaken 1,983 escort missions, 1,310 close-support missions, 511 air cover missions, and 2,557 fighter sweep missions.

In the meantime, the Saetta was being progressively improved and new variants of the basic Macchi Castoldi were being evolved. The totally enclosed cockpit of the initial production series of Saetta

fighters was quickly discarded, and several arrangements were tried on different production series, ranging from a completely open cockpit with faired headrest to an arrangement in which two perspex flaps were hinged on each side so that only the top of the pilot's head was exposed. The M.C.200 A.S. (the suffix indicating *Africa Settentrionale*, or North Africa) featured sand filters and other equipment to suit it for desert operation, and the M.C.200 C.B. (*Caccia Bombardiere* or Fighter-Bomber) had under-wing racks for eight 33-lb. or two 110-lb., 220-lb., or 352-lb. bombs, or two 22 or 33 Imp. gal. (26.4 or 39.6 U.S. gal.) drop tanks. An armoured seat and armour protection for the pilot's head and shoulders were progressively introduced, together with improved equipment, such as an Allocchio Bacchini B.30 R/T set. Late production aircraft were fitted with identical wings to those of the M.C.202 Folgore with provision for two 7.7-mm. Breda-SAFAT machine guns with 500 r.p.g.

The installation of additional equipment, armament and armour resulted in progressive increases in weights, the empty and normal loaded weights of the prototype Saetta of 3,902 lb. and 4,850 lb. respectively eventually rising to 4,451 lb. and 5,597.5 lb. in the final production (Serie XXI) Saetta. A typical production Saetta with empty and normal loaded weights of 4,175 lb. and 5,121 lb., attained a maximum speed of 312 m.p.h. at 14,750 ft. An altitude of 3,280 ft. was reached in 1 min. 3 sec., 9,840 ft. took 3 min. 24 sec., and 16,400 ft. took 5 min. 52 sec. Service ceiling was 29,200 ft., and normal range was 354 mls. at 283 m.p.h., although this could be increased to 540 mls. by the addition of two 33 Imp. gal. (39.6 U.S. gal.) drop tanks.

A late-production M.C.200 Saetta with perspex side flaps which partly enclosed the pilot's cockpit. Some late Saettas had identical wings to those of the M.C.202 Folgore with provision for two 7.7-mm. Breda-SAFAT guns with 500 r.p.g.

MACCHI-CASTOLDI SERIES

Towards the end of 1938, the Ministero dell' Aeronautica had begun to consider a potential replacement for the Saetta based on the use of the new Fiat A.76 R.C.40 air-cooled radial which, rated at 1,000 h.p., was then under test. Mario Castoldi endeavoured to meet the new requirements by refining his basic design. He had never been happy about the characteristic humped-back of the Saetta which had been imposed upon him by official demands, and as these had been modified in the meantime, he now took the opportunity to discard the "hump" and thus reduce fuselage drag. The refined Saetta received the designation M.C.201, but during the construction of the prototype (MM 436) it had been decided to abandon further work on the A.76 engine and, in consequence, when flight trials began in August 1940, a standard A.74 R.C.38 was installed. Apart from the lowering

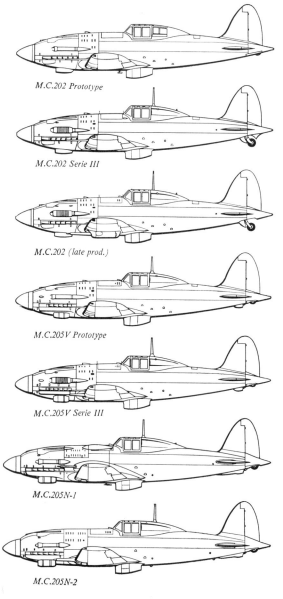

M.C.202 Prototype

M.C.202 Serie III

M.C.202 (late prod.)

M.C.205V Prototype

M.C.205V Serie III

M.C.205N-1

M.C.205N-2

of the upper fuselage decking which necessitated the semi-external mounting of the twin Breda-SAFAT guns in the nose, and the provision of a redesigned cockpit canopy, the M.C.201 differed little from its predecessor, and although a maximum speed of 342 m.p.h. was anticipated with the more powerful A.76 R.C.40 engine, with the A.74 installed the performance improvement over the Saetta was insufficient to warrant the disruption of production deliveries that would have resulted had the M.C.201 been introduced, despite the retention of the same basic airframe.

Another factor motivating against the adoption of the M.C.201 was the appearance of the infinitely superior M.C.202 which had flown for the first time on August 10, 1940. Again, the basic airframe remained relatively unchanged, apart from some further improvement in the fineness ratio of the fuselage and local strengthening, but the installation of an imported Daimler-Benz DB 601A-1 liquid-cooled engine radically changed the appearance of the fighter. The combination of Italian airframe and German power plant was an instantaneous success. The delightful symmetry of line which had characterised Castoldi's racing seaplanes had reappeared; the re-engined fighter had lost little of the agility and none of the finger-light handling qualities for which the Saetta was already renowned, and maximum speed exceeded 370 m.p.h. So successful were initial trials that Breda's Sesto S.Giovanni plant was instructed to begin immediate preparations for the quantity production of the M.C.202, and by making use of most of the jigs and tooling already in use for Saetta production, the first deliveries of the improved fighter were made only eight months after the prototype had begun testing.

The Daimler-Benz engine was immediately placed in production by the Alfa Romeo company as the R.A.1000 R.C.41-I Monsoni (Monsoon), the Italian-built version of this twelve-cylinder inverted-Vee liquid-cooled engine being rated at 1,175 h.p. and driving a Piaggio P.1001 constant-speed airscrew. Early production M.C.202's received DB 601A engines surplus to Luftwaffe requirements. The M.C.202's structure was essentially similar to that of the Saetta, the vertical and horizontal tail surfaces being identical as were also the wings, apart from the installation of 8.8 Imp. gal. (10.57 U.S. gal.) fuel tanks in each of the inboard wing sections, these supplementing the fuse-

FINISH AND INSIGNIA: *The Macchi C.202 Folgore illustrated on the opposite page belonged to the 6o Gruppo of the 1o Stormo Caccia and was the seventh aircraft of the 79a Squadriglia operating in North Africa. The upper surfaces employed "Desert" pattern camouflage comprising sand brown overall with irregular patches of spinach green. Under surfaces were pale blue-grey, and the asces insignia on the upper and lower surfaces of the wings appeared in black silhouette. The "Sagittario" emblem of the 1o Stormo was painted in black on the white "combat identification" band which encircled the rear fuselage, the arms of the House of Savoy appeared in the centre of the white Cross of Savoy on the vertical tail surfaces, and the fascist emblem appeared on the fuselage sides ahead of the cockpit, this comprising a silver axehead protruding from a brown bundle of faggots on a circular blue field. The spinner and extreme forward portion of the engine cowling were painted white and the unit and individual aircraft identification numerals were painted in black.*

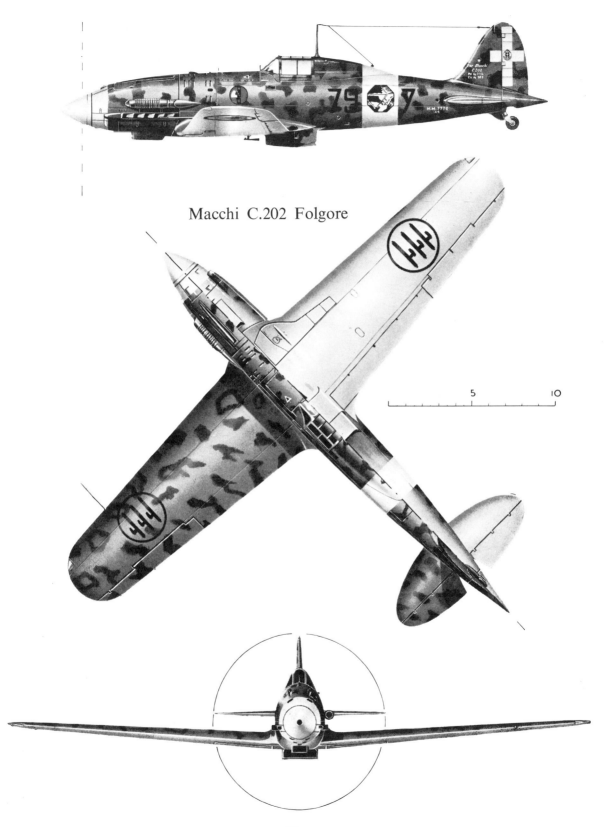

Macchi C.202 Folgore

5   10

The M.C.202 Folgore *reached operational service late in* 1941, *early production fighters such as that illustrated having no wing guns.*

lage tanks which had been slightly increased in capacity to 59 Imp. gal. (70.85 U.S. gal.) and 17.6 (21 U.S. gal.). The glazed panels aft of the pilot's headrest featured by the prototype were deleted on the production model as the extremely slim aft fairing rendered these unnecessary, and the anti-turnover structure aft of the pilot's head was supplanted by a strengthened canopy frame. Early production series machines retained the original Saetta armament of twin 12.7-mm. Breda-SAFAT guns, ammunition capacity being increased to 400 r.p.g., but later production series (e.g., Serie IX-XI) also carried a 7.7-mm. gun with 500 rounds in each wing, while one batch carried a 20-mm. Mauser MG 151 cannon (with 200 r.p.g.) under each wing. The moulded armour-plate seat was somewhat lighter than comparable Allied seats, and no armour-glass windscreen

was provided on early M.C.202s, although this was introduced at a later stage. The M.C.202 A.S. was equipped with anti-dust filters and other equipment for desert operation, and late-production aircraft had underwing racks for similar loads to those carried by the M.C.200 C.B.

In service, the M.C.202 was dubbed Folgore (Lightning), and the first fighters of this type reached Libya on November 25, 1941, being operated by the 1° Stormo and supplementing the Saettas which were now largely transferred to the fighter-bomber and escort roles. After the failure of the second British offensive in the Western Desert, the Regia Aeronautica had two Folgore-equipped Gruppi in Libya, the 6° Gruppo at Ara Fileni and the 17° Gruppo at Tamet, and three Saetta-equipped Gruppi, the 8° Gruppo at En Nofilia and the 3° and 150° Gruppi at

The prototype M.C.202 Folgore (MM 445), *below, flew for the first time on August* 10, 1940, *with an imported Daimler-Benz DB* 601A-1.

Ara Fileni. As the British forces retreated in front of Rommel, the Folgore and Saetta bases were progressively moved forward, the Folgores undertaking fighter sweeps and, together with the Bf 109E and Bf 109F fighters of the Luftwaffe, endeavouring to maintain air superiority over the battle area, and the Saettas escorting Fiat C.R.42 fighter-bombers and Ju 87B dive-bombers and performing close-support missions. It was during this period that the Folgore was truly blooded in action, establishing a marked ascendancy over the Hurricane. In fact, the Folgore could turn inside all the fighters by which it was opposed, including the Spitfire which was the only Allied fighter that could outclimb the Macchi-Castoldi. In May 1942, the 1º Stormo was supplemented by the 4º Stormo, also equipped with the Folgore, and the Italo-German offensive of May 26th began with an attack by fifty-nine Folgores on Gambut airfield where twenty-four British aircraft were claimed to have been destroyed or seriously damaged. From the beginning of the offensive until the capture of Bir Hacheim during the first week of June, the Folgores flew 1,093 sorties as compared with 480 by the Saettas and C.R.42 Falcos.

The Saetta was progressively relegated to the fighter-bomber role, and one of the most noteworthy exploits of the Saetta while performing this task took place on September 14, 1942 when the 13º Gruppo Assalto attacked a British force attempting a landing in the vicinity of Tobruk, sinking the destroyer H.M.S. *Zulu* and leaving four motor torpedo boats on fire. Despite the superiority of the Folgore, production of the Saetta had continued owing to the extreme shortage of liquid-cooled engines. Few were forthcoming from Germany, and Alfa Romeo rarely succeeded in delivering more than fifty engines per month, some of these being diverted to Reggiane for installation in the Re.2001. The 21º Gruppo fighting on the Russian Front had made urgent requests for Folgores to replace their worn Saettas, but all available fighters of this type were needed for the North African Front, and it was not until the beginning of September 1942 that the first Folgores reached Russia. By the beginning of the Russian winter offensive of November 1942, only thirty-two Saettas and eleven Folgores remained in Russia, and two months later, on January 17, 1943, they carried out their last operational sortie of the Russian campaign, the survivors thereafter being withdrawn from operations. After the Italo-German retreat to the El Agheila-Tauorga line, the activities of the Saettas and Folgores in Libya were constantly reduced by shortages of fuel and spares, and in January 1943, the 3º Stormo was transferred with its Folgores to Tunisia, taking over the surviving aircraft of the 4º Stormo which had been recalled to Italy, together with the 13º Gruppo which possessed two Saetta-equipped Squadriglie and one Folgore-equipped Squadriglia.

Mario Castoldi and his team were not content to rest on the laurels gained with the Folgore for, on April 19, 1942, a further development of the basic

(Above) An M.C.202 A.S. (Africa Settentrionale) Serie III (MM 7806).

(Above) A late-production M.C.202 (MM 91974) with underwing cannon.

(Above) A late-production M.C.202 (MM 9044) with 7.7-mm. wing guns.

(Above) An M.C.202 Serie IX of the 353º Squadriglia (51º Stormo).

fighter was flown for the first time. This, the M.C. 205V Veltro (Greyhound), differed from the M.C.202 in having a Daimler-Benz DB 605 engine rated at 1,475 h.p. for take-off. The prototype did, in fact, employ a Folgore airframe with some local strengthening, and apart from the use of the Fiat-built version of the DB 605A engine, which was known as the R.A.1050 R.C. 58 Tifone (Typhoon), there were few differences between the late-production series of the M.C.202 and the initial production M.C.205, armament remaining two 12.7-mm. and two 7.7-mm. guns. The Serie III version of the Veltro relinquished the wing-mounted 7.7-mm. guns in favour of a pair of 20-mm. Mauser MG 151 cannon with 250 r.p.g., and

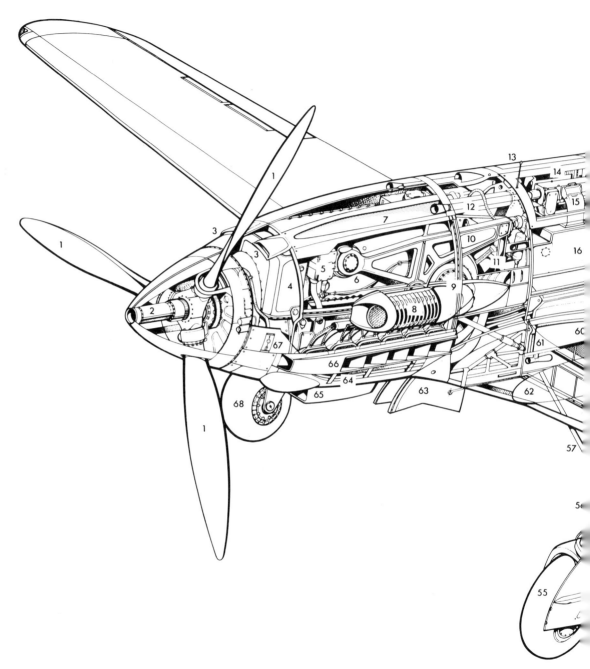

Macchi C.202 Folgore Serie XI Cutaway Key

1 Piaggio P.1001 constant-speed airscrew of 9ft 10$\frac{1}{2}$in (3.05 m) diameter
2 Airscrew shaft
3 Cooling scoops
4 Alfa Romeo R.A.1000 R.C.41-1 Monsoni 12-cylinder inverted-vee liquid-cooled engine
5 Header tank
6 Anti-vibration engine mounting pad
7 Port fuselage gun trough

8 Dust filter housing for supercharger air intake
9 Supercharger
10 Forged light alloy engine bearer
11 Oil tank of 7.9 Imp gal (36 1)capacity
12 Machine-gun barrel shroud
13 Secondary ring-and-bead sight (offset to port)
14 Ammunition tray
15 Port 12.7mm Breda-SAFAT machine-gun
16 Main fuselage fuel tank of 59.4 Imp gal (270 1) capacity

17 Instrument panel
18 San Giorgio reflector sight (offset to starboard)
19 Non-armoured windscreen
20 Sideways-hinging cockpit canopy
21 Pilot's headrest incorporating armour plate
22 Pilot's adjustable seat
23 Hydraulic reservoir for flap actuation
24 Hydraulic reservoir for undercarriage actuation

25 Overload fuel tank of 17.6 Imp gal (80 1) capacity
26 Rear-view cup-out (centre spine strengthening)
27 Fuel filler cap
28 Aerial mast
29 Aerial
30 Allocchio Bacchini B.30 receiver-transmitter
31 Fin construction
32 Metal-framed fabric-skinned rudder
33 Tail cone navigation light

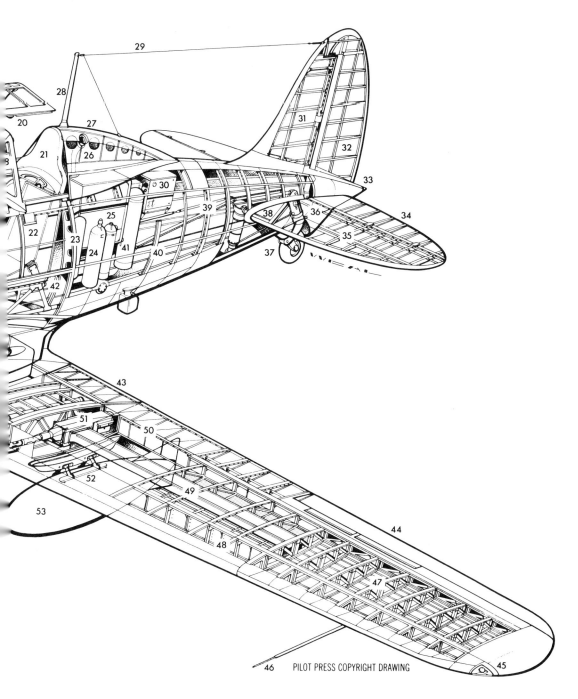

PILOT PRESS COPYRIGHT DRAWING

34 Port fabric-skinned
   elevator
35 Port tailplane
36 Tailwheel fairing
37 Non-retractable
   tailwheel
38 Tailwheel shock-absorber
   strut
39 Rudder and elevator
   push-pull rod control
   linkage
40 Semi-monocoque
   fuselage construction
41 Compressed air bottle
42 Seat support frame

43 Hydraulically-operated
   flaps
44 Fabric-covered statically
   and dynamically
   balanced aileron
45 Port navigation light
46 Pitot tube
47 Two-spar wing
   construction
48 Mainspar
49 Ammunition feed tray
50 Rear spar
51 Wing-mounted 7.7-mm
   Breda-SAFAT
   machine-gun

52 Underwing bomb/
   auxiliary tank shackle
53 Auxiliary tank of 22 Imp
   gal (100 l) capacity
54 Mainwheel fairing door
55 Port mainwheel
56 Mainwheel Oleo-
   pneumatic leg
57 Mainwheel retraction
   jack
58 Mainwheel retraction
   pivot point
59 Ventral radiator bath

60 Port wing-root fuel tank
   of 8·8 Imp gal (40 l)
   capacity
61 Fuselage centre section/
   wing steel attachment
   forgings
62 Mainwheel well
63 Centreline mainwheel
   fairing plates
64 Cooling lines
65 Air intake
66 Ejector exhausts
67 Cowling quick-release
   clip
68 Starboard mainwheel

(Left and above) An M.C.205V Veltro of the Italian Co-Belligerent Air Force.

(Below) The prototype M.C.205V Veltro (MM 9287) which flew for the first time on April 19, 1942 with the DB 605 engine.

having empty and loaded weights of 5,691 lb. and 7,514 lb. respectively, this model attained a maximum speed of 399 m.p.h. at 23,620 ft., and a maximum cruising speed of 310 m.p.h. An altitude of 3,280 ft. was reached in 53 sec., 9,840 ft. in 2 min. 40 sec., and 22,965 ft. in 7 min. 6 sec., and service ceiling and range were 36,090 ft. and 646 mls. respectively. Underwing racks could be fitted for two 110-lb., 220-lb., or 353-lb. bombs, and the Veltro bore comparison with the best fighters of any air arm, being one of the few Axis aircraft capable of matching the redoubtable P-51D Mustang.

The Veltro was considered by Castoldi as very much an interim development for production while he was working on a more refined version of the fighter

capable of making full use of the DB 605 engine. For the first time, wing span and area which had remained constant throughout the development life of the Macchi-Castoldi fighter at 34 ft. 8½ in. and 180.83 sq. ft., were increased, these becoming 36 ft. 10⅞ in. and 204.514 sq. ft. respectively. The tail surfaces and undercarriage were essentially similar to those of the Veltro, but the fineness ratio of the fuselage was again improved, and all armament was removed from the wings. This new model was designated M.C.205N Orione (Orion), and two prototypes were built, the first of these flying on November 1, 1942. This aircraft, the M.C.205N-1 (MM 499), carried four 12.7-mm. guns grouped in the forward fuselage plus an engine-mounted 20-mm. cannon. Two of the machine guns were housed in fairings over the wing roots. The second prototype, the M.C.205N-2, which first flew on May 19, 1943, reverted to wing-mounted armament, the 12.7-mm. guns over the wing roots being supplanted by a 20-mm. MG 151 cannon within each wing, total armament thus comprising three 20-mm. cannon and two 12.7-mm. machine guns.

Production priority was allocated to the Veltro as this fighter could be built almost entirely on the jigs and tools used in Folgore production whereas the Orione demanded much new tooling. In any case, the Orione offered no major performance advantage over the Veltro, the M.C.205N-1 version attaining maximum speeds of 367 m.p.h. at 13,120 ft., 372 m.p.h. at 16,400 ft., 385 m.p.h. at 19,685 ft., and 390 m.p.h. at 22,965 ft., the M.C.205N-2 being approximately 2 m.p.h. slower at all altitudes.

By February 12, 1943, there were fifty-five service-able Folgores and twenty-five Saettas in Tunisia, the 384° Squadriglia with Saettas at Tunis, and the 6° Gruppo with Folgores at Sfax and Gannert in the Northern Sector, and the 3° Stormo with both Folgores and Saettas at El Hamma, the 13° Gruppo with Saettas also at El Hamma, and the 16° Gruppo with Folgores at K34 and K41 airfields in the Southern Sector. These were actively engaged against the

British and American forces between the Mareth line and Medenine, but by May few aircraft remained serviceable, and the last Macchi-Castoldi fighters were withdrawn from North Africa.

During the Battle of Pantelleria, M.C.205V Veltro fighters were employed operationally for the first time, fifteen aircraft of this type escorting torpedo-bombers and Saetta fighter-bombers attacking Allied warships shelling the Pantelleria defences on July 8, 1943. On July 9th, after the first Allied landings on Sicily, eight Folgores from the 3º Stormo and ten Veltros from the 51º Stormo were hurriedly flown to the island from Cerveteri and Sardinia, but the Italian fighters were soon overwhelmed. When, on September 8, 1943, Marshal Badoglio's government capitulated, the Regia Aeronautica had only thirty-three Saettas, fifty-three Folgores and thirty-five Veltros in serviceable condition, the total numbers of these fighters on charge being fifty-two, one hundred and twenty-two and sixty-six respectively. Twenty-three of the Saettas and six each of the Folgores and Veltros reached the Allied-occupied airfields. These included all the serviceable Saettas of the 8º Gruppo which began operations as a part of the Italian Co-Belligerent Air Force the day after the Armistice, escorting the Italian Fleet sailing from La Spezia to Malta. The other Macchi-Castoldi fighters served with the Iº and IIº Gruppi Caccia of the Aviazione della RSI when that force was organised after the formation of the Repubblica Sociale Italiana, continuing to fight alongside the Luftwaffe.

When production of the Macchi-Castoldi fighters terminated, approximately 1,000 Saettas and 1,500 Folgores had been manufactured, and of these 395 Saettas and 392 Folgores had been produced by the parent company. In addition, 262 Veltro fighters were built. These quantities were small indeed by comparison with the numbers of fighters produced by the other major combatants, but despite the existence of many well-equipped plants, the Italian aircraft industry had never been mobilised for mass production on modern lines. Almost entirely dependent on imports for the supply of raw materials for aircraft production, Italy was forced to rely on Germany for supplies, and the limitations of German assistance and the enforced emigration of large numbers of skilled workers to German factories kept Italian production at a figure far below the essential minimum to sustain intensive operations. Had it been possible to build the Macchi-Castoldi fighters in really *large* numbers, the air war over North Africa and the Mediterranean could well have followed a different course. The M.C.200 Saetta of 1937 bore little resemblance to the M.C.205V Veltro of 1943 at first sight, but in fact the latter was essentially a progressive development of the former with no major structural changes, and a U.S.A.A.F. pilot's comment after flight testing a captured Folgore may be considered descriptive of all the Macchi-Castoldi fighters—"Gee, that's a honey of an airplane!"

Macchi C.202 Folgore (Serie IX-XI)

Dimensions:	Span, 34 ft. 8½ in.; length, 29 ft. 0½ in.; height, 9 ft. 11½ in.; wing area, 180.83 sq. ft.
Armament:	Two 12.7-mm. Breda-SAFAT machine guns with 400 r.p.g. in the fuselage and two wing-mounted 7.7-mm. Breda-SAFAT guns with 500 r.p.g., plus two 110-lb., 220-lb., or 353-lb. bombs.
Power Plant:	One Alfa Romeo R.A.1000 R.C.41-I Monsoni (licence-built Daimler-Benz DB 601A-1) twelve-cylinder inverted-Vee liquid-cooled engine rated at 1,175 h.p. at 2,500 r.p.m. for take-off and 1,400 h.p. at 2,400 r.p.m. Maximum internal fuel capacity, 76.6 Imp. gal. (91.85 U.S. gal.).
Weights:	Empty, 5,181 lb.; normal loaded, 6,459 lb. maximum, 6,636 lb.
Performance:	Maximum speed, 309 m.p.h. at sea level, 324 m.p.h. at 3,280 ft., 352 m.p.h. at 9,840 ft., 370 m.p.h. at 16,400 ft., 363 m.p.h. at 22,965 ft.; time to 3,280 ft., 39 sec., to 6,560 ft., 1 min. 28 sec., to 9,840 ft., 2 min. 28 sec., to 13,120 ft., 3 min. 32 sec., to 16,400ft., 4 min. 4 sec.; service ceiling, 37,730 ft.; normal range 475 mls.

The prototype M.C.205N-1 Orione which flew for the first time on November 1, 1942. The M.C.205N-2 differed principally in the type and arrangement of its armament.

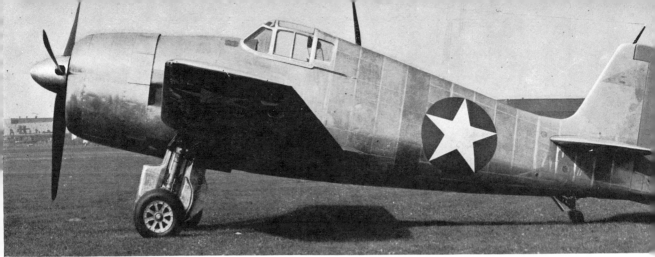

Above and below, left) The second prototype Hellcat, the XF6F-3, which flew for the first time on July 30, 1942.

THE
GRUMMAN HELLCAT

The Hellcat was unquestionably the most importa
Allied shipboard fighter of the Second World W
and to this aircraft more than to any other went t
distinction of turning the tide in the air war over t
Pacific. By 1944, when the U.S. Navy had fina
gained the initiative over the Japanese, the Hell
had become the mainstay of U.S. carrier aviati
while the Corsair was the mainstay of the Nav
shore-based fighter elements. The Hellcat norma
made the initial contact with the opposing enemy f
mations in amphibious operations and engaged in
major attacks against enemy surface vessels, the C
sair taking over as soon as shore bases had be
secured, the two fighters becoming known as
"Terrible Twins."

(Above, left and below) The first prototype Hellcat, the XF6F-1, which flew with the R-2600 engine on June 26, 1942

The XF6F-3 seen in late March 1943 *after modification to production F6F-3 standard with the exception of the undercarriage which remained unchanged. No armament was installed.*

Until the operational début of the Hellcat, the Mitsubishi Zero-Sen had enjoyed a definite ascendancy over U.S. carrier-borne fighters, whose pilots, invariably at a disadvantage, were forced to rely on superior tactics to offset the inferior speed, climb rate and manoeuvrability of their aircraft. The appearance of the Hellcat in the late summer of 1943 changed the situation virtually overnight, however, and the Grumman fighter was to be credited with no fewer than 4,947 of the 6,477 enemy aircraft claimed to have been destroyed in the air by U.S. Navy carrier pilots. With the scores of shore-based Hellcat units added, the Hellcat was to claim the destruction of no less than 5,156 enemy machines, the ratio of "kills" to losses exceeding nineteen to one!

Between the invasion of Poland and the attack on Pearl Harbour a little more than two years later, the U.S. Navy's knowledge of the tactics and weapons of aerial warfare was expanded on the basis of the experience of the combatants, despite the fact that the European conflict was essentially a land war with few naval aircraft participating. Nevertheless, the general lessons were, in many cases, applicable to carrier-based fighter aircraft, and the U.S. Navy observers found Europe a fruitful field for investigation. They learned that speed, climb rate, adequate armour protection and firepower, pilot visibility and manoeuvrability were primary requirements in that order, and to these desirable attributes the shipboard fighter had to add ample fuel and ammunition capacity. At this time the Grumman Wildcat was entering service with the U.S. Navy, and it was obvious that, from the performance standpoint at least, it did not compare favourably with land-based European contemporaries. The XF4U-1 Corsair prototype was undergoing trials, but the U.S. Navy considered it advisable to order the development of another fighter as an insurance against the failure of the Chance Vought design. Accordingly,

The XF6F-2 was originally to have had a turbo-supercharged R-2600 Cyclone but was eventually flown in January 1944 *with a turbo-supercharged R-2800-21 (below).*

The F6F-3 (above) went into action for the first time on August 31, 1943 during a strike on Marcus Island.

the Grumman Aircraft Engineering Corporation was asked to proceed with the design of a version of the Wildcat fitted with the larger, more powerful Wright R-2600 Cyclone fourteen-cylinder radial air-cooled engine rated at 1,600 h.p. at 2,400 r.p.m.

A contract for two prototypes under the designation XF6F-1 was awarded Grumman on June 30, 1941, but the design team, headed by Leroy R. Grumman and William T. Schwendler, already had its own ideas on the form that the Wildcat's successor should take, having canvassed U.S. Navy pilots for their opinions on the subject. So many changes were evolved that, in the end, the more powerful development of the Wildcat originally envisaged by the U.S. Navy only served as a basis for the creation of an entirely new design; one bearing little more than a vague family resemblance to its predecessor. Substantial increases had been made in both fuel and ammunition capacity and a sixty per cent increase in weight over that of the earlier fighter necessitated what was to be the largest wing area of any wartime U.S. single-engined production fighter in order to keep wing loading within reasonable bounds. This wing was mounted at the minimum angle of incidence to obtain the least drag in level flight, but as a comparatively large angle of attack was required, a negative thrust line was adopted for the Cyclone engine, resulting in a tail-down flight attitude. This negative thrust line also aided pilot visibility by improving forward view, and all-round visibility was enhanced by positioning the cockpit at the highest point amidships, the pilot being seated over the fuel tanks. Aesthetically, the design lacked

A total of 252 F6F-3s was delivered to the Royal Navy, these being known initially in that service as Gannet Is.

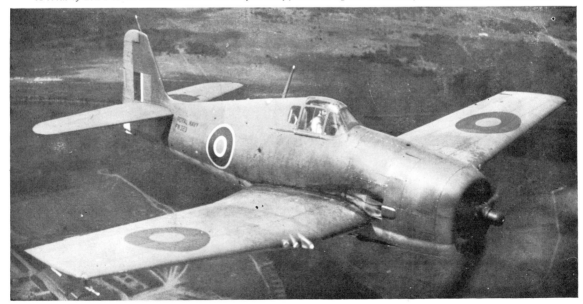

An F6F-3 under test in March 1945 with non-standard cockpit canopy and dummy MK 13-2 torpedo.

elegance, but its sturdy lines were in keeping with its immensely strong structure which was to endow the fighter with a reputation for absorbing punishment and staying in the air.

Design and prototype construction progressed with startling rapidity, although, during the gestation of the fighter, encounters with the Mitsubishi Zero-Sen, with its marked performance superiority over the Wildcat, logically resulted in the question of whether American designers ought not to emulate their Japanese contemporaries, and produce fighters of extremely light construction. But the Japanese, with their fatalistic and ruthless disregard for expenditure of human life, could reduce safety elements to the minimum in order to achieve a low weight, and the U.S. Navy was unwilling to accept the loss of versatility of attack

and increased vulnerability that would have been the penalties of improved speed, climb and manoeuvrability obtained in this way. Nevertheless, the best possible performance was demanded without compromising structural strength, armour protection and firepower, and the Grumman team spent the critical first months of the Pacific War in wrestling with these problems. The result of their toil was to be a shipboard fighter of unparalleled lethal efficiency.

The first XF6F-1 was flown on June 26, 1942 by Selden A. Converse, but shortly after the Battle of Midway (June 3–6, 1942), Leon A. Swirbul, Grumman's president, had flown to Pearl Harbour where he met leading naval fighter pilots, including Lieut.-Comm. John S. Thach, the U.S. Navy's authority on combat tactics. The preponderance

An experimental F6F-3 under test with two 1,000-lb. bombs and a 137 Imp. gal. (165 U.S. gal.) ventral drop tank.

FINISH AND INSIGNIA: *The F6F-3 Hellcat illustrated on the opposite page was operational in the Pacific during the late summer of 1943, and was finished in non-specular blue-grey overall upper surfaces and pale grey over the under surfaces. The individual aircraft number "22" appeared in white ahead of the national insignia and on the vertical fin and in black on the hinged upper flaps of the undercarriage doors. The national insignia appeared on the upper surfaces of the port wing, lower* *surfaces of the starboard wing and fuselage sides. The presentation of the national insignia shows an interesting variation to the standard style at this stage of the war. The additional white horizontal bar adopted on June 28, 1943 was outlined in red on the fuselage sides in accordance with the new insignia specification (the red outline being discarded on September 14, 1943 in favour of a blue outline), but no outline had been added to the insignia on the wing surfaces.*

of opinion insisted that, to counter the Zero-Sen, more climb and speed were needed than were expected from the XF6F-1, and the result of these meetings was the finalising of a decision already contemplated to abandon the R-2600 Cyclone in favour of the Pratt and Whitney R-2800 (B) Double Wasp eighteen-cylinder engine which, adopted for the Corsair, offered a twenty-five per cent increase in power. This engine was installed in the second prototype airframe from the outset, this second aircraft receiving the designation XF6F-3 and flying for the first time on July 30, 1942, the new fighter being dubbed, appropriately enough as it was to transpire, Hellcat.

As the Hellcat and Corsair were designed for the same purpose, it was inevitable that rivalry between Grumman and Chance Vought should be keen, a fact not lost upon U.S. Navy Bureau of Aeronautics representatives, and when the XF6F-3 prototype was

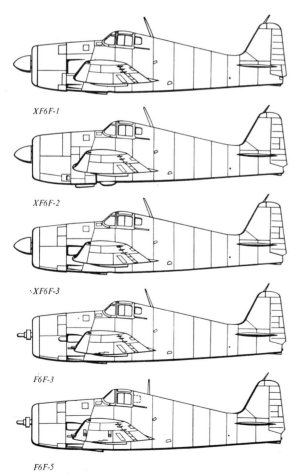

XF6F-1

XF6F-2

·XF6F-3

F6F-3

F6F-5

undergoing its initial trials in the summer of 1942, impressed by the excellent cockpit vision and ground handling characteristics of the Hellcat, they made the tentative suggestion, undoubtedly with tongue in cheek, that Corsair production should be cancelled in favour of the Grumman fighter! The result was that Chance Vought, already committed to an extensive programme of modifications to suit their fighter for operational service, redoubled their efforts to overcome the Corsair's poor cockpit vision and ground handling.

Initial flight trials with the Hellcat prototypes were generally satisfactory, although the fighter suffered from excessive longitudinal stability, and excessive trim change between flaps up and flaps down, and airspeed in a dive had to be limited to 525 m.p.h. owing to flutter. These shortcomings were easily corrected, however, and changes were held to a minimum in order to expedite delivery of the initial production F6F-3 Hellcats which were being built on a pre-production line at Bethpage while a new plant specifically for Hellcat production was under construction. The principal modifications were the replacement of the Curtiss Electric airscrew by a Hamilton Standard unit, the discarding of the airscrew spinner, and the redesign of the main undercarriage wheel fairings.

Production of the Hellcat had been ordered on May 23, 1942, and the speed with which deliveries began was one of the highlights of the fighter's history, the first production F6F-3 flying on October 4, 1942, ten having been completed by the end of the year. Apart from some elevator buffeting, the first F6F-3 passed its preliminary acceptance trials without revealing any serious shortcomings, but during arrester trials late in November, an arrester hook was pulled out of the fuselage, and in the following month a complete fuselage failure occurred. The fuselage was hurriedly strengthened and the trials were completed satisfactorily. Work on the plant intended for Hellcat production had begun in August 1942, and in order to avoid the inevitable delays while the U.S. Navy awaited the necessary priorities for the issue of the required steel, Leon A. Swirbul purchased the steel as scrap from New York's old Second Avenue elevated railway, and the first production jigs were set up in October, fighters starting down the assembly line while the plant was still under construction!

The F6F-3 was powered by an R-2800-10 engine with a maximum rating of 2,000 h.p. at 2,700 r.p.m., and self-sealing fuel cells beneath the cockpit floor housed 195.6 Imp. gal. (235 U.S. gal.). These could be supplemented by a 125 Imp. gal. (150 U.S. gal.) drop

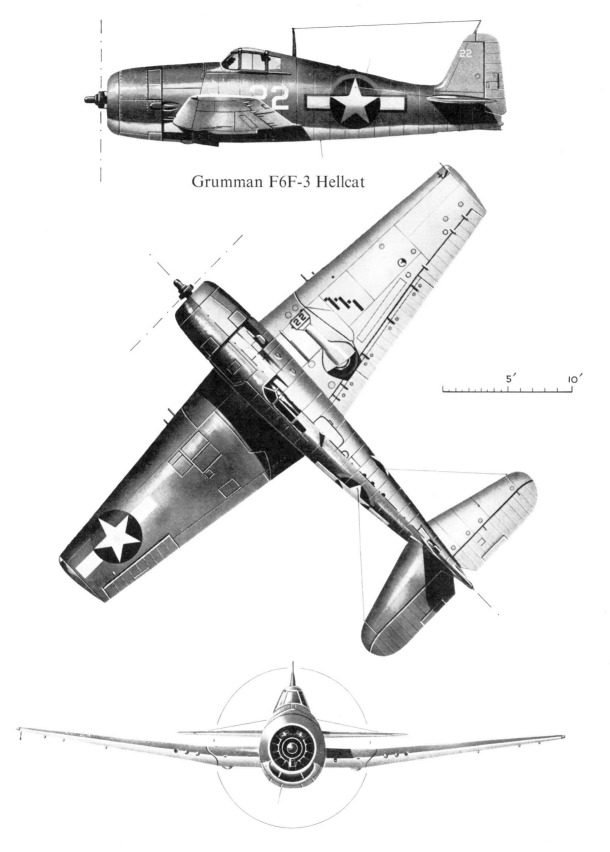

Grumman F6F-3 Hellcat

5′   10′

(Above and left) The XF6F-3N night-fighter prototype with radar housing attached to the starboard wing.

stringers completing the basic structure. The aluminium alloy skinning was applied in lateral strips and flush riveted. Mounted in low-mid position, the three-spar wing comprised five principal assembles; the section traversing the fuselage beneath the cockpit and housing the self-sealing tanks, two stub centre sections providing the attachment points and accommodation for the main undercarriage members, and the detachable outer panels arranged to swivel at the forward spar and fold aft along the fuselage sides. All control surfaces were metal framed, the rudder and elevators being fabric-covered. Split flaps were provided between the ailerons and fuselage, and the fully retractable main undercarriage members retracted aft, turning through 90° to lie flush within the centre-section wells.

On January 16, 1943, the first production F6F-3 Hellcats were delivered to the U.S. Navy's Fighter

tank. Armament comprised six 0.5-in. Colt-Browning machine guns with a maximum of 400 r.p.g., three guns being mounted immediately outboard of each wing fold point, and 212 lb. of armour was provided to protect the pilot, the oil tank and the oil cooler. The fuselage was an all-metal monocoque with vertical keels positioned either side of the centre-line. The pressed flange aluminium alloy frames were riveted to these keel members, extruded aluminium alloy

A total of one hundred and forty-nine F6F-3N night fighters was delivered to the U.S. Navy.

Squadron VF-9 aboard the U.S.S. *Essex*, although the distinction of first taking the new fighter into action was to go to VF-5 on August 31, 1943, this squadron operating from the U.S.S. *Yorktown* with Task Force 15 during the second strike on Marcus Island. The Hellcats of VF-9 aboard the *Essex* also participated in the action later in the day. Only fourteen months had elapsed between the first prototype's inaugural flight and the first operational sortie of the fighter, the corresponding time for the Corsair having been more than thirty-two months!

The F6F-3 now rapidly supplanted the Wildcat aboard the principal U.S. Navy carriers, production tempo building up quickly, 2,555 machines having been completed by the end of 1943. Initial combat experience stressed the ruggedness, reliable performance and ease of maintenance of the Hellcat, the only serious criticisms being concerned with excessive tyre wear and other undercarriage troubles, and reduced vision resulting from the curved plexiglas windscreen being easily scratched and dust collecting between it and the inner armoured glass screen. In combat with the A6M2 and A6M3, the Hellcat pilots considered their mount to possess a definite advantage over its opponents, although the manoeuvrability of the Japanese fighters was generally superior. But the superior speed, dive and altitude capabilities of the American fighter more than compensated for this inferiority, permitting its pilots to acquire an advantage of position and thus enabling them to adopt tactics whereby the Mitsubishi fighters could be destroyed without the dog-fighting for which they had been conceived. Generally, the F6F-3 had no difficulty in staying with the earlier models of the Zero-Sen through most manoeuvres, but the Grumman could not follow its opponent in a tight loop, and, often, when following a Zero-Sen in a tight turn, the F6F-3 was forced to roll out to avoid a stall. A manoeuvre frequently adopted by the Japanese pilots to evade an F6F-3 on their tail was a snap split-S to port at low altitude, pulling through over the water at a safe margin. Once on the tail of a Zero-Sen, the F6F-3 could usually turn with the Japanese fighter long enough to get in a good burst, although it could not stay with the Zero-Sen for more than 90° of the turn. When the positions were reversed, the F6F-3 could usually elude its opponent by diving and twisting with the ailerons. In level flight the F6F-3 could usually pull away, and its rugged structure stood up well to the 7.7-mm. guns of the Zero-Sen, whereas the sextette of .50-in. guns of the Grumman could destroy the Japanese fighter with a relatively small expenditure of ammunition, the Zero-Sen burning readily.

From January 1944, sixty per cent of all production F6F-3s were equipped with the R-2800-10W engine in which water injection boosted emergency power to 2,200 h.p., and from the beginning of April, all new Hellcats were so equipped. On the 21st of that month production of the F6F-3 terminated with the 4,402nd machine, and the improved F6F-5 began to roll off

the line. Prior to this event, however, several other versions of the Hellcat had made their appearance. The XF6F-2 had originally been proposed in parallel with the XF6F-1, this having provision for an R2600-Cyclone with a turbo-supercharger. In mid-December 1943, the engine had been changed to a turbo-supercharged R-2800-21, the XF6F-2 flying for the first time with this power plant in January 1944, but the aircraft was later modified to production configuration and delivered as an F6F-3. The original XF6F-1, which had been converted as the second XF6F-3, was further modified as the XF6F-4 by the installation of a two-speed R-2800-27 engine, flying in this form for the first time on October 2, 1942, and being accepted by the U.S. Navy six months later.

Sub-variants of the F6F-3 included the -3E and -3N radar-equipped fighters. Early in 1941, specifications had been drawn up for a radar set to be carried by single-seat fighters and, owing to the extensive development work that had gone into the Corsair, this became the first single-seat radar-equipped fighter used in combat by the U.S. Navy, but it was soon supplemented by the Hellcat which made, from the viewpoints of operation and maintenance, a much better night fighter. Night vision of the Hellcat was poor, however, and in an attempt to reduce this shortcoming red lights were installed for the instrument panels to cut down cockpit glare, and the outer plexiglas windscreen was eliminated to provide a flat-fronted screen. Eighteen F6F-3E Hellcats were produced from standard -3 airframes by the installation of early AN/APS-4 radar in a fairing which, attached to the starboard wing, did not disturb the fighter's normal structure, but the principal radar-equipped model was the F6F-3N which differed from the -3E in having the later AN/APS-6 radar. The first such installation was completed in July 1943, this aircraft, designated XF6F-3N, commencing trials at Quonset Point shortly afterwards. One hundred and forty-nine F6F-3N night fighters were delivered to the U.S. Navy, these having the AN/APN-1 radar altimeter, AN/APX-21FF, a redesigned instrument panel and landing lights. The first use of Hellcat night fighters from carriers took place during the occupation of the Gilbert Islands in November 1943, the first nocturnal sortie being undertaken on the 24th without contact being made, but during a second sortie on the 26th, two Hellcats operating with an Avenger from the U.S.S. *Enterprise* and led by Lieut.-Comm. Edward H. O'Hare, engaged an enemy bombing formation, disrupting its attack and saving the task group from damage.

With the R-2800-10W engine, the empty weight of the radar-equipped F6F-3N was increased from the 9,042 lb. of the original production -3 to 9,331 lb., normal and maximum gross weights being 13,015 lb. and 14,074 lb. respectively. The increased drag resulting from the radar fairing reduced maximum speed to 360 m.p.h. at 18,000 ft. and 305 m.p.h. at sea level, and initial climb rate and service ceiling were 3,090 ft./min. and 38,100 ft.

The Royal Navy received 930 F6F-5s which entered service as Hellcat IIs (above) plus eighty F6F-5N night fighters which were designated Hellcat N.F.II (left).

Although the Hellcat was markedly faster than Japanese shipboard fighters, the striving for still greater speeds continued unabated, and by the end of January 1944, a specially "cleaned-up" version of the F6F-3 had attained a speed of 410 m.p.h. in level flight at 21,000 ft. Some of the modifications introduced on this aircraft, together with the progressive improvements made during production of the F6F-3 as well as changes arising from the F6F-3N programme, were incorporated in the F6F-5 which flew for the first time on April 4, 1944. The F6F-5 retained the R-2800-10W engine, the principle changes in the new model being the adoption of the flat-fronted windshield as standard and, on some machines, the deletion of the windows aft of the sliding canopy,

red instrument panel lighting, a redesigned, close-fitting engine cowling, spring tab ailerons, an increase to 242 lb. in total armour weight, a strengthened tail assembly, provision for racks for two 1,000-lb. bombs beneath the centre section and for six 5-in. rocket projectiles beneath the wings, and a special smooth finish. The new model had an empty weight of 9,238 lb., normal and maximum gross weights being increased to 12,740 lb. and 15,413 lb., but despite the greater weight, maximum speed was increased to 380 m.p.h. at 23,400 ft., although initial climb rate fell off from 3,500 ft./min. to 2,980 ft./min. Some late production F6F-5s had a pair of 20-mm. cannon in the wings in addition to four wing-mounted 0.5-in. guns.

By comparison with the Mitsubishi A6M5, the F6F-5 had a speed advantage of 45 m.p.h. at 10,000 ft. and 75 m.p.h. at 25,000 ft. Climb rate was inferior by about 600 ft./min. to that of the Japanese fighter up to 9,000 ft., after which the advantage fell off until the two aircraft were equal at 14,000 ft., at higher altitudes the F6F-5 having the advantage, varying from 500

The F6F-5, which first flew on April 4, 1944, possessed a marked speed advantage over the Mitsubishi A6M5 but low-level climb rate and manoeuvrability were inferior.

ft./min. better at 20,000 ft. to 250 ft./min. better at 30,000 ft. Manoeuvrability of the A6M5 was generally superior to the F6F-5 at low speeds, particularly in turns at low and medium altitudes, but the F6F-5 compared favourably at 30,000 ft. In slow speed turns, the A6M5 gained one turn in three-and-a-half at 10,000 ft. In competitive trials with the F4U-1D Corsair, the F6F-5 attained 323 m.p.h. at 500 ft. compared with the Corsair's 328 m.p.h., and both aircraft were even at 349 m.p.h. at 10,000 ft., above which the Corsair maintained a speed advantage up to 30,000 ft.

Early in 1943, F6F-3 Hellcats had been made available to the Fleet Air Arm under Lend-Lease, 252 being delivered. These were known initially as Gannet Is in British service until standardisation of names resulted in the F6F-3 in the F.A.A. being renamed Hellcat I. The Hellcat I entered service with No. 800 Squadron on July 1, 1943, supplanting that unit's Sea Hurricanes, and made its operational début in December of that year from the light escort carrier *Emperor* during anti-shipping strikes off the Norwegian coast. No. 800 Squadron's Hellcat Is provided fighter cover for an attack on the *Tirpitz* in Kaafiord in April 1944, and a similar task was undertaken four months later by the Hellcat Is of No. 1840 Squadron operating from the *Furious*, but the Grumman fighter's service with the F.A.A. was principally with the British Pacific Fleet in the Far East where the bulk of the 930 F6F-5 Hellcat IIs supplied to Britain were employed until Japan's defeat, ten squadrons being equipped with the fighter on V-J Day, of which eight were operational. Hellcat IIs played a major role in the F.A.A.'s first large-scale action against the Japanese when, in January 1945, the oil refineries in Sumatra were attacked. In that month, Hellcats had begun to supplant the Wildcat aboard Britain's light escort carriers in preparation for the invasion of the Japanese home islands. In addition to the ten F.A.A. squadrons equipped with Hellcat IIs, two squadrons, Nos. 891 and 892, had been equipped with the night-

fighting Hellcat N.F.II by V-J Day, although neither unit saw operational service before the end of the war. Eighty night fighters of this type were supplied, bringing the total number of Hellcats diverted to the F.A.A. to 1,262.

The Hellcat N.F.II was the equivalent of the U.S. Navy's F6F-5N which employed the same equipment as the earlier -3N, 1,434 night fighters of this type being delivered in addition to the eighty for Britain, these seeing extensive service in the Pacific. The F6F-5N possessed a much better climb rate than U.S.A.A.F. night fighters available early in 1945, and on one occasion at Leyte, a P-61 Black Widow squadron was withdrawn and replaced by a U.S. Navy F6F-5N unit.

Surprisingly few major changes were introduced in the Hellcat during its production life, performance and adaptability being improved by progressive refinement. However, soon after the F6F-3 had

(*Above*) *An experimental F6F-5N with twin radomes and an armament of two 20-mm. and four 0.5-in. guns.*

(*Above, right and below*) *An experimental F6F-5 with two 11.75-in. rockets and a 125 Imp. gal. (150 U.S. gal.) drop tank beneath the fuselage and six high-velocity 5-in. rockets beneath the wings.*

H

(Above) An F6F-5P high-altitude photographic reconnaissance aircraft, deliveries of which to the U.S. Navy began during 1944. The few delivered to the Royal Navy were designated Hellcat F.R.II.

The XF6F-6 which flew for the first time on July 6, 1944.

entered production, Pratt and Whitney had redesigned the R-2800 (B) engine to strengthen critical parts and improve cooling. The resulting engine, the R-2800 (C), offered 2,100 h.p. for take-off without water injection. In 1943, Grumman decided to complete two experimental Hellcats with this engine before committing themselves to installing it in production models. These experimental models received the designation XF6F-6, the first flying on July 6, 1944. This was powered by an R-2800-18W driving a four-blade Hamilton Standard airscrew, the maximum rating of 2,100 h.p. being boosted to 2,450 h.p. by water injection, and 1,800 h.p. being offered at 21,900 ft. The XF6F-6 proved to be the fastest of all Hellcats, attaining 417 m.p.h. at 22,000 ft. Before trials with the XF6F-6 had been completed, however, Hellcat production had terminated. A less radical modification was the installation of cameras, aircraft so modified being designated F6F-5P. Long focal length cameras were installed in the fuselage aft of the pilot for high-altitude photo reconnaissance, but the aircraft did not differ in any other respect from the standard F6F-5. A number of F6F-5s delivered to the F.A.A. were also fitted with cameras as Hellcat F.R.IIs.

Production of the Hellcat was finally completed in November 1945, 3,578 machines being delivered in that year to bring the total number of all versions of the fighter to 12,274, including prototypes, production orders for a further 1,677 F6F-5s having been cancelled on V-J day. In April 1944, the Corsair had been finally cleared for use aboard U.S. Navy fast carriers, although its introduction in the following December to shipboard operations had supplemented rather than replaced the Hellcat in the final campaigns of the war. Perhaps the highlight of the Grumman fighter's operational career had been the Battle of the Philippine Sea (June 19–20, 1944) when Hellcats completely smashed the Japanese attack on the first day of the battle, accounting for the bulk of the three hundred aircraft lost by the enemy force. From its appearance over the Pacific, the Hellcat had evinced sufficient margin over the Zero-Sen to turn the tide of the conflict, and although Japanese fighters of superior performance made their operational début, they were introduced too late to wrest the aerial ascendancy from the U.S. Navy established largely by this outstanding Grumman fighter.

Grumman F6F-3 Hellcat

Dimensions :   Span, 42 ft. 10 in. ; span folded, 16 ft. 2 in. ; length, 33 ft. 7 in. ; height, 11 ft. 3 in. ; wing area, 334 sq. ft.

Armament :   Six 0.5-in. Colt-Browning machine guns with 400 r.p.g.

Power Plant :   One Pratt and Whitney R-2800-10 Double Wasp eighteen-cylinder radial air-cooled engine rated at 2,000 h.p. for take-off, 1,800 h.p. at 15,700 ft., and 1,650 h.p. at 21,000 ft. Maximum fuel capacity, 195.6 Imp. gal. (235 U.S. gal.)

Weights :   Empty, 9,042 lb. ; normal loaded, 12,186 lb.; maximum overload, 13,221 lb.

Performance :   Maximum speed (at 11,381 lb.), 376 m.p.h. at 22,800 ft., 324 m.p.h. at sea level, (at 12,186 lb.), 373 m.p.h. at 23,700 ft., 303 m.p.h. at sea level, (at 13,221 lb. with 125 Imp. gal. drop tank), 359 m.p.h. at 23,700 ft., 294 m.p.h. at sea level; range (maximum internal fuel), 1,085 mls. at 179 m.p.h., (with 125 Imp. gal. drop tank), 1,620 mls. at 177 m.p.h.; initial climb rate, 3,240 ft./min.; time to 15,000 ft., 7.7 min., to 25,000 ft., 14 min.; service ceiling, 37,500 ft.

Late-production Yak-1 fighters with the M-105PF engine driving a VISh-105 SV airscrew. The Yak-1 began to reach the V.-V.S. in quantity during the late spring of 1942.

THE YAKOVLEV SERIES

Of the many types of warplane employed by the Soviet Air Forces during the Second World War, the most celebrated were undoubtedly the fighters evolved by the design bureau or collective led by Alexander Sergeivich Yakovlev. Lacking many of the refinements of their western contemporaries and possessing only the most rudimentary equipment, they nevertheless commanded the respect of their antagonists. Simple to build in quantity, rugged and possessing superlative flying characteristics, they were excellent low-to-medium altitude fighters, at their best near to the ground where they could out-turn and out-climb any opponent. The Soviet Union's lack of really powerful liquid-cooled engines suitable for fighter installation had necessitated concentration on light structures, a task rendered the more difficult by extremely limited supplies of metal alloys. Lightly armed for the most part, and limited by the poor altitude performance of their engines, the rated altitudes of which seldom exceeded fifteen thousand feet, they were still supremely successful, and were built in greater quantities than the fighters of all other Russian designers combined, providing the bulk of the 30,000 aircraft of Yakovlev design manufactured in Russia during the war years. From the outset, Yakovlev and his team adopted a policy of progressively refining the one basic design, and adapting it to undertake a variety of tasks, rather than evolving new and possibly superior designs whose introduction would have disrupted output while the factories retooled. The success of this policy may be judged by the fact that the Yakovlev series of fighters more than any other weapons provided the standard by which Russia's wartime achievements were judged.

During 1938 the governmental department concerned with aircraft development announced its requirements for a new single-seat fighter which was to be selected on a competitive basis from the prototypes produced by a number of design bureaux. At that time, Alexander Yakovlev was thirty-two years of age and unknown outside the Soviet Union. In fact, he was little known in his own country, despite the highly successful sporting and training aircraft in which he had specialised. However, his entry in the fighter contest, the I-26, promptly adjudged the most promising competitor, earned for him on April 27, 1939, within a few weeks of the prototype's maiden flight, the Order of Lenin, a 100,000-rouble prize and a Zis automobile, and seventeen months later the title of "Doctor of Technical Science" followed, in October 1941, by that of "Hero of Socialist Labour"!

The I-26 was, like its closest competitor, the LaGG-1 (later to be redesignated LaGG-1), a low-wing cantilever monoplane with a fully retractable undercarriage and an M-105PA twelve-cylinder vee liquid-cooled engine with a single-stage two-speed supercharger evolved from the French Hispano-Suiza 12Y by V. Ya. Klimov. The prototype was flown for the first time in March 1939 by Yakovlev's chief test pilot, Yv. I. Pyontkovsky, and soon proved to possess an appreciably better performance and superior flying characteristics to the I-22 which flew for the first time on the 30th of that month. Work on a pre-production batch of fighters for simultaneous development work and service evaluation was begun immediately, the aircraft receiving the designation Yak-1 shortly afterwards. At this time the Soviet Union was pitifully short of light metal alloys for aircraft construction, necessitating the extensive use of wood and welded steel tube, and the one-piece, two-spar wing of the Yakovlev fighter was built entirely of wood with a plywood skin, while the fuselage was a welded steel-tube structure, the forward portion of which was

This Yak-1 was flown by one of the V.-V.S.'s most successful female operational pilots, Lieutenant Lily Litvyak, who claimed several victims in aerial combat.

covered by detachable metal panels and the aft section by plywood and, finally, doped fabric. The control surfaces were metal framed and fabric-covered, and the retractable undercarriage was operated hydraulically. A considerable saving in weight would undoubtedly have resulted from the use of stressed skin construction, but such demanded a standard of manufacture far beyond that of the Soviet aircraft industry, and the welded fuselage had the advantages of being simple to produce and to repair, and was lighter than the wooden fuselage of the I-22. The Yak-1 was thus a compromise. The M-105PA engine (the "P" suffix indicating provision for a *pushka*, or cannon, firing through the airscrew shaft) driving a three-blade metal VISh-61P airscrew with

hydraulic pitch control was rated at 1,100 h.p. for take-off and 1,050 h.p. at 13,120 ft. and armament comprised one 20-mm. ShVAK cannon and two 7.62-mm. ShKAS machine guns in the upper decking of the forward fuselage.

Various modifications were introduced on the pre-production Yak-1. The carburettor air intake was transferred from beneath the nose to the wing roots, the ventral radiator bath was reduced in size, the oil cooler intake was moved forward beneath the nose, and the retractable tailwheel was replaced by one of fixed type. The Yak-1 suffered its share of teething troubles, one of the most serious being excessive engine vibration. This resulted in fractures of the fuel and oil lead connections and several fires in the

Yak-1 fighters leaving the main Yakovlev assembly plant in the Urals during the late summer of 1942.

air until it was finally suppressed by redesign of the engine mount. The undercarriage well doors and oleo legs were extensively modified, and troubles were experienced with the hydraulic system, but most defects had been rectified by early 1941, and in June of that year the Yak-1 passed its final acceptance trials at the State and V.-V.S. test centres and was cleared for mass production. Sixty-four Yak-1 fighters had been completed during 1940, and the first of these had been delivered to a special service test squadron responsible for wringing out the new fighter's "bugs". Incidentally, this unit participated in the 1940 May Day fly-past over Moscow and, on November 7, 1940, was again present during an Air Fête held near Moscow, appearances which did not pass unnoticed by German intelligence agents.

The main Yak-1 production line was situated at a factory in Moscow, but no fighters of this type had been delivered to operational V.-V.S. units by the time the German invasion of the Soviet Union began. The bulk of the Russian aircraft industry was situated in the western part of the Soviet Union. Some factories were quickly overrun by the advancing German forces while others were threatened, and the progress of the armoured spearheads soon began to endanger the Russian capital. Preparations for the transfer of much of the armaments industry East of the Urals had begun more than a year earlier, but the German attack had taken the Russians completely by surprise, and none of the jigs or tools for aircraft manufacture had been transferred to the new plants. In September it was decided to move the Yakovlev plant to Kamensk/Uralsk, and all personnel and tooling for the Yak-1 fighter were immediately sent to the new location. Yakovlev himself left Moscow on October 16th. The remarkable drive with which this move was carried out can be gauged from the fact that the first Yak-1 rolled off the assembly line at the new plant exactly three weeks after the arrival of the first jigs and tools, and monthly production rate exceeded that of the original Moscow factory within three months. Another production line for the Yak-1 had been started at a new factory in Siberia, but owing to mismanagement, very few fighters had been delivered by the Siberian plant by the end of 1941, and thus the Yak-1 did not begin to reach operational units of the V.-V.S. in worthwhile quantities until the late spring of 1942.

The first production model of the Yak-1 was powered by the 1,100 h.p. M-105PA with which it attained maximum speeds of 311 m.p.h. at sea level and 363 m.p.h. at 15,740 ft. Economical cruising speed was 155 m.p.h. at sea level and 149 m.p.h. at 9,840 ft., and maximum range was 510 mls., the fuel tanks between the wing spars having a total capacity of 89 Imp. gal. (107 U.S. gal.). Empty and loaded weights were 5,137 lb. and 6,217 lb. respectively, and armament comprised one 20-mm. ShVAK cannon with 120 rounds and two 7.62-mm. ShKAS machine guns with 375 r.p.g. Six 25-lb. RS-82 rocket missiles could be carried beneath the wings and, later, some

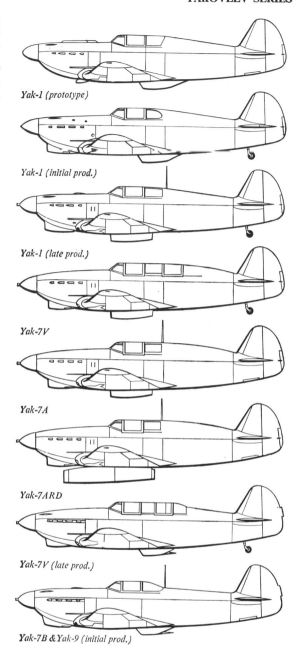

Yak-1 (prototype)

Yak-1 (initial prod.)

Yak-1 (late prod.)

Yak-7V

Yak-7A

Yak-7ARD

Yak-7V (late prod.)

Yak-7B & Yak-9 (initial prod.)

Yak-1s were fitted with underwing racks for two 110-lb. or 220-lb. bombs. Cockpit equipment was austere, and all instrument flying had to be done on primary instruments alone as no gyroscopic instruments were installed. The gunsight was a rudimentary affair resembling early British reflector sights, a simple R/T set of high-frequency type working on one channel was provided, and the pilot had 9-mm. armour protection to the rear.

As production progressed, a number of modifications were introduced, one of the most important changes being the installation of the M-105PF engine which drove an automatic VISh-105 SV airscrew.

The initial production version of the Yak-9 (above) was not externally distinguishable from the Yak-7B, the essential internal difference being the use of light alloy spars in place of wooden spars in the later production model.

This power plant provided 1,210 h.p. for take-off, but had the disadvantage that the second speed of the supercharger engaged at 8,860 ft. as compared with 13,120 ft. for the earlier M-105PA. With the introduction of the new engine, the ventral radiator bath was deepened and moved forward to a point just aft of the mainwheel wells, and shortly afterwards the twin 7.62-mm. weapons were supplanted by a single 12.7-mm. Beresin UBS machine gun, the 20-mm. hub cannon being retained. With these modifications loaded weight rose to 6,382 lb., and time to 16,400 ft. was increased from 4.5 to 5.4 mins., but maximum speed was raised to 372 m.p.h. at 11,150 ft.

Bearing previous V.-V.S. experience with the Polikarpov-designed I-16 fighter in mind, the Yakovlev design bureau had evolved a tandem two-seat conversion training variant of the Yak-1 at an early stage in the fighter's development, and, as the UTI-26, this flew for the first time in 1940, entering production early in the following year as the Yak-7V. Apart from repositioning the radio and other equipment aft of the original cockpit to provide space for the instructor's seat, the Yak-7V was initially identical to the Yak-1 fighter. However, a number of improvements were made to the controls, minor changes were introduced in the structure, and the M-105PF engine was installed, and the modifications made on the Yak-7V two-seater, together with the progressive

(Below) A Yak-7A shot down at Pitkäranta on the North-East shore of Lake Laatokka, Finland, on February 12, 1943. The Yak-7A was externally almost indistinguishable from the late production Yak-1 apart from the upper contours of the rear fuselage, and appeared in service with the V.-V.S. during 1942.

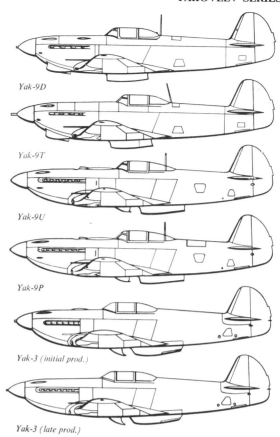

Yak-9D

Yak-9T

Yak-9U

Yak-9P

Yak-3 (initial prod.)

Yak-3 (late prod.)

improvements introduced during Yak-1 production, were standardised in a new single-seat fighter model, the Yak-7A. Externally, this differed little from the late production Yak-1, apart from slightly modified upper fuselage contours aft of the cockpit. At the end of 1941 a further change was made in the two-seat Yak-7V. The rear fuselage was cut down to improve rear vision. At this time, the Yak-7A fighter was undergoing some refinement during which the internal ducting was redesigned and the ventral bath improved aerodynamically and returned to its original position further aft. With these changes and the first all-round-vision cockpit canopy to be used by a Yakovlev fighter, the Yak-7A became the Yak-7B, and the result was a net gain of 8 m.p.h. in maximum speed which was increased to 381 m.p.h. Armament was the same as that of late production Yak-1s, and the internal fuel capacity of 91 Imp. gal. (109 U.S. gal.) provided a maximum range of 516 miles. The loaded weight of the Yak-7B was increased to 6,636 lb.

During the summer of 1942 supplies of steel alloys and light metals began to improve, and the wooden spars in the Yak-7B wing were replaced experimentally by light alloy spars, although the wooden ribs and plywood skin were retained. The adoption of metal spars resulted in an appreciable saving in weight and provided more space within the wing for fuel. This modified variant was initially known as the Yak-7DI (*Dalnii Istrebitel*—Long-range Fighter), but this designation was changed to that of Yak-9 when the new model entered quantity production. By comparison with the Yak-7B, the Yak-9's useful load was increased by 324 lb., although normal loaded weight rose by only 110 lb. to 6,746 lb. Fuel capacity was raised by 7.7 Imp. gal. (9.25 U.S. gal.), increasing range to 565 miles. The Yak-9 was placed in large-scale production in the late summer of 1942, and appeared operation-

ally over the Stalingrad front during that October. The M-105PF engine was retained, and maximum speed was 367 m.p.h. at 16,400 ft., and at a loaded weight of 6,334 lb. an altitude of 16,400 ft. was attained in 4.9 min., range at this weight being 528

The Yak-9DD (below) was a special long-range version of the fighter developed specifically to provide escorts for U.S.A.A.F. heavy bombers on shuttle raids between the United Kingdom, the Soviet Union and Italy. Aircraft of this type operated from Bari, Italy, in support of Yugoslav partisans.

G

The Yak-9D (above) was the first long-range version of the basic Yak-9 fighter and featured enlarged wing fuel cells with a total capacity of 143 Imp. gal. (172 U.S. gal.). The Yak-9D appeared in operational service during 1943.

miles. Armament of the initial production version of the Yak-9 remained one 20-mm. cannon and one 12.7-mm. gun, but the Yak-9M (the "M" suffix indicating *Modificatsion*—Modification) featured an increase in firepower, a second 12.7-mm. gun being mounted in the forward fuselage, while the Yak-9B ("B" indicating *Bombardirovshchik*—Bomber) had the lower portion of the second fuselage bay adapted as a bomb-bay with racks for an 880-lb. internal bomb load.

The principal task of the Yak-9 was army co-operation, supporting the ground forces by keeping the air clear of the Luftwaffe, and bombing and strafing enemy troops. The Yak-9s also served as escorts for

(Left and below) The Yak-9T differed externally from earlier Yak-9 models in having the cockpit mounted further aft. Various weapons were installed between the engine cylinder banks, the Yak-9T illustrated having a 12.7-mm. gun in this position.

FINISH AND INSIGNIA: *The Yak-3 illustrated on the opposite page belonged to the Normandie-Niémen Regiment. The upper surfaces were finished high-gloss dark olive overall and the under surfaces were pale blue. The nationality of the pilot was indicated by the red-white-blue (blue to the fore) spinner and the white Cross of Lorraine on the vertical fin. The five-pointed red star appeared on the under wing surfaces and fuselage sides only, those on the fuselage sides being outlined in white. The divisional insignia comprised a white lightning flash along the fuselage sides. After the presentation of the Yak-3s to the Armée de l'Air and their arrival at Le Bourget in June 1945, the rudders of the fighters were painted red-white-blue.*

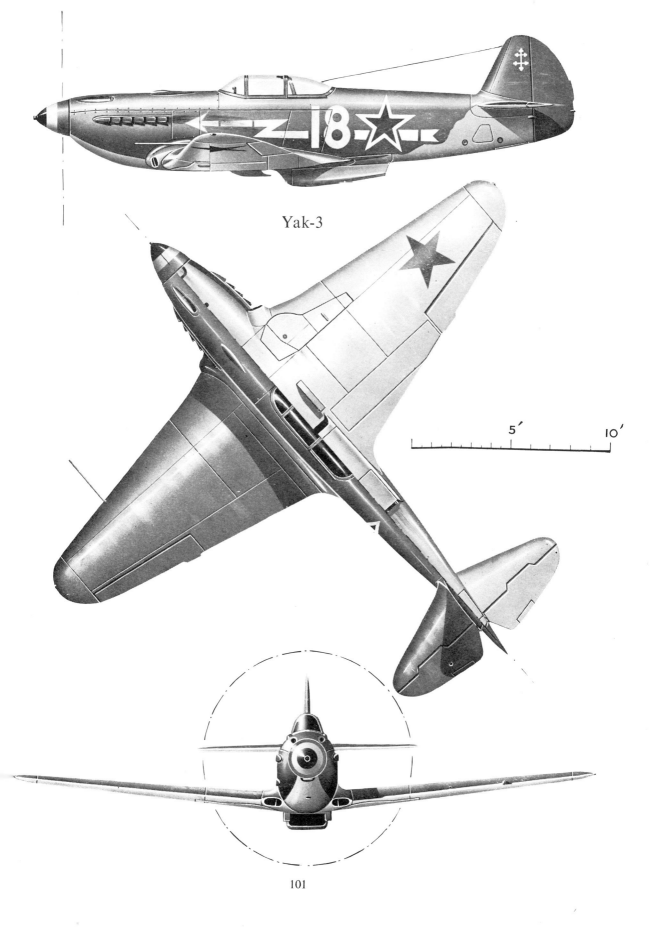

Yak-3

5´   10´

The Yak-3 (Above and left) was evolved from the experimental Yak-1M as a high-performance light fighter, and made its operational début in August 1943 during the German Kursk offensive.

and low altitude manoeuvrability was the forté of the Yakovlev, many a Bf 109G stalling and crashing when trying to follow the Russian fighter in a tight turn. One problem which manifested itself over the Kursk battle area in May 1943, however, was a tendency for the wing skinning to peal away under the stresses of high-*g* manoeuvres. The cause was eventually traced to inefficient adhesives. The French Normandie-Niémen Group which had been formed on Yak-1 fighters at Ivanovo in December 1942, and had begun operations on the Russian Front on March 24, 1943, quickly exchanged its Yak-1s for Yak-9s, operating these with considerable success until re-equipped with Yak-3s in October 1944, and the first Russian-trained Polish fighter squadron, which became operational on Yak-1s in July 1943 from Grigorjevskoje, some ninety miles south of Moscow, soon received Yak-9Ms. This unit, together with a second Polish squadron formed on August 10, 1944, continued to operate Yak-9Ms and Yak-9Ts until the end of the war, taking an active part in the "Battle of Berlin", and flying 1,400 operational sorties.

Despite the gradual increase in range of the basic Yakovlev fighter, it still possessed insufficient endurance to provide with adequate air cover ground forces operating at some distance from the nearest airfield or armoured spearheads fighting deep within enemy-held territory. Nor could it escort bombers on any but short-distance raids. Therefore, early in 1943, still larger fuel cells were installed in the wings, these having a total capacity of 143 Imp. gal. (172 U.S. gal.) and providing a maximum range of 882 mls. at 17:

the Il-2 and Pe-2 bombers, and as intruders, making sweeps over Luftwaffe airfields in the forward areas. They rarely operated much above 15,000 ft, and below this altitude the Yak-9 was faster than the Messerschmitt Bf 109G-2 which it met for the first time in the vicinity of Stalingrad during the closing months of 1942. It also enjoyed a better climb rate than the German fighter, attaining 16,400 ft. in 4 min. 54 sec. as compared with the 5 min. 18 sec. of the Bf 109G-2, m.p.h. at 3,280 ft., or 655 mls. at 248 m.p.h. at 9,840 ft. This model, which had a loaded weight of 6,834–7,055 lb., entered production as the Yak-9D, but in 1944 even longer ranges were demanded in order to provide escorts for U.S.A.A.F. heavy bombers on planned shuttle raids between the United Kingdom, the Soviet Union and Italy, and Soviet bombers attacking targets far behind the enemy lines. Thus, a further variant was evolved, the Yak 9DD (*Dalnii Deistviia*—Ultra Long Range), in which the maximum fuel load was raised to 187 Imp. gal. (224.5 U.S. gal.) and maximum range to 1,245–1,365 mls. In 1944 a group of Yak-9DD fighters flew from a Ukrainian base to Bari in Italy, making the 1,120-mile flight non-stop and operating from Bari in support of the Yugoslav partisans.

During 1943, in parallel with the long-range Yak-9D, the Yakovlev design bureau had been developing a special close-support model of the fighter with a new hub-mounted 37-mm. Type 11-P-37 cannon with thirty-two rounds of ammunition. To accommodate this large cannon it was necessary to move the cockpit aft by 1 ft. 3¾ in. to the second fuselage bay. The 12.7-mm. gun was retained for aiming purposes, and this new variant entered production as the Yak-9T (the "T" suffix indicating *Tyazholy*, or Heavy, and referring to the cannon). With a 77 Imp. gal. (92.5 U.S. gal.) fuel capacity, the Yak-9T had a range of 273 mls. at 292 m.p.h. at 3,280 ft., and 516 mls. at 186 m.p.h. at the same altitude. It proved particularly efficacious against Mk. 3 or Mk. 4 tanks, armoured troop carriers and self-propelled guns, and was also employed for anti-shipping strikes in the Baltic. Later the Yak-9T was also built with the 20-mm. MPSh-20, 23-mm. MP-23-VV and even the 12.7-mm. UBS gun in place of the 37-mm. weapon, being used for the combined low-level interception and close-support roles, and frequently using the RS-82 rocket projectiles for the latter task. The 37-mm. cannon of the

Yak-9T did not prove effective against the armour of the Tiger and Panther tanks, however, and in 1944 the Yak-9K appeared with a hub-mounted cannon of no less than 45-mm. calibre. Some V.-V.S. units were equipped with a mixture of Yak-9T and Yak-9K aircraft.

Throughout the early war years, Vladmir Klimov had been striving to improve the basic M-105 engine which was seriously wanting in high-altitude performance. A two-speed supercharger had been used from the outset, and considerable attention was paid to providing the engine with a two-stage supercharger in order to increase substantially the rated altitude of the M-105. A two-stage supercharger was fitted to a variant of the engine designated M-105PD, but this offered only 1,100 h.p. for take-off and showed a marked increase in weight, and therefore Klimov concentrated on refining and improving the basic single-stage two-speed engine, and the result was the M-107A. This featured injection-type carburettors, and each cylinder had four valves, through one of which pure air was passed from the supercharger to improve scavenging, increasing the efficiency of the intake stroke and reducing fuel consumption. The M-107A provided 1,620 h.p. for take-off, and began bench trials in 1942.

It was decided to install the new engine in a variant of the Yak-9 in place of the standard M-105PF, and to take full advantage of the increase in power a lighter, all-metal structure was adopted, duralumin ribs supplanting the wooden ribs in the wing, and a light metal skin replacing the plywood. Simultaneously, the lines of the fighter were improved, the fineness ratio of the fuselage being increased, and the oil cooler intake was transferred from under the nose to the port wing root, the starboard wing root being occupied by the carburettor air intake. A cockpit canopy of improved aerodynamic form was introduced, and the prototype of the new model, which

The last production version of the basic Yak-9 to see wartime service was the extensively revised Yak-9U which began to reach operational units during the last few months of 1944, and was thus enabled to participate in the final stages of the battle on the Eastern Front. The aircraft illustrated was one subsequently supplied to Poland.

During the October of 1944, the Yak-3 entered service with the French Normandie-Niémen Group, the unit having reportedly selected this type in preference to all other available fighters.

received the designation Yak-9U (the "U" suffix indicating *Usilennui*—Strengthened, and referring to the increased power of the engine), was completed in December 1943 and flew for the first time in January 1944. During flight trials, the Yak-9U achieved a speed of 434 m.p.h. at 18,045 ft., and was thus more then 60 m.p.h. faster than the M-105PF-powered model. The M-107A-powered version also had a greatly superior climb performance, attaining an altitude of 16,400 ft. in 3 min. 36 sec.

The Yak-9U began to reach operational units during the last few months of 1944, and was able to participate in the final stages of the battle on the Eastern Front. Probably the first Russian fighter to compare favourably from the structural viewpoint with its western counterparts, the Yak-9U carried an armament of one 20-mm. hub-mounted ShVAK cannon with 100 rounds and two 12.7-mm. Beresin BS machine guns with 250 r.p.g. Provision was made for two 220-lb. bombs beneath the wings, and all fuel was housed in four wing tanks with a total capacity of 132 Imp. gal. (158.5 U.S. gal.). The maximum speed of the production model at 415 m.p.h. at 16,400 ft. was somewhat less than that of the prototype but still represented a notable step forward in Russian fighter performance, range was 506 mls. at 300 m.p.h. and 575 mls. at 242 m.p.h., service ceiling was 34,000 ft., and empty and normal loaded weights were 5,100 lb. and 6,985 lb. respectively. Purely post-war developments of the Yak-9U included the Yak-9P which differed externally in having a transparent panel in the rear fuselage covering a D/F loop.

From 1942 the Yakovlev design bureau began work on a second line of development which, based on the Yak-1, aimed at obtaining the highest possible performance with the M-105PF engine. In fact, the V.-V.S. required a high-performance light fighter capable of maintaining aerial superiority over the battlefield. Various aerodynamic improvements were embodied in an experimental aircraft, the Yak-1M, which began trials in 1942. The rear fuselage was cut down in the style of that of the Yak-7B, and an all-round-vision cockpit canopy fitted, the wing span and area were reduced from 32 ft. 9¾ in. and 184.5 sq. ft. to 30 ft. 2¼ in. and 159.95 sq. ft. respectively, and loaded weight was reduced by 660 lb. Trials with the experimental Yak-1M led, in the spring of 1943, to the design of the Yak-3 which was placed in production during the following summer. Having the smaller wing of the Yak-1M, the Yak-3 was powered by an M-105PF-2 engine rated at 1,222 h.p. for take-off, the oil cooler intake for which was transferred to the port wing root, and the radio mast was eliminated. An exceptionally fine finish was obtained on the wings by applying a thick layer of polish which proved to stand up extremely well to service use. Performance was superior to that of the early production versions of the Yak-9 in several respects, a maximum speed of 403 m.p.h. being attained at 16,400 ft., and an altitude of 16,400 ft. being reached in 4.1 mins. Range was 506 mls. at 305 m.p.h., 456 mls. at 341 m.p.h., and 560 mls. at 193 m.p.h., and loaded weight was 5,864 lb. The handling characteristics of the Yak-3 were excellent, and pilots that flew both the Russian fighter and early versions of the Spitfire claimed that the Yak-3 was lighter on the ailerons and smoother to fly although the wing loading at 36.56 lb./sq. ft. was on the high side, stalling speed was relatively high, and take-off and landing could present the novice with difficulties. Armament comprised one 20-mm. ShVAK cannon with 120 rounds and two 12.7- mm. Beresin machine guns with 250 r.p.g.

The Yak-3 made its operational début during the German Kursk offensive, the failure of which placed the initiative in Russian hands in August 1943, and by the early spring of 1944 several V.-V.S. fighter regiments had re-equipped with the type, and such was the success of the Yak-3 that Luftwaffe fighter pilots received instructions to "avoid combat below five thousand metres with Yakovlev fighters lacking an oil cooler intake beneath the nose!" According to Russian records, on July 14, 1944, a formation of eight Yak-3s fought a running battle with a formation of sixty Ju 87 dive-bombers and escorting Bf 109Gs, destroying three Ju 87s and four Bf 109s without loss, and on the following day, eighteen Yak-3s encountered a force of thirty Luftwaffe fighters, destroying fifteen of their number for the loss of only one Russian aircraft. During the summer of 1944 the French Normandie-Niémen Group was reportedly offered its choice of Russian fighters or Lend-Lease British or American machines, and selected the Yak-3 with which they re-equipped in October 1944, subsequently scoring a considerable number of their 273 victories while flying this type.

At the beginning of 1944 the M-107A engine which was then undergoing trials in the prototype Yak-9U, was also installed in a Yak-3 airframe, and during State acceptance trials carried out between February and May, the M-107A-powered Yak-3 attained a speed of 447 m.p.h. at 18,865 ft. At 16,400 ft., the re-engined Yak-3 was 60–70 m.p.h. faster than the Bf 109G-2 or Fw 190A-4, and the official report on the acceptance tests stated, "The experimental Yak-3 powered by the M-107A engine and designed by Comrade Yakovlev appears to offer the best performance of all indigenous and known foreign fighters, being superior in horizontal speed, rate of climb and manoeuvrability." Production of the Yak-3 with the M-107A engine began late in 1944, but it reached operational units too late to see action.

During the war years, various experiments aimed at boosting performance for short periods were undertaken with Yakovlev fighters, and a Yak-7A fighter was flown with a Merkulov ramjet beneath the fuselage, this reportedly boosting maximum speed by 33 m.p.h. This experimental aircraft was designated Yak-7ARD (the "RD" suffix indicating *Reaktivnii Dvigatyel*, or Reaction Propulsion). A two-seater, the Yak-7VRD was tested with two smaller Merkulov ramjets beneath the wings, this aircraft being flown by S. N. Anohin. These boosted maximum level speed by 37 m.p.h. to 56 m.p.h., according to the altitude, but the advantages of the ramjets were negated by their drag when not in use, and the experiments were abandoned. Early in 1945, an experimental mixed-power interceptor was produced based on the M-105-engined Yak-3. An auxiliary liquid fuel rocket motor was installed in the extreme rear fuselage, and during trials a maximum speed of 487.7 m.p.h. was attained with both power plants operating.

The Yak-3 was lighter on the ailerons and smoother to fly than early versions of the Spitfire.

There is no doubt that the Yakovlev series of fighters made the largest contribution to Russian fighter strength during the last two years of the war in Europe. Their conception was entirely orthodox and lacked originality, but they were evolved at a time when the Soviet Union could ill afford to experiment and with an eye on the materials and labour available. Competently designed, they were flown by such Russian fighter aces as N. Goulayev with fifty-three victories and D. Glinka with thirty-eight victories, and all Yakovlev fighters had three things in common: excellent stability under all flying conditions, good controllability at high angles of attack, and extremely pleasant handling characteristics. By contemporary standards they lacked firepower and their altitude performance was poor, but they were easily maintained under the most trying conditions provided by the Eastern Front, operating in circumstances that would have grounded their more refined western contemporaries.

Yakovlev Yak-9D

Dimensions:	Span, 32 ft. 9¾ in.; length, 28 ft. 0½ in.; height, 8 ft. 0 in.; wing area, 185,676 sq. ft.
Armament:	One 20-mm. ShVAK cannon with 120 rounds firing through the airscrew shaft and one 12.7-mm. Beresin BS machine gun with 220 rounds in the port side of the forward fuselage.
Power Plant:	One Klimov M-105PF twelve-cylinder Vee liquid-cooled engine rated at 1,210 h.p. at 2,600 r.p.m. for take-off and 1,260 h.p. at 2,700 r.p.m. at 2,600 ft.
Weights:	Empty, 6,060 lb; normal loaded, 6,834 lb.; maximum, 7,055 lb.
Performance:	Maximum speed, 310 m.p.h. at sea level, 332 m.p.h. at 7,220 ft., 359 m.p.h. at 16,400 ft.; range at maximum speed at 7,220 ft., 447 mls., at 267 m.p.h. at 3,280 ft., 590 mls., at 248 m.p.h. at 9,840 ft., 665 mls., at 174 m.p.h. at 3,280 ft., 870 mls.; maximum endurance, 4 hr. 37 min.; time to 16,400 ft. (at 6,540 lb.), 5 min. 23 sec.; service ceiling, 32,300 ft.

(Left) An early Ju 88C-6 night fighter prior to the installation of the 20-mm. MG 151 cannon. The first C-model to be manufactured in substantial numbers, the Ju 88C-6 began to appear during 1942.

THE JUNKERS JU 88 SERIES

In 1939, with a full-scale European conflict imminent, none of Germany's leaders was thinking defensively. Dazzled by the prospect of a single-front war and a lightning decision, they viewed the newly created Luftwaffe purely as an offensive force. They had become reckless gamblers with a marked disinclination to face distasteful facts. A glance at the map of Europe should have revealed forcibly the vulnerability of Germany from the air, but home defence depended solely on the Flak regiments; the undeniably efficient force of anti-aircraft artillery and searchlight batteries that had prompted Hermann Goering's famous boast that no foreign aircraft would ever penetrate the Ruhr. The possibility of enemy aircraft making nocturnal sorties in strength over the Third Reich was too unpalatable a thought to be entertained by the German Supreme Command. A night interceptor arm had no place in Germany's short-term plan to win the approaching conflict, and Goering considered defeatist the provision of such a safeguard which common prudence should have insisted upon.

The failure to provide the Luftwaffe with a night fighter force was a dangerous gamble; a gamble which

appeared to have been fully justified until the night of May 15–16, 1940. On that night, R.A.F. bombers appeared over Germany and a ground haze robbed the Flak units of the possibility of effective action. The provision of a night interceptor arm now became imperative, but it was too late for Germany's night defences to make good the leeway that had resulted from early neglect. Nevertheless, one aircraft, the ever tractable Junkers Ju 88, came within an ace of saving the situation brought about by Goering's short-sightedness.

Although conceived solely as a *schnellbomber*—a medium bomber with the speed of a fighter—the "eighty-eight" was to provide the backbone of the most efficient night fighter arm ever created; a force offering a formidable and flexible defence against strategic night bombing and which, until overtaken by military events, rendered R.A.F. Bomber Command's nocturnal sorties most costly operations. Indeed, by midsummer 1944, the night fighter arm comprised no less than fifteen per cent of the Luftwaffe's total first-line strength, and it was by no means unusual for this force to inflict casualties amounting to eight per cent of the aircraft engaged on a particular night mission. More potent night fighters than the Ju 88 were evolved by the German aircraft industry, but none of these reached operational units in sufficient quantities to have any serious effect on the outcome of the nocturnal conflict in German skies,

A Ju 88C-6 day fighter of one of the units attached to the Fliegerfuehrer Atlantik. The "World-in-a-Ring" emblem used by many such units may be perceived beneath the cockpit.

A Ju 88C-6b *fighter fitted with the* FuG 212 Lichtenstein C-1 *radar in place of the* FuG 202 *normally installed.*

and the "eighty-eight", possessing a remarkably good performance for such a large aircraft, excelled in the night interception role.

Such a task was far from the minds of the design team responsible for the conception of the Ju 88 in 1936, but nor were many of the other roles that this outstandingly versatile aircraft was called upon to fulfil in the overstrained and severely depleted German defences as the war progressed. It is doubtful if any one basic design has ever before, or, for that matter, ever will again be adapted to undertake so many widely varying duties. A continual process of power and weight increases and equipment changes kept the "eighty-eight"—still recognizable if somewhat distorted in its final variants—constantly in production and first-line service throughout the war years. Manufactured as a bomber in greater numbers than all other German bombers combined, the Ju 88 was the best medium bomber serving any of the combatants during the early war years, but it was even more successful in the heavy fighter role for which nearly four thousand machines were produced.

German medium bomber design reigned supreme in the mid 'thirties, but the Ju 88 owed nothing to any previous German design. In fact, it was not of pure German descent, a matter which the Junkers Flugzeug und Motorenwerke were at great pains to conceal, owing much to design and construction techniques evolved by the U.S. aircraft industry and the product of two engineers that had worked in the U.S.A. before entering Junkers employ. The R.L.M. requirement to which the Ju 88 was designed had called specifically for a bomber, but such was the performance evinced by the aircraft during its earliest prototype trials that its potential value as a *Zerstörer*, or heavy fighter, was seen at an early development stage, and on September 27, 1938, twenty-one months after the Ju 88's first flight and before the first pre-production Ju 88A-0 bomber had left the assembly line at Bernburg, trials of a fighter prototype, the Ju 88V7, began.

Like the fifth prototype, the Ju 88V5, which, six months later, was to establish a 1,000-km. closed-circuit record with a 2,000-kg. payload at an average speed of 321.25 m.p.h., the Ju 88V7 was powered by a pair of Junkers Jumo 211B-1 twelve-cylinder inverted-vee liquid-cooled engines with direct fuel injection, two-speed superchargers and annular radiators, and rated at 1,100 h.p. at 2,400 r.p.m. for take-off. The Ju 88V7 differed from its immediate predecessor, the Ju 88V6 production prototype for the A-series bomber, in having the "beetle's eye" of optically-flat transparent panels in the extreme nose supplanted by a "solid" nose cone which enclosed the barrels of two 7.9-mm. MG 17 machine guns and two 20mm. MG FF cannon which protruded through a circular 11-mm. armoured bulkhead. Unlike the bomber variant which provided accommodation for four crew members, the Ju 88V7 carried only three—pilot, radio operator (operating a second 7.9-mm. gun which fired from the rear of the raised cabin superstructure) and observer. The Ju 88V7 attained a maximum level speed of 312 m.p.h. at 13,120 ft., and such was the success of initial trials that, at the begin-

The Lichtenstein C-1 *antennae of the Ju* 88C-6b.

ning of 1939, plans were prepared for the production of the *Zerstörer* model as the Ju 88C. No thought had been given to the use of the aircraft as a night fighter at this time, the Ju 88C being envisaged as a long-range intruder, anti-shipping aircraft and close-support machine. However, highest priority was allocated to the Ju 88A bomber, and as the fighter could only be produced at the expense of the more urgently needed version of the design, little effort was applied to the development of the Ju 88C.

From the outset of design work the possibility of installing both liquid-cooled and air-cooled engines in the same basic airframe had been carefully considered, and this flexibility, never equalled by the

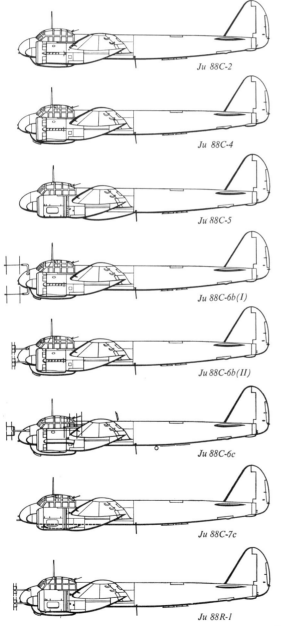

Ju 88C-2

Ju 88C-4

Ju 88C-5

Ju 88C-6b(I)

Ju 88C-6b(II)

Ju 88C-6c

Ju 88C-7c

Ju 88R-1

Allies, was to prove of utmost importance in the years that followed. In view of considerable demands upon supplies of the Jumo 211B engine for the Ju 88A bomber, a variant powered by BMW 801 air-cooled radials, the Ju 88B, was proposed in parallel with the Jumo-powered model, and as adequate supplies of the radial engine were expected to be available by the beginning of 1940 when production of the "eighty-eight" fighter was scheduled to begin, it was intended that the Ju 88C-1 should receive two 1,600 h.p. BMW 801MA engines with which a maximum speed of 355 m.p.h. was anticipated. Apart from the power plant installation and some local strengthening, the airframe of the Ju 88C-1 was to have been identical to that of the Ju 88A-1 bomber, and armament was to have been similar to that of the Ju 88V7. Several early production Ju 88A-1 airframes were modified to take fighter armament during July and August 1939, and these machines, designated Ju 88C-0 and intended for service evaluation, were actually used operationally during the Polish campaign, their principal task being that of "train-busting".

Delays in deliveries of the BMW engine and the priority in its supply enjoyed by the Fw 190A resulted in a decision to abandon the Ju 88C-1 in favour of a straightforward conversion of the Ju 88A-1 bomber powered by Jumo 211B-1 engines, this being the Ju 88C-2 which began to appear in the summer of 1940. The Ju 88C-2 carried a fixed forward-firing armament of one 20-mm. MG FF cannon and three 7.9-mm. MG 17 machine guns, and was immediately considered as an interim night fighter. The Luftwaffe's night fighter organisation had come into being in June 1940 when the crews of ZG.1, together with their Messerschmitt Bf 110Cs, had been transferred to Düsseldorf for training in night fighting tactics. Provisionally known as the Nacht und Versuchs Staffel (Night and Experimental Squadron), the unit was redesignated Gruppe I of the Nachtjagdgeschwader 1 (I/NJG.1) on July 20, 1940, and a second Gruppe was formed shortly afterwards, receiving the first twenty Ju 88C-2 conversions. These enjoyed some successes over R.A.F. bombers passing through coastal searchlight belts, but most of the sixty-two Ju 88A-1 bomber airframes converted to C-2 standards during the course of 1940 were equipped as fighter-bombers, carrying a 1,100-lb. bomb load internally and undertaking day and night intruder sorties over the British Isles. Rear-firing armament comprised one 7.9-mm. MG 15 machine gun in the upper position and, weighing 24,250 lb. without bomb load, the Ju 88C-2 attained a maximum speed of 298 m.p.h. at 18,040 ft. Maximum range and service ceiling were 1,895 miles and 28,200 ft. respectively.

The Ju 88C-3 was an experimental BMW 801-powered model which did not attain production, and the first variant to be built for the fighter role from the ground up was the Ju 88C-4. This differed from the earlier C-2 principally in having an airframe similar

A Ju 88C-6 night fighter without radar but with the so-called "Schräge Musik" installation of two obliquely-firing 20-mm. cannon in the fuselage just forward of the wing trailing edge, and (right) a close-up photograph of the installation.

to that of the Ju 88A-4 bomber, the most important structural change being a six-foot increase in overall wing span from 59 ft. 10¾ in. to 65 ft. 10½ in. Armour protection for the crew was increased, the aft-firing gun mountings being armoured, the undercarriage was strengthened, and a rear-firing machine gun (MG 15) was reintroduced in the under-fuselage gondola. This gun was virtually useless as inadequate space was available for its effective operation. Attachment points were retained for four external carriers between the engine nacelles and the fuselage, these sometimes being fitted with a pair of WB 81 pods each housing six 7.9-mm. MG 81 machine guns and their ammunition for the close-support role. The guns in these containers were inclined downward at an angle of 15° in order to clear the airscrew discs. The first production Ju 88C-4s retained the Jumo 211B-1 engines, but during 1942 the Ju 88C-4/R was introduced with Jumo 211J engines offering 1,410 h.p. for take-off. Only sixty-six Ju 88C fighters were delivered in 1941, despite the urgent demands of the night fighter units, and many of these were employed in the fighter-reconnaissance role, a camera installation replacing the twin 20-mm. MG FF cannon in the lower gondola of some late production machines. The Ju 88C-5 was limited to a pre-production batch of approximately a dozen machines, these having 1,700 h.p. BMW 801D fourteen-cylinder air-cooled radials and the forward gondola supplanted by a ventral gun pack inserted in the bomb-bay and housing two 7.9-mm. MG 15 machine guns.

By the early months of 1942, with the Allied air offensive gaining momentum, it was becoming increasingly necessary to expand the Luftwaffe's night fighter arm, and output of the Ju 88C was boosted. The original night fighter unit, NJG.1, had been brought up to full Geschwader strength of three Gruppen, and by mid-1942 three more Geschwader (NJG.2, 3 and 4) had been added to the embryo "Kammhuber Line", the system of night fighter

(Above) A Ju 88C-4 night fighter and (below) an early production Ju 88C-6.

boxes designed to straddle the bomber routes from the British Isles and commanded by General Kammhuber, the *General der Nachtjagd*. The whole system was supported by a network of early warning radar installations, and by 1943 R.A.F. bombers were being compelled to make extensive detours or take extremely hazardous routes through the dangerous

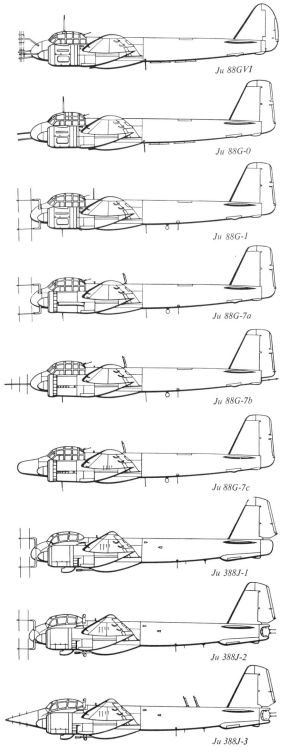

Ju 88GVI

Ju 88G-0

Ju 88G-1

Ju 88G-7a

Ju 88G-7b

Ju 88G-7c

Ju 388J-1

Ju 388J-2

Ju 388J-3

defence belt. However, airborne radar was essential if the "Kammhuber Line" was to be fully effective.

The night fighters could be guided to the intruding bomber formations with the help of *Freya* and *Würzburg* ground radar, but the maintenance of contact with the enemy was by no means assured. Trials had been conducted with an infra-red device, the *Spanner-Anlage*, this being, in effect, an infra-red spotlight, the sighting screen, known as *Q-Rohr*, being mounted in front of the pilot and used in conjunction with a Revi C 12/D gunsight. This equipment did not produce any practical results, but by the summer of 1941 Telefunken had evolved relatively efficient radar suitable for aircraft installation and known as FuG 202 *Lichtenstein BC*. It had a range of 2.5 miles and provided useful D/F in azimuth and elevation by the use of a rotating phase switch which actuated the different antennae in rapid succession. This set, which proved to be satisfactory only under certain conditions, was later to be augmented by FuG 220 *Lichtenstein SN-2* on a two-metre wavelength, but with the progressive improvement in the close-range location ability of the SN-2 to 650 ft., the original BC equipment was dispensed with. However, the SN-2 equipment was not available for installation in the early C-series. Early in 1942 *Lichtenstein BC* was mounted in four of NJG.1's Ju 88C-4 fighters. The cumbersome aerial array reduced maximum speed by some 25 m.p.h., and initially the reactions of the night fighter crews were unfavourable. After Hauptmann Becker, one of the most successful of the Luftwaffe's night fighter pilots, achieved positive success with the radar, the highest priority was given to production of *Lichtenstein* which markedly reduced the dependence of the night fighters on ground guidance and substantially increased the effectiveness of the Luftwaffe's night fighter arm.

A total of 257 Ju 88C fighters was delivered in 1942, in which year really large-scale production began. Such was the importance of the Junkers Ju 88 series of aircraft to the Luftwaffe that, by 1941, the type was being produced by Heinkel at Oranienburg, Arado at Brandenburg, Siebel at Halle, Henschel at Berlin, Dornier at Wismar, and ATG at Leipzig, as well as by Junkers at Bernburg. During 1942, the Ju 88C-6 powered by the Jumo 211J engine attained production, this being the first C-model to be manufactured in really substantial numbers.

The Ju 88C-6 was intended for both day and night fighting roles, and armament comprised three 7.9-mm. MG 17 machine guns with 2,800 rounds and one 20-mm. MG FF/M cannon with 120 rounds in the nose and two 20-mm. MG FF/M with 120 r.p.g. in the gondola. For rear defence two 7.9-mm. MG 81 guns with 900 r.p.g. were mounted in the upper

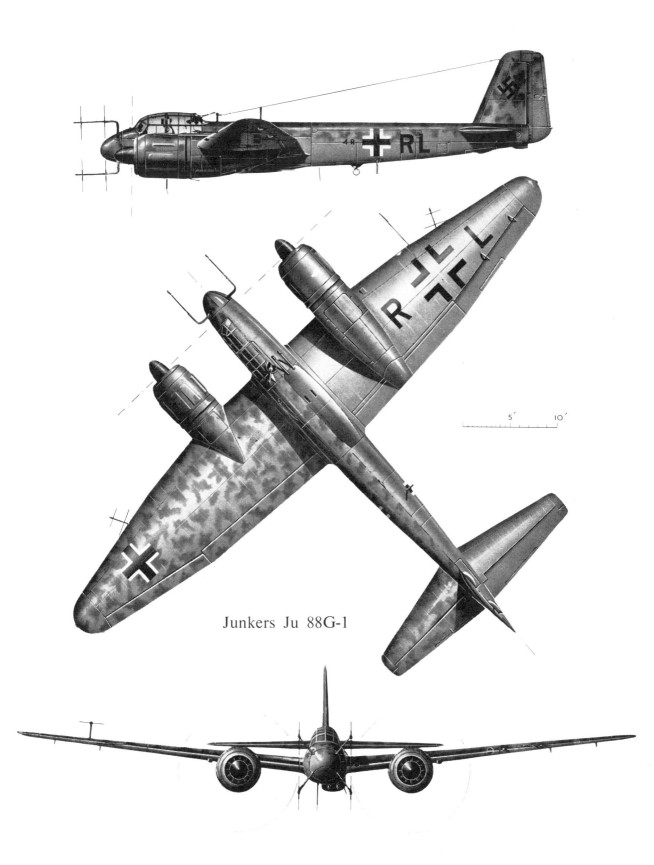

Junkers Ju 88G-1

5' 10'

A captured Ju 88R-2 under test. The Ju 88R-2 normally carried both FuG 202 and FuG 212 radar.

position, and a similar gun with 1,800 rounds was supposed to be installed in the lower position, although this was usually omitted. The Ju 88C-6a was essentially a day fighter, and was operated extensively from Bordeaux-Merignac and other airfields along the Atlantic coastline under the control of the *Flieger-fuehrer Atlantik* on anti-shipping operations. It was also used to protect coastal shipping from the depred-ations of R.A.F. Coastal Command Beaufighters.

The Ju 88C-6b was the night fighting equivalent of the C-6a, and many aircraft of this type had the standard armament augmented by a pair of 20-mm. MG 151 cannon which were remotely controlled and arranged to fire upward at an oblique angle, this installation being known as *Schräge Musik* (Jazz Music). It was retroactively fitted with *Lichtenstein BC* (FuG 202), the use of a lighter aerial array reducing its detrimental effect on the aircraft's performance. However, the use of metal foil strips adjusted to the wavelength of the *Lichtenstein* and dropped by R.A.F. night bombers seriously handi-capped the fighters during the last few months of 1943. The dangers presented by known British interest in metal foil strips as a radar counter-measures device had been recognised in Germany at an early date, but Goering had forbidden any mention

of *Düppel*, as the strips were dubbed in Germany (the foil having first been found at Düppel, a town near the Danish border), preventing the testing of any antidote, and it was not until *Düppel* was used on a large scale by the R.A.F. during an attack on Hamburg on July 25, 1943 that serious attempts were made to overcome the problems that it offered. The only defence against jamming was to change the frequency, and in October 1943 the Ju 88C-6c night fighter appeared with the FuG 212 *Lichtenstein* C-1, and a single 13-mm. MG 131 machine gun firing aft from the upper position. The Ju 88C-6c attained a maximum speed of 311 m.p.h. at 19,685 ft., and maxi-mum and normal cruising speeds of 282 m.p.h. and 264 m.p.h. Initial climb rate was 1,770 ft./min., maxi-mum ceiling was 32,480 ft., and maximum range was 2,131 miles with maximum external fuel. Empty and normal loaded weights were 18,871 lb. and 26,125 lb. respectively. Some machines were fitted with Jumo 211H engines and TK 11a superchargers which boosted maximum speed to 335 m.p.h. at 30,180 feet.

The final production C-series model was the Ju 88C-7 which was essentially a day fighter and intruder. Powered by Jumo 211J engines, the Ju 88C-7a carried a 1,100-lb. bomb load internally and a jettisonable ventral gun pack, while the Ju 88C-7b

Instability during take-off as a result of the installation of BMW 801 engines in the Ju 88R led directly to the adoption of Ju 188 tail surfaces in the G-series fighters. The photograph below depicts a Ju 88R-2.

The Ju 88G-1 was the first model to receive FuG 220 radar which necessitated the removal of nose-mounted cannon.

had underwing racks between the fuselage and engine nacelles, these raising the total permissible bomb load to 3,300 lb. A pure day fighter variant with no provision for bombs was the Ju 88C-7c with BMW 801MA radial engines, but only a pre-production batch of this variant was completed, the principal radial-engined model being the Ju 88R night fighter. Possessing a similar airframe to the Ju 88C-6 and carrying a forward-firing armament of three 7.9-mm. MG 17s, one 20-mm. MG 151 and two 20-mm. MG FF cannon, and FuG 202 *Lichtenstein BC* radar, the Ju 88R-1 was powered by two BMW 801MA engines initially, these later being replaced by BMW 801Cs, the Ju 88R-2 differing only in having BMW 801Ds and additional radar equipment which included FuG 212 *Lichtenstein C*-1 with additional tail warning. FuG 350 *Naxos Z* which was used against bombers with the British H2S 9-cm. equipment or the American H2S 3-cm. unit was installed in some machines.

During 1943 production of the Ju 88C and Ju 88R fighters rose to 706 aircraft, and in the following year, when these models were phased out in favour of the greatly improved Ju 88G, no fewer than 2,518 Ju 88 fighters were delivered. Constant increases in equipment in the Ju 88 night fighter had adversely affected

performance but, more important, the low-speed characteristics of the aircraft had deteriorated seriously, and losses from accidents during take-off and landing were rising alarmingly. To improve stability, the Ju 88G was fitted with the more angular vertical tail surfaces of the Ju 188 bomber, and the asymmetrical gondola was eliminated, forward-firing armament being installed in a ventral bulge. A Ju 88C-5 was used to test the equipment and armament of the G-model, becoming the Ju 88GV1. This aircraft retained the earlier tail surfaces and, in addition to four 20-mm. MG 151 cannon in a ventral housing had two similar weapons in the starboard side of the nose. Radar equipment included FuG 212 *Lichtenstein C*-1, and the pre-production Ju 88G-0, which was powered by two BMW 801D radials, differed from the Ju 88GV1 apart from the tail surfaces, in having forward-firing armament reduced to the four MG 151 cannon in the ventral housing, these being provided with 200 r.p.g. The reason for the removal of the nose-mounted cannon was to provide space for the new FuG 220 *Lichtenstein SN*-2 radar, although several pre-production Ju 88G-0 aircraft were delivered without interception radar and with the nose cannon installed. One rearward-firing 13-mm. MG 131 machine gun with 500

A Ju 88G-1 of Gruppe I of the Nachtjagdeschwader 2. The Ju 188-type tail surfaces were adopted to rectify instability experienced with the similarly-powered Ju 88R.

The Ju 88G-7a (above) featured Junkers Jumo 213E engines with MW 50 methanol-water injection.

A Ju 88G-1 on a compass-swinging table.

rounds was installed in the rear of the cockpit, and total fuel capacity was 624 Imp. gal. (749 U.S. gal.). The Ju 88G-1 was the production version of the Ju 88G-0.

The Ju 88G-1 appeared in action in the summer of 1944 by which time the German night fighter defences had attained the peak of their success, and such were the casualties that they were inflicting that it was generally believed in the Luftwaffe that R.A.F. Bomber Command would be forced to abandon its large-scale night attacks. Some of the most impressive results of the German night defences were those achieved on the nights of March 24–25 and 30–31, 1944, when seventy-two out of 810 bombers attacking Berlin and ninety-four out of 795 aircraft attacking Nuremburg were destroyed, representing losses of 8.8 and 11.8 per cent respectively! The Ju 88G-1, with its maximum speed of 379 m.p.h. at 21,325 ft., heavy firepower and relatively efficient radar equipment, promised even greater successes. Unfortunately for the Luftwaffe, with the Allied advance across France to the borders of Germany and the steady approach of the Russian forces from the opposite direction, the night fighter arm gradually dwindled in strength. Although the aircraft industry made good attrition despite constant attack on its facilities by day and night, replacement crews were not so easily obtained and some night fighter units were diverted to the Eastern Front for close-support operations by day.

In the meantime, development of the Ju 88 fighter continued without pause, and the Ju 88G-1 was

succeeded in production by the Ju 88G-6, the G-2 to G-5 having been projected models with equipment changes. The Ju 88G-6a was similar to the G-1 apart from having BMW 801G engines, and the G-6b had additional radio and radar equipment, an additional 81 Imp. gal. (97 U.S. gal.) internal fuel, and two 20-mm. MG 151 cannon with 200 r.p.g. in a *Schräge Musik* installation. A third variant powered by Jumo 213A engines rated at 1,750 h.p. for take-off was designated Ju 88C-6c, this model attaining a maximum speed of 331 m.p.h. at 19,700 ft., or 344 m.p.h. with the flame dampers removed. Initial climb rate was 1,850 ft./min., an altitude of 19,700 feet was attained in eleven minutes and service ceiling was 32,800 ft. Endurance (with 705 Imp. gal.—847 U.S. gal. internal fuel) was 3.75 hours at maximum continuous cruising speed at 19,700 ft., and 5.19 hours at maximum economical cruising speed at the same altitude, these endurances including one hour at combat rating. The final G-series production model, the Ju 88G-7, differed from its predecessor in having Jumo 213E engines with MW 50 methanol-water injection which boosted power in an emergency to 1,800 h.p. at 26,000 ft. The Ju 88G-7a had FuG 220 *Lichtenstein, the* G-7b had the improved FuG 228 *Lichtenstein SN-3*, some machines having the *Morgenstern* antennae enclosed by a pointed cone in an attempt to reduce drag, and *Naxos* built into the *Morgenstern* compartment, and the C-7c having FuG 240 *Berlin N-1* centimetric radar enclosed by a wooden radome. Only twenty-five complete *Berlin N-1* sets were built and of these only ten were installed in the Ju 88C-7c by the end of the war.

One other version of the basic Ju 88 that had, in fact, preceded the G-series was the Ju 88H long-range variant produced by the conversion of A- and D-series airframes. The H-series was characterised by an elongated fuselage which resulted from the introduction of two additional bays, one forward and one aft of the wing main spar, housing additional fuel tanks. The Ju 88H-1 had been a long-range photo-reconnaissance aircraft with search radar and three cameras, but the Ju 88H-2 powered by two BMW 801D radials and carrying a forward-firing armament of six 20-mm. MG 151 cannon, featured a similar nose and gun tray to the Ju 88G and was a long-range heavy day fighter intended primarily for anti-shipping duties. Only ten of each H-model were produced, and these saw service over the Atlantic during 1942–43.

The proposed G-series of night fighters ranged to the Ju 88G-12. The G-12 employed not only the rear fuselage and tail of the Ju 188 bomber but the wings as well, and was eventually redesignated Ju 188R. Three prototypes were built and flown, the Ju 188R-01 and -02 having a forward-firing armament of four 20-mm. MG 151 cannon, and the Ju 188R-03 having two 30-mm. MK 103 cannon. One of these prototypes was flown to Sweden by its crew in 1944. The Ju 88G-8 was a projected model in which the elongated fuselage of the Ju 88H-2 was to have been employed.

An indirect development of the "eighty-eight" intended to succeed the earlier aircraft in production was the Ju 388 which was the final variant of this prolific series stemming from the original Ju 88 of 1936 to reach the assembly lines before Germany's defeat brought further work to a halt. The second prototype of this new model, the Ju 388V2, was intended to serve as a prototype for the Ju 388J *Strötebeker* high-altitude night-fighter. Based on the final developments of the Ju 188 bomber which had featured pressure cabins for high-altitude operations, the Ju 388 employed a similar basic airframe to that of the earlier type but was fitted with BMW 801TJ radial engines with exhaust-driven turbo-superchargers and offering 1,800 h.p. for take-off and 1,890 h.p. at 9,850 ft. The initial production model, the Ju 388J-1, had a forward-firing armament of two 20-mm. MG 151 cannon with 180 r.p.g. and two 30-mm. MK 103 or MK 108 cannon with 110 r.p.g. in a ventral tray offset to port, and rear defence was provided by a remotely controlled FDL 131Z tail barbette housing twin 13-mm. MG 131 machine guns with 300 r.p.g. In the event, delays in the delivery of the tail barbette resulted in the only three Ju 388J-1 fighters to leave the assembly line being completed with this item of equipment omitted. Performance included a maximum speed of 362 m.p.h. at 40,300 feet and 249

m.p.h. at sea level, and normal and maximum loaded weights were 30,700 lb. and 32,350 lb. respectively. Radar equipment was similar to that installed in the Ju 88G-7a, and the projected Jumo 213E-powered Ju 388J-3 was to have featured a pointed wooden nose cone enclosing the *Morgenstern* antennae for FuG 228 *Lichtenstein SN-3*, and two additional MG 151 cannon in a *Schräge Musik* installation.

The Ju 88 was considered by many to be the backbone of the Luftwaffe; it was certainly the backbone of Germany's night fighter arm. This ubiquitous warplane was an exceptional machine by any standards and can lay claim to having been one of a score or so truly outstanding combat aircraft to serve with one or other of the opposing sides during the Second World War. To the Ju 88 more than to any other aircraft type in Luftwaffe service went the distinction of rendering the R.A.F. night bomber offensive a very costly undertaking; an undertaking that came near to being defeated.

Junkers Ju 88G-7b

Dimensions:	Span, 65 ft. 10½ in.; length, 54 ft. 1½ in.; height, 15 ft. 11 in.; wing area, 590 sq. ft.
Armament:	Four forward-firing 20-mm. MG 151 cannon with 200 r.p.g. in ventral housing, one rear-firing swivelling 13-mm. MG 131 machine gun with 500 rounds, and two fixed 20-mm. MG 151 cannon with 200 r.p.g. firing obliquely upward.
Power Plants:	Two Junkers Jumo 213E twelve-cylinder inverted-vee liquid-cooled engines each rated at 1,880 h.p. at 3,250 r.p.m. for take-off, 1,420 h.p. at 3,000 r.p.m. at 27,000 ft., and 2,250 h.p. (emergency) with water-methanol injection at sea level. Internal fuel capacity: 335 Imp. gal. (402 U.S. gal.) in fuselage and 370 Imp. gal. (444 U.S. gal.) in wings.
Weights:	Normal loaded, 28,900 lb.; maximum overload (with 198 Imp. gal.—238 U.S. gal. drop tank), 32,350 lb.
Performance:	Maximum speed (clean), 270 m.p.h. at sea level, 363 m.p.h. at 33,500 ft., (with water-methanol injection), 389 m.p.h. at 29,800 ft.; initial climb rate, 1,655 ft./min.; time to 30,200 ft., 26.4 min.; service ceiling, 32,800 ft.; endurance (including one hour at emergency power with water-methanol injection), 3 hr. at maximum continuous power at 29,800 ft., 3.72 hr. at maximum economical power, (with 198 Imp. gal. drop tank) 4.14 hr. at maximum continuous power, 5.2 hr. at maximum economical power.

One of the ten Ju 88G-7c fighters fitted with FuG 240/1 Berlin N-1 radar enclosed by a wooden nose radome.

(*Above*) *The Ki.43-IIb, or Type* 1 *Fighter Model 2B, was outclassed by most Allied fighters that it encountered from 1943, but it was exceptionally manoeuvrable and suffered no serious vices. The Ki.43-Ib (below) was essentially an interim production version of the Hayabusa, differing from the initial model solely in having one of the fuselage-mounted 7.7-mm. guns replaced by a 12.7-mm. weapon. The début of the Hayabusa came as a complete surprise to the Allies in the Pacific.*

THE
NAKAJIMA HAYABUSA

Every major air arm participating in the Second World War had its workhorse; a fighter serving when hostilities began and still operational when they terminated, amenable to adaptation for a variety of roles and encountered in every theatre of war in which was engaged the air force it served. Such an aircraft was the Nakajima Type 1 Fighter, or Hayabusa (Peregrine Falcon), which, numerically, was the most important Japanese Army Air Force fighter of the conflict.

The Hayabusa was, in several respects, a transitional type, bridging the gap between the lightly loaded fighter monoplanes of the late 'thirties, with their fixed undercarriages, and the high-powered, heavy fighters that began to appear in the early 'forties. As such it was in a class of its own; either far superior to or completely outclassed by the Allied fighters that it was to encounter during its operational career. Despite the fact that when the Pacific War began, on December 7, 1941, the Japanese Army Air Force possessed only forty Hayabusa fighters, this warplane appeared in startling succession over Malaya, Burma, Sumatra and Java during the first six months of the conflict, and remained in production until Japan's final defeat. Virtually every J.A.A.F. fighter pilot flew the Hayabusa at one time or another, and most of the Japanese Army's "Aces" established the larger part of their scores while mounted in this warplane.

The career of the Hayabusa began at the beginning of 1938, when the Nakajima Hikoki K.K. received a development contract for a single-seat fighter to which was allocated the Kitai number Ki.43. Nakajima was one of the oldest and most important of aircraft manufacturers, having served its apprenticeship in the customary Japanese manner by producing foreign aircraft under licence, and gradually evolving an independent line of development. A little over a year before the receipt of the Ki.43 development contract, the company had won the closely-contested Type 97 Fighter competition with its Ki.27 which, possessing exceptional powers of manoeuvre, was the first indigenous Japanese fighter design to compare favourably with contemporary foreign fighters. The successful outcome of the Type 97 Fighter's service evaluation led the J.A.A.F. to think in terms of a more ambitious fighter fully capable of meeting the challenge offered by the new fighters being evolved abroad, and as an indication of its satisfaction with the company's earlier fighter, a contract for a more advanced fighter was awarded Nakajima virtually at the same time that the Ki.27 was making its service début.

The placing of a direct contract was an innovation insofar as the J.A.A.F. was concerned for, previously, development contracts had been awarded to all interested manufacturers, the resulting prototypes being pitted one against another in comparative trials to determine the best aircraft for production. However, this competitive method led to friction and a lack of co-operation between aircraft companies, and with the signs that the Sino-Japanese conflict was to be a long and fierce struggle, the J.A.A.F. was most anxious that petty jealousies within the industry should not impede its ambitious expansion and modernisation programme. The requirements of the Ki.43 specification necessitated a substantial advance in design technique by comparison with the Ki.27. The role of the aircraft was outlined in the specification as an interceptor fighter capable of destroying enemy attack bombers, equally suitable for use as an escort fighter and possessing a combat performance superior to that of enemy interceptors that it was likely to encounter. While manoeuvrability and cockpit vision had to be comparable with or superior to these features of the Ki.27, speed, climb rate, and range had to better the outstanding individual characteristics of all known fighters then under development.

Engineer Hideo Itokawa, the designer of the earlier Ki.27, immediately began work on the new fighter, although it was obvious that the specification exceeded appreciably aeronautical engineering standards previously attained in Japan. The specification did not demand pilot protection or self-sealing fuel tanks, and this omission, although to be regretted later by the J.A.A.F., eased Itokawa's task in striving for manoeuvrability. The specified armament consisted of two 7.7-mm. Type 89 machine guns, then standard on all Japanese fighters, an extreme policy of weight saving was rigidly adhered to, much care was devoted to drag reduction, and the choice of a power plant was a foregone conclusion—Nakajima's new Ha.25 Sakae (Prosperity) two-row fourteen-cylinder radial rated at 950 h.p. Basically, the Ki.43 was a small, low-wing cantilever monoplane of all-metal construction, the

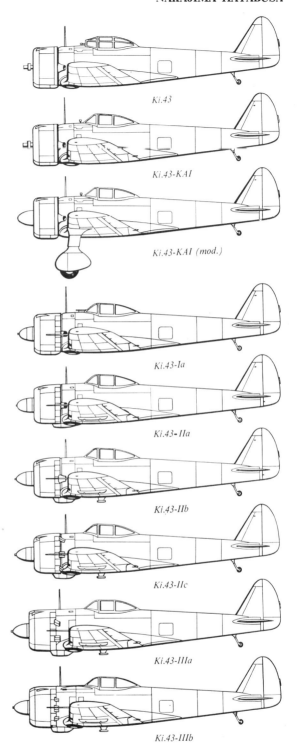

Ki.43

Ki.43-KAI

Ki.43-KAI (mod.)

Ki.43-Ia

Ki.43-IIa

Ki.43-IIb

Ki.43-IIc

Ki.43-IIIa

Ki.43-IIIb

three-spar wing being built in a single piece and possessing substantial area to keep loadings to the minimum. The fuselage was exceptionally slim, the whole being covered by a metal stressed-skin, all control surfaces being metal-framed and fabric-covered. The fully retractable main undercarriage

(*Above*) *The mock-up of the Ki.43 Hayabusa fighter at Nakajima's Ota plant in 1938, and (left) the twelfth pre-production Ki.43-Ia after suffering an undercarriage failure.*

members represented an innovation in Japanese fighter design, although a similar feature had been adopted by the Navy's 12-*Shi* fighter which was being developed in parallel by Mitsubishi.

The Nakajima team found it exceedingly difficult to fulfil the contradictory requirements of extreme speed and maximum manoeuvrability, the ultimate in one being attained only at the expense of the other. In consequence, the Ki.43 had to be a compromise. Three Ki.43 prototypes were built at Nakajima's Ota factory, located in the eastern part of Ota in the Gumma Prefecture, about fifty miles north-west of Tokyo, and the first of these was completed in January 1939, being closely followed by the second and third

machines. After brief manufacturer's trials, the prototypes were taken over by J.A.A.F. test pilots for evaluation and acceptance trials, and their reaction was immediate—and bad! By comparison with the earlier Ki.27, the manoeuvrability of the Ki.43 left much to be desired, and its response to the controls was sluggish. Agility in aerial combat was considered to be of paramount importance by the J.A.A.F. The Army had for long been a firm adherent of the classic dog-fighting method of fighter-versus-fighter combat. Its pilots had been trained to excel in the manoeuvres demanded by such combat, and they did not take kindly to the Ki.43's inferior manoeuvrability. In fact, the J.A.A.F.'s fighter concepts were already undergoing radical changes, the first indication of which had come with the placing of a development contract for the Ki.44 in which speed and climb rate were stressed at the expense of manoeuvrability, but the Ki.43 had been envisaged as an extrapolation of the Ki.27; coupling the earlier fighter's manoeuvrability with greater speed and climb!

In the opinion of the Army test pilots the new

FINISH AND INSIGNIA: *The Ki.43-Ic Hayabusa illustrated on the opposite page belonged to the 1st Chutai (Flight) of the J.A.A.F.'s 64th Fighter Sentai. A jungle green dapple was applied over the natural metal finish of the upper surfaces, and the under surfaces were left natural metal. The national Hinomaru was outlined in white on the fuselage sides but not on the wing surfaces. A white "combat stripe" was painted around the* *rear fuselage, and the Sentai tail emblem was also painted in white, indicating the 1st Chutai. The 2nd Chutai had the emblem painted in red and the 3rd had it painted in yellow. A black anti-dazzle panel stretched from the front of the cockpit over the engine cowling, and the airscrew spinner was painted red.*

Nakajima Ki. 43-Ic Hayabusa

The Ki.43-IIa Hayabusa, the first production model of the fighter to employ the more powerful Ha.115 engine and pilot armour.

fighter did not measure up to the Ki.27 already in service! An urgent programme of redesign was immediately instituted in an attempt to improve the characteristics of the Ki.43. Some pilots considered the retractable undercarriage to be a dispensable luxury in view of the weight of the retraction mechanism, and one of the Ki.43-KAI prototypes subsequently evaluated was, in fact, fitted with a fixed undercarriage. Trials soon proved, however, that the saving in weight did not adequately compensate for

the increased drag. Ten Ki.43-KAI prototypes were built, the first of these being completed in November 1939. The wing span was increased slightly from 37 ft. 6¼ in. to 37 ft. 10¾ in., minor structural changes were made, the cockpit canopy was slightly modified to improve pilot vision, and some alterations were made to the controls, but the most important change was the introduction of the so-called "combat" or "battle" flap which, extended in action, provided additional lift, increased the turn rate and improved control response. By means of this innovation, the Ki.43 became one of the most manoeuvrable fighters extant, J.A.A.F. trials were resumed at the beginning of 1940, and the test pilots' reaction to the Ki.43-KAI was the exact reverse to that expressed so forcibly when the initial prototypes of the fighter had been evaluated. It was found that the Ki.43-KAI was completely devoid of any vicious characteristics, all controls being extremely sensitive, and quantity

The Ki.43-Ic was the first Hayabusa variant to attain large-scale production. (Left) A Ki.43-Ic with a Hucks type starter such as was in vogue during the First World War.

The Ki.43-IIa Hayabusa represented a marked improvement over the earlier production models of the Nakajima fighter.

production began at Nakajima's Ota plant, the first model receiving the designation Type 1 Fighter, Model 1A (Ki.43-Ia).

With the acceptance of the Ki.43, a companion project which had been evolved in parallel with this fighter to safeguard against its failure, the Ki.27-KAI, was abandoned, and dubbed Hayabusa, the Type 1 Fighter, Model 1A began to reach J.A.A.F. fighter units in October 1941, only eight months after production had begun at Ota. The Model 1A variant of the Hayabusa carried an armament of two 7.7-mm. machine guns in the forward fuselage upper decking, and power was provided by an Ha.25 Sakae (later to be known as the Ha.35/12 under the unified J.A.A.F./ J.N.A.F. designation system) offering 975 h.p. for take-off and possessing a military rating of 955 h.p. at 11,100 ft. Performance included a maximum speed of 304 m.p.h. at 13,120 ft., a cruising speed of 199 m.p.h.

(Right and below) The Ki.43-IIa served in virtually every theatre of operations to which the J.A.A.F. was committed, and although slower than most Allied fighters, it enjoyed particularly rapid acceleration.

at 8,200 ft., a range of 620 miles, and the ability to reach 9,840 ft. in 2 min. 50 sec., and 16,400 ft. in 4 min. 50 sec. Empty and loaded weights were 3,307 lb. and 4,630 lb. respectively. The Model 1A was rapidly supplanted on the assembly line at Ota by the Model 1B (Ki.43-Ib) in which a 12.7-mm. Ho 103 machine gun similar to the Colt-Browning supplanted one of the 7.7-mm. weapons, while the Model 1C, the first

large-scale production version of the Hayabusa, carried an armament of two 12.7-mm. guns. It could also be fitted with racks for two 33-lb. bombs or an 8.8. Imp. gal. (10.5 U.S. gal.) drop tank. By comparison with the Navy's A6M2 Zero-Sen fighter which had a basically similar Sakae engine and constant-speed airscrew, the Model 1C Hayabusa had a substantially lower wing loading (18.4 to 23 lb./sq. ft.) and power loading (4.3 to 5.5 lb./h.p.) but was, nevertheless, slightly inferior to the shipboard fighter in overall manoeuvrability. The A6M2 manifested a decided superiority over the Hayabusa in zoom climb, although in a steady climb to 16,400 ft. the Nakajima fighter possessed a slight edge over its Mitsubishi contemporary.

The Hayabusa quickly supplanted the earlier Type 97 Fighter as standard J.A.A.F. first line equipment, and soon manifested an ascendancy over the Allied fighters that it encountered, its success dispelling the last doubts of its pilots who, until the Hayabusa had proved itself in combat, were suspicious of its retractable undercarriage and other innovations. There is no doubt that much of this early success was also due in no small part to the fact that many of the Allied fighter pilots, on the defensive and operating under conditions of enemy air superiority, lacked the élan of their Japanese opponents. Japanese military security had maintained an effective cloak of secrecy over the Type 1 Fighter, the début of which had come as a complete surprise to the Allies, but with the opening of the Pacific War and the subsequent press publicity given to the Navy's A6M2 Zero-Sen, the J.A.A.F. decided that it too should have public recognition of its new fighter, and thus, in April 1942, the Hayabusa was publicly revealed for the first time.

Despite the Hayabusa's early successes, the J.A.A.F. was soon forced to admit that it had made a serious mistake in excluding a demand for pilot protection and self-sealing fuel tanks from the original specification, and a rudimentary form of self-sealing fuel tank was introduced together with 13-mm. armour plate head and back protection for the pilot, and these changes, together with an improved version of the Sakae engine, the Ha.115 rated at 1,105 h.p. for take-off and possessing a military rating of 1,085 h.p. at 9,200 ft., were embodied in a new variant of the fighter, the first of five prototypes of which was completed in February 1942. As the Type 1 Fighter Model 2A (Ki.43-IIa), the modified Hayabusa entered production at Ota, the earlier Model 1 being progressively phased out until the 716th and last aircraft of this type left the assembly line in February 1943. As the Model 1 was succeeded by the Model 2 in the operational units, the lower-powered version was assigned to advanced fighter training schools, and others were delivered to the Royal Thai Air Force, Thailand then being ostensibly allied to Japan, these being destined to remain in Thai service until late in 1949.

From the wreckage of several Model 2A Hayabusas found at Lae, New Guinea, in September 1943, one complete fighter was rebuilt at Brisbane and flown in mock combat with various Allied types. Close evaluation and study of the new fighter, which had been allocated the Allied code-name of *Oscar*, divulged its secrets, and it was learned that the Nakajima fighter was surprisingly below western standards. The knowledge acquired from trials of the fighter gave Allied fighter pilots a decided tactical edge over the Hayabusa. Allied pilots who flew the Japanese fighter were unanimous in their praise for its sensitive controls and extreme manoeuvrability. As one American pilot put it, the Hayabusa was an aircraft which could definitely be flown by "the seat of the pants". However, they were equally unanimous in declaring the Japanese fighter outclassed by the P-47 Thunderbolt, the P-38 Lightning, the Spitfire, and even by the later models of the P-40 Warhawk providing their pilots had a knowledge of the Hayabusa's capabilities and weaknesses. The consensus of opinion was that the Hayabusa had no vicious characteristics; its turn and stall characteristics were superior to those of any Allied fighter; it handled well in the air and could be looped and Immelmanned at airspeeds of 170 m.p.h. or lower; take-off and landing characteristics were good, and the "battle" flaps effective, and Allied fighters would do well to stay clear of the Japanese fighter at low airspeeds as it could accelerate from 150 m.p.h. to 250 m.p.h. with extreme rapidity. Conversely, the Hayabusa lacked firepower; it was appreciably slower than most Allied fighters, and could usually be evaded by diving.

The Model 2A Hayabusa had been placed in production by the Tachikawa Hikoki K.K. in May 1943, and prior to this the 1st Army Air Arsenal (Tachikawa Dai-ichi Rikugun Kokusho) had also commenced the manufacture of the type, but the latter concern was not equipped to solve the numerous problems provided by quantity production of the fighter, and in November 1943 the programme was abandoned, only forty-nine aircraft having been completed.

Despite the inadequacy of the armament of the early Hayabusas, the Model 2A retained the twin 12.7-mm. guns with 250 r.p.g. introduced by the Model 1C, but a reflector sight was installed and provision made for two bombs of up to 550-lb. under the wings. The carburettor air intake was transferred to the upper lip of the engine cowling, the oil cooler was moved back under the nose, and the Ha.115 engine drove a three-blade constant-speed airscrew in place of the two-blader of earlier Hayabusas. Maximum speed rose to 320 m.p.h. at 19,685 ft., and the inclusion of two additional wing tanks increasing the overload internal fuel capacity from 87 Imp. gal. (104.5 U.S. gal.) to 123 Imp. gal. (148 U.S. gal.), increased normal range from 620 mls. to 1,006 mls. Minor equipment changes marked the Model 2B (Ki.43-IIb), but the Ki.43-II-KAI, three prototypes of which were built between June and August 1942, introduced clipped wingtips which reduced overall span to 35 ft. 6¾ in. The Ki.43-II-KAI entered service in the summer of 1943 as the Ki.43-IIc, serving over every theatre to which the J.A.A.F. was committed.

(Above) Ki.43-IIa Hayabusa fighters of the Akeno Fighter Training School where most J.A.A.F. fighter pilots received training before being posted to an operational unit.

The Model 2 Hayabusa was a formidable fighter in many respects but it was unable to withstand the heavier firepower of the less manoeuvrable Allied fighters, and often disintegrated in the air when hit. It served from the North in the defence of Paramushiru to the southern Pacific, from the Manchurian mainland to the India-Burma theatre. The majority of the J.A.A.F. fighter *sentais* (roughly equivalent to a U.S. squadron and comprising approximately thirty-six aircraft) flew the Model 2, these including the 1st., 11th., 13th., 17th., 18th., 19th., 20th., 23rd., 24th., 25th., 26th., 30th., 31st., 33rd., 48th., 50th., 54th., 59th., 64th., 65th., 71st., 72nd., 73rd., 77th., 101st., 102nd., 103rd., 104th., 112th., 203rd., 204th., and 248th *sentais*. Many of the leading J.A.A.F. fighter pilots applied colourful markings to their Hayabusas, and one of the most famous individual emblems to appear on a fighter of this type was the red eagle insignia of Lieut. Col. Tateo Kato who failed to return from a sortie over the Bay of Bengal after scoring his fifty-eighth victory. The Hayabusa played a major part in the J.A.A.F.'s last serious challenge to Allied air power in Burma, in May 1944, when sweeps of twenty to thirty Hayabusas were sent into the Imphal area to provide cover for the Japanese troops participating in the Kohima drive. Later, the Hayabusa was used in the disastrous Philippines campaign, forming the bulk of the J.A.A.F. fighter units defending these islands from the beginning of October 1944.

Despite the obsolescence of the Hayabusa's basic design, development continued, and as late as December 1944, production began of an improved version, the Model 3A (Ki.43-IIIa) with the Ha.115-II Sakae

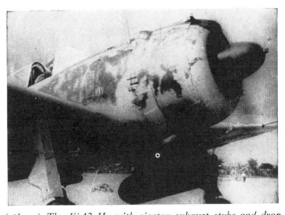

(Above) The Ki.43-IIc with ejector exhaust stubs and drop tank.

engine rated at 1,230 h.p. and employing individual exhaust stacks to provide a certain amount of exhaust thrust augmentation. Maximum speed was increased to 354 m.p.h. at 13,120 ft. and 363 m.p.h. at 19,190 ft., an altitude of 16,400 ft. was attained in 5 min. 19 sec., and 26,250 ft. was reached in 10 min. 54 sec. The short-span wing first introduced on the Ki.-43-II-KAI was retained as was also the armament of two 12.7-mm. guns, and production of the Model 3A was undertaken by both Nakajima and Tachikawa, the fighter being assigned to units defending Tokyo and other major Japanese cities, and also being used in the suicide attacks which characterised the final phases of the Pacific conflict, serving with the J.A.A.F.'s *Taiatari* (Suicide) elements.

The Ki.43-IIc was the most widely used variant of the Hayabusa fighter and played a major part in the J.A.A.F.'s last serious challenge to Allied air power in Burma. Despite its obsolescence, production was maintained until the end of the Pacific War.

The ultimate development of the Hayabusa series was the Model 3B (Ki.43-IIIb) evolved by Tachikawa. This was the first variant of the fighter to mount large calibre armament, a pair of 20-mm. Ho-5 cannon supplanting the 12.7mm. guns in the upper decking of the forward fuselage, and extensive modifications were made to the fuselage and wing structure as well as further changes to the exhaust system, and overall wing span was similar to that of the Model 3A at 35 ft. 6¾ in. However, only two prototypes of the Model 3B had been completed when the termination of hostilities brought further work to a standstill.

Although the Hayabusa was not an exceptional fighter by world standards, more aircraft of this type were produced during the war years than any other operational J.A.A.F. type, total production being 5,751 machines. It had proved amenable to adaptation for roles other than those for which it was originally envisaged, and it had served throughout the conflict ; participating in the great victories of the first six months of the war and finishing its career as a suicide aircraft in Japan's final débâcle.

Nakajima Type 1 Model 2B Hayabusa (Ki.43-IIb)

Dimensions :	Span, 37 ft. 6½ in. ; length, 29 ft. 2½ in. ; height, 10 ft. 1½ in. ; wing area, 236.806 sq. ft.
Armament :	Two 12.7-mm. Type 1 machine guns with 250 r.p.g., and two 550-lb. bombs.
Power Plant :	One Nakajima Ha.115 (Ha.35/21) fourteen-cylinder two-row radial air-cooled engine rated at 1,105 h.p. for take-off and 1,085 h.p. at 9,200 ft. Maximum internal fuel capacity, 123 Imp. gal. (148 U.S. gal.) plus two 45 Imp. gal. (54 U.S. gal.) drop tanks.
Weights :	Empty, 3,812 lb. ; normal loaded, 5,320 lb. ; maximum overload, 5,874 lb.
Performance :	Maximum speed, 320 m.p.h. at 19,680 ft., 288 m.p.h. at sea level ; economic cruising speed, 214 m.p.h. at 13,125 ft. ; range (on internal fuel), 1,006 mls., (with maximum external fuel), 1,865 mls. ; maximum endurance, 7.6 hrs. ; initial climb rate, 3,240 ft./min. ; time to 16,400 ft. (clean), 5 min. 49 sec. ; service ceiling, 36,800 ft.

Most of the leading J.A.A.F. fighter pilots established the bulk of their scores while flying the Hayabusa. This photograph depicts the Ki.43-IIa model.

The prototype Type 300 Spitfire (K5054) with Merlin "C" engine and two-blade fixed-pitch airscrew.

THE SUPERMARINE SPITFIRE

The Supermarine Spitfire was much more than just a highly successful fighter. It was the material symbol of final victory to the British people in their darkest hour, and it was probably the only fighter of the Second World War to achieve a truly legendary status. Certainly no other fighter is more deserving of its place among the famous. In its forty major variants, it was built in greater numbers than any other British aeroplane; it flew operationally on every front between 1939 and 1945, and it was engaged in every major air action fought by the R.A.F. in that time.

The success which attended the Spitfire from its earliest days was no accident. Like most of the world's really great aeroplanes, the Spitfire was both an inspired design *and* the outcome of a lengthy process of technical development. Its sires, if less widely known, bore names hardly less illustrious—such as the Supermarine S.6B which, in 1931, won the Schneider Trophy outright for Britain, and went on to raise the world air speed record to 406.99 m.p.h., nearly 50 m.p.h. faster than the record set two years earlier by its immediate predecessor, the S.6. In few warplanes was evolution more clearly discernible, and with such a distinguished pedigree nothing less than a true thoroughbred could result.

The creation of one of the most brilliant designers Britain has produced, Reginald J. Mitchell, the Spitfire was the culmination of a line of development initiated in 1925 at a time when streamlining was more a theoretical exercise than an engineering possibility. These ancestors of the Spitfire remain aesthetically to this day among the most pleasing aircraft designs ever evolved.

Before the final Schneider Trophy contest Mitchell turned his attention to fighter design for the first time in response to the official F.7/30 specification. Drawing though he did on his experience in the design of high-speed floatplanes, the performance of Mitchell's first fighter was unspectacular, thanks to the untried and unsuccessful Rolls-Royce Goshawk engine and the rigidity of the official specification. But Mitchell went on to put down on paper his own ideas of what a fighter could look like if unhampered by official requirements. He gave his design an enclosed cockpit and a retractable undercarriage, but he was still restricted by the lack of a really suitable engine. In 1934, however, Rolls-Royce promised 1,000 h.p. from production models of their new PV-12 liquid-cooled twelve-cylinder engine. In the same year, specification F.5/34 asked officially for the first time for a fighter armed with eight machine-guns and possessed of just the advanced features that Mitchell had envisaged—a retractable undercarriage and an enclosed cockpit.

By a process of development and refinement, Mitchell took his private-venture fighter design, now based on the PV-12 engine, and with four machine-guns in each wing, far beyond the requirements of F.5/34. It was, in essence, the smallest and simplest fighter which could be designed around the engine and armament. While the lines first evolved for the Schneider Trophy racers reappeared in the fuselage contours, the wing was of a new elliptical planform, the aerodynamic advantages of which far outweighed the production difficulties that it presented. Submitted to the Air Ministry, this design, the Type 300, was accepted in January 1935 for prototype construction, and specification F.37/34 was written

125

The High Speed Spitfire intended for a World Air Speed Record attempt.

round the fighter for contractual purposes. Work on a mock-up had already started when this contract was placed, and the final mock-up conference was held at Woolston on March 26, 1935. Almost exactly a year later the prototype Spitfire, bearing the serial K5054, was complete, and on March 5, 1936, Captain J. "Mutt" Summers, chief test pilot of the Vickers and Supermarine companies, took it on a successful first flight at Eastleigh Airport, Hampshire. The PV-12 engine was by then known as the Merlin, the first prototype Spitfire being powered by one of the early versions, the Merlin C, which endowed it with a top speed of 349.5 m.p.h.

Meanwhile plans had been laid to adopt this brilliant new fighter on a production basis, and specification F.16/36 was drawn up to cover further development and production. On June 3, 1936, the first production contract for 310 Spitfire Is was placed with the Supermarine company. It was followed by a contract for a further 200 machines during 1937, but in that year its

designer, R. J. Mitchell, died and was succeeded as chief designer by Joseph Smith.

Deliveries of production Spitfire Is began in June 1938, two years after the first production contract had been placed. In those two years Supermarine laid out their Woolston factory for large-scale production and organized one of the largest sub-contract schemes ever envisaged in Britain until that time, as it was becoming increasingly obvious that there was no limit to the likely demand for the Spitfire. It was also obvious that one factory alone was not going to be able to meet the demand, even with sub-contracting on a large scale, and plans were laid during 1937 for the construction by the Nuffield Group of a large new "shadow" factory at Castle Bromwich, near Birmingham, for Spitfire production. On April 12, 1938, a contract was placed for 1,000 Spitfires to be built at this new factory, the actual construction of which had not then even begun. In the following year further contracts were placed with Supermarine—on April 29 for 200 Spitfires and on August 9 for 450—so that when Britain went to war on September 3, 1939, a total of 2,160 Spitfires were already on order.

Structurally the Spitfire was a straightforward design, with a light alloy monocoque fuselage and a single spar wing, with stressed-skin covering and fabric-covered control surfaces. To preserve the clean nose-cowling lines originally conceived by Mitchell for his F.7/30 design, the radiator was located beneath the starboard wing, with the smaller oil cooler causing some asymmetry beneath the port wing, and the carburettor air intake under the centre fuselage. A de Havilland two-blade wooden fixed-pitch airscrew was employed by the prototype, and the first Spitfire Is had the Airscrew Company's wooden fixed-pitch two-blader. Later, a de Havilland three-blade two-position airscrew was adopted after trials on the first prototype. The new airscrew gave a 5 m.p.h. increase in speed. In 1940 de Havilland three-blade constant-

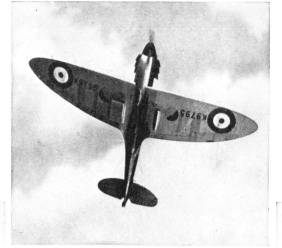

(Left) The ninth production Spitfire I (K9795), and (below) the seventh production Spitfire I fitted experimentally during the early months of 1939 with a three-blade de Havilland variable-pitch airscrew.

speed airscrews were substituted. Production Spit-fires had a fixed tailwheel and triple ejector exhaust manifolds. The 880 h.p. Rolls-Royce Merlin II, and later the Merlin III, was fitted.

During 1938 plans had been prepared for an attempt on the world air speed record with a specially modified Spitfire, the Type 323, which became known as the "High Speed Spitfire". It was, in fact, K9834, ex-tracted from the initial Supermarine production batch and renumbered N17 for its trial flights. The cockpit enclosure was specially streamlined, wing span was reduced to 33 ft. 8 in., flush riveting was used and a high-gloss finish was applied. The engine was a strengthened Merlin III, operating on 100-octane fuel and giving 2,160 h.p. through an Airscrew Company four-blade fixed-pitch propeller. It was expected that N17 would achieve 420 m.p.h., but before any attempt on the record could be made the Heinkel He 100V8 had raised the record to 463.92 m.p.h., and immedi-ately afterwards the Me 209V1 further increased the record to 469.22 m.p.h., and as there was little likeli-hood of the Spitfire bettering such speeds plans for the attempt on the record were abandoned. Re-engined with a Merlin XII, it later became one of the first photographic-reconnaissance Spitfires.

Before the outbreak of war various foreign govern-ments planned to purchase the Spitfire, and export versions were designed for Greece (Type 335), Portugal (Type 336), and Turkey (Type 341). Seven-teen Spitfires from the third Supermarine production order were in fact exported. In June 1938 No. 19(F) Squadron of Fighter Command, based at Duxford near Cambridge, received the first Spitfires, and was completely equipped by the end of July. Deliveries to the R.A.F. maintained a steadily increasing tempo, and when war broke out nine squadrons of the R.A.F. and Aux.A.F.—Nos. 19, 41, 54, 65, 66, 72, 74, 602 and 611—were equipped with Spitfires, and two more Auxiliary squadrons—Nos. 603 and 609—had been partially equipped with the new fighter. On October 16, 1939, the Spitfire's guns were fired in anger for the first time when aircraft of Nos. 602 and 603 Squadrons engaged German bombers over the Firth of Forth; the two Heinkel He 111s then destroyed were the first enemy aircraft to be shot down over the British Isles since 1918.

In the form in which it first entered service, the Spitfire I weighed 5,280 lb., had a wing loading of 24 lb./sq. ft., and a fuel capacity of 85 Imperial gallons. Its maximum speed was 362 m.p.h., its maximum diving speed was 450 m.p.h., its initial climb rate was 2,500 ft./min., and it took 9.4 minutes to climb to 20,000 feet. Its combat range was 395 miles and its roll rate was 140 deg./sec. Standard armament in what was subsequently to become known as the "A" wing was eight 0.303-in. Browning machine-guns with 300 rounds of ammunition. The speed of the Spitfire I was marginally higher than that of its principal opponent, the Luftwaffe's Messer-schmitt Bf 109E, and it was infinitely more manœuv-rable than the German fighter, although the Bf 109E

could outclimb and outdive the British fighter, and its shell-firing cannon were longer-ranging than the Spitfire's machine-guns.

From 1938 onwards the Spitfire had been the sub-ject of an intensive development programme which was to remain the major preoccupation of the Super-marine design team for several more years and pre-cluded the introduction of any other Supermarine

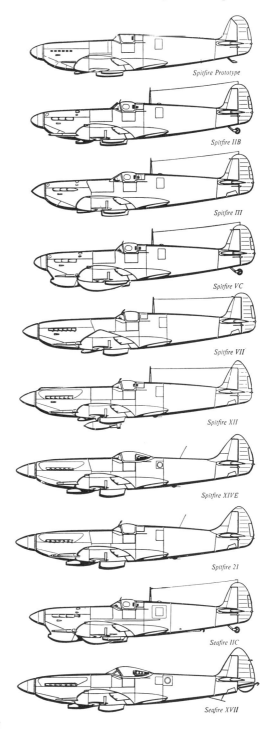

Spitfire Prototype

Spitfire IIB

Spitfire III

Spitfire VC

Spitfire VII

Spitfire XII

Spitfire XIVE

Spitfire 21

Seafire IIC

Seafire XVII

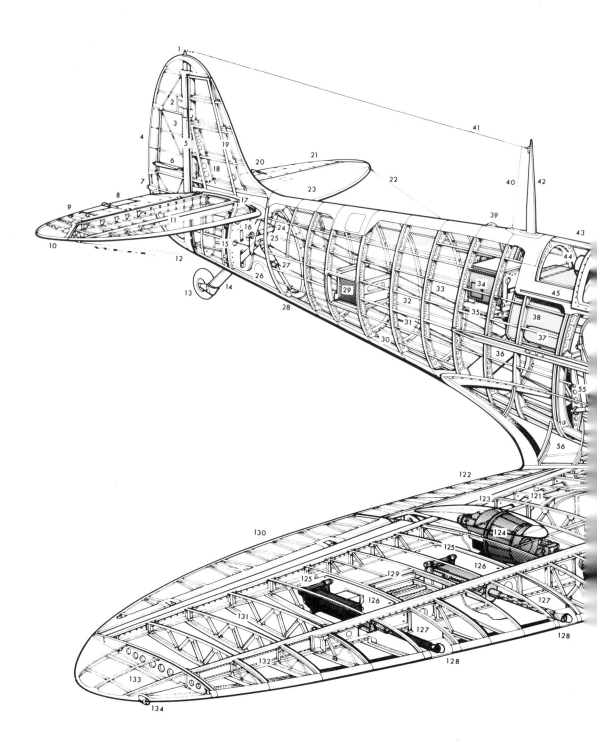

Supermarine Spitfire VB
Cutaway Key

1 Aerial stub attachment
2 Rudder upper hinge
3 Fabric-covered rudder
4 Rudder tab
5 Sternpost
6 Rudder tab hinge
7 Rear navigation light
8 Starboard elevator tab
9 Starboard elevator structure
10 Elevator balance
11 Tailplane front spar
12 IFF aerial
13 Castoring non-retractable tailwheel
14 Tailwheel strut
15 Fuselage double frame
16 Elevator control lever
17 Tailplane spar/fuselage attachment
18 Fin rear spar (fuselage frame extension)
19 Fin front spar (fuselage frame extension)
20 Port elevator tab hinge
21 Port elevator
22 IFF aerial

33 Rudder control cables
34 Radio compartment
35 Radio support tray
36 Flare chute
37 Oxygen bottle
38 Auxiliary long-range fuel tank (29 gal/132 litre)
39 Dorsal formation light
40 Aerial lead-in
41 HF aerial
42 Aerial mast
43 Cockpit aft glazing
44 Voltage regulator
45 Canopy track
46 Structural bulkhead
47 Headrest
48 Plexiglas canopy
49 Rear-view mirror
50 Entry flap (port)
51 Air bottles (alternative rear fuselage stowage)
52 Sutton harness
53 Pilot's seat (moulded Bakelite)
54 Datum longeron
55 Seat support frame
56 Wingroot fillet
57 Seat adjustment lever
58 Rudder pedal frame
59 Elevator control connecting tube
60 Control column spade grip
61 Trim wheel

70 Fuselage lower fuel tank (37 gal/168 litre)
71 Firewall/bulkhead
72 Engine bearer attachment
73 Steel tube bearers
74 Magneto
75 "Fishtail"/exhaust manifold
76 Gun heating "intensifier"
77 Hydraulic tank
78 Fuel filler cap
79 Air compressor intake
80 Air compressor
81 Rolls-Royce Merlin 45 engine
82 Coolant piping
83 Port cannon wing fairing
84 Flaps
85 Aileron control cables
86 Aileron push tube
87 Bellcrank
88 Aileron hinge
89 Port aileron
90 Machine-gun access panels

104 Main engine support member
105 Coolant pipe
106 Exposed oil tank
107 Port mainwheel
108 Mainwheel fairing
109 Carburettor air intake
110 Stub/spar attachment
111 Mainwheel leg pivot point
112 Main spar
113 Leading-edge ribs (diagonals deleted for clarity)
114 Mainwheel leg shock-absorber
115 Mainwheel fairing
116 Starboard mainwheel
117 Angled axle
118 Cannon barrel support fairing
119 Spar cut-out
120 Mainwheel well
121 Gun heating pipe
122 Flap structure
123 Cannon wing fairing
124 Cannon magazine drum (120 rounds)

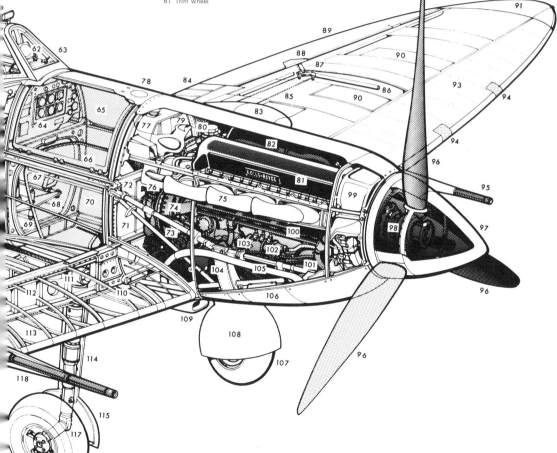

23 Port tailplane
24 Rudder control lever
25 Cross shaft
26 Tailwheel oleo access plate
27 Tailwheel oleo shock-absorber
28 Fuselage angled frame
29 Battery compartment
30 Lower longeron
31 Elevator control cables
32 Fuselage construction

62 Reflector gunsight
63 External windscreen armour
64 Instrument panel
65 Main fuselage fuel tank (48 gal/218 litre)
66 Fuel tank/longeron attachment fittings
67 Rudder pedals
68 Rudder bar
69 King post

91 Port wingtip
92 Port navigation light
93 Leading-edge skinning
94 Machine-gun ports (projected)
95 20mm cannon muzzle
96 Three-blade constant-speed propeller
97 Spinner
98 Propeller hub
99 Coolant tank
100 Cowling fastening
101 Engine anti-vibration mounting pad
102 Engine accessories
103 Engine bearers

125 Machine-gun support brackets
126 Gun access panels
127 0.303in machine-gun barrels
128 Machine-gun ports
129 Ammunition boxes (350 rpg)
130 Starboard aileron construction
131 Wing ribs
132 Single-tube outer spar section
133 Wingtip structure
134 Starboard navigation light

(Left) A standard production Spitfire IIA (P7508), and (right) a Spitfire II with experimental flush-fitting overload tanks.

(Left) Sole Spitfire III in its original form with clipped wing-tips, and (right) the same aircraft (N3297) after the installation of a Merlin XX and the fitting of standard wing-tips. The Spitfire III was designed to employ the Merlin XX.

combat aircraft during the war. Development followed several lines simultaneously: to improve aerodynamic efficiency and thereby performance; to take advantage of increases in engine power offered by Rolls-Royce; to increase the armament; to increase the fuel capacity; and to adapt the basic design for alternative roles, particularly those of photographic-reconnaissance and shipboard fighter. The first major developments were engine changes. At Hucknall, Rolls-Royce received the second production Spitfire I, K9788, and employed it to test various early experimental and production models of the Merlin—the RM2S, RM4S, RM5S and Merlin III, VIII and XII. Subsequently, two other Spitfire Is went to Rolls-Royce for similar purposes: N3053, which flew with the RM4S, RM5S and Merlin 45 and 46, and was also tested with a Heine airscrew from a captured Bf 109E; and R6889, which was flown with RM3S, RM5S, Merlin III, XII, XIII, 45 and 60 engines.

The 1,175 h.p. Merlin XII was adopted as the standard power plant in the Type 329 Spitfire II with a Rotol three-blade airscrew and 73 lb. of armour protection, but this variant was otherwise similar to the Spitfire I. Deliveries commenced in 1940, the Spitfire II having followed the Mark I on the production lines and becoming the first major production variant to be delivered from Castle Bromwich. In 1941 the Merlin 45 series of two-stage single-speed engines was adopted, and the Type 349 Spitfire V so powered followed the Mark II into production and service. Loaded weight had crept up to 6,417 lb. and maximum speed to 369 m.p.h. The first squadron to fly the Spitfire V was No. 92, and in March 1942 fifteen Spitfire VBs which had been shipped to Malta on H.M.S. *Eagle* became the first Spitfires to serve outside Europe. Spitfires of this Mark were later to serve in the Western Desert, and the Pacific and Burma areas.

In the meantime important armament and fuel developments had taken place. The first re-design of the wing was to accommodate a 20-mm. Hispano cannon in place of two of the Browning machine-guns. This cannon-wing was designated "B" wing (Type 331) to distinguish it from the machine-gun-housing "A" wing. Some cannon-armed Spitfires were operational during the "Battle of Britain" in 1940, and the first operational success with a cannon-armed Spitfire was recorded as early as March 1940, although the cannon armament was looked upon with mixed feelings by Spitfire pilots, for the gun was not without its share of teething troubles. Of the 920 Spitfire IIs built, 170 were completed as Mark IIBs with cannon armament, and a number of older Spitfire Is were converted to Mark IB standard. The next step was to produce a universal wing (the "C" wing, Type 346) which could take either two Hispano cannon, one cannon and two machine-guns, or four machine-guns. This was first introduced on the Mark VC which differed from the Marks VA and VB in having a strengthened undercarriage with the wheels moved two inches forward, and a further increase in armour from 129 lb. on the Mark VA and 152 lb. on the VB, to 193 lb. Later Spitfire VCs also had extended horn balances on the elevators, and still later Mark Vs in general had metal-covered ailerons.

The quest for greater range began early in the war, and showed itself in various experiments conducted on the Spitfire II. One aircraft had a flush-fitting long-range fuel tank beneath each wing outboard of the wheel wells, and an enlarged oil tank which deepened the nose cowling contours. During 1941 three squadrons, numbers 66, 118 and 152, flew Spitfire IIAs with a 40-gallon long-range tank on the starboard wing (Type 343). What was to become the standard drop-tank, however, was the "slipper" type fitted flush under the centre section. This was manufactured in 30-gallon, 45-gallon, and 90-gallon versions, more than 300,000 of these tanks subsequently being manufactured for the Spitfire. For ferrying duties a 170-gallon "slipper" tank was also produced, and, later, 45-gallon and 90-gallon "finger" cylindrical tanks

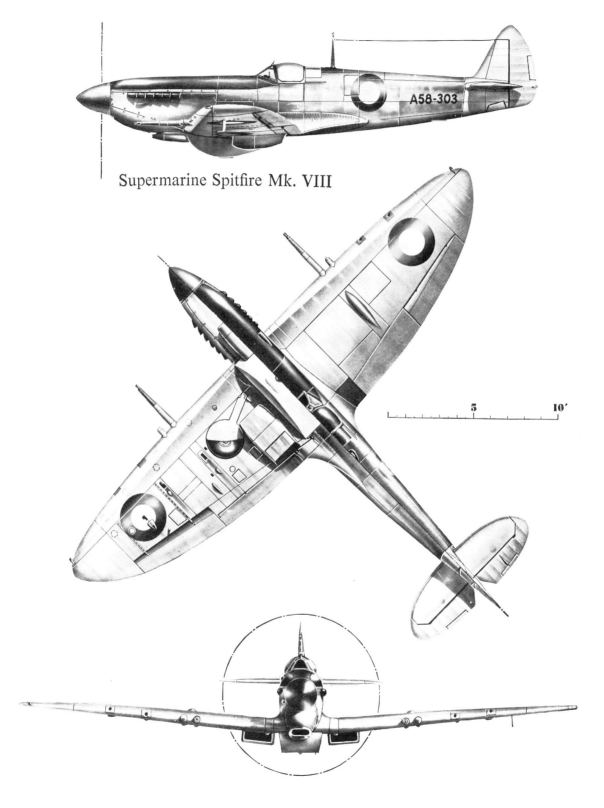

Supermarine Spitfire Mk. VIII

5   10'

(Above) A standard production Spitfire VB. (Left) A standard tropical Spitfire VA, (left, centre) a Spitfire VC fitted with an experimental overload tank and featuring a deeper nose to accommodate a larger oil tank, and (left, bottom) a captured Spitfire VB (EN830) employed for comparative tests by Daimler-Benz with a 1,475 h.p. DB 605A engine.

(Above) The Spitfire IV (later XX), DP845, with a six-cannon wing mock-up and experimental flaps.

engine and featured several aerodynamic and structural refinements such as a strengthened fuselage, an internal bullet-proof windscreen, a retractable tail-wheel, strengthened main undercarriage with wheels set forward, and 88 lb. of armour. To improve low-level performance the wing-tips were removed, reducing the span to 30 ft. 6 in. and the area to 220 sq. ft. The prototype, N3297, was a converted Mark I from the second Supermarine contract and appeared in 1939. It later reverted to the full-span wing and was the first Spitfire to have the "universal" wing with cannon armament. Subsequently it was taken over by Rolls-Royce for engine development, being flown with the Merlin VIII, 45, 60, 61 and RM2SM. Its maximum all-up weight was 7,300 lb. and, with the Merlin 61, it achieved 351.5 m.p.h. at 12,000 feet in October 1941. In October 1940 a contract had been placed with the Castle Bromwich factory for 1,000 Spitfire IIIs, but these were eventually completed as Spitfire Vs and IXs, and a further 120 Spitfire IIIs ordered from Supermarine at the same time were subsequently cancelled. The Spitfire IV, development of which had commenced simultaneously with that of the Mark III, was intended to take advantage of the additional power available from the new Rolls-Royce Griffon engine, preliminary information on the single-stage Griffon II becoming available in 1940. The Spitfire IV (Type 337) embodied extensive airframe re-design, and included many features of the Mark III. At one stage in the design, plans were made for the installation of six 20-mm. Hispano cannon, and a mock-up wing of this type was produced. However, before the prototype Spitfire IV (DP845) had flown, the Spitfire P.R.IV had entered production, and the Griffon-engined prototype was redesignated Spitfire XX to avoid confusion.

were used in place of the "slipper"-type tanks to reduce drag.

While these various improvements were being made, work had also been initiated on two further Spitfire variants, the Marks III and IV. Parallel development of these two machines was undertaken, and although neither achieved production status they provided valuable information for incorporation in later models. The Spitfire III (Types 330 and 348) was designed to make use of the 1,390 h.p. Merlin XX

In the normal course of development, means were sought to increase the altitude performance of the

(*Above*) *A production Spitfire VII (AB450). (Right) A Spitfire F.VIII with long-span wing and standard rudder, (centre, right) a Spitfire L.F.VIII with standard wing and tall rudder, and (bottom, right) a Spitfire F.VIII with tall rudder and standard wing in South-East Asia Command insignia.*

Spitfire which was inferior to that of the Bf 109E. This called for two principal modifications—the introduction of a pressurized cabin, and the use of an engine suitably rated for higher altitude. The first version of the Spitfire so equipped was the Mark VI, derived directly from the Mark VB as a result of work on pressure cabins at the Royal Aircraft Establishment and Supermarine during 1940–41. At the R.A.E., R7120 was fitted with a Merlin 47 (the high-rated version of the Merlin 45) with a four-blade Rotol airscrew with Jablo blades, and a pressure cabin. The same engine was employed by the 100 Spitfire VI (Type 350) fighters built by Supermarine, the first two of these, AB176 and X4942, serving as prototypes. The production Spitfire VI also had an increase in wing area to improve controllability at high altitudes, the wing being of "pointed" planform with a span of 40 ft. 2 in. The pressure cabin was contained between the bulkheads fore and aft of the cockpit, and a special non-sliding hood was fitted to simplify the sealing problem. A Marshall blower provided a cabin differential of 2 lb./sq. in., reducing apparent altitude from 40,000 feet to 28,000 feet. In other respects, including armament, the Spitfire VI was similar to the Mark VB.

The Spitfire VII (Type 351) was a more extensive re-design for high-altitude work and was the first of the Spitfire series intended to make use of the two-speed Merlin 60 series of engines. These two-stage engines were coupled with a re-designed cooling system which showed itself in the enlarged air intake under the port wing, matching that to starboard. The wing outline remained similar to that of the Spitfire VI, but the ailerons were reduced in span. The chord and area of the rudder were increased and the elevator horn balance was extended. Structural changes were made to the fuselage to take the increased engine loads, and a double-glaze sliding hood was fitted to

(*Immediately above*) *A Spitfire VIII with experimental rear-view hood and cut-down rear fuselage.*

the cockpit. The retractable tailwheel first developed for the Spitfire III was applied in production for the first time on the Mark VII, and the "universal" "C"-type wing was employed. Maximum speed jumped by 44 m.p.h. to 408 m.p.h., and normal loaded weight climbed to 7,875 lb.

The Spitfire VI was restricted to home defence during 1942–43, being flown by five squadrons. One hundred and forty Spitfire VIIs (commencing with AB450) were built, and these were used to equip

133

(Left) A Spitfire VIII (*JK535*) *with an experimental contraprop installation.* (*Right*) *A standard Spitfire L.F.IX with Merlin 66 engine and* "*C*" *wing.*

nine squadrons at home and in the Middle East from 1942 onwards. With the exception of the pressure cabin itself, most of the modifications introduced on the Spitfire VII were applicable to the standard range of aircraft, and a new production series was accordingly planned to take full advantage of these improvements. This version became known as the Spitfire VIII (Type 359) and was in essence the complement of the Mark VII for operation at lower altitudes. It was produced in three main versions: the F.VIII with a Merlin 61 or 63 engine, the H.F.VIII with a Merlin 70, and the L.F.VIII with the lower altitude-rated Merlin 66. All versions had a Vokes Aero Vee tropical filter on the air intake fitted as standard. Earlier versions of the Spitfire serving in the Middle and Far East had to use a larger and clumsier filter developed at Abu Sueir to adapt the temperate air intake. A total of 1,658 Spitfire VIIIs of all versions was built. The first production series, including F. and H.F. types, had the extended span wing; later Mark VIIIs had the standard wing and enlarged rudder.

The Spitfire F.VIII entered service in the Mediterranean theatre in August 1943, several squadrons flying them in Italy and elsewhere. Number 155 Squadron operated Spitfire VIIIs for a time in Russia later in 1943, and the type remained operational, principally overseas, until 1945. Several experimental versions of the Mark VIII were flown, including JF299 with the first 360° vision cockpit canopy and cut-down rear fuselage, and JK535 (Type 376) with a contraprop version of the Merlin 60 series.

While the Spitfires VII and VIII were still under development the need for a higher performance than that offered by the Spitfire V was becoming a matter of vital urgency. The Spitfire V was having difficulty in combating the newest versions of the Bf 109 fighter, and it was completely outclassed by the new Focke-Wulf Fw 109A which was appearing in constantly increasing numbers. To achieve the desired performance improvement with the least possible delay, it was decided to install the Merlin 60 series engine in the basic Spitfire VC airframe. This marriage of convenience resulted in the Spitfire IX (Type 361), which was essentially an interim type until the Mark VIII became available, but its maximum speed was 402 m.p.h. Apart from the changes necessary to accommodate the two-speed two-stage Merlin which drove a four-blade Rotol airscrew, no modifications were made to the Mark VC airframe. Depending on the particular version of the Merlin fitted, the Spitfire IXs

were categorized as L.F., F., or H.F. (low-, medium-, or high-altitude fighters) but no external changes distinguished these variants. The first Spitfire IXs reached No. 64 Squadron in July 1942, and this version substantially reduced—although failed to eliminate—the margin of ascendancy over the Spitfire gained by the Fw 190A. At the usual combat range it was impossible for enemy pilots to distinguish between the Spitfire IX and the inferior Mark V, and this fact gave the British fighter's pilots some tactical advantage at first.

At first the Spitfire IXs had the "universal" or "C" wing, but by 1944 the fire power had again been boosted by the introduction of the "E" wing, which had the two 0.303-in. Brownings replaced by a 0.5-in. Browning. This was mounted in what had been the inner cannon bay on the "C" wing, while the 20-mm. cannon was moved to the outboard position. Later in its life the Spitfire IX was adapted for use principally in the ground-attack role, having been replaced as an interceptor fighter by the Griffon-engined versions. For this role it carried a 500-lb. bomb beneath the fuselage and a 250-lb. bomb beneath each wing. Since these operations were invariably conducted at low altitudes, the wings were frequently clipped to a span of 32 ft. 7 in. Another later modification was the introduction of a rear-fuselage fuel tank of 72 Imperial gallons capacity, and the large rudder also became standard, together with metal-covered elevators. Although the Spitfire IX was an interim type, with the Mark V, it was produced in larger quantities and was more widely used than any other Spitfire variant. Total production reached 5,609 aircraft.

The Spitfire was essentially a short-range fighter. It had been designed primarily for defensive duties, and R. J. Mitchell never envisaged the relatively long-range sweeps that the Spitfire would be called upon to make. Several experiments were made on Spitfire IXs with the aim of extending the fighter's limited range; EN314 had a torpedo-shaped tank slung beneath the fuselage, while another Spitfire IX had Mustang-type tanks attached underwing. Possibly the greatest range ever achieved by a Spitfire was the flight across the Atlantic from Newfoundland to Ireland by a much modified Mark IX which carried nearly 500 gallons of fuel.

One of the many ways in which the U.S.A. made a direct contribution to the British war effort was the production of very large numbers of Merlin engines for British-built aircraft. Produced by Packard

Motors, they were not interchangeable with their British
equivalents and, consequently,
aircraft powered by Packard-
built Merlins were separately
designated. Thus it was that
the Spitfire L.F.XVI (Type 361)
appeared—a close relative of
the Mark IX but with a low-
rated Packard Merlin 266.
Initially, the Spitfire XVIs, like
the Mark IXs, were produced
with "C" wing armament, but
usually they featured clipped
wing-tips. Later, a change was
made to the "E" wing, the
enlarged rudder was introduced,
and at about the same time the
rear-view hood was adopted as
standard for this Mark. From
1944 onwards 1,054 Spitfire XVIs
were delivered, the type going
into service with the 2nd T.A.F.
as a ground-attack fighter.

(Above) A production Spitfire XII with bomb. (Below) The original Spitfire IV
(DP845) in a later form as the prototype Spitfire XII.

Reference has already been
made to the Spitfire IV powered
by the Griffon engine and redesignated Mark XX to avoid
confusion with the P.R.IV. The
original intention was that the
XX series Spitfires would all be
Griffon-powered, but this plan
was not adhered to when the
interim Marks XII, XIV, and

XVIII were produced. Like the Spitfire III, the Spitfire
IV, alias XX, was made the subject of production contracts during the time the prototype was under development. For instance, 750 were ordered from the Castle
Bromwich factory on August 23, 1941, but, in fact,
none was produced in this form; although when, in
1942, the need arose suddenly for a high-performance
low-altitude fighter to combat the Fw 190, experience
with DP845, the Mark IV/XX prototype, was used to
produce the Mark XII (Type 366). This was a Mark
VC airframe with a Griffon II engine, strengthened
fuselage, clipped wings and, in some cases, a retractable tailwheel. Top speed was 393 m.p.h. One
hundred were built and were used on home-defence
duties by Nos. 41 and 91 Squadrons, and particularly
for flying-bomb patrols during 1944.

A second Griffon-engined prototype, ordered at the
same time as the Mark IV and serialled DP851, was
developed to take the two-stage Griffon 61 series of
engines, and featured several other important changes,
principally concerning the wing. A later prototype
(PP139) was also used to develop these modifications.
The extended-span wing of the Spitfires VI and VII was
further modified in form for this aircraft, four 20-mm.
cannon were fitted, the undercarriage was lengthened
and its track increased, and larger fin and rudder were
fitted. In this guise, the Spitfire became the Mark 21

(Type 356) and just too late to see operational service
during the war. The Spitfires 22 and 24 derived from
the Mark 21 were exclusively post-war variants.

In order to gain experience with the two-stage
Griffon for the Spitfire 21, six Mark VIII airframes,
JF316 to JF321 inclusive, were allocated for flight
development (JF321 with a contraprop). Experience
with these prototypes indicated the practicability of
producing such a version in quantity and led to the
Spitfire XIV (Type 372). The Spitfire XIV as initially
produced was a standard Mark VIII airframe strengthened to take the Griffon 65 and its five-blade Rotol
airscrew. The vertical tail surfaces were enlarged to
compensate for the additional area forward, and the
"C" wing armament was used. A later production
series had the "E" wing, and the last few Mark XIVs
built had the rear-vision hood and cut-down rear fuselage. A separate production batch, with the designation F.R.XIVE, featured an oblique camera in the rear
fuselage and clipped wings. This served as a low-level
tactical reconnaissance fighter in Europe. Combined
production of Spitfire XIVs totalled 1,055 aircraft.

Operationally, the Spitfire XIV had several distinc-
tions, and perhaps the most noteworthy incident
involving a Spitfire of this type was the destruction
of the first Messerschmitt Me 262 turbojet-driven
fighter, this achievement going to a Spitfire XIV of

(Above) A Spitfire VIII with Griffon 65 engine.

(Above) A standard Spitfire XIV

(Above) A standard Spitfire XIVE.

No. 401 Squadron on October 5, 1944. Spitfire XIVs entered service—with No. 610 Squadron—on January 1, 1944, and this Mark was the most successful of all Spitfire variants in destroying flying bombs. Twenty squadrons of the 2nd T.A.F. were equipped with the Mark XIV, and the type was fast entering service in the Far East as the war terminated. Experimental Spitfire XIVs included RB144, which flew with a de Havilland contraprop driven by a Griffon 85, and others fitted with Rotal contraprops.

To consolidate the Mark XIV type, Supermarine developed a further version, the Spitfire XVIII (Type 394), in which the fuselage and undercarriage were strengthened once again to permit the all-up weight to be increased, this latter being consequent upon the introduction of additional fuel tanks in the wings and rear fuselage. Versions both with and without an oblique camera in the fuselage, designated F.R. and F.XVIII respectively, were produced, but contracts were cut at the end of the war, actual production totalling only 300 (100 F.XVIIIs and 200 F.R.XVIIIs). The type was earmarked for service in the Far East but never became operational.

Apart from the special and experimental versions of the Spitfire mentioned in the foregoing narrative, many others existed—produced either as part of the planned development programme by Supermarine or used by the engine, airscrew and equipment manu-

facturers, or at service establishments for special duties. One experiment of particular interest was made in Germany during 1944, using the airframe of Spitfire VB EN830 which had been captured intact after a forced landing. This Spitfire was fitted, for comparative purposes, by Daimler-Benz with a 1,475 h.p. DB 605A engine. Flown at a weight of 6,000 lb. (all armament having been removed), this Spitfire achieved 379 m.p.h. at 22,000 feet as compared to the 385 m.p.h. attained by the similarly-powered Bf 109G at the same altitude.

Another Spitfire, a Mark VC, BR372, had split, trailing-edge dive brakes, and AB457 was flown at the Royal Aircraft Establishment with liquid oxygen injection to boost the performance. A Spitfire I (P7674) was fitted, in 1941, with a mock-up of the Rolls-Royce 26P1 two-stroke diesel engine, and plans were laid for an Exe-engined version, although neither of these projects materialised. In the Middle East, in 1942, two Spitfire VCs were modified to undertake an epic series of high-altitude flights, without pressurization, to combat the high-flying, pressurized Ju 86P and 86R bomber and reconnaissance aircraft. One of these modified Spitfires eventually attained an altitude of nearly 50,000 feet—an incredible performance by both machine and pilot in view of the lack of special high-altitude equipment.

Another series of experiments concerned the adaptation of the Spitfire as a float seaplane. Such an adaptation was first considered in 1940 in relation to the Norwegian campaign, during which such a float-plane might have been of immense value. A Spitfire I was adapted to take a pair of floats similar to those fitted to the third Blackburn Roc two-seat naval fighter, but the marriage, which was given the Type 342 designation, had not been consummated by the time the Norwegian campaign had terminated. In 1942 the project was revived, and Supermarine designed a set of floats for the Spitfire VB, having a reserve buoyancy of 90 per cent. Made by Folland Aircraft, who also completed the conversion, these floats were attached by cantilever struts to the wing spars some five feet from the aircraft centre line. After successful hand-line trials with the prototype, the Type 355 (W3760), Folland built twelve sets of these floats, and converted two more Spitfire Vs, one of which was flown for a time in the Mediterranean area. During 1943 Folland produced one further floatplane, this time based on a Spitfire IX, MJ892 (Type 385). A characteristic of all the Spitfire floatplanes was additional fin area, and the attachment of an under fin to counteract the destabilizing effect of the floats.

Reference has been made to the use of the Spitfire in the photo-reconnaissance role. These versions, including a series known as the Spitfire A to G inclusive, and the P.R.IV, VII, X, XI, XIII, and XIX, were for the most part unarmed counterparts of the various Merlin- and Griffon-engined fighters.

By 1941, when the war at sea had reached a highly critical phase, the Fleet Air Arm still lacked a ship-board fighter with a performance comparable with contemporary land-based aircraft. It was proposed, therefore, to "navalise" the Spitfire, although upper-most among numerous technical difficulties was the question of landing speed—the 85 m.p.h. at which the Spitfire landed was then considerably in excess of normal deck-landing requirements. Nevertheless, the Spitfire's docile stalling characteristics did much to offset the disadvantage of speed, and towards the end of 1941 a production Spitfire VB was fitted with an A-frame arrester hook and completed a series of deck-landing trials aboard H.M.S. *Illustrious*, the pilot, Cdr. P. H. Bramwell, having earlier spent two weeks practising dummy deck landings. The result of these trials was an order for a batch of forty-eight "hooked" Spitfires, henceforth known as Seafires.

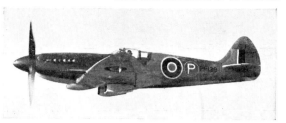

(*Above*) *The first prototype Spitfire* 21 *with re-designed fin and rudder and four cannon.*

These were produced by Air Service Training at Hamble by converting existing Spitfire VB airframes which were known as Seafire IBs (Type 340). Apart from the arrester hook and catapult spools, plus some local strengthening of the fuselage, the Seafire IB differed little from the Spitfire VB. Its wings did not fold and it could not, therefore, be struck down below decks on the existing lifts of Navy carriers, but a further quantity of Seafire IBs was built, increasing the total to over 100. The first Seafire squadron, and the first to embark on a carrier, was No. 807, com-manded by Lieut. A. B. Fraser-Harris. This squadron joined H.M.S. *Furious* which was carrying a quantity of Spitfires to Malta, and subsequently joined in the assault against North Africa, in November 1942. The Seafires' first action was against Vichy French fighters that attempted to intercept the Fairey Albacore torpedo-bombers, and the first recorded "kill" by a Seafire was attained during the North African landings, Lieut. G. C. Baldwin destroying a Dewoitine D.520.

(*Above*) *A production Spitfire* 21 *with five-blade airscrew.*

A similar conversion of the Spitfire VC produced the Seafire IIC (Type 351), and this was the first major production Seafire variant, 262 being built by Super-marine with the Merlin 45, 46, 50, 55 or 56 engine of 1,300 h.p., although some of these were later fitted with the low-rated Merlin 32 driving a Rotol four-bladed airscrew as Seafire L.IICs (Type 375), and a few became P.R.IICs, fitted with several cameras. Seafire IIs embarked on H.M.S. *Formidable*, joining Force H in the Ionian Sea to participate in the in-vasion of Sicily. Comprehensive operational deploy-ment of the Seafire called for the introduction of wing folding, and the considerable technical difficulties of such a feature in a wing as thin as that of the Spitfire were successfully over-come in the Seafire III (Type 358). The wing-tips folded down and the main panels folded up. After prototypes had been built by converting Spitfire VCs, the Seafire III was placed in production by Cunliffe-Owen Aircraft, which company built 350, and by Westland Aircraft who built a further 948. The Seafire F.R.III had one vertical and one oblique camera in the rear fuselage, and the L.F.III had the low-rated Merlin 45 series engine or the Merlin 32.

The Seafire is undoubtedly best remembered for its part in the Allied landing at Salerno, on September 9, 1943, when it provided close support for the invading

(*Above*) *A Seafire II (BL676) with Merlin* 45 *engine.*

troops virtually unaided for the first four critical days of the battle. Seafire squadrons operated with the Desert Air Force, and with the introduction of the Seafire III there was little doubt that, as Mr. A. V. Alexander said at the time, the Fleet Air Arm had acquired "the best naval fighter in existence anywhere in the world". On D-Day, June 6, 1944, Seafires were in the forefront of the battle, with the important task of target finding and "spotting" for the heavy guns of the Navy's ships, and as 1944 drew to a close the Seafire was embarked for the Far East, where it commenced operations on January 24, 1945, with a full-scale attack against oil targets in Sumatra. Paralleling Spitfire development, a Griffon-engined Seafire was next produced, the Type 377 or Mark XV. This had the naval features of the Seafire III combined with a Griffon VI engine and some features of the Spitfire XII. Deck-landing characteristics were improved by fitting a new form of arrester hook, known as the sting hook, and an exactly similar variant with the rear-vision hood was designated Seafire XVII (Type 384). Cunliffe-Owen built 134 Seafire XVs and 20 Seafire XVIIs, while Westland built 256 Seafire XVs and 169 Seafire XVIIs. Naval equivalents of the Spitfire 21 and 22, designated Seafire 45, 46 and 47, were entirely post-war developments.

For an aircraft which originated as a pure short-range interceptor, the Spitfire proved remarkably

(*Top*) *A Seafire III with wings folded, and* (*immediately above*) *a Griffon-powered Seafire F.XV.* (*Immediately below*) *The Type 385 Spitfire IX floatplane produced in 1943, and* (*bottom*) *the prototype Spitfire VB floatplane developed in 1942.*

amenable to adaptation. From the beginning to the end of the war it was in the forefront of the fighting. Spitfires fought over the beaches of Dunkirk and above the D-Day landings four years later. They supported the 14th Army in Burma; they took part in the invasion of Greece; and earlier, in 1943, they repulsed Japanese attacks on Darwin, Australia. They flew in the Solomon Islands, Borneo and New Guinea—in fact the Spitfire operated everywhere that the R.A.F. was committed, and was flown at one time or another by nearly all the R.A.F.'s leading wartime fighter pilots. It was paid many tributes by friend and foe alike; but perhaps the greatest tribute to the Spitfire came from Germany's General Adolf Galland, who was later to become the Luftwaffe's General of Fighters. While on a visit to Luftwaffe fighter squadrons based on the Channel coast, Reichmarschall Goering complained bitterly of the losses being experienced by Luftwaffe bomber formations in attacks on England. Goering said that the fighters must give the bombers closer protection. He then asked Galland what his fighter requirements were, and Galland replied, "I should like a Staffel of Spitfires for my Gruppe!"

More than 22,000 Spitfires and Seafires were built. The Spitfire's design epitomized technical resourcefulness and no combat aircraft has ever better served the country of its birth. The Spitfire was undoubtedly the one truly immortal warplane to emerge from the Second World War.

Supermarine Spitfire I

Dimensions :	Span, 36 ft. 10 in. ; length, 29 ft. 11 i n. ; height, 11 ft. 5 in. (airscrew vertical) ; wing area, 242 sq. ft.
Armament :	Eight 0.303-in. Browning machine-guns with 300 rounds of ammunition.
Power Plant :	One Rolls-Royce Merlin II or III twelve-cylinder 60° Vee liquid-cooled engine developing 880 h.p. at 3,000 r.p.m. for take-off, 990 h.p. at 2,600 r.p.m. at 12,250 ft., and 1,440 h.p. at 3,000 r.p.m. at 7,750 ft. Fuel capacity, 85 Imp. gal. internally.
Weights :	Normal loaded, 5,280 lb. ; wing loading, 24 lb./sq. ft.
Performance :	Maximum speed, 362 m.p.h. at operational height ; maximum rate of climb, 2,500 ft./min. ; time to 20,000 ft., 9.4 min. ; range (including allowance for take-off, climb and 15 minutes' combat), 395 miles; maximum range, 575 miles.

The XF4U-1 was the first U.S. fighter of any type to exceed 400 m.p.h. in level flight, a speed of 404 m.p.h. being attained on October 1, 1940.

THE CHANCE VOUGHT CORSAIR

"Sweetheart of Okinawa" to the U.S. Marine Corps, "Whistling Death" to the Japanese, and "Bent-winged Bird" to the American ground forces that sheltered under the massive umbrella of ordnance which it delivered in the Pacific, the Corsair was universally acknowledged to be the finest naval fighter of the Second World War. Many people, and particularly its pilots, went further and claimed it to be the best single-seat fighter of any nation to emerge from that conflict.

Despite its formidable quality, however, and the fact that it was expressly designed for shipboard operations, the Corsair spent most of its wartime career confined to land bases, and it was not until the end of 1944 that it made its first operational sorties from American carriers in the Pacific. But the same problems which kept it from the U.S. Navy's carrier decks for two years after its introduction to operational service provided it with the opportunity to prove its superiority, at the eager and capable hands of U.S. Marine Corps pilots, to all enemy and, for that matter, friendly fighters in the South-West Pacific.

Operating from airstrips on Guadalcanal and the Solomon Islands, the U.S. Marines forged the Corsair into an air supremacy weapon, meeting the Japanese Navy's Zero-Sen fighters on more than equal terms for the first time in the Pacific conflict, smashing them into the sea and jungle alike, and helping turn the tide of air combat permanently in favour of the Allied forces. Most of the twenty-eight victories achieved by Major "Pappy" Boyington, the top-scoring U.S. Marine Corps fighter pilot, were gained from the cockpit of a Corsair, as were also the majority of the "kills" of the runner-up, Captain Joe

Foss, with twenty-six victories, and other aces such as Majors Ken Walsh and Marion Carl, Commander Thomas Blackburn, Lieutenants Ike Kepford and Bob Hanson. Within six months of its introduction all Marine Corps fighter squadrons in the South Pacific were Corsair-equipped, but to Britain's Royal Navy was to go the distinction of first introducing the remarkable Chance Vought fighter to carrier service.

The Corsair stemmed from a U.S. Navy design contest of February 1, 1938, the requirements specifying a single-seat shipboard fighter offering a particularly good service ceiling, and a speed which encouraged Chance Vought's design team to aim at producing the fastest fighter ever built. The Engineering Department of Chance Vought Aircraft, led by Rex B. Beisel, prepared several design studies to meet the Navy's requirements and, eventually, submitted two proposals during the following April. These were designated V-166A, a fighter powered by a Pratt and Whitney R-1830 Twin Wasp, then one of the most powerful production engines available to the U.S. aircraft industry, and V-166B, a more advanced design with the revolutionary Pratt and Whitney XR-2800-2 Double Wasp. As the most powerful engine available in the forseeable future, the 2,000 h.p

(Left) The first production F4U-1 Corsair which flew for the first time on June 25, 1942, and (above) an early production F4U-1 in flight.

Double Wasp was an obvious choice, except for the fact that it was still very much in the experimental stage, and its manufacturers were under considerable pressure from the U.S. Army Air Corps to concentrate all their facilities on the development and production of liquid-cooled engines. Since the Air Corps had backed the liquid-cooled inline engine, it was inevitable, in view of the strong inter-service rivalry, that the Navy should have favoured the air-cooled radial. While proponents of the liquid-cooled power plant pointed out the immediate advantages of streamlining possible with inline engines, air-cooled radials were claimed to be appreciably lighter, less complex and less vulnerable to battle damage. In the case of the Corsair, adherence to the air-cooled formula was to be fundamental to the success of this warplane.

The Navy contest had resulted in four promising proposals differing widely one from another, and of these the V-166B was the most conventional and the most impressive, being the smallest possible airframe designed around the largest and most powerful air-cooled radial which drove the largest airscrew ever considered for a fighter. Approval was received from the U.S. Navy on June 11, 1938, together with a contract for a prototype aircraft designated XF4U-1. Wind tunnel models were built to finalise the design configuration, and a mock-up of the complete aircraft

was ready for Navy inspection by February 10, 1939. The fighter's characteristic inverted gull wing arrangement was a neat solution to the problem of accommodating the massive power plant with its enormous airscrew while keeping undercarriage length and ground angle to a mimimum, and simultaneously obtaining the optimum right angle for minimum drag at the junction of the wing and fuselage.

The wing was built in three sections, the centre section being integral with the fuselage, and was of single-spar type, the outer panels being fabric-covered aft of the mainspar, and the fuselage was a semi-monocoque structure built up in four sections, these being assembled individually with heavy, pressed flange bulkheads, extruded stiffener section stringers and heavy sheet skin. The combination of heavy frames and thick skin drastically reduced the number of longitudinal members and simplified construction. A new spot-welding technique evolved jointly by Chance Vought and the Naval Aircraft Factory resulted in an exceptionally smooth external finish. The mainwheel legs folded straight aft, with the wheels rotating through ninety degrees to lie flat in the wings where they were each completely enclosed by twin doors. Even before the XF4U-1 had been completed and flown, it had become the yardstick by which the Navy judged other aircraft and the goal that other manufacturers strove to attain.

The prototype was fitted with an XR-2800-4 engine affording 1,805 h.p. for take-off and 1,460 h.p. at 21,500 ft., armament comprising one 0.3-in. gun and one 0.5-in. gun in the upper decking of the forward fuselage, and a single 0.5-in. gun in each wing, and there was also a receptacle in each wing for ten light bombs which were to be dropped on bomber formations. The idea of bombing enemy formations, although to be abandoned in the production Corsair, was subsequently used with some success by the Luftwaffe against American bomber formations over Germany. The first flight of the XF4U-1, with Lyman A. Bullard Jnr. at the controls, took place on May

29, 1940 at Stratford, Connecticut, and the sensational performance of the new fighter was immediately apparent, although more than a year was to elapse before its manufacturers received their first production contract.

Further flight testing confirmed the remarkable capabilities of the XF4U-1 which, during a flight from Stratford to Hartford on October 1st., attained a speed of 404 m.p.h., thus becoming the first U.S. fighter of any type to exceed the 400 m.p.h. mark in level flight. The Corsair was accorded much publicity for this flight, although the precise figure attained was not to be revealed for some years, and it was indirectly responsible for Pratt and Whitney being given permission by General H. H. Arnold, chief of the U.S. Army Air Corps, to abandon their liquid-cooled engine programme. Weighing 7,505 lb. empty and 9,357 lb. in normal loaded condition, the XF4U-1 possessed an initial climb rate of 2,660 ft./min. and a service ceiling of 35,200 ft., but suffered several shortcomings, including poor lateral stability and unsatisfactory spin recovery characteristics. On October 24, 1940, the XF4U-1 was flown to Anacostia for preliminary flight testing by Navy pilots, and on November 28th the manufacturers received a request for proposals for a productionised design to be designated F4U-1. In the meantime the prototype continued its long flight development programme, and was not, in fact, to be delivered finally to the U.S. Navy until December 1942, some time after the 100th production Corsair had been accepted!

In the light of European combat experience extensive modifications to the design were called for to improve the fighter's operational capabilities. The need for heavier armament unrestricted by airscrew synchronisation was clearly apparent, and the first move was to place two additional 0.5-in. guns with greatly increased ammunition capacity in each outer wing panel, and remove the fuselage guns. To make room for this wing armament, the integral fuel tanks in the wing leading edges had to be removed, and to compensate for this loss of fuel capacity, a single 197 Imp. gal. (237 U.S. gal.) self-sealing tank had to be housed in the fuselage. This tank had to be positioned as nearly as possible on the aircraft's c.g. to avoid trim changes as fuel was consumed, and this entailed moving the pilot's cockpit a full three feet aft to provide the necessary space. Not unnaturally, the repositioning of the cockpit resulted in a greatly inferior forward view for the pilot who had an enormous length of fuselage obscuring his vision, and this was to become one of the primary reasons for the Corsair's initial unsuitability for shipboard operations.

The U.S. Navy issued a letter of intent for the F4U-1 production contract on March 3, 1941, following the final acceptance demonstrations of the prototype at Anacostia on February 24–25th., and a firm initial contract for 584 F4U-1s was placed on June 30, 1941, but such was now the Navy's confidence in the fighter that four months later, on November 1st., the Brewster Aeronautical Corporation was designated as an associate contractor to supplement the parent company's production, and in December the Goodyear Aircraft Corporation also became an associate contractor in the Corsair programme.

In the F4U-1, armour protection weighing 150 lb. was added around the cockpit and oil tank, the number of frames in the sliding cockpit canopy, which was made jettisonable, was reduced to improve vision, and rearward view was increased by the addition of transparent panels aft of the cutaway head-rest. Changes were made to the tailwheel and arrester hook retraction system, IFF (Identification, Friend or Foe) radar responder gear was installed, aileron span was increased to improve roll rate, a small flap section in each outer wing being eliminated, and to compensate for the inevitable increase in gross weight to the new figure of 11,093 lb., the R-2800-8(B) was installed, this offering 2,000 h.p. for take-off. By comparison with the original prototype, the F4U-1 was longer

The first Royal Navy Corsair squadron, No. 1830, was formed on June 1, 1943, and the accompanying photograph depicts one of the ninety-five F4U-1s (JT126) delivered as Corsair Is prior to the introduction of bulged front hood.

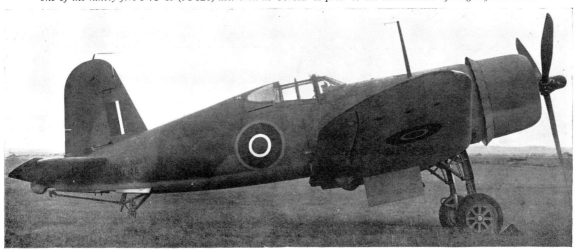

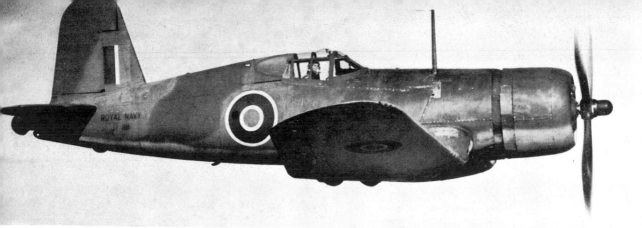

A Corsair I of the Royal Navy (JT118) with the bulged front hood which improved forward view by permitting the pilot to raise his seat. Provision was later made for a ventral drop tank and underwing rocket rails.

overall, length being increased from 31 ft. 11 in. to 33 ft. 4 in., an interim armament of four 0.5-in. Browning guns were installed in the wings, although this was increased to six at an early stage with a total of 2,350 rounds, and another early modification was the provision of two 51.6 Imp. gal. (62 U.S. gal.) unprotected fuel tanks in the wing leading edges outboard of the guns, normal loaded weight in clean condition being raised to 12,694 lb.

The first production F4U-1 Corsair flew for the first time on June 25, 1942, at a time when the Allies were on a crumbling defensive throughout the entire Pacific. The Japanese Navy's Zero-Sen fighter had come as a shattering surprise to the western nations, and there was an immediate outcry for fighters capable of besting the Mitsubishi. The Corsair promised to do just that, but it took time to eliminate its teething troubles and introduce it into service, albeit a remarkably short time. The U.S. Navy received its first F4U-1 on July 31, 1942, and the first Navy squadron to receive the new fighter, VF-12, began to take delivery of its aircraft on October 3rd., but the U.S. Marine Corps had priority, and by September sufficient Corsairs had been delivered to equip VMF-124 which had been formed on September 7th from the remnants of VMF-122. As an essential accompaniment to the operational units, a combat modification centre was set up at Air Base Group Two, Fleet Marine Force West Coast, in November, and despite an extended spell at this centre, after less than three months in service, the twenty-two F4U-1s of VMF-124 were declared combat ready on December 28th., by which time a total of 178 Corsairs had rolled off the assembly line. The Marine Corps pilots had each completed only some twenty hours flying in their new mounts when they were sent post-haste to join the beleagured American forces on Guadalcanal. Twelve Corsairs were in the first batch of VMF-124 to arrive on Guadalcanal on February, 12 1943, their pilots logging nine hours flying to further their familiarisation before the day was over.

The first combat mission flown by the Corsair in the Second World War took place on the next day,

February 13, when VMF-124 flew escort to a formation of Navy PB4Y Liberators in a raid on Bougainville. Fortunately, perhaps, for the inexperienced pilots of VMF-124, no combat ensued, but their luck did not hold out during the following day when some fifty Zero-Sen fighters from Bougainville intercepted the formations, shooting down the entire top cover of four P-38 Lightnings, two escorting P-40 Warhawks, two of the PB4Y Liberators, and two of the Marine Corps F4U-1 Corsairs, all for the loss of only four Japanese fighters. Once familiar with the formidable potential of their mounts, however, the Marine Corps pilots soon established decisive air superiority over the Japanese in that combat theatre, and within six months all Marine Corps fighter squadrons in the South Pacific were Corsair-equipped.

In the meantime, the first ten F4U-1s of the Navy's VF-12 had been pronounced combat-ready on January 14, 1943, and the unit's establishment had been increased to twenty-two aircraft by January 22. The Corsair was not without its share of troubles at this stage, however, the aircraft of VF-12 suffering from low engine power output at altitude because of air leakage in the induction system. Carrier trials, too, had been disappointing, dating from the initial qualification tests undertaken aboard the U.S.S. *Sangamon* in Chesapeake Bay, on September 25, 1942. These tests were undertaken by Lieut.-Com. S. Porter with the seventh production F4U-1, and only four landings and take-offs were made. The principle trouble was encountered during deck landing, the long nose of the Corsair seriously interfering with forward view in the three-point attitude. The fighter also tended to swing badly on touchdown, was prone to bounce on slamming into the deck owing to the rigidity of the landing gear, and the windscreen and cockpit were contaminated by oil from the hydraulically-operated cowl flaps and the valve push-rod mechanism. The last-mentioned difficulty persisted until mechanical cooling gills were fitted, and the top section of the engine cowling permanently closed.

Exploratory steps were taken to cure the more fundamental difficulties of Corsair deck-landing in

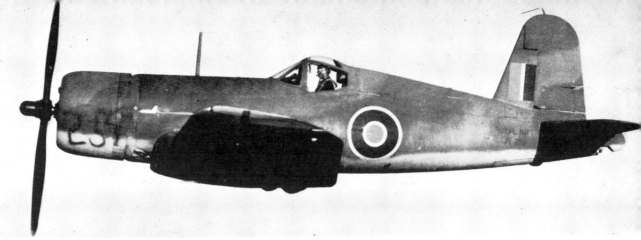

The Royal Navy received 510 F4U-1As as Corsair IIs, one of which (JT259) is illustrated above and right. Some sixteen inches were clipped from the wingtips to permit below-deck stowage in the smaller British carriers.

December 1942, and to improve forward view, the cabin of the fifth production F4U-1 was raised by seven inches and a frameless clear-view-type canopy fitted. This modification was introduced on the 689th aircraft which became the first F4U-1A in mid-1943, and directional stability for landing was improved by increasing the height of the tailwheel leg, changing its tyre from one of solid to one of pneumatic type, and adding a small spoiler on the starboard wing leading edge. The inflatable tailwheels were tested on the 81st and 154th production F4U-1s on the Navy's first Corsair squadron, VF-12, during carrier trials aboard U.S.S. *Core* on March 4, 1943. These trials displayed some improvement in deck handling, although the pneumatic tailwheel tyres tended to blow out on severe impact, and the entire squadron became deck-qualified in April 1943.

The U.S. Navy still considered the Corsair as unsuitable for carrier operations, and its first operational Corsair squadron, VF-17, formed on April 19, 1943, under Lieut.-Com. J. T. Blackburn, although attached to the U.S.S. *Bunker Hill*, was land-based on reaching the New Georgia area in September. This squadron was the first to receive the "high-cabin" F4U-1As which it flew with conspicuous success in the Pacific, claiming the destruction of 154 Japanese aircraft in seventy-nine days of combat, and the inclusion of no fewer than twelve aces among its pilots. Other famous pilots forming Corsair squadrons between April and July 1943 were Marine Corps Majors John L. Smith, Marion Carl, and Joseph Foss. The U.S. Navy's first Corsair squadron, VF-12, however, handed over its aircraft to the Marine Corps at Espiritu Santo to re-equip with F6F-3 Hellcats for carrier operations.

The fact that the Corsair *could* be deck-landed by experienced pilots was demonstrated by VF-17's F4U-1As in November 1943 when they provided high cover for two carriers during a naval strike against Rabaul. Running short of fuel after shooting down all eighteen aircraft of an attacking Japanese torpedo-bomber force, the Corsairs of VF-17 all landed safely on the *Essex* and the *Bunker Hill* after combat. The

Royal Navy showed that even the original F4U-1 was capable of deck operations, even from ships as small as escort carriers on which the first British Corsair squadrons were based. Under Lend-Lease arrangements, the Fleet Air Arm took delivery of ninety-five F4U-1s as Corsair Is followed by 510 F4U-1As as Corsair IIs. On June 1, 1943, No. 1830 Squadron was formed at Quonset, and before the end of the year seven more F.A.A. squadrons were working up on Corsair Is and IIs.

In Fleet Air Arm service the Corsairs underwent several modifications, and some sixteen inches were clipped from their wingtips to permit below-deck stowage in the smaller British carriers. The Corsair Is were also fitted with bulged front hoods to improve the forward view by enabling the pilot to raise his seat. Rocket rails were attached beneath the wings, and the early machines were quickly given provision for a ventral drop tank beneath the fuselage.

CHANCE VOUGHT CORSAIR

By the end of 1943, 1,958 Corsairs had been delivered by the parent company, the 1,550th machine (the 862nd F4U-1A) introducing the R-2800-8W engine with water injection, and to these had been added 377 Goodyear-built and 136 Brewster-built Corsairs. The Goodyear-built model, which was designated FG-1 and FG-1A, was intended for land-based Marine Corps units and was essentially similar to the F4U-1 and F4U-1A but lacking wing folding and equipment associated with shipboard operation. The first FG-1 flew on February 25, 1943, and two FG-1As were experimentally fitted by Goodyear with an all-round-vision "bubble" canopy; but although these aircraft were evaluated at the Naval Air Test Centre at Patuxent River, the modification

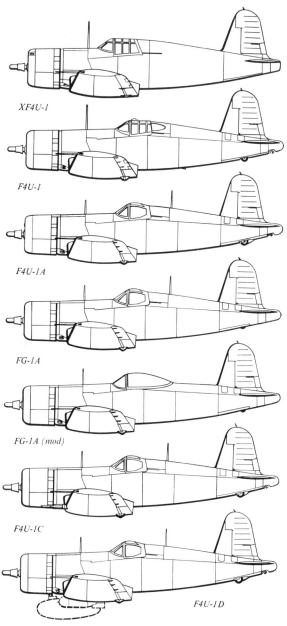

XF4U-1

F4U-1

F4U-1A

FG-1A

FG-1A (mod)

F4U-1C

F4U-1D

was not introduced on the production line. The Brewster-built Corsair received the designation F3A-1, and the first fighter of this type flew on April 26, 1943.

Soon after the acceptance of the 1,000th Corsair to be produced by the parent company, on August 22, 1943, a modified version was handed over on August 30, the F4U-1C with a new armament of four 20-mm. M-2 cannon supplanting the sextette of 0.5-in. weapons. The muzzles of the long-barrelled Hispano cannon protruded well forward of the wing leading edges, and the F4U-1C proved particularly potent for ground strafing, and production of the cannon-armed Corsair continued alongside the version with the earlier machine gun armament. However, most American combat pilots preferred the 0.5-in. guns, and after the completion of the original U.S. Navy order for two hundred cannon-armed machines no further F4U-1C Corsairs were produced. On October 5, 1943, the first Corsair with a centreline drop tank fitted was accepted by the U.S. Navy, and the next month, on November 25, an F4U-1A with an R-2800-8W engine incorporating water injection was delivered, and both of these modifications were featured by the next production model, the F4U-1D.

In January 1943 the Chance Vought and Sikorsky Aircraft Divisions of the former Vought-Sikorsky Division of the United Aircraft Corporation had been reconstituted as separate manufacturing divisions to enable Chance Vought to devote all their energies to the development and production of combat aircraft, and the F4U-1D went into production with the reorganized concern in April 1944. The new model was also produced by Goodyear and Brewster as the FG-1D and F3A-1D respectively. The F4U-1D differed from the F4U-1A in having the unprotected outboard 51.6 Imp. gal. (62 U.S. gal.) wing tanks deleted, twin pylons provided beneath the centre section for two 1,000-lb. bombs or a 133 Imp. gal. (160 U.S. gal.) drop tank, and attachment points beneath the outer wing panels for an alternative external load of eight 5-in. rockets. Water injection boosted the maximum take-off power of the R-2800-8W engine to 2,250 h.p. Some weight saving had resulted in a reduction in the empty weight from 8,873 lb. to 8,694.6 lb., normal loaded and overload weights being 12,039 lb. and 13,120 lb. respectively. Initial climb rate was boosted from 2,890 ft./min. to 3,120 ft./min., maximum speed ranged from 328 m.p.h. at 500 ft. to 349 m.p.h. at 10,000 ft. and 425 m.p.h. at 20,000 ft., and range with a 2,000-lb. bomb load was 500 miles.

By the end of 1943, when the U.S. Navy signed contracts for no less than 4,699 Corsairs, the service still refused to accept the aircraft for shipboard operation. In fact, in March 1944 the Chief of Naval Air Operational Training, Jacksonville, Florida, drew up a statement condemning the Corsair's deck-landing characteristics, stressing the fighter's tendency to bounce dangerously on landing, particularly in the hands of inexperienced pilots! To prevent this statement being promulgated, Chance Vought initiated a

The F4U-1A (above), photographed early in 1944, was flown by U.S. Navy ace Lieutenant J. G. Ira C. Kepford who was awarded the Distinguished Flying Cross. Lieut. Kepford was a member of VF-17, the "Skull and Crossbones" squadron led by Lieut.-Com. J. T. Blackburn, and won this decoration for outstanding skill displayed during operations in the New Georgia area between October 27 and December 1, 1943.

final development scheme—one of four presented by the company's engineers—to eliminate once and for all the Corsair's built-in bounce, the scheme being known as "Programme Dog". The undercarriage oleo legs were redesigned to provide a long stroke with low rebound ratios, and the results of test flights made by Cdr. T. K. Wright and Lieut. Col. J. Dobbins were so encouraging that carrier trials aboard the U.S.S. *Gambier Bay* followed immediately. These were performed in April 1944 by VF-301 whose Corsairs completed 113 landings with excellent results. All Corsair oleos were similarly modified, and the F4U-1 was finally cleared for shipboard service with the U.S. Navy.

Surprisingly, the Corsair had been cleared by the Royal Navy for operation from carriers some nine months earlier, and the first operational sorties with the F.A.A. were undertaken by the Corsair IIs of No. 1834 Squadron from H.M.S. *Victorious* on April 3, 1944, when these aircraft provided fighter cover for torpedo-bombers attacking the German battleship *Tirpitz*. Lend-Lease F4U-1s supplied to Britain were designated F4U-1B by their manufacturer, but in addition to the ninety-five Chance Vought-built F4U-1s and 510 F4U-1As supplied to the Royal Navy, this service also received 430 Brewster-built F3A-1Ds as Corsair IIIs and 977 Goodyear-built FG-1Ds as Corsair IVs, Britain thus receiving 2,012 Corsairs which equipped nineteen squadrons. A

further 370 F4U-1Ds were delivered to the R.N.Z.A.F., these being operated by three squadrons in the Pacific early in 1944.

During all the development work on the basic F4U-1, other work was proceeding on a number of experimental Corsair projects. Early in 1941 specifications had been drawn up for a radar set for installation in single-seat fighters, and just before Pearl Harbour, on November 8, 1941, the Navy had requested a design study for a night fighter development of the Corsair under the designation XF4U-2. The study was submitted on January 6, 1942, and a mock-up of the proposed design was inspected twenty-two days later, but after finalisation, pressure of work on the standard model prevented further development of the night fighter by Chance Vought. Instead, the necessary modifications were incorporated in twelve standard F4U-1s by the Naval Aircraft Factory at Philadelphia, an early mark of airborne interception radar being installed in a radome on the starboard wing, two guns being deleted, and an autopilot being provided. After brief trials, six of the F4U-2s were formed into a specialist night fighter unit, VFN-75, at Munda, New Georgia, while the other six went to VFN-101 on board the U.S.S. *Essex*, this unit also operating from the *Hornet* and the *Intrepid*. These specially-equipped Corsairs could claim the distinction of being the first radar-carrying single-seat fighters in history, and their pilots pioneered all subsequent solo night operations with their arrival in the Pacific. Apart from the technical difficulties occasioned by radar interception, flying a "hot" fighter at night demanded a high level of experience which was provided in VFN-75 by veteran pilots under Cdr. W. J. Widhelm, each with a minimum of two thousand flying hours. The Japanese made widespread use of nuisance bombers over the Allied airstrips at night, including light aircraft dubbed by the sleepless Americans as "Washing Machine Charlies", but their activities were rudely and successfully interrupted by the handful of radar-equipped F4U-2s, one of these making the Navy's first successful radar-guided interception over New Georgia on October 31, 1943.

As far back as June 14, 1941, the Navy had requested a design study for a high-altitude version of the Corsair equipped with a new two-stage supercharger developed by the Turbo-Engineering Company of Trenton, New Jersey. Designated XF4U-3 and having a 1009A turbo-supercharger on its XR-2800-16-(C) engine which was thus enabled to maintain its 2,000 h.p. up to 40,000 ft., the high-altitude fighter project got under way in July 1943 when work began on the conversion of three F4U-1 airframes to serve as prototypes. Work on the conversion of a further twenty-seven airframes by Goodyear as FG-3s was also initiated. The first XF4U-3 flew for the first time on April 26, 1944, but many teething troubles arose

early in the test programme, and the number of FG-3s on order was cut back to thirteen, these subsequently being used for high-altitude operational test work. One of the XF4U-3s was further developed as the XF4U-3B. The XF4U-3 and FG-3 were characterized by a large scoop under the engine cowling for the supercharger intake.

Further development of the Corsair resulted in the XF4U-4, the progenitor of the final wartime production model of the fighter. Pratt and Whitney had been steadily refining the Double Wasp engine and, from the R-2800(B) series, had evolved the R-2800(C) in which critical components had been strengthened and cooling improved, boosting the normal maximum rating for take-off to 2,100 h.p. This output was further raised in the R-2800-18W engine of the XF4U-4 by the use of water-methanol injection, no less than 2,450 h.p. being available. Chance Vought elected to use the new (C)-series engine in production at once, and received a Navy letter of intent for development of this more powerful model on January 25, 1944. The conversion of five F4U-1 airframes to serve as prototypes for the F4U-4 began immediately and the first two of these, designated F4U-4XA and F4U-4XB and flown for the first time on April 19 and July 12, 1944 respectively, only featured the new engine employing a downdraught carburettor, the intake ducts for which were moved from the wing leading edges to beneath the engine cowling, this

The Royal Navy received 977 Goodyear-built FG-1Ds as Corsair IVs, one of these (KD178) being illustrated below.

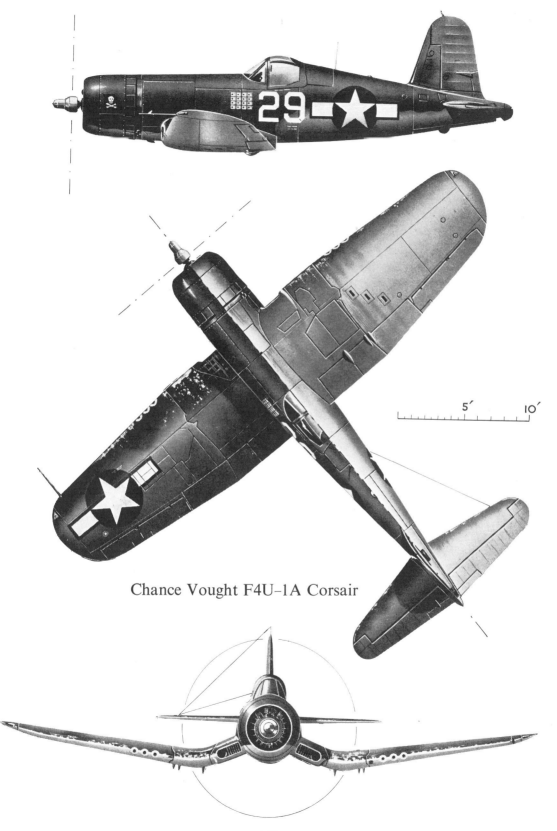

Chance Vought F4U–1A Corsair

(*Above*) *An F4U-1D* (*Bu. No. 57707*) *with late-production-style cockpit canopy, and* (*left*) *the cannon-armed F4U-1C Corsair.*

becoming a characteristic feature of the production F4U-4. The remaining three aircraft, which were designated XF4U-4, also embodied a redesigned cockpit with a revised canopy, a new armour-plated bucket seat, re-grouped instruments and improved access to the radio equipment by means of a folding seat back, and the first of these flew on October 7, 1944, being accepted by the U.S. Navy on the last day of the month.

Five hundred production F4U-4 Corsairs had been delivered by Chance Vought by the following April, these carrying a total of 197 lb. of armour and later being fitted with zero-length stubs beneath each outer wing panel for a total of eight high-velocity rockets. The F4U-4B was the designation allocated to F4U-4s that were to have been delivered to the British Navy, although none were in fact received by that service, and three hundred F4U-4Cs were produced, these, ordered on January 10, 1945, having an armament of four 20-mm. M-2 cannon. The normal gross weight of the standard F4U-4 was increased from the 11,093 lb. of the early F4U-1 to 12,399 lb., maximum overload weight being 14,670 lb., but with an initial climb rate of 3,870 ft./min., a service ceiling of 41,500 ft., and

a maximum speed ranging from 381 m.p.h. at sea level to 446 m.p.h. at 26,200 ft., the -4 version of the Corsair was a powerful answer to the best Japanese aircraft that were appearing in the Pacific area. Complete F4U-4 production and engineering data had been passed to Goodyear who produced two hundred similar aircraft as FG-4s.

Towards the end of 1944 the Corsair finally achieved its original design aim of shipboard operation when, on December 28th, VMF-124 began operations from the U.S.S. *Essex*. This unit and VMF-213 were the first Marine Corps fighter squadrons to operate from fast carriers in combat. The threat of Japanese *Kamikaze* attacks had resulted in a Pacific Fleet High Command conference at Pearl Harbour during November 24–26, 1944, and a decision had been taken to increase the number of fighters aboard aircraft carriers for *Kamikaze* interception, and to ensure the procurement of the highest performing combat types. This inevitably meant extensive re-equipment with the Corsair since, earlier that year, on May 16th, after a series of comparative trials between the F6F-3 Hellcat and the F4U-1D Corsair, a Navy evaluation board had concluded: "It is the opinion of the board that generally the F4U is a better fighter, a better bomber and equally suitable carrier aircraft compared with the F6F. It is strongly recommended that the carrier fighter and/or bomber complements be shifted to the F4U type."

This confirmed previous evaluations of the Corsair, including one early in 1944 against a North American P-51B Mustang to determine the possible suitability of the A.A.F. fighter for Naval use. Matched against an F4U-1 and an F4U-1A, the P-51B weighed in at 9,423 lb. as compared with 12,162 lb. for the Corsairs, but the Chance Vought fighter, with an equal range, showed eighty-six per cent greater firepower. The

F4U-1 proved the faster of the two Corsairs, being superior to the Mustang from sea level to 13,600 ft., slightly inferior from that altitude to 16,000 ft., markedly superior up to 24,200 ft., and markedly inferior at higher altitudes. At 30,000 ft. the P-51B achieved a T.A.S. of 450 m.p.h. while the F4U-1 attained 432 m.p.h. at 20,000 ft. The Corsairs offered better climb rate to 20,000 ft., above which the P-51B was superior, but the Chance Vought fighters were all over the Mustang under all conditions in level flight acceleration, manoeuvrability and response, with better take-off performance and lower stalling speeds. Apart from level speed at extreme altitudes, the only marked superiority of the Mustang was to be found in its dive acceleration. North American had studied the possibility of converting the Mustang to a shipboard fighter with folding wingtips, but its lateral control at low speeds was inadequate for carrier operation, and forward visibility over the nose in the three-point attitude was extremely poor. For these and other reasons, the Mustang was rejected by the Navy.

In competitive tests with an F6F-5 Hellcat, an F4U-1D at overload weights up to 13,120 lb. with two drop tanks, and with internal fuel only at 12,039 lb., achieved 328 m.p.h. at 500 ft. in the latter configuration compared with 323 m.p.h. for the Hellcat, and both aircraft were even at 349 m.p.h. at 10,000 ft. Average rates of climb were 2,645 ft./min. for the Corsair and 2,460 ft./min. for the Hellcat. The F4U-1D maintained its speed advantage up to 30,000 ft., after which the Hellcat was marginally faster.

A little-known research venture involving a Corsair at this stage was the installation of a Westinghouse Model 19A turbojet beneath the fuselage of a Goodyear-built FG-1. The aircraft was delivered to the Naval Air Material Centre at Philadelphia on August 1, 1943, the turbojet following on October 8th., and the modified FG-1 was delivered to the Flight Test section on December 30th. During the first month or so

of flight testing nine flights were made with the turbojet operating, and these were the first air tests of this early American jet engine. Some trouble was experienced with aircraft test instrumentation, however, and subsequent difficulties with the engine led to its return to the Naval Air Material Centre on June 3, 1944. Another experimental installation was the use of a six-bladed 12 ft. 7 in. Aero Products contra-prop on one of the XF4U-4s for a vibration and performance survey on this type of airscrew. These tests were run between June 6 and August 22, 1945, and the 864-lb. contra-prop was evaluated against the normal 667-lb. four-blade airscrew. At 26,000 ft. the contra-prop displayed a 10 m.p.h. decrease in maximum speed, and climb rate was inferior at sea level by 300 ft./min. As a result of these tests, the four-blade airscrew was retained because of its lower drag and weight.

Less radical modifications to the Corsair resulted in a tactical reconnaissance version carrying cameras in the fuselage while retaining its normal armament, and aircraft thus adapted were designated F4U-1P and F4U-4P. In mid-1944, in the Pacific, Charles A. Lindbergh, famed trans-Atlantic pilot, then acting as a civilian technical representative in combat areas, pioneered the process of doubling the Corsair's bomb load from 2,000 to 4,000 lb. This gave the Corsair the same offensive capability as the Mosquito bomber, and after Lindbergh had proved the weight-lifting capabilities of the F4U-1D in a 65° dive-bombing attack on Wotje Island, Corsairs played an increasing role in tactical support. In a seven-week period Corsairs dropped more than 200,000 lb. of bombs on

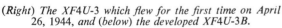

(Right) The XF4U-3 which flew for the first time on April 26, 1944, and (below) the developed XF4U-3B.

Japanese installations in the Marshalls, and Corsairs of the Royal Navy were equally active in operations from the four large carriers of the British Pacific Fleet.

By the end of 1944 Chance Vought were turning out 300 Corsairs per month, or one aircraft every eighty-two minutes, and the parent company had completed 4,631 machines while Goodyear had delivered a further 2,485, although the badly managed Brewster production line had closed down during the previous July after completing 735 Corsairs. On April 7, 1945, cannon-equipped F4U-1C Corsairs went into action for the first time with Marine Air Group 31 which was catapulted from the carriers *Sitkoh* and *Breton* to intercept a *Kamikaze* attack. On April 18th,

(Above) The F4U-4XA and (below) the F4U-4XB which were flown for the first time on April 19 and July 12, 1944, respectively.

Napalm, or jellied petroleum, was added to the Corsair's armoury, and the Chance Vought fighter earned its soubriquet of "Sweetheart of Okinawa" soon afterwards when the Marine Corps' "Death Rattler" squadron shot down 124.5 Japanese aircraft in that area without loss to itself. The Corsairs in this action included the first operational F4U-4s which had started to reach Okinawa in May 1945.

By the end of the Okinawa campaign, nearly every U.S. carrier was equipped with Corsairs, which, in the Pacific, were to be credited with the destruction of 2,140 enemy aircraft in aerial combat by V-J Day for the loss of 189 F4Us. Operational sorties from February 13, 1942 comprised 64,051, 54,470 being from land bases and 9,581 from carriers. Further F4U losses included 349 from anti-aircraft fire, 230 from other causes, 692 on non-operational flights, and 164 in crashes on carriers or airfields. In Royal Navy service the Corsair also took its attack into the heart of Japan before V-J Day with strikes in the Tokyo area and elsewhere. During one of these sorties Lieut. R. H. Gray, R.C.N.V.R. of No. 1841 Squadron was awarded a Victoria Cross posthumously for sinking a destroyer at Shiogama before being shot down.

Other Corsair developments during the later stages of the war included radar-equipped models of the F4U-4—the F4U-4E with APS-4 radar and the F4U-4N with APS-6 in a radome projecting from the starboard wing. Cannon-armed, these aircraft were too late to play an active part in the Japanese campaign although they were to figure prominently in Korean operations many years later.

The increasing threat of *Kamikaze* attack early in 1944 resulted in Goodyear being asked to evolve a special low-altitude version of the Corsair with a Pratt and Whitney R-4360 twenty-eight cylinder four-row radial, this being intended for U.S. Marine Corps use as a specialised interceptor for low-flying

(Below) The last production variant of the Corsair to see extensive wartime service was the F4U-4 which embodied numerous refinements and a more powerful engine.

The Goodyear-developed F2G-1 (above) displayed poor lateral control and insufficient speed to warrant quantity production, and of 418 machines of this type originally ordered only five were completed.

suicide aircraft. The R-4360 had already been flight-tested in an early F4U-1, and a standard FG-1 airframe was also adapted to flight test the immense engine as the XF2G-1 although this installation differed appreciably from that in the F4U-1 test bed. In March 1944, Goodyear was awarded contracts for 418 rigid-wing F2G-1s intended for operation from land bases and ten F2G-2s equipped to operate from carriers. The fuselage of the F2G was extensively redesigned to make full use of the fifty per cent increase in take-off power afforded by the new engine, and an all-round-vision bubble-type cockpit canopy was adopted. It was proposed to install a water injection system to boost the engine's emergency rating to 3,650 h.p., and with the aid of this system a maximum speed of 450 m.p.h. was anticipated at 16,500 ft. Alternative wing-mounted armaments comprised four or six 0.5-in. machine guns and eight 5-in. rocket projectiles or two 1,000-lb. or 1,600-lb. bombs. Internal fuel capacity was increased substantially to 257 Imp. gal. (309 U.S. gal.) and this could be augmented by two 125 Imp. gal. (150 U.S. gal.) drop tanks. Unfortunately, difficulties in developing the engine upset the original production schedule, and when the first F2Gs were tested they displayed poor lateral control and insufficient speed to warrant continuation of development, and thus, in May 1945, contracts were cut back and only five F2G-1s and five F2G-2s were completed. These were powered by the R-4360-4 engine, and the shipboard F2G-2 attained a maximum speed of 399 m.p.h. at sea level and 431 m.p.h. at 16,400 ft. Initial climb rate was 4,400 ft./min., and normal and maximum ranges were 1,190 and 1,955 mls. respectively.

Many other more minor developments took place in Corsair design during the Second World War, such as a study for the installation of the R-2800(E) two-stage supercharged engine, and the introduction of special Metalite tailplanes on several hundred F4U-4s. While the Pacific air war was battling to its close, yet another Corsair development was projected in a

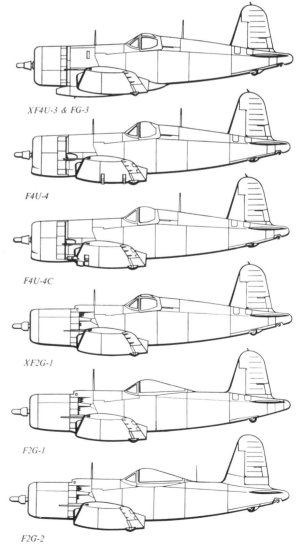

XF4U-3 & FG-3

F4U-4

F4U-4C

XF2G-1

F2G-1

F2G-2

(*Above*) *The F2G-2 was a shipboard version of the fixed-wing F2G-1.* (*Left*) *One XF4U-4 was tested with an Aero Products contraprop.*

cockpit. The cannon bays and pitot head were electrically heated, the tailwheel was made completely retractable, and the nose cowling was lowered some two degrees to further improve forward visibility. It was perhaps fortunate for the Japanese that the F4U-5 did not materialise until after the cessation of hostilities.

A total of 1,912 F4U-4s had been built by V-J Day which reduced contracts for this version of the Corsair from 3,149 to 2,356 machines, but another seven-and-a-half years were to elapse before the last example of this outstanding Chance Vought fighter was to roll off the new Dallas production line, and the Corsair was to enjoy a distinguished post-war career, the highlight of which was the Korean campaign, its first-line service stretching into the 'sixties. During its long life the Corsair underwent 981 major modifications and some 20,000 minor changes, but the airframe remained basically unaltered throughout, and such were its qualities that it was destined to gain the distinction of being the last airscrew-driven fighter built in the United States, having outlived all its contemporaries, both land- and carrier-based.

further attempt to maintain technical supremacy over the latest Japanese types. This variant was designated XF4U-5, and a mock-up inspection was made on February 24, 1945, although the prototype was not to fly until December 21st of that year. The principal change was the installation of the Pratt and Whitney R-2800-32(E) engine with the double supercharger and developing a maximum of 2,450 h.p. This had automatic control for the blowers, the cowl flaps, the intercooler doors and the oil cooler. The combat power system was also automatic. The new power plant was distinguishable externally by the cheek inlet ducts flanking each side of the lower cowling. Aerodynamic modifications included, for the first time in the F4U series, metal-covered outer wing panels, and it is astonishing that the Corsair, as one of the fastest wartime fighters, had managed for so long with fabric aft of the wing spars on the outboard panels! Spring tabs were introduced on the elevators and rudder to reduce pilot effort by as much as forty per cent—very necessary at the increased maximum of 462 m.p.h. at 31,400 ft. Pilot comfort was emphasized to a high degree in a completely modernized

Chance Vought F4U-1A Corsair

Dimensions :	Span, 40 ft. 11¾ in. ; span folded, 17 ft. 0⅝ in. ; length, 32 ft. 9½ in. ; height (tail down), 12 ft. 2 in., (tail up), 15 ft. 3⅞ in.
Armament :	Six 0.5-in. Browning MG 53-2 machine guns with 2,350 rounds (total).
Power Plant :	One Pratt and Whitney R-2800-8 Double Wasp eighteen-cylinder radial air-cooled engine rated at 2,000 h.p. at 2,700 r.p.m. for take-off, 1,755 h.p. at 5,400 ft., and 1,650 h.p. at 21,000 ft. Maximum internal fuel capacity, 300 Imp. gal. (361 U.S. gal.) plus one 145.6 Imp. gal. (175 U.S. gal.) drop tank.
Weights :	Empty, 8,873 lb. ; maximum loaded (clean), 12,694 lb. ; maximum overload, 13,846 lb.
Performance :	Maximum speed (at 11,149 lb.), 395 m.p.h. at 23,000 ft., 341 m.p.h. at sea level ; initial climb rate, 2,890 ft./min. ; time to 10,000 ft., 3.9 min., to 20,000 ft., 8.4 min. ; service ceiling, 37,900 ft. ; maximum range (at 12,694 lb.), 1,596 mls. at 179 m.p.h. at 5,000 ft., (at 13,846 lb. with 145.6 Imp gal. drop tank), 2,215 mls. at 178 m.p.h. ; combat radius (clean), 386 mls.

The I-16 was the most widely used of Russian fighters during the first year of conflict on the Eastern Front, and remained in first-line service until mid-1943. The photograph above depicts a late-production M-62-powered version of the fighter.

THE POLIKARPOV I-16

During the early 'thirties the biplane configuration, offering slow landing and extreme manoeuvrability, dominated the fighter scene, but its heyday was passing. In their search for increased performance by means of improved aerodynamic efficiency, fighter designers all over the world were following in the wake of their bomber contemporaries and turning to the low-wing monoplane. Few believed that, without an inordinately heavy structure, the fully cantilever wing was capable of withstanding the extreme stresses to which a fighter was subjected in combat, however, and much of the advantage offered by the monoplane configuration was cancelled out by the retention of drag-producing external struts and wire bracing, while such refinements as retractable undercarriages and enclosed cockpits were viewed with the utmost suspicion by fighter pilots.

At this time the Russians were labelled as copyists. It was fashionable to claim, not without some justification, that all products of Soviet industry were inferior copies of obsolescent western designs. But it should be remembered that little more than a decade had passed since the revolution and the first attempts to establish a modern, industrialised State. The Russians

had discovered a natural aptitude for things mechanical and a genius for copying the basic designs of others and adapting them to their own requirements and more primitive production methods. The aircraft industry absorbed the foreign influence more rapidly than other industries, and by the late 'twenties was evincing considerable creative ability. Russian aircraft designers were among the first to see the potential advantages of the low-wing monoplane configuration for fighters, and whereas in most other countries the transition from be-strutted, wire-braced biplane to the fully cantilever monoplane with retractable undercarriage and enclosed cockpit was made in stages, Russian design teams began work on such fighters as early as 1932.

One single-seat fighter first conceived in that year, the I-16, was to gain the distinction of becoming the first low-wing interceptor with a fully retractable undercarriage to enter service anywhere in the world. Yet, paradoxically, the Soviet Union, although the first major air power to introduce fighters of such advanced concept, was the last to relinquish the fighter biplane! The I-16 was deserving of considerably more credit than it was later to receive in the West. Despite

153

(Above and left) The I-16 Type 10 entered operational service in Spain late in 1937, and featured a more powerful engine and a heavier armament than employed by earlier I-16 variants.

some crudity of construction and equipment by western standards appertaining at the time, it was a rugged and extremely manoeuvrable fighter, appreciably faster than any true contemporary, easily maintained in the field and offering some armour protection for its pilot at a time when such "luxuries" were not generally considered to be necessary.

It was to be claimed on many occasions that the designer of the I-16 had found his inspiration in the Boeing P-26A, this fallacy first being perpetrated during the Spanish Civil War and perpetuated ever since, but not only did the I-16 bear no resemblance to the American fighter, it was actually under test before the first P-26A had been delivered to the U.S. Army Air Corps. Built in tens of thousands, the I-16 did more to raise Russian combat aircraft design techniques to world standards than any other single type, but unfortunately for the Soviet Union, the

fighter's development peak had been attained rather earlier than that of its principal opponent during the Luftwaffe offensive of 1941–42, the Messerschmitt Bf 109, and in consequence the I-16 was outclassed in fighter-versus-fighter combat. Nevertheless, it was destined to bear the brunt of the early fighting on the Eastern Front, and it had not been completely supplanted in first-line fighter units until mid-1943.

Late in 1932 a design bureau of Andrei N. Tupolev, one of Russia's veteran aircraft designers at the Central Aero and Hydrodynamic Institute, or TsAGI, and the Central design bureau of the Aviatrust, or TsKB, headed by Nickolai N. Polikarpov, began work simultaneously on designs for advanced low-wing cantilever fighter monoplanes with retractable undercarriages and enclosed cockpits. The construction of prototypes of the designs evolved by both teams began early in 1933, and the first to fly was the I-14, or ANT-31, which began trials during October of that year. Designed by Pavel Sukhoi, the I-14 was powered by an imported Bristol Mercury VS-2 nine-cylinder radial air-cooled engine offering 570 h.p. at 16,075 ft., and carried what was for its time the remarkably heavy armament of two 20-mm. cannon in the wings and two 7.62-mm. PV-1 machine guns in the upper decking of the forward fuselage, synchronised to fire through the airscrew disc. The structure was principally of wood, although both fuselage and wings were clad with a light alloy skin, a sliding cockpit canopy was provided, and the retractable main undercarriage members had oleo shock absorber legs and wheel brakes.

During flight trials the I-14 attained a speed of 238.5 m.p.h. in level flight at 16,400 ft., and effected a 180° turn in twelve seconds, but this performance was not greatly in advance of that of the more orthodox I-15, or TsKB-3, fighter biplane which, designed by Polikarpov's team, had made its début during the same month. The biplane was appreciably more manoeuvrable than the I-14, and at 9,840 ft. was marginally faster! It was decided, therefore, to place the I-15 in production immediately for the Army's Military-Aviation Forces (Voenno-Vozdushnye Sily), or V.-V.S., and continue development work on the monoplane. Shortly after this decision had been taken, the competitive Polikarpov fighter monoplane, the I-16, or TsKB-12, had begun tests. First flown on December 31, 1933, the I-16 was, like the I-14, a snub-nosed, barrel-like little aircraft. It featured very small overall dimensions, extremely small inertia moments around all three axes, and a very small margin of longitudinal static stability when gliding. The fuselage was a circular-section wooden monocoque, and the abbreviated nose housed an M-22 (licence-built Gnôme-Rhône Jupiter) nine-cylinder radial rated at 450 h.p. at sea level. The cockpit was enclosed by a sliding canopy into which was built the windscreen which slid forward with the canopy. The wing structure comprised two chrome-steel spars with duralumin ribs and was fabric covered, the centre section being built integral with the fuselage. Split flaps were provided, and armament comprised two of the new 7.62-mm. ShKAS machine guns which, developed by B. M.

Shpitalny and I. A. Komaritsky, offered nearly twice the fire rate of the standard PV-1. These were mounted immediately outboard of the main undercarriage attachment points. The mainwheels retracted manually into wells in the centre section.

The I-16 attained 224 m.p.h. at sea level and had superior powers of manoeuvre to those of the I-14, and on the strength of initial trials, factories No. 1 and No. 21 at Moscow and Gorki respectively began tooling up for production of the fighter as the I-16 Type 1. The production model had an uprated M-22 engine of 480 h.p., and weighed 2,965 lb. in normal loaded condition, wing and power loadings being 18.8 lb./sq. ft. and 6.25 lb./h.p. respectively. Maximum speeds were 225 m.p.h. at sea level and 202 m.p.h. at 13,120 ft., and an altitude of 16,400 ft. was attained in 9.4 minutes. Deliveries of the I-16 Type 1 to V.-V.S. squadrons began during the second half of 1934, and the new fighter was displayed publicly for the first time during the 1935 May Day celebrations, formations of I-16s being flown over Red Square. At this time, the R.A.F. had still to order the Gladiator fighter biplane into production, in Germany the Heinkel He 51 fighter biplane was just being delivered to the Jagdgeschwader Richthofen, the Dewoitine D.500 series of fighter monoplanes with their fixed, braced undercarriages, were entering service with the Armée de l'Air, while in the U.S.A. the Curtiss Design

(*Right and below*) *The I-16 Type 6, illustrated in the markings of the Spanish Nationalist Fighter Group 1W, was the last variant built in quantity with a cockpit canopy.*

75, forerunner of the Hawk 75A and P-36, had still to make its first flight. Yet, despite the design innovations displayed by the I-16, its appearance passed unnoticed outside the Soviet Union. During the impressive autumn manoeuvres held near Kiev that year, the I-16 once again appeared in quantity and was seen by a number of foreign observers, but it was not until more than two years later, when the fighter appeared in Spanish skies, that the existence of the I-16 became generally known.

While preparations were being made for the production of the I-16 Type 1, second prototypes of both the I-14 and I-16 had been completed, these being powered by the M-25 engine, the Soviet version of the Wright Cyclone 9, a nine-cylinder radial rated at 700 h.p. The first of the two M-25-powered prototypes to fly was the I-14bis which began trials on February 12, 1934. During the course of flight testing it became evident that at high angles of attack and particularly when spinning, the elevators were blanketed by the tailplane, becoming ineffective. This problem and other teething troubles seriously delayed the completion of flight trials, and series production of the I-14bis, ordered before these defects had revealed themselves, was progressively postponed until finally, in 1936, it was cancelled completely.

The M-25-powered second prototype of the I-16 (TsKB-12bis) had flown for the first time four days later than the I-14bis, on February 18, 1934, and this enjoyed considerable success from the outset of flight testing. The test pilot was Valerii P. Chkalov, one of the best-known of Russia's pre-war pilots who was to lose his life in December 1938 when testing a later experimental variant of the I-16, and during the second flight the new prototype achieved 282 m.p.h. at 9,840 ft., a greater speed than attained by any fighter flown at that time. Despite the outstanding performance of the M-25-powered I-16, some eighteen months were to elapse before the decision was taken to place this type in production. The reason for the delay was the small size of existing Russian fighter airfields. The new version of the fighter had take-off and landing runs of 985 ft. and 755 ft. respectively, considerably more than were acceptable for operational fields, but in July 1935 an official decision was taken to enlarge all fighter airfields and, simultaneously, the M-25-powered model was ordered into production as the I-16 Type 4.

The advances introduced by the I-16 had been accompanied in service by their full share of problems, for the fighter was no novice's aircraft and casualties during conversion training assumed serious proportions as increasing numbers of the machine were delivered to the V.-V.S. The limited static stability under most conditions of flight and marked instability during climbing and turning made the aircraft unpopular. The oleo legs provided inadequate shock absorbing, the wheel brakes were ineffective, and there was a tendency to bounce indefinitely after touching down, a dangerous nose-up attitude being adopted. The nose also rose alarmingly as soon as the

flaps were lowered for landing, and it was difficult to wind up the undercarriage. The process of retraction called for forty-four turns of a handcrank which became progressively stiffer as the wheels came up. An undulating climb-out following a take-off was characteristic, the cranking motion being transmitted from the hand winding up the mainwheels through the pilot's body to the hand holding the control column. The undercarriage frequently stuck when partially retracted, and a cable-cutter was therefore a standard item of cockpit equipment, enabling the pilot to sever the undercarriage cables in an emergency!

The introduction of the heavier and more powerful I-16 Type 4 aggravated the situation, and the evolution of a two-seat training model became vital. This, the UTI-4 (later known as the I-16UTI), was built on the same assembly lines as the fighter, every fourth machine being a trainer. The UTI-4 was produced by inserting a second cockpit for the pupil in front of the normal cockpit, the main fuel tank aft of the engine firewall being redesigned and reduced in size to provide the necessary space. The undercarriage was locked in the extended position, the retraction mechanism being removed. The UTI-4 successfully versed pilots in the idiosyncrasies of the fighter, although it was officially admitted that the I-16 could be something of a handful by comparison with the biplanes that had preceded it. Later, some early production I-16s were converted as two-seaters for advanced training and liaison roles, these retaining the retractable undercarriage.

The I-16 Type 4 retained the twin-ShKAS armament of the initial production model. Normal loaded weight was 3,135 lb., wing loading was increased to 20.1 lb./sq. ft., and power loading was reduced to 4.5 lb./h.p. The M-25 engine had a maximum output of 700 h.p. at 2,300 ft. and drove a two-blade AV-1 airscrew, and maximum speed ranged from 248 m.p.h. at sea level to 279 m.p.h. at 8,530 ft. and 283 m.p.h. at 9,840 ft. An altitude of 16,400 ft. was attained in 5.9 mins., a 180° turn could be effected at 3,280 ft. in 14.3 seconds, service ceiling was 30,440 ft., and maximum cruising speed and range were 224 m.p.h. and 510 mls. respectively. The Type 4 was followed by the Type 5 in which 9-mm. seat armour became standard and minor revisions were made to the equipment, and the Type 6 which switched to the M-25A engine rated at 730 h.p. The last-mentioned model was to become the first of the I-16 series to see active service.

Despite the success of the I-16, the fighter biplane still had its adherents in the V.-V.S., although increasing confidence in the capabilities of the monoplane was indicated by the fact that, during 1936, of the total fighter output of the Russian aircraft industry, twenty-five per cent comprised I-15 biplanes and the remainder I-16 monoplanes.

The advent of the Spanish Civil War on July 18, 1936, provided the Russian government with an admirable opportunity to evaluate under true operational conditions its latest combat equipment, and

(Above and right) The I-16 Type 10 had been largely supplanted by M-62-powered models by 1941. The fighter was markedly unstable during climbing and turning.

by the following September, some two hundred V.-V.S. pilots and about 1,500 ground personnel, together with disassembled aircraft, had reached Cartagena aboard the Russian vessels *Rostock*, *Neva*, and *Volga*. Both I-15 and I-16 fighters were shipped to Spain, the latter making its operational début on November 5th in support of the offensive against the Nationalist troops advancing in Valdemoro, Seseña and Esquivias. The I-16 fighters were flown and maintained by V.-V.S. personnel seconded to the Spanish government on a six-month duty rota, and not by members of the *Brigadas Internacionales* as was generally believed at the time.

The first I-16 fighters despatched to Spain were Type 6 models with the 730 h.p. M-25A engine and two 7.62-mm. ShKAS wing-mounted machine guns with 750 r.p.g. The loaded weight of this version had increased to 3,660 lb., empty weight being 2,790 lb., and wing and power loadings were 23.4 lb./sq. ft. and 5.07 lb./h.p. Climb rate was reduced slightly, 6.2 mins. being required to attain an altitude of 16,400 ft. With the reorganisation of the Republican air arm in March 1937, the I-16s and their Russian personnel formed Fighter Group 31, the statutory strength of this unit being seven squadrons of fifteen aircraft. The I-16 was dubbed *Mosca* (Fly) by the Republicans and *Rata* (Rat) by its Nationalist opponents, and the latter nickname was to cling to the fighter throughout the remainder of its career, although, for obvious reasons, it was never used by the Russians.

While faster than any other fighter in Spanish skies and clearly the master of the Heinkel He 51 then being operated by the *Legión Cóndor*, the I-16 Type 6 experienced difficulty in combating the extremely nimble Fiat C.R.32 operated by the Italian *Aviación Legionaria*, as its pilots persisted in employing the

classic dog-fighting tactics in which the I-16 did not excel. The Russian fighters usually flew in large, tight formations, and their pilots tried to get above the opposing fighters, plunging through their formation and then zoom-climbing back to a suitable altitude for a further attack, similar tactics being employed some six years later by the U.S. Navy's Wildcats in combat with the Japanese Zero-Sen. The diving speed was inferior to that of the C.R.32, although the climb rate and level speed of the I-16 were both superior to those of the Italian fighter, permitting the Russian pilot to break off combat at will.

The patently obvious inferiority of the I-16 to the Fiat C.R.32 in the classic dog-fighting style of combat provided the adherents of the biplane in the V.-V.S. with ammunition with which to reinforce their arguments for the continued development and production of fighter biplanes, and at the end of 1936 the decision was taken to boost fighter biplane production by the Russian aircraft industry, and the improved I-15bis (TsKB-3bis) was placed on the assembly lines. At the same time, work proceeded on improving the qualities of the basic I-16 in the light of lessons

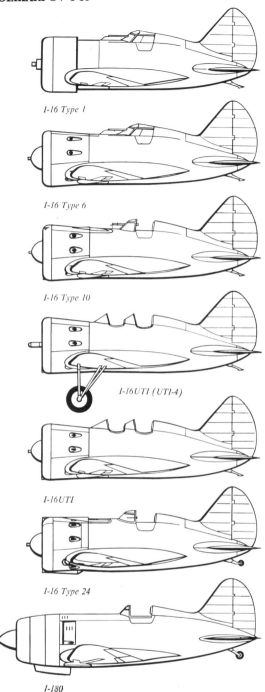

I-16 Type 1

I-16 Type 6

I-16 Type 10

I-16UTI (UTI-4)

I-16UTI

I-16 Type 24

I-180

in Spain was its inadequate firepower, and thus, in 1937, the I-16 Type 10 entered production with two additional 7.62-mm. ShKAS guns mounted in the upper decking of the forward fuselage and synchronised to fire through the airscrew disc. These were provided with 450 r.p.g., and although the Type 10 initially retained the tubular collimator gun sight, later machines had an early form of reflector sight. The new production model was fitted with an M-25V engine rated at 750 h.p. at 9,500 ft., and the engine bearers were modified to reduce the high vibration level which had had a detrimental effect on the fighter's capability as a firing platform. In Spain, pilots invariably flew with their cockpit canopies open as these tended to jam shut in the event of a forced landing and also impaired vision in combat, so the canopy was removed on the Type 10, and a fixed windscreen introduced.

The I-16 Type 10 reached Spain late in 1937, and before the end of the year had encountered the Messerschmitt Bf 109B fighters of the *Legión Cóndor* in combat. There was little to choose between Russian and German fighter in speed, and while the Bf 109B had an edge in rate of turn, the I-16 enjoyed a superior rate of climb and heavier firepower. Thus, the outcome of a combat between the two fighter types was largely dependent on the relative quality of the opposing pilots. On one occasion, one of the Legion's finest pilots, Lieut. Balthasar, performed the remarkable feat of destroying four I-16s in six minutes! The I-16 Type 10 had a loaded weight of 3,783 lb., and wing and power loadings were 24.35 lb./sq. ft. and 5 lb./h.p. An altitude of 16,400 ft. was attained in 6.5 mins., service ceiling was 26,245 ft., and maximum range was 497 mls.

No fewer than 475 I-16 fighters were sent to Spain from the Soviet Union, but during the autumn of 1938 the V.-V.S. personnel were withdrawn and replaced by Spanish personnel most of whom had received training on the I-16 at various schools in Russia. The I-16s operating over Spain were repaired at various plants in the vicinity of Alicante, and the actual production of both I-16 Type 10 fighters and UTI-4 trainers was initiated in Spain, although only between fifteen and twenty fighters and some ten trainers had been completed when fighting terminated. During the closing stages of the conflict, the successful Nationalist blockade of Republican ports resulted in the I-16 airframes being shipped to Bordeaux or Le Havre from where they were sent to Catalonia by rail. Some of these airframes were fitted with American-built Wright R-1820-F54 Cyclone engines after their arrival in Spain. The Nationalist forces formed

learned during the opening stages of the conflict.

Among the shortcomings of the I-16 Type 6 revealed

FINISH AND INSIGNIA: *The I-16 Type 24 illustrated on the opposite page was operational on the Eastern Front during the spring of 1942. All upper surfaces were painted a non-gloss dark green and under surfaces were pale blue. The national insignia was not outlined. The numeral "4" was painted in white on the rudder and did not indicate the position of the aircraft in the Eskadrilya (Squadron) as it was Russian practice to allocate such numbers consecutively to all aircraft of one type based on a particular airfield. The tip of the vertical tail surfaces was painted yellow, indicating that the pilot led a Tryohzvonnie Eskadrilya (Small Squadron), other colours indicating the leaders of each Zveno (Flight or Cluster) within the unit. In pre-war years no individual or unit emblems or decorations were permitted, the application of such being considered defacing state property. During the war years this rule was unofficially relaxed, and many I-16s bore patriotic slogans such as "Za Stalina!" (See page 13).*

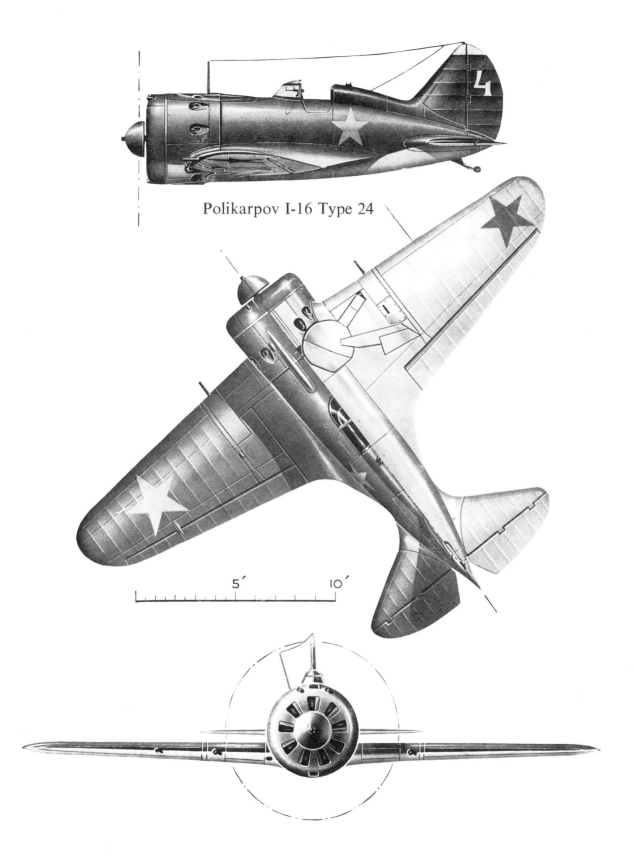

Polikarpov I-16 Type 24

5′ 10′

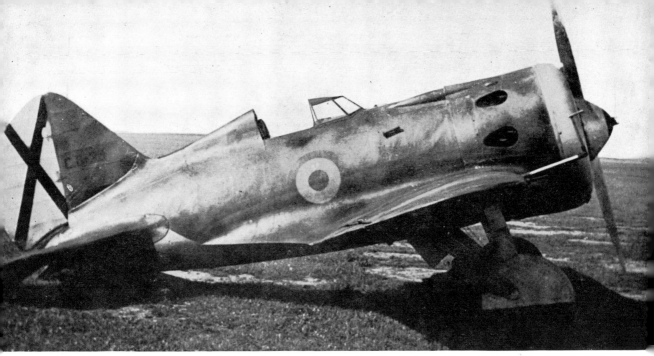

This I-16 Type 10 (C.8-25) was probably the last airworthy example of the fighter, serving with the Fighter School at Moron, Spain, until June 1952. It retained its original M-25V but the curved windscreen was replaced by flat panels in Spanish service.

Fighter Group 1W in Baleares with eighteen I-16 fighters shortly after the end of the Civil War, and later, a further fifteen I-16s were assembled at Jerez de la Frontera from finished components found at Alicante. Together with the surviving I-16s of Group 1W, these equipped a new squadron formed at Tablada as late as May 1943.

Despite developments abroad during the late 'thirties which underlined the basic rightness of the I-16's concept, the V.-V.S. believed increasingly in the need for both high-speed, heavily-armed fighter monoplanes *and* lighter, more nimble biplanes. Analysis of experience over Spain was partly responsible for this belief in the need to retain the biplane, but more important were the results of combat in the Far East. On August 29, 1937, the Chinese government had entered into a Non-Aggression Pact with the Soviet Union, and soon after the pact had been concluded, four hundred combat aircraft were supplied to China, including I-15bis and I-16 fighters. Russia also despatched two bomber and four fighter squadrons of the V.-V.S. to China in the guise of volunteers, and these were to remain in China until the late summer of 1939. The appearance of the Mitsubishi A5M2a fighter monoplane over China came as a shock to the Russians for the Japanese fighter outperformed the I-15bis biplane on all counts. It could even out-climb the I-16 Type 10 (attaining 16,400 ft. in 5 min. 54 sec. compared to 6 min. 30 sec. for the Russian fighter) and was infinitely more agile, only maximum speed being inferior (252 m.p.h. as against 281 m.p.h.). It was obvious that greater agility than that of the A5M2a could only be achieved with a biplane. Thus, a member of Polikarpov's design bureau, A. J. Scherbakov, was charged with the task of severely refining the basic I-15 biplane to produce a fighter capable of besting the A5M2a in speed,

manoeuvrability and climb rate. Scherbakov reverted to the gull-type upper wing employed by the original I-15 and introduced fully-retractable main undercarriage members, and with a 750 h.p. M-25V, the prototype flew for the first time in 1938. This engine was quickly replaced by an M-63 rated at 1,100 h.p. for take-off, and with this power plant the biplane entered production in 1939 as the I-153.

In July 1938 fighting had broken out between Russo-Mongolian and Japanese forces on the ill-defined Mongolian-Siberian-Manchurian border. After a month of fighting a compromise was reached, but early in May 1939 a further clash developed into a full-scale war which was waged bitterly for four months. By June as many as two hundred aircraft were engaged at one time in battle over the Koronbail Plain, the Japanese Army's Kawasaki Ki.10 fighter biplanes and Nakajima Ki.27 fighter monoplanes being opposed by the I-15bis and the I-16. It was during this conflict that RS-82 rocket missiles, which were to be extensively used by I-16s and other Russian fighters during the Second World War, were first employed in action, and a batch of newly completed I-153 biplanes was hurriedly sent to the area to participate in the fighting. According to Russian sources, the I-153s approached the combat area at cruising speed with their undercarriages extended and, as was anticipated, were mistaken for the earlier I-15bis fighters by the Japanese. As the Ki.27 fighters approached, the Russian pilots retracted their undercarriages, opened their throttles fully, and were through the Japanese formation before their startled opponents could take evasive action. The early successes enjoyed by the I-153 in combat with the Japanese over the Khalkiïn Gol led to a substantial increase in production of this biplane, and, thus, the Soviet Union, which had been the first nation to introduce into service the cantilever fighter monoplane with retractable undercarriage, became the *last* to relinquish the fighter biplane!

Although less manoeuvrable than its opponents, the I-16 Type 10's speed and firepower had given the Japanese a healthy respect for the Russian fighter which they dubbed *Abu* (Gadfly), and it was with understandable elation that they greeted a young Mongolian seeking political asylum when he landed a fighter of this type at Arutaukou in eastern Manchuria. The I-16 was immediately sent to the Tachikawa Army Aeronautical Engineering Institute near Tokyo for thorough evaluation, and flight trials were conducted by one of the J.A.A.F.'s leading pilots, Major G. Yamamoto, in the spring of 1940. While praising the I-16's armament and pilot protection, Major Yamamoto considered the fighter's c.g. to be too far aft, this resulting in serious elevator heaviness. It was insensitive by comparison with Japanese fighters, and landing characteristics were bad.

However, the Type 10 was already obsolescent, for more powerful, more heavily armed variants of the I-16 had entered production in the Soviet Union some eighteen months earlier. Experiments aimed at increasing the fighter's firepower by the inclusion of cannon in its armament had begun in 1938. An experimental model, the I-16P or TsKB-12P evolved in close co-operation with the armament specialist, B. M. Shpitalny, had two 20-mm. cannon in the fuselage synchronised to fire through the airscrew, and in the same year the I-16 Type 17 appeared in production, this variant retaining the twin ShKAS machine guns in the fuselage first introduced on the Type 10 but replacing the wing machine guns with two 20-mm. ShVAK cannon which raised loaded weight to 3,990 lb. Another experimental model intended for the close-support role, the TsKB-18, carried six 7.62-mm. PV-1 machine guns, four of which were installed in the fuselage, underwing racks for a 220-lb. bomb load and armour to protect the engine and pilot from ground fire.

In an attempt to rectify shortcomings stemming from the manually-operated flaps and undercarriage, the TsKB-29 was flown with pneumatically-operated flaps and undercarriage, and experiments were conducted with the I-16SPB intended for the dive-bombing role. The I-16SPB was built in limited numbers, and in August 1941, some aircraft of this type attacked and destroyed a bridge across the Danube after being carried half way to their target beneath the wings of TB-3 bombers. Greatest attention, however, was given to improving the performance of the basic fighter by introducing new and progressively more powerful engines. As early as 1937 it was becoming obvious that constant increases in weight without any truly commensurate increases in power were having detrimental effects on both performance and handling characteristics. The M-25 engine had reached the limit of its development but A. D. Shvetsov had evolved a new engine based on the M-25, and in 1937 this was installed experimentally in an I-16 airframe. Designated M-62, this power plant had a two-speed supercharger and offered 1,000 h.p. at 2,200 r.p.m. for take-off and had a nominal rating of 850 h.p. at 2,100 r.p.m. at 5,000 ft. With the M-62 installed, the I-16 reached a speed of 328 m.p.h. at sea level and 288 m.p.h. at 15,750 ft. The first production model to be equipped with the M-62 engine was the I-16 Type 18 which appeared in 1939. Loaded weight rose to 4,034 lb., despite a drastic reduction in the capacity of the fuselage fuel tank (from 93.5 to 56 Imp. gal.—112 to 67 U.S. gal.), but provision was made for two 22 Imp. gal. (26.4 U.S. gal.) drop tanks. Armament comprised four 7.62-mm. ShKAS machine guns, but the similarly-powered I-16 Type 24 had two fuselage mounted 7.62-mm. guns and two wing-mounted 20-mm. cannon, the last-mentioned variant of the fighter being built in larger quantities than any other.

Another modification of the basic fighter was the

Some early production M-25-powered models of the I-16 had their undercarriages fixed in extended position and served in the fighter-trainer and liaison roles during the Second World War. That illustrated (above, right) was captured by Finnish forces on the Russo-Finnish Front. The M-62-powered I-16s below bear the inscriptions Za Stalina (For Stalin!) and Za SSSR (For USSR!) and are believed to have been operated by one of the 'do-or-die' squadrons formed from fanatical young Communists (Komsomoltsi). Others carried such inscriptions as Za Rodynu (For Our Fatherland!) and Za Lenina (For Lenin!).

(Above and immediately below) The I-16 Type 24 was frequently operated on skis during the fighting on the Russo-Finnish Front in the winter of 1941–42.

(Above) An I-16 Type 18 fighter on the Eastern Front early in 1942.

I-180 which was first tested in 1938. Employing an airframe essentially similar to that of the standard I-16, the I-180 was powered by a fourteen-cylinder two-row M-88 radial derived from the French Gnôme-Rhône 14K series of engines and rated at 1,100 h.p. at 13,100 ft. and 1,000 h.p. at 19,650 ft. Primarily a bomber engine, the M-88 weighed some 400 lb. more than the M-62, but its smaller frontal area reduced drag, and a maximum speed of 342 m.p.h. was attained. A small series of fighters of this type was produced in 1940, but the newer fighters with liquid-cooled engines being evolved by the design bureaux of the Mikoyan-Gurevich team, Yakovlev and Lavochkin appeared more promising. One other power plant was installed in the I-16, this being the M-63 first installed in the I-153 biplane and offering 1,100 h.p. for take-off, 1,000 h.p. at 5,900 ft., and 900 h.p. at 14,760 ft. This engine drove a VV-1 two-blade airscrew, and M-63-powered I-16s were produced in parallel with the M-62-powered Type 24, attaining a maximum speed of 326 m.p.h. at 15,750 ft. Some machines were fitted with a single 12.7-mm. Beresin BS machine gun between the ShKAS weapons in the fuselage and had the wing guns deleted, three RS-82 rocket missiles being carried on racks beneath each wing, and a

number of M-63-powered machines reintroduced the sliding cockpit canopy discarded with the I-16 Type 10.

Used during the Russo-Finnish War in the winter of 1939–40, the M-62 and M-63-powered I-16s bore the brunt of the fighting on the Eastern Front and remained in widespread service until the Russian counter-offensive in the Stalingrad area began at the end of October 1942. Although completely outclassed by the Messerschmitt Bf 109E and F, the I-16 did enjoy some success against unescorted German bomber formations, and one unit in particular, the 1st Fighter Regiment, was awarded the coveted title of "Guards Regiment" for its operations against the Luftwaffe with I-16s. The fighter was affectionately known in the V.-V.S. as the *Ishak* (Donkey), and was the first type to be used for the so-called *Taran* method of attack, a special steel-clad airscrew being used to slice off the tail surfaces of German bombers. The first V.-V.S. pilots to score with this "close-combat" method were awarded the "Golden Star" (Hero of the Soviet Union). I-16s were also used for straight-forward ramming attack by special "do-or-die" units formed by fanatical young communists. The rotund Polikarpov fighter continued in first-line service until mid-1943, being largely relegated to the Finnish Front, where it operated on skis, to home defence duties around industrial centres outside the range of Luftwaffe fighters, and to the Asiatic borders of Russia during the closing stages of its operational career.

The I-16 had passed its development peak long before the Soviet Union became embroiled in the Second World War, and this veteran of the Spanish and Sino-Japanese conflicts rarely found itself fighting on equal terms with its Luftwaffe opponents over the Eastern Front, having been long since surpassed in speed and climb rate. Its designer never succeeded in overcoming the poor take-off and landing characteristics that had plagued it from its birth, yet once its undercarriage was tucked up it handled pleasantly enough, and there is no doubt that it taught the Soviet air forces and aircraft industry much that was eventually used to good effect in later fighters. The I-16 was the precursor of a new style in fighter design, a style favoured until the advent of the turbojet, and as such it possesses a unique place in the history of fighter development.

Polikarpov I-16 Type 24

Dimensions :	Span, 29 ft. 6½ in. ; length, 20 ft. 1¼ in. ; height, 8 ft. 5 in. ; wing area, 161 sq. ft.
Armament :	Two 7.62-mm. ShKAS machine guns with 450 r.p.g. and two 20-mm. ShVAK cannon with 90 r.p.g., plus six RS-82 rocket missiles.
Power Plant :	One Shvetsov M-62 (R) nine-cylinder radial air-cooled engine rated at 1,000 h.p. at 2,200 r.p.m. for take-off and 850 h.p. at 2,100 r.p.m. at 5,000 ft. Normal fuel capacity, 56 Imp. gal. (67 U.S. gal.) plus two 22 Imp. gal. (26.4 U.S. gal.) drop tanks.
Weights :	Empty, 3,285 lb. ; normal loaded, 4,215 lb. ; maximum overload, 4,546 lb.
Performance :	Maximum speed, 326 m.p.h. at sea level, 286 m.p.h. at 14,765 ft.; economical cruising speed, 186 m.p.h. ; range (clean), 248 mls. at 199 m.p.h. at 3,280 ft., (with two 22 Imp. gal. drop tanks), 435 mls. at 186 m.p.h. ; time to 16,400 ft., 5.8 min. ; service ceiling, 29,530 ft.

The Ki.84-Ia Hayate made its operational début in August 1944 in China. That illustrated above belonged to the 104th Fighter Sentai activated in November 1944 as a home defence unit and photographed at Ohta in 1945.

THE NAKAJIMA HAYATE

"Forget it, it's a Frank!" This comment was made frequently by U.S.A.A.F. Mustang pilots participating in the most popular of "indoor pastimes" on Okinawa during the closing weeks of the Pacific War—radar watching. The object was to sit in wait for a likely target to appear on the radar screen and then scramble the Mustangs to intercept the intruder, but the rapidity with which this blip moved across the screen could only mean that its originator was a "Frank", the Nakajima Type 4 Fighter which had been so named by the Allies for identification purposes, and the American pilots knew that they would be wasting their time in attempting to catch this outstanding Japanese warplane!

Dubbed Hayate (Gale) by the Japanese Army Air Force, the Type 4 was the culmination of a line of original fighter monoplane development initiated by the Nakajima Hikoki K.K. in 1935 with the Ki.27,

and from its operational début over China in August 1944, the new fighter proved itself the most troublesome J.A.A.F. type insofar as the Allies were concerned. The Hayate was a formidable foe which possessed none of the shortcomings of the earlier generation of Japanese fighters. Extremely sturdy and possessing adequate firepower and protection for both pilot and fuel tanks, it compared favourably with the best of its antagonists, out-climbing and out-manoeuvring both the P-51H Mustang and P-47N Thunderbolt, the ultimate developments of these excellent American fighters, and like all thoroughbreds

(Right and below) One of the pre-production Ki.84 Hayate fighters tested late in 1943.

163

*One of the prototypes of the Ki.84 Hayate assigned to the
J.A.A.F. for service testing.*

it was amenable to adaptation, serving in the high-,
medium-, and low-altitude interception, close-support
and dive-bombing roles.

The Hayate was conceived in the Spring of 1942, at a
time when the J.A.A.F. was experiencing a series of
easy victories. The Type 1 Fighter, or Hayabusa, was
establishing an impressive score of "kills" over the
semi-obsolescent Allied fighters by which it was
opposed, but the J.A.A.F. was sufficiently realistic to
see that its ascendancy could not be maintained
indefinitely unless superior warplanes were introduced.
The Type 2 Shoki interceptor was being readied for
combat at this time, but this new aircraft was restricted
in application, and a "third generation" penetration
fighter would obviously be demanded for what might
well be years of conflict ahead. Nakajima, anxious to
consolidate their position as the principal supplier of
single-seat fighters to the J.A.A.F., were successful in
obtaining a development contract for the new warplane which was allocated the Kitai designation Ki.84.
The specification demanded the manoeuvrability of
the Ki.43 Hayabusa coupled with the speed and climb
of the Ki.44 Shoki, and to these qualities was to be
added a heavy armament. In fact, the J.A.A.F.
required a fighter superior to those that intelligence
reports and study of contemporary western aviation
journals indicated were under development in the
U.S.A. and Britain.

Design work began in 1942 under the direction of
Engineer T. Koyama, and the basic design work
applied to the earlier Nakajima Ki.62 light fighter, a
project for a Ki.44 replacement powered by a liquid-
cooled engine and abandoned in favour of Kawasaki's
Ki.61 Hien, was utilized. This earlier project contributed the exceptionally fine lines which were to
characterize the Hayate, together with the tail surfaces
and the all-round-vision cockpit canopy. The power
plant selected for the new fighter was a J.A.A.F.
version of the Navy's NK9A Homare, an eighteen-
cylinder two-row radial air-cooled engine rated at
1,850 h.p. and produced by Nakajima as the Ha.45.
The all-metal airframe structure followed the common Japanese practice of building the wing integral
with the centre fuselage in order to save the weight

of heavy attachment points, but the fighter was very
much sturdier than its predecessors. The fuselage was
of oval-section with flush-riveted stressed skin, and
the two-spar wing carried metal-framed, fabric-
covered ailerons with hydraulically-operated Fowler
flaps inboard. Fuel tanks aft of the cockpit and in the
wing, inboard of the main undercarriage members,
had a total capacity of 183 Imp. gal. (220 U.S. gal.), and
the pilot was protected by a 70-mm. armoured windscreen and by 13-mm. armour plate in the cockpit
floor and aft. All three undercarriage members were
hydraulically retractable, armament comprised two
12.7-mm. Type 103 machine guns in the forward
fuselage upper decking with 350 r.p.g., and two
wing-mounted 20-mm. Type 5 cannon with 150 r.p.g.,
and underwing racks were provided for two 550-lb.
bombs or auxiliary fuel tanks.

Work on the prototypes progressed rapidly, and the
first of these was completed in March 1943. The first
prototypes were assigned to the J.A.A.F. for service
testing under the direction of combat-experienced
pilots, and all modifications recommended were
incorporated in the fourth prototype which, in tests
conducted at Tachikawa by Lieut. Funabashi, revealed a maximum speed of 394 m.p.h. at 21,800 ft.
During dive tests the aircraft attained a speed of
496 m.p.h. at which point the pilot experienced
difficulty with his oxygen mask.

While prototype construction was progressing the
power plant itself was being developed for production,
and although the Homare had already displayed
several design faults and offered a number of maintenance problems, it was believed that such deficiencies
could be eradicated while production built up
momentum. Experimental models of the engine had
been test run as early as May 1941, but few Homare
power plants were available for installation until
August 1943, and experimental production did not
commence until late in that year at Nakajima's
Musashi engine factory, full-scale production beginning in April 1944 as the Type 4 engine with a rating
of 1,900 h.p. Production at Musashi was hampered
by many setbacks which were mostly the result of
inadequate preparation. In consequence, when full-
scale production was ordered, severe shortages of jigs,
tools and skilled personnel became apparent. Only
sixty-six Ha.45 engines were completed in 1943, and a
production rate exceeding one hundred engines per
month could not be attained until April 1944.

Production of the Hayate had begun at Nakajima's
Ota plant in August 1943, rapidly ousting the Ki.43
Hayabusa as the principle fighter built at the factory,
and supplanting the earlier fighter at Ota completely
in September 1944. The first production model was
the Type 4 Fighter Model 1A (Ki.84-Ia) with the
Ha.45/11 engine and an armament of two fuselage-
mounted 12.7-mm. guns and two 20-mm. wing guns,
and this version of the Hayate made its operational
début against the U.S.A.A.F. in August 1944 with the
22nd Fighter Sentai based at Hankow, China. The
introduction of the Hayate to this theatre soon proved

costly to the U.S. 13th Air Force, and in addition to the penetration and interception roles, the aircraft was used as a fighter-bomber and dive-bomber. The detachable racks installed under each wing outboard of the gun ports normally carried either 66-lb. or 110-lb. bombs for dive-bombing, the dive normally being made at an altitude of 5,000 feet, the bombs being released at 2,000 ft. at an airspeed of 340 m.p.h., the diving angle being 60° with wing flaps lowered 5°.

The Hayate proved simple to fly and pilots with a minimum of training could be assigned to the type, the majority of the new pilots converting to the fighter with only some two hundred flying hours, a training level regarded as decidedly sub-standard by the Allies but one tolerated by the J.A.A.F. in order to maintain an adequate supply of pilots. However, the generally attractive flying characteristics of the Hayate were in part responsible for a high training attrition rate, for the fighter did possess certain poor control characteristics, and the pilot unfamiliar with these idiosyncrasies could find himself in difficulties. Taxying and ground handling were generally poor, and once the tail came up pressure had to be maintained on the starboard rudder pedal to counteract a tendency to swing to port. In flight the controls were somewhat sluggish by comparison with those of the Hayabusa, and the elevators tended to be heavy at all speeds. The ailerons were excellent up to about 300 m.p.h., after which they too became rather heavy, and the rudder was mushy at low speeds for angles near neutral, but most pilots became accustomed to these characteris-

tics. Climb rate was exceptionally good, 16,400 feet being attained in 5 min. 54 sec., or 6 min. 26 sec. with maximum internal fuel, providing the Hayate with a decided edge over opposing Allied fighters, although this advantage was to be lost later as the performance of the Type 4 fell away as a result of slipping control of production quality.

The model 1A Hayate was followed in production by the Model 1B (Ki.84-Ib) armed with four 20-mm. cannon and the Model 1C (Ki.84-Ic) with two 20-mm. and two 30-mm. weapons, the latter being mounted in the wings. Unfortunately for the J.A.A.F. the performances of the various Hayate models varied greatly from aircraft to aircraft owing to the general lowering of manufacturing standards as the war progressed, and decreases in Ha.45 power ratings. Other problems encountered resulted from the poorly-designed hydraulic and fuel pressure systems, untrustworthy brakes, and inadequately hardened metal in the landing gear struts which were liable to snap at any time. Thus, many Hayate fighters were written off as a result of crash landings after a mission despite having suffered no damage in action! Even more difficulties were provided by the power plant which continually suffered from drops in fuel and oil pressure, limiting the delivered power and seriously reducing performance. The Ha.45 also offered more than its share of maintenance problems which, together with the Hayate's other shortcomings, placed an impossible burden on maintenance personnel in the field, this steadily reducing the number of fighters available for operations.

A late-production Ki.84-Ia Hayate. The Hayate was one of the most formidable fighters to be introduced by the J.A.A.F. during the Pacific conflict, but the gradual lowering of manufacturing standards adversely affected performance during the final stages of the war.

FINISH AND INSIGNIA: *The Ki.84-Ia Hayate illustrated on the opposite page belonged to the J.A.A.F.'s 52nd Fighter Sentai which was activated in April 1944 and participated in the Battle of Leyte in the Philippines. The upper surfaces were finished in a jungle green and khaki dapple and the under surfaces were natural metal. The Hinomaru on the upper wing surfaces and fuselage sides was outlined in white, and the Sentai marking on the vertical tail surfaces was painted in yellow to indicate the 3rd Chutai. The airscrew spinner was also yellow.*

After proving the capabilities of the Hayate in China, the 22nd Fighter Sentai was moved to the Philippines where it was joined by the 1st, 11th, 21st, 51st, 52nd, 55th, 200th and 246th, all similarly equipped, and pitted against the massive American forces in these islands in the decisive battles at Leyte. Although the Hayates again proved themselves formidable foes, their importance in the Philippines steadily declined as a result of combat losses, lack of supplies and maintenance problems, but they fought well against a variety of American fighter types, including the U.S. Navy's F6F Hellcats, the U.S. Marine Corps' F4U Corsairs and the U.S.A.A.F.'s P-38 Lightnings. Hayate-equipped units participating in the Battle of Okinawa were the 101st, 102nd and 103rd Hikō Sentais.

The production Hayate was powered by a never-ending succession of Type 4 engine models, commencing with the Ha.45/11 which was later replaced by the Ha.45/12 and Ha.45/21, but late production fighters were ultimately fitted with the Ha.45/23, a low-pressure fuel-injection model of the Ha.45/21 intended to overcome the fuel pressure difficulties experienced with the earlier engines. While the problems that

plagued production of the engine were serious enough in themselves, Musashi became the most frequently bombed factory in the Japanese aircraft industry, and B-29 Superfortresses of the U.S. 20th Air Force were to hit the plant on twelve occasions between November 24, 1944 and August 8, 1945. But despite aerial attacks, Musashi somehow managed to maintain production of the Ha.45 until April 20, 1945, when all assembly operations came to a standstill, these being transferred to an underground plant at Asakawa where production continued until the end of the war. Production of the Ha.45 engine at Musashi and Asakawa to the end of the Pacific War was to total 4,066 units, substantially less than the J.A.A.F. orders placed during the period. Production of the Ha.45 was also initiated at Nakajima's Hamamatsu engine works in January 1945, this plant completing 353 engines, and plans for the engine to be manufactured by Kawasaki were prepared but had not materialised by the time the conflict ended.

While engine production lagged, airframe production increased steadily until the Hayate was numerically the most important fighter in production. A pre-production programme began in 1943 with twenty-four machines being delivered in that year, this climbing to 1,670 aircraft in 1944 and a further 992 up to August 1945. These figures were far below J.A.A.F. requirements for the type. Orders for 1944 alone totalled 2,565 machines, almost a thousand more than actually delivered. The difference between the quantity ordered and the number delivered was partly accounted for by the failure of sub-contractors to maintain an adequate supply of components, but Allied air attacks on Japanese industry had an increasingly important effect during the last months of the year. The first direct attack on the Hayate assembly plant came on February 10, 1945, when eighty-four B-29 Superfortresses seriously damaged Nakajima's Ota facilities, damaging or destroying some seventy-four Hayates on the assembly lines. Two attacks by U.S. carrier aircraft further damaged the plant to such an extent that the dispersal programme had to be accelerated with, in consequence, a sharp drop in production.

Production of the Hayate also began at Nakajima's Utsunomiya airframe factory in May 1944, this facility producing 727 fighters by July 1945, less than half the 1,606 scheduled during this period, bringing total Nakajima production of the Hayate to 3,413 machines. Construction of the Hayate was also assigned to the Mansyu Hikoki Seizo K.S. (Manchurian Aircraft Manufacturing Company) at Harbin, Manchuria, in the spring of 1945, more than a hundred being built to raise the total production of the Hayate by all factories to 3,577.

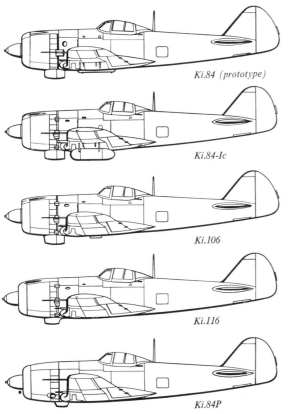

Ki.84 (prototype)

Ki.84-Ic

Ki.106

Ki.116

Ki.84P

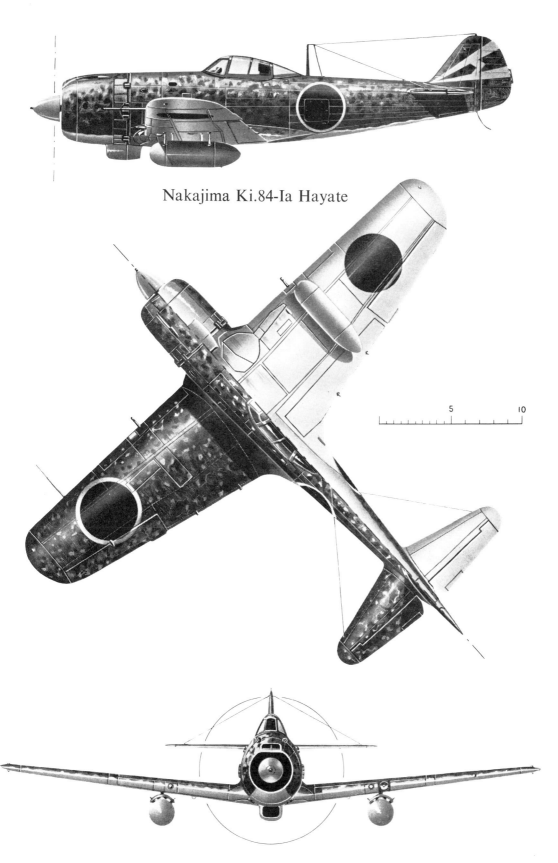

Nakajima Ki.84-Ia Hayate

(*Left and above*) *The Ki.84-Ic featured twin 30-mm. wing-mounted cannon in place of the earlier 20-mm. weapons.*

While manufacture of the standard Hayate continued, experimental work was being undertaken on several projects intended to improve the fighter's performance and, simultaneously, make more extensive use of non-strategic materials. It was hoped that these new models could be introduced into Hayate-equipped squadrons without demanding the retraining of the personnel. Experimental production of a Hayate variant with wooden components was attempted at the Ota factory in the early summer of 1945 as the Type 4 Fighter Model 2 (Ki.84-II). Wooden sub-assemblies were constructed at the dispersed Tanuma plant and delivered to Ota for final assembly. These included all-wood rear fuselage sections, fittings, control rods and wingtips, the remainder of the aircraft being built in the conventional manner. The Model 2 performed well under test, but the extensive use of wood in place of light alloys increased the total weight well beyond expectations, and the project was abandoned. The next Hayate project was the Model 3 (Ki.84-III), an adaptation of the Model 1 powered by an advanced 2,000 h.p. version of the Ha.45 fitted with a turbo-supercharger and known as the Ha.45ru. It was hoped that the installation of the turbo-supercharged engine would boost the service ceiling of the Hayate sufficiently to permit it to intercept Superfortresses with ease, but no Model 3 fighters had been completed when Japan capitulated.

At one time plans had been prepared for the Tachikawa Hikoki K.K. to build the standard Hayate, but although these did not see fruition, the company undertook the redesign of the entire structure of the fighter for wooden construction as the Ki.106, and

late in 1944 the construction of three prototypes of the wooden Hayate was subcontracted to Ohji Koku (Prince Aircraft) which concern, using largely unskilled labour, completed the aircraft at Ebetsu, the actual design work involved in the conversion from metal to wood having been undertaken by Engineers Shinagawa and Nakagawa. The Ki.106 retained the external characteristics of the normal Hayate, apart from minor revisions of the vertical tail surface contours, and a superlative external finish was obtained by applying a thick coat of polish to the plywood skin. The first prototype Ki.106 was powered by an Ha.45/21 engine and was flown for the first time in July 1945 by Major Yasuhiko Kuroe, one of the most prominent J.A.A.F. combat pilots. The use of wood had raised normal loaded weight to 8,598 lb., an increase of some 600 lb., and this had an adverse effect on climb rate and manoeuvrability, an altitude of 26,240 ft. being attained in 13 min. 5 sec., this being 1 min. 25 sec. more than was required by the standard Hayate, but owing to its exceptionally fine finish, the Ki.106's maximum speed of 384 m.p.h. at 24,000 ft. compared closely, and studies were initiated immediately to determine means of reducing the fighter's weight.

During trials with the first prototype, the plywood skinning failed in flight and began to rip away from the wing surfaces. The aircraft was landed safely, however, and modifications made in order to anchor the skin more firmly. The first prototype had carried an armament of four 20-mm. cannon, but the second prototype, which was flown to Fukuo, near Tokyo, on August 13, 1945, carried only two cannon to reduce weight, although flight trials had only just commenced when the end of the war brought with it the end of development of the Ki.106.

A further attempt to conserve light alloys in Hayate production had been made earlier by Nakajima who had attempted to make use of steel in as many sub-assemblies as possible. Assigned the designation

One of the Ki.84-Ia Hayate fighters evaluated by the South-West Pacific Area Technical Air Intelligence Unit. Allied pilots were impressed by the handling characteristics and performance of the fighter.

Ki.113 during the autumn of 1944, the fighter employed steel sheet skinning, and the cockpit section, ribs and bulkheads were made of carbon steel. The prototype retained the Ha.45 engine and an armament of four 20-mm. cannon, and was nearing completion in January 1945. However, difficulties experienced in manufacturing the steel sections and, as might have been expected, a substantial increase in weight which would have seriously reduced the performance of the Ki.113 led to its abandonment without flight trials.

No effort on the part of Nakajima had been able to turn the Ha.45 into a thoroughly reliable power plant, and in view of the successful adaptation of the Kawasaki Ki.61-II Hien airframe to take the Mitsubishi Ha.112-II engine, the J.A.A.F. evinced interest in a suggestion that the Ha.45 problem might be solved by supplanting this with the Mitsubishi power plant in the Hayate. Orders were therefore issued to the Mansyu Hikoki to make a trial installation, and the Ha.112-II engine was accordingly installed in the fourth Ki-84-Ia airframe from the company's Harbin production line, the test machine being designated Ki.116. Rated at 1,500 h.p., the fourteen-cylinder Ha.112-II Type 4 (Ha.33/62) engine, an Army version of the Navy's Kinsei 62, was substantially lighter than the Ha.45 that it replaced. In consequence, the engine mounts had to be lengthened to maintain the c.g. position, and to compensate for this additional length, the tail surfaces had to be enlarged. A standard three-blade airscrew from a Mitsubishi Ki.46-III reconnaissance aircraft was fitted, and the Ki.116 proved to weigh 4,850 lb. empty—a 1,000 lb. reduction on the empty weight of the standard Ki.84-Ia! A further two hundred pounds could have been pared from the fighter by careful attention to detail design. Unfortunately for the J.A.A.F., the Ki.116 had only just entered the test phase at the time of the final collapse. In consequence, no detailed performance figures were recorded, although the performance of the Ki.116 approximated closely to that of the Ki.100,

The Ki.84-Ia compared favourably with the P-51H and P-47N, and could out-climb and out-manoeuvre both U.S.A.A.F. fighters.

and during its limited flight testing its pilots were extremely enthusiastic concerning its characteristics.

The Hayate had been designed primarily as a general-purpose and penetration fighter at a time when combat at the altitudes at which the B-29 Superfortresses operated had not been considered. By June 1945 the lowering of manufacturing standards had cut the climb rate of the fighter so severely that the Hayate was virtually impotent at altitudes above 30,000 feet. A conference was therefore held on the fourth of that month to determine means of adapting the Hayate as a specialised high altitude interceptor, and a direct result of this meeting was the launching of three new Hayate projects known respectively as the Ki.84R, Ki.84N and Ki.84P. Design work was started immediately, the highest possible priority being awarded the programme. The Ki.84R was based on the use of the vastly improved Army Ha.45/44 engine of 2,000 h.p. fitted with a mechanically-driven two-stage three-speed supercharger, while both the Ki.84N and Ki.84P were to utilise the powerful Nakajima Ha.219 (Ha.44/13), a 2,500 h.p. eighteen-cylinder two-row radial also built experimentally for the Navy as the NK11 series. The first test engines had been completed late in 1944, and development work was being rushed in order to make the power plant available for several advanced J.A.A.F. projects.

Design work on the Ki.84R was eighty per cent complete when the war ended, but neither the Ki.84N or Ki.84P attained more than the initial design stage. The Ki.84N, which had been assigned the Kitai number Ki.117, was to have featured a redesigned wing with a 16 sq. ft. increase in gross area, while the wing of the Ki.84P was to have had a gross area of 263.4 sq. ft.

During the closing stages of the Pacific War the Hayate was active over Okinawa, and in one sortie eleven Hayates of the 100th Fighter Sentai made a surprise attack on American airfields on Okinawa. This sortie, which took place on April 15, 1945, was extremely successful, severely damaging installations and destroying a substantial number of aircraft on the ground, but eight of the Hayates were destroyed, and another made a forced landing on a small islet near Kyushu. The Hayate was assigned to the defensive role over the Japanese home islands during the last weeks of the struggle, operating with the 10th Division responsible for the defence of the Tokyo area, and its importance as an interceptor largely prevented its use

in the suicide role, a fate which befell so many other J.A.A.F. types. Hayate units employed for home defence were the 47th, the 73rd, the 111th, the 112th and the 246th.

The Hayate typified the changing fighter requirements of the J.A.A.F. during the war years. Its original concept as an advanced aircraft capable of maintaining the air superiority gained by the J.A.A.F. during the opening phases of the conflict was nullified by the technical advances made in Allied aircraft sent to the Pacific to oppose it. Although never completely outclassed by its opponents, the Hayate spent most of its operational life in the defensive role and, thus, at a constant disadvantage. There was rarely an opportunity to use the Hayate in the role for which it was best suited, offensive penetration, but during the final phases of the Pacific War it was numerically the most important J.A.A.F. fighter, and certainly the most potent available in quantity. As such, it is probably the best remembered Japanese aircraft of the war insofar as the Allied pilots who participated in the final assault on Japan are concerned.

Nakajima Type 4 Model 1A Hayate (Ki.84-Ia)

Dimensions :	Span, 36 ft. 10½ in. ; length, 32 ft. 6½ in. ; height, 11 ft. 1¼ in. ; wing area, 226 sq. ft.
Armament :	Two 12.7 mm. Type 103 machine guns with 350 r.p.g. in the fuselage and two 20-mm. Type 5 cannon with 150 r.p.g. in the wings, plus a maximum bomb load of up to 1,100 lb. on underwing racks.
Power Plant :	One Nakajima (Ha.45/11) Type 4 eighteen-cylinder radial air-cooled engine rated at 1,900 h.p. for take-off, 1,790 h.p. at 5,900 ft., and 1,700 h.p. at 21,000 ft. Maximum internal fuel capacity, 183 Imp. gal. (220 U.S. gal.)
Weights :	Empty, 5,864 lb. ; normal loaded, 7,965 lb. ; maximum overload, 9,194 lb.
Performance :	Maximum speed, 388 m.p.h. at 19,680 ft. ; maximum cruising speed, 254 m.p.h. ; range (internal fuel), 1,025 mls. at 178 m.p.h., (maximum external fuel), 1,815 mls. at 173 m.p.h. ; range at maximum cruising speed, 780 mls. at 1,500 ft. ; time to 16,400 ft., 5 min. 54 sec., to 26,240 ft., 11 min. 40 sec. ; service ceiling, 34,450 ft.

Although externally similar to the Ki.84, the Ki.106 (below) had an entirely redesigned structure for wooden construction.

The Focke-Wulf Fw 190V1 (FO+LY), first flown on June 1, 1939.

THE FOCKE-WULF Fw 190

No combat aircraft has ever achieved perfection, but at the time of its début the Fw 190 probably came as near to this elusive goal as any fighter. It was a brilliant design in which weight consciousness and simplicity were keynotes, although they had not been allowed to affect structural strength. But this beautifully proportioned fighter was not merely a pilot's aeroplane : it had been conceived with a careful eye to the problems of both produceability and maintenance in the field. It was highly praised, both by its pilots and by their opponents, and its appearance in action gave the Luftwaffe a decided, if temporary, ascendancy over its adversaries. Its ease of control and the incredible aileron turns which it performed at speeds which would have torn the wings from most of its contemporaries commanded immediate respect from R.A.F. fighter pilots and alarm at Britain's Air Ministry.

When, in June 1942, a Luftwaffe deserter fortuitously presented the Allies with his Fw 190A fighter intact, the detailed examination of this remarkable product of the Focke-Wulf Flugzeugbau profoundly influenced fighter thinking in Britain. It directly result in the issue of specification F.2/43 to which was designed the Hawker Fury, embodying numerous features directly copied from the Fw 190A, and F.19/43 which produced the Folland Fo.118 fighter project, also owing much to the design of the Fw 190A. What higher tribute could have been paid to what was undoubtedly the finest warplane to which Germany gave birth.

In the autumn of 1937 the Reichluftministerium placed an order with the Focke-Wulf Flugzeugbau for the design development of a new single-seat fighter to supplement the Messerschmitt Bf 109—a second "iron in the fire" as R.L.M. officials referred to the order at the time. The contract was placed with Focke-Wulf primarily because this company was not extensively committed to the development of other combat aircraft and possessed a highly qualified design team headed by Dipl.Ing.Kurt Tank. Tank's design team prepared two proposals ; one based upon the use of the Daimler-Benz DB601 liquid-cooled engine and the other upon the use of a large air-cooled radial engine. At that time the radial engine was not favoured as a fighter power plant owing to its drag and the restrictions that its bulk placed upon forward view during taking-off and landing, and, in consequence, General Ernst Udet's decision to proceed with the development of the radial-engined fighter came as a profound surprise to Tank and his colleagues.

Allocated the R.L.M. type number "Fw 190", detail design work on the new fighter project was initiated in the summer of 1938. The design team, directed by Kurt Tank, was supervised by Oberingenieur Blaser, who had been primarily responsible for the design of the Fw 159 single-seat fighter, which had been built to compete with the Bf 109, and the Fw 187 Falke (Falcon) twin-engined fighter, which had also been designed originally as a single-seater. Work on the Fw 190 progressed rapidly and within ten months the first prototype was being readied for flight testing. It was a combination of simple yet sturdy construction, the underlying theory of the entire design being the reduction of field maintenance time to a minimum combined with the possibility of widespread manufacture by dispersed sub-contracting plants. Essentially a low-wing monoplane with a wide-track undercarriage, it possessed aesthetically appealing contours in which the blending of the bulky radial engine was little short of a masterpiece of ingenuity.

The Fw 190V5k, the third prototype, flown in the spring of 1940.

Fw 190V1

Fw 190V2

Fw 190A-1

Fw 190A-3

Fw 190A-4/U8

Fw190A-5/U15

Fw 190A-8/R3

Fw 190A-8/U1

The first prototype, the Fw 190V1, was flown on June 1, 1939, by Focke-Wulf's chief test pilot, H. Sander, immediately proving itself to be a delightful machine in the air with beautifully balanced controls and an excellent turn of speed. The prototype was powered by a 1,550 h.p. B.M.W. 139 radial engine with fan cooling housed in a closely fitting, low-drag cowling. Its wings spanned 31 ft. 2 in. and had an area of 160 sq. ft., and loaded weight was 3,968 lb. After a series of only five flight tests the Fw 190V1 was transferred to the Luftwaffe test centre at Rechlin, where the prototype was flown by such well-known test pilots as Franke, Thoenes and Beauvais, all of whom were highly enthusiastic about the fighter's characteristics. During these tests a maximum level speed of 370 m.p.h. was attained.

In the meantime a second prototype, the Fw 190V2, was being completed. This differed from its predecessor in having a large spinning nose ring attached to the airscrew hub and experimental armament comprising one 7.9-mm. MG 17 and one 13-mm. MG 131, both firing through the airscrew arc. The Fw 190V2 weighed 4,410 lb. loaded and was first flown in October 1939. It was flown both with and without the cooling fan for the B.M.W. 139 engine, but without the fan the engine overheated quickly. Early in 1940 Marshal Goering visited the Focke-Wulf factory and inspected the Fw 190V2. He was very impressed and told Tank that he "must turn these new fighters out like so many hot rolls!" After the inspection the Fw 190V2 was flown to Tarnewitz for armament tests and then transferred to Rechlin, where, after some fifty hours of flight testing, it crashed when the crankshaft broke.

A third prototype, the Fw 190V3, had also been under construction, but in June 1939 further work on this machine was stopped and development of the Fw 190V4 abandoned as the entirely new B.M.W. 801 engine was giving satisfactory results during bench running and held promise of more power than was within the capabilities of the B.M.W. 139. Therefore no further prototype construction work was to be undertaken until the new power plant became available for installation. The B.M.W. 801 was a considerably heavier engine than its predecessor, although the overall dimensions differed little, and necessitated a stiffer engine mount and extensive structural strengthening. The re-design involved gave Blaser an opportunity to rectify one of the few faults that had manifested themselves in the first prototype. Test pilots had objected to proximity of the engine to the cockpit which resulted in extremely high cabin temperatures, sometimes reaching 55°C. (131°F.), which, as Sander said, felt as though he had his "feet in the fireplace". In addition, exhaust gases

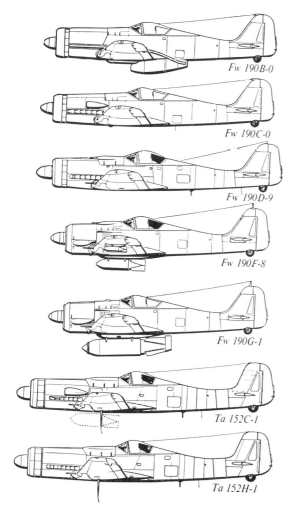

Fw 190B-0

Fw 190C-0

Fw 190D-9

Fw 190F-8

Fw 190G-1

Ta 152C-1

Ta 152H-1

radial engine while taxying. The Fw 190V5g was completed soon after the V5k. It proved to be about 6 m.p.h. slower than the smaller prototype but the larger wing area was beneficial to manœuvrability. This prototype, incidentally, was later to be used to test a variety of engines, including the B.M.W. 801D and E, the Jumo 213A and F, and the DB 603A and G. The Fw 190V6 was similar to the V5g and was flown early in October 1940.

While awaiting the delivery of the B.M.W. 801C engines for installation in the V5k and V5g, preparations had been made for the construction of a pre-production batch of eighteen Fw 190A-0 fighters for service evaluation. The first seven of these (Werk Nrs. 0008 to 0014 inclusive) were fitted with the short span wings used by the Fw 190V5k, but the remaining pre-production machines and the production model, the Fw 190A-1, were fitted with the wings of larger span. At the beginning of the winter of 1940-41, deliveries of the pre-production Fw 190A-0 fighters to Luftwaffe service test centres commenced, and by the end of the year the first production Fw 190A-1 fighters had begun to leave the assembly lines at Focke-Wulf's Bremen and Hamburg plants.

Most of the Fw 190A-0s were sent to Rechlin-Roggenthin for pre-service tests. During intensive flight testing it was discovered that the engine cowlings frequently flew off at high speeds, and internally stressed cowlings with stronger locks were requested. Some re-stressing was also proved necessary, and it was found that above 250 m.p.h. the cockpit canopy could not be released in an emergency. The latter problem was solved by fitting two standard 20-mm. cartridges which blew the rear end of the canopy backward far enough to let the slipstream get under it and pull it away. Pilots also complained that there was a serious risk of hitting the tail assembly when baling out and requested the fitting of some form of ejector seat which would throw them clear. However, in view of the serious weight penalty imposed by an ejector seat, the engineers refused to install this equipment, resulting in a serious disagreement between the test pilots and the manufacturers. The B.M.W. 801 engine tended to overheat, but this fault was rectified by improvements to the cooling fan and, in general, the Fw 190A was highly praised by the test pilots. They particularly favoured the wide-track undercarriage which tremendously improved ground stability as compared with the Bf 109, but one of the

found their way into the cockpit and necessitated the continuous use of an oxygen mask. Therefore in the next prototypes the cockpit was relocated further aft, a move also suggested by the c.g. problems presented by the heavier engine.

The next two prototypes were designated Fw 190V5k (the "k" suffix indicating *klein* or small) and Fw 190V5g (the "g" indicating *gross* or large). The V5k was fitted with similar wings to those of the first two prototypes, but the V5g's wings spanned 34 ft. 5½ in. and had an area of 196.98 sq. ft. Both prototypes were powered by the B.M.W. 801C engine providing 1,600 h.p. for take-off, and both were fitted with an armament of four 7.9-mm. MG 17 machine-guns, two installed above the engine and two in the wing roots. The Fw 190V5k was flown during the early spring of 1940, but was destroyed towards the end of August when the aircraft collided with a tractor during a take-off—the first accident caused by the limited forward view over the large

The initial production model, the Fw 190A-1.

E

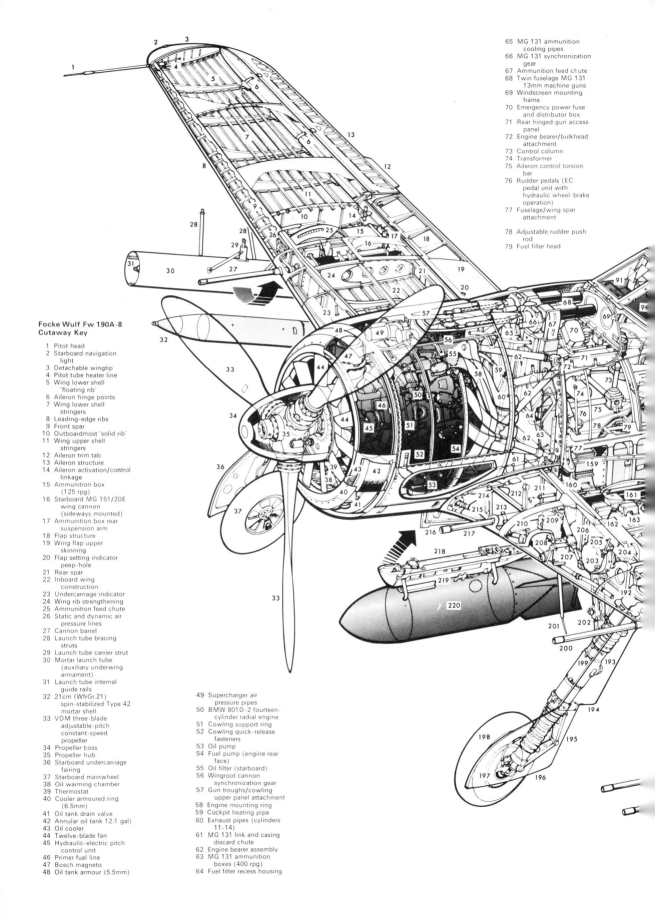

Focke Wulf Fw 190A-8 Cutaway Key

1 Pitot head
2 Starboard navigation light
3 Detachable wingtip
4 Pitot tube heater line
5 Wing lower shell 'floating rib'
6 Aileron hinge points
7 Wing lower shell stringers
8 Leading-edge ribs
9 Front spar
10 Outboardmost 'solid rib'
11 Wing upper shell stringers
12 Aileron trim tab
13 Aileron structure
14 Aileron activation/control linkage
15 Ammunition box (125 rpg)
16 Starboard MG 151/20E wing cannon (sideways mounted)
17 Ammunition box rear suspension arm
18 Flap structure
19 Wing flap upper skinning
20 Flap setting indicator peep-hole
21 Rear spar
22 Inboard wing construction
23 Undercarriage indicator
24 Wing rib strengthening
25 Ammunition feed chute
26 Static and dynamic air pressure lines
27 Cannon barrel
28 Launch tube bracing struts
29 Launch tube carrier strut
30 Mortar launch tube (auxiliary underwing armament)
31 Launch tube internal guide rails
32 21cm (WfrGr.21) spin-stabilized Type 42 mortar shell
33 VDM three-blade adjustable-pitch constant-speed propeller
34 Propeller boss
35 Propeller hub
36 Starboard undercarriage fairing
37 Starboard mainwheel
38 Oil warming chamber
39 Thermostat
40 Cooler armoured ring (6.5mm)
41 Oil tank drain valve
42 Annular oil tank 12.1 gal)
43 Oil cooler
44 Twelve-blade fan
45 Hydraulic-electric pitch control unit
46 Primer fuel line
47 Bosch magneto
48 Oil tank armour (5.5mm)

49 Supercharger air pressure pipes
50 BMW 801D-2 fourteen-cylinder radial engine
51 Cowling support ring
52 Cowling quick-release fasteners
53 Oil pump
54 Fuel pump (engine rear face)
55 Oil filter (starboard)
56 Wingroot cannon synchronization gear
57 Gun troughs/cowling upper panel attachment
58 Engine mounting ring
59 Cockpit heating pipe
60 Exhaust pipes (cylinders 11-14)
61 MG 131 link and casing discard chute
62 Engine bearer assembly
63 MG 131 ammunition boxes (400 rpg)
64 Fuel filter recess housing

65 MG 131 ammunition cooling pipes
66 MG 131 synchronization gear
67 Ammunition feed chute
68 Twin fuselage MG 131 13mm machine guns
69 Windscreen mounting frame
70 Emergency power fuse and distributor box
71 Rear hinged gun access panel
72 Engine bearer/bulkhead attachment
73 Control column
74 Transformer
75 Aileron control torsion bar
76 Rudder pedals (EC pedal unit with hydraulic wheel-brake operation)
77 Fuselage/wing spar attachment
78 Adjustable rudder push rod
79 Fuel filler head

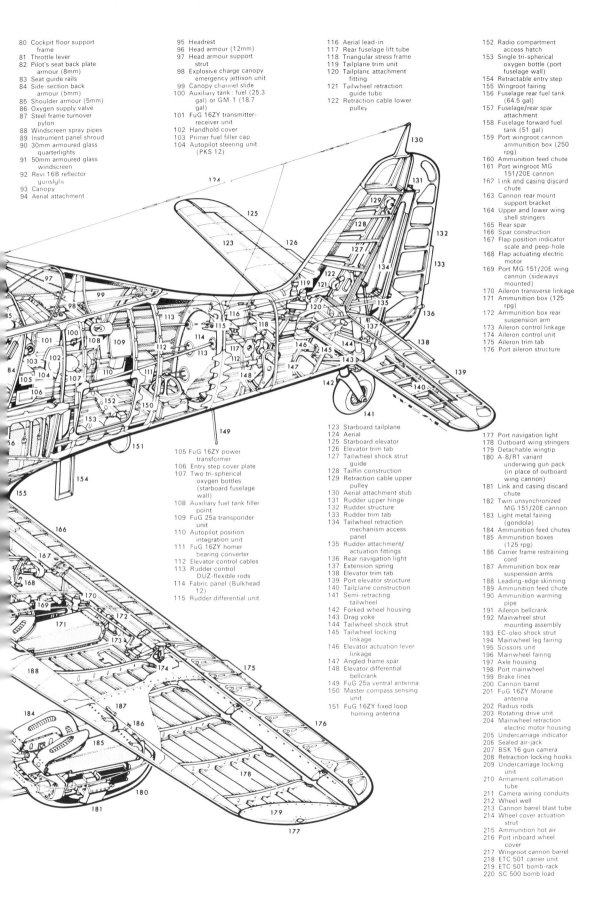

80 Cockpit floor support frame
81 Throttle lever
82 Pilot's seat back plate armour (8mm)
83 Seat guide rails
84 Side-section back armour (5mm)
85 Shoulder armour (5mm)
86 Oxygen supply valve
87 Steel frame turnover pylon
88 Windscreen spray pipes
89 Instrument panel shroud
90 30mm armoured glass quarterlights
91 50mm armoured glass windscreen
92 Revi 16B reflector gunsight
93 Canopy
94 Aerial attachment

95 Headrest
96 Head armour (12mm)
97 Head armour support strut
98 Explosive charge canopy emergency jettison unit
99 Canopy channel slide
100 Auxiliary tank: fuel (25.3 gal) or GM-1 (18.7 gal)
101 FuG 16ZY transmitter-receiver unit
102 Handhold cover
103 Primer fuel filler cap
104 Autopilot steering unit (PKS 12)

105 FuG 16ZY power transformer
106 Entry step cover plate
107 Two tri-spherical oxygen bottles (starboard fuselage wall)
108 Auxiliary fuel tank filler point
109 FuG 25a transponder unit
110 Autopilot position integration unit
111 FuG 16ZY homer bearing converter
112 Elevator control cables
113 Rudder control DUZ-flexible rods
114 Fabric panel (Bulkhead 12)
115 Rudder differential unit

116 Aerial lead-in
117 Rear fuselage lift tube
118 Triangular stress frame
119 Tailplane trim unit
120 Tailplane attachment fitting
121 Tailwheel retraction guide tube
122 Retraction cable lower pulley

123 Starboard tailplane
124 Aerial
125 Starboard elevator
126 Elevator trim tab
127 Tailwheel shock strut guide
128 Tailfin construction
129 Retraction cable upper pulley
130 Aerial attachment stub
131 Rudder upper hinge
132 Rudder structure
133 Rudder trim tab
134 Tailwheel retraction mechanism access panel
135 Rudder attachment/ actuation fittings
136 Rear navigation light
137 Extension spring
138 Elevator trim tab
139 Port elevator structure
140 Tailplane construction
141 Semi-retracting tailwheel
142 Forked wheel housing
143 Drag yoke
144 Tailwheel shock strut
145 Tailwheel locking linkage
146 Elevator actuation lever linkage
147 Angled frame spar
148 Elevator differential bellcrank
149 FuG 25a ventral antenna
150 Master compass sensing unit
151 FuG 16ZY fixed loop homing antenna

152 Radio compartment access hatch
153 Single tri-spherical oxygen bottle (port fuselage wall)
154 Retractable entry step
155 Wingroot fairing
156 Fuselage rear fuel tank (64.5 gal)
157 Fuselage/rear spar attachment
158 Fuselage forward fuel tank (51 gal)
159 Port wingroot cannon ammunition box (250 rpg)
160 Ammunition feed chute
161 Port wingroot MG 151/20E cannon
162 Link and casing discard chute
163 Cannon rear mount support bracket
164 Upper and lower wing shell stringers
165 Rear spar
166 Spar construction
167 Flap position indicator scale and peep-hole
168 Flap actuating electric motor
169 Port MG 151/20E wing cannon (sideways mounted)
170 Aileron transverse linkage
171 Ammunition box (125 rpg)
172 Ammunition box rear suspension arm
173 Aileron control linkage
174 Aileron control unit
175 Aileron trim tab
176 Port aileron structure

177 Port navigation light
178 Outboard wing stringers
179 Detachable wingtip
180 A-8/R1 variant underwing gun pack (in place of outboard wing cannon)
181 Link and casing discard chute
182 Twin unsynchronized MG 151/20E cannon
183 Light metal fairing (gondola)
184 Ammunition feed chutes
185 Ammunition boxes (125 rpg)
186 Carrier frame restraining cord
187 Ammunition box rear suspension arms
188 Leading-edge skinning
189 Ammunition feed chute
190 Ammunition warming pipe
191 Aileron bellcrank
192 Mainwheel strut mounting assembly
193 EC-oleo shock strut
194 Mainwheel leg fairing
195 Scissors unit
196 Mainwheel fairing
197 Axle housing
198 Port mainwheel
199 Brake lines
200 Cannon barrel
201 FuG 16ZY Morane antenna
202 Radius rods
203 Rotating drive unit
204 Mainwheel retraction electric motor housing
205 Undercarriage indicator
206 Sealed air-jack
207 BSK 16 gun camera
208 Retraction locking hooks
209 Undercarriage locking unit
210 Armament collimation tube
211 Camera wiring conduits
212 Wheel well
213 Cannon barrel blast tube
214 Wheel cover actuation strut
215 Ammunition hot air
216 Port inboard wheel cover
217 Wingroot cannon barrel
218 ETC 501 carrier unit
219 ETC 501 bomb-rack
220 SC 500 bomb load

(Above) The Fw 190A-4/U8 (in foreground).

(Above) The Fw 190A-4/R6 with WG 21 rocket-launching tubes, and (below) the second prototype Fw 190A-8/U1 dual-control trainer used by Jagdgeschwader 103 for training former Ju 87D pilots in July 1944.

unusual features of the fighter commented on by test pilots was the fact that, at high altitude and high speed, the B.M.W. 801 engine produced a pair of contrails which started immediately behind the exhaust exits and completely hid the wings.

By the late spring of 1941 the initial production batch of 100 Fw 190A-1 fighters had been completed, and these were being tested under operational conditions by Luftwaffe fighter units. The main complaint was inadequate fire power. This fault had already been foreseen, and the Fw 190A-1 had been succeeded by the A-2 on the production lines in which the MG 17 machine-guns mounted in the wing roots had been replaced by MG FF (Oerlikon-type) cannon of 20-mm. calibre. Loaded weight was increased from 7,055 lb. to 7,716 lb., and maximum speed was 389 m.p.h. at 18,000 feet. In May 1941, after tests at Rechlin-Roggenthin, the first Fw 190A-2s were delivered to a fighter unit based on Le Bourget, near Paris, but this fighter was to see its first action in July and August 1941 with Jagdgeschwader 26 based on the Channel coast and commanded by Adolf Galland, later to become General of Fighters. The Fw 190A immediately established its superiority over the Spitfire V which was then standard equipment with R.A.F. Fighter Command, a superiority that it was to maintain for nearly two years. While the Fw 190 could

not compete with the Spitfire's superlative turning circle, it could outfly its British opponent on almost every other count, and its superior speed enabled it to break off combat at will.

Under service conditions several faults manifested themselves. The slow-firing MG FF cannon that had replaced the wing-mounted MG 17s were not entirely satisfactory and armament was supplemented by a further pair of MG 17s. The B.M.W. 801C engine also gave a considerable amount of trouble. Therefore, after the completion of only a small number of Fw 190A-2 fighters, a new version was introduced on the assembly lines in the autumn of 1941. This, the Fw 190A-3, had the improved B.M.W. 801Dg engine of 1,700 h.p. for take-off, and a further increase in armament. The twin MG 17 machine-guns mounted over the engine were retained but the pair of 20-mm. MG FF cannon were moved outboard in the wing and their place taken in the wing roots by two faster-firing MG 151 cannon, also of 20-mm. calibre. The pilot was protected from frontal attack by the engine and a bulletproof windscreen and by 8-mm. and 14-mm. armour to the rear. By the end of 1941 a total of 210 Fw 190A-1, A-2, and A-3 fighters had been delivered.

An extensive production programme for the Fw 190 had been prepared, and gradually, over the next two years, numerous plants were brought into the programme. Those engaged in the assembly of the Fw 190 were to include the Focke-Wulf factories at Tutow/Mecklenburg and Marienburg, the Ago factory at Oschersleben, the Fieseler factory at Kassel-Waldau, and plants at Gydnia-Rahmel, Sorau/Silesia, Cottbus, Halberstadt, Neubrandenburg, Schwerin, Wismar, Einswarden and Eschwege, while many other plants produced components for this fighter. While production had been gaining momentum many of the pre-production Fw 190A-0 machines had been returned to Focke-Wulf for use as development prototypes, and by mid-1942 the Fw 190A-4 had made its appearance. This differed from its predecessor primarily in having a supplementary fuel injection system (MW 50) fitted to its B.M.W. 801D-2 engine which boosted power to 2,100 h.p. for short periods, and increased maximum speed to 416 m.p.h. at 20,600 feet. A tropicalized version for use in the Mediterranean theatre was the Fw 190A-4/Trop with tropical filters and with a rack for a 550-lb. bomb under the fuselage. The A-4/R6 had no MW 50 power-boost equipment but could carry a WG 21 rocket missile tube under each wing, and the A-4/U8 was a long-range fighter-bomber variant which carried a single 1,100-lb. bomb under the fuselage and a 300-litre drop-tank under each wing. Armament was reduced to two 20-mm. MG 151 cannon in the wing roots.

The year 1942 saw the delivery of 1,850 Fw 190A-3 and A-4 fighters and sixty-eight Fw 190A-4/Trop and A-4/U8 fighter-bombers to the Luftwaffe. The next production model, the Fw 190A-5, was essentially similar to the A-4 but featured a ree-dsigned engine

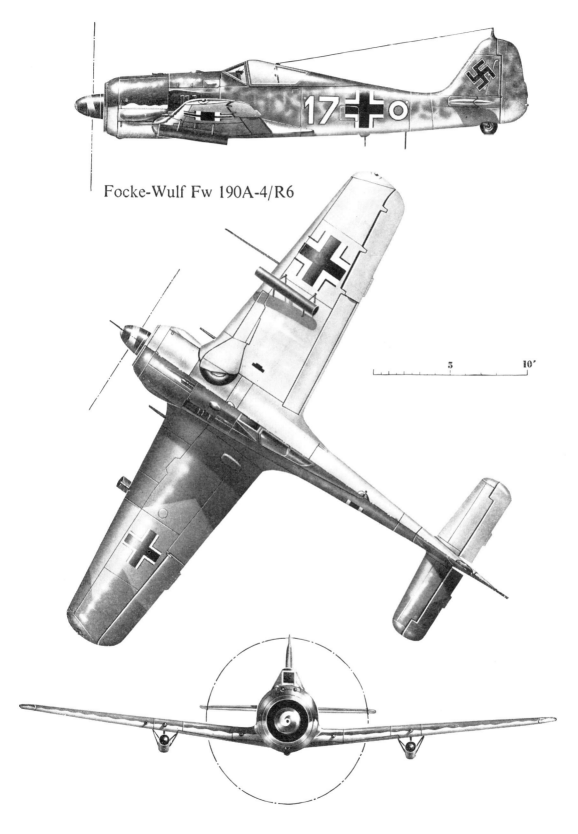

Focke-Wulf Fw 190A-4/R6

5   10'

The Fw 190D-9 which became operational with the Jagdgeschwader Udet in the winter of 1943–44.

mounting which resulted in the engine being moved forward 5.9 inches. By this time, the summer of 1943, night attacks on the Reich were assuming alarming proportions, and in July the Geschwader Herrmann (later expanded to three Geschwäder), led by an ex-bomber pilot, Major Herrmann, and staffed by other ex-bomber pilots, was equipped with a special night-fighter variant of the Fw 190A-5, the A-5/U2. The Fw 190A-5/U2 was equipped with anti-glare shields and flame-shrouders over the exhaust outlets, and was used for Wilde Sau (Wild Boar) tactics—a form of free-lance night fighting with the aid of searchlights. The successes achieved by Major Herrmann's pilots had resulted in their being considered as national heroes by September 1943, but with the onset of winter losses rose rapidly; and as wastage on the scale attained could not be continued indefinitely, the Fw 190A-5/U2 night fighters were withdrawn and the three Geschwäder re-trained for day fighting.

The Fw 190A-5/U3 was a fighter-bomber variant carrying two 550-lb. bombs and one 1,100-lb. bomb; the A-5/U8 was a long-range version with underwing auxiliary tanks; the A-5/U11 was a close-support fighter with the outboard MG FF cannon replaced by two 30-mm. MK 103 cannon which appeared in November 1943; the A-5/U15 was a special torpedo-fighter with armament reduced to two MG 151 cannon, a special rack to carry a single 2,090-lb. LT 950 torpedo and a long tailwheel yoke to enable the torpedo to clear the ground during take-off (three aircraft of this type were produced in November 1943, one having two 30-mm. MK 103 cannon fitted outboard), and the A-5/U16 bomber-destroyer with two 30-mm. MK 108 cannon in place of the outboard MG FF cannon.

The Fw 190F-9 "Panzerblitz" with racks for six R4M rockets under each wing.

The Fw 190A-6 was similar to the A-5 but the elderly MG FF cannon fitted outboard had finally given place to the later MG 151 cannon, and the A-6/R2 was a fighter-bomber variant with underwing racks for two 550-lb. bombs in place of the outboard cannon. The Fw 190A-7 denoted a further armament change, the paired machine-guns in the engine cowling becoming 13-mm. MG 131s, and a strengthened undercarriage. The A-7/R2 had 30-mm. MK 108 cannon fitted outboard and the A-7/R3 reverted to the standard armament but had shackles under the fuselage for a 300-litre tank.

The Fw 190A-8, introduced at the end of 1943, had its internal fuel tankage increased by 25 gallons; the A-8/R1 had four 20-mm. MG 151 cannon mounted in pairs underwing in place of the single outboard cannon; the A-8/R3 was a ground-support variant with two wing-mounted MK 103 cannon, and the A-8/R11 was a "dirty weather" fighter with special radio equipment and an automatic pilot (FuG 16Ze and FuG 25a). On January 23, 1944, the first of two prototypes of the Fw 190A-8/U1 was flown. This was a tandem two-seat development intended to train former Ju 87D dive-bomber pilots for ground-support tasks. The prototypes were to serve as patterns for forward maintenance units which were to rebuild a limited number of airframes of current Fw 190A-8 fighters for the training role. Only one such conversion was actually completed. The A-8/U11 was another fighter-bomber variant which carried one 550-lb. bomb and four 110-lb. bombs, and served with Ju 87Ds in mixed ground-assault units. The Fw 190A-9 differed from the A-8 only in having a B.M.W. 801F engine with different supercharger gear ratios and 2,000 h.p. available for take-off. The A-9/R11 was a "dirty weather" fighter similar to the A-8/R11 but fitted with a B.M.W. 801TS with an exhaust-driven turbo-supercharger. A similar engine was fitted in the Fw 190A-10 which carried a bomb load of 3,860 lb.

The Fw 190V13 was the prototype for the proposed Fw 190B series of high-altitude fighters. This had a pressurized cockpit and GM 1 power boost for its B.M.W. 801C engine. Nine further prototypes were built and fitted with Daimler-Benz DB 603 engines with large belly-mounted superchargers. The final six prototypes (the V18/U1, the V29 to V33) were intended for service evaluation as Fw 190B-0s. The Fw 190C was similar to the Fw 190B but lacked the supercharger and embodied an extended wing spanning 35 ft. 7 in. and having an area of 209.896 sq. ft. However, only one prototype for the Fw 190C was built, and further development of both B- and C-models was abandoned owing to the extraordinary promise shown by the Fw 190V17 and V19, prototypes for the Fw 190D series which was to be dubbed the "long-nose" when encountered over the Continent.

The small batches of Fw 190D-0 and D-1 fighters for service evaluation were delivered and tested during the spring and summer of 1943. These were powered by the Junkers Jumo 213A-1 twelve-cylinder inverted-Vee liquid-cooled engine rated at 1,776 h.p. for take-off, but this could be boosted to 2,240 h.p. by recourse to water/methanol injection. The Jumo had a nose radiator in a short annular duct, and it substantially improved the fighter's performance, maximum speed being 432 m.p.h. for the Fw 190D-1. To compensate for the lengthened nose, the rear fuselage was also lengthened, overall length becoming 33 ft. 11 in. The vertical fin was increased in width by $5\frac{1}{2}$ inches and in area by 2.5 sq. ft. The standard Fw 190A wings and tailplane were retained, and armament comprised two 13-mm. and two 20-mm. guns.

The first service version of the D-series, the Fw 190D-9, became operational with the Jagdgeschwader Udet stationed at Detmold in the winter of 1943–44, and soon R.A.F. fighters engaged on sweeps across the Channel were encountering increasing numbers of "long-noses". The Fw 190D-9 was even faster than the service test D-0 and D-1 fighters, attaining 440 m.p.h. at 37,000 feet. The Fw 190D-12 and D-13 were both ground-attack versions, the former having a 30-mm. MK 108 cannon in the engine Vee and firing through the airscrew hub, and the latter having a 30-mm. MK 103 in a similar position. Both of these sub-types were powered by the Jumo 213F which was not fitted with the three-stage supercharger and provided 2,060 h.p. for take-off.

In the autumn of 1943, with the Fw 190D's capabilities proven by flight testing, Kurt Tank decided that the series should be redesignated to give an indication of its originator. Thus the next variant in the Jumo-powered series was redesignated Ta 152A ("Ta" indicating "Tank"). However, development of the radial-engined Fw 190 had not ceased with the successful trials of the versions powered by the liquid-cooled engine, although all subsequent work was devoted to fighter-bomber, close-support and dive-bomber variants with the B.M.W. 801.

The designation "Fw 190E" was not allocated, and the next B.M.W. 801-powered version was the Fw 190F for close-support duties. Fitted with the strengthened undercarriage first employed by late production A-series machines, the Fw 190F saw the introduction of a new, clear-vision blown hood which was generally known as the "Galland Hood". This new hood was necessitated by the introduction of a new type of suspended armour plate to provide rear protection for the pilot's head. The Fw 190F-0 and F-1 were, like subsequent versions of this sub-type, powered by the B.M.W. 801D-2, and carried an armament of two 13-mm. MG 131 machine-guns and four 20-mm. MG 151 cannon. One SC 250 bomb rack for a 550-lb. bomb was fitted under the fuselage, and four SC 50 racks for 110-lb. bombs were fitted underwing. The Fw 190F-2 was similar but had the outboard cannon removed; the F-3 carried a built-in armament of only two MG 151 cannon; the F-8 carried additional radio equipment (FuG 16Ze and FuG 25a) for operation in bad weather; and the Fw 190F-9 was a "Panzerblitz" or "Panzerschreck" type, carrying twelve R4M rockets for tank busting.

The Fw 190G actually preceded the F-model, being virtually the Fw 190A with all the modifications made on the A-5/U3 variant as standard. It was intended to perform both the fighter-bomber and dive-bomber roles; the G-0 carried a 2,200-lb. bomb under the fuselage, but the first production version, the Fw 190G-1, could carry a single 3,970-lb. bomb. This version had the strengthened undercarriage later fitted to the Fw 190F, and the large bomb had cropped fins in order to clear the ground during take-off. The G-3 (two MG 17 and two MG 151) and G-4, G-5, G-6, and G-7 (the latter was tested with a torpedo-size 900-litre drop-tank and had a lengthened tailwheel yoke to provide the necessary ground clearance) were similar apart from the types of bomb racks fitted, and the Fw 190G-8 had GM 1 power boost and only two 20-mm. MG 151s.

Numerous further prototypes were produced, including the V34, V35, V36 (with the B.M.W. 801F), V45, V47 (with B.M.W. 801T and GM 1 power-boost equipment), and V55 for engine tests, and the V72 which tested the PKS 12 automatic controls, most of these being converted from early A-series fighters.

As previously mentioned, in the autumn of 1943 the Fw 190D series was redesignated Ta 152, and the initial production machines differed from the Fw 190D-9 in several respects. The flap and undercarriage operating systems were changed from electric to hydraulic, and armament was increased by the addition of a 30-mm. MK 108 firing through the airscrew hub. The pre-production Ta 152A-0 and the initial production Ta 152A-1 both employed the Jumo 213A-1 engine with MW 50 power boost, weighed 9,700 lb. loaded, and attained 429 m.p.h., but the Ta 152B-0 and B-1 had a Jumo 213E-1 which had a

The Fw 190G-3 fighter-bomber and dive-bomber.

The tenth production Ta 152H-1—the last completed before the war's end.

three-speed two-stage supercharger and induction cooler, and delivered 1,750 h.p. for take-off. Neither the Ta 152A or B was produced in large numbers, production of these having commenced at Sorau/ Silesia on August 31, 1944, and initial battle experience resulted in the radically modified Ta 152C, which was the first sub-type to go into series production towards the end of 1944. The pre-production batch of Ta 152C-0s employed a considerable proportion of Fw 190 components and the Daimler-Benz DB 603E engine which provided 1,800 h.p. for take-off. The initial production model, the Ta 152C-1, employed a DB 603LA engine with two-stage supercharger and aftercooler, and was classed as a medium-altitude fighter, although it was used primarily as a ground strafer and could carry a 1,100-lb. bomb under the fuselage. Armament comprised four 20-mm. MG 151 cannon and one 30-mm. MK 108. Span had been increased to 36 ft. 1 in. (as compared with 34 ft. 5 in.

(Above) A pre-production Ta 152-C-0 built at Sorau/Silesia.

(Above) The third Ta 152H-0, rebuilt from an Fw 190A-1 airframe and under test at Hannover-Langenhagen between April 4 and November 9, 1943. (Below) The fifth production Ta 152H-1 at Cottbus.

for the A- and B- sub-types) and performance included a maximum speed of 463 m.p.h. at 34,400 feet with MW 50 boost. The Ta 152C-3 was similar but had the MK 108 cannon replaced by an MK 103. The loaded weight of the latter at 12,125 lb. was the heaviest of any of the series.

The Ta 152E-0 and E-1 were reconnaissance fighters with reduced armament and the Jumo 213F-1 or -2, but did not enter service, and the Ta 152E-0 was similar but had the Jumo 213E-1, and wing span increased to 47 ft. 6¾ in. The final production variant was the Ta 152H high-altitude fighter. The first prototype had been under test since January 1943, but production did not commence until November 21, 1944, at Cottbus. The Ta 152H had a pressure cabin and an entirely re-designed wing of even greater span.

The Ta 152 H reverted to the Jumo 213 engine, and its high aspect ratio wing spanned 48 ft. 7½ in. Armament comprised one 30-mm. MK 108 cannon and two 20-mm. MG 151 cannon. A few pre-production Ta 152H-0 fighters were delivered for service testing, but only ten production Ta 152H-1 machines had been completed by the end of the war. The Ta 152H-1 attained maximum speeds of 465 m.p.h. at 30,000 feet, and 472 m.p.h. at 41,000 feet. Normal and maximum loaded weights were 10,472 lb. and 11,508 lb. respectively. The Ta 152R-2 was an experimental long-range sub-type with increased internal fuel capacity and shackles for a drop-tank. The performance of the Ta 152H-1 was such that it could escape any Allied fighter with ease, and Kurt Tank himself has related how easily he pulled away from a flight of P-51D Mustangs that jumped him during a test flight.

During the war years, apart from prototypes, 13,367 Fw 190 fighters and 6,634 Fw 190 fighter-bomber and close-support aircraft were produced, plus sixty-seven Ta 152s. The Fw 190 commenced its career by wresting from the R.A.F. the slim margin of superiority that it had gained in fighter-versus-fighter combat and, in the ground-attack role, it subsequently proved its ability to absorb considerable punishment.

Focke-Wulf Fw 190A-8

Dimensions :	Span, 34 ft. 5½ in. ; length, 29 ft. 0 in. ; height, 13 ft. 0 in. ; wing area, 196.98 sq. ft.
Power Plant :	One B.M.W. 801D-2 fourteen-cylinder air-cooled two-row radial engine with methanol/ water injection (MW 50), rated at 1,700 h.p. for take-off (2,100 h.p. with MW 50 boost), and 1,440 h.p. at 18,700 ft.
Armament :	Two 13-mm. MG 131 machine-guns in upper cowling ; two 20-mm. MG 151 cannon in wing roots ; and two 20-mm. MG 151 cannon mounted in the wing.
Weights :	Empty, 7,000 lb. ; normal loaded, 9,750 lb. ; maximum, 10,800 lb.
Performance :	Maximum speed, 408 m.p.h. at 20,600 ft., 402 m.p.h. at 18,000 ft., 355 m.p.h. at sea-level ; normal cruising speed, 298 m.p.h. ; range (internal fuel only), 500 miles ; initial climb rate, 2,350 ft./min. ; time to 10,000 ft., 4.5 min., to 20,000 ft., 9.9 min. ; service ceiling, 37,400 ft.

The prototype Gloster Gladiator (K5200) after the replacement of the Watts two-blade wooden airscrew by a Fairey Reed three-blade metal airscrew and prior to the introduction of a cockpit canopy.

THE GLOSTER GLADIATOR

When the first shots of the Second World War were fired, the Gloster Gladiator single-seat fighter biplane was an anachronism. It was the last of a generation of combat aircraft whose era had passed with the mid 'thirties, and it was not the unqualified success that its long and adventurous career might suggest. It appeared in service at a time when the biplane had already been eclipsed by the monoplane, and it achieved wartime fame despite a manifest unsuitability for the conflict in which it found itself; fame derived from the heroism of pilots who flew it rather than from its own intrinsic qualities; pilots who, out-gunned, out-performed and, in most cases, out-numbered, flew the old Gladiator in some of the most dramatic battles of the early war years.

The Gladiator was perhaps symbolic of the Air Ministry's reluctance to relinquish in favour of the monoplane the tried and tested biplane formula which had dominated the British fighter scene for more than two decades. Although the Gladiator was universally acknowledged to be responsive and well-behaved under all conditions, opinions as to its capabilities as a fighting vehicle were never unanimous. Some pilots decried it for its low performance; others vigorously defended it, lauding its extreme manoeuvrability. In fact, the Gladiator will remain forever a subject for controversy, but one thing is certain: this little biplane represented a victory for the conventionalists in their war with the visionaries.

Although the imminent demise of the biplane as a fighter was already an accepted fact by 1935, in British official circles there existed considerable pre-

judice against the monoplane. Apart from its cockpit canopy, the Gladiator's only concession to modernity was its use of hydraulically-operated flaps. Its concept was thoroughly traditional. In fact, it was a direct decendant of the S.E.5 fighter of the First World War. Yet the Gladiator was conceived to meet the demands of one of the most imaginative fighter requirements issued; a specification which should have presaged a really high-performance, heavily-armed aircraft. Instead, it resulted in the Gladiator, a fighter which, despite undeniable qualities, was a mediocrity by standards appertaining at the time of its service début, and obsolescent within the year.

This specification, F.7/30, was framed in 1930 and called for a single-seat fighter capable of 250 m.p.h. and carrying four rifle-calibre machine guns, doubling the armament standard on R.A.F. fighters for so many years. The specification insisted originally that the cocking handles of all four guns be within reach of the

The Gladiator prototype in its original form as the Gloster F.7/30 private-venture fighter.

The initial production batch of Gladiators on delivery to the R.A.F. in the spring of 1937. *The aircraft in the foreground* (*K6143*) *was the fifteenth production machine.* (*Below, left*) *The second production Gladiator* (*K6130*) *with the original armament of twin fuselage-mounted Vickers and twin wing-mounted Lewis guns.*

pilot in flight, although this requirement was later waived, and the aircraft had to be suitable for both day and night operation, particular stress being placed on a wide field of view for the pilot with freedom from exhaust glare, and excellent landing characteristics. It was intimated that "sympathetic consideration" would be given to designs employing the new Rolls-Royce Goshawk engine, and, attracted by the possibility of substantial production orders, many aircraft manufacturers entered the contest.

The Gloster Aircraft Company, whose chief designer, H. P. Folland, had been responsible for a number of successful single-seat fighters, including the Grebe and Gamecock, were concentrating on developing the S.S.18 and S.S.19 fighters as potential replacements for the Bristol Bulldog in R.A.F. service when the Air Ministry issued specification F.7/30, and the company did not immediately participate in the contest. Late in 1933, however, the S.S.19B was selected for production for the R.A.F. as the Gauntlet, and with the take-over of the Gloster company by Hawker Aircraft early in the following year, and the rationalization of the company's production methods coupled with the introduction of Hawker-type structural methods, Folland's team began the aerodynamic refinement of the Gauntlet as the S.S.37, and this became a late private-venture entry in the F.7/30 contest.

Gloster's fighter was one of the most conventional of the many contenders for the R.A.F. order. Other relatively conventional biplanes produced to meet the F.7/30 requirements were the Goshawk-powered Hawker P.V.3 and the Bristol Type 123. Certain manufacturers had placed emphasis on distinct features of the specification and, in particular, pilot vision, examples being the unorthodox Goshawk-powered Blackburn and Westland biplanes. In order to provide the best possible view for the pilot, the cockpit of the Blackburn fighter was positioned above the upper wing, while, to place the pilot as far forward in the nose as possible, the Westland fighter had its engine mounted amidships, the airscrew being driven by a long extension shaft. Others endeavoured to meet the requirements with low-wing monoplanes, Supermarine producing the Goshawk-powered Type 224, and Vickers tendering the Jupiter VIIF-powered Jockey III. A private venture interpretation of the specification by the Bristol company, the Type 133, even featured retractable main undercarriage members, and this Mercury VI-powered monoplane was generally believed to be favourite in the contest until, shortly before it was due to be flown to Martlesham Heath for official trials, it was totally destroyed. All the Goshawk-powered fighters were seriously handicapped by the weight and complexity of their engine's steam cooling system, and no amount of design ingenuity could prevent them from falling far short of the requirements of the specification. Only the Gloster S.S.37 was capable of meeting the official requirements, the prototype having attained 253 m.p.h. during official evaluation, and much to the relief of the traditionalists, it was adjudged the winner.

Flown for the first time in September 1934, the S.S.37 retained the fuselage and tail assembly of the S.S.19B Gauntlet, together with the 645 h.p. Bristol

Mercury VIS.2 nine-cylinder radial air-cooled engine, but the two-bay wing cellules of the earlier fighter were discarded in favour of a single-bay arrangement, and a cantilever single-strut undercarriage utilizing Dowty internally-sprung wheels was adopted. The twin fuselage-mounted 0.303-in. Vickers Mk.V machine guns with 600 r.p.g. were supplemented by a pair of Lewis guns of similar calibre housed in trays beneath the lower wing and firing outside the airscrew disc, each having a 97-round drum. The result was an extremely attractive, compact warplane which brought fighter biplane design in Britain to its peak. The prototype was eventually taken on charge by the Air Ministry on April 3, 1935, and allocated the serial number K5200, and during the following July, twenty-three aircraft were ordered to specification F.14/35, the name Gladiator thereupon being adopted. Five years had elapsed since the issue of the original specification; five years which had seen the beginnings of a revolution in fighter design, for prototypes of the Hurricane and Spitfire which were to totally invalidate the 1930 fighter philosophy were within a few months of flying!

Trials with the prototype progressed satisfactorily, and the aircraft was returned to Gloster Aircraft to have the Mercury VIS engine replaced by a Mercury IX engine which offered a maximum output of 840 h.p. at 2,750 r.p.m. at 14,000 ft. and 825 h.p. at 2,650 r.p.m. at 13,000 ft. A Fairey Reed three-blade light metal airscrew was fitted for comparison purposes but, on October 23, 1935, after being flown back from Hucclecote to Martlesham Heath for further handling trials, the port cantilever undercarriage leg failed on landing, resulting in some damage to port and star-

board lower planes and to the airscrew. Subsequent investigation revealed that the cantilever leg had failed owing to faulty material, a fracture having developed on the inner side of the tube. At that time, K5200 had completed 108 flying hours and made some 300 landings throughout which the cantilever under-carriage had proved to be outstandingly efficient.

After repairs, K5200 undertook an extensive series of airscrew comparison trials. The original Fairey Reed metal unit was damaged when the spinner came off in flight, and the replacement was stiffened to overcome the rough running reported with its pre-decessor at maximum r.p.m. Although the second airscrew showed some improvement, there was still a slight but noticeable period of rough running coinciding approximately with maximum r.p.m. Further tests were made with both sheathed and un-sheathed Watts two-blade wooden airscrews, and at the same time a sliding cockpit canopy operated by a chain and sprocket gear from within the cockpit was fitted, K5200 previously having an open cockpit with a small windscreen and a head fairing. The airscrew trials revealed that on climb the performance was virtually the same for both metal and wooden air-screws, but that the level speed at full throttle with the Fairey Reed airscrew was 4-5 m.p.h. in excess of the speed with the Watts airscrew. Take-off performance was better with the latter, but at all engine speeds up to the maximum the Mercury ran more smoothly with the three-bladed than with the two-bladed airscrew. With the Fairey Reed airscrew, K5200 was flown at a weight of 4,471 lb., took-off in 220 yards, clearing 50 ft. in 450 yards, and attained a maximum speed of 253 m.p.h. at 14,500 ft. By comparison, with

The seventy-second Gladiator I of the first major production batch (K7964), below, was used at Martlesham Heath in July 1937 for trials with a fixed-pitch Fairey Reed airscrew and a Mercury engine in which the gear ratio was changed from 0.5 to 0.572.

the unsheathed Watts two-blade wooden airscrew and at a weight of 4,402 lb., K5200 took-off in 165 yards, clearing 50 ft. in 330 yards, and attained a maximum speed of 248 m.p.h. at 14, 400 ft.

The Gladiator I, as the first production model was to become known, embodied most of the modifications incorporated in K5200 during more than two years of evaluation. The 840 h.p. Mercury IX engine with a 0.5 reduction gear ratio was standardised, this being housed in a cowling of broader chord and driving a Watts two-blade fixed-pitch wooden airscrew. The fuselage fuel tank was of 83 Imp. gal. (100 U.S. gal.) capacity, and the production specification called for an armament of four 0.303-in. Browning machine guns, two mounted in troughs in the sides of the fuselage with 600 r.p.g., and two mounted below the lower wing with 400 r.p.g., one on either side of the fuselage and firing outside the airscrew disc. In the event, there were delays in the delivery of the Browning guns, products of the Colt Automatic Weapon Corporation which were being produced under licence in Britain by B.S.A., owing to the need to redesign the breech mechanism and to change the calibre. When the first production Gladiator I (K6129) was taken on charge on February 16, 1937, what Browning guns were available were required for installation in the first Hurricanes. In consequence, the Gladiator was forced to retain the armament of the original prototype which comprised twin fuselage-mounted Vickers Mk.V guns and two wing-mounted Lewis guns. In fact, the first Gladiator to be delivered with Browning armament was the seventy-first aircraft off the production line (K7939), although some earlier machines were retroactively fitted with these guns. Ten aircraft (K.7929-K7938) were fitted with one Vickers K gas-operated gun with 100 rounds under each wing, and during 1937, as a safeguard against the failure of the eight-gun Hurricane and Spitfire, a contract was issued to cover the investigation of the possibility of providing the Gladiator with six- or eight-gun armament. As part of this investigation K7919 had the fuselage guns removed and four Brownings with 400 r.p.g. installed in the lower wing.

The structure of the Gladiator was orthodox, the wing comprising two Hawker-type high-tensile steel spars with duralumin former ribs, the whole covered by fabric, and the fuselage was a rectangular-section tube structure with Warren-girder bracing in the side bays and faired to an oval section, skinning comprising detachable metal panels forward and fabric aft over a light metal structure in the form of hoops and stringers. The tail assembly was a fabric-covered, steel-tube and duralumin structure, and the tailplane was of variable-incidence type. The wing centre section was carried above the fuselage by splayed-out struts, and there was one pair of parallel struts on either side of the fuselage. An unusual feature of the production model was the introduction of small trailing-edge flaps on both upper and lower wings, these being operated by an hydraulic pump and serving to increase drag rather than lift, steepening the

approach angle during landing. The sliding cockpit canopy first tested on the prototype was standardised, although this was greeted with some misgivings on the part of service pilots who, appreciative of the increased comfort, nevertheless considered it a potential menace to clear vision in combat.

Three months after the placing of the initial order for twenty-three Gladiators (K6129-51), an order was placed for a further 180 machines (K7892-8055 and L7608-23). In the event, three of these (K8005-7) were allocated to the Royal Iraqi Air Force, the training of which was being supervised by R.A.F. personnel, but they never reached Iraq, being retained by the R.A.F. and taken on charge by No. 33 Squadron at Mersa Matruh in 1939. Weighing 3,511 lb. empty and 4,750 lb. in maximum loaded condition, the Gladiator I attained maximum speeds of 202 m.p.h. at sea level, 232.5 m.p.h. at 10,000 ft., and 245.5 m.p.h. at 14,200 ft. Initial climb rate was 1,920 ft./min., an altitude of 3,000 ft. was attained in 1.5 min., 10,000 ft. in 4.35 min., and 15,000 ft. in 6.8 min., and service ceiling was 32,900 ft.

The first squadron to commence re-equipping with the Gladiator I was No. 72 at Tangmere, closely followed by No. 3 Squadron at Kenley, and other units soon began to receive the new Gloster fighter. Although the Gladiator was, in general, well liked by service pilots, many preferred its predecessor, the Gauntlet, in all respects apart from performance. Some rough running of the Mercury IX engine and airscrew vibration at certain r.p.m. necessitated prolonged investigation. In an attempt to obtain smoother running, in July 1937 trials were conducted at Martlesham Heath with K7964 in which the gear ratio of the Mercury engine had been changed to 0.572 and a three-blade fixed-pitch Fairey Reed airscrew fitted. The original prototype, K5200, was used for comparative trials, having the standard 0.5 gear ratio, and being flown with both the three-blade metal and two-blade wooden airscrews. It was concluded that performance was substantially the same with the metal airscrew and 0.572 gear reduction as with the wooden airscrew and 0.5 gear reduction. However, further tests were made in December 1937 with two Martlesham Gladiators (K7964 and K8049) with the increased gear ratio and three-blade metal airscrews, and two standard aircraft (K6130 and K7934) from No. 72 Squadron. Similar tests were conducted in January 1938 with two standard Gladiators (K6148 and K7900) from No. 3 Squadron, and it was concluded that, from the standpoint of vibration, the three-blade metal airscrew used in conjunction with the 0.572 gear ratio was generally superior, and as was expected, the increased gear ratio reduced the take-off run, although maximum level speed was also marginally reduced.

Only twenty-eight additional Gladiator Is (L8005-32) were built to Air Ministry contracts, bringing the total production of this model, apart from direct export contracts, to 231 machines, subsequent aircraft being Gladiator IIs to specification F.36/37. The

Gladiator II standardised on the three-blade Fairey Reed metal airscrew, although some early production machines were delivered with three-blade wooden airscrews owing to shortages of the metal unit, and its Mercury VIII or VIIIAS (the latter being shadow factory-produced) engine had a 0.572 gear ratio. The Mercury VIIIA offered a similar performance to the Mercury IX of the Gladiator I but featured an auto-matic-mixture-control carburettor and a Hobson control box. An accumulator was provided for electric starting from the cockpit, and a Vokes air cleaner and sand filters were standardised to suit the Gladiator for desert operation. Another feature introduced on the Mk. II was a flying-instrument panel with a vacuum pump. This panel was first tested on a Gladiator I (K7919) and comprised a Hughes rate of ascent and descent meter, Sperry directional gyro and artificial horizon, a Reid and Sigrist turn and bank indicator, an airspeed indicator and a Kollsman altimeter.

Before Gladiator production switched to the Mk. II model in 1938, however, Gloster Aircraft had com-pleted a substantial number of Mk. Is for export. The early demonstrations of the Gladiator had aroused much interest abroad and, despite the urgency of the R.A.F. expansion scheme, Gloster were able to accept contracts from several foreign governments. The first such contract was received from Latvia in 1937, this country ordering twenty-six machines from the proceeds of a public lottery. Neighbouring Lithuania followed suit, purchasing fourteen machines, four were delivered to the Irish Army Air Corps, two were purchased privately as a gift for the Royal Hellenic Air Force, and thirty-six were ordered by the Chinese government. The year 1937 also saw orders from Belgium for twenty-two machines and from Sweden for thirty-seven (the latter country ordering eighteen Gladiator IIs in the following year). Six Gladiator Is delivered to Norway in the summer of 1937 brought

total production of this model to 380 machines.

With the completion of the last Gladiator Is further Air Ministry orders were for Mk. IIs, contracts calling for 350 machines of this model to bring total production of the Gloster fighter to 748 aircraft. However, sixty aircraft on Gladiator II contracts (N5500-5549 and N5565-74) were officially transferred to the Admiralty on May 24, 1939 as Sea Gladiators. At the end of 1938 the Navy had begun to evince interest in a shipboard conversion of the Gladiator II as a replacement for its Hawker Nimrods which had served since 1932. While the necessary modifications were being made to suit the Sea Gladiators for ship-board operations, fourteen machines from the first production batch of fifty Gladiator IIs (N2265-3214) were transferred to the Admiralty together with a few additional machines loaned by the Air Ministry, these being employed for familiarization, etc., and were referred to officially as the Sea Gladiator (Interim). Although they carried hooks they were not intended for operational use aboard carriers. Two Gladiator Is were used for Sea Gladiator development purposes. One of these, K6129, the first production aircraft, was used between January 27 and February 9, 1939 for trials with special ammunition box lids and a modified cartridge case and link ejector system to Navy requirements. The standard Gladiator included used cartridge case collectors for the two fuselage guns, but the fitting of a dinghy in a fairing beneath the fuselage between the undercarriage legs of the Sea Gladiator necessitated the extension of the chutes so that cases and links could be ejected externally. The belt box lids of the fuselage gun installation had to be shortened so that they could be withdrawn and refilled in the aircraft in accordance with Navy requirements. During February 1939, the other Gladiator I (K8039) was used for trials intended to determine the best type of airscrew for the Sea Gladiator. A special Watts two-bladed airscrew with

A Gladiator I seen in 1939 sporting the early type camouflage finish and red-blue fuselage roundels, and prior to the application of unit code markings. The starboard underwing surfaces were painted white and the port underwing surfaces were black.

The Royal Swedish Air Force ordered thirty-seven Gladiator Is in 1937, these being powered by the Nohab-built Mercury VIS.2 engine and entering service under the designation J 8. During the following year, eighteen Mercury VIII-powered Gladiator IIs were ordered, these being designated J 8A. The photograph above depicts Gladiators of Flygflottilj 8, three of the aircraft being J 8As and the third aircraft in the line-up being a J 8.

weighted boss and a Fairey Reed airscrew retwisted to a finer pitch were tested, but although it was concluded that the Watts airscrew was much superior for shipboard operations, it was decided to standardise on the Fairey Reed. It was also decided to increase the armament of the Sea Gladiator by making pro-

(Above) Sixty Gladiator IIs were modified for shipboard use in 1939 as Sea Gladiators, this photograph depicting the eighteenth aircraft (N5517) with arrester hook extended. (Below) One of fifteen Air Ministry contract Gladiator IIs transferred to Portugal.

vision for two additional Browning guns in the upper wing outboard of the airscrew disc. These had 300 r.p.g. Apart from the collapsible dinghy, the modified armament, ammunition box lids and case ejection system, the only differences between the Sea Gladiator and the Gladiator II were provided by the installation of a deck arrester hook and catapult points, and the first aircraft (N5500-17) were embarked in May 1939 aboard H.M.S. *Courageous* with No. 801 Squadron.

The Air Ministry took the last Gladiator IIs on charge on August 30, 1939, although many were delivered straight into storage. Gladiators Is or IIs had served with Nos. 3, 6, 25, 33, 46, 54, 56, 65, 72, 73, 79, 80, 85, 87, 94, 112, 127, 141, 152, 247, 261, 263, 521, 602, 603, 605, 607, and 615 squadrons at home and overseas, and thirteen of these units were still equipped with the Gloster biplane at the beginning of the Second World War. Incidentally, thirty-nine Gladiator Is (L8005-32, N2303-6 and N2308-14) were brought up to Mk.II standards. A substantial number of Air Ministry contract machines had been exported to foreign air forces, however, these including fifteen Gladiator IIs (N5835-49) for Portugal and an additional six (N5919-24) for Norway. Eighteen (N5875-92) were allocated to Egypt but were not taken on charge, being returned to the R.A.F. as (L9030-47). In December 1939, thirty Gladiator IIs were taken from No. 4 Maintenance Unit where they had been held in storage and supplied to the Finnish government. Previously, in April 1939, eighteen Gladiator Is (L8005 and L8012–28) had been supplied to Egypt, and in December 1940, nineteen Gladiator Is were transferred to the Greeks. The transfer of eleven Gladiator IIs from No. 94(B) Squadron to the South African Air Force in April 1941, brought the total number of air arms in which the Gladiator had served to no less than fourteen, a record not to be equalled by any fighter until the post-war years.

The first Gladiators to fire their guns in anger were those purchased by the Chinese government then engaged in resisting the invading Japanese. The thirty-six Gladiators were accompanied by a Gloster test pilot and a number of technicians, and as international regulations forbade the assembly of combat aircraft for either of the warring countries in Hongkong, the crated fighters were ferried from there by junk to Canton. The Gladiators were erected in the open, mostly in graveyards to evade aerial attack, being flown off from the nearest roadway. The first four Gladiators were written off in taxying accidents, and others were either stalled into the ground or flown through the nearest hedge by their inexperienced Chinese pilots. However, those that did survive the machinations of their own pilots gave a good account of themselves in combat with the Japanese, some being used to protect the aircraft assembly plant at Siuchow.

No. 33 Squadron collected its first four Gladiators from Aboukir on February 26, 1938 while based at Ismailia, and was subsequently heavily engaged in army co-operation duties against Arabs in Palestine during the autumn, its task being to isolate Arab villages while the Palestine police went into action on the ground. During these operations several Gladiators were lost or forced down by rifle fire.

The next Gladiators to see combat were, surprisingly enough, Swedish machines! In Swedish service, the Gladiator I was designated J 8, the thirty-seven machines mostly having the 645 h.p. Nohab-built Mercury VIS.2. The eighteen Gladiator IIs were known as J 8As and were powered by the 840 h.p. Mercury VIIIS.3 driving a three-blade Fairey-Reed airscrew. Two flights of the Swedish Air Force's Flygflottilj 8 at Barkarby each had nine J 8 Gladiators and one flight had J 8As. When the Soviet Union attacked Finland, the Swedish government authorized the formation of a voluntary fighter squadron and a light bomber flight to be sent to the aid of the Finns. The volunteers came from the F 8, which contributed twelve J 8A Gladiators and 104 men to the force, and the F 4, which contributed four Hawker Hart bombers and eighty-four men, the balance being made up from various other units. Commanded by Major Hugo Beckhammar and designated Flygflottilj 19, the force began operations from the frozen lake of Kemi on January 11, 1940. The Swedish Gladiators found themselves opposed by Polikarpov I-15bis fighter biplanes which possessed a slightly inferior performance to the Gloster fighter but enjoyed the advantage of armour protection for the pilot. The Swedish unit was in action for sixty-two days, during the coldest winter recorded in northern Finland for fifty years, destroying six Russian fighters and six bombers for the loss of three Harts and three Gladiators, one of the latter being lost as a result of an accident. The Gladiators remained in first-line service with the Swedish Air Force until supplanted in 1941–42 by the Reggiane Re.2000 Falco.

The thirty Gladiator IIs despatched to Finland reached that country between mid-January and mid-February 1940, in time to participate in the closing stages of the first Russo-Finnish conflict. Dubbed *Gelli* by the Finns, the Gladiator II served principally with HLeLv 26, and although Finnish pilots appreciated its excellent handling qualities, its lack of firewall, armour protection and self-sealing fuel tank, and relatively low performance and light firepower did not make for popularity. It proved ineffective

Twelve of the Royal Swedish Air Force's Gladiator IIs (J 8As) equipped the fighter element of Flygflottilj 19 formed to assist the Finns in their struggle against the invading Russian forces.

against Russian bombers and no match for the I-153 and I-16 fighters, and in the few weeks before, on March 13, 1940, the Finnish government accepted Russian surrender terms, thirteen of the Gladiators had been lost in combat.

Two Gladiator squadrons of the R.A.F., Nos. 607 and 615, flew to France in December 1939 as part of the Advanced Air Striking Force, although these saw no action until the start of the main German offensive in May 1940 when they were based at Abbeville. The Gladiators were credited with a number of confirmed victories, although they proved relatively ineffectual against the faster Luftwaffe bombers and more heavily armed fighters, and on May 22nd the remains of the squadrons were evacuated. When Germany attacked Belgium on May 10, 1940, the Belgian Air Force's 1st Squadron, the Escadrille Comete, had fifteen Gladiators on strength, but these were rapidly overwhelmed by the Luftwaffe.

Prior to this, on April 9, 1940, German forces had invaded Norway, and the Norwegian Army Air Force's fighter squadron based at Fornebu for the defence of Oslo, the Norwegian capital, had nine Gladiators on strength, only seven of these being serviceable. Norway had received six Gladiator Is in the summer of 1937 and six Gladiator IIs late in 1939. Three Gladiators had been lost in accidents before the German invasion. The Gladiators succeeded in destroying a number of Luftwaffe aircraft and damaging many more, and only one was actually lost in aerial combat, but the others were destroyed on the ground or in forced landings when the German forces occupied Fornebu. However, on April 22nd., the Gladiators of No. 263 Squadron were flown aboard H.M.S. *Glorious* off Scapa Flow for ferrying

to Norway. Fighter cover was provided during the crossing by the Sea Gladiators of No. 804 Squadron, and on the 24th., No. 263 Squadron's eighteen Gladiators landed on the frozen Lake Lesja. Operating under the most primitive conditions, the Gladiators fought for two-and-a-half days, the lake being constantly bombed and strafed by the Luftwaffe. The Squadron claimed fifteen confirmed victories without losing one machine in aerial combat, but thirteen of the Gladiators had been destroyed on the ground and, as supplies of petroleum were completely exhausted on the 27th., the remaining five Gladiators were set alight by their ground crews who, together with the eighteen pilots, were evacuated to Britain to re-equip.

Hastily issued with new Gladiators, No. 263 Squadron was on its way back to Norway within three weeks, its destination being Bardufoss in the Arctic Circle. Only sixteen of the Squadron's eighteen Gladiators reached Bardufoss, two having crashed into a mountain in bad visibility. These fought continuously until June 7th., claiming a further twenty-six confirmed victories, and the survivors successfully landed back aboard H.M.S. *Glorious* the next day. By a cruel quirk of fate, however, the carrier, which was proceeding independently of the main convoy owing to shortage of fuel, was sighted by the *Scharnhorst* and the *Gneisenau* and sent to the bottom of the Atlantic, together with the remaining Gladiators of No. 263 Squadron.

Only one home-based R.A.F. unit, No. 247 Squadron, was still officially flying Gladiators operationally during the "Battle of Britain", but No. 141 had ostensibly some half-dozen on first-line strength, and about six first-line squadrons showed Gladiators on their second-line strengths. With eighteen pilots and

One of the thirty Gladiator IIs supplied to Finland early in 1940. *The Gladiator was not popular with the Finns owing to its lack of armour protection, firewall and self-sealing fuel tank. In Finnish service it was dubbed "Gelli".*

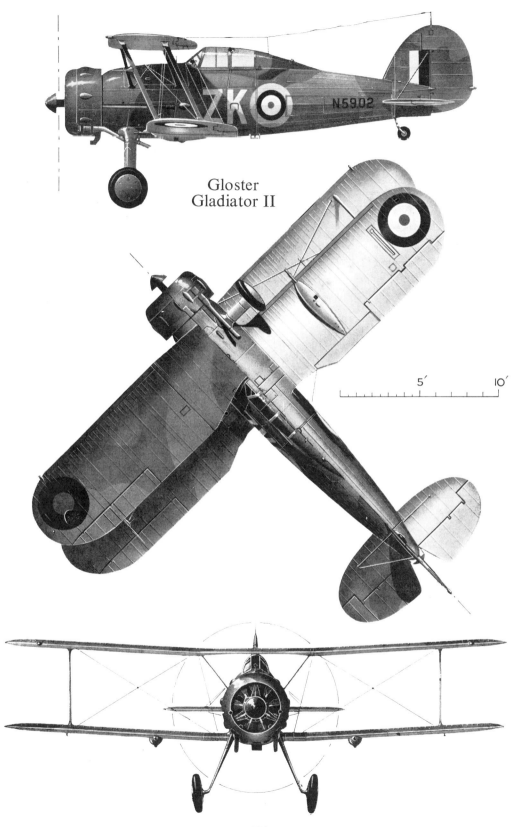

Gloster
Gladiator II

5′   IO′

twelve Gladiators No. 247 Squadron flew from Roborough in defence of the Royal Naval Dockyards at Plymouth from July 1940, and overseas the Gladiator was extremely active. Gladiators had first arrived in the Middle East in February 1938 with Nos. 33 and 80 Squadrons, and five Gladiator-equipped R.A.F. squadrons were operational in this theatre when, on June 10, 1940, Benito Mussolini declared war on the Allies. Now began an action for which the Gladiator was to achieve immortality, the defence of Malta.

The operations of the Gladiator in Maltese skies in June 1940 received a tremendous amount of publicity in the years that followed, and a fictionalized account of the action has come to be accepted as fact. The story of the indomitable trio of Gladiators, dubbed *Faith*, *Hope* and *Charity*, whose pilots flew them continuously at maximum boost with their throttles "right through the gate" day after day to provide the island's sole defence, made romantic if not strictly accurate reading! Eighteen Sea Gladiators (N5518-35) had been allotted to Kalafrana, Malta, on May 24, 1939, and Admiralty records indicate that at least six but not more than ten of these were taken aboard H.M. carriers between October 1939 and February 1940, leaving a minimum of eight or a maximum of twelve aircraft at Kalafrana. There is no record of any carrier restocking with Sea Gladiators after this. A naval seaplane tender collected another Sea Gladiator (N5513) from H.M.S. *Courageous* and a second from H.M.S. *Glorious* and delivered these two to Maleme in crates early in 1940, these subsequently being assembled and taken over by No. 33 Squadron in the battle for Crete. In May 1940, Pilot Officer Collins of the Aircraft Repair Section at Kalafrana received instruction to erect four of the crated Sea Gladiators (N5519-20, N5524 and N5531). H.M.S. *Glorious* was scheduled to call at Malta for new aircraft during the summer but, as already recorded, this carrier was to be sunk in June while ferrying the Gladiators of No. 263 Squadron back to the United Kingdom. N5519 was seriously damaged during the first week of June, and another of the Sea Gladiators was damaged during the following week, but battle order strength figures submitted on June 14, 1940, list four Sea Gladiators as fully serviceable, these including N5523 and N5529, indicating that two additional Gladiators had then been assembled.

On the morning of June 11 the Regia Aeronautica mounted the first bombing attack on Malta, but the bombing force was intercepted and broken up by two Gladiators. Owing to the shortages of ammunition links, and fuel, and the danger of straying too far from Malta, the pilots of the Gladiators appear to have been instructed to avoid dogfights with the Regia Aeronautica fighters and not to chase retreating bombers, concentrating on diving through enemy bomber formations when over the island to disrupt the aim of their bombardiers. However, the Italians mounted only three actual raids on the island between the 11th and 21st! The remaining Gladiators other

than the six made airworthy were cannibalized for spares, and a Mercury engine with three-blade variable-pitch airscrew from a Blenheim bomber was installed in one of the fighters. Fitted with this power plant, N5519 flew on June 22nd but was shot down in action two days later. Another of the sextet, N5520, was destroyed on the 26th, but on the 28th the surviving Gladiators were supplemented by four Hurricanes which had reached Malta on the 21st, had stood idle until the 26th when they were flown to North Africa from where they returned two days later! At the end of June, N5523, N5524, N5529 and N5531 were still flying operationally, two of these being lost in mid-July, and on August 2, 1940, twelve Hurricanes were flown off H.M.S. *Argus* and landed on Malta to participate in the defence of that island, No. 261 Squadron being formed.

Insofar as the legend of *Faith*, *Hope* and *Charity* is concerned, it appears probable that the R.A.F. succeeded in keeping no more than three of the six available Sea Gladiators serviceable at any one time, and none of these was, in fact, named *Faith*, *Hope* or *Charity*, these appellations first appearing in a Maltese newspaper some months after the action.*

Four Gladiator-equipped squadrons, Nos. 33, 80, 94, and 112, fought the Regia Aeronautica over the Western Desert, and with the invasion of Greece in October 1940, Nos. 80 and 112 squadrons were sent to that country to aid the Royal Hellenic Air Force. The R.A.F. squadrons began operations over Greece in November, and initially they were opposed primarily by the Fiat C.R.42 Falco biplanes of the 363°, 364° and 365° Squadriglie of the 150° Gruppo which operated from Tirana, Valona and Argirocastro in Albania. For the first time the Gladiator was having a fair crack of the whip against a fighter of its own generation. The Italian fighter was faster than the Gladiator which it could out-dive and out-climb, but there was little to choose between the two fighters in manoeuvrability, and neither succeeded in establishing an ascendancy over the other. During December 1940, nineteen of the surviving Gladiators were transferred to the R.H.A.F., but almost all had been destroyed on the ground at Paramythia within a week of the transfer.

The South African Air Force had received one Gladiator I (K7922) for evaluation, and on April 18, 1941, eleven Gladiator IIs were transferred to the S.A.A.F. from No. 94(B) Squadron, some of these serving with No. 1 Fighter Squadron in the Sudan and others with No. 2 Fighter Squadron alongside

* *The so-called* Faith *presented to Malta, even assuming that one of the Sea Gladiators on the Island in 1940 was so-named displays no evidence of ever having been flown at all. The wing attachment points are still inhibited by the manufacturer's red lead, the stringers are in mint condition, and the engine has obviously been fitted afterwards. It shows no battle damage whatsoever, and the constructor's number which should appear on the fuselage frames and cabane struts has been carefully sandpapered off and painted over! According to the plaque accompanying the aircraft, this Sea Gladiator was N5520 (lost on June 26th), but other sources have referred to* Faith *as N551_ (lost two days earlier), and yet the popularly accepted account states that* Faith *was the last survivor of the "trio".*

The last Gladiator II was taken on charge by the Air Ministry on August 30, 1939, and that depicted above (N5902) was the twenty-eighth machine of the last production batch which called for fifty machines (N5875–5924). In the event, the last six Gladiator IIs (N5919–5924) were not taken on charge by the Air Ministry, being delivered instead to the Norwegian government. The Gladiator II illustrated belonged to No. 25 Squadron which operated from Northolt and North Weald.

Hawker Furies and Hurricanes in East Africa. No. 94 Squadron's Gladiators had been charged with the air defence of Aden and provided a spirited defence against Italian bombing attempts. The Royal Iraqi Air Force received three Gladiator Is (K6140-1 and K6147), but these were destroyed in that year when the R.A.F. took action against the R.I.A.F. during the German-instigated rising. Three replacement Gladiator Is (K7907, K7928 and K7989) were supplied to Iraq on December 6, 1942, and on March 1, 1944, five Gladiator IIs were received by the R.I.A.F. Gladiator Is and IIs served with Nos. 2 and 5 squadrons of the Royal Egyptian Air Force but these took no active part in the aerial defence of Egypt. During 1942, the last operational Gladiators with the R.A.F. were withdrawn, and subsequently a number of aircraft were modified for meteorological duties, being fitted with Lorenz blind-flying equipment and de-icing gear, serving in this role until 1945.

The Gladiator marked the end of the era of the single-seat fighter biplane in the R.A.F. and the F.A.A. Britain was not alone in believing that such warplanes still had a place in the modern air arm when the Second World War began, both Italy and the Soviet Union having placed new fighter biplanes in production as late as 1938, but the heyday of the biplane, with its struts and bracing wires, had passed with the

mid 'thirties. Had the Gladiator been introduced two or three years earlier it might well have found a place among the greatest aircraft of all time. In fact, it was already obsolescent when first delivered to the squadrons, and although it acquitted itself well, an unfair share of responsibility was vested in its pilots during those critical first years of the Second World War.

Gloster Gladiator II

Dimensions: Span, 32 ft. 3 in. ; length, 27 ft. 5 in. ; height, 10 ft. 4 in. ; wing area, 323 sq. ft.

Armament: Two 0.303-in. Browning machine guns in the fuselage and firing through the airscrew disc, and two additional Browning guns mounted beneath the lower wing.

Power Plant: One Bristol Mercury VIIIA or VIIIAS nine-cylinder radial air-cooled engine rated at 840 h.p. at 2,750 r.p.m. at 14,000 ft., and 825 h.p. at 2,650 r.p.m. at 13,000 ft. Maximum internal fuel capacity, 83 Imp. gal. (100 U.S. gal.).

Weights: Empty, 3,745 lb. ; loaded, 4,790 lb. ; maximum, 5,420 lb.

Performance: Maximum speed, 231 m.p.h. at 10,000 ft., 241 m.p.h. at 13,000 ft., 246 m.p.h. at 14,500 ft., 245.5 m.p.h. at 15,430 ft. ; maximum cruising speed, 212 m.p.h. at 15,500 ft. ; range, 410 mls. ; initial climb rate, 2,430 ft./min. ; maximum climb rate, 2,460 ft./min. at 6,500 ft. ; time to 3,000 ft., 1.3 min., to 5,000 ft., 2.1 min., to 10,000 ft., 4.1 min., to 15,000 ft., 6.5 min., to 20,000 ft., 9.7 min. ; service ceiling, 32,900 ft. ; absolute ceiling, 33,800 ft.

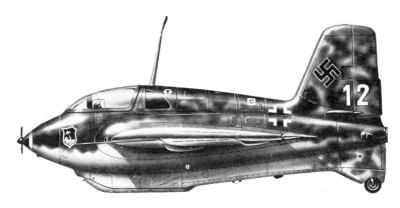

Messerschmitt Me 163B–1a Komet

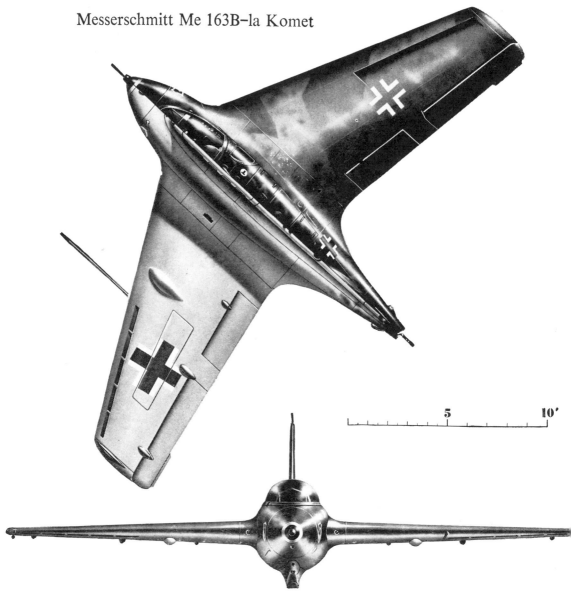

The Me 163V1 high-speed research aircraft at Peenemünde in the summer of 1941.

THE MESSERSCHMITT Me 163 KOMET

The application of the liquid-fuel rocket motor to aircraft propulsion was not purely the result of war-time expediency, although the stress of war undoubtedly resulted in its premature realization. Its unique properties possessed a magnetic attraction for the designer of the short-range interceptor fighter, although inordinately high fuel consumption presented an apparently insoluble problem, while the hazards of handling and storing rocket fuels lent rocket propulsion the air of a highly dangerous stunt rather than that of a practical means of propelling an aircraft. But despite the scepticism surrounding any combination of rocket motor and manned aircraft, the Deutsche Versuchsanstalt für Luftfahrt evinced interest in rocket propulsion from an early date. Nevertheless the rocket-powered fighter was not a German concept, although Germany was the only nation to succeed in bringing such a combat aircraft to operational status, for several of the major warring powers were simultaneously attempting to bring rocket fighters to fruition.

In Russia the design of three rocket-driven fighters was initiated in 1939, and all (the BI-1 designed by Berezniak and Isaev, the Malyutka designed by Polikarpov, and the Type 302 designed by Tikhonravov) were tested with limited success in 1942. In the U.S.A. the year 1944 saw the commencement of flight testing of the MX-324 by Northrop Aircraft, a proposed forerunner to a rocket-driven fighter designed specifically for ramming attack, while even Japan conducted tests, based largely on earlier German development work, with the J8M1 Shusui.

Germany's rocket-propelled fighter, the Me 163B Komet, was remarkable both for the audacity of its concept and the design innovations that it displayed. Its birth was due, indirectly, to a contract placed by the D.V.L. with Hellmuth Walter in the mid 'thirties for a small, well-calibrated, 90 lb. thrust liquid-fuel rocket for testing the dynamic characteristics in roll of various aircraft. The rocket was to be fired on one wing-tip

and the time history of the roll displacement recorded. At that time Walter was mainly concerned with the development of a hydrogen-peroxide/potassium-manganate system for underwater propulsion, but the success of the small rocket, also tested as a means of boosting the climb rate of a light plane, resulted in the ideas of using such rockets to assist the take-off of heavily loaded bombers and as prime movers for high-speed research aircraft.

The latter project was initiated by the D.V.L. in 1937 under the leadership of Dr. A. Baeumker. In order to explore the full potentialities of the rocket motor, the airframe in which it was installed had obviously to be of advanced design. Professor A. M. Lippisch, working at the D.F.S., or Deutsche Forschungsanstalt für Segelflug (German Research Institute for Sailplanes), had earlier developed several aerodynamically advanced machines of tailless type, such as the Pobjoy-powered two-seat DFS 39 Delta IVc, and was currently working on the even more advanced Argus-powered DFS 40 Delta V which featured a prone position for the pilot. Dr. Baeumker's assistant, Dr. Lorenz, therefore approached Professor Lippisch with the proposal that he should design and build a suitable airframe to serve as a rocket-motor test vehicle and for high-speed research.

The DFS 39 had possessed good flight characteristics and it was decided that a similar wing should be employed for the new aircraft. However, free-flight model tests and extensive wind-tunnel investigations at Göttingen proved that directional stability and yaw-roll characteristics would be considerably improved by using a basically similar wing without dihedral and with central vertical tail surfaces in place of the wing-tip rudders, which tended to cause flutter at high speeds. The aerodynamic performances obtained

The DFS 194 for low-speed flight tests.

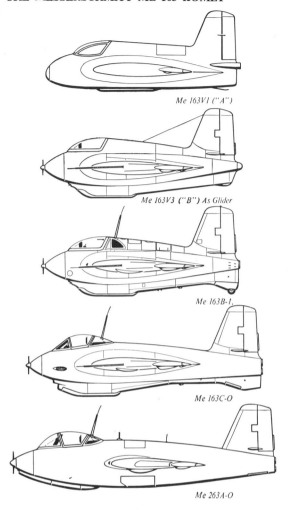

Me 163V1 ("A")

Me 163V3 ("B") As Glider

Me 163B-1.

Me 163C-O

Me 263A-O

during wind-tunnel tests were exceptional and indicated that with a rocket of 1,650 lb. thrust a speed of 620 m.p.h. could be attained at 13,100 feet.

Since the D.F.S. did not possess extensive facilities, and in view of the secrecy attached to the project, it was decided that only the wings should be built at the D.F.S., the fuselage being built by the Ernst Heinkel A.G. The programme, which had been dubbed "Projekt X", proceeded slowly, largely due to security restrictions. Professor Lippisch had decided to build a glider of similar configuration to the proposed high-speed aircraft, the DFS 194, to provide advance information on the low- and medium-speed flight characteristics, and construction of this began in 1938, but he soon realized that further development could not be carried out successfully at the D.F.S., and therefore, in January 1939, Lippisch and twelve of his assistants joined the Messerschmitt A.G., being installed at Augsburg as "Section L".

The transition from a research-institute project to an aircraft-industry project brought the programme under the control of the Aircraft Development Department of the Luftwaffe. The high-speed aircraft was given the R.L.M. designation "Me 163" and Herr

Antz was placed in charge. In order to make preliminary tests the nearly completed airframe of the DFS 194 was taken over by the Messerschmitt A.G., the proposal being that, with slight modifications, this could be used as a test vehicle for a smaller rocket, the Walter HWK R.I of 660 lb. thrust.

The outbreak of war delayed the completion of this scheme and the DFS 194 with its rocket motor was not completed until early 1940. The DFS 194 was taken to the experimental centre of Peenemünde-Karlshagen, where Flugkapitän Heini Dittmar began flight trials in the following summer. The airframe of the DFS 194 had not been built for high speeds and the maximum speed attained was only 340 m.p.h., but the general characteristics of the aircraft, particularly in climbing, exceeded all estimates. The airframes of the two high-speed prototypes, the Me 163V1 and V2 ("A" sub-type), were completed in the spring of 1941, but since security restrictions did not permit rocket-powered flights to be made in the vicinity of Augsburg, all the preliminary flight tests were made without the rocket motor installed. Piloted by Dittmar, the Me 163V1 was towed into the air by a twin-engined Bf 110 and usually cast off from the tow-plane at about 13,000 feet. In diving tests extremely high speeds were obtained, although, during early dives, Dittmar experienced some rudder vibration which was traced to faulty mass-balancing. The aircraft performed extremely well as a glider, and in spite of the low aspect ratio wing (1 : 4.4) the best gliding angle was 1 : 20 and the drag coefficient and small lift coefficients were 0.011. This made it possible to glide around Augsburg for quite long periods.

In 1940, when Germany had expected a speedy termination of the war, Adolf Hitler had issued an order that all technical dvelopments not likely to reach fruition within eighteen months were to be indefinitely shelved, but General Ernst Udet, chanced to see one of Dittmar's gliding demonstrations of the Me 163V1 during a visit to Augsburg, and he immediately put his full influence behind the project.

In the summer of 1941 the Me 163V1 was transferred to Peenemünde-Karlshagen, where a more powerful Walter engine than that installed in the DFS 194, the HWK R.II of 1,650 lb. thrust, was fitted, flight testing beginning in August 1941. The HWK R.II rocket motor was highly unreliable. Nevertheless it was considered to be sufficiently developed to permit flight testing to proceed. Heini Dittmar, therefore, commenced a high-speed flight programme.

On his fourth powered flight he surpassed the existing world air speed record (which, at that time, stood at 469.22 m.p.h.), and a higher speed was attained on each successive flight with the aim of exceeding the 1,000 km./hr. mark. The exact speed attained on each flight was registered on the ground by six Ascania kinotheodolites, but Dittmar discovered that when he reached the 920 km./hr. (570 m.p.h.) mark he had exhausted the limited fuel carried. He then conceived the idea of conserving fuel by means of an air tow to the altitude at which the high-speed runs were being made. Accordingly, on October 2, 1941, the Me 163V1 was towed to 13,000 feet. Dittmar cast off from the tow-plane, fired the rocket motor and attained a level speed of 623.85 m.p.h. (1,002 km./hr.) within two minutes. At this speed, which corresponded to a Mach number of 0.84, the compressibility effects in the transonic range caused a sudden change in pitch stability and the aircraft went into an uncontrollable dive. However, Dittmar succeeded in regaining control by cutting the motor. Since the wing of the Me 163V1 was still essentially the same as that of the DFS 39, which had a considerable wash-out, the wing-tips had a compressibility stall in the negative lift range.

Until this time the Me 163 had been looked upon almost entirely as a high-speed research aircraft, but the success of the Peenemünde tests led to an Air Ministry proposal that the basic design should be developed as a rocket-propelled interceptor. The HWK R.II burned T-stoff (hydrogen-peroxide and water) and used calcium permanganate as a catalyst. This tended to clog the jets and, with insufficient quantities of the catalyst being supplied, the pressure and thrust fluctuated considerably. It was therefore suggested that a motor to employ a different catalyst known as C-stoff (hydrazine hydrate and methyl alcohol) and to run at higher temperatures should be developed.

Lippisch's engineers began the re-design of the Me 163 at Augsburg in December 1941. Provision was to be made for increased fuel capacity, armament and other operational equipment, and the first prototype of the fighter version was to be ready for flight testing by May 1942, Hellmuth Walter having promised to deliver the new "hot" rocket motor by that time. In the meantime the Wolf Hirth glider factory at Göttingen was awarded a contract to build ten gliders essentially similar to the Me 163V1. These were to be used for training purposes and were designated Me 163A. They were to be towed off the ground and the weight of the engine and fuel tanks would be compensated for by water tanks. Simultaneously, the Messerschmitt factory at Regensburg was instructed to prepare for the manufacture of an initial series of seventy Me 163B pre-production and production fighters.

The prototype fighter, the Me 163V3, was ready to receive its rocket motor on schedule, but, owing to difficulties with throttling, the new Walter engine, the HWK 509, did not arrive until the summer of 1943! Meanwhile, gliding tests were conducted with the Me 163V3, but as these progressed the aircraft was found to be virtually uncontrollable in a spin. To rectify this problem Lippisch designed adjustable slots which were fitted along 40 per cent of the wing leading edges. These were later replaced by special low-drag fixed slots, the so-called "C" slots, which proved highly successful. With these fitted the Me 163 could not be spun. With crossed controls the aircraft merely side-slipped. Several members of Germany's glider pilot élite, including Hanna Reitsch and Wolfgang Späte, flew the Me 163 as a glider and reported that its handling characteristics were better than those of any conventional aircraft. Heini Dittmar suffered serious

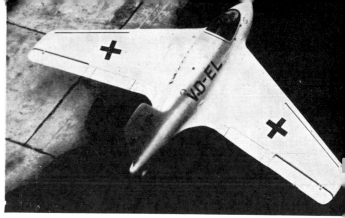

The Me 163V3 in May 1942.

injuries in a crash with one of the early prototypes and was replaced by Rudolf Opitz.

In the early part of 1943 friction that existed between Professors Lippisch and Messerschmitt concerning the further handling of the Me 163 project had developed into open antagonism, and Lippisch, having completed as much test work on the Me 163B as could be done without the engine, left Augsburg to take over the Aeronautical Research Institute in Vienna. Lippisch's engineers were absorbed by Messerschmitt's normal projektbüro and by the end of 1942 the Regensburg plant had completed eight further airframes. All the pre-production Me 163B-0 fighters and more than half the initial production Me 163B-1s had been completed and were awaiting their motors by the time the first HWK 509 arrived from the Walter Werke for installation in the Me 163V3 at Peenemünde. The first powered flight was made in August 1943, and trials progressed favourably, but the whole programme was overshadowed by Professor Messerschmitt's aversion to the rocket fighter since it was not his original design, and the Air Ministry took little convincing that the Messerschmitt group was committed to the development of too many varied types of aircraft and should hand Lippisch's fighter to another manufacturer. Accordingly, after the completion of the seventy airframes production was handed over to the Hans Klemm Flugzeugbau. Design development, however, continued at Augsburg.

It was not until the late autumn of 1944 that Major Wolfgang Späte formed the first operational test group equipped with Me 163B-1 interceptors at Brandis, near Leipzig. The specific task of this unit was to provide additional protection for the Leuna synthetic fuel plants which were being attacked frequently by U.S. bombers. Another group was stationed at Stargard, near Stettin, to protect the large synthetic fuel plant at Pölitz. The service début of the Me 163B-1, which by this time had been appropriately dubbed "Komet", considerably alarmed the Allies and posed entirely new problems in defending large bomber formations.

The Komet-equipped groups each protected an area with a radius of fifty miles. With the approach of an enemy bomber formation the Komets would take off, climb in loose formation on a course provided by a radar-equipped ground directing post until some 3,000 feet above the bombers, then glide until the enemy aircraft were in a favourable position for attack. The speed of the Komet necessitated the evolution of new tactics, and among the most popular methods of attack were dives on the bomber formation from immediately above, low approaches from five o'clock, barrel-rolling up through the formation, or roller-coasting attacks through the formation and then turning and reversing the procedure. The latter tactics were developed by Kapitän Olejnik, who commanded one group of Komets, and employed with great success. On one occasion, over Altenburg in Thuringia, he destroyed three B-17 Fortresses in quick succession by these means.

Accidents on take-off were frequent, although most occurred on landing, when shocks on the fighter's landing skid often exploded any fuel remaining in the tanks. In fact more Komets were destroyed in landing accidents than in combat. The loaded weight of the Me 163B was originally to have been 7,400 lb., but it actually came out at 9,500 lb. and, in consequence, solid-propellant rockets had to be employed to boost power for take-off. Apart from the seventy machines built at Regensburg, less than a further 300 Komets had been completed at the time of Germany's collapse.

A characteristic of the liquid-fuel rocket motor is its loss of efficiency at low outputs, and this led the Walter Werke to develop an auxiliary cruising chamber which gave 660 lb. thrust in addition to the 3,750 lb. thrust provided by the main chamber. The first engine to employ this auxiliary chamber was the HWK 509C and this was installed for testing in the Me 163V6 in the summer of 1944. The Me 163V6 took off and climbed with both chambers operating at full thrust, but for cruising flight the auxiliary chamber alone provided more thrust for a lower fuel consumption than would have been possible by throttling back the main chamber. Powered flight endurance was increased from eight to twelve minutes. Preparations were made at the end of 1944 for the production of a version using the new engine and designated Me 163C. Apart from the new engine, the Me 163C was slightly larger than its predecessor, overall span and length being increased to 32 ft. 2 in. and 23 ft. 1 in. respectively. Normal take-off weight was increased to 11,280 lb., and a pressure cabin with a blister-type canopy was fitted. Maximum speed was 590 m.p.h. between 13,000 and 40,000 feet, and service ceiling was 52,500 feet, but only a few pre-production Me 163C-0 fighters were completed.

An even more advanced development was initiated at Augsburg, the Me 163D. This was intended to employ a similar HWK 509C motor to that used by the "C" sub-type but provided tankage for approximately one-third more fuel and featured a retractable tricycle landing gear in place of the jettisonable take-off trolly and landing skid. At an early design stage the Me 163D was handed over to the Junkers design staff at Dessau, where a team headed by Professor Hertel undertook further re-design. For a brief period this development was re-designated Ju 248 but was subsequently designated Me 263. The prototype, the Me 263V1, was completed at Dessau in August 1944, and several towed flights were made before the rocket motor was installed. In the late autumn of 1944 development of the Me 263 was handed back to the Messerschmitt A.G., and powered flight tests were made. For these the undercarriage of the Me 263V1 was fixed in the down position. The wing of the Me 263 was similar to that of the Me 163B but suitably modified to accommodate larger C-stoff tanks, and the fin and rudder were standard Me 163B components.

The fuselage of the Me 263 was completely re-designed and of better aerodynamic shape than those of its predecessors. All effort was directed towards improving the range and the ground-handling characteristics. A total of 352 gallons of C-stoff and 185 gallons of T-stoff was carried, and it was estimated that the production Me 263A-1 would have a top speed of 590 m.p.h., cruise at 495 m.p.h. for fifteen minutes and climb to 32,800 feet in three minutes.

The series of rocket-propelled target-defence fighters stemming from the original Me 163V1 high-speed research aircraft of 1941 held promise of solving the immense problem which faced Germany's war leaders of protecting important centres from mass air attack, but too few were available and too late.

Messerschmitt Me 163B-1 Komet

Dimensions :	Span, 30 ft. 7 in. ; length, 18 ft. 8 in. ; height, 9 ft. ; gross wing area, 211 sq. ft.
Armament :	Two 30-mm. MK 108 cannon with sixty rounds per gun.
Power Plant :	One Walter HWK 109-509A-2 bi-fuel, liquid-rocket motor developing 3,750 lb. thrust. Maximum fuel capacity, 226 Imp. gal. T-stoff and 110 Imp. gal. C-stoff.
Weights :	Empty, 4,200 lb. ; loaded, 9,500 lb.
Performance :	Maximum speed, 596 m.p.h. at 30,000 ft.. 515 m.p.h. at sea-level ; endurance after climb. 2.5 min. ; initial climb rate, 16,000 ft./min. ; time to 30,000 ft., 2.6 min., to 39,500 ft., 3.35 min. ; ceiling, 54,000 ft. ; stalling speed, 140 m.p.h.

(Left) The Me 163V8 production prototype for B-series. (Right) The Me 163V6 with auxiliary cruising chamber.

THE KAWANISHI SHIDEN

It was characteristic of the improbabilities of the air war in the Pacific theatre that one of the finest *land-based* fighters employed operationally by Japan was a *naval* machine, and, stranger yet, a fighter evolved from a *floatplane*. This aircraft, the Kawanishi N1K2-J Shiden-Kai, was undoubtedly among the finest combat aircraft developed by the Japanese aircraft industry during the Second World War, and superior in most respects to the U.S. Navy's shipboard fighters by which it was largely opposed. However, it was no mere chance that one of the finest Japanese *land-based* fighters should be developed for the Japanese Naval Air Force.

The Japanese Naval Air Force was assigned an air responsibility that would have been regarded as impossible by the naval air arms of other powers. As a naval force possessing a large fleet of aircraft carriers, prime emphasis in the J.N.A.F. was placed on the training of shipboard pilots. This training included much long-range flying as well as specialized training in night-flying missions. The war against China, however, limited the active use of aircraft carriers, although long-range flying by day and night was a necessary role of Japanese air combat units committed to the Chinese mainland. The Japanese Army Air Force lacked the necessary training in long-range missions and, consequently, the bulk of such tasks devolved on the naval air groups. In addition to these responsibilities the J.N.A.F. was in sole charge of the air defence of its own bases, a duty that was to demand an extensive use of land-based interceptor fighters as defensive needs increased.

These duties were never re-evaluated, and the J.N.A.F. entered the Second World War with a range of tasks far surpassing its capabilities. With the sweeping victories achieved in the initial stages of the conflict by Mitsubishi's A6M Zero-Sen shipboard fighter, Japan began to believe herself invincible in the air. Little thought was given to purely defensive operations, and much less to the possibility that these future operations would have to be conducted from land bases as a result of the almost total destruction of her carrier forces. Thus it was not until the appearance of the prototype Kawanishi Shiden in the middle of 1943 that Japan possessed an interceptor fighter capable of meeting Allied fighters on a basis of equality, and in some cases superiority.

Development of the Shiden fighter really commenced in the early months of 1940. Facing the possibility of future military operations in the Pacific, the Japanese Navy issued a specification for a water-based fighter to provide air cover during amphibious landing operations prior to the capture of airfields by the ground forces. Nakajima was assigned the responsibility of producing an interim floatplane fighter based on Mitsubishi's A6M2, resulting in the A6M2-N Suisen, but Kawanishi was awarded a development contract for what was intended to be the most powerful and advanced water-based fighter in the world.

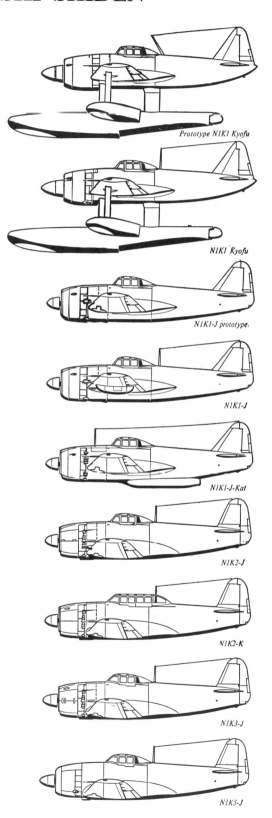

Prototype N1K1 Kyofu

N1K1 Kyofu

N1K1-J prototype.

N1K1-J

N1K1-J-Kai

N1K2-J

N1K2-K

N1K3-J

N1K5-J

(Left) The first prototype Kyofu with contraprops. (Right) The Kawanishi N1K1 Kyofu Model 11.

Initially known as the 15-Shi floatplane fighter (being ordered in the fifteenth year of the Showa reign or era, 1940), it was later assigned the name Kyofu (Mighty Wind) when the J.N.A.F. adopted popular names for its aircraft in 1942. Over two years of design and development went into the 15-Shi project before the first prototype was completed at Kawanishi's Naruo factory in August of 1942.

In its original form the Kyofu was powered by a special model of the Mitsubishi Kasei (Mars) engine geared for contra-rotating airscrews. Known as the MK4D Kasei 14, and also as the Ha.32/14 under the unified J.N.A.F./J.A.A.F. designation system, this engine was a fourteen-cylinder two-row air-cooled radial developing 1,460 h.p. The contra-props were selected to offset the airscrew torque expected from such a powerful engine mounted in the relatively small airframe and resulting in a tendency to snake during take-off. A mid-wing configuration was adopted to clear the water spray during take-off and landing, and a laminar-flow aerofoil section was selected after extensive wind-tunnel tests. The original plans called for retractable stabilizing floats, but retraction was abandoned in view of its increased weight and complexity, fixed floats being standardized. Two prototypes were built, the second being completed in October 1942, but experience with the Kasei 14 engine showed that the complexities of the gearing necessary for the contra-props outweighed the advantages that these airscrews offered, and the design was modified to employ the 1,460 h.p. Kasei 13 (Ha.32/13). This was similar to the Kasei 14 but drove a single, three-bladed airscrew via an extension shaft. Further prototypes were tested with the new power plant and, carrying an armament of two 20-mm. cannon and two 7.7-mm. machine-guns, the 15-Shi type was accepted by the Japanese Navy as the N1K1 Kyofu 11 (dubbed "Rex 11" by the Allies).

The Kyofu proved to be a rugged and highly efficient floatplane with a maximum speed of 302 m.p.h. at 18,700 feet, a cruising speed of 230 m.p.h. at 13,120 feet, a service ceiling of 34,645 feet and a range of 1,060 miles. Empty and maximum loaded weights were 4,850 lb. and 7,407 lb. respectively. Later production models of the N1K1 Kyofu were powered by the MK4E Kasei 15 (Ha.32/15), which differed only in minor details from the Kasei 13. Although developed as an offensive fighter, the Kyofu was

never to be employed in this capacity. The situation in the Pacific had changed so drastically between the time that the prototype had flown and production aircraft were available that the aircraft was impressed as a defensive *interceptor* fighter.

Production started slowly but the tempo began to increase in June 1943. Construction was undertaken at the Naruo factory, reaching a production peak in December 1943, when fifteen machines were completed. By that time, however, the Japanese Navy was no longer faced with mediocre Allied fighters, and a floatplane fighter, no matter how exceptional its performance, was no match for the Allied single-seat fighters. Production continued at a modest rate until it was finally terminated in March 1944, the total number completed amounting to ninety-seven. At the time production was halted, an advanced model known as the Kyofu-Kai was in the development stage. Power was provided by the greatly improved 1,900 h.p. Mitsubishi MK4R Kasei 23 (Ha.32/23).

The Kyofu was allocated to operational units as rapidly as possible. A number were sent to the South Pacific, but their operations were limited owing to the rapidly changing combat conditions. They fought well in the Balik Pakan area of the Dutch East Indies, and later, at the close of the war, one unit was stationed on the inland Lake Biwa, on the Japanese home island of Honshu.

Soon after the completion of the prototype 15-Shi the J.N.A.F. faced the need for a high-altitude fighter to combat the later Allied fighters and bombers that were beginning to appear in increasing numbers in the Pacific theatre. Prototypes of the short-range Mitsubishi 14-Shi Raiden (J2M1) were flying, and Mitsubishi was also working on the 17-Shi (J3K1) project, but these designs were plagued with the prospect of time-consuming development programmes, and the Navy needed a high-performance Type "B" fighter without delay. The Type "B" fighter class was intended for the land-based interceptor role as opposed to the Type "A" shipboard fighter, and in November 1942 it was suggested to Kawanishi that a landplane fighter might well be derived from the Kyofu.

This project, undertaken under the project name Shiden (Violet Lightning), was assigned the 1,990 h.p. Nakajima NK9H Homare 21 (Ha.45/21) eighteen-cylinder twin-row radial engine which had been accepted for production before the completion of its

(Left) The first prototype Shiden, the Model X-1, and (right) the N1K1-J Shiden Model 11.

final tests. In consequence it was plagued with teething troubles. Nevertheless the Kawanishi design staff entered into the Shiden project with enthusiasm. Work on Mitsubishi's J3K1 was suspended in favour of the landplane adaptation of the 15-Shi floatplane, and, known as the Model X-1 fighter, the first prototype was completed at Naruo in July 1943, only nine months after the project was initiated. A number of modifications had, of course, been made to the basic N1K1 airframe, and the Shiden was a compromise between rapid produceability and operational requirements. One of the most difficult problems facing its design staff was the development of a retractable undercarriage of sufficient length to permit mounting of a large-diameter airscrew to make full use of the available power, yet fit within the limitations of the mid-wing configuration. The design team had to adopt exceptionally lengthy legs and solve the problem of stowing these units in the wings by a system of double retraction. The legs were lowered and then extended, and when retracting they contracted as they folded into the wing wells.

The wing and tail surfaces of the Kyofu were adopted without any major changes, but the mounting of the smaller-diameter Homare 21 engine entailed extensive modification to the fuselage. The aft portion was deepened to give more vertical stabilizing area and include a retractable tailwheel. An outstanding feature of the Shiden was its exceptional manœuvrability, this being due in no small measure to its unique "Combat Flap" installation. These surfaces changed their angle automatically with changes in "g" value during manœuvres, supplying additional surface when a high lift coefficient was required. The flaps were operated by electricity and hydraulic pressure, were light in weight and simple to maintain. Automatic operation took the responsibility out of the pilot's hands during combat and eliminated the possibility of stalling at a time when such might well prove fatal.

An armament of two 7.7-mm. machine-guns in the fuselage and four 20-mm. cannon (two in the wings and two suspended under the wings in gondolas) was installed in the prototype, and flight tests commenced immediately. Prior to this event the new fighter had been ordered into quantity production "off the drawing board" under the designation N1K1-J (the "J" indicating that it was a landplane development of

the original N1K1), and three further prototypes were completed before the end of July 1943. Although full production was attained less than a year after the Shiden's inception, it did not allow time to eliminate the teething troubles that manifested themselves in the prototypes. A total of eight N1K1-J prototypes was produced, and the testing of these proceeded concurrently with that of the first production model, known as the Shiden 11. Consequently the production lines were continually inflicted with design changes and modifications suggested by flight testing.

The Shiden 11 (dubbed "George 11" for identification purposes by the Allied forces) originally entered production at the Naruo factory, but in December 1943 it also entered production at Kawanishi's Himeji plant. One Shiden was produced at Himeji in December 1943, 353 in 1944, and 112 from January to June 1945. Production at Naruo, beginning in July 1943, was seventy in that year, and 471 in 1944. U.S. bombing terminated production at Himeji, and the N1K1-J was phased out at Naruo in December 1944 in favour of the more advanced Shiden-Kai. Total N1K1-J Shiden production was thus 1,007 aircraft, including prototypes.

The N1K1-J was produced in three basic models. The first was known as the Shiden 11, being the production model of the original "X-1". This was followed by the N1K1-Ja Shiden 11a with four Type 99 20-mm. cannon mounted in the same manner as those of the N1K1-J, and the N1K1-Jb Shiden 11b with all four cannon mounted internally in the wings and calling for a major re-design of the wing structure. Late production N1K1-Jb fighters had completely re-designed, square-tipped vertical tail surfaces. Another late modification was the fitting of six rocket bombs on the underside of the fuselage. Late in 1944 a Shiden 11 was modified as the N1K1-J-Kai with a supplementary rocket unit to increase available power for short periods. The rear portion of the fuselage was modified to mount a power rocket unit, and several machines received this modification. But although flight tests gave encouraging results the rocket-boosted model did not attain operational status.

A further modification was the Shiden Special Attack aircraft—a variant for suicide attack carrying a heavy bomb load. Between the last weeks of December 1944 and the end of January 1945 four Shiden 11s were modified for this suicidal attack role,

The Kawanishi N1K2-J Shiden Model 21, *the prototype of which was first flown on December* 31, 1943.

but, although extensively tested, the Special Attack Shiden was not adopted.

Production models of the Shiden 11 had maximum speeds of 362 m.p.h. at 17,715 feet and 334 m.p.h. at 9,840 feet. Service ceiling was 39,700 feet and range was 888 miles at 230 m.p.h. at 13,120 feet. The Shiden entered service with the Japanese Navy early in 1944 and soon gained for itself a reputation among Allied fighter pilots as one of the toughest and most troublesome Japanese fighters to be met in combat. It was an exceptional aircraft in the hands of a capable pilot, and was regarded by J.N.A.F. pilots as more than a match for the majority of the U.S. shipboard fighters. The Grumman Hellcat in particular was regarded as an easy "kill" to a pilot of any experience. The Shiden was first met in numbers over Formosa and the Philippines. The first large unit of Shidens to face the U.S. forces was the 341st Air Corps which arrived on Luzon from Formosa on October 20, 1944, as part of the J.N.A.F. Second Air Fleet. A total of 100 Shiden fighters was attached to this unit, but although they fought well they were soon impotent as a fighting force owing to lack of spares for the machines not lost in combat.

Following the U.S. successes in the Philippines, the Shiden was met in large numbers during the invasion of Okinawa, and continued to be used over these islands after their occupation by American forces. A Japanese naval communiqué of the time reported an engagement over Amami Oshima island in this group in which a unit of thirty-four Shidens met a superior force of seventy Allied fighters, destroying twenty with a loss of only twelve aircraft. Shidens also equipped the 343rd Air Corps of the First Air Fleet based at Tinian, and later at Mitsuyama Airfield at Shikoku in Japan in defence of the home islands during the spring of 1945.

Although the Shiden was in many respects an outstanding fighter, it suffered several serious faults. Its Homare 21 engine was unreliable, and the wheel brakes were so bad that the Shiden was often landed on rough ground alongside a runway to reduce the length of the landing run. To rectify these and other failings a complete re-design was undertaken by Kawanishi in the middle of 1943, and the result was the Shiden-Kai—undoubtedly the finest J.N.A.F. production fighter type of the war.

The Shiden-Kai was completely re-designed with an eye to simplification of production and the use of non-critical materials. It made use of only 43,000 parts, excluding nuts and bolts, as compared to the 66,000 required by the original Shiden. Another step towards simplification was the use of pre-formed sheet construction, a process developed under the guidance of engineer Franz Paul, who had been loaned to the J.N.A.F. by the Henschel company. The Homare 21 was retained owing to its immediate availability.

Work on the Shiden-Kai proceeded rapidly, and the design staff was augmented by personnel released from the N1K1-J and 18-Shi Jimpu (J6K1) projects which had been abandoned in favour of the Shiden-Kai. The first prototype was completed in December 1943, and the aircraft was accepted by the J.N.A.F. as the N1K2-J Shiden 21. On December 31, 1943, the prototype was flown at Naruo airfield. The service armament of four 20-mm. cannon mounted internally in the wings was fitted to the first as well as subsequent prototypes. A further seven prototypes had been completed by June 1944. In March 1944 the Naruo plant began to tool up for the quantity production of the Shiden-Kai, but once again, as with the original Shiden, test results were applied directly to production aircraft on the assembly lines, resulting in confusion and delays. To make matters worse, the prototypes began to experience a long series of teething troubles which proved difficult to eliminate. Planned production quotas proved impossible to meet, and the Shiden-Kai production programme entered the autumn of 1944 behind schedule to

A modified N1K2-J with re-designed engine cowling and cockpit.

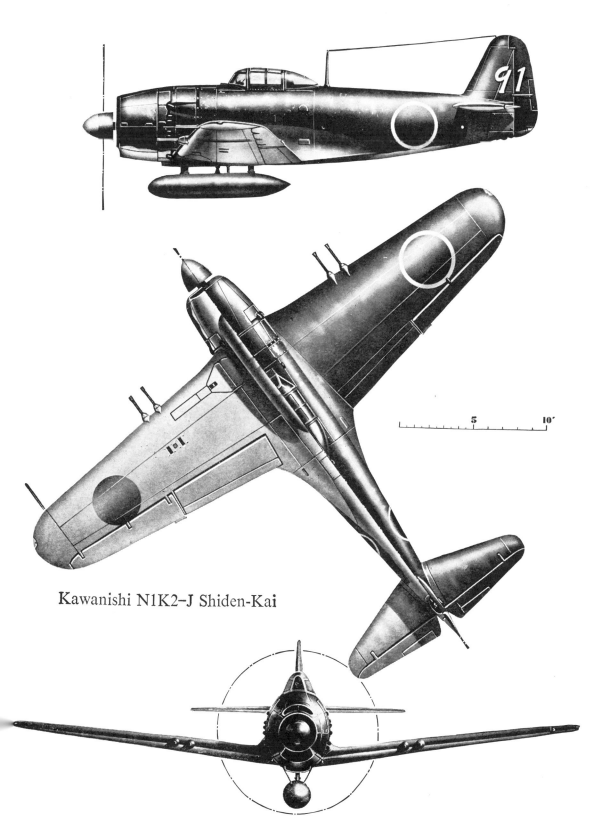

Kawanishi N1K2–J Shiden-Kai

5   10'

be met by the strategic bombing of the B-29 Super-fortress aircraft of the U.S.A.'s 20th Air Force. Although direct attack on N1K2-J production lines did not begin immediately, the attacks against the factories of Kawanishi's sub-contractors led to shortages of Homare engines, steel forgings, aluminium extrusions, sheet stock, and landing-gear assemblies, forcing the production of completed aircraft to a crawl. The Naruo factory produced only sixty Shiden-Kai fighters between July and the end of 1944, and only 294 subsequently. Production at Himeji did not begin until March 1945, and here too shortages of materials held up production, only forty-four being completed.

As a result of the Japanese Navy's decision to standardize on the N1K2-J, construction of this type was also assigned to Mitsubishi's 7th airframe plant (where nine were produced between March and August 1945), to the Ettoku factory of Aichi (where only one was completed, in July 1945), to Showa at its Shinonoi plant (only one being completed, in August 1945), and to the Naval Air Arsenals at Hiro (one completed), Omura (ten completed), and Atsugi (none completed). Japanese Navy production quotas planned for 1946 totalled 9,240 Shiden-Kai fighters, giving an indication of the importance attached to this aircraft. Actual production by all manufacturers up to the end of the war totalled only 428 machines.

The Shiden 21 was fast, powerful and manoeuvrable, and in the hands of an average pilot was the equal of any Allied fighter that it was called upon to face, even the later models of the North American P-51 Mustang that appeared over Japan in the spring of 1945. As the tide of the air war swung directly over the Japanese home islands the N1K2-J was still under operational test by the Yokosuka Air Corps. On one occasion a Shiden 21 piloted by Flight Warrant Officer Kinsuke Muto was "jumped" by twelve Grumman F6F Hellcat fighters. A pilot of exceptional skill, Muto succeeded in shooting down four of the American fighters before they broke off the engagement to return to their carrier. Muto was successful in returning to Yokosuka airfield in his badly damaged Shiden 21.

The Shiden 21 was also built in small numbers as a two-seat advanced trainer under the N1K2-K designation. Known as the Shiden-Rensen, this trainer model was produced to conform to the Japanese Navy practice of ordering a two-seat version of all new single-seat fighter types. The N1K2-K was fitted with dual controls and the combat armament of four 20-mm. cannon in the wings, as well as two additional 7.9-mm. machine-guns in the fuselage. Racks were also fitted for four 132-lb. or two 550-lb. bombs.

The N1K2-J was extensively modified and re-designed to conform to the dictates of the ever-changing air war. One of the first major revisions was the N1K3-J Shiden 31. This represented an attempt to move the centre of gravity slightly by moving the Homare 21 engine forward some six inches. Armament was increased by the addition of two 13-mm. guns in the fuselage. A shipboard version, the N1K3-A Shiden 41, was also proposed, but neither the N1K3-J nor N1K3-A was built. Late in 1944 work began on a new modification, the N1K4-J, which was intended to overcome some of the operational problems attendant on using the still unreliable NK9H Homare 21 engine. The N1K4-J employed a NK9H-S Homare 23 engine which was a low-pressure fuel injection model and rated at 2,000 h.p. Three experimental prototypes of the N1K4-J, known as the Shiden 32, were completed at Naruo, and numerous modifications were made during their test programme. Simultaneously, work was undertaken on a shipboard version known as the N1K4-A. Similar to the N1K4-J, the first prototype was finished on September 20, 1944, and the second in the first week of October. The aircraft was accepted for production as the Shiden 42 but abandoned with the complete destruction of Japan's carrier forces.

Although the Shiden 21 proved to be an outstanding fighter in fighter-versus-fighter combat, it was a great disappointment to the Japanese Navy in the one category in which it was most sorely needed, that of the high-altitude bomber interceptor. It had proved ineffective against the B-29 Superfortress owing to its poor climbing ability, and numerous suggestions were made in attempts to combat this fault. One of the first attempts was the N1K5-J of early 1945. In this the Homare 21 was replaced by the 2,200 h.p. Mitsubishi MK9A (Ha.43/11) radial. Design work was nearly completed and construction actually begun at Himeji when the plant was destroyed during B-29 raids in June 1945. During joint Industrial-Military conferences held at Yokosuka in April and May 1945, it was decided that the only way a high operational altitude coupled with high speed and manoeuvrability at the heights at which the B-29s operated could be obtained with the Shiden was by installing the new Homare 44 (Ha.45/44) engine which, developing 2,200 h.p., was fitted with a mechanically-driven, two-stage, three-speed supercharger. The new model was immediately assigned top production priority but the war had ended before the project could be realized.

Unique among land-based fighters of the Second World War in beginning its life as a floatplane, the Shiden was more than a competent fighter; it was exceptional. Had large numbers of Shidens been available to the Japanese Navy during the air battles of 1944–45, their outcome might well have been different and the war in the Far East lengthened.

Kawanishi N1K2-J Shiden 21 (Shiden-Kai)

Dimensions :	Span, 39 ft. 3¼ in. ; length, 30 ft. 8 in. ; height, 13 ft. ; wing area, 253 sq. ft.
Armament :	Four 20-mm. Type 99 cannon ; provision for four 132-lb. or two 550-lb. bombs on underwing racks.
Power Plant :	One Nakajima NK9H Homare 21 (Ha.45/21) eighteen-cylinder two-row air-cooled radial developing 1,990 h.p. for take-off.
Weights :	Empty, 5,858 lb. ; loaded, 9,039 lb. ; wing loading, 33.07 lb./sq. ft.
Performance :	Maximum speed, 370 m.p.h. at 18,370 ft., 359 m.p.h. at 9,840 ft. ; time to 19,685 ft., 7 min. 22 sec. ; range, 1,069 miles at 219 m.p.h. at 9,840 ft.

(*Above*) *The second of two Mustangs delivered to the U.S.A.A.F. under the designation XP-51. The machine illustrated (Serial No.* 41-039) *is actually the tenth production Mustang, the first XP-51 (41-038) being the fifth production machine.* (*Right*) *The first production Mustang (AG345) which was retained by North American Aviation for flight development.*

THE NORTH AMERICAN MUSTANG

Unquestionably the finest of all American wartime fighters and ranking in merit with the best of any other combatant, the North American P-51 Mustang was an inspired design evolved almost by accident. It outperformed all other U.S.A.A.F. types in speed, range and manœuvrability and, although produced in slightly smaller numbers than the P-47 Thunderbolt, it eventually re-equipped all but one Eighth Air Force Thunderbolt group and established itself as the principal Allied strategic fighter. Its reputation with the U.S.A.A.F. was made in the last two years of the war, the first combat group arriving in the United Kingdom in November 1943, and after the cessation of hostilities General "Hap" Arnold frankly admitted that it had been "the U.S.A.A.F.'s own fault" that this excellent fighter had not been employed operationally very much earlier. In fact it was only by chance that the Mustang was accepted by the U.S.A.A.F. at all.

The Mustang owed its origin to the British Air Purchasing Commission, which, in April 1940, requested a substitute for the Curtiss P-40 which it considered unsuitable for European combat conditions. North American Aviation was consulted by the Commission on the possibility of manufacturing a fighter meeting the requirements that it had formulated but the Commission stipulated that, in view of the serious war situation, a prototype must be completed within 120 days. North American's president, J. H. "Dutch" Kindelberger, had followed accounts of air combat over Europe assiduously and had already conceived the broad outlines of a fighter such as was required. A useful amount of technical data was obtained from the Curtiss-Wright Corporation, North American's only previous experience in fighter design and construction being limited to the NA-50A which

(*Above, top to bottom*) *The second production Mustang I (AG346), the first to arrive in the United Kingdom. An early production P-51 (41-37427) with cannon armament, and a P-51A-NA with Allison V-1710-81 engine.*

had been designed in 1939 for Siam, and headed by Raymond Rice and Edgar Schmued, the latter having formerly worked with Fokker and Messerschmitt, the design team started work. By a near superhuman effort the first prototype fighter, known by its manufacturer's designation NA-73, was pushed out of the assembly shed in 117 days—although lacking an engine and having wheels borrowed from an AT-6 basic trainer. Several modifications were made before the aircraft flew six weeks later, in October 1940, but

The first production model of the Mustang for the U.S.A.F., the P-51.

the phenomenal endeavour on the part of the North American engineering team was to be more than recompensed.

Very few snags were encountered during the flight test programme, and production started almost immediately, albeit on a minor scale to fulfil the relatively modest British orders as Lend-Lease had not then been instituted and all military equipment had to be purchased with hard cash or gained by barter. The NA-73 was one of the first fighters to employ a laminar-flow wing which had its maximum thickness well aft and resulted in greatly reduced drag. Drag was further minimized by positioning the intake for the then shallow radiator for the 1,100 h.p. Allison V-1710-39 (F3R) engine beneath the rear fuselage and keeping the fuselage cross-section to the least depth possible. A beautifully clean airframe resulted, although the NA-73 differed from nearly all contemporary fighter designs in having square-cut tips to both wing and tail surfaces. The air of austerity introduced by these had virtually no effect on performance and simplified production.

The first production Mustang, as the fighter had already been dubbed by the R.A.F., flew within a

year of the prototype. This machine was allocated the serial number AG345 but was retained by North American for flight development. The second production Mustang (AG346) had arrived in the United Kingdom by November 1941. U.S.A.A.F. fighter policy at that time hinged mainly on the P-38 Lightning and the P-47 Thunderbolt, and there was thus little official American interest in the Mustang. When North American had first initiated development of the new fighter, all that had been stipulated by the U.S. authorities was that, should the design attain production, two machines should be delivered without charge to the U.S.A.A.F. for evaluation. Therefore the fifth and tenth production Mustangs were sent to Wright Field under the designation XP-51 (Serial Nos. 41-038 and 41-039). These early Mustangs had a gross weight of 8,400 lb., and their maximum speed of 382 m.p.h. was higher than nearly all contemporary fighters, including the Spitfire.

As soon as the first Mustang arrived in the United Kingdom it was recognized as being outstandingly superior to any previous American fighter type, but the low-rated altitude of the Allison engine rendered it unsuitable for normal fighter duties. Nevertheless, its armament of two 0.5-in. MG 53-2 Browning machine-guns mounted below the engine and firing through the airscrew disc, plus one 0.5-in. MG 53 and two 0.3-in. MG 40 guns in each wing, gave the Mustang a good ground-attack potential, while its high speed at low altitude rendered it ideal for tactical reconnaissance. An F.24 camera was therefore mounted obliquely behind the pilot's seat to point downward behind the port wing, and the Mustang I entered service with Army Co-operation Command. Its first operational sortie was on July 27, 1942, and on August 19 Mustangs took a major part in the costly Dieppe operation, supporting the assault troops. In all, 620 Mustang Is and IAs, the latter having four 20-mm. M-2 wing cannon in place of the entire machine-gun armament, were delivered to the R.A.F., and operated by Nos. 2, 4, 13, 16, 26, 63, 116,

(Above, left) One of the first Mustang Is for the R.A.F. (AG351). (Above, right) A Mustang I (AG357) fitted with eight rocket projectiles. (Below, left) A Mustang II (FR 901) with special deep-section fuel tanks, and (below, right) a Mustang I (AM106/G) fitted experimentally with two 40-mm. Vickers "S" guns.

168, 225, 239, 241, 268, 309, 315, 400, 414, 430, 485 and 613 Squadrons. In R.A.F. service the Mustang achieved the distinction of becoming the first single-engined fighter based in the United Kingdom to penetrate beyond the German border, the internal fuel capacity of 180 U.S. gallons in two self-sealing tanks providing a maximum range of up to 1,000 miles.

(Above) One of the first Merlin conversions, a Mustang I (AM208) with a "beard" radiator. (Below) A Mustang III (P-51B) with Malcolm hood.

After conducting extremely successful trials with the two XP-51s the U.S.A.A.F. began to evince a little interest in the North American fighter, ordering 150 P-51s under the name Apache, armed with four 20-mm. cannon and equivalent to the R.A.F. Mustang IA. This order was followed by another for 310 P-51As. Initially, this new designation covered a change in armament to four wing-mounted 0.5-in. machine-guns, but later P-51As had the Allison V-1710-81 (F20R) engine which developed 1,200 h.p. for take-off and increased maximum speed to 390 m.p.h. In the R.A.F. the P-51A was known as the Mustang II, and fifty were delivered late in 1942. Apart from the engine and armament, the P-51A differed principally from the first production model in having two underwing racks for carrying either 500-lb. bombs or 75- or 150-gallon drop-tanks. The latter load brought the take-off weight up to 10,600 lb., but provided a ferrying range of no less than 2,350 miles.

In Britain the early Mustangs were used extensively for various experimental purposes, and one machine (AM106/G) was fitted successively with eight rocket projectiles on zero-length launchers, special long-range fuel tanks and, eventually, two 40-mm. Vickers "S" guns in underwing mountings. A Mustang II (FR901) was fitted with special deep-section fuel tanks beneath the wings for ultra-long-range flying. The experiment which was to bring the Mustang to fruition as an all-round fighter *par excellence*, however, was made by Rolls-Royce. Major Thomas Hitchcock, then U.S. military attaché in London, reported to Washington in the autumn of 1942 that the P-51 was one of the best, if not *the* best, fighter airframes developed at that date, and advised its development as a high-altitude fighter by cross-breeding it with the Merlin 61 engine. This opinion was endorsed by such authorities as Eddie Rickenbacker and Air Marshal Sir Trafford Leigh-Mallory, and four Mustangs were delivered to Rolls-Royce for conversion.

A Mustang I (AM 208) was fitted with a Merlin 65, and a Mustang IA (AL 975-G) received a Merlin 61. These aircraft, together with AM203 and AL963, had four-bladed airscrews to absorb the extra power, and featured small "chin"-type radiators of varying shape while retaining the ventral radiators originally fitted. These four machines were known as Mustang Xs. A Rolls-Royce project which called for the installation of a Griffon engine aft of the pilot's cockpit, driving the airscrew via an extension shaft, progressed no further than the mock-up stage. The Merlin installations were completed and the Mustang Xs successfully flown within six weeks, and the data provided by flight tests with these machines was sufficient for the North American company to initiate a complete redesign of the Mustang for production with the Packard-built 1,520 h.p. Merlin 61, the V-1650-3,

A standard P-51B-15-NA (42-106767) with underwing bomb shackles.

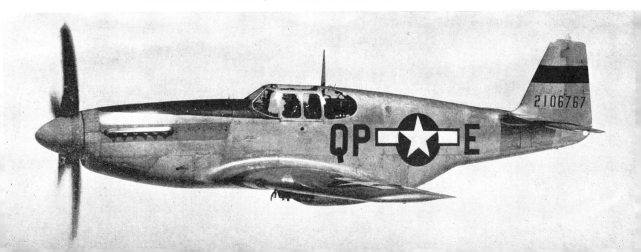

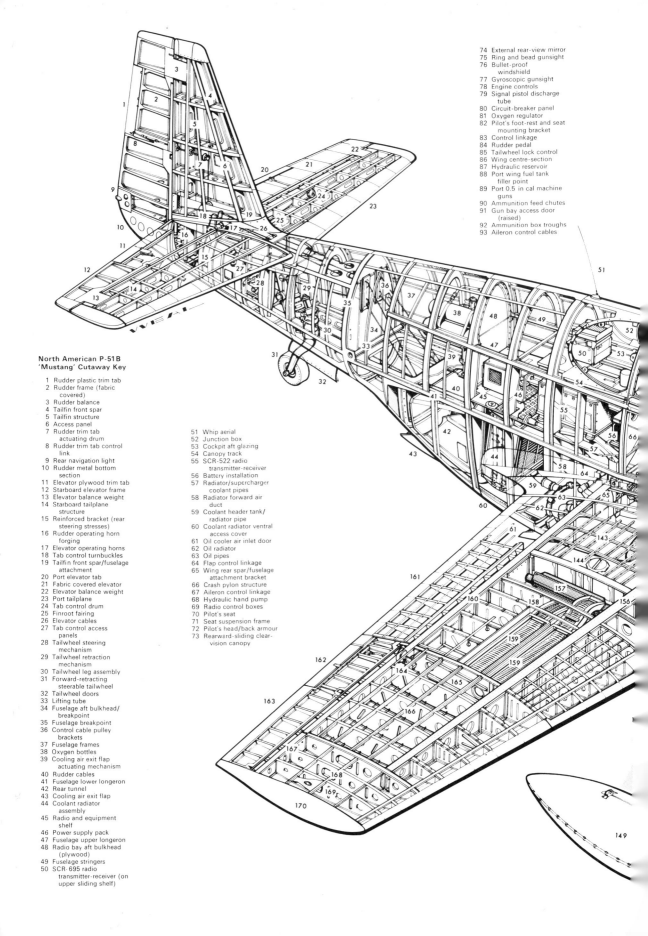

74 External rear-view mirror
75 Ring and bead gunsight
76 Bullet-proof
    windshield
77 Gyroscopic gunsight
78 Engine controls
79 Signal pistol discharge
    tube
80 Circuit-breaker panel
81 Oxygen regulator
82 Pilot's foot-rest and seat
    mounting bracket
83 Control linkage
84 Rudder pedal
85 Tailwheel lock control
86 Wing centre-section
87 Hydraulic reservoir
88 Port wing fuel tank
    filler point
89 Port 0.5 in cal machine
    guns
90 Ammunition feed chutes
91 Gun bay access door
    (raised)
92 Ammunition box troughs
93 Aileron control cables

North American P-51B 'Mustang' Cutaway Key

1 Rudder plastic trim tab
2 Rudder frame (fabric
   covered)
3 Rudder balance
4 Tailfin front spar
5 Tailfin structure
6 Access panel
7 Rudder trim tab
   actuating drum
8 Rudder trim tab control
   link
9 Rear navigation light
10 Rudder metal bottom
   section
11 Elevator plywood trim tab
12 Starboard elevator frame
13 Elevator balance weight
14 Starboard tailplane
   structure
15 Reinforced bracket (rear
   steering stresses)
16 Rudder operating horn
   forging
17 Elevator operating horns
18 Tab control turnbuckles
19 Tailfin front spar/fuselage
   attachment
20 Port elevator tab
21 Fabric covered elevator
22 Elevator balance weight
23 Port tailplane
24 Tab control drum
25 Finroot fairing
26 Elevator cables
27 Tab control access
   panels
28 Tailwheel steering
   mechanism
29 Tailwheel retraction
   mechanism
30 Tailwheel leg assembly
31 Forward-retracting
   steerable tailwheel
32 Tailwheel doors
33 Lifting tube
34 Fuselage aft bulkhead/
   breakpoint
35 Fuselage breakpoint
36 Control cable pulley
   brackets
37 Fuselage frames
38 Oxygen bottles
39 Cooling air exit flap
   actuating mechanism
40 Rudder cables
41 Fuselage lower longeron
42 Rear tunnel
43 Cooling air exit flap
44 Coolant radiator
   assembly
45 Radio and equipment
   shelf
46 Power supply pack
47 Fuselage upper longeron
48 Radio bay aft bulkhead
   (plywood)
49 Fuselage stringers
50 SCR-695 radio
   transmitter-receiver (on
   upper sliding shelf)

51 Whip aerial
52 Junction box
53 Cockpit aft glazing
54 Canopy track
55 SCR-522 radio
   transmitter-receiver
56 Battery installation
57 Radiator/supercharger
   coolant pipes
58 Radiator forward air
   duct
59 Coolant header tank/
   radiator pipe
60 Coolant radiator ventral
   access cover
61 Oil cooler air inlet door
62 Oil radiator
63 Oil pipes
64 Flap control linkage
65 Wing rear spar/fuselage
   attachment bracket
66 Crash pylon structure
67 Aileron control linkage
68 Hydraulic hand pump
69 Radio control boxes
70 Pilot's seat
71 Seat suspension frame
72 Pilot's head/back armour
73 Rearward-sliding clear-
   vision canopy

94 Flap lower skin (Alclad)
95 Aileron profile (internal aerodynamic balance diaphragm)
96 Aileron control drum and mounting bracket
97 Aileron trim tab control drum
98 Aileron plastic (Phenol fibre) trim tab
99 Port aileron assembly
100 Wing skinning
101 Outer section sub-assembly
102 Port navigation light
103 Port wingtip
104 Leading-edge skin
105 Landing lamp
106 Weapons/stores pylon
107 500-lb bomb
108 Gun ports
109 Machine-gun barrels
110 Detachable cowling panels
111 Firewall/integral armour
112 Oil tank
113 Oil pipes

114 Upper longeron/engine mount attachment
115 Oil tank metal retaining straps
116 Carburettor
117 Engine bearer assembly
118 Cowling panel frames
119 Engine aftercooler
120 Engine leads
121 Packard-Rolls-Royce Merlin V-1650 engine
122 Exhaust fairing panel
123 Stub exhausts
124 Magneto
125 Coolant pipes
126 Cowling forward frame
127 Coolant header tank

128 Armour plate
129 Propeller hub
130 Spinner
131 Four-blade Hamilton Standard Hydromatic propeller
132 Carburettor air intake integral with
133 Engine mount front frame assembly
134 Intake trunking
135 Engine mount reinforcing tie
136 Hand crank starter
137 Carburettor/trunking vibration-absorbing connection

138 Wing centre-section front bulkhead
139 Wing centre-section end rib
140 Starboard mainwheel well
141 Wing front spar/fuselage attachment bracket
142 Ventral air intake (radiator and oil cooler assemblies)
143 Starboard wing fuel tank
144 Fuel filler point
145 Mainwheel leg mount/pivot
146 Mainwheel leg rib cut-outs
147 Main gear fairing doors

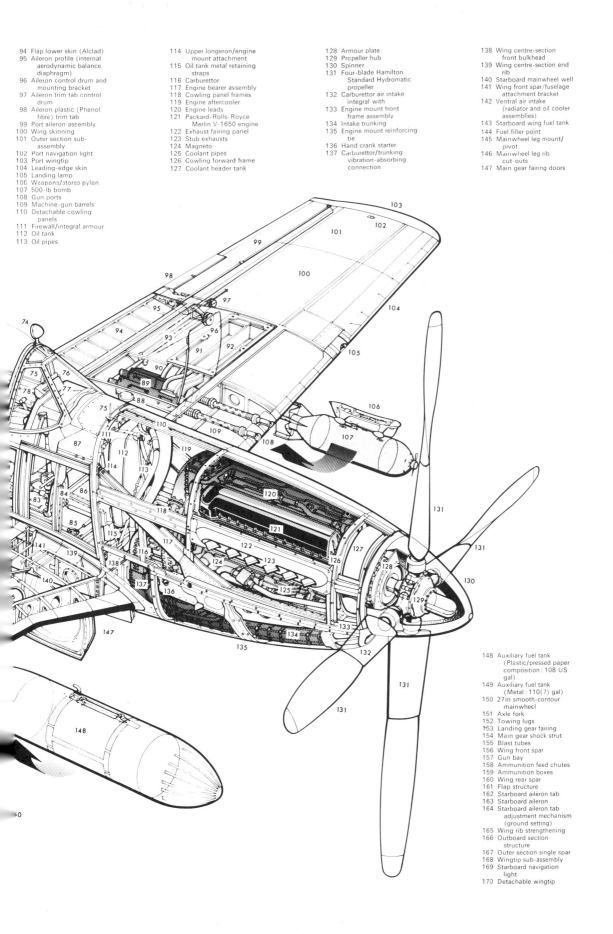

148 Auxiliary fuel tank (Plastic/pressed paper composition: 108 US gal)
149 Auxiliary fuel tank (Metal: 110(?) gal)
150 27in smooth-contour mainwheel
151 Axle fork
152 Towing lugs
153 Landing gear fairing
154 Main gear shock strut
155 Blast tubes
156 Wing front spar
157 Gun bay
158 Ammunition feed chutes
159 Ammunition boxes
160 Wing rear spar
161 Flap structure
162 Starboard aileron tab
163 Starboard aileron
164 Starboard aileron tab adjustment mechanism (ground setting)
165 Wing rib strengthening
166 Outboard section structure
167 Outer section single spar
168 Wingtip sub-assembly
169 Starboard navigation light
170 Detachable wingtip

(Above) A P-51B-1-NA (43-12094) with long-range tanks, and (below) a P-51C-1-NT.

production models delivered to the U.S.A.A.F. were modified for tactical reconnaissance, following the R.A.F. precept. In 1942 some fifty-seven P-51s were each fitted with two K-24 cameras under the designation F-6A, and these became the first of a substantial series of photo-reconnaissance Mustangs, including thirty-five F-6Bs modified from P-51As.

Two production lines for the Merlin-engined Mustangs began to roll in 1943, building identical aircraft at Inglewood, California (P-51B), and Dallas, Texas (P-51C). The first Merlin-Mustangs were delivered to the U.S. Eighth Air Force in the United Kingdom on December 1, 1943, and, with two 92 U.S. gallon wing tanks and either two 75-gallon or 150-gallon external tanks, flew their first long-range escort mission on December 13—490 miles to Kiel and back,

with two-speed, two-stage supercharger and intercooler.

Two P-51s were fitted with the Packard-built Merlin in the U.S.A., and after a brief period as XP-78s were eventually redesignated XP-51B. Their airframes were strengthened in order to make full use of the increased power available; the ventral radiator was deepened; the carburettor intake was moved from above to below the nose for the Merlin's up-draught induction system; new ailerons were fitted and the underwing racks increased in capacity to take two 1,000-lb. bombs or their equivalent weight in fuel. Before the two XP-51Bs, which were to show a level speed improvement of 51 m.p.h. to 441 m.p.h., had even flown, General Arnold was able to report to President Roosevelt that approximately 2,200 Merlin-powered P-51Bs had been ordered for the U.S.A.A.F.

The time was then November 1942, and it was to be a year before the first group of P-51B Mustangs (this name having also been adopted by the U.S.A.A.F. in preference to the Apache) were to be available for combat. In the meantime a new version of the P-51A had been evolved specifically for dive-bombing in the spring of 1942, fitted with wing-mounted airbrakes, a 1,325 h.p. Allison V-1710-87 engine, and designated A-36A. Five hundred of these were delivered to the U.S.A.A.F., with which they were the first Mustangs to see combat, equipping two groups in Sicily and Italy in 1943. The dive-bombing equipment of the A-36A increased gross weight to 10,700 lb. and reduced maximum speed to 356 m.p.h., and the type was only moderately successful. The dive brakes proved unsatisfactory and were eventually wired shut. Many fighters were subsequently to be adapted for the dive-bombing role, and some—notably the Spitfire—proved highly successful, but only without the weight of extraneous equipment and by retaining their versatility. One A-36A (EW998) was supplied to the R.A.F. in March 1943 for experimental purposes.

The Mustang's inherent versatility was beginning to manifest itself even before the introduction of the Merlin-powered P-51B, and a number of the earlier

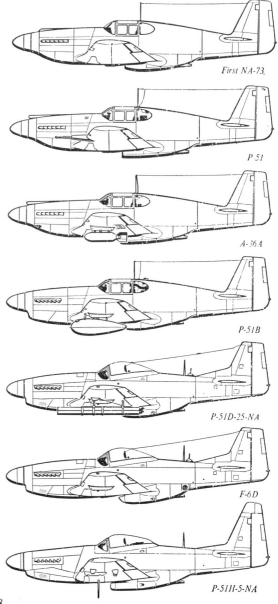

First NA-73

P 51

A-36A

P-51B

P-51D-25-NA

F-6D

P-51H-5-NA

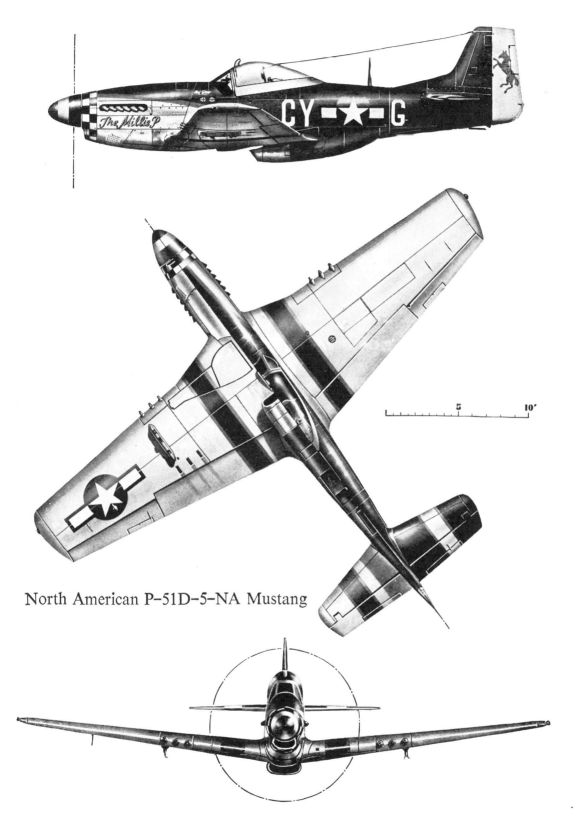

North American P-51D-5-NA Mustang

(Above) A P-51D-10-NA (44-14214) with dorsal fin extension, and (immediately below) a P-51D-5-NA (Mustang IV) without dorsal fin. (Bottom) An F-6D-1 converted from a P-51D-10-NA.

U.S. gallon fuselage fuel tank, bringing the total internal fuel capacity to 269 U.S. gallons and the normal range to 1,300 miles. This modification was also made in the field to earlier P-51Bs and Cs. The armament in all cases remained either four or six 0.5-in. machine-guns in the wings with a total of 1,260 rounds of ammunition.

Some 250 P-51Bs and about 637 P-51Cs were supplied to the R.A.F., which operated them as the Mustang III, and equipped numerous units, including Nos. 19, 65, 66, 94, 112, 118, 122, 126, 129, 165, 249, 260, 306, 309, 315, 316 and 345 Squadrons. These aircraft were supplied under Lend-Lease with the original sideways-hinging and close-fitting cockpit canopy which restricted rearward view, and was unacceptable to the R.A.F. for European combat. A bulged sliding frameless hood, similar to the Spitfire canopy, was therefore designed by R. Malcolm and fitted to most R.A.F. Mustang IIIs, plus a number of the U.S.A.A.F.'s P-51Bs and Cs and F-6s. Tactical reconnaissance variants included seventy-one P-51Bs and twenty P-51Cs modified into F-6Cs and carrying several K-17, K-22 and K-24 cameras in the rear fuselage. These had a gross weight of about 10,000 lb. and could carry full armament. Maximum speed was 430 m.p.h.

In the early months of 1944 U.S. Mustangs began operating in Burma in support of airborne troops attacking Japanese lines of communication 200 miles behind the Assam-Burma front. P-51Bs were also introduced in the Fifteenth Air Force in Italy at this time, and on May 5, 1944, R.A.F. Mustangs accompanied by Kittyhawks, and operating from Eastern Italy, smashed the great Pescara Dam by bombing. Not one Mustang was lost on this operation, which was a remarkable feat to be accomplished by single-engined fighters.

Despite the highly favourable ratio of successes in the European theatre against the Luftwaffe, the U.S.A.A.F. was evincing as much concern as the R.A.F. about rearward view. The Malcolm hood was but a temporary measure to improve this fault, and by 1944 a major re-design was under way in order to fit a beautifully streamlined "bubble" canopy on a cut-down rear fuselage. A new version of the Mustang, the P-51D, was already on the production lines, having the more powerful Packard Merlin V-1650-7 and six 0.5-in. machine-guns with 270 or 400 r.p.g., and after the completion of the first four aircraft the new "bubble" hood was introduced onto the production line.

The P-51D was to become the most widely produced variant of all Mustangs, 6,502 being built at Inglewood and 1,454 at Dallas. It was quickly delivered to U.S.A.A.F. squadrons in both Europe and the Pacific, and P-51Ds were to make the first land-based

which established a record at that time. Whatever shock this was to the Luftwaffe was nothing compared with that a few months later when, in March 1944, Merlin-powered Mustangs accompanied B-17 Fortress and B-24 Liberator bombers all the way on the 1,100-mile round trip to Berlin. It is true to say that the introduction of the P-51B and C, capable of accompanying bombing formations to their targets and still meeting the Luftwaffe on equal terms after jettisoning nearly empty external tanks, imposed a severe tactical problem on the German defence system, while adding tremendous impetus to the American daylight offensive. The long-ranging fighters, weaving over the massed formations of bombers, were soon christened "little friends" by the hard-pressed crews of the Fortresses and Liberators, and many crippled bombers owed their return to the protection of escorting Mustangs.

Between 1942 and 1943, 1,988 P-51Bs and 1,750 P-51Cs were built, initially with the Packard Merlin V-1650-3 and later with the V-1650-7, the Merlin 68. The V-1650-7s in The P-51B-15-NA and P-51C-5- to 10-NT had a war emergency rating of 1,695 h.p. at 10,300 feet and conferred a maximum speed of 439 m.p.h. at 25,000 feet. The sea-level climb rate was 3,900 ft./min., and the maximum weight with a 2,000-lb. bomb load was 11,200 lb. The last 550 P-51Bs became P-51B-7 to -10 with the addition of an 85

fighter strikes against Tokyo on April 7, 1945. The fuselage fuel tank had by this time become standard, and the underwing racks were augmented by twin zero-length launching stubs for 5-in. rocket missiles on the last 1,100 P-51D-25-NA fighters. Some Mustangs in Europe had previously carried a cluster of three Bazooka-type rocket-launching tubes beneath each wing and on returning from fighter escort frequently engaged in ground-strafing sorties, using either rockets or machine-guns. An enormous number of vehicles, trains and dispersed aircraft were destroyed by marauding Mustangs before and after D-Day in France and Germany.

(*Above*) *A P-51K-5-NT with Aeroproducts airscrew.* (*Immediately below*) *A P-51H-1-NA, and* (*bottom*) *one of three lightweight XP-51F experimental fighters.*

High-altitude escort and combat remained the Mustang's forte, however, and it was superior in speed and manœuvrability to all Luftwaffe piston-engined fighters above 20,000 feet. Luftwaffe pilots considered the Mustang to be rather vulnerable to cannon fire, however. Among the many pilots who flew Mustangs from bases in the United Kingdom over Germany was Colonel "Chuck" Yeager. Mustangs were the only Allied fighters with sufficient range to accompany heavy bombers on their "shuttle" missions, in which landings were made in North Africa and Russia after deep-penetration targets had been attacked from United Kingdom bases.

As production of the P-51D got into its stride a dorsal fin was introduced to compensate for the loss of keel surface on the rear fuselage, and tail warning radar was added. U.S. Eighth Air Force pilots were among the first to wear the new anti-"g" suits which inflated automatically around the calves, thighs and lower body during tight turns and when pulling out from a dive, restricting the blood from draining from the head and trunk and thus delaying "black-out". This device had to be used with caution, however, as the pilots found that they could then take more "g" than their Mustangs. On a number of occasions after dog-fights, Mustangs landed with several more degrees wing dihedral than when they had taken off, plus a number of popped rivets where the wings had bent.

Only 280 P-51Ds were supplied to the R.A.F., by which service they were known as the Mustang IV, since the U.S.A.A.F. demanded as many fighters of this type as it could obtain for the Pacific campaign. The Mustang's extreme range made it a natural choice for bomber-escort and fighter sweeps over the broad wastes of the Pacific, and after the capture of Iwo Jima, in February 1945, P-51Ds began aiding the B-29 Superfortress force in its assault against Japanese targets. With external tanks giving a total of 489 U.S. gallons of fuel, the P-51D was comparatively light at 11,600 lb., and had an absolute range of no less than 2,080 miles—an endurance of 8½ hours.

While in R.A.F. service the Mustang IV equipped Nos. 19, 64, 65, 112, 118, 122, 213, 249, 303, 442 and 611 Squadrons, as well as No. 8 Squadron R.A.A.F. In February 1944 the Australian Commonwealth Aircraft Corporation began tooling up for the licence production of the P-51D, but the first of eighty aircraft assembled from imported components did not fly until May 1945 and was too late to participate in the final assault on Japan.

The tactical reconnaissance version of the P-51D was the F-6D, 136 being converted at Dallas with several hatches for oblique and vertical cameras in the rear fuselage and additional radio, including D/F equipment. Another modification of this series resulted in the TP-51D trainer, ten of which were built. These had the radio equipment re-located and an additional seat, with full dual control, behind the normal seat. The extra seat was accommodated within the standard "bubble" canopy. One of the TP-51Ds was further modified for use as a high-speed observation post for the Supreme Allied Commander, General Eisenhower, with which to inspect the Normandy beach-heads in June 1944.

Following immediately on the P-51D, and differing only in the replacement of the Hamilton-Standard airscrew by one of Aeroproducts type, came the P-51K, 1,337 of which were built at Dallas. Weighing 11,000 lb. loaded, the P-51K was not fitted with rocket stubs

G

(Above) The XP-51G, and (below) the XP-51J.

and had a slightly inferior performance to that of the P-51D. Its tactical reconnaissance variant was the F-6K, 163 being converted from P-51Ks. Meanwhile at Inglewood development continued with the XP-51F, which represented the first attempt to produce a lightweight Mustang. With the same Packard Merlin V-1650-7 engine, the XP-51F was an extensive re-design in which loaded weight had been reduced to 9,060 lb. through the simplification of the structure, the deletion of some equipment, and the use of new materials, including plastics. A new low-drag wing was employed, and by fitting smaller wheels, with the new disc brakes, to a simplified undercarriage the "cranked" inner wing that had characterized all previous Mustangs was eliminated. To reduce drag a longer "bubble" hood was fitted, together with a modified radiator fairing, the oil cooler being replaced by a heat exchanger. Two of the six 0.5-in. guns were removed, and the fuel system was re-designed around two 105 U.S. gallon wing tanks, while more weight was saved with the three-bladed Aeroproducts hollow-steel airscrew. The net result was the saving of about one ton in weight and the attainment of a maximum speed of 466 m.p.h. Three XP-51F Mustangs were built, one (FR409) being supplied to the R.A.F.

With similar airframes, two further lightweight Mustangs were produced, designated XP-51G. These were fitted with the 1,500 h.p. Rolls-Royce Merlin 145 which drove a five-bladed Rotol airscrew, and the XP-51G, which weighed only 8,879 lb., attained a maximum speed of 472 m.p.h., one (FR410) being supplied to the R.A.F. The designation P-51E was unassigned, but the development work on the lightweight Mustang materialized in the production P-51H which emerged towards the end of 1944, 555 being completed by V-J Day out of an original contract for 1,445 machines. The P-51H had a Packard Merlin V-1650-9 which delivered a maximum of 2,218 h.p. at 10,200 feet under war emergency conditions, and the wing tanks of the XP-51F were supplemented by a 50-gallon fuselage tank, bringing the total internal fuel capacity to 255 U.S. gallons. The maximum range

was then just over 1,000 miles, but this could be extended to 1,530 miles by the use of two 75-gallon external drop-tanks.

The P-51H was generally similar in appearance to the XP-51F, except for a shorter "bubble" hood, a four-blade Aeroproducts airscrew, a dorsal extension to the taller fin and rudder, and an increase in overall length to 33 ft. 4 in. It had the same shallower carburettor air intake and modified cowling, with integral engine mounting, and had provision for normal external stores, including rockets. Either four or six 0.5-in. machine-guns could be carried, as in the P-51D, and the overload gross weight of 10,500 lb. was only a few hundred pounds less than the "D". Nevertheless the P-51H was the fastest Mustang variant of all, with a maximum speed of 487 m.p.h. at 25,000 feet. One P-51H was supplied to the R.A.F. with the serial number KN987. The P-51H appeared too late to take part in operations in Europe, but a number of fighter groups in the Pacific re-equipped with this variant. It proved to be the last production version of the Mustang, although several more development aircraft appeared.

The final experimental models included two XP-51Js which were similar to the lightweight XP-51F except for the 1,500 h.p. Allison V-1710-119 power plant, giving a fuselage length of 32 ft. 11 in. and a loaded weight of 9,141 lb. The XP-51J had its carburettor air intake incorporated in the ventral radiator. Because of the end of the war the 1,700 P-51Ls, which were to have been similar to the P-51H but have more powerful V-1650-11 engines, were cancelled, not even a prototype being completed, but one P-51M was flown. This was the Dallas-built version of the P-51H, with a 1,400 h.p. Packard V-1650-9A. A total of 1,628 were to have been built.

Even under the stress of war it takes a considerable time to apply the lessons of experience to a completely new design, but the rapid genealogical processes through which the Mustang passed were phenomenal by any standard. The Mustang created records from the day of its inspired conception and ended the war as probably the best all-round single-seat piston-engined fighter to be employed by any of the combatants.

North American P-51D Mustang

Dimensions :	Span, 37 ft. 0 in. ; length, 32 ft. 3 in. ; height, 13 ft. 8 in. ; gross wing area, 233 sq. ft.
Armament :	Four or six 0.5-in. Browning MG 53-2 machine-guns with 270 or 400 r.p.g., and up to two 1,000-lb. bombs on underwing racks or ten 5-in. High-velocity Aircraft Rockets.
Power Plant :	One Rolls-Royce/Packard Merlin V-1650-7 twelve-cylinder liquid-cooled Vee engine with two-speed, two-stage supercharging, developing 1,450 h.p. for take-off, and 1,695 h.p. under war emergency conditions at 10,300 ft.
Weights :	Empty, 7,635 lb. ; combat, 10,100 lb. ; maximum loaded, 11,600 lb.
Performance :	Maximum speed, 437 m.p.h. at 25,000 ft., 413 m.p.h. at 15,000 ft., 395 m.p.h. at 5,000 ft. ; initial climb rate, 3,475 ft./min. ; service ceiling, 40,000 ft.

The Curtiss XP-40, originally the tenth production P-36A, with the coolant radiator under the rear fuselage.

THE CURTISS P-40

The Curtiss P-40 was undoubtedly one of the most controversial fighters to serve in quantity during the Second World War. It was praised and abused, lauded and vilefied, but the fact remains that, as the first American single-seat fighter to be manufactured on a mass-production basis, it bore much of the brunt of the air warfare over several battlefronts. Its performance was inferior to the performances of the majority of its antagonists, but this shortcoming was partly compensated for by its tractability and its sturdiness which enabled it to withstand a considerable amount of punishment. It was amenable to adaptation and it was available when most sorely needed.

To understand the requirements which gave birth to the P-40 it is necessary to appreciate the U.S. strategic thinking in the early 'thirties. Between the two world wars fighter development in the U.S.A. fell behind international standards, principally because of the U.S. Army Air Corp's preoccupation with the long-range bomber which had prior claim on the limited air appropriations. At that time there was a very slim performance margin between the bomber and the fighter, and it was believed that the defensive armament of the larger aircraft would prove more than a match for the destructive ability of the smaller.

This belief in the "ascendancy of bombardment over pursuit" was rife in 1937 when the Curtiss P-40 was first envisaged, and it is a sobering thought that, with the Bell P-39 Airacobra, this product of such a school of thought constituted more than half the strength of all U.S.A.A.F. fighters until July 1943. Prior to September of that year the P-39 and P-40

also comprised more than half the U.S.A.A.F. fighters committed overseas. However, by July 1945 only one P-40 group remained operational.

When the requirements for the P-40 were formulated, no prospect of high-altitude enemy attack against the U.S.A. was envisaged, so that coastal defence and ground attack were the main tasks indicated. Low-altitude flying qualities and rugged construction therefore received priority, and, in fact, the P-40 was subsequently to prove itself an excellent ground-attack weapon. But at the time of the Japanese attack on Pearl Harbour this fighter was already approaching obsolescence, despite having been in production for less than two years. Nevertheless,

One of the three initial production P-40s used for service testing.

(*Left*) *A Curtiss Hawk H-81-A of the initial French contract, and* (*right*) *a Tomahawk IIB (P-40C), or Hawk H-81-A3, of the R.A.F.*

between 1940 and 1944, when acceptances were terminated, a total of 13,738 P-40 fighters were delivered to the U.S.A.A.F., the peak number in service being 2,499 in April 1944.

The P-40 was initially designed around the Allison V-1710 liquid-cooled inline engine which offered better streamlining, more power per unit of frontal area, and better specific fuel consumption than did air-cooled radials of comparable power. Unfortunately, the rated altitude of the Allison engine was only some 12,000 feet, rendering combat above 15,000 feet a completely impracticable proposition. The P-40's ancestry dated back as far as 1924; the famed Curtiss Hawk fighters being in the forefront of all U.S. warplanes. But its development was hindered from the start. The overall limitations of its design were such that the addition of multi-speed superchargers was considered inadvisable in view of the pending production of superior fighter designs. The achievements of the P-40 were therefore all the more creditable.

The prototype XP-40, the Curtiss Hawk Model 81, owed its origin to the earlier Model 75 of 1935 vintage. With the standardization of the Allison V-1710, the P-36 design was reworked to incorporate this engine, becoming the XP-37 which was equipped with a General Electric turbo-supercharger, and featured numerous other modifications, including a rearward-positioned cockpit. Thirteen YP-37s were built for service evaluation; but, with increasingly ominous signs of an approaching war, development of this fighter was abandoned in favour of a less complex and more direct conversion of the P-36 for the Allison engine, the XP-40. This was, in fact, the tenth production P-36A with an integrally-supercharged 1,160 h.p. Allison V-1710-19 (C13) engine, and first flew with its new power plant in the autumn of 1938. Successful in a U.S. Army Pursuit Contest staged at

Wright Field, in May 1939 it was awarded what was at that time the largest-ever production order for a U.S. fighter, totalling nearly thirteen million dollars.

Weighing 6,780 lb. all-up, the XP-40 was subsequently modified by the removal of the coolant radiator from under the rear fuselage to the nose. An intake for an inlet for the single-speed supercharger above the nose was introduced on the production P-40, the Curtiss Model H-81-A, three of which were used for service testing, there being no YP-40. These differed from the prototype also in having the main-wheel fairing plates removed and the production Allison V-1710-33 (C15) of 1,040 h.p. installed.

The P-40 was a relatively clean design, and was unusual for its time in having a fully retractable tail-wheel. One hundred and ninety-seven P-40s were built in 1939-40 for the U.S.A.A.F., and many more were sold abroad to Britain and France. In the R.A.F., which service purchased 140 outright, it was known as the Tomahawk Mk. I, IA, and IB, and carried two 0.303-in. Browning machine-guns in place of the 0.30-in. calibre guns fitted in U.S.A.A.F. machines. It retained the standard synchronized armament of two 0.5-in. calibre machine-guns in the top nose decking. With many of the machines taken over from French orders still bearing Continental instrumentation and cockpit lettering, the Tomahawk Is were used primarily for training, possessing little in the way of operational equipment, and most of them eventually served as hacks for airframe instruction. For a time, however, they equipped Nos. 2, 13, 26, 94, 112, 171, 239, 250, 268, 400, 403 and 414 R.A.F. Squadrons.

The first really combat-worthy model was the P-40B (the P-40A model designation not being assigned), the Curtiss Model H-81-A2, which benefited from reports of air combat in Europe, and embodied armour protection for the pilot, an armour-glass wind-screen, and self-sealing fuel tanks. The wing armament was increased from a total of two to four 0.3-in. calibre guns, and these were retained on the version supplied to the R.A.F. as the Tomahawk Mk. II. No fewer than 1,041 Tomahawk IIs were purchased by Britain, although 100 of these were diverted to China for use by the American Volunteer Group, 146 were re-shipped to the U.S.S.R., and the last forty-nine on British contract were shipped direct to Russia. The modifications made

A Curtiss RP-40 converted from the initial production P-40.

to the P-40B increased gross weight from 7,215 lb. to 7,645 lb., but reduced the official maximum speed by 15 m.p.h. to 352 m.p.h. Only 131 P-40Bs were built for the U.S.A.A.F., and this fighter took the weight of the opening air action of the U.S. entry into the war at Pearl Harbour. In Hawaii every single fighter was destroyed in the initial Japanese attack, including sixty-two P-40Bs and eleven P-40Cs.

In the middle of 1941 General Claire Chennault began recruiting for his Volunteer Group—better known as the Flying Tigers—to fight the Japanese from China, for which 100 P-40s were ordered for purchase through a loan from the U.S. Government. Ninety aircraft, mostly P-40Bs, were actually delivered, sufficient for three squadrons, plus a few spares. At the time of the U.S.A.'s entry into the war there were eighty American pilots in the Volunteer Group, and shortly after arriving at Kunming the P-40s drew first blood, six out of ten attacking Japanese bombers being destroyed by two of the A.V.G. squadrons on December 20. There were no American casualties on this occasion, but the third squadron, left behind at Mingaladon, Burma, was less fortunate, and lost two pilots on their first interception, on December 23, 1941. The American pilots had underestimated the manoeuvrability of the lightly built Japanese fighters, and failed to utilize their superior speed and diving ability to advantage. It was soon the cardinal rule that a P-40 should always avoid mixing it individually with a Japanese fighter, owing to the Curtiss machine's inferior climb rate and manoeuvrability, but the P-40 substantiated a reputation for ruggedness that it was already acquiring with the R.A.F. in the Middle East, and its armour protection saved many A.V.G. pilots in subsequent combat.

Meanwhile the R.A.F. Tomahawks were far from being outdone in aerial combat ; and although outclassed by the Bf 109, the Tomahawk more than held its own in the hands of such pilots as Neville Duke. Of course much of its opposition was provided by obsolescent fighter biplanes, and underpowered, lightly armed fighter monoplanes, of the Regia Aeronautica. Wing-Commander Clive "Killer" Caldwell, R.A.A.F., scored more than twenty victories while flying the P-40 in the Middle East. Towards the end of 1941 the Tomahawk did its share of strafing the retreating Axis troops in North Africa, where its ability to absorb punishment became almost legendary. R.A.F. variants of the P-40B included the Tomahawk IIA with British radio, and the IIB with U.S. equipment, and these operated with Nos. 2, 26, 73, 112, 136, 168, 239, 241, 250, 403, 414, 430 and 616 Squadrons. In the United Kingdom it was used principally for tactical support duties at low altitudes.

Minor production changes in 1941, including improved self-sealing fuel tanks and revised internal equipment, resulted in the P-40C which had a gross weight of 8,058 lb. and a maximum speed of only 340 m.p.h. One hundred and ninety-three of these fighters were built. The first major change in design

came with the development of the P-40D, the Curtiss Model H-87-A2. This had the 1,150 h.p. Allison V-1710-39 (F3R) engine. The external spur airscrew reduction gear of this unit shortened the engine and raised the thrust line, enabling the overall length to be reduced by six inches, the cross-section of the fuselage reduced and the undercarriage shortened. The radiator was increased in size and moved forward, and the fuselage guns were removed, wing armament

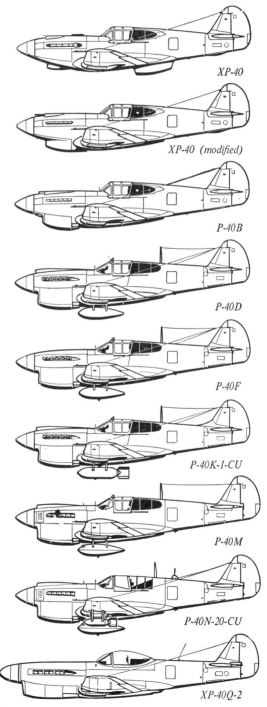

XP-40

XP-40 (modified)

P-40B

P-40D

P-40F

P-40K-1-CU

P-40M

P-40N-20-CU

XP-40Q-2

The first Kittyhawk I (P-40D or Hawk H-87-A2) for the R.A.F. (AK571).

The P-40E, generally similar to the P-40D but having two additional 0.5-in. guns.

The P-40F-1-CU, the first production version with the Packard-Merlin.

The P-40F-3-CU with rearward-positioned radiator.

(Above) The P-40K-1-CU with the short fuselage of the P-40E. (Below) The modified P-40K-10-CU with "beard" radiator replaced by radiators level with the wing leading edges.

being increased to four 0.5-in. calibre machine-guns with new hydraulic chargers. Provision was made for a ventral drop-tank or a 500-lb. bomb, and for small bomb-racks under the wings. Gross weight of the D-model was increased to 8,670 lb., and the official maximum speed became 260 m.p.h., but the climb rate and ceiling remained poor.

Only twenty-two P-40Ds were supplied to the U.S.A.A.F., but 560 were ordered for the R.A.F., by whom it was designated Kittyhawk I as its external appearance differed considerably from that of the Tomahawk. This variant paved the way for the first major production model, the P-40E, or Curtiss Model H-87-A3. Generally similar to the D-model, and known in the R.A.F. as the Kittyhawk IA, the P-40E had two additional 0.5-in. wing guns, bringing the total to six, with 281 rounds per gun, and a further increase in gross weight to 8,840 lb., bringing the maximum speed down to 354 m.p.h. Two thousand three hundred and twenty were built, including a number of P-40E-1s with minor modifications. At this stage in its development the P-40 had a maximum fuel capacity of 201 U.S. gallons (167 Imp. gals.), including a 52-gallon drop-tank, and could carry a bomb load of up to 700 lb., although there were no wing racks on early production aircraft. A few P-40Es were converted as two-seat trainers by the removal of a fuselage fuel tank and the installation of a second seat, while at least one "E" was fitted with an additional belly shackle permitting two 500-lb. bombs to be carried in tandem.

Both the Flying Tigers in China and the R.A.F. squadrons in the Middle East had their P-40Bs replaced by P-40Es. The American Volunteer Group, after continuous operation, was down to some twenty P-40Bs by March 1942, when some thirty P-40Es were ferried to China by air from Accra, in Africa. The improved performance offered by these more potent P-40s was found to be extremely valuable against the Mitsubishi A6M Zero-Sen fighters which, first introduced in the Chinese theatre in 1940, were becoming increasingly numerous. The ground-attack potential of the P-40E was also much superior. The A.V.G. pilots had resorted to carrying 30-lb. incendiary and fragmentation bombs in the flare chutes of their P-40Bs, but it was questionable whether this was not more hazardous to the attackers than to the attacked. But some indication of the P-40's capabilities in resolute hands is given by the fact that from its inception in December 1941 until July 4, 1942, when it was absorbed by the U.S.A.A.F., the A.V.G. was officially credited with the destruction of 286 Japanese aircraft for the loss of eight pilots killed in action, two pilots and one crew chief killed during ground attack, and four pilots missing. The top-scoring A.V.G. pilot, Robert H. Neale, was credited with the destruction of sixteen enemy aircraft while flying the P-40, and eight other pilots claimed ten or more victories.

The P-40s continued operating with the U.S.A.A.F. in the Far East, where Colonel David "Tex" Hill claimed eighteen Japanese aircraft destroyed while flying P-40s, and R.A.F. Kittyhawks spearheaded the

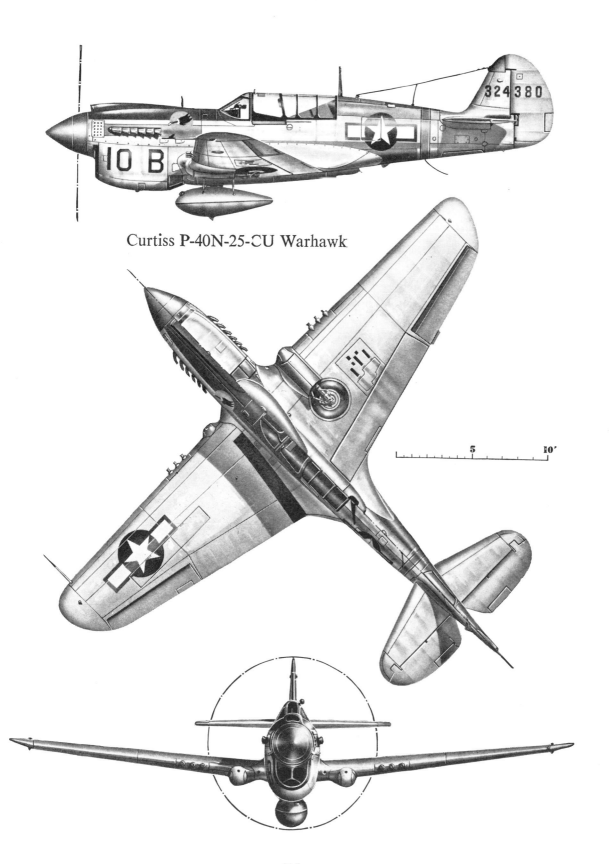

Curtiss P-40N-25-CU Warhawk

324380

10 B

5   10'

The P-40L-5-CU with the standard "long" fuselage.

The P-40N-20-CU with revised cockpit hood and V-1710-99 engine.

The TP-40N-30-CU two-seat trainer adaptation.

attack against Rommel's Afrika Korps in the Western Desert, participating in the combat until the last German forces had been cleared from the tip of Cape Bon, then proceeding to Sicily and, eventually, Italy. In these battles they operated alongside similarly equipped squadrons of the U.S.A.A.F., four of which took part in the massacre of German transport aircraft off Cape Bon. Other P-40-equipped squadrons in the Middle Eastern theatre were Nos. 2, 4, and 5 Squadrons of the S.A.A.F. Elsewhere these aircraft were being operated by the R.C.A.F., the R.N.Z.A.F. and the Soviet Air Force.

One of the most significant steps in P-40 development came in 1941, when a British-built Rolls-Royce Merlin 28 engine with a single-stage, two-speed supercharger was installed in a Kittyhawk I airframe to improve its high-altitude performance. The Curtiss H-87-D, or XP-40F, as the Merlin-powered prototype became known, then had 1,300 h.p. available for take-off, and 1,120 h.p. at 18,500 feet, which offered vast improvements over earlier models and endowed a maximum speed of 373 m.p.h. This was reduced slightly in the YP-40F, which, like later variants, had the Packard-built Merlin V-1650-1 and revised cooling, the air intake above the cowling being incorporated in the radiator scoop. Gross weight climbed to 9,870 lb.

Known as the Warhawk in the U.S.A.A.F. and Kittyhawk II in the R.A.F., 1,311 P-40Fs were subsequently built. Armament was similar to that of its immediate predecessor, but heavier external loads of bombs or drop-tanks could be carried—with a 170 U.S. gallon (141.5 Imp. gal.) external tank the total fuel load became 327 U.S. gallons (272 Imp. gal.). The P-40F-1-CU had the same 31-foot fuselage as the

E-model, but subsequent machines had overall length increased to 33 ft. 4 in., moving the fin and rudder rearward of the tailplane and improving directional stability, particularly during take-off and landing.

Prior to the introduction of the Warhawk, the sixty-sixth production P-40 (Serial No. 39-221) was modified to carry six 0.5-in. calibre guns in the wings, and fitted with operational armour and self-sealing tanks to become the sole P-40G. The designation P-40H was not assigned, but the P-40J was a 1942 project to boost the altitude performance of the Allison engine by the addition of a turbo-supercharger. With the introduction of the Merlin this project was abandoned.

Despite the introduction of the Packard-Merlin, Allison-engined P-40 development continued, and the P-40K Warhawk, known as the Kittyhawk III in R.A.F. service, appeared simultaneously with the P-40F. This model had the more powerful Allison V-1710-73 (F4R) engine which developed 1,325 h.p. for take-off, but its rated power was still well below that of the Merlin. The initial production P-40K-1 to K-5 batches had the short fuselage of the P-40E, but with the extra power there was a tendency to swing during take-off, and a dorsal fin was added to correct this fault, while the P-40K-10 to K-15 production batches embodied the lengthened fuselage introduced on the P-40F. The P-40K also had an automatic manifold pressure altitude regulator, an American term for automatic boost control which had been long standard on British aircraft. The gross weight of this variant was 10,000 lb., and many P-40K-10s and K-15s were "winterized" for service in Alaska and the Aleutians with both the U.S.A.A.F. and the R.C.A.F. The XP-40K was actually a modified P-40K-10 airframe.

In a further attempt to improve performance for short-range combat, the Packard-Merlin-powered P-40F was modified by the removal of some equipment, two wing guns, armour and fuel, and was commonly referred to as the "Gypsy Rose Lee", having been partially stripped. Designated P-40L, the production model which incorporated these changes only saved about 250 lb. in weight, and the official maximum speed was increased by a mere 4 m.p.h. at rated altitude. Nevertheless, 700 P-40Ls with the 1,300 h.p. Packard V-1650-1 were built. The P-40L-1-CU was virtually identical externally to the P-40F, but later variants up to the P-40L-20-CU had the standard "long" fuselage. Like the F-model, the P-40L was designated Kittyhawk II by the R.A.F.

Developed from the P-40L, and also serving with the U.S.A.A.F. in the Middle and Far East as well as with the R.A.F. as the Kittyhawks III and IV, the P-40M (production blocks M-1 to M-10) reverted to the Allison engine, but this was of the V-1710-81 (F20R) version which provided only 1,200 h.p. for take-off but had a greatly increased altitude rating to 17,300 feet. The P-40M was otherwise similar to the P-40K-20, except for the introduction of a cooling grill forward of the exhaust stubs. Six hundred were built, and the P-40M equipped No. 5 Squadron of the South African Air Force serving in Italy.

The largest series of all P-40s began to appear in 1943 in the form of the lightweight P-40N—also designated Kittyhawk IV by the R.A.F. The first production batches (P-40N-1-CU to N-15-CU), which amounted to 1,977 aircraft, had the M-model's high-rated Allison V-1710-81, but introduced an extensive weight-saving programme. Two of the six wing guns were originally removed, together with the front wing tank, and aluminium oil coolers and radiators were incorporated, as well as lighter wheels, reducing combat weight to 8,850 lb. and increasing maximum speed to 378 m.p.h.—the highest speed attained by any P-40 production model. Having been removed in the P-40L, the head armour was reintroduced in the P-40N, which also had in its later production form a modified cockpit canopy with a frameless sliding hood, and a deeper, rectangular aft section to improve rearward view. After the first few hundred P-40N-1s had been built the full six-gun armament was restored, together with the 137 U.S. gallon (114 Imp. gal.) wing tank, and the external stores capacity was increased to 1,500 lb. from 300 lb. This raised the maximum weight to 11,400 lb., and as the Kittyhawk F.B. IV it served with several R.A.F. units in Italy, including Nos. 250 and 450 Squadrons, as a fighter-bomber.

The most widely-built variant of all was the P-40N-20-CU to -35-CU of 1943. This had the 1,200 h.p. Allison V-1710-99 (F26R) engine, and was produced to the tune of 3,022 aircraft. Generally similar to the earlier P-40Ns, this series was shipped to many Allied air forces under Lease-Lend, and did most of its operational flying in the Pacific in fighter-bomber or escort roles. Like earlier variants, the P-40N was adapted in small numbers as a two-seat tandem trainer, one such modification being designated TP-40N-30-CU. The last production P-40 Warhawk was the P-40N-40-CU. This again marked a straightforward engine change to the V-1710-115 (F3R). Other features of these aircraft (220 P-40N-40s were completed in 1944, and another 780 cancelled) included improved non-metallic self-sealing fuel tanks, new radio and oxygen equipment, and flame-damping exhausts.

Following experiments in cooling-drag reduction in 1943 with a P-40K-10-CU which had its "beard" radiator removed to wing installations, and in rear-vision improvements by installing a "bubble" canopy on a standard P-40L, a general "clean-up" programme was initiated, resulting in the sole XP-40Q. With a 1,425 h.p. Allison V-1710-121 engine, the XP-40Q was modified from the first P-40K-1 to have a "bubble" canopy and cut-down rear fuselage, wing radiators and, eventually, clipped wing-tips. A four-blade airscrew was fitted, and water injection installed. With a weight of only 9,000 lb., the XP-40Q attained a maximum speed of 422 m.p.h. This was still less than the speed attained by contemporary production Mustangs and Thunderbolts, however, and the XP-40Q did not achieve production.

The final designation in the Warhawk series was the P-40R, this distinguishing some 300 P-40F and P-40L fighters which had their Packard-Merlins

The XP-40Q with revised radiators and four-blade airscrew.

(Above) The XP-40Q-1 (originally a P-40K-1-CU) with revised air intakes and "bubble" canopy. (Below) The XP-40Q-2 (a modification of the "Q-1") with clipped wing-tips.

replaced by the less powerful Allison V-1710-81 (F20R) engines due to a shortage of Merlin spares in some theatres at a certain stage in the war. All P-40Rs had the "long" fuselage.

Good, bad or indifferent, the U.S.A.A.F. had only the P-40 available when it went to war. More than 14,000 P-40s were delivered during its six-year production life. It will be remembered as a "best second choice", but the majority of its pilots viewed it with affection. It rarely out-performed the fighters that it opposed, but it was one of the sturdiest fighters produced during the Second World War, and innumerable pilots owe their lives to its rugged quality.

Curtiss P-40N-20/35-CU Warhawk

Dimensions : Span, 37 ft. 4 in. ; length, 33 ft. 4 in. ; height, 12 ft. 4 in. ; wing area, 236 sq. ft.

Armament : Six 0.5-in. Browning machine-guns with 281 rounds per gun ; provision for a total of three 500-lb. bombs.

Power Plant : One Allison V-1710-99 liquid-cooled Vee-twelve engine developing 1,200 h.p. for take-off, and 1,125 h.p. at 17,300 ft., with a single-speed supercharger. Maximum fuel capacity, including two 225 U.S. gal. (187 Imp. gal.) drop-tanks, 611 U.S. gals. (508 Imp. gals.).

Weights : Empty, 6,700 lb. ; combat, 8,400 lb. ; maximum permissible, 11,400 lb. ; wing loading, 48.3 lb./sq. ft.

Performance : Maximum speed, 325 m.p.h. at 25,000 ft., 343 m.p.h. at 15,000 ft., 308 m.p.h. at 5,000 ft. ; initial climb rate, 2,120 ft./min. ; climb at 25,000 ft., 900 ft./min. ; service ceiling, 30,000 ft. ; maximum range (full ferry tanks), 2,800 miles at 10,000 ft. ; normal range, 750 miles at 10,000 ft. ; take-off run to clear 50 ft. (combat weight), 2,700 ft. ; landing run, 1,850 ft.

The first prototype Defiant (K8310) is seen above after the installation of the turret, the introduction of a tailwheel and the removal of the lower segments of the wheel fairings from the undercarriage legs.

THE BOULTON PAUL DEFIANT

During the half-decade preceding the Second World War, the views held by the British Air Ministry on fighter armament were undergoing radical change. With the aid of the more imaginative of Britain's aircraft designers, schemes destined to revolutionize fighter concepts were crystallizing. The philosophy of the single-seat single-engined fighter mounting a battery of wing guns was born, and was eventually to be proved tactically correct, but official policy also embraced another development which was not to prove so successful; the single-engined two-seat fighter with all armament concentrated in a massive power-operated turret and exemplified by the Boulton Paul Defiant.

The Defiant was a competently-designed aircraft which more than fulfilled the requirements to which it was produced, but it was a failure. It failed through

no fault in the work of the Boulton Paul design team headed by J. D. North; its failure was partly due to the fact that no designer, however ingenious, could evolve a fighter handicapped by the weight and drag of a bulky powered turret yet capable of matching the agility and speed of contemporary single-seaters employing the same power plant. Its biggest shortcoming, however, and the most serious error in its concept lay in the division of responsibility between pilot and gunner. The Defiant possessed no fixed forward-firing armament, and while the pilot had to think in abstract terms of his gunner's likely line of sight, it was all too easy for an enemy fighter to creep in under cover of the blind spot beneath the tail and deliver the coup de grâce.

The idea of a single-engined two-seat fighter as represented by the Defiant was in some ways a throw-

The first prototype Defiant (K8310) was initially flown on August 11, 1937 without the power-operated turret installed, ballast being carried for the turret and second crew member. The single-seat configuration was later reverted to when, in 1940 a single-seat fixed-gun variant of the Defiant was proposed.

The second prototype Defiant (K8620), which flew on May 18, 1939, introduced a revised engine cowling with ejector exhausts and an enlarged carburettor air intake, mid-crew transparent panels, a multi-panel curved cockpit roof and single-panel curved windscreen.

back to the thinking of the First World War when such two-seaters as the Sopwith 1½-Strutter and the Bristol Fighter had achieved considerable success in the fighter role. As speeds increased, the extra drag of the second cockpit and its exposed guns became prohibitive, widening the performance gap between single- and two-seater to an unacceptable degree. By the end of 1934 a Demon two-seat interceptor biplane had been fitted with a prototype of a Frazer-Nash hydraulically-operated turret with a segmented folding shield, as part of a series of attempts by Hawker Aircraft to provide protection from the slipstream for the gunner. The so-called "lobster-back" of the turret also reduced drag, and Boulton Paul, who were manufacturing the Demon under licence and also developing a compact four-gun turret intended for the defensive armament of bombers, began to consider the idea of designing a small two-seat fighter around their turret.

Development of the Boulton Paul turret inevitably led to a revival of official interest in the two-seat fighter concept, in the belief that a gunner possessing no responsibility for flying the fighter, and having control of a battery of guns with a 360° traverse, had more chance of hitting the enemy than a pilot who had to point the whole aircraft in the direction in which he wished to fire. How fallacious was this belief was to be revealed all too forcibly several years later, but in 1935 it enjoyed sufficient support for the Air Ministry to conceive a requirement for a two-seat interceptor fighter to supplant the turret-equipped Demon then approaching obsolescence. This requirement was written into specification F.9/35 which called for a two-seat fighter with the main armament concentrated in a revolving turret and a speed capability comparable with the forthcoming generation of single-seat interceptors.

The extent to which official views were fluctuating

The first production Defiant I (L6950) was flown on July 30, 1939, and is seen below with the underwing racks for eight light bombs which were fitted for close-support trials. The Defiant was also evaluated in the close-support, dive-bombing and army co-operation roles during 1939–40.

One of the first production Defiant I two-seat fighters in standard day fighter camouflage. This aircraft possessed very few vices, apart from a tendency to swing to port during take-off, and enjoyed excellent handling characteristics.

in these years immediately prior to the Second World War may be gauged from the fact that, while, in 1935, the official mind could contemplate with equanimity a fighter powered by a single Rolls-Royce Merlin engine and carrying two crew members and a 600 lb. turret, eighteen months later a proposal to produce a Merlin-powered Hurricane single-seater with four 20-mm. wing-mounted cannon was rejected on the grounds that such an armament was "too heavy for a *single*-engined aircraft", and this pronouncement was not referring to the weight of fire!

At least five aircraft manufacturers submitted proposals to meet the Air Ministry's specification, and two of these proposals were selected for prototype construction. The successful contenders were the designs submitted by Hawker Aircraft and Boulton Paul, and one prototype of each company's project was ordered in the Autumn of 1935.

The Hawker fighter was basically a redesign of a two-seat light bomber, construction of which had started at Kingston some three months earlier and which was eventually to emerge as the Henley.

Bomb stowage facilities beneath the wing were deleted, and the aft movement of the centre of gravity resulting from the installation of the turret necesitated extensive changes to the wing, the centre section of which was moved forward four inches. Like those of the Henley, the outer wing panels of the fighter were built on Hurricane primary jigs, although the fabricated Warren truss of the single-seater allowing for the batteries of wing guns had to be replaced by a cast truss, the ribs were rearranged, and the rear spar was shortened to give a 3.5° sweep to the outer panels. An entirely new cockpit section was introduced, and the increased side area of the cockpit superstructure and turret necessitated slight modifications to the fin contours. The name Hotspur was applied to the fighter, but owing to the company's Hurricane commitments, prototype construction did not commence until 1937.

The prototype Hotspur (K8309) was flown by P. G. Lucas for the first time on June 14, 1938, but by that time the competitive Boulton Paul fighter had been flying for almost a year, and A. V. Roe, who it had been

Defiant Is of No. 264 Squadron, two sections of which became operational on March 20, 1940. During one of its first offensive patrols, the squadron's "B" Flight lost five of its six aircraft to Messerschmitt Bf 109Es. Thereafter the Defiant was restricted largely to the anti-bomber role over the Channel.

planned would produce the Hotspur, were fully committed to the production of other designs. The Hawker two-seater was tested at Martlesham where it was found to be both lighter and faster than its Boulton Paul contemporary. The results of these tests were only of academic interest, however, and no far-reaching comparative trials between the two fighters were undertaken, but carrying ballast for the second crew member and the four-gun turret (only a wooden mock-up of the turret having been fitted), though not for the ammunition, the Hotspur attained 316 m.p.h. at 15,800 ft., this being some 14 m.p.h. faster than the maximum speed attained by the Boulton Paul prototype when carrying similar ballast, a superiority primarily due to a substantially lower structural weight.

Boulton Paul's design to the requirements of F.9/35, the P.82 and later to be named officially Defiant, was generally similar in overall size and design to the Hurricane, with its ventral radiator and inward-retracting undercarriage. Its construction was conventional for its period, one of the few unusual features being the method of attaching the light alloy fuselage and wing skins to the stringers and ribs, and then attaching these to the fuselage frames and wing spars. In this way, the need to pre-form the skins was avoided, and by riveting the skins while flat and using countersunk holes, an exceptional surface finish was obtained. The closest attention was given to aerodynamic cleanliness in an attempt to counter to some extent the drag of the turret. The fuselage was built in two sections, the forward section being built up of four L-section longerons and several massive bulkheads, and the rear section consisting of three units—two side panels and top decking. The rear section accommodated the turret, fore and aft of which were fairings of spruce and three-ply which were operated by pneumatic jacks actuated by cams fitted to the turret, and hinged downwards automatically to allow the guns to traverse. The pilot was seated in the forward section immediately over the wing centre section, the upper surface of which formed the floor of the cockpit. A slightly unorthodox feature of the cockpit was the mounting of the control column on the pilot's seat frame so that the column had a constant effective length no matter how the seat was adjusted.

The wing, described as a compromise between straight taper and the ideal elliptical shape, was a two-spar structure in five components—centre section, two outer panels, and two detachable tips. The outboard extremities of the wing centre section housed the self-sealing fuel tanks, these containing a total of 104 Imp. gal. (125 U.S. gal.), the hydraulically-actuated undercarriage with Lockheed Airdraulic shock-absorbers being accommodated inboard. Split trailing edge flaps extended across the whole of the wing between the Frise-type ailerons, except where interrupted by the glycol radiator. The oil cooler and the carburettor air intake were grouped together further forward.

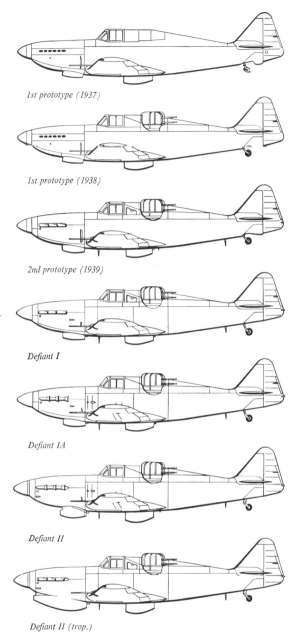

1st prototype (1937)

1st prototype (1938)

2nd prototype (1939)

Defiant I

Defiant IA

Defiant II

Defiant II (trop.)

The Boulton Paul A.Mk.IID turret was a removable self-contained unit mounting four 0.303-in. belt-fed Browning guns with 600 r.p.g., and its entire hydraulic system formed an integral part of the turret itself, being independent of any other hydraulic system in the aircraft. The bare turret weighed 361 lb. to which was added the 88 lb. of the four Browning guns, 106 lb. for ammunition, and some 35 lb. for gunner's oxygen equipment, sights, etc. This turret was not installed when the first prototype, K8310, made its inaugural flight at Wolverhampton on August 11, 1937, with Boulton Paul's chief test pilot, Cecil Feather, at the controls. Design work on the Defiant had begun at Norwich, but the company was in process of moving

(*Above*) *This Defiant I night fighter (T4106), the 114th aircraft of an order for 150 machines placed at the end of December 1939, was shipped to the U.S.A. and evaluated at Wright-Patterson Field. (Left) The sixty-second production Defiant I (L7012) with the black (port) and white (starboard) underwing finish applied to this type during its early service. The first Defiant production order calling for eighty-seven machines (L6950–7036) was placed in March 1937.*

to a new plant at Wolverhampton, and it was here that the prototype had been built. The initial flight trials of the Defiant were conducted as a single-seater with the turret "well" faired over and at a loaded weight of 7,500 lb. A Rolls-Royce Merlin I engine was installed, and a speed of 302 m.p.h. was attained. The increased side area resulting from the installation of the turret necessitated a slight increase in vertical tail surface area, the tail skid was supplanted by a wheel, and the folding lower segments of the wheel fairings were detached from the undercarriage legs, but its flying characteristics were generally satisfactory, and the Defiant was pronounced an excellent flying machine, with few vices. Stability was very satisfactory, and there was practically no change of trim when the undercarriage or flaps were lowered. There was a tendency to swing to port during take-off, but this was easily corrected, and with flaps and undercarriage up one wing dropped to a vertical position when the aircraft was stalled, this usually developing into a gentle flick roll if the control column was held back. In most respects, however, the Defiant handled like the lady she was.

With the decision to abandon production of the competitive Hotspur fighter, a second prototype of the Defiant (K8620) had been ordered, and a contract for eighty-seven production Defiants had been placed

in March 1937, production drawings beginning to reach the shops before the end of the year. Some delay resulted in the completion of the second prototype owing to the decision to supplant the Merlin I by the Merlin II, and to incorporate production changes, such as undercarriage fairing segments on the centre line of the fuselage, these completely enclosing the mainwheels, a multi-panel curved cabin-roof, additional glazed panels aft of the pilot's canopy and other refinements, and this aircraft flew for the first time on May 18, 1939. Earlier, the first prototype had been fitted with an enlarged carburettor air intake, a single-panel curved windscreen, and retractable radio masts, these features also appearing on the second prototype. The Merlin III engine had been selected for the production Defiant, this having a standardised shaft for de Havilland or Rotol constant-speed airscrews and offering a similar 1,030 h.p. output at 16,250 ft., and the first production aircraft followed closely on the heels of the second prototype, flying on July 30, 1939.

In parallel with the production of the Defiant I, Boulton Paul initiated the design of a dual-control training version with a semi-enclosed rear cockpit replacing the turret, but this was cancelled when design work was eighty per cent complete in 1938. The year 1938 also saw the placing of further production contracts for the standard fighter, 202 being

FINISH AND INSIGNIA: *The Defiant I of No. 256 Squadron illustrated on the opposite page had an overall matt black finish with light grey unit code letters (dull red was later standardised). "B" type red-blue roundels appeared on the upper wing surfaces, and "A" type red-white-blue roundels with broad yellow outline appeared on the fuselage sides, and a standard red-white-blue flash with equal division of colours appeared on the fin. The serial number was painted in dull red. Some Defiant night fighters were later given "B" type red-blue roundels on the fuselage sides or "C1" type roundels with narrow white portion and narrow yellow outline.*

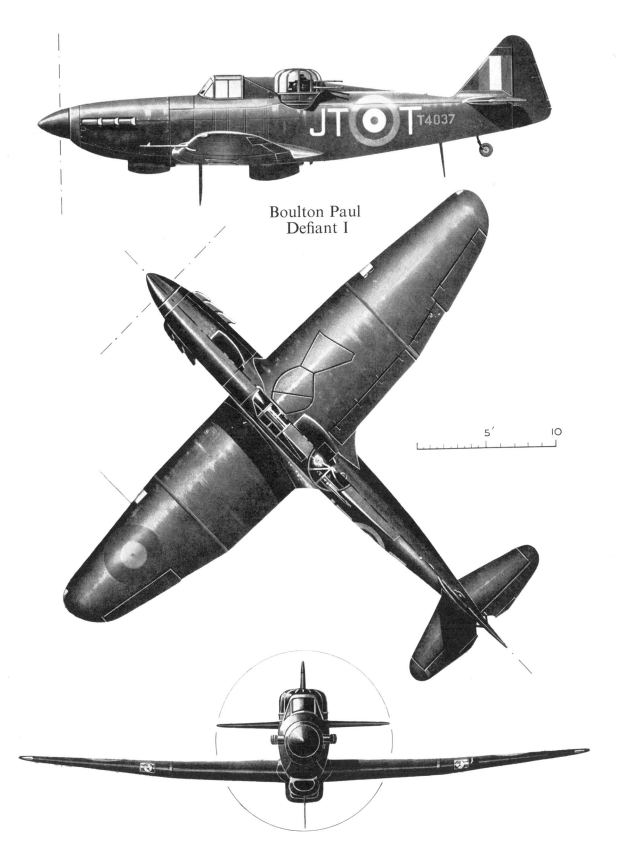

Boulton Paul
Defiant I

5′   10

ordered in February and 161 in May. The Defiant I weighed 8,318 lb. in normal loaded condition and had a maximum permissible loaded weight of 8,350 lb. It thus weighed some seventeen hundred pounds more than the similarly powered Hurricane, yet the gross wing area of the two-seater at 250 sq. ft. was less than that of the single-seater, and thus both wing loading at 33.27 lb./sq. ft. and power loading at 8.07 lb./h.p. were substantially higher. It was hardly to be expected, therefore, that the Defiant would be able to compete on the score of level speed, climb rate, or manoeuvrability. In fact, maximum level speed of the production aircraft was only 304 m.p.h. at 17,000 ft. Comparative trials between the Defiant and the Hurricane were undertaken by No. 111 Squadron at Northolt in October 1939, and in his report on the trials, the squadron's commanding officer gave it as his opinion that any average pilot flying a Hurricane could carve up an aircraft with the power/weight ratio of the Defiant, and that the Boulton Paul fighter would suffer badly if it came up against a German fighter for a *second* time! He obviously considered the Defiant's philosophy to be outmoded, and his comments were to prove prophetic when the Defiant eventually saw combat a few months later.

Deliveries of the Defiant had proceeded quickly after the first aircraft had come off the line and, despite the unfavourable results of the Defiant-versus-Hurricane trials, No. 264 (Madras Presidency) Squadron, which had been formed at Sutton Bridge during the same month as the trials took place, was designated as the first unit to re-equip with the new fighter and, after moving to Martlesham, received its first two Defiants on December 8, 1939. There

followed the essential period of training and working up, during the course of which the Defiant was grounded for a short period while Rolls-Royce and Lockheed teams investigated a series of engine failures and malfunctioning of the hydraulics. The ban was lifted during the first week of February 1940, and the first night flying trials were carried out on the fifteenth of that month, the Defiant having been intended from the outset for both day and night roles. In the meantime, trials to determine the Defiant's suitability for roles other than interception were being carried out. The first production Defiant (L6950) had been fitted with underwing racks for light bombs for close-support trials shortly after its appearance, dive-bombing trials were conducted at Orfordness, and an early Defiant (L6968) was used for army co-operation trials. In fact, No. 2 Squadron did eventually receive a few Defiants for army co-operation duties in August 1940, although the unit never flew operationally with these machines which were quickly withdrawn.

With the outbreak of war, orders for the Defiant were substantially increased, a contract for 150 aircraft in December 1939 being supplemented by contracts for fifty and 280 Defiants in February and July 1940, bringing total orders for the fighter to 930 machines. Although the tactical problems offered by the Defiant had still to be resolved satisfactorily, on March 20, 1940, two sections of No. 264 Squadron, each having three aircraft, were considered operational, and these moved to Wittering for operational duty two days later. Led by Squadron Leader Philip Hunter as commanding officer, the Defiants of what was known as No. 264 Squadron Detachment first operated on convoy patrols at the end of March and continued in this role for most of April. On May 10th the entire Squadron was transferred to Duxford, and two days later the six Defiants of "A" Flight flying from Horsham St. Faith patrolled along the Dutch coast in company with the Spitfires of No. 66 Squadron's "B" Flight which flew top cover. After strafing ground targets in the vicinity of the Hague, the Defiants succeeded in intercepting and destroying a Ju 88A engaged in attacking a destroyer, thus drawing first blood. The next day the Defiants of "B" Flight undertook a similar patrol during which they encountered a formation of Ju 87B dive bombers, claiming the destruction of four of the enemy. Unfortunately for the Squadron, "B" Flight was bounced by Messerschmitt Bf 109Es which had been covering the dive bombers, and the German fighters were not apparently misled by the Defiant's superficial resemblance to the Hurricane, for only one of the six Boulton Paul fighters survived. Thereafter, offensive patrols were cancelled, and the Defiant was largely restricted to the anti-bomber role over the Channel.

The Defiant was still to enjoy its brief hour of glory, however, despite the inauspicious start to its operational career. Between the 27th and 31st of May, the exigencies of the times necessitated despatching No. 264 Squadron's Defiants across the Channel to patrol over Dunkirk. During this period, the Squadron claimed fifty-seven "kills", of which no fewer than thirty-seven were claimed during the course of two patrols over Dunkirk on May 29th! One of the reasons for this startling success was, according to the Squadron's commanding officer, that "the enemy mistook us for Hurricanes". If this is so, the Luftwaffe was not to make the same mistake again, but the claims, fully accepted at the time, were subsequently to prove considerably exaggerated. For instance, on May 29th., the day on which No. 264 Squadron claimed its thirty-seven victims, official Luftwaffe records were to show that only *fourteen* aircraft were lost in action! However, at the time it appeared that the philosophy of the Defiant's design had been fully vindicated, and the fighter enjoyed considerable favourable publicity. The rapidity with which the

Luftwaffe discovered the most effective means of engaging the Defiant may be judged from the fact that, on May 31st., no less than seven of No. 264's Defiants were lost.

The battle-weary unit spent June and July working up again to squadron strength, and No. 264 carried out a few patrols along the East Coast without engaging the enemy. Similar patrols were also being conducted by a second Defiant unit, No. 141 Squadron, which had become operational on June 3rd. In July No. 141 Squadron had transferred to Hawkinge for the defence of coastal targets, and by this time its Defiants, like those of No. 264 Squadron, had been fitted with de Havilland constant-speed airscrews in place of the Rotol units. On July 19th nine of No. 141's Defiants patrolling South of Folkestone were "bounced" by Bf 109E fighters whose pilots were certainly labouring under no misapprehension as to the identity of their opponents for, after shooting down two of the Defiants in a firing pass from out of the sun, they promptly used the Defiant's principal blind spot for their next attack, approaching from below and dead astern. Four more of the Defiants were despatched in this manner, although No. 141 Squadron claimed four of the Bf 109Es. This disastrous action resulted in the Squadron being released from operations and withdrawn to Prestwick two days later, taking no further part in the "Battle of Britain".

(Right) A Defiant IA with the "arrow-head" type aerial on the starboard wing leading edge and "H"-type fuselage aerial. On the port wing the "arrow-head" aerial was mounted at mid-chord. (Below) A Defiant II night fighter (AA436) of No. 151 Squadron. Delivery of this version of the fighter began in February 1941.

This was only a foretaste of what was to befall No. 264 Squadron whose Defiants had, in the meantime, undertaken the first night interception sorties from Kirton. On August 22nd the Squadron was moved South and, two days later, lost four of its aircraft. On the 28th two more Defiants were lost and four damaged, the Squadron being left with only three serviceable fighters and also withdrawn from the "Battle". The operation of the Defiant by day was obviously too costly to continue, and it was now clear that the concept of the turret-armed fighter was wrong for the kind of aerial warfare prevailing in 1940. The pilot always had to think in terms of his gunner's firing arc and this was impracticable in the type of mêlée taking place almost every day of the "Battle". Again, the Defiant was always at a disadvantage when opposed by a single-seater owing to the high-power loading and turret drag which were inevitable in a fighter of this type. But by this time Defiant production was in full swing and, in 1940, the R.A.F. could not afford to waste aircraft of any kind, so the fighters were assigned to the night interception role. Flame-damper exhausts were fitted and the mid-crew perspex panels were deleted.

Both Nos. 141 and 264 Squadrons participated in the development of night fighting techniques, and with the commencement of the Luftwaffe's night offensive against London both squadrons were transferred to bases from which they could operate in defence of the British capital, the first night "kill" being claimed by No. 141 on December 22nd when the destruction of an He 111 bomber was confirmed. No. 307 Squadron, which had begun to form as a day fighter unit with Defiants in September 1940, was the only new night fighter squadron operating the Boulton Paul fighter to be operational at the beginning of 1941, but thereafter the Defiant night fighter force expanded rapidly, and a further four squadrons were using Defiants by May (Nos. 96, 151, 255, and 256), the crews for these having been trained at No. 54 Operational Training Unit at Church Fenton, although three of the units still had a few Hurricanes on strength. Other units to receive the Defiant I were Nos. 85, 125, 153, 409, 410 and 456 Squadrons, and in the Autumn of 1941 the first radar-equipped Defiant IAs began to appear, No. 264 Squadron being the first to employ these operationally. The Defiant IA was equipped with the early A.I.Mk.4 radar with an "arrow-head" type aerial on the starboard wing and "H"-type aerials on the sides of the fuselage. The A.I.Mk.4 had minimum and maximum ranges of 600 ft. and four miles, and although possessing many shortcomings, substantially improved the Defiant's effectiveness as a night fighter. The Mk.IA was also delivered to Nos. 96, 125, 256 and 410 Squadrons.

Long before the Defiant had embarked upon its nocturnal career, Boulton Paul were endeavouring to further exploit the basic design and, in 1940, a single-seat fixed-gun variant was proposed. It was intended to remove the turret and install two 0.303-in. Browning guns in each wing, and the original prototype (K8310)

was modified to participate in the development programme, rear fuselage decking similar to that with which the prototype made its first test flights being reintroduced. It was anticipated that performance would be slightly superior to that of the Hurricane, but the scheme did not find official favour. At the same time, Boulton Paul were developing the Defiant II which featured redesigned engine mountings for a 1,280 h.p. Merlin XX engine, a pressurized fuel system, additional fuel tankage, and redesigned deeper radiator and lengthened engine cowling. The wing centre section housed two 52 Imp. gal. (62.4 U.S. gal.) main fuel tanks which were augmented by auxiliary tanks in the outer panels, 27 Imp. gal. (32.4 U.S. gal.) to port and 28 Imp. gal. (33.6 U.S. gal.) to starboard, total fuel capacity being 159 Imp. gal. (191 U.S. gal.). These changes were accompanied by a slightly larger rudder, and normal loaded weight rose to 8,424 lb., empty weight being 6,282 lb. The performance increase resulting from these changes was only marginal, maximum speed being raised to 303 m.p.h. at 12,000 ft., 315 m.p.h. at 16,000 ft., and 313 m.p.h. at 19,000 ft. Economical cruising speed was 160 m.p.h. at 20,000 ft., and the speed for maximum rate of climb was 140 m.p.h. up to that altitude.

The Merlin XX was first tested in two Defiant Is (N1550 and N1551), the first of which flew on July 20, 1940, and the contract placed earlier that month for 280 Defiants was amended to sixty-three Mk. Is and 210 Mk. IIs. Seven Mk. Is were also converted to Mk. II standards on the production line, and deliveries of the Mk. II began in February 1941, production of this variant being completed eleven months later. Like the Defiant IA, the Mk. II was initially fitted with A.I.Mk.4 radar, although this was soon supplanted by the refined A.I.Mk.6, and the type served with Nos. 96, 125, 141, 151, 153, 264 and 410 Squadrons. At one period, the Defiant IIs of No. 264 Squadron operating from Hunsdon collaborated with Turbinlite-equipped Douglas Havocs on night patrols, but by mid-1942 the Defiant had already largely given place to later, twin-engined night fighters, and the last two squadrons to operate this type in the night interception role, Nos. 153 and 256, had re-equipped by the end of the year, although a flight of No. 515 (Special Duties) Squadron retained Defiants until mid-1943.

As Defiants were released from the night fighter role they were handed over to R.A.F. Fighter Command air-sea rescue units, largely supplanting the Lysander. Two "M"-type rescue dinghies were carried in containers beneath the wings, and the fifty or so Defiants converted for the air-sea rescue role served with Nos. 275, 276, 277, 278 and 281 Squadrons. Their suitability for the role was questionable as their wide turning circle and high stalling speed were distinct disadvantages on A.S.R. operations. However, maintenance problems necessitated their withdrawal after some six months. Defiant production ended with a run of 140 examples of a target-towing variant ordered in July 1941 as the T.T.Mk.I. The turret was removed and replaced by a fixed canopy over the winch operator's cockpit, and a "B" or "E" type winch was attached to the side of the fuselage and driven by a "windmill" on the fuselage starboard side, and target sleeves were carried in a pack under the rear fuselage. Based on the Defiant II, the first T.T.Mk.I (DR863) was completed at the end of 1941, and deliveries occupied most of 1942. The last forty Mk. II fighters were also converted as T.T.Mk. Is and, subsequently, 150 Defiant Is with Merlin III engines were converted as target tugs following a successful trial conversion of N3488 in mid-1942, and designated T.T.Mk. III. The designation T.T.Mk. II was reserved for a proposed production variant with a 1,620 h.p. Merlin 24 engine. The Defiant performed the unglamorous but vital task of target tug throughout the remainder of the war years, serving at air gunnery training schools and many fighter and bomber O.T.U.s. Some sixty Defiant target tugs were transferred to the Royal Navy.

The Defiant was an aircraft of exceptional qualities and an excellent flying machine, and as the world's first fighter to have an enclosed power-driven turret it made its mark on history. It was hardly to be expected that the Defiant, penalised by the weight and high drag of even such a compact turret as that evolved by Boulton Paul and possessing a motor of only the same power as that of the very much lighter Hurricanes and Spitfires, would compete in performance and agility with contemporary single-seaters, and it was not the fault of the design team that their product was born of an outmoded philosophy. The Defiant failed by day, but when the Luftwaffe turned to night operations, presenting the R.A.F. with a formidable problem, it found its forté,

filling a gap in Britain's defences until more advanced night interceptors became available.

(*Above*) *The first Defiant T.T.Mk.I target tug (DR863) photographed during the winter of 1942-43. One hundred and forty T.T.Mk.Is were ordered in July 1941, and the last forty Mk.II fighters were completed to similar standards.*

Boulton Paul Defiant I

Dimensions :	Span, 39 ft. 4 in. ; length, 35 ft. 4 in. ; height, 11 ft. 4 in. ; wing area, 250 sq. ft.
Armament :	Four 0.303-in. Browning machine guns with 600 r.p.g. in a Boulton Paul A.Mk.IID hydraulically-operated turret.
Power Plant :	One Rolls-Royce Merlin III twelve-cylinder Vee liquid-cooled engine rated at 880 h.p. at 3,000 r.p.m. for take-off, 990 h.p. at 2,600 r.p.m. at 12,250 ft., and 1,030 h.p. at 3,000 r.p.m. at 16,250 ft. Internal fuel capacity: 104 Imp. gal. (125 U.S. gal.)
Weights :	Empty, 6,078 lb. ; normal loaded, 8,318 lb. ; maximum permissible loaded (day fighter), 8,350 lb., (night fighter), 8,600 lb.
Performance	Maximum speed, 304 m.p.h. at 17,000 ft., 298 m.p.h. at 12,000 ft., 250 m.p.h. at sea level ; cruising speed, 259 m.p.h., at 15,000 ft. ; range, 465 mls. at 259 m.p.h. ; endurance, 1.78 hrs. ; initial climb rate, 1,900 ft./min. ; time to 15,750 ft., 8.5 min. ; service ceiling, 30,350 ft.

The Defiant II (AA370) illustrated below was, in fact, the first Mk.II model to be built from the ground up, although it was preceded by seven Mk.Is (AA363–369) which had been converted to Mk.II standards on the production line. One of the most important changes in the Mk.II was the introduction of two auxiliary fuel tanks—27 Imp. gal. to port and 28 Imp. gal. to starboard—to supplement the two 52 Imp. gal. main tanks.

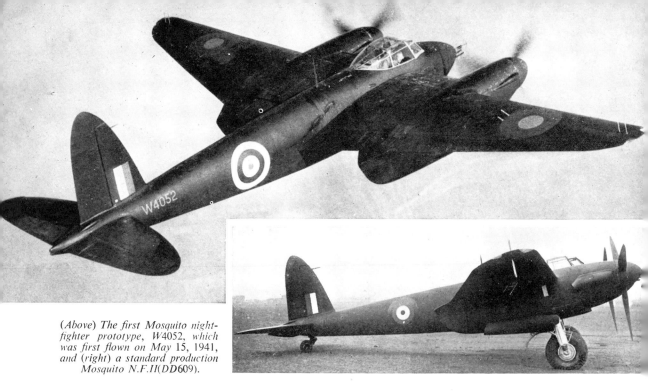

(Above) The first Mosquito night-fighter prototype, W4052, which was first flown on May 15, 1941, and (right) a standard production Mosquito N.F.II(DD609).

THE DE HAVILLAND MOSQUITO

It is one of the paradoxes of aircraft development that some of the world's greatest aeroplanes have achieved their fame doing jobs other than the one for which they were originally designed. No better example of this could be found than the Mosquito, which, conceived as a bomber, became one of the war's most potent fighters. More than this, indeed, it was probably the most successfully versatile of any twin-engined type built between 1939 and 1945, for, contrary to the old adage, "Jack-of-all-trades and master of none", it excelled in all the widely varied roles for which it was found to be amenable. Its repertoire included the duties of low-level and high-attack day and night bomber, long-range photo-reconnaissance, minelayer, pathfinder, high-speed military transport, long-range day and night fighter, and fighter-bomber. It served in Europe, the Middle and Far East and on the Russian front. In fact the ubiquitous Mosquito reigned supreme among General Purpose types; and of the grand total of 7,781 Mosquitos built, 6,710 were delivered during the war years.

The story of the Mosquito commenced during the summer of 1938, the year of the Munich crisis, when the de Havilland organization first gave thought to the possibilities of a high-speed bomber. The essence of de Havilland's bomber conception was the reliance on speed rather than armament for defence, and it was this emphasis on performance upon which the Mosquito's success as a fighter was subsequently to be built. As a bomber it was designed to outperform existing fighters. Therefore as a fighter it was bound to be outstanding. By the end of 1938 a number of proposals had been considered by the design office,

and that regarded as potentially the most promising was a twin-Merlin monoplane of wooden construction, having a crew of two and no defensive armament. Speeds of 400 m.p.h. were envisaged, combined with a 1,500-mile range with a 1,000-lb. bomb load. The Air Ministry viewed the project with academic rather than practical interest, although the Member for Research, Development and Production on the Air Council, Sir Wilfred Freeman, was enthusiastic from the outset.

Germany's invasion of Poland and Britain's declaration of war changed the atmosphere at the Air Ministry, and interest in the D.H.98, under which type number the project designs had been studied, hardened. On December 29, 1939, the Air Ministry accepted the de Havilland proposal for the bomber. At the same time the company pointed out the potentialities of the design in the photographic-reconnaissance and fighter roles; the former was the subject of some official interest, the latter of scarcely any, but de Havillands designed from the outset with a view to the later installation of four 20-mm. cannon under the cockpit floor.

On March 1, 1940, the first contract was placed, for fifty D.H.98 bombers (including prototypes) to be built to specification B.1/40 which had been written around de Havilland's proposals, and the name Mosquito was approved. The period was an inauspicious one for the initiation of so radical a design; with the war going against Britain the tendency was to concentrate on existing designs. With the fall of France and the Dunkirk evacuation the Mosquito was actually dropped from Ministry of Aircraft

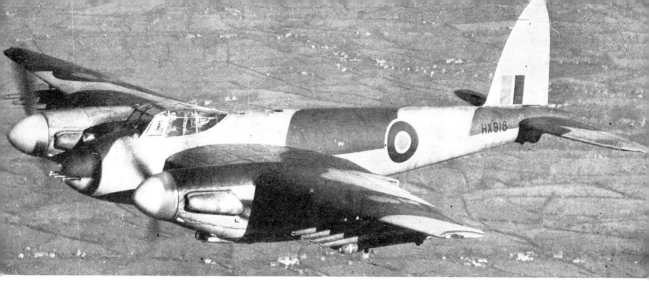

A Mosquito F.B.VI with rocket-launching rails fitted outboard of the engine nacelles.

Production programmes at one stage, setting back the ordering of materials. But permission to proceed was later given again, although de Havillands were told that their Tiger Moth and Oxford production were to take priority. Had it not been that the Mosquito used "non-strategic" wood for its construction, it might well never have been reinstated.

Construction of the prototype was pressed ahead through the difficult months of 1940, while the "Battle of Britain" was fought out overhead; bombs fell within a mile of the Hatfield factory on one day in every five, and nearly 25 per cent of the working hours, day and night, were spent in air-raid shelters. Despite all these vicissitudes, the prototype (W4050) made its first flight on November 25, 1940, only ten months and twenty-six days after detailed design work had commenced. The pilot was Geoffrey de Havilland, Jnr. Meanwhile, inevitably, requirements had been changing. There was some loss of confidence in the high-speed bomber, while the heavily armed long-range fighter grew in favour. The contract was, therefore, changed to twenty bombers and thirty fighters, necessitating the modification of a number of parts already manufactured. Construction of a fighter prototype proceeded at Salisbury Hall, London Colney, which served as a dispersal for the Hatfield design office and experimental shop. Two days before this prototype (W4052) was ready to fly, a German agent was dropped by parachute close to Salisbury Hall, in plain clothes and with a portable radio. He was captured next day, and the day after, May 15, 1941, Geoffrey de Havilland flew the fighter prototype from a 450-yard field beside the shed in which it had been built.

Already, on February 19, 1941, the bomber prototype had been handed over for official trials, which were eminently successful. Between the prototype and the production stages only one important aerodynamic modification was required—the extending aft of the nacelle fairings to improve airflow around them. By July the Mosquito was known to be a

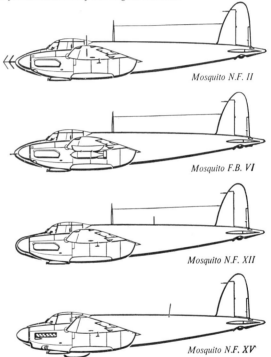

Mosquito N.F. II

Mosquito F.B. VI

Mosquito N.F. XII

Mosquito N.F. XV

winner and de Havillands were told to prepare for large-scale production in their own factories and elsewhere, and also to make plans for production in Canada. On June 10, 1941, the last of the three prototypes (W4051) was flown as an unarmed photographic-reconnaissance variant, and the division of the initial batch of fifty Mosquitos was finally agreed at ten P.R.Mk.I photo-reconnaissance aircraft, thirty F.Mk.II fighters and ten B.Mk.IV bombers (the Mark III was by this time a proposal for a dual-control trainer variant which was ordered on a later contract). The first Mosquitos went to the R.A.F. in July 1941, and the first operational sortie, a reconnaissance flight at 20,000 feet over Bordeaux, Brest and La Pallice, was made on September 19 by a Mosquito P.R.I (W4055).

(Above) The prototype night-fighter fitted with a Bristol B.XI turret, and (below) the same machine fitted with a circular, segmented air brake.

(Above) A Mosquito N.F.XII, the first to carry centimetric A.I radar, and (below) the N.F.XIII with the more powerful Merlin 25 engines.

As production mounted, bomber and fighter squadrons were formed throughout the winter of 1941-42; twenty Mosquitos had been delivered by the end of 1941, the first fifty by March 1942. In May, No. 23 Squadron at Ford and No. 157 Squadron at Castle Camps became operational with Mosquito fighters and quickly made their presence felt on the enemy. Production, which had been put in hand at Hatfield, was assisted from an early date by the output of de Havilland's Second Aircraft Group at Leavesden. This factory was built by the company in 1940–41 at M.A.P. request for the shadow production of Wellington bombers, this plan being dropped in favour of Mosquito production. Hatfield and Leavesden were jointly to produce 4,444 Mosquitos up to August 15, 1945, the date of Japan's surrender. This figure is broken down as follows: Hatfield, 1941 (21) ; 1942 (389) ; 1943 (806) ; 1944 (1,203) ; 1945 (635). Leavesden, 1942 (53) ; 1943 (379) ; 1944 (585) ; 1945 (373). Additionally, in Britain the Standard Motor Company was called in to assist with production in 1942, producing 916 machines up to V-J Day.

Percival Aircraft built 198 Mosquitos during 1944–45, and Airspeed Limited produced a further twelve.

Two de Havilland engineers arrived in Canada in September 1941 to establish a Mosquito production line at the company's Toronto plant. This venture called for the shipment from Britain to Canada of very large quantities of jigs and tools, sample aircraft and components, and tens of thousands of drawings. Despite the difficulties, less than 2 per cent of the shipments were lost en route, and the first Canadian-built Mosquito flew in 1943, just a year after the first drawings arrived from Hatfield. In 1943 the Toronto factory turned out 90 Mosquitos, 419 in the following year, and a further 523 between January 1 and August 15, 1945. Australia, too, became a source of Mosquitos with the establishment of a production line at the de Havilland factory in Sydney. The pattern followed that used for the initiation of production in Canada, and the first Australian Mosquito also flew a year after the drawings arrived, taking to the air on July 23, 1943, a total of 107 further machines being delivered before V-J Day.

The basic fighter Mosquito introduced into squadron service in 1942 was the N.F.Mk.II, equipped primarily as a night-fighter and used for home defence alongside the Bristol Beaufighter. Its armament comprised four 20-mm. cannon in the front fuselage belly and four 0.303-in. Browning machine-guns in the extreme nose. It carried A.I.Mk.IV or A.I.Mk.V "arrowhead" radar and a G-45 cine gun. Its matt-black overall finish, incidentally, reduced its maximum speed by 16 m.p.h. Power was provided either by two Merlin 21 engines giving 1,280 h.p. for take-off and 1,480 h.p. at 12,250 feet, or two Merlin 23 engines giving 1,390 h.p. for take-off and the same maximum power at 12,250 feet.

On the night of May 28–29, 1942, Mosquito N.F.IIs scored their first "probable", and in the following three years Mosquito night-fighters racked up a score of approximately 600 enemy aircraft over the British Isles, and also destroyed 600 flying bombs in a two-month period. They later operated in the bomber-support role, their task being to defend the main heavy bomber streams over enemy territory. Of the 466 Mark II Mosquito fighters produced, some of the later aircraft had day-fighter finish and, with the A.I. radar removed, operated over Malta, Italy, Sicily and North Africa from the end of 1942 onwards.

Apart from the general development of the Mosquito in its various roles, the type rapidly became the subject of all sorts of experiments, the Mark II figuring in several of these. The prototype fighter, W4052, itself had a chequered career, and was at one time flown with a bellows-operated segmented air brake fitted around the fuselage aft of the wing. This was intended to facilitate rapid deceleration during interceptions, and the time taken to decelerate from 250 m.p.h. to 150 m.p.h. in level flight was reduced by a third. However, this reduction was not considered sufficient to warrant the adoption of the brake operationally. The same aircraft was also fitted, for a time, with a Bristol B.XI four-gun dorsal turret immediately behind the cockpit, but defensive armament for the Mosquito was never really considered necessary and the scheme was abandoned.

One Mosquito II was fitted with a Helmore Turbinlite, an airborne searchlight with a candlepower of 2,600 million, intended to illuminate enemy bombers for the benefit of patrolling fighters. The development of more efficient, centimetric A.I. radar for the Mosquito rendered

The high-altitude Mosquito N.F.XV with extended wing and machine-guns in a ventral blister.

it unnecessary to pursue this scheme. Another experiment involving a Mosquito F.II (DD723) was the attachment of chin radiators to its Merlin 23 engines in place of the standard wing leading-edge type.

Operational experience with the Mosquito II in its day-fighter and intruder roles led to the development of the F.B.VI, a potent fighter-bomber which came into service during the early months of 1943. It had been discovered that the Mosquito was able to accommodate a much greater warload than that for which it had been designed, and thus the Mark VI, with a strengthened wing for external loads which later became known as the "basic" wing, carried a full complement of cannon and machine-guns, two 500-lb. bombs in the rear half of the bomb bay (the front half containing the cannon breeches) and two 500-lb. bombs under the wings. Actually, the full 2,000-lb. bomb load was only carried by the Mark VI Series 2 which took advantage of the 1,620 h.p. available from the Merlin 25 for take-off, the first 300 machines being F.B.VI Series 1 Mosquitos with Merlin 21s or 23s and carrying two 250-lb. bombs internally.

The first squadron to be equipped with the Mosquito F.B.VI, No. 418, became operational in May 1943. Early in 1944 the Mosquito VI also entered service with R.A.F. Coastal Command for anti-shipping strikes. In this role it usually carried eight 60-lb. rocket projectiles under the wings in lieu of bombs or fuel tanks. The performance of the Mosquito F.B.VI was fairly representative of the earlier Marks of this aircraft. It attained a maximum speed of 378 m.p.h. at 13,200 feet, possessed an initial climb rate of 1,870 ft./min., and had a range of 1,120 miles cruising at 250 m.p.h. at sea-level. The F.B.VI Series 2 was produced in larger numbers than any Mosquito variant, with over 1,000 built by de Havilland and Standard Motors, remaining in service until the end of the war and being used as a day and night intruder by the 2nd T.A.F. in Europe as well as seeing service in the Far East, where it made its operational début at the beginning of 1944. Before the end of 1943 a variant of the F.B.VI had been produced specifically for R.A.F. Coastal Command. This was the Mosquito F.B.XVIII—sometimes known as the "Tsetse"—which carried a 57-mm. (six-pounder) Molins gun in place of the four 20-mm. cannon. Two 500-lb.

bombs or eight rocket projectiles could also be carried, and this variant first went into action on November 4, 1943. Although only twenty-seven were produced, the Mosquito F.B.XVIII proved particularly efficacious against shipping, submarines and shore installations.

An entirely separate line of development from the Mosquito N.F.II produced a series of night-fighting variants which were primarily used for home-defence purposes. The first of these was the N.F.XII, plans to produce the N.F.VI with Merlin 21s and the "basic" wing, and the N.F.X with Merlin 61s and the "basic" wing, having been abandoned. The Mosquito N.F.XII became the first British aircraft to carry centimetric A.I. radar. This form of radar introduced the spinning-dish scanner with greatly improved performance compared with the earlier "arrow-head" type, but it resulted in some singularly unattractive nose contours on the aircraft in which it was carried. The centimetric radar supplanted the four machine-guns in the fuselage nose, reducing the armament to four 20-mm. Hispano cannon. To expedite its service début, the Mosquito XII was based directly on the Mark II and ninety-seven machines were converted by the installation of the new radar.

Almost concurrently, the Mosquito N.F.XIII was placed in production. With generally similar characteristics to the N.F.XII, including the A.I. Mk.VIII radar, this model used the "basic" wing and Merlin 25 engines which permitted an increase in loaded weight from the 18,720 lb. of the N.F.XII to 21,100 lb., total range being extended by means of underwing fuel tanks. A total of 270 was built, but a high-altitude variant with Merlin 72 engines was abandoned.

Soon after production of the Marks XII and XIII had been initiated, American centimetric radar became available to supplement British production. This equipment was known as SCR720 and 729, and was designated A.I.Mk.X in Britain. Its performance was rather better than that of the A.I.Mk.VIII, but it was not installationally interchangeable with the British equipment. Therefore 100 Mosquito N.F.IIs were converted to take the American radar and redesignated N.F.XVII, while the N.F.XIX was placed in production as the equivalent of the N.F.XIII but carrying A.I.Mk.X equipment. A total of 220 Mosquito N.F.XIX night-fighters was built.

F

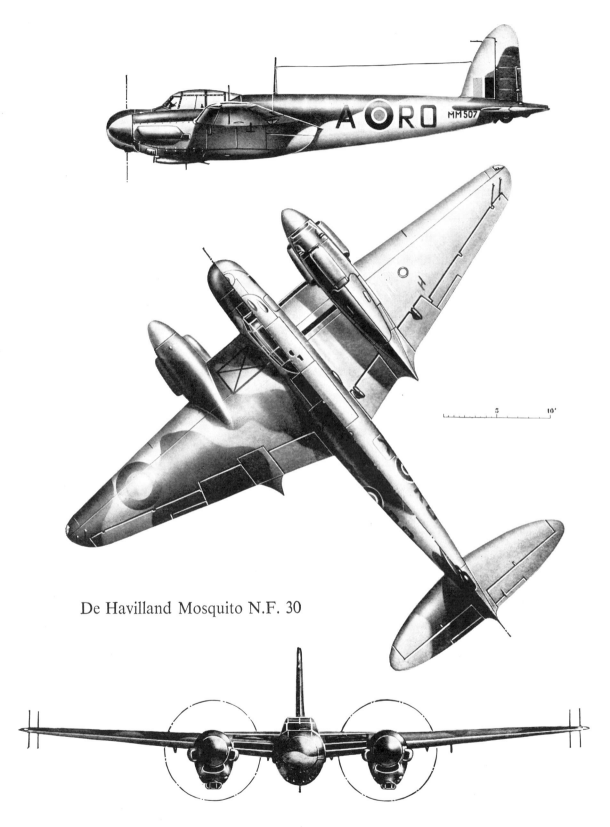

De Havilland Mosquito N.F. 30

During 1944 a further night-fighter variant came into production to replace the Mosquito N.F.XIX. Equipped with similar radar, this new version was the Mosquito N.F.30 which differed from its predecessors primarily in having a higher-altitude ability derived from the use of the Merlin 72 (in the first seventy production aircraft) and subsequently the Merlin 76 or the Merlin 113. The latter power plant had a take-off rating of 1,535 h.p., a combat rating of 1,690 h.p. at 13,000 feet, and 1,430 h.p. at 27,250 feet, and the increased power substantially improved the Mosquito's performance and operational ceiling, which was increased from 28,000 feet to 36,000 feet. Production of between 800 and 900 Mosquito N.F.30s was scheduled but curtailed to between 300 and 400 with the end of the war. Apart from serving with home-defence squadrons, the Mosquito N.F.30 was operational as a night-fighter from European bases in 1944–45, and also flew escort duties with No. 100 Bomber Support Group in operations over Germany.

One other night-fighter mark was produced, the high-altitude N.F.XV. This version had an interesting origin in 1942 when de Havilland Aircraft were asked to produce at short notice a very high-flying Mosquito fighter to combat the Ju 86P bomber which was flying unmolested over Britain at altitudes above 40,000 feet. Such a sortie had been observed over Hatfield on September 4, 1942. Two days later work commenced on the conversion of a special Mosquito bomber (MP469), which had high-rated Merlin 60 engines and the first pressure cabin fitted to a Mosquito, to perform the interceptor role. The conversion took one week and involved the extension of the wing span, the fitting of smaller wheels, the removal of some tankage and armour, and the installation of four machine-guns in the nose. The weight was reduced by 2,300 lb. and an altitude of 43,500 feet was achieved. However, little subsequent demand arose for this fighter and the high-altitude Spitfires soon became available.

As a safeguard against enemy high-altitude operations by night, MP469 was then used as the basis for a night-fighter variant in which the machine-guns were moved to a blister under the fuselage and A.I.Mk.VIII was fitted in the nose. Five aircraft of this type, designated Mosquito N.F.XV, were converted from B.Mk.IV airframes, having Merlin 77 engines and an all-up weight of 17,600 lb.

Of the Mosquitos built in Canada, the F.B.26 was one of the chief variants, the design of which was based upon that of the F.B.VI. With the same armament as its British counterpart, it had Packard Merlin 225 engines and weighed 21,473 lb. The sole F.B.24 was similar but had Packard Merlin 69s, while the F.B.21, of which only three were built, had Packard Merlin 31 or 33 engines. Australian production was also based initially on the fighter-bomber, the F.B.40 being similar to the F.B.VI but having Packard Merlin 31 (first hundred production machines) or 33 (last seventy-eight) engines. One F.B.40 was re-engined with Packard Merlin 69s and re-designated Mosquito

(*Above*) *The Mosquito N.F.XVII, and* (*below*) *the Mosquito N.F.XIX.*

(*Above*) *The Mosquito F.B.XVIII or "Tse-tse" with a 57-mm. Molins gun in the forward fuselage.* (*Below*) *The Mosquito N.F.30, the last night-fighter variant to see service in World War II.*

F.B.42, but no production of this version was undertaken.

No fewer than twenty-seven different versions of the Mosquito went into service during the war years, and some of the most spectacular operations of the air war stood to its credit. The Mosquito carried phenomenal loads over extremely long distances, performing feats out of all proportion to the specification originally envisaged by its designers. In short, the Mosquito was an outstanding warplane on every count.

De Havilland D.H.98 Mosquito N.F.XIX

Dimensions : Span, 54 ft. 2 in. ; length, 41 ft. 2 in. ; height, 15 ft. 3 in. ; wing area, 454 sq. ft.

Armament : Four 20-mm. British Hispano cannon.

Power Plants : Two Rolls-Royce Merlin 25 twelve-cylinder 60° Vee liquid-cooled engines each providing 1,620 h.p. for take-off, and 1,500 h.p. at 9,500 ft.

Weights : Empty, 15,970 lb. ; normal loaded, 20,600 lb. ; maximum loaded, 21,750 lb.

Performance : Maximum speed, 378 m.p.h. at 13,200 ft. ; cruising speed, 295 m.p h. at 20,000 ft. ; initial climb rate, 2,700 ft./min. ; operational ceiling (climb rate 500 ft./min.), 28,000 ft. ; still-air range (with 453 Imp. gal.), 1,400 miles. (with 616 Imp. gal., including two 50-gal. drop-tanks), 1,905 miles.

(Above) The Grumman XF4F-2 as flown during the spring of 1938. The prototype suffered a series of teething troubles and several accidents during the trials held at the Anacostia Naval Air Station. The fuselage and undercarriage were eventually retained for the XF4F-3.

THE GRUMMAN WILDCAT

The XF4F-2 (above) was flown for the first time on September 2, 1937, and delivered to the Anacostia Naval Air Station on December 23rd. As depicted by this photograph, the engine cowling has been redesigned and the fuselage gun blast tubes modified.

(Above and below) The XF4F-2 in its initial form with close-cowled engine and protruding fuselage gun barrels. During its test programme, the XF4F-2 suffered a number of crankshaft bearing failures and several engine changes were necessitated.

When the United States entered the Second World War, the Grumman Wildcat was the standard single-seat fighter serving with the U.S. Navy's shipboard squadrons, and remained so throughout the crucial first half of the Pacific conflict. The first really successful western shipboard fighter monoplane, and the first fighter in the world to enter service with a two-stage supercharged engine, the Wildcat was, nevertheless, an undistinguished warplane from the performance aspect. To keep pace with the changing needs of warfare, additional equipment and armour were progressively added during the fighter's career, still further reducing a mediocre performance, and in speed, climb rate and manoeuvrability, the Wildcat was markedly inferior to its principal opponent, the Mitsubishi Zero-Sen. But it compensated to some extent for these shortcomings with its tractability, sturdy structure, and superior fire-power and internal protection, and its American pilots soon proved themselves adept in turning the Wildcat's strong points against the enemy's weaknesses; evolving combat tactics which minimized the advantages held by the Japanese fighter. Thus, this pugnacious little warplane was enabled to establish an enviable operational record, flying from shore bases and carriers, large and small alike, and making a significant contribution to Allied victory.

The Grumman Aircraft Engineering Corporation had received an order on March 2, 1936 for the design and development of a single-seat shipboard fighter biplane under the designation XF4F-1, a continuation of the line of carrier-borne fighters founded some four years earlier with the XFF-1. The XF4F-1 was conceived around the 900 h.p. Wright XR-1670-2 radial engine with the 875 h.p. Pratt and Whitney XR-1535-92 as an alternative. Either twin 0.3-in. guns or one 0.5-in. and one 0.3-in. gun could be mounted in the forward fuselage decking, and estimated performance included a maximum speed of 264 m.p.h. at 10,500 ft.

the ability to climb to 15,000 ft. in 7.6 mins., and a range of 853 miles.

However, while design work on the XF4F-1 biplane was proceeding, radical changes were taking place in U.S. Navy thinking, and the conclusion had been reached that shipboard fighter design concepts were lagging seriously behind those of land-based aircraft ; that greater speeds and heavier firepower would be vital in the years ahead, and that such could only be obtained by supplanting the biplane, which had dominated naval aviation since the First World War, with the monoplane. Almost simultaneously, it was realised that, by installing a 950 h.p. Wright R-1820-22 engine in place of the 700 h.p. Pratt and Whitney R-1535-84 in the airframe of the F3F-1 then being delivered to the U.S. Navy, a performance comparing closely with that anticipated for the XF4F-1 could be obtained!

The net result was that Grumman abandoned further work on the XF4F-1 design on July 28, 1936, initiating the development of a fighter monoplane under the designation XF4F-2 as a direct competitor to the Brewster Aeronautical Corporation's shipboard fighter monoplane project ordered by the U.S. Navy a month earlier, on June 22, 1936, as the XF2A-1. Whereas Brewster were designing their fighter around the single-row nine-cylinder Wright R-1820 Cyclone engine, the Grumman team elected to use Pratt and Whitney's fourteen-cylinder two-row R-1830 Twin Wasp for their fighter.

Retaining the characteristic rotund fuselage of the naval biplanes that had preceded it, the XF4F-2 was

The XF4F-3 as initially flown in February 1939 (above).

(Above and below) The XF4F-3 as it appeared after modifications late in 1939.

The photograph below depicts the XF4F-3 after tail fin area had been increased and the rudder horn balance enlarged, wing dihedral increased and ailerons reduced in area. During trials, the XF4F-3 attained a speed of 333.5 m.p.h., slightly more than guaranteed by the manufacturers.

The first production F4F-3 (BuA No. 1844) seen above prior to flight trials in February 1940. This aircraft, together with the second production machine, retained the twin fuselage-mounted guns of the prototype, but these were deleted in subsequent aircraft. The second production F4F-3 was initially flown with an airscrew spinner.

of all-metal construction with fabric-covered control surfaces. The mid-mounted wing employed the newly-developed NACA 230-series aerofoil, and comprised a broad centre section built integral with the fuselage and two non-folding outer panels. The Pratt and Whitney R-1830-66 Twin Wasp radial with single-stage, single-speed supercharger, drove a Hamilton Standard three-blade constant-speed airscrew, and developed 1,050 h.p. for take-off. This engine was housed in an NACA cowling with a rectangular carburettor air intake on top of the forward fuselage, and was fed from a 91.6 Imp. gal. (110 U.S. gal.) fuel tank beneath the cockpit. A 16.6 Imp. gal. (20 U.S. gal.) reserve tank was also provided.

The retractable undercarriage was basically similar to that employed by previous Grumman fighters, the main members retracting into wells provided in the fuselage immediately aft of the engine, the wheels being raised and lowered by means of a handcrank, and armament comprised two 0.5-in. Browning machine guns with 200 r.p.g. in the upper decking of the forward fuselage. Provision was made for the installation of a 0.5-in. gun in each wing or, alternatively, two 100-lb. bombs could be attached to underwing racks.

The XF4F-2 was flown for the first time on September 2, 1937, at Bethpage by Robert L. Hall, some three months before the competitive Brewster design was to leave the ground for the first time. After the completion of initial manufacturers trials which appeared to augur well for the fighter in what was undoubtedly to be an intensely fought contest ahead, the XF4F-2 was flown to the Anacostia Naval Air Station where it arrived on December 23rd for official evaluation and eventual comparison with the XF2A-1 and a third competitor, the Seversky NF-1, a shipboard adaptation of the Army Air Corps' P-35.

Ill fortune now appeared to dog the Grumman prototype. Its Twin Wasp engine suffered a number

of crankshaft bearing failures which kept the XF4F-2 on the ground for considerable periods, and on February 14, 1938, a fire occurred in the aft fuselage while the aircraft was flying at 10,000 ft. Fortunately, damage was slight, and the prototype had resumed trials within two days, accumulating sixteen hours in the air by March 11th. Rigorous comparative tests were conducted with the three prototypes by the U.S. Navy, but on April 11th misfortune again singled out the XF4F-2 as its target, for during a simulated deck landing the engine cut, and in the ensuing forced landing, the aircraft suffered severe damage to the undercarriage, engine cowling, airscrew, starboard wingtip and tail surfaces. The prototype was shipped back to Bethpage where repairs were completed within two weeks and the XF4F-2 once again flown to Anacostia for a resumption of the official trials.

By the end of April 1938, the NF-1 had been eliminated from the contest as trials had indicated a maximum speed of only 250 m.p.h. under test conditions and, in addition to its disappointing performance, the Seversky prototype suffered some lateral instability. By comparison, the measured speed of the XF4F-2 was 290 m.p.h. at 10,000 ft., 10 m.p.h. greater than that of the XF2A-1 at the same altitude. However, tests conducted with the XF2A-1 in the full-scale wind tunnel at Langley Field during May indicated that maximum speed could be increased by 30 m.p.h. by improving the contours of the air intakes and exhaust outlet ducts, modifying the fairings around the fuselage guns, and installing undercarriage well covers. These wind tunnel tests were the first of their type, and as such formed a highlight in the development of U.S. naval aircraft, and although it proved impracticable to make all the recommended changes, those that were made were destined to raise the maximum speed of the Brewster fighter by 20 m.p.h. The results of the wind tunnel tests coupled with the teething troubles suffered by the Grumman fighter during the evaluation programme undoubtedly influenced the U.S. Navy in its choice of the XF2A-1 as the winner of the contest, and on June 11, 1938, Brewster were awarded a production contract for fifty-four F2A-1s.

Despite this inauspicious start which might have been expected to terminate the Grumman fighter's career there and then, an event which would have resulted in serious consequences for the U.S. Navy a few years later, it was admitted that none of the XF4F-2s troubles had been of a fundamental nature, and the U.S. Navy had found the fighter's performance to be sufficiently impressive to award a development contract to Grumman in October 1938 for a more advanced version of the basic design under the designation XF4F-3.

The next five months were spent in detail design and the reconstruction of the original prototype, although, in fact, only the fuselage and undercarriage of the XF4F-2 were retained, the remainder of the fighter being entirely new. One of the most important changes was the adoption of an XR-1830-76 Twin Wasp with a two-stage supercharger. Driving a Curtiss Electric airscrew, this power plant offered 1,200 h.p. for take-off, 1,050 h.p. at 11,000 ft., and

1,000 h.p. at 19,000 ft. It was appreciably heavier and more complex than the R-1830-66 of the XF4F-2, and adequate engine cooling and maintenance accessibility afforded many problems, but the new engine was finally installed in the prototype airframe late in January 1939, and the first test flight took place on February 12th. Apart from its power plant, the XF4F-3 differed from its predecessor in many respects. The redesigned wing had been increased in overall span and gross area from 34 ft. to 38 ft. and from 232 to 260 sq. ft., the tips of all surfaces were square-cut, fuselage length had increased from 26 ft. 5 in. to 28 ft., and loaded weight had risen by some 600 lb. over the original XF4F-2's 5,386 lb. Armament comprised twin 0.3-in. guns in the fuselage and a pair of 0.5-in. guns in the wings.

Following initial manufacturer's trials at Bethpage, the XF4F-3 was flown to Anacostia in March for official evaluation tests, and during the next six months numerous modifications were made of both major and minor nature. Tail fin area was increased and the rudder horn balance enlarged; wing dihedral angle was slightly increased and the ailerons reduced in area; various engine cowling flap arrangements were tested to improve cooling, particularly at high

Two F4F-3 Wildcat fighters photographed during the early months of the Pacific War. The red-and-white rudder striping, introduced shortly before the beginning of hostilities in the Pacific, was deleted shortly after this photograph was taken.

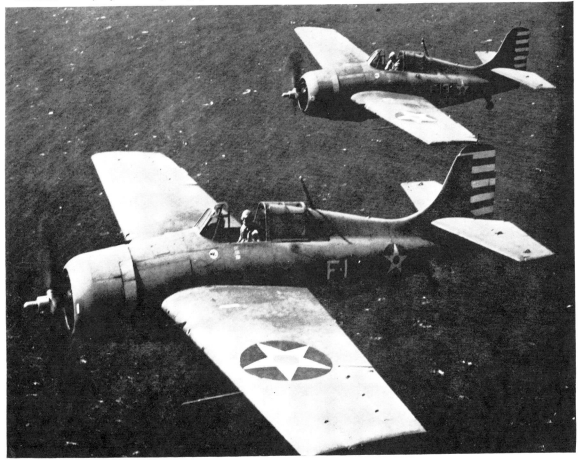

Grumman F4F-4 'Wildcat' Cutaway Key

1 Starboard navigation
   light
2 Wingtip
3 Starboard formation
   light
4 Rear spar
5 Aileron construction
6 Fixed aileron tab
7 All riveted wing
   construction
8 Lateral stiffeners
9 Forward canted main
   spar
10 'Crimped leading edge
   ribs
11 Solid web forward ribs
12 Starboard outer gun
   blast tube
13 Carburettor air duct
14 Intake

33 Bearer assembly welded
   cluster joint
34 Main beam
35 Lower cowl flap
36 Exhaust stub
37 Starboard mainwheel
38 Undercarriage fairing
39 Lower drag link
40 Hydraulic brake
41 Port mainwheel
42 Detachable hub cover
43 Low-pressure tyre
44 Axle forging
45 Upper drag link
46 Oleo shock strut
47 Ventral fairing
48 Wheel well
49 Pivot point
50 Landing light
51 Main forging
52 Compression link
53 Gun camera port
54 Counter balance

71 Pilot's adjustable seat
72 Instrument panel shroud
73 Undercarriage manual
   crank
74 Control column
75 Rudder pedals
76 Fuselage/front spar
   attachment
77 Main fuel filler cap
78 Seat harness attachment
79 Back armour
80 Oxygen cylinder
81 Reserve fuel filler cap
82 Alternative transmitter/
   receiver (ABA or IFF)
   installation
83 Battery

84 IFF and ABA dynamotor
   units
85 Wing flap vacuum tank
86 Handhold
87 Turnover bar
88 Rearward-sliding
   Plexiglas canopy
89 Streamlined aerial mast
90 Mast support
91 One-man Mk.IA
   life-raft stowage
92 Upper longeron
93 Toolkit
94 Aerial lead-in

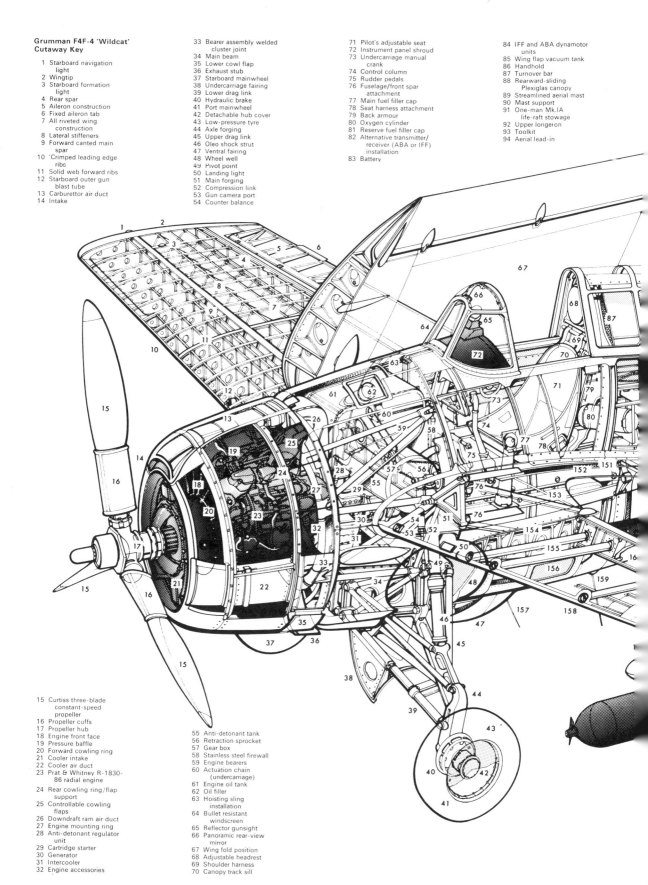

15 Curtiss three-blade
   constant-speed
   propeller
16 Propeller cuffs
17 Propeller hub
18 Engine front face
19 Pressure baffle
20 Forward cowling ring
21 Cooler intake
22 Cooler air duct
23 Prat & Whitney R-1830-
   86 radial engine
24 Rear cowling ring/flap
   support
25 Controllable cowling
   flaps
26 Downdraft ram air duct
27 Engine mounting ring
28 Anti-detonant regulator
   unit
29 Cartridge starter
30 Generator
31 Intercooler
32 Engine accessories

55 Anti-detonant tank
56 Retraction sprocket
57 Gear box
58 Stainless steel firewall
59 Engine bearers
60 Actuation chain
   (undercarriage)
61 Engine oil tank
62 Oil filler
63 Hoisting sling
   installation
64 Bullet resistant
   windscreen
65 Reflector gunsight
66 Panoramic rear-view
   mirror
67 Wing fold position
68 Adjustable headrest
69 Shoulder harness
70 Canopy track sill

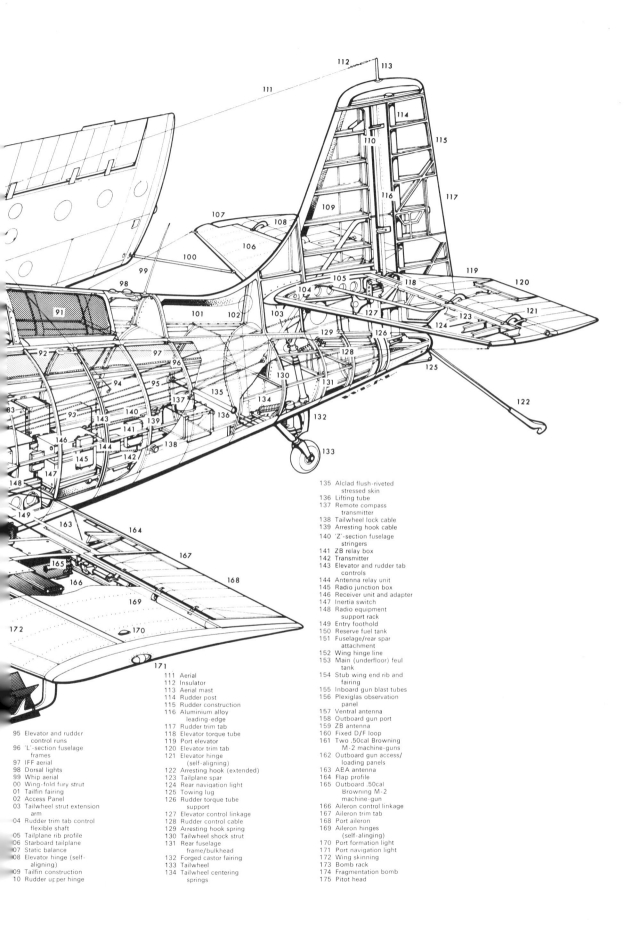

112
113
111
114
110
115
116
117
107
109
108
106
100
119
99
105 118 120
98
104 121
91
101 102 103 127 123
92 129 126 124 125
97 96 128
94 95 131 122
135
137 134 130
83 136 132
93 143 140 139
146 144 138 133
141
145 142
147
148
135 Alclad flush-riveted
149 stressed skin
163 136 Lifting tube
164 137 Remote compass
transmitter
167 138 Tailwheel lock cable
165 139 Arresting hook cable
166 168 140 'Z'-section fuselage
stringers
169 141 ZB relay box
142 Transmitter
172 170 143 Elevator and rudder tab
controls
171 144 Antenna relay unit
145 Radio junction box
146 Receiver unit and adapter
147 Inertia switch
148 Radio equipment
support rack
149 Entry foothold
150 Reserve fuel tank
151 Fuselage/rear spar
attachment
152 Wing hinge line
153 Main (underfloor) feul
tank
154 Stub wing end rib and
fairing
155 Inboard gun blast tubes
156 Plexiglas observation
panel
157 Ventral antenna
158 Outboard gun port
159 ZB antenna
111 Aerial 160 Fixed D/F loop
112 Insulator 161 Two .50cal Browning
113 Aerial mast M-2 machine-guns
114 Rudder post 162 Outboard gun access/
115 Rudder construction loading panels
116 Aluminium alloy 163 ABA antenna
leading-edge 164 Flap profile
117 Rudder trim tab 165 Outboard .50cal
118 Elevator torque tube Browning M-2
119 Port elevator machine-gun
95 Elevator and rudder 120 Elevator trim tab 166 Aileron control linkage
control runs 121 Elevator hinge 167 Aileron trim tab
96 'L'-section fuselage (self-aligning) 168 Port aileron
frames 122 Arresting hook (extended) 169 Aileron hinges
97 IFF aerial 123 Tailplane spar (self-alinging)
98 Dorsal lights 124 Rear navigation light 170 Port formation light
99 Whip aerial 125 Towing lug 171 Port navigation light
00 Wing-fold fury strut 126 Rudder torque tube 172 Wing skinning
01 Tailfin fairing support 173 Bomb rack
02 Access Panel 127 Elevator control linkage 174 Fragmentation bomb
03 Tailwheel strut extension 128 Rudder control cable 175 Pitot head
arm 129 Arresting hook spring
04 Rudder trim tab control 130 Tailwheel shock strut
flexible shaft 131 Rear fuselage
05 Tailplane rib profile frame/bulkhead
06 Starboard tailplane 132 Forged castor fairing
07 Static balance 133 Tailwheel
08 Elevator hinge (self- 134 Tailwheel centering
aligning) springs
09 Tailfin construction
10 Rudder upper hinge

altitudes; various airscrew spinners were fitted and wide-chord blade cuffs were tried. However, although minor problems remained to be solved, performance was sufficiently promising for the U.S. Navy to place a production contract with Grumman on August 8, 1939 for fifty-four F4F-3 fighters. During Navy trials the XF4F-3 had attained a speed of 333.5 m.p.h., a slight increase on the 330 m.p.h. guaranteed by the manufacturer, this speed being attained at 20,500 feet. Initial climb rate was 2,800 ft./min., service ceiling was 33,500 feet, and range was 907 miles.

The first production F4F-3 was flown in February 1940, this being powered by an R-1830-76 Twin Wasp,

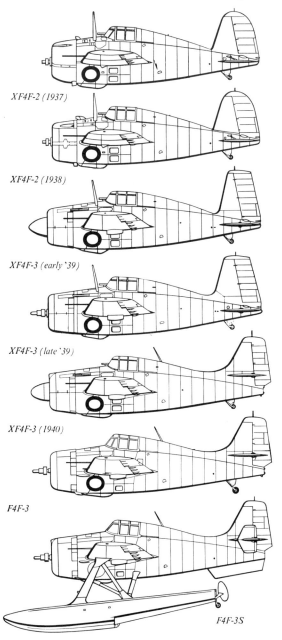

XF4F-2 (1937)

XF4F-2 (1938)

XF4F-3 (early '39)

XF4F-3 (late '39)

XF4F-3 (1940)

F4F-3

F4F-3S

the second production aircraft following in July. The armament of these two machines was similar to that of the XF4F-3, but subsequent F4F-3s had the 0.3-in. fuselage guns deleted, four 0.5-in. guns being installed in the wings. The fifth and eighth production machines featured strengthened undercarriages and some armour protection for the pilot, and were absorbed by the evaluation and test programme, and after the completion of the first official tests, the first production F4F-3 was transferred to Pratt and Whitney for engine development purposes. Trials with the F4F-3 proceeded relatively smoothly, and the Navy found the aircraft to be eminently satisfactory, although the maximum speed of 331 m.p.h. at 21,300 ft. was well below the manufacturer's guarantee of 350 m.p.h.

The principle criticisms were concerned with some longitudinal instability, difficulties with ammunition feed during high-G manoeuvres, excessive carbon monoxide seepage in the cockpit and inadequate cockpit ventilation, the close proximity of the fuel valves to the flap controls, some canopy vibration, inadequate tailwheel strength, and insufficient cylinder cooling. The second production F4F-3 was flown from Anacostia to Langley Field where the N.A.C.A. attempted to improve engine cooling by means of various cowling and cowl flap arrangements, eventually devising a satisfactory solution to the cooling problem which was embodied by later production F4F-3s.

In the meantime, the French government, anxious to obtain a suitable shipboard fighter for operation from the 18,000-ton carriers *Joffre* and *Painlevé* then under construction, had placed an order for eighty-one fighters basically similar to the U.S. Navy's F4F-3. Given the company's designation G-36A, the French fighter utilized the Wright R-1820-G205A-2 Cyclone with a single-stage two-speed supercharger and rated at 1,200 h.p. for take-off and 1,000 h.p. at 11,500 feet. The French contract specified six wing-mounted 7.5-mm. Darne machine guns, an OPL 38 gunsight, Radio-Industrie-537 R/T equipment, metric-calibrated instrumentation, and a throttle operating in the reverse direction to that standard in U.S. aircraft. The first French Cyclone-powered G-36A flew on May 11, 1940, one day after the Germans had opened their campaign for the conquest of France. With the fall of France, the contract for Grumman fighters was quickly transferred to Britain, and with four 0.5-in. wing guns and the throttle modified to operate in conventional fashion, the first aircraft was delivered on July 27, 1940.

The G-36A was allocated the name Martlet I in British service, and by the end of October the remaining eighty aircraft on the original French contract had been delivered, the first of these entering service in that month with No. 804 Squadron based at Hatston, superseding the unit's Sea Gladiators. The Martlet Is were shore-based, lacking folding wings and other equipment considered to be necessary for carrier operation by the British Navy, and to these went the distinction of becoming the first U.S. aircraft in

British service to shoot down a German aircraft in the Second World War. This event took place on December 25, 1940, when a flight of No. 804 Squadron's Martlet Is patrolling Scapa Flow intercepted and destroyed a Junkers Ju 88A bomber attempting to attack the Home Fleet base.

Production of the F4F-3 for the U.S. Navy had been proceeding in parallel with that of the Martlet I, but troubles were still being experienced with the two-stage Twin Wasp, and in April 1940 the U.S. Navy had ordered the installation of a single-stage R-1820-40 Cyclone (the equivalent of the Martlet I's R-1820-G205A) in the third and fourth production F4F-3s which had been delivered during the summer of 1940 as XF4F-5s. The XF4F-5 attained 306 m.p.h. at 15,000 ft., and the two aircraft were to be further modified during 1942–3, the first by the installation of an R-1820-54 engine with a turbo-supercharger, and the second by the installation of a two-stage XR-1820-48.

Another F4F-3 was fitted with an R-1830-90 Twin Wasp with a single-stage two-speed supercharger and, redesignated XF4F-6, this aircraft began trials at Anacostia in November 1940, attaining 319 m.p.h. at 16,100 ft. The possibility of delays in deliveries of two-stage Twin Wasps was still worrying the Navy at this time, leading to a limited production order for this model as the F4F-6, the designation being changed to F4F-3A prior to delivery. Soon after the invasion of Greece by Italian forces in November 1940, a Greek delegation sought combat aircraft from the U.S.A., and the Navy agreed to the first thirty production F4F-3As being diverted to Greece, the aircraft being despatched to that country in the Spring of 1941. When Greek resistance collapsed in April, the F4F-3As had only reached Gibraltar. They were therefore purchased from Lend-Lease funds and taken over by the Fleet Air Arm as Martlet IIIs. A further ten F4F-3As were transferred to Britain in lieu of the first ten folding-wing G-36B Martlet IIs from a batch of one hundred machines ordered for shipboard use by the British Purchasing Commission in mid-1940. Only nine of the F4F-3As were actually shipped as one was retained by Grumman for development purposes. Most of the remaining fifty-five F4F-3As produced during 1941 were delivered to U.S. Marine Corps squadrons.

Like the F4F-3A, or Martlet III, the G-36B Martlet II was powered by a single-stage Twin Wasp (S3C4-G equivalent to the R-1830-90) owing to the shortage of two-stage engines, but its folding wings mounted six 0.5-in. guns, catapult spools were fitted, and a larger tailwheel was provided. Fifty Martlet IIs were delivered during the Autumn of 1941, thirty-six of these being shipped to the United Kingdom and the others, together with the remaining forty machines of the order produced early in 1942, were sent to the Far East, although some of these were lost en route. By virtue of its folding wings, the Martlet II was the first version of the Grumman fighter to be embarked in British carriers, and on September 20, 1941, fighters

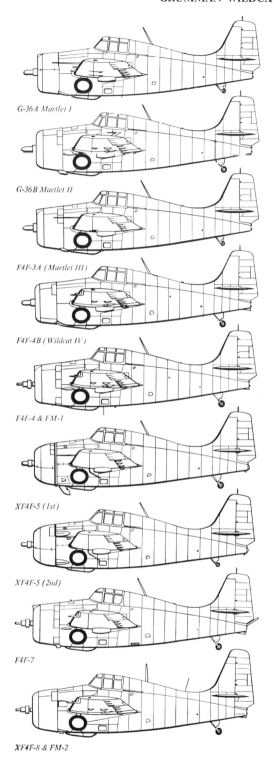

G-36A Martlet I

G-36B Martlet II

F4F-3A (Martlet III)

F4F-4B (Wildcat IV)

F4F-4 & FM-1

XF4F-5 (1st)

XF4F-5 (2nd)

F4F-7

XF4F-8 & FM-2

of this type operated by No. 802 Squadron from the small escort carrier *Audacity* destroyed an Fw 200C Condor that had been shadowing the convoy escorted by the carrier. During the next voyage of the *Audacity*, No. 802's Martlets accounted for no fewer than four of the Condors.

(*Above and left*) *The F4F-3A Wildcat with the R-1830-90 Twin Wasp with single-stage two-speed supercharger. The F4F-3A illustrated above belonged to VMF-121 and is seen in the non-specular pale grey overall finish adopted on December 30, 1940 and retained until October 13, 1941.*

By that time the Grumman fighter had been officially named Wildcat, and during 1941 the 185th and last F4F-3 then on order had been delivered, and the first five folding-wing F4F-4s had left the assembly line. However, no folding-wing Wildcats had reached U.S. Navy squadrons when, on December 7, 1941, Japanese forces attacked Pearl Harbour. The first delivery of the F4F-3 had been made to VF-41 a year earlier, on December 4, 1940, and in addition to U.S. Navy squadrons, several U.S. Marine Corps units were operating the fixed-wing Wildcat at the time of the Japanese onslaught, including VMF-121 and -211 with F4F-3s and VMF-111 with F4F-3As. During the first stage of the Japanese attack, Zero-Sen fighters surprised a line-up of eleven F4F-3s of VMF-211 at Ewa, in South-West Oahu, destroying or severely damaging nine of the aircraft before any of the Marine Corps fighters could get into the air. Nevertheless, although first blood had gone to the Japanese, VMF-211 was to have a chance to even the score and was to become the first unit to employ the Wildcat against the enemy.

A few days earlier, twelve of the squadron's F4F-3s led by Major Paul Putnam had arrived at lonely Wake Island, and the epic defence of this tiny outpost was to become legendary. Few of the Marine Corps pilots had done more than cursory familiarization flights in the Wildcat, only two of the aircraft had self-sealing fuel tanks, the 100-lb. bombs available on the island did not fit the Wildcat's bomb racks, no shelters or revetments were available, and there was little or no ground handling equipment. In the first Japanese attack on Wake Island on December 8, 1941, eight of the Wildcats were destroyed on the ground, and another was damaged, although later repaired with the aid of components cannibalised from the irreparable fighters. The remaining Wildcats fought heroically for two weeks, breaking up a number of air attacks and routing one seaborne invasion attempt during which they sank a Japanese destroyer and damaged a medium transport with 100-lb. bombs. But, finally, on December 22nd., the last two Wildcats were destroyed, and shortly afterwards a new invasion was launched and the defences of the island overwhelmed.

During the first U.S. carrier offensive action at the beginning of February 1942, when Task Forces 8 and 17 built around the carriers *Enterprise* and *Yorktown* attacked Japanese installations in the Marshall and Gilbert Islands, F4F-3s of VF-6 were credited with destroying two Japanese aircraft in the first attack, and on February 20th, Lieut. Edward H. O'Hare of VF-42 flying an F4F-3 from the *Lexington* encountered a formation of Mitsubishi G4M1 land-based bombers, destroying five of the enemy aircraft within the space

FINISH AND INSIGNIA: *The F4F-3 Wildcat illustrated on the opposite page employed the finish adopted for all U.S. Navy shipboard aircraft on October 13, 1941, which comprised non-specular blue-grey upper surfaces and pale grey under surfaces, definite lines of demarcation being avoided by the use of wavy lines and blending. The national insignia appeared on the fuselage sides and on the top port and under starboard wing surfaces, this arrangement being adopted on February 26, 1941, at which time all coloured tail markings, engine cowling bands, chevrons, pennants, etc., were eliminated. On January 5, 1942, thirteen red and white horizontal stripes were adopted as the standard rudder. The "F" (indicating Fighter) and individual aircraft number (i.e., "13") were painted in white on the fuselage sides ahead of the national insignia, and the aircraft number was repeated on the engine cowling and on the wing centre section (both to port and starboard of the fuselage).*

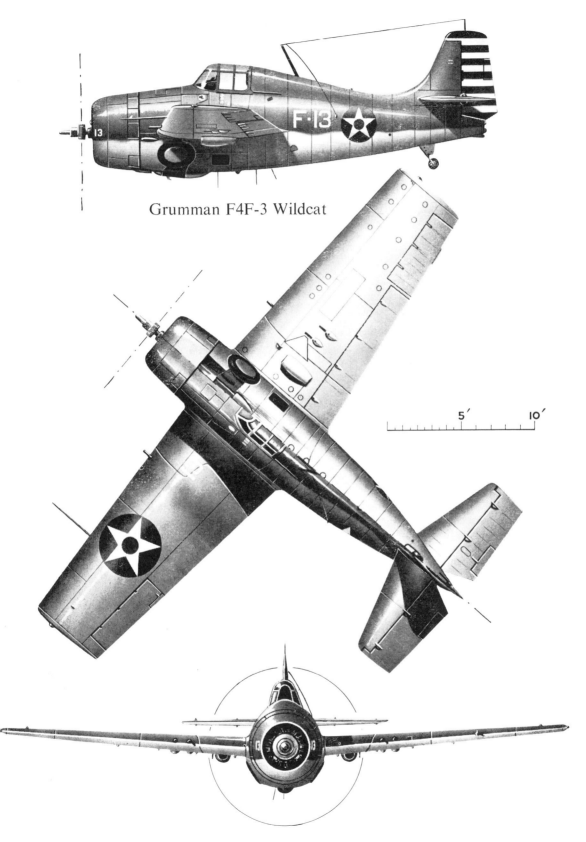

Grumman F4F-3 Wildcat

5′   10′

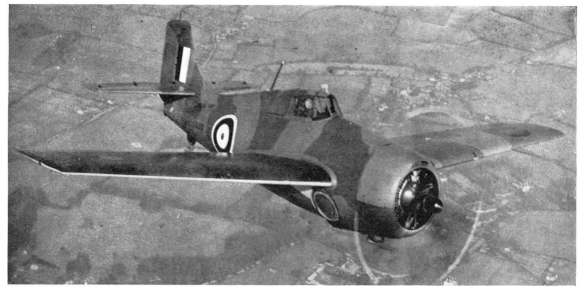

(*Above*) *A Martlet I (BJ556), one of the original French contract G-36As transferred to Britain with the defeat of France, and (left) the first G-36A with the French Navy insignia in which it was originally completed. This aircraft flew for the first time on May 11, 1940.*

of a few minutes! Two months later F4F-3s of VF-2 from the *Yorktown* and VF-42 from the *Lexington* participated in the Battle of the Coral Sea, the first naval engagement in history fought without the opposing ships making contact. When the Battle of Midway was fought at the beginning of June, the folding-wing F4F-4 Wildcat made its operational début in strength, being flown by VF-3 from the *Yorktown*, VF-6 from the *Enterprise*, and VF-8 from the *Hornet*, and it was during this engagement that Wildcats first employed a tactic known as the "Thach Weave" which, evolved by Lieut.-Comdr. John S. Thach, commander of VF-3, was to be employed throughout the remainder of the Pacific War.

The F4F-4, the first version of the Wildcat to be built in really substantial numbers and also the first U.S. Navy model of the fighter to feature wing folding, began to reach the U.S. Navy late in November 1941, and 1,169 F4F-4s had been manufactured for the U.S. Navy and Marine Corps when production of this variant was completed at the end of 1942. The prototype, the XF4F-4, had flown for the first time on April 14, 1941, and had undergone handling trials with VF-42 aboard the *Yorktown*. The wings of the XF4F-4 consisted of a stub centre section and two outer panels arranged to swivel at the forward spar and fold aft along the fuselage sides. Hydraulic folding mechanism was installed, but it was concluded that the added weight and complexity of this system was not justified and, thus, the wings of the production F4F-4 were folded and spread manually.

Power was furnished by a 1,200 h.p. R-1830-86 Twin Wasp similar to that installed in the last production F4F-3s, this driving a Curtiss Electric constant-speed airscrew. Two fuel tanks were provided, a 97 Imp. gal. (117 U.S. gal.) main tank and a 22.5 Imp. gal. (27 U.S. gal.) reserve tank, and provision was made for the attachment of two 41.6 or 48 Imp. gal. (50 or 58 U.S. gal.) drop tanks beneath the stub wing centre section. Armament comprised three 0.5-in. M-2 Browning machine guns in each outer wing panel with 240 r.p.g., and the pilot was protected by a 25-lb. armoured windscreen, a 45-lb. armour plate immediately in front of the oil tank, and ninety-four pounds of armour aft of his seat.

A version with an R-1830-90 engine and designated F4F-4A was contemplated but not built, and 220 examples of a further version, the F4F-4B, were produced for Britain and designated Martlet IV. This variant differed from its U.S. Navy counterpart, the F4F-4, principally in having a Wright GR-1820-G205A-3 Cyclone driving a Hamilton Standard Hydromatic airscrew. Weighing 7,904 lb. loaded and armed with six 0.5-in. Browning M-53A guns, the Martlet IV had a somewhat lower performance than the Twin Wasp-powered F4F-4, maximum speed being only 298 m.p.h., and service ceiling being 30,100 ft. The first F.A.A. squadron to re-equip with this type was No. 892 which took delivery of its Martlet IVs on July 15, 1942, and subsequently embarked on the escort carriers *Archer* and *Battler*. Among the more noteworthy actions in which the Martlet IV participated were the landings on Madagascar during which Nos. 881 and 882 squadrons operated from *Illustrious*, and the Allied invasion of North Africa during which a Martlet of No. 882

Squadron operating from *Victorious* took the surrender of the French fighter airfield at Blida! Martlets even operated in the Western Desert with No. 805 Squadron based at Dekheila.

By the end of 1942 all U.S. Navy shipboard fighter squadrons were equipped with the F4F-4 Wildcat, but it had been appreciated from the beginning of the Pacific War that, from the performance aspect, the American fighter was outclassed by the A6M2 Zero-Sen. The Japanese fighter was superior in speed and climb to the F4F-4 at all altitudes above a thousand feet, and was the better of the two in both service ceiling and range. In a dive the two aircraft were equal, but the turning circle of the Zero-Sen was very much smaller than that of the Wildcat by reason of its lower wing loadings and, in consequence, lower stalling speed. However, by concentrating on the two-plane fighter element and evolving tactics such as the "Thach Weave" in which two Wildcats criss-crossed back and forth, each thus covering the other's tail, the American pilots took the measure of their more nimble opponents, and made full use of the Grumman fighter's superior firepower and internal protection, and structural integrity. Whenever possible, the Wildcat pilots endeavoured to get above the enemy, then plunge through the Japanese formation in a firing pass, continuing their dive until they were able to zoom-climb back to a favourable altitude for another attack, and avoiding a dog-fight in which the Zero-Sen would have been in its element.

From mid-1941, Grumman had been working on the Wildcat's successor, the heavier and more powerful Hellcat, and in order to facilitate production of the new fighter and yet maintain deliveries of the Wildcat which was in growing demand for operation from the expanding fleet of light escort carriers, early in 1942 it had been decided to transfer production of the F4F-4 to the Eastern Aircraft Division of General Motors which, made up of five plants formerly engaged in

automobile manufacture, had been established officially on January 21, 1942. On April 18, 1942, the Linden, New Jersey, plant of General Motors was awarded a contract for 1,800 F4F-4s which were to be produced under the designation FM-1, and the first General Motors-built Wildcat flew on August 31, 1942, a further twenty being accepted by the end of the year in addition to the first two of 311 similar aircraft for Britain as the Martlet V. The FM-1 differed from the F4F-4 solely in having an armament of four 0.5-in. guns with 430 r.p.g., and a 75-lb. increase in loaded weight, and a total of 839 was delivered to the U.S. Navy and U.S. Marine Corps by late 1943.

Before production of the Wildcat was turned over entirely to General Motors, however, Grumman were responsible for the construction in 1942 of twenty-one F4F-7s and, early in 1943, an additional batch of one hundred fixed-wing F4F-3s required for training purposes. The F4F-7 was a long-range photographic-reconnaissance variant, the fixed wing of which housed no less than 452 Imp. gal. (555 U.S. gal.) of fuel, total fuel capacity being 570 Imp. gal. (685 U.S. gal.), the reserve tank being replaced in the fuselage by a

(Below and right) The first G-36B Martlet II. This was the first model for The Royal Navy to feature wing folding, the outer panels swivelling at the forward spar on the stub centre section and folding aft.

An early production F4F-4 of VF-41, one of the first U.S. Navy squadrons to receive the folding-wing Wildcat. Whereas the XF4F-4 had featured hydraulic wing folding, the wings of the production F4F-4 were folded and spread manually.

camera. No armament was installed, all pilot protection was deleted, an automatic pilot was fitted, and loaded weight reached an all time high for Wildcats at 10,328 lb., but maximum range was 3,700 miles. The F4F-7 was first flown on December 30, 1941, and at one time orders for this aircraft exceeded a hundred machines, but, in the event, only twenty-one were completed and it is believed that these were eventually converted as standard F4F-4s.

(Above) The F4F-4 equipped all U.S. Navy shipboard fighter units by the end of 1942. That illustrated is one of the initial production batch.

(Above) The XF4F-5 with the R-1820-40 Cyclone. The third and fourth production F4F-3s were completed as XF4F-5s. (Below) The R-1830-90 Twin Wasp-powered XF4F-6, prototype for the F4F-3A.

Several interesting experiments were conducted with Grumman-built Wildcats, one of these being a twin-float fighter which resulted from U.S. Navy interest in a fighter capable of operating from sheltered waters and capable of providing air cover until land bases became available. The Edo Corporation designed a special pair of floats and fitted these to an F4F-3 which flew in floatplane form as the F4F-3S for the first time on February 28, 1943. By this time, however, the U.S. Navy's construction units had demonstrated their ability to lay airstrips in a remarkably short time, rendering a float fighter superfluous. Weighing 7,506 lb. in normal loaded condition, the F4F-3S attained a maximum speed of 266 m.p.h. at 20,300 ft., an initial climb rate of 2,460 ft./min., and a service ceiling of 33,500 ft. Maximum range was 600 miles at 132 m.p.h. Another experimental Wildcat was an F4F-4 fitted with electrically-operated full-span flaps. This programme was abandoned after the system malfunctioned, only one flap came down and the aircraft crashed out of control. Other Wildcats were towed behind A-20s and B-17s in experiments aimed at increasing the ferry range of small fighters, and one Wildcat participated in trials with frangible wing-tips, these being designed to break away from the wing at a specified high-G loading. Each of the frangible wingtips spanned 3.5 ft., and in theory the use of such tips could save several hundred pounds in wing structural weight. This feature was later to be incorporated in Grumman's last piston-engined fighter, the F8F-1.

By the summer of 1943 the Wildcat was in process of being replaced aboard the U.S. Navy's principal carriers by the F6F-3 Hellcat, and the General Motors-built FM-1 Wildcats were seeing increasing use from light escort carriers which had become a vital factor in the war against submarines in both the Atlantic and the Pacific. The bulk of the FM-1s supplied to Britain as Martlet Vs served in this role, working in collaboration with Swordfish rocket-firing aircraft in attacks on U-boats. But the possibility of a lighter version of the Wildcat intended specifically for operation from the short flight decks of the smaller carriers had been under consideration from mid-1942, and as part of this programme, an R-1820-56 Cyclone with a single-stage

A General Motors-built FM-1 Wildcat V (JV336) of the Royal Navy. Martlet Vs collaborated with rocket-firing Swordfish aircraft in attacks on U-boats. Three hundred and eleven Martlet Vs were delivered to the Royal Navy.

two-speed supercharger had been installed in an F4F-4 airframe. Featuring new forged cylinder heads, this version of the Cyclone engine was some 230 lb. lighter than the F4F-4's Twin Wasp, and offered 1,350 h.p. for take-off, 150 h.p. more than the Pratt and Whitney engine. Designated XF4F-8, the first experimental aircraft flew at Bethpage on November 8, 1942, being followed shortly by a second machine.

The XF4F-8 carried only four 0.5-in. guns, and slotted flaps were fitted, although these were later replaced by standard split flaps, and the second XF4F-8 was eventually fitted with enlarged vertical tail surfaces to counteract the increased torque of the more powerful engine. The empty weight of the XF4F-8 was some 530 lb. less than that of the standard F4F-4, initial climb rate was increased by nearly a thousand feet per minute, and service ceiling was boosted from 34,000 to 36,400 ft. Early in 1943 a contract was awarded General Motors for the production of 1,265 Wildcats similar to the XF4F-8 under the designation FM-2, and by the end of the year 310 aircraft of this type had been accepted, no less than 4,437 having been delivered to the U.S. Navy when production terminated in August 1945. In addition, 340 were delivered to the Fleet Air Arm as the Wildcat VI, the name "Martlet" having been abandoned in January 1944 to conform with U.S. Navy nomenclature, earlier models being renamed retroactively. The first F.A.A. squadron to re-equip with the Wildcat VI was No. 881 which became operational with this type aboard H.M.S. *Pursuer* in July 1944. Late in 1943 some FM-2 Wildcats were organised into composite squadrons with Avenger torpedo aircraft, and operating from escort carriers, these were particularly effective in the Pacific where they gave close air support to the forces ashore.

The FM-2 Wildcat was normally powered by the R-1820-56 or -56A Cyclone rated at 1,350 h.p. for take-off and having military ratings of 1,300 h.p. at 4,000 ft. and 1,000 h.p. at 17,500 ft., but some machines had the -56W or -56WA with water injection. The main 97 Imp. gal. (117 U.S. gal.) fuel tank was retained, but the reserve tank was deleted, and the 2,401st and subsequent FM-2s had an enlarged tank of 105 Imp. gal. (126 U.S. gal.) capacity. Maximum

range on internal fuel was 780 miles at 164 m.p.h. at 5,000 feet, but this could be increased to 1,350 miles at 153 m.p.h. by means of two 48.3 Imp. gal. (58 U.S. gal.) drop tanks. Maximum speed was 320 m.p.h. at 16,800 ft., initial climb rate was 2,890 ft./min., and altitudes of 10,000 and 20,000 feet were attained in 3.7 and 8.0 minutes respectively. The 3,301st and subsequent FM-2s had provision for six 5-in. rockets under the wings.

(Above) A Martlet V during tests with Blackburn Aircraft who were responsible for the modification of fighters of this type prior to their delivery to the Royal Navy.

(Above and below) The first XF4F-8, predecessor of the FM-2, photographed at Bethpage on November 12, 1942, four days after its initial flight test.

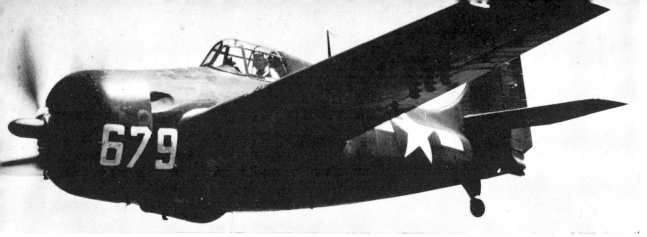

A late-production General Motors FM-2 Wildcat. Built in larger numbers than any other version of the Wildcat, 4,437 being delivered to the U.S. Navy and 340 to the Royal Navy, the FM-2 was a lighter, more powerful fighter intended specifically for operation from the smaller carriers.

Excluding prototypes, a total of 7,898 Wildcats was produced during the fighter's six-year production life, 5,927 of these being built by General Motors, and U.S. Navy statistics credited the Wildcat with the destruction of 905 enemy aircraft in aerial combat for the loss of only 178 during the period 1941–3, while the ratio of victories to losses for the entire war was claimed as 6.9 : 1—not bad for a fighter which rarely outperformed those by which it was opposed! The Wildcat fought in all major naval battles of the Pacific War, and its battle honours included such memorable names as Wake, Midway, Guadalcanal, Coral Sea and the Solomons. It was succeeded in fast carrier operations by more potent fighters which established higher "kill" ratios, but none made a greater contribution to victory in the Pacific than the portly little Wildcat.

Grumman F4F-4 Wildcat

Dimensions : Span, 38 ft. 0 in.; span folded, 14 ft. 4 in.; length, 29 ft. 0 in.; height (tail down), 8 ft. 11 in., (tail up), 12 ft. 1⅜ in.; wing area, 260 sq. ft.

Armament : Six 0.5-in. Browning M-2 machine guns with 240 r.p.g. and two 100-lb. bombs.

Power Plant : One Pratt and Whitney R-1830-86 fourteen-cylinder two-row radial air-cooled engine rated at 1,200 h.p. at 2,700 r.p.m. for take-off, 1,150 h.p. at 2,700 r.p.m. at 11,500 ft., and 1,040 h.p. at 2,550 r.p.m. at 18,400 ft. Maximum fuel capacity, 120 Imp. gal. (144 U.S. gal.) plus two 48 Imp. gal. (58 U.S. gal.) drop tanks.

Weights : Empty, 5,895 lb.; normal loaded, 7,975 lb.; maximum overload, 8,762 lb.

Performance : Maximum speed, 284 m.p.h. at sea level, 320 m.p.h. at 18,800 ft.; range, 830 mls. at 161 m.p.h. (with one external tank), 1,050 mls. at 157 m.p.h. (with two external tanks), 1,275 mls. at 153 m.p.h.; initial climb rate, 2,190 ft./min.; time to 10,000 ft., 5.6 min., to 20,000 ft., 12.4 min.; service ceiling, 34,000 ft.

FM-2 Wildcats such as that depicted below gave effective close support to ground forces in the Pacific.

THE HEINKEL HE 219 UHU

The history of military aviation has seen many highly successful warplanes conceived not as the results of officially-inspired specifications but from the vision of aircraft designers capable of foreseeing operational requirements long before they have been officially formulated. It has also seen many warplanes that have achieved fame performing tasks not envisaged at the time of their conception. The Heinkel He 219 Uhu, or Owl, can lay claim to membership of the first category, having been born as a private venture; it also found its true métier in a role unforseen at the time of its birth.

Intended as a multi-purpose machine for daytime operation, the He 219 became one of the finest, if not *the* finest, night fighting aircraft evolved by any of the Second World War's combatants. Few combat aircraft enjoyed a more auspicious operational début, for when tested under service conditions for the first time, on the night of June 11–12, 1943, its pilot, Major Streib, succeeded in destroying five R.A.F. Lancaster bombers during a single sortie! Yet, despite this spectacular trial, the quirks of fate denied the He 219 the fame which it might justifiably have expected, and prevented its widespread usage which could have had such a radical effect on the nocturnal air war over Germany.

In the early summer of 1940 the Ernst Heinkel A.G. found themselves with more design capacity than could be usefully employed on existing contracts, and in order to use this surplus the company initiated a design study for a fast twin-engined multi-purpose aircraft suitable for the roles of long-range escort and heavy fighter, fighter-bomber, and dive-, level-, or torpedo-bomber. The promise indicated by the initial feasibility study led to a more detailed design which, allocated the type designation "He 219", embodied several novel and advanced features, such

as remotely-controlled dorsal and ventral gun barbettes for defence. The cockpit was pressurized, and a nosewheel undercarriage was employed. The design was submitted to the German Air Ministry, or Reichsluftfahrtministerium, but little interest was displayed in Heinkel's proposals. No official requirement existed for such an aircraft and, at that stage in the war, there was every reason to suppose that the Luftwaffe could bring the conflict to a successful conclusion with the aircraft which it already possessed. It was admitted that several features of the He 219 were worthy of further investigation, but the nosewheel undercarriage was looked upon as an impracticable "American innovation" which could provide endless trouble on service airfields. Thus, the He 219 project was shelved.

"Night fighting! It will never come to that!" With these words German service chiefs had dismissed a proposal to evolve specialised night fighters a few weeks before the outbreak of the Second World War, and in the Summer of 1940 they still subscribed to this view, despite an obvious tendency on the part of R.A.F. Bomber Command towards night attack, and intelligence reports indicating the increasing effort being given by the British aircraft industry to the development of four-engined heavy bombers. A memorandum on the subject was prepared and presented to the R.L.M., this stressing the inadequacy of Germany's night defences, pointing out the poor results obtained with the Messerschmitt Bf 110 and bombers, such as the Dornier Do 17Z and Junkers Ju 88, converted for the night interception role, and suggesting the re-examination of the He 219 project as a potential specialized night fighter. The R.L.M. studied the memorandum but took no action in the matter. A year passed and, in the meantime, R.A.F. night attacks on northern and western Germany

The He 219V1 (below) was flown for the first time on November 15, 1942. Remotely-controlled dorsal and ventral gun barbettes were originally to have been installed.

H*

The He 219V5 (above) had the lengthened fuselage introduced on the V3 but was the first prototype to have the upper fuselage "step" faired over.

became something more than the mere pin pricks that German propagandists were dismissing as unimportant.

At the end of 1941 even the R.L.M. could no longer shut their eyes to the increasing dangers of R.A.F. Bomber Command's nocturnal sorties, and the Ernst Heinkel A.G. was requested to evolve a night fighter version of the He 219 project with all possible speed. The new night fighter, designated He 219A, was to be powered by two Daimler-Benz DB 603 liquid-cooled engines, carry two crew members and feature an armament of six fixed 20-mm. MG 151

cannon and paired 12.7-mm. MG 131 machine guns in remotely-controlled dorsal and ventral barbettes. Provision was to be made for a 4,410-lb. bomb load to enable the aircraft to participate in intruder operations. After a careful investigation of the needs of the night fighter units, redesign of the He 219 began at Rostock-Marienehe in January 1942, and, in an attempt to make up the lost eighteen months, the drawings were passed to the experimental shop so that prototype construction could proceed in parallel with detail design.

The He 219V11 (below) was the first prototype to test two 30-mm. MK 108 cannon in a Schräge Musik installation. This aircraft was later evaluated at Farnborough.

By March eighty per cent of the drawings had been completed, but in that month the Heinkel fighter suffered the first of a series of setbacks which were to punctuate a checkered development and production career—an R.A.F. attack on Rostock resulting in the destruction of three-quarters of the completed drawings! A second attack during the following month destroyed the remaining drawings, but the partly built first prototype survived both raids unscathed, and the draughtsmen, together with their drawing boards, moved into the experimental shop to work alongside the prototype. However, the constant threat of R.A.F. attack soon resulted in the transfer of the design office to Vienna-Schwechat where it was proposed to establish the principal He 219A assembly line. General Kammhuber, the *General der Nachtjagd*, who had been largely responsible for framing the requirements to which the He 219A was being built, watched development of the fighter closely, and on August 17, 1942, during a visit to Rostock-Marienehe, he stated his anxiety to have the first He 219A-equipped *Nachtjagdgruppe* in operational service by April 1, 1943! The manufacturers considered such a demand to be totally unrealistic. One hundred and thirty pre-production aircraft had been ordered instead of the usual ten or a dozen, but they felt that deliveries could not possibly commence before August 1943.

A number of problems were already being encountered, not least of which were those posed by the DB 603G engines with which it was proposed to power the fighter and which had still to complete bench running. In fact, the R.L.M. had been toying with the idea of abandoning the He 219A and, instead, adapting the Focke-Wulf Fw 187A Falke twin-engined fighter for the night interception role! The Focke-Wulf fighter had begun trials in the summer of 1937 as a single-seat day fighter, and six prototypes and three pre-production models had been completed, later machines being two-seaters. The possibility of resurrecting the design as a night fighter was quickly discarded, however, as a result of the evaluation report of the Chief of Department C-E2. This stated, ". . . There can be no doubt that the Fw 187 was and still is an excellent aircraft, but it can be of little use as a night fighter. It is too small and accommodation is too cramped to permit the installation of all the necessary instrumentation and equipment demanded by the night-fighting role, and there is no possibility of installing rearward defensive armament!" Thus, at a meeting held at the R.L.M. on August 18, 1942, it was decided to maintain the existing priority on He 219A development, and install the lower powered DB 603A engine pending availability of the DB 603G. Although R.L.M. enthusiasm for the Heinkel fighter had apparently waned, it was certainly waxing once more by September 4th, when, during a conference held by the Technical Branch of the R.L.M., or *Technisches Amt*, at which General Kammhuber was present, it was proposed that the He 219 could also be used as a fast bomber, supplant-

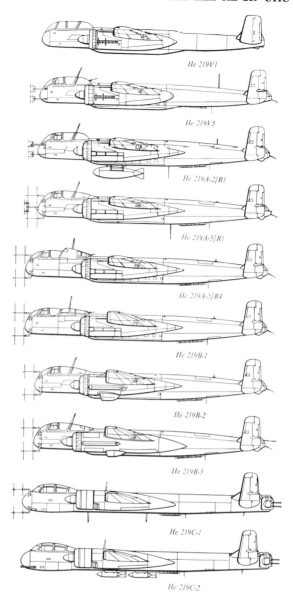

He 219V1

He 219V5

He 219A-2/R1

He 219A-5/R1

He 219A-5/R4

He 219B-1

He 219B-2

He 219B-3

He 219C-1

He 219C-2

ing the Bf 110G and the Ju 88. Kammhuber protested strongly at this proposal, stating that he would need all available He 219s for the *Nachtjagdgeschwader*!

In the meantime, a number of changes had been taking place in the design of the fighter. The system of remotely-controlled gun barbettes which had functioned so perfectly on ground test rigs had presented some insoluble problems during flight tests. The hydraulic system had proved to have inadequate power to counter the effects of airflow at high speeds with the result that the guns invariably pointed in a different direction to that indicated by the gun sight. The periscopic sight itself offered inadequate view, and the complexity of the system with its potential maintenance problem under service conditions, added to the inordinate weight of the barbettes with their adverse affect on performance, had resulted in the decision to abandon the whole installation and provide a single hand-operated 12.7-mm. MG 131 machine gun for rear defence. It had been originally proposed to install four of the forward-firing 20-mm. cannon in the wing roots and the remaining two in a tray which had terminated in the ventral barbette. The deletion of this barbette now provided adequate space to accommodate in the ventral tray four cannon of any calibre from 15-mm. to 30-mm., and the number of cannon installed in the wing roots was reduced to two, the ammunition tanks for all six weapons being housed in the wing centre section.

Despite aerial attack and the vacillation of the R.L.M., the first prototype of the new night fighter, the He 219V1, was completed in little more than eleven months from the receipt of the development contract, flying for the first time on November 15, 1942, a second prototype following a month later. Both prototypes were powered by 1,700 h.p. DB 603A engines, and initial trials were generally very satisfactory apart from some slight directional and lateral instability, and some tail oscillation. The nose-wheel undercarriage, which had been accepted with bad grace by the R.L.M., proved trouble-free, the fighter enjoying excellent take-off and landing characteristics. Flight trials progressed so rapidly that, during December, the He 219V1 was delivered to Peenemünde for armament trials, two MG 151 cannon being mounted in the ventral tray. The MG 151 was an extremely accurate weapon with a high muzzle velocity and fire rate, and interchangeable barrels and breech-blocks for 15-mm. or 20-mm. calibre ammunition, but two other cannon were favoured at this time, the MK 103 and MK 108, both of 30-mm. calibre. The MK 103 was a long-barrelled weapon with a high muzzle velocity and a very flat trajectory, whereas the MK 108 was a short-barrelled weapon with a very limited effective range but suited to mass production techniques. The breech-block components were mostly die-pressed sheet metal welded together, and during violent manoeuvres the MK 108 tended to seize as a result of the centrifugal forces. Despite the shortcomings of this weapon, a battery of four MK 108 cannon was installed in the ventral tray of the He 219V1 for trials in February 1943. It was proposed to collect the links and cases within the tray which was riveted to the fuselage and had no ejector chutes. The tremendous gas forces generated when firing four 30-mm. cannon had been overlooked, however, and during the first test the tray was bulged out of shape by the pressure. A ventilation system was promptly incorporated, but during subsequent trials the tray constantly parted company with the fuselage! The second, third and fourth prototypes were equipped

with six forward-firing 20-mm. MG 151 cannon with substantially better results, although a decision regarding the armament of production models was delayed.

On January 8, 1943, the first comparison flights between the He 219V2 and the Ju 188 were made, both types clocking 273 m.p.h. at sea level, but more extensive comparative trials took place on March 25 when the Heinkel fighter competed with the Dornier Do 217N and the Ju 188S, the latter being the forerunner of the Ju 388K. The Do 217N retired from the competition at an early stage, but a closely fought battle ensued between the Ju 188S flown by Colonel Lossberg and the He 219 flown by Major Streib, from which the Heinkel emerged the victor, proving more manoeuvrable and some 15 m.p.h. faster than its rival. The outcome was an increase in the pre-production order for the He 219A to three hundred machines in April. By this time, five prototypes had been completed and flown, the fuselages of four of these having been manufactured at Milec in Poland and then transported in Me 323 transports to Vienna-Schwechat for mating with the wings, empennages and other components. The He 219V3 and all subsequent aircraft had a lengthened fuselage (from 47 ft. $6\frac{7}{8}$ in. to 50 ft. $11\frac{3}{4}$ in.) and enlarged vertical tail surfaces, the He 219V4 was the first machine to carry FuG 202 Lichtenstein SN-2 radar, and the "step" in the upper rear fuselage contour, originally for the dorsal barbette, was faired over on the He 219V5 and later machines.

In May 1943 four 30-mm. MK 103 cannon were installed in the ventral tray and tested for the first time and, combined with two 20-mm. MG 151 cannon in the wing roots, this armament proved extremely efficacious. Although all aircraft completed at that time bore *Versuchs* (Experimental) numbers, they were also He 219A-0 pre-production machines, and a complex series of suffixes were applied to the designation to indicate armament and equipment changes. Aircraft with four tray-mounted MK 108 cannon became He 219A-0/R1's while those with MK 103s were He 219A-0/R2's. Minor variations in radar equipment led to the He 219A-0/R1-U1, A-0/R2-U2 and A-0/R2-U3. The He 219A-0/R3 could have 15-mm. MG 151 or 30-mm. MK 103s or 108s.

During April Director Frydag of the Ernst Heinkel A.G. had reported that, in the circumstances, it was impossible to deliver more than ten He 219A fighters per month, but in order to expedite service introduction, the first of several *Versuchs* machines to be delivered to the Luftwaffe for evaluation reached Venloe in Holland during that month for tests with the first Gruppe of Nachtjagdgeschwader 1. The first operational sortie was made from Venloe on the

---

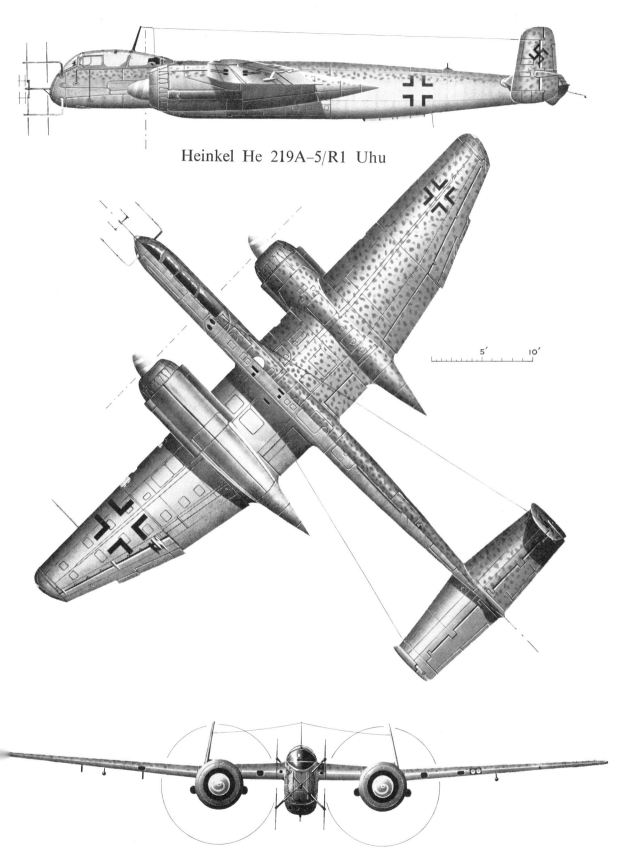

Heinkel He 219A–5/R1 Uhu

5′   10′

The He 219A-O/R3, the production prototype for the He 219A-2, carried four 30-mm. MK 103 cannon and two 20-mm. MG 151 cannon.

night of June 11–12 and, as already recounted, an He 219A-0 flown by Major Streib accounted for five R.A.F. bombers. During the following ten days He 219A-0s flown by NJG.1 pilots accounted for a further twenty R.A.F. bombers, including six Mosquitos which, until that time, had been considered invulnerable! General Kammhuber immediately demanded two thousand He 219s, but the General Luftzeugmeister called for a monthly output of only two dozen machines. Even this small output was to prove impracticable, and production did not attain ten per month before December 1943. The plan called for the completion of the three hundred pre-production He 219A-0 fighters by the summer of 1944, large-scale production beginning at the Heinkel-controlled plants at Milec and Buczin in Poland in January 1944. This plan was to be frustrated by lack of personnel and machine tools at the Polish factories, and in the meantime, General Milch, who favoured the Junkers Ju 88G, was to start a campaign aimed at bringing about the cancellation of the entire He 219 programme.

During a conference held at the R.L.M. on June 15, 1943, a few days after Major Streib's success, Milch commented: "The He 219 appears to be excellent.

During a single sortie he (Streib) destroyed five bombers. They (the pilots of NJG.1) are most enthusiastic about the fighter, but perhaps Streib would have shot down as many of the enemy when using another aircraft type!" Six months later, at an R.L.M. Technical Branch production planning conference, the General Luftzeugmeister was obviously yielding to pressure from Milch to abandon the He 219 in favour of the Ju 88G, but at the crucial moment the Junkers fighter which was then undergoing trials revealed a major defect. After examining the situation, the Technical Branch considered three alternatives: (1) Complete the current production run of He 219 fighters and then switch Heinkel-North to the Ju 88G and Heinkel-South to the Do 335; (2) Reduce the planned He 219 production rate from one hundred to fifty aircraft per month, Heinkel-North switching to the production of the Ju 88G; (3) Continue production of the He 219 as planned. In the event, the third alternative was chosen, despite Milch's protestations, and production of the Heinkel fighter continued, although air attack by the R.A.F. and the U.S.A.A.F. on the Heinkel plants and those of He 219 subcontractors was now threatening to do exactly what Milch had failed to do.

In July 1943, the first batch of He 219As with revised armament and equipment had left the Vienna-Schwechat assembly line, these being designated He 219A-2/R1's, the production prototype for this model being designated He 219A-0/R3. The He 219A-2/R1 was supposed to receive two 20-mm. MG 151 cannon in the wing roots, two 30-mm. MK 108 cannon in the ventral tray and two additional MK 108 cannon in the fuselage aft of the fuel tanks and mounted obliquely to fire upward and forward at an angle of 65°, this installation being known as *Schräge Musik*. In fact, the *Schräge Musik* installation was not tested until the He 219V19 flew in August 1943, and the obliquely-mounted guns were fitted to the He 219A-2/R1 retroactively. Owing to the erratic deliveries of the MK 108 cannon most aircraft were delivered, in fact, with twin MG 151s in the ventral tray. Forty He 219A-2/R1 fighters were built and these were mostly delivered to NJG.1. Powered by 1,750 h.p. DB 603A engines housed in annular cowlings, this model attained a maximum speed of 376 m.p.h. at 36,100 feet, cruised at 292 m.p.h. over a range of 1,370 miles, and had an initial climb rate of 1,712 ft./min. Empty and loaded weights were 19,952 lb. and 27,006 lb. respectively.

By August full production was running at Rostock-Marienehe in parallel with the He 111H-20 bomber, and in order to accelerate production of the He 219 at Milec component production for the He 177 was stopped. The He 219A-2 gave place to the He 219A-5 (the intervening suffix numbers being, like the He 219A-1, proposed high-speed reconnaissance-bomber variants which progressed no further than the drawing board) which, in its initial form, retained the DB 603A engines. The rear portion of the cockpit-canopy was refined and lowered, the provision for a rear-firing 12.7-mm. MG 131 machine gun which had been fitted on some machines was deleted, ammunition capacity was reduced, and an additional 86 Imp. gal. (103 U.S. gal.) of fuel was accommodated in the rear of each engine nacelle. The first production variant. the He 219A-5/R1, had an armament of two 20-mm, MG 151s in the wing roots, two 30-mm. MK 108s in the ventral tray, and two similar guns in a *Schräge Musik* installation, and this armament was also carried by the He 219A-5/R2 which differed principally in having 1,800 h.p. DB 603E engines, these having been tested by the converted He 219V16 and the He 219V20. The He 219A-5/R2-U2 featured a further increase in power, having 1,900 h.p. DB 603G engines and 20-mm. MG 151 cannon in the ventral tray, and the similarly armed He 219A-5/R3 had 1,800 h.p. DB 603Aa engines.

Until the appearance of the DB 603E-powered He 219A-5/R4, all production versions of the Uhu had been two-seaters. In an attempt to combat the increasing night fighter opposition being encountered over Germany, the R.A.F. had begun to send Mosquito night fighters with its bomber formations, and a number of He 219s had been lost to these marauders. Some form of rear defence was considered necessary and, thus, the He 219A-5/R4 carried a third crew member armed with a single rear-firing 12.7-mm. MG 131 machine gun. The additional crew member was enclosed by a raised canopy but it was discovered that this canopy's drag reduced maximum speed by some 22 m.p.h., and it was decided that another means of combating the Mosquito menace would have to be found. A special "anti-Mosquito" version of the fighter was hurriedly evolved. A few He 219A-2/R2 fighters were fitted with 1,750 h.p. DB 603L engines, stripped of all armour and, with an armament of four forward-firing 20-mm. MG 151 cannon, entered service as the He 219A-6. Loaded weight was reduced to 26,345 lb., and maximum speed and initial climb rate were increased to 404 m.p.h. and 1,810 ft./min.

The He 219V16 was originally flown with DB 603A engines but was later fitted with DB 603Es as the He 219A-5/R2.

Improved deliveries of the 1,900 h.p. DB 603G resulted in the final A-series production model of the Uhu, the He 219A-7 which became operational in January 1944. The most important service version of the Heinkel fighter, the He 219A-7 was produced in several versions, the principal prototypes of which were the He 219V25, V26 and V27, the last-mentioned aircraft being the first Uhu to be tested with tail warning radar. Externally, the He 219A-7 differed little from the A-5, apart from having enlarged supercharger air intakes of improved aerodynamic form. All sub-types were intended for high-altitude operations and were heavily-armed pressurized two-seaters, their operational ceilings being of the order of 41,600–42,650 ft. The first variant, the He 219A-7/R1, carried two 30-mm. MK 108 cannon in the wing roots, two 30-mm. MK 103 and two 20-mm. MG 151 cannon in the ventral tray, and two obliquely-mounted 30-mm. MK 108s, and empty and loaded weights were 24,692 lb. and 33,730 lb. respectively. Maximum speed was 416 m.p.h. and range was 1,240 mls. The He 219A-7/R2 had MK 108s in place of the MK 103s in the ventral tray, and in addition to this change, the A-7/R3 had the MK 108 cannon in the wing roots supplanted by 20-mm. MG 151s. The He 219A-7/R4 with a forward-firing armament of four 20-mm. MG 151s was the first production model to feature tail warning radar, and six airframes were fitted with 1,900 h.p. Junkers Jumo 213E engines with methanol-water injection for anti-Mosquito operations. These, carrying a similar armament to that of the A-7/R3, were known as He 219A-7/R5's.

During the production of the He 219A the radar equipment had been progressively improved, FuG 220 Lichtenstein SN-2 replacing the older FuG 202 Lichtenstein BC-1 and FuG 212 Lichtenstein C-1, and fully operational after only seven months of experimental flying, the Heinkel fighter had proved to offer excellent maintenance accessibility. The fixed forward-firing armament was highly concentrated and effective even when the smallest calibre cannon were installed, and ammunition capacity was adequate, provision being made for 300 rounds for each of the 15-mm. or 20-mm. weapons and 100 rounds for all 30-mm. cannon. The crew, engines, fuel and ammunition tanks and radiators were all well protected, and the He 219A was the first operational aircraft to feature ejector seats, a field in which the Heinkel concern had undertaken much pioneer work. Fully loaded, the fighter enjoyed an ample surplus of power, and an engine cutting immediately after take-off or during an approach presented little danger. In fact, an instance was recorded of a pilot making an emergency take-off in an He 219A on one engine with his undercarriage locked in the "down" position and flaps fully extended! Aircrew and ground personnel alike were unanimous in their praise for the Heinkel fighter. Yet General Milch's efforts to curtail production of the He 219 continued unabated.

At a special conference held on May 25, 1944, Milch finally succeeded in persuading the R.L.M. to order the cancellation of He 219 production in favour of two new night fighters, the Focke-Wulf Ta 154 and the Junkers Ju 388J. The former had only flown for the first time ten months earlier, on July 7, 1943, but making extensive use of wood in its structure, it suggested a solution to the problem of diminishing metal alloy production. At the time of the conference seven Ta 154 prototypes had been completed and flown, but although an exceptionally promising night fighter, its career was to be terminated as a result of a series of crashes caused by *unsuitable glue bonding*! The plant producing the glue originally intended for use in the Ta 154 programme was burned down in an R.A.F. attack on Wuppertal, and the substitute proved to contain too much acid which weakened the joints which then failed. The Ju 388J, the prototype of which had begun trials only a few months earlier, was markedly slower than the Mosquito and featured an extraordinarily complex hydraulic system destined never to be perfected.

The order to abandon He 219 production was promulgated despite the protests of such leading Luftwaffe night fighter experts as Colonel Lossberg, Lieut. Colonel Knemeyer, Major Streib, and Captain Modrow, the latter alone having destroyed twenty four-engined bombers and one Mosquito at night while flying the Heinkel fighter. However, Heinkel tacitly ignored the R.L.M. directive, and production and development of the fighter continued unabated! In fact, such was the demand for the He 219 by operational units that one Luftwaffe maintenance unit succeeded in assembling six He 219As from its stock of spares and components! These aircraft were unique in that they bore no Werk-Nrs., and their existence was carefully withheld from the R.L.M.

Despite the order cancelling He 219 production that had been issued in May 1944, the R.L.M. evidently reconsidered their decision very quickly, for in June the Rechlin Experimental Establishment had joined "Operation He 219" which was aimed at improving the fighter without disrupting the production lines, and introducing the twenty-four cylinder multi-bank Junkers Jumo 222 rated at 2,500 h.p. for take-off. Unfortunately, this large and complex engine was suffering numerous teething troubles, and so few production engines had left the assembly lines that orders had to be given to all Luftwaffe "Special Commandos" to bring in every damaged enemy aero engine that could be found to boost material supply to the Junkers plants for "Operation Jumo 222"! Two Jumo 222s were installed in an He 219A airframe for test purposes, and this aircraft, designated He 219A-7/R6, clocked 435 m.p.h. during trials.

It was proposed to install the Jumo 222 in a high-altitude three-seat model, the He 219B-1, but the non-availability of the Junkers engines necessitated the installation of DB 603Aa engines in the sole example of this variant completed and tested. The designation He 219B had been allocated to a projected long-range high-altitude fighter powered by Daimler-Benz DB 614 engines which, proposed in

258

The He 219 V14 was employed as a test-bed for the BMW 003 turbojet as part of the He 162 development programme.

1942, had failed to progress further than the initial feasibility study. The new He 219B-1 had an aerodynamically refined cockpit, a lengthened fuselage of 53 ft. 7¼ in., and an extended wing spanning 72 ft. 4½ in., gross wing area being 538.196 sq. ft., but the starboard undercarriage leg collapsed during the second landing of this aircraft which suffered extensive damage and was completely written off. The He 219B-2 stemmed from the stripped-down He 219A-6 and, like its predecessor, was intended specifically for anti-Mosquito operations. First flown with the DB 603Aa, the few He 219B-2s completed and hurriedly placed in service were two-seaters powered by DB 603L engines and armed with two 20-mm. MG 151s and two 30-mm. MK 108s, the latter mounted as a *Schräge Musik* installation. The final B-series model was the He 219B-3 two-seater with a forward-firing armament of four 20-mm. MG 151s and two 30-mm. MK 108s. For initial flight trials DB 603L engines were installed, but before tests could begin, a directive was received which instructed Heinkel to await the arrival of Jumo 222 engines. In the event, the Junkers power plants never arrived and the He 219B-3 never left the ground.

In May 1944 the project office at Vienna-Schwechat had begun work on two radically modified versions of the basic fighter design, the He 219C-1 night fighter and the He 219C-2 fighter-bomber. Although the wing and tail assembly were similar to those of the He 219B, the fuselage was entirely redesigned. The forward section of the fuselage was of improved aerodynamic form and housed three crew members, the ventral tray was eliminated and two 30-mm. MK 108 cannon were installed beneath the cockpit in the C-1 model, MK 103s being used by the C-2. The former also had a pair of MG 151 cannon in the wing roots and twin obliquely-mounted MK 108s, and the centre and aft fuselage portions of both versions were of near-constant section throughout and terminated in a pressurized Rheinmetall-Borsig tail turret armed

with four 13-mm. MG 131 machine guns. This hydraulically-operated turret was heavily armoured but of exceptionally small dimensions and capable of accommodating only the smallest gunners. The He 219C-2 fighter-bomber had provision for three 1,100-lb. bombs on racks beneath the fuselage, and prototypes of both models were completed, but like the He 219B-3, they fell victims to the Jumo 222 engines with which they were to be powered, and were still awaiting the arrival of their power plants when the conflict ended. The He 219C-1 and C-2 were expected to attain maximum speeds of 419 m.p.h. and 429 m.p.h. respectively.

Several other developments of the basic He 219 design reached various stages before the end of the Second World War, these including the He 419 and Hütter Hü 211. During 1942 the Ernst Heinkel A.G. was working on a parallel design to that of the He 219 which received the designation He 319. This was a night fighter variant of the twin-engined Projekt 1065 multi-purpose aircraft, and a full-scale mock-up of the He 319 was completed and the first metal was being cut on the prototype at Rostock-Marienehe when, in November 1942, the plant was once again extensively damaged by air attack. It was then decided to abandon work on the He 319 in favour of the proposed He 419 high-altitude fighter. A prototype was built under the designation He 419A-0, and this employed the fuselage and tail assembly of an He 219A-5, two DB 603G engines and an extended, redesigned wing with a gross area of 597 sq. ft. Six further A-5 airframes were converted as He 419B-1/R1's, and these had extended wingtips to increase gross area to 635 sq. ft., and exhaust-driven turbo-superchargers for their DB 603G engines. It was originally intended to fit the He 419 with a single fin-and-rudder assembly similar to that designed for the He 319, but in the event standard He 219 components were employed. The He 419B-1/R1 carried four 30-mm. MK 108 cannon in the ventral tray and two 20-mm. MG 151 cannon in

The He 219A-7/R4 was the first production model of the Uhu to feature tail warning radar. Forward-firing armament comprised four 20-mm. MG 151 cannon.

the wing roots, and endurance was 2.15 hours at 44,600 ft. Proposed versions which did not materialise were the He 419B-1/R2 with four MG 212 cannon in the ventral tray, and the B-1/R3 with four MK 103 cannon in the tray.

In an attempt to produce an effective high-speed long-range reconnaissance aircraft, Dr. Hütter began work in 1944 on adapting a high aspect ratio (15:1) wooden wing for use with the He 219 fuselage, this development being designated Hü 211. Employing a laminar-flow aerofoil section, the wing housed 798 Imp. gal. (955 U.S. gal.) of fuel and two 39.5 Imp. gal. (47.5 U.S. gal.) methanol-water tanks for the MW 50 boost system. A camera was installed in the fuselage and two further cameras were mounted in the rear of each engine nacelle, and defensive armament comprised two fixed forward-firing and two fixed rearward-firing 20-mm. MG 151 cannon. The wing had a span and gross area of 80 ft. 6 in. and 430 sq. ft., and empty and loaded weights were 20,880 lb. and 38,600 lb. Power was to have been provided by two Jumo 222 engines with which maximum speeds of 386 m.p.h. at sea level and 445 m.p.h. at 24,000 ft. were anticipated. Range at economical cruising speed at 23,000 ft. was 3,810 mls. Two prototypes of the Hü 211 had reached an advanced stage of construction when, in December 1944, they were totally destroyed in an air raid.

Among the numerous experimental models of the He 219 was one employed as a test-bed for the BMW 003 turbojet which was intended as the power plant of the diminutive He 162, popularly known as the *Volksjäger*. The aircraft selected for these tests was the He 219V14 which, with ventral tray removed and the BMW 003 mounted beneath the fuselage, began flying trials at Vienna-Schwechat in July 1944.

When, in the Autumn of 1944, the "Fighter Emergency Programme" was promulgated, eliminating all twin-engined fighters from the production programme, the only exceptions being the Do 335 and Me 262, it appeared that construction of the He 219 was at last

to come to a standstill. But again the Ernst Heinkel A.G. ignored the order, and production of the He 219 continued until the plants producing the fighter were finally overrun by the Russians. By that time only 268 pre-production and production He 219s had been completed, 195 of these in 1944 and sixty-two in 1945. In addition, twenty *Versuchs* machines were employed operationally, and six further aircraft had been assembled unofficially from spare components, bringing the total to 294 machines.

In one of the last situation reports from the General Luftzeugmeister before the final collapse of German resistance, it was stated that the He 219 was without doubt an excellent aircraft with few of the teething troubles that haunted virtually all other new types. But the R.L.M. had been too late in acknowledging the qualities of the Heinkel fighter, and the damage done to its production career by vacillation and bickering within the R.L.M. was completed by R.A.F. and U.S.A.F. attacks on the factories building this ill-fated warplane.

Heinkel He 219A-7/R1 UHU

Dimensions:	Span, 60 ft. 8⅛ in.; length, 50 ft. 11¾ in.; height, 13 ft. 5½ in.; wing area, 478.994 sq. ft.
Armament:	Two 30-mm. MK 108 with 100 r.p.g. in wing roots, two 30-mm. MK 103 cannon with 100 r.p.g. and two 20-mm. MG 151 cannon with 300 r.p.g. in ventral tray, and two 30-mm. MK 108 cannon in the rear fuselage mounted at an oblique angle.
Power Plants:	Two Daimler-Benz DB 603G twelve-cylinder inverted-vee liquid-cooled engines rated at 1,900 h.p. at 2,700 r.p.m. for take-off and 1,560 h.p. at 24,200 ft. Internal fuel capacity (fuselage), 572 Imp. gal. (687 U.S. gal.), (engine nacelles), 172 Imp. gal. (206.5 U.S. gal.).
Weights:	Empty, 24,692 lb.; loaded, 33,730 lb.
Performance:	Maximum speed, 416 m.p.h. at 22,965 ft.; maximum cruising speed, 391 m.p.h.; economical cruising speed, 335 m.p.h.; range at maximum continuous cruising speed, 960 mls., at economical cruising speed, 1,243 mls.; initial climb rate, 1,810 ft./min.; time to 19,685 ft., 11.5 min., to 32,810 ft., 18.8 min.; maximum ceiling, 41,660 ft.

(*Above*) *The Bf* 110*V*1, *first prototype of Germany's long-range escort fighter, powered by two early Daimler-Benz DB* 600 *engines and first flown on May* 12, 1936. (*Right*) *The Bf* 110*A*-0 *with* 610 *h.p. Junkers Jumo* 210*B engines, revised cockpit canopy and re-designed endplate fins.*

THE MESSERSCHMITT BF 110

The long-range multi-seat escort fighter is possibly the most difficult of combat aircraft to design. Certainly no entirely successful machine in this category emerged from the Second World War, and when Professor Willy Messerschmitt began design studies for such a warplane towards the end of 1934 at the Bayerische Flugzeugwerke at Augsburg his problems would have seemed insurmountable had he possessed a full knowledge of interceptor fighter development trends abroad. Such a machine as was required by Marshal Goering to equip the élite "zerstörer" formations that he envisaged had to be capable of penetrating deep into enemy territory, possessing sufficient range to accompany bomber formations. The fuel tankage necessary presented a serious weight penalty and called for the use of two engines if the "zerstörer" was to achieve a performance approaching that of the lighter interceptor fighter by which it would be opposed. Yet it had to be manœuvrable if it was to successfully fend off the enemy's single-seaters. One requirement could only be fulfilled at the expense of the other, and compromise invariably results in a mediocre aircraft. The Bf 110 was such a compromise, but was the first serious attempt to produce a strategic fighter.

The strategic fighter conception was far-sighted, but the solution was not to be found in the heavy, twin-engined multi-seater which could never match the single-engined single-seater on the score of manœuvrability. The U.S.A.A.F. toyed with the idea of using heavy long-range escort fighters, and issued a requirement for such a machine in 1936, resulting in the slow and unwieldy Bell XFM-1 Airacuda, but only Germany persisted in this line of development.

Messerschmitt possessed no previous experience with twin-engined military aircraft when he commenced work on the Bf 110. Indeed, his first warplane, the single-seat Bf 109, had been conceived only the previous summer. At the time, the most powerful aero engine of national design available was the Junkers Jumo 210A of 610 h.p. It was obvious from the outset that a pair of such engines would be inadequate to provide the power needed for the relatively large and heavy fighter envisaged. However, the Daimler-Benz Aktiengesellschaft was actively engaged in developing a new twelve-cylinder liquid-cooled inverted-vee engine, the DB 600, which held promise of 1,000 h.p.; and on the premise that such engines would be available for his prototypes, Messerschmitt began the design of the Bf 110.

The result was a slim, rakish, low-wing cantilever

The Bf 110*B*-0 *after being re-engined with DB* 600*A units.*

(Above) The Bf 110C-1 in night-fighter finish, and (below) a pre-production Bf 110C-0.

which was superior to that of the Bf 109B-1 single-seater then being supplied to the Richthofen Jagdgeschwader. The Bayerische Flugzeugwerke was ordered to proceed with the construction of four Bf 110A-0 fighters for service evaluation. These were to carry an armament of four 7.9-mm. MG 17 machine-guns in the upper half of the nose and a free 7.9-mm. MG 15 in the rear cockpit. The airframes were completed between August 1937 and March 1938, but Daimler-Benz had yet to bring its DB 600 engine to production status owing to teething troubles and 610 h.p. Junkers Jumo 210B engines were therefore installed in place of the Daimler-Benz units, driving two-blade variable-pitch airscrews. With these engines the Bf 110A-0 was seriously underpowered, and with a loaded weight of 12,346 lb. it attained a maximum speed of only 267 m.p.h. at 12,470 feet.

However, in the spring of 1938 the first deliveries of the 960 h.p. DB 600A engine began, and in the following summer two further airframes which had been tested with 670 h.p. Jumo 210G engines and were designated Bf 110B-0, the first having flown on April 19, 1938, were re-engined with the DB 600A to serve as test vehicles for the initial production model, the Bf 110B-1. The B-0 and B-1 embodied a heavier offensive armament than that installed in the A-0, two 20-mm. MG FF cannon being installed in the lower half of the nose beneath the cockpit and four MG 17s fitted in the upper half of the nose. It was planned that the small production batch of Bf 110B-1 fighters would be transferred to the Condor Legion for testing under operational conditions, but the Spanish Civil War, the invaluable "test conflict", had terminated by the time the twin-engined fighters were ready, and they were therefore diverted to Luftwaffe test centres where they were intensively flown by service pilots in order to reveal any faults which could be corrected on the Augsburg assembly line.

monoplane with an all-metal stressed-skin structure, a retractable undercarriage and twin fins and rudders in order to provide a reasonable arc of fire for the rear gunner. The construction of three prototypes was commenced at Augsburg in 1935; and with the delivery of a pair of pilot production DB 600 engines from Daimler-Benz in the spring of 1936, the first prototype, the Bf 110V1, was completed and flown successfully on May 12, 1936. With a total of 1,800 h.p. available from its DB 600 engines, the Bf 110V1 attained 316 m.p.h. in level flight during its first test flights, and this compared closely, according to intelligence reports, with the maximum speed attained by the prototype of Britain's new Hawker Hurricane which had first flown six months earlier. Similarly powered to the first prototype, the second and third machines, the Bf 110V2 and V3, were flown respectively on October 24 and December 24, and on January 14, 1937, the Bf 110V2 went to the Luftwaffe test centre at Rechlin for flight testing.

While the service test-pilots were unimpressed by the fighter's powers of manœuvre and sluggish acceleration compared with smaller single-seat fighters, they were highly enthusiastic regarding the Bf 110's speed,

Bf 110C-4 long-range escort fighters. One of the first variants to be mass-produced.

Several shortcomings were revealed during this concentrated evaluation programme. The tail assembly tended to vibrate severely under certain flight conditions and the rigidity of the rear fuselage had to be increased, and considerable turbulence was experienced around the underslung radiator baths, which were moved outboard of the nacelles forward of the flaps. Meanwhile, development of the DB 600 engine had been abandoned in favour of the more promising DB 601 which incorporated a direct fuel-injection system and improved supercharging capacity.

Embodying extensive structural strengthening, two 1,100 h.p. DB 601A engines driving VDM three-bladed controllable-pitch fully-feathering airscrews, and a revised cockpit enclosure, the fighter became the Bf 110C and the first C-0 pre-production machines were delivered to Luftwaffe test centres in February 1939, closely followed by the fully operational Bf 110C-1 with which Marshal Goering founded his "zerstörer" units which he saw as the strategic fighter élite of the Luftwaffe. The Bf 110C differed from earlier models in having clipped wing-tips to simplify manufacture, reducing overall span from 55 ft. 5$\frac{3}{8}$ in. to 53 ft. 4$\frac{7}{8}$ in. The Bf 110C-2 was generally similar to the initial production C-1 apart from radio equipment (FuG-10) and revised electrical systems, while the C-3 and C-4 were similar respectively to the C-1 and C-2 but carried improved MG FF cannon.

By the time Germany invaded Poland on September 1, 1939, ten Luftwaffe Gruppen had been equipped with the heavy fighter. Owing to the limited aerial opposition the Bf 110C was largely employed in the ground-support role, and after the fall of Poland little was heard of this much-vaunted machine until, on December 14, 1939, it was encountered by a formation of twelve Wellingtons over the Heligoland Bight. But it was not until it was to come up against R.A.F. fighters in 1940 that the Bf 110C was to receive its first real trial in combat and to be found wanting.

By the end of 1939 approximately 537 Bf 110C fighters had been delivered to the Luftwaffe. A typical early sub-type, the Bf 110C-4, had a maximum speed of 349 m.p.h. at 22,965 feet and a maximum cruising speed of 301 m.p.h. at the same altitude, at which, on internal fuel capacity alone (280 Imp. gal.), range was 565 miles. At sea-level maximum speed was 294 m.p.h. and maximum cruising speed was 263 m.p.h., at which a range of 481 miles was attained. By the beginning of 1940 the basic aircraft had been adapted to undertake several alternative roles. The Bf 110C-4/B had bomb-racks for 550-lb. bombs fitted under the centre section, each side of the fuselage, to suit it for the fighter-bomber role, and the C-5 was a special reconnaissance version, a camera replacing the two 20-mm. cannon in the lower part of the fuselage nose.

As a long-range escort fighter the Bf 110C received a disastrous mauling at the hands of the more nimble Hurricane and Spitfire during the "Battle of Britain". Rather than protecting the bombers under escort, the Bf 110C formations usually found that they were hard put to defend themselves, and the farcical situation

developed in which single-seat Bf 109E fighters were having to afford protection to the escort fighters. The complete failure of the Bf 110C in the role for which it had been conceived led to its eventual withdrawal from the Channel coast but did not result in any reduction in its production priority. Several attempts were made to adapt it for specialized roles: the Bf 110C-6 carried a 30-mm. Mk 101 cannon in a fairing beneath the fuselage for bomber destroyer duties, while the C-7 featured a specially strengthened undercarriage to enable it to take off with two 1,100-lb. bombs. Some of the late production C-models were re-engined with 1,200 h.p. DB 601N power plants, and a number of the initial production machines were rebuilt as Bf 110C-1/U-1 tugs for towing heavy transport gliders.

Generally similar to the Bf 110C, the D-series were intended originally as long-range escort fighters with

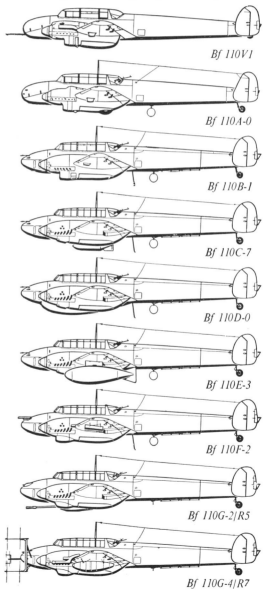

Bf 110V1

Bf 110A-0

Bf 110B-1

Bf 110C-7

Bf 110D-0

Bf 110E-3

Bf 110F-2

Bf 110G-2/R5

Bf 110G-4/R7

(Above) A Bf 110C-4/B fighter-bomber, and (below) a Bf 110C-5 reconnaissance-fighter.

improved range capabilities. The pre-production Bf 110D-0 had its offensive armament reduced by the removal of the two 20-mm. MG FF cannon and featured a large supplementary fuel tank under the fuselage. This tank was not jettisonable and resembled a large fairing, resulting in the D-0 sub-type being dubbed "pot belly". It contained some 230 Imperial gallons of fuel and, with two 900-litre-capacity external wing tanks, brought the total fuel tankage up to a phenomenal 907 gallons. However, the Bf 110D-0 demanded an exceptionally long take-off run and was unwieldy in the air, and the production version, the Bf 110D-1, carried no belly tank but retained provision for a pair of underwing drop-tanks ranging from 300- to 900-litre capacity. The D-1 also reverted to the cannon armament. The Bf 110D-2 was similar but had shackles for two 1,100-lb. bombs and had the rearward-firing defensive armament increased to two 7.9-mm. MG 17 machine-guns. The D-3 was similar to the D-1 but could carry bomb shackles.

(Below) The Bf 110E-1 fighter-bomber with racks outboard of the radiator baths

Both the C- and D-models had almost disappeared from the European theatre by the summer of 1941, although they were being used extensively on the Russian front and in the Middle East. Production during 1940 had risen to 1,083 machines, but with the impending introduction of the Me 210 only 784 machines were produced in the following year. With the introduction of the Bf 110E-0 and E-1, provision was made for carrying four 110-lb. bombs on additional racks under the outer wings; and with the standardization of the DB 601N engine for the E-2 maximum bomb load was increased from 2,645 lb. to 4,410 lb. The Bf 110E-3 was a reconnaissance version of the E-2 with reduced armament and two 900-litre drop-tanks. The F-model denoted a switch to the 1,300 h.p. DB 601F engine and, apart from the engine change, the Bf 110F-0, F-1 and F-3 were identical to the E-0, E-1, and E-3, but the Bf 110F-2 was a heavy bomber interceptor which could carry four 21-cm. WG. 21 rocket missile tubes underwing.

In July 1940 General Kammhuber had formed a night-fighter Gruppe which comprised two Staffeln of Bf 110Cs and one Staffel of Dornier Do 17Z-10. This Gruppe was intended to develop night-fighting tactics, which were then in their infancy. As General der Nachtjagd, Kammhuber developed a system of close-range interception with the aid of searchlights, known as "Helle Nachtjagd" (illuminated night-fighting), the guiding principle of this technique being ground control. However, the German High Command resisted all Kammhuber's attempts to have a proportion of the Bf 110 output equipped as specialized night-fighters, although the demands he made for equipment with which to develop an efficient G.C.I. technique eventually bore fruit in the form of the Wurzbürg Riese radar for the guidance of fighters and the Lichtenstein airborne radar. By the beginning of 1942 a procedure had been developed known as "Himmelbett" ("place in the heaven") which embodied G.C.I. controlled fighters in "boxes" covering the area affected by the raid. The night-fighters were vectored towards the enemy bombers as they approached the "boxes" until such a time as the enemy was picked up by the Lichtenstein radar. The Bf 110's characteristics made it especially suitable for "Himmelbett" operations, and the first version to be built especially for night-fighting was the Bf 110F-4, which, initially carrying no radar, had a position for a third crew member and two 30-mm. MK 108 cannon in a ventral tray.

By the end of 1942, in which year 580 Bf 110s were produced, production of this aircraft had again been stepped up as, on April 17, production of the Me 210 was cancelled after numerous accidents, thus leaving a serious gap in the Luftwaffe's fighter and fighter-bomber production programme. To fill the gap an improved version

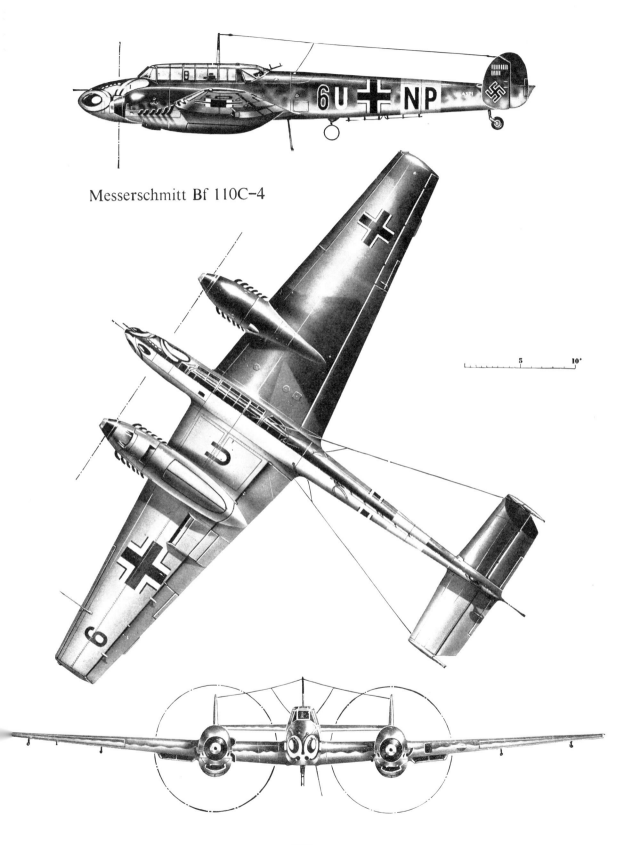

Messerschmitt Bf 110C-4

5   10'

(*Top*) *Bf* 110G-2 *fighter-bomber.* (*Immediately above*) *A Bf* 110G-4/R3 *night fighter, and* (*below*) *a Bf* 110G-4/R7.

of the Bf 110 was introduced, the G-series with the DB 605 engine which provided 1,475 h.p. for take-off and 1,355 h.p. at 18,700 feet. The pre-production Bf 110G-0 fighter-bomber was delivered for service evaluation late in 1942, and from early in 1943 G-series machines were encountered in increasing numbers. Apart from its engines the first production model, the Bf 110G-1, was similar to earlier fighter-bomber variants, and the G-2 differed principally in the armament installed: two or four 20-mm. MG 151 cannon and four 7.9-mm. MG 17 in the nose plus two 7.9-mm. MG 81 in the rear cockpit. The G-2/R1 carried a 37-mm. Flak 18 (BK 3.7) cannon with seventy rounds in place of the 20-mm. guns; the G-2/R3 was similar apart from having GM 1 (nitrous-oxide) power boost equipment; the G-2/R4 carried a nose armament of two 30-mm. MK 108 cannon and the 37-mm. Flak 18 gun; and the G-2/R5 was similar but embodied GM 1 power boost. The Bf 110G-3 was a long-range reconnaissance variant with one Rb 50/30 camera and one Rb 75/30 camera, and the G-3/R3 was a reconnaissance-fighter which carried a similar armament to the G-2/R4.

With the build-up of the R.A.F.'s night offensive against Germany increasing priority was given to the production of night-fighters, and all subsequent variants of the Bf 110G were built to fulfil this role. The first of these, the Bf 110G-4, which carried a forward-firing armament of either two or four 20-mm. 151 cannon and four MG 17 machine-guns, carried no radar, and the G-4/U7 and G-4/U8 were respectively versions with GM 1 power boost and shackles for two 300-litre drop-tanks to increase patrol endurance, but despite some success it was becoming

apparent that successful night-fighting could only be conducted with the aid of airborne radar.

From time to time Bf 110G night-fighters were used on day operations. They were first employed as close escort to the *Scharnhorst* and the *Gneisenau* off the Dutch coast and Heligoland Bight, and in the summer of 1943 they fought American day-bomber formations whenever the latter flew unescorted. The Bf 110G groups sustained heavy losses during these actions owing to their pilots, trained in night-fighting tactics, going in close before attacking and being met by the heavy defensive fire of the bombers. They were no match for the Thunderbolts escorting American bombers over Berlin.

The first version of the Bf 110 to be built from the outset as a radar-carrying night-fighter was the G-4/R3 which carried an additional crew member to operate the Lichtenstein SN 2 radar. Forward-firing armament comprised two 30-mm. MK 108 cannon and two 20-mm. MG 151 cannon. Loaded weight was 22,050 lb. and maximum speed was 342 m.p.h., range being 1,305 miles. The operational altitude of the Bf 110G-4/R3 was limited, but its performance was adequate for dealing with the standard R.A.F. heavy bombers. The G-4/R6 and G-4/R7 were similar but had GM 1 boost and provision for drop-tanks respectively. In 1943 production of the Bf 110G was treble that of the previous year, 1,580 machines being produced, and a further 1,525 machines were delivered in 1944, although by the end of the year production was being tapered off in favour of later night-fighters such as the He 219A Uhu and the Focke-Wulf Ta 154A, and only forty-five Bf 110Gs were produced in 1945.

The Bf 110's powers of manœuvre proved inadequate in combat with opposing single-seat interceptors and its range was insufficient to enable it to perform the role of bomber escort effectively. Consequently it became virtually the "maid-of-all-work" of the Luftwaffe and eloquent testimony to the rule that in combat aircraft design à compromise between two entirely conflicting requirements must result in a mediocrity.

Messerschmitt Bf 110G-4

Dimensions : Span, 53 ft. 4⅞ in. ; length, 41 ft. 6¾ in. ; height, 13 ft. 1¼ in. ; wing area, 413 sq. ft.

Armament : Two 30-mm. MK 108 cannon and two 20-mm. MG 151 cannon in nose and two flexible 7.9-mm. MG 81 machine-guns in rear cockpit.

Power Plants : Two Daimler-Benz DB 605B twelve-cylinder inverted-Vee liquid-cooled engines rated at 1,475 h.p. at 2,800 r.p.m. for take-off and 1,355 h.p. at 2,800 r.p.m. at 18,700 ft.

Weights : Empty, 10,970 lb. ; maximum loaded, 21,800 lb.

Performance : Maximum speed, 342 m.p.h. at 22,900 ft., 311 m.p.h. at sea-level; climb to 18,000 ft., 7.9 min. ; service ceiling, 26,000 ft. ; range with maximum internal fuel, 1,305 miles.

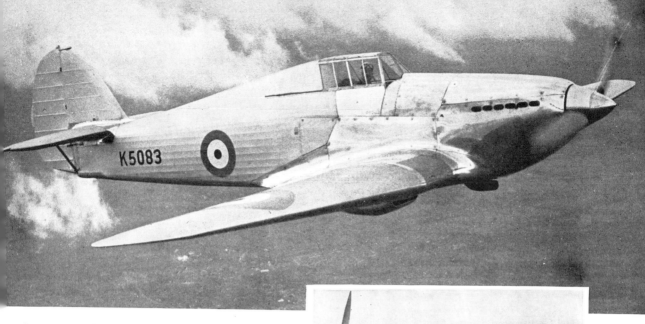

The prototype of the Hurricane, K5083, was first flown on November 6, 1935, with the experimental Merlin "C" engine. The success of initial flight trials was such that the directors of Hawker Aircraft felt justified in tooling up and ordering material for 1,000 machines before any official production order had been placed. More than 14,000 were subsequently built and the Hurricane proved one of the most versatile aircraft ever to serve with the R.A.F.

THE HAWKER HURRICANE

The synthesis of many years' intimate experience of fighter biplane design translated into the modern formula; a compromise between tradition and requirements born of a new era in air warfare—such was the Hawker Hurricane. The first fighter monoplane to join the Royal Air Force and the first combat aircraft adopted by that arm capable of exceeding 300 m.p.h. in level flight, the Hurricane shouldered the lion's share of Britain's defence during the "Battle of Britain", and was largely responsible for the successful outcome of this conflict for the defending forces, equipping more than three-fifths of R.A.F. Fighter Command's squadrons. The Hurricane also proved to possess an astounding propensity for adaptation, and the multifarious roles that it undertook earned for it the distinction of being the most versatile of single-seat warplanes to emerge from the Second World War.

Some aircraft manufacturers excel in the diversity of their products; others build success upon the unwavering pursuit of a single idea. Both methods possess their advantages and both have led to the production of good aeroplanes, but no more outstanding example of singleminded purpose in an aircraft manufacturer can be found than that provided by Hawker Aircraft Limited. This company, which evolved from the Sopwith concern, had spent its entire life in developing single-engined warplanes. As a result of this specialization the Hawker name was coupled with many illustrious aircraft types but none was to achieve more fame than the Hurricane.

The early history of the Hurricane is an interesting parallel in many ways with that of the Supermarine Spitfire with which it was to form an immortal partnership; but while the Spitfire was an entirely new conception based on specialized experience, the Hurricane was the logical outcome of a long line of fighting aircraft. Thus, although the two aeroplanes met broadly the same requirements, they represented entirely different approaches to the same problem. The two approaches were reflected to an interesting degree in their respective appearances; the Hurricane workmanlike, rugged and sturdy, the Spitfire slender and ballerina-like. One was the studied application of experience, the other a stroke of genius.

Early in 1934 Sydney Camm, chief designer of Hawker Aircraft, learned of the work being undertaken by Rolls-Royce to develop a powerful new engine, then known as the PV-12. At that time the Hawker design team had been working on a fighter project known as the Fury Monoplane which had been designed around the 660 h.p. Rolls-Royce Goshawk steam-cooled engine. As the new engine offered a substantial improvement in performance, the projected fighter was re-designed for the new power plant. In view of Air Ministry interest, project design work was rapidly completed, stressing commencing in March 1934, and work on detail drawings beginning in May.

Official views on single-seat fighter performance requirements were revised in 1934, and these changes resulted in the issue of specification F.5/34, the first

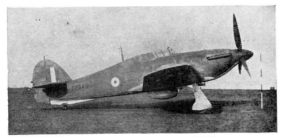

A late production Hurricane I (Z2346).

to envisage an eight-gun fighter. This specification was investigated by Hawkers and a new design prepared, but the earlier design clearly held greater promise, and this was recognized by the Air Ministry when specification F.36/34 was written around it. The detailed design was submitted to the Air Ministry on September 4, 1934; and with an official order in the offing, drawings were issued to the Experimental Shop for the construction of a prototype to begin on October 17th. By December the estimated all-up weight had risen to 4,800 lb., but Rolls-Royce promised 1,025 h.p. at 15,000 feet from the new engine.

Following an official inspection of the mock-up of the new fighter at Kingston-on-Thames, Surrey, on January 10, 1935, the Air Ministry contracted for the construction of one "high-speed monoplane". This contract was dated February 21, 1935—a date that was subsequently to have particular significance for both the Hawker company and the Royal Air Force. At this time the armament was envisaged as two Vickers Mk. V machine-guns in the fuselage and two Browning guns in the wings, and this proposed armament was retained until July 20, 1935, when the contract was amended to include an armament of eight wing-mounted machine-guns. The estimated weight crept up to 5,200 lb. with this armament, which was, in fact, fitted to the prototype and became standard on production aircraft.

On October 23, 1935, the prototype fighter, bearing the serial number K5083, was moved from Kingston to Brooklands for its first flight, which was effected on November 6 with P. W. S. "George" Bulman, the company's chief test pilot, at the controls. As measured at Brooklands, the prototype's loaded weight was 5,416 lb. The Hawker monoplane was a clean aircraft. Its tubular metal construction and fabric covering were similar to those of the earlier Fury fighter biplane, and many of its contours, particularly the tail surfaces, were characteristic of earlier Camm designs. The continued adherence to fabric covering was viewed with misgivings by some, and was, in fact, soon to be supplanted by metal skinning for the wings; but this seemingly dated feature was linked with what were for that time ultra-modern items such as a fully retractable under-carriage and a sliding cockpit canopy. For its first flight the fighter was powered by a Merlin "C", the name that had earlier been bestowed upon the PV-12, which drove a Watts two-bladed, fixed-pitch wooden airscrew.

In February 1936 the prototype was delivered to the A. & A.E.E. at Martlesham Heath for official trials at an all-up weight of 5,670 lb. Its maximum speed was 315 m.p.h. at 16,200 feet, service ceiling was 34,000 feet, and an altitude of 20,000 feet could be attained in 8.4 minutes. These trials proved the new fighter to be a most efficient and tractable mount, and Hawker Aircraft's directors, led by T. O. M. Sopwith, decided to initiate a large-scale production programme on their own authority, convinced that quantity orders from the Air Ministry would soon be forthcoming, and that any time to be saved in turning out production aircraft might later prove of vital importance in view of the ominous developments on the Continent. While production drawings were commenced in March, plans went quietly ahead for the production of 1,000 of the new fighters. This was an unprecedented step in the history of British aviation, but it was vindicated three months later when, on June 3rd, the Air Ministry placed an initial production contract for 600 aircraft. On June 27, 1936, the name Hurricane was approved by the Air Ministry, and production aircraft were to meet specification F.15/36 which had been drawn up to cover Hurricane development and production.

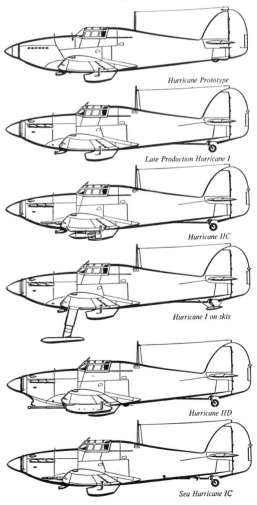

Hurricane Prototype

Late Production Hurricane I

Hurricane IIC

Hurricane I on skis

Hurricane IID

Sea Hurricane IC

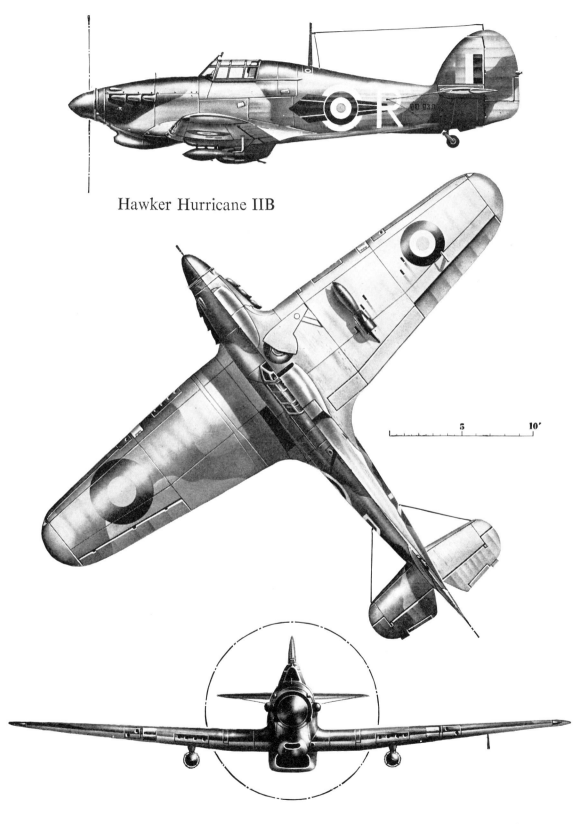

Hawker Hurricane IIB

5   10'

One of the Hurricane's multifarious roles was that of night-fighter. The photograph depicts a Hurricane IIC (BE500) in matt black night finish

mander personally demonstrated the prowess of the Hurricane by flying from Edinburgh to Northolt at an average speed of 408 m.p.h. Even with a stiff tail-wind this was a remarkable performance. Squadrons were rapidly equipped with the Hurricane—thanks to the foresight of the Hawker Aircraft directors—and at the time war was declared, on September 3, 1939, just short of 500 Hurricanes had been delivered and eighteen squadrons had been equipped. These were all of the Mark I type, armed with eight 0.303-in. machine-guns but having alternative airscrew installations: a Merlin II engine driving a Watts two-blade fixed-pitch wooden airscrew, or a Merlin III of similar power having a standardized shaft for de Havilland or Rotol three-blade metal airscrews. The Hurricane I, at 7,127 lb. all-up weight, possessed a maximum speed of 325 m.p.h. at 17,500 feet, a range of 700 miles at 200 m.p.h. at 15,000 feet, a service ceiling of 36,000 feet, and the ability to climb to 20,000 feet in 9 minutes.

Progressive development of the basic Hurricane design had, of course, been initiated at an early stage in the fighter's life. As far back as July 1935 the design office had commenced the investigation of metal stressed skin outer wing panels, and in 1937 serious development of these had been inaugurated. Flight tests with metal wings (on L1877) were begun in April 1939. Schemes for a slotted wing and for fitting a Merlin VIII engine were investigated in 1938, although these did not reach fruition. However, high priority was allocated to work on front armouring and the provision of a bullet-proof windscreen. As part of an attempt to increase fire power, one Hurricane I (L1750) was fitted with a 20-mm. cannon slung under each wing, and flew in this form on May 24, 1939. On June 17, 1939, another Hurricane I (L1856) flew with a Merlin XII engine, although this installation never became standard. To assist in development flying, and for demonstration purposes, Hawker Aircraft built a Hurricane for themselves—registered G-AFKX—and, fitted with a Merlin III, it flew on January 24, 1939.

In the meantime steps had been taken to boost Hurricane production. A second contract, for 1,000 machines, had been placed on November 1, 1938, and plans had been completed for the production of Hurricane fighters by Gloster Aircraft. The latter company produced its first Hurricane (L2020) on October 27, 1939, and had built 1,000 by the end of 1940, a peak output of 130 machines per month having been achieved. In January 1939 the Air Ministry issued further instructions for the production of Hurricanes in Canada by the Canadian Car and Foundry Company, this production being intended primarily for the R.A.F.

Production drawings began to reach the machine shops that same month, and work proceeded smoothly until December when a change from the Merlin I (the production equivalent of the experimental Merlin "C" installed in the prototype) to the Merlin II had to be made as it had been decided to discontinue plans to manufacture the earlier model. The Merlin II, with a different cylinder block, called for changes to be made in the cowling shape and fairing lines. Other items affected were the air intake, the airscrew, the engine controls and mounts, the hand-starter gear, and the header tank and its mounting. However, by the following April the re-design work had been completed and a production Merlin II had been delivered by Rolls-Royce for installation in the first production Hurricane. This machine (L1547) was moved to Brooklands in September and made its first flight there on October 12, 1937.

After the initial flight test stage various detail modifications were made, including the fitting of ejector exhausts in November, and the introduction of a larger rudder with horn balancing, together with a small ventral fin and fixed tailwheel in January 1938. Now weighing 6,017 lb., the production Hurricane went to the A. & A.E.E. at Martlesham Heath in June 1938. No aeroplane can have been brought into operational service use more rapidly after the commencement of production deliveries than was the Hurricane. Deliveries were being made to No. 111 Squadron at Northolt before the end of 1937, less than *two months* after the first flight of L1547. This was a remarkable demonstration of faith in the Hurricane on the part of Service chiefs—also a reflection on the growing international tension which made the Hurricane so eagerly sought.

Under the command of Sqn. Ldr. J. W. Gillan, No. 111 Squadron quickly settled down with its new monoplanes, and on February 10, 1938, the com-

Much interest in the Hurricane had been aroused abroad and particularly in those countries where Hawker biplanes had for long been in service. Export orders were soon received, although these were largely curtailed by the war and the overriding requirements of the R.A.F. Nevertheless, three export versions of the Hurricane were in fact produced: for Yugoslavia (first flown on March 23, 1939), for Belgium (first flown May 13, 1939), and for Iran (first flown May 10, 1940). By arrangement with the R.A.F., Hurricane Is were also exported to Turkey and Rumania. All of these were standard machines except for those supplied to Belgium, which carried one 0.5-in. machine-gun in each wing. This type was also built in small numbers in Belgium under licence in 1939–40.

Following the outbreak of war the Hurricane was quickly in action with Nos. 1 and 73 Squadrons, which were the first to be posted to France as part of the Advanced Air Striking Force, and a Hurricane registered its first confirmed victory over the Western Front on October 30, 1939. Until at least the end of 1940 the Hurricane was numerically the most important British fighter in service. During its early combat months some epic operations were conducted by the Hurricanes of No. 46 Squadron which were flown off H.M.S. *Glorious* in order to operate from Norwegian

bases and landed *back on* the carrier when Norway was evacuated. At the time of the invasion of Norway Hawkers had been asked to produce a Hurricane floatplane with all possible speed. This was designed, using a set of Blackburn Roc floats, and construction was commenced but abandoned at the termination of the short-lived Norwegian campaign. The floatplane had an estimated speed of 273 m.p.h. at 16,800 feet at an all-up weight of 7,650 lb. A similar fate was suffered by the two seat Hurricane trainer which was designed and partially built in 1939.

When the "Battle of Britain" commenced, the R.A.F. order of battle included thirty squadrons of Hurricanes and nineteen squadrons of Spitfires. It was the Hurricane, therefore, that bore the brunt of the fighting between July and November 1940. However, the Hurricane was too slow (Lord Dowding later revealed that the average speed of production Hurricanes was only 305 m.p.h.) to deal adequately with the Luftwaffe's Bf 109E fighters, so that top cover, fighter-versus-fighter combats were largely the responsibility of the faster Spitfire, while the Hurricanes tackled the bombers. Nevertheless, despite its inferior performance, the Hurricane proved itself capable of more than holding its own against the faster Messerschmitts by virtue of its superior manoeuvrability. It could take a remarkable amount of punishment and had several outstanding qualities. It offered a good view for its pilot, it was less sensitive to an excessive approach speed than the Spitfire, and its wide track undercarriage permitted greater liberties to be taken while landing—all qualities of extreme importance to less experienced pilots. It was against the background of the epic "Battle of Britain" that the only Fighter Command Victoria Cross was won—by Flt. Lt. J. B. Nicholson of the Hurricane-equipped No. 249 Squadron.

Until the middle of 1940 all Hurricane production had centred on the basic Mark I variety, with the eight-gun fabric-covered wings and Merlin II or III engine.

(Above, left) An experimental Hurricane II (Z2415) photographed in February 1942 with prototype rocket launching rails. (Left) A Hurricane IIA photographed in March 1942 with SBC (Small Bomb Container) equipment. (Below) A Hurricane IIC with underwing bombs.

Hawker Hurricane Mk 11C Cutaway Key

1 Starboard navigation light
2 Starboard wingtip
3 Aluminium alloy aileron
4 Self-aligning ball-bearing aileron hinge
5 Aft wing spar
6 Aluminium alloy wing skinning
7 Forward wing spar
8 Starboard landing light
9 Rotol three-blade constant-speed propeller
10 Spinner
11 Propeller hub
12 Pitch-control mechanism
13 Spinner back Plate
14 Cowling fairings
15 Coolant pipes
16 Rolls-Royce Merlin XX engine

37 Magneto
38 Two-stage supercharger
39 Cowling panel attachments
40 Engine RPM indicator drive
41 External bead sight
42 Removable aluminium alloy cowling panels
43 Engine coolant header tank
44 Engine firewall (armour-plated backing)
45 Fuselage (reserve) fuel tank (28 Imp gal/127 l)
46 Exhaust glare shield
47 Control column
48 Engine bearer attachment
49 Rudder pedals
50 Control linkage
51 Centre-section fuel tank
52 Oil system piping
53 Pneumatic system air cylinder
54 Wing centre-section/front spar girder construction
55 Engine bearer support strut

75 Bullet-proof windscreen
76 Rear-view mirror
77 Rearward-sliding canopy
78 Canopy frames
79 Canopy handgrip
80 Plexiglas canopy panels
81 Head/back armour plate
82 Harness attachment
83 Aluminium alloy decking
84 Turnover reinforcement
85 Canopy track
86 Fuselage framework cross-bracing
87 Radio equipment (TR9D/TR133)
88 Support tray
89 Removable access panel
90 Aileron cable drum
91 Elevator control lever
92 Cable adjusters
93 Aluminium alloy wing/fuselage fillet
94 Ventral identification and formation-keeping lights
95 Footstep retraction guide and support rail
96 Radio equipment (R3002)
97 Upward-firing recognition apparatus

98 Handhold
99 Diagonal support
100 Fuselage fairing
101 Dorsal identification light
102 Aerial mast
103 Aerial lead-in
104 Recognition apparatus cover panel
105 Mast support
106 Wire-braced upper truss
107 Wooden fuselage fairing formers
108 Fabric covering
109 Radio antenna
110 All-metal tailplane structure
111 Static and dynamic elevator balance
112 Starboard elevator
113 Tailfin metal leading-edge
114 Fabric covering
115 Tailfin structure
116 Diagonal bracing struts
117 Built-in static balance
118 Aerial stub
119 Fabric-covered rudder
120 Rudder structure
121 Rudder post
122 Rear navigation light

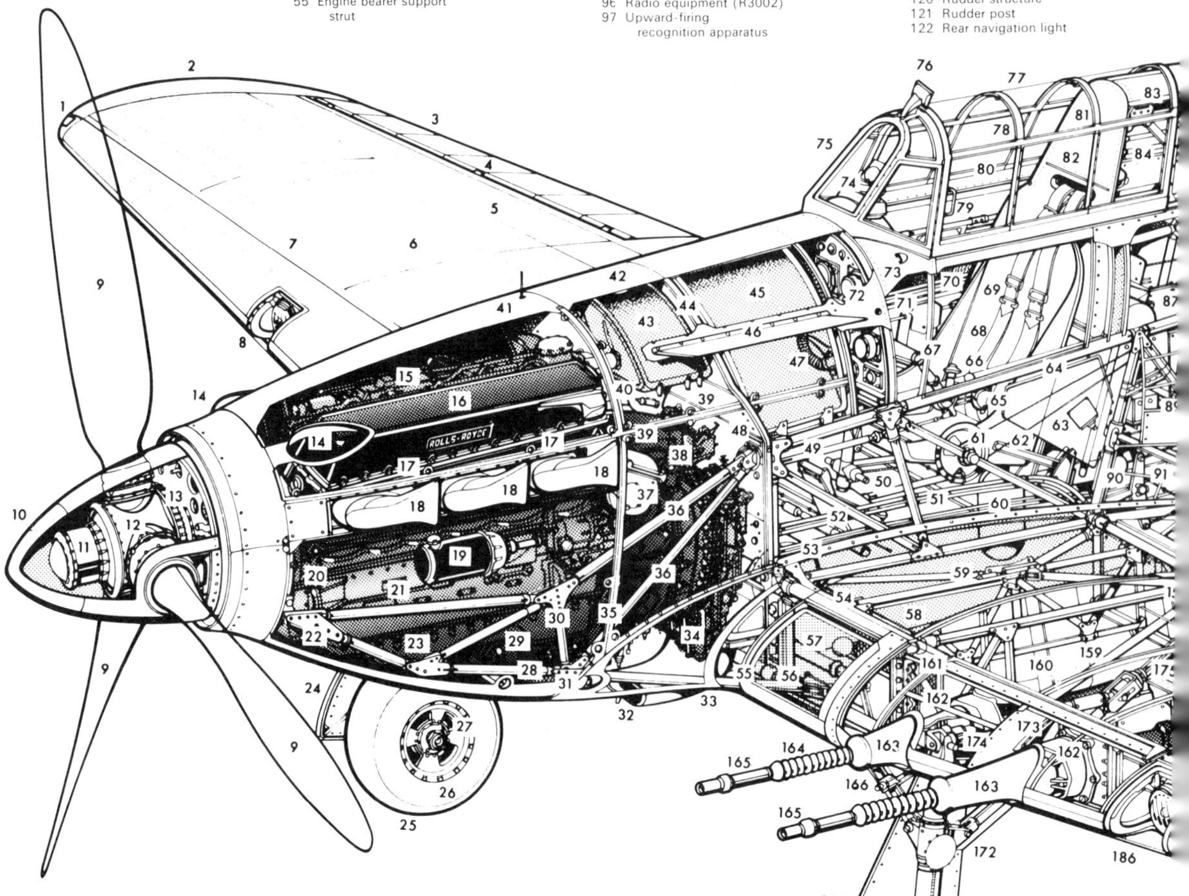

17 Cowling panel fasteners
18 "Fishtail" exhaust pipes
19 Electric generator
20 Engine forward mounting feet
21 Engine upper bearer tube
22 Engine forward mount
23 Engine lower bearer tubes
24 Starboard mainwheel fairing
25 Starboard mainwheel
26 Low pressure tyre
27 Brake drum (pneumatic brakes)
28 Manual-type inertia starter
29 Hydraulic system
30 Bearer joint
31 Auxiliary intake
32 Carburettor air intake
33 Wing root fillet
34 Engine oil drain collector/breather
35 Fuel pump drain
36 Engine aft bearers

56 Oil tank (port wing root leading-edge)
57 Dowty undercarriage ram
58 Port undercarriage well
59 Wing centre-section girder frame
60 Pilot's oxygen cylinder
61 Elevator trim tab control wheel
62 Radiator flap control lever
63 Entry footstep
64 Fuselage tubular framework
65 Landing lamp control lever
66 Oxygen supply cock
67 Throttle lever
68 Safety harness
69 Pilot's seat
70 Pilot's break-out exit panel
71 Map case
72 Instrument panel
73 Cockpit ventilation inlet
74 Reflector gunsight

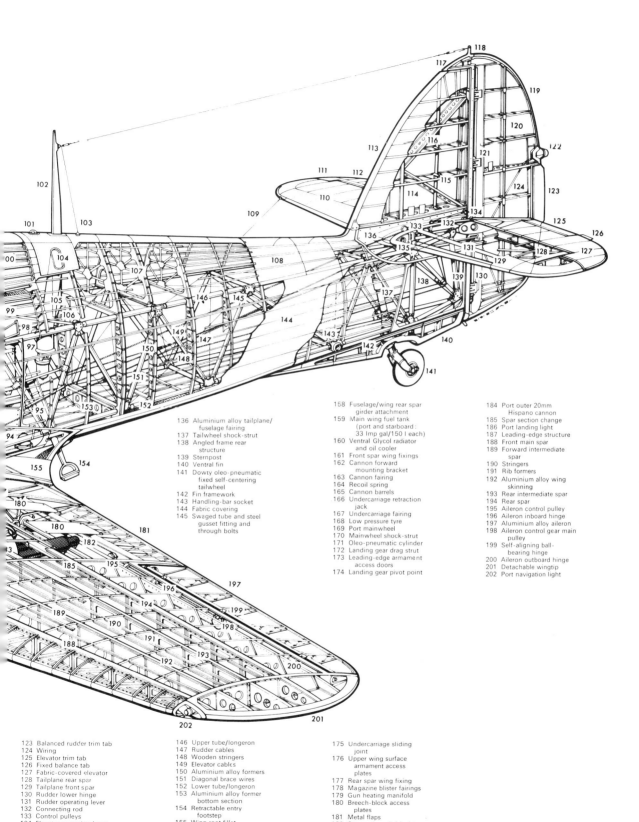

136 Aluminium alloy tailplane/ fuselage fairing
137 Tailwheel shock-strut
138 Angled frame rear structure
139 Sternpost
140 Ventral fin
141 Dowty oleo-pneumatic fixed self-centering tailwheel
142 Fin framework
143 Handling-bar socket
144 Fabric covering
145 Swaged tube and steel gusset fitting and through bolts

158 Fuselage/wing rear spar girder attachment
159 Main wing fuel tank (port and starboard: 33 Imp gal/150 l each)
160 Ventral Glycol radiator and oil cooler
161 Front spar wing fixings
162 Cannon forward mounting bracket
163 Cannon fairing
164 Recoil spring
165 Cannon barrels
166 Undercarriage retraction jack
167 Undercarriage fairing
168 Low pressure tyre
169 Port mainwheel
170 Mainwheel shock-strut
171 Oleo-pneumatic cylinder
172 Landing gear drag strut
173 Leading-edge armament access doors
174 Landing gear pivot point

184 Port outer 20mm Hispano cannon
185 Spar section change
186 Port landing light
187 Leading-edge structure
188 Front main spar
189 Forward intermediate spar
190 Stringers
191 Rib formers
192 Aluminium alloy wing skinning
193 Rear intermediate spar
194 Rear spar
195 Aileron control pulley
196 Aileron inboard hinge
197 Aluminium alloy aileron
198 Aileron control gear main pulley
199 Self-aligning ball-bearing hinge
200 Aileron outboard hinge
201 Detachable wingtip
202 Port navigation light

123 Balanced rudder trim tab
124 Wiring
125 Elevator trim tab
126 Fixed balance tab
127 Fabric-covered elevator
128 Tailplane rear spar
129 Tailplane front spar
130 Rudder lower hinge
131 Rudder operating lever
132 Connecting rod
133 Control pulleys
134 Elevator operating lever
135 Tailplane spar attachments

146 Upper tube/longeron
147 Rudder cables
148 Wooden stringers
149 Elevator cables
150 Aluminium alloy formers
151 Diagonal brace wires
152 Lower tube/longeron
153 Aluminium alloy former bottom section
154 Retractable entry footstep
155 Wing root fillet
156 Flap rod universal joint
157 Aileron cables

175 Undercarriage sliding joint
176 Upper wing surface armament access plates
177 Rear spar wing fixing
178 Magazine blister fairings
179 Gun heating manifold
180 Breech-block access plates
181 Metal flaps
182 Cannon breech-blocks
183 Ammunition magazine drum

A Hurricane IV carrying eight rocket projectiles underwing. The Mark IV had the more powerful Merlin 24 or 27 engine.

In February 1940, however, Hawker Aircraft had proposed the introduction of a new variant, the Mark II with a Merlin XX and an armament of six 0.303-in. Browning guns in each wing. This scheme, which found favour, was to lead the way to a much wider exploitation of the Hurricane's capabilities. The first stage in this development was the introduction of the Hurricane IIA Series I which differed from the Mark I only in having the 1,185 h.p. Merlin XX, the eight-gun armament being retained. The first Hurricane

(*Above*) *A Hurricane IID (KZ320), and* (*below*) *a Hurricane IV (LB774).*

(*Below*) *One of the two Hurricane Vs built (KZ193).*

IIA (P3269) flew on June 11, 1940, at an all-up weight of 6,738 lb. Two new sets of wings were designed for the Hurricane II at the outset, one set having twelve Browning machine-guns and the other having four 20-mm. Hispano cannon, the latter installation being an extension of the trials conducted in 1939 with L1750. These wings were also intended to support two 250-lb. or 500-lb. bombs, and strengthened fuselage longerons were required in association with these changes.

The Hurricane IIA Series 2 was a further interim production version with the strengthened fuselage to permit conversion to a later Mark but fitted initially with the eight-gun armament. Aircraft fitted with the twelve machine-guns were designated Hurricane IIB, and those with four cannon became the Hurricane IIC (first delivered in October 1940). Paralleling armament development, engine development continued in the Hurricane G-AFKX. This flew with an experimental Merlin RM4S on June 9, 1940, and later with a Merlin 45. Delivery of Hurricane IIAs to R.A.F. units began in August 1940, but the more heavily armed IIB and IIC did not reach the squadrons until 1941. By this time the Hurricane was in the forefront on other war fronts. The first deployment of Hurricanes overseas, following the withdrawals from the European mainland in the spring of 1940, was in Malta where No. 261 Squadron arrived in August 1940, flying off H.M.S. *Argus*.

In 1940 the first attempts were made to increase the range of the Hurricane for ferry purposes, and on May 10, 1940, the first Hurricane I to be fitted with long-range tanks was flown. At this stage the tanks were not jettisonable, and each contained only 44 gallons. More unorthodox methods of extending the Hurricane's range were also investigated. One of these schemes, worked out by Flight Refuelling Limited, was for an aircraft to be towed by a Wellington bomber. This plan was abandoned, however, when it was found that the engine, oil and coolant systems of the fighter tended to freeze during the tow, and the engine could not, therefore, be restarted when the Hurricane's pilot came to cast off. Later, two 45 or 90-gallon drop-tanks were fitted as standard.

The use of the Hurricane I in the Western Desert necessitated the introduction of a tropical version which had a larger coolant radiator than that of the standard aeroplane, and a Vokes air cleaner over the air intake. Desert equipment was fitted, and provision was made for the pilot to control the air supply inside the cockpit. The first tropical Hurricane I (L1669) flew on May 17, 1939, and tropical Hurricane IIs followed in 1941. It was also largely for use in the Western Desert that the Hurricane fighter-bomber, or "Hurribomber" as it was dubbed, was developed. As already mentioned, the Hurricane IIB and IIC wing could carry bombs or, alternatively, an SBC (Small Bomb Container) installation or SCI (Smoke Curtain Installation). The "Hurribomber" went into action over Occupied France in October 1941 and was operational in the Western Desert in the following month.

Six months later the Hurricane IID made its operational début in the Western Desert. This variant was a Mark II with yet another type of wing, one designed to carry a 40-mm. cannon for tank-busting. The cannon, either a Vickers Type S with fifteen rounds per gun or a Rolls-Royce B.F. with twelve rounds per gun, was slung under the wing, while the wing itself contained a 0.303-in. Browning gun for aiming purposes. Apart from the first few production machines, all Hurricane IIDs had additional armour to protect pilot, radiator and engine from small-arms fire. Only one squadron of Hurricane IIDs was employed in Europe, the others being deployed in the Western Desert and in Burma. The guns and their mountings reduced the maximum speed of the Mark IID to 286 m.p.h. at 18,800 feet, but this sturdy warplane soon became the scourge of Rommel's armoured units. In the Far East the Hurricane IIC first saw service in 1943, initially as a night-fighter. Its sturdiness suited it perfectly to the harsh operating conditions existing in Burma and India, and it remained the principal British fighter opposing the Japanese until the end of the war.

The year 1943 saw two important developments in the Hurricanes history—the introduction of the Mark IV and the adoption of the Hurricane to fire rocket missiles or, as they were initially known, "unrifled projectiles". The Hurricane IV differed from the Mark II in two respects: it used a Merlin 24 or 27 which developed 1,620 h.p. for take-off, and it featured "low attack" or universal armament wings. These wings were derived from those fitted to the Hurricane IID and could carry the 40-mm. Vickers or Rolls-Royce cannon, bombs, drop-tanks or rocket projectiles. The Hurricane IV was in service by March 1943 and was operational in the Middle and Far East theatres until the end of the war, and in Europe until the end of 1944. The development of the aircraft rocket had introduced a new factor in the use of aircraft as ground-assault weapons, and the Hurricane IIB and IIC were the first single-seaters to employ the

rockets operationally. After extended trials at the A. & A.E.E. and elsewhere with rockets launched from Hurricanes (commencing with Z2415 which was fitted with three launching rails under each wing early in 1942), No. 137 Squadron took its rocket-carrying Hurricanes into action for the first time at the beginning of September 1943. Hurricane IIBs, IICs, and IVs were fitted with four rockets under each wing.

A close relative of the Hurricane IV, the Mark V, differed only in the type of engine a 1,600 h.p. Merlin 32 driving a four-blade airscrew. Only two Hurricane Vs were built (KZ193 and NL255), the first appearing late in 1943.

Early experience with the operation of Hurricanes from aircraft carriers led to the introduction of several variants specifically for naval use. The first of these were based on the land-based Hurricane I, with a Merlin II or III, and were named Sea Hurricane I. Several sub-variants were produced, the first, the Sea Hurricane IA, being a specially strengthened version for catapult launching and possessing no deck arrester hook. Popularly known as the "Hurricat", the Sea Hurricane IA was intended to combat the Focke-Wulf Fw 200C Condor maritime reconnaissance bombers that were inflicting heavy casualties on Atlantic convoys. The fighters were intended for catapult launching from certain merchant ships in each convoy known as CAM-ships (Catapult Aircraft Merchantmen). The plan was proposed in 1940 and expedited by Winston Churchill, who, on March 6, 1941, issued a directive which stated: "Extreme priority will be given to fitting out ships to catapult, or otherwise launch, fighter aircraft against bombers attacking our shipping."

The first of the CAM-ships, the s.s. *Michael E*, put to sea on May 27, 1941, it being proposed that the Sea Hurricane would be launched at the discretion of the master of the ship and abandoned at the end of the sortie, the pilot baling out in order to be picked up by one of the convoy's escort vessels. The *Michael E* was sunk by a torpedo before it could launch its fighter; but despite the first failure some sixty R.A.F. pilots were trained for CAM-ship duties, and the first recorded victory of a "Hurricat" came on August 3, 1941. However, as the weather in the Atlantic deteriorated with the approach of winter, CAM-ship operation was brought to a temporary standstill, not being resumed until the following year. In all, thirty-five ships were fitted out with catapults, fifty Hurricanes

A Hurricane I fitted with skis for use in Canada.

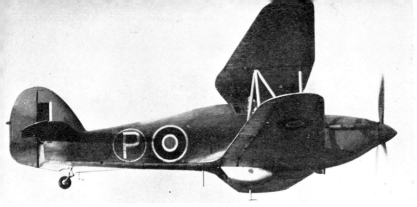

*An experiment in improving take-off with overload, the Hurricane fitted with
an auxiliary wing which could be discarded at will.*

were allocated from R.A.F. Fighter Command, and a
further fifty were earmarked from Canadian production, although all were not employed for this role.

In the Sea Hurricane IB a V-frame arrester hook
was added to permit normal carrier operations, and
this was the principal variant to serve with the Fleet
Air Arm. Produced in 1941, it was the first British
single-seat fighter monoplane to perform the shipboard role, becoming operational in June 1942. The
later Sea Hurricane IC was similar but had the four-
cannon armament of the Hurricane IIC. Navalized
versions of the Hurricane II were also produced.
Some of these variants were known as "Hooked Hurricanes" as they had an arrester hook and a position
indicator for it in the cokpit, but retained R.A.F.
radio equipment. The Sea Hurricane IIB and IIC had
full Fleet Air Arm radio equipment and stowage
for signal pistol and cartridges in the cockpit. In 1940
designs had been prepared for a folding-wing version
of the Hurricane, but this variant never materialized.

Plans for the production of the Hurricane in Canada
had originated at the beginning of 1939, and the first
Canadian-built Hurricane flew in January 1940,
being delivered to Britain in the following month.
Production mounted rapidly, and over 1,400 were
built by Canadian Car and Foundry in addition to
spares equal to another thousand machines. At first,
Canadian-built Hurricanes were similar in all respects
to British-built Hurricane Is, but from the end of 1941
onwards Packard-built Merlin engines became available, and these were adopted for all subsequent
Canadian production machines. This changeover led
to a new series of Mark numbers. The Hurricane X,
with a Packard Merlin 28 and Hamilton Standard
Hydromatic airscrew but otherwise corresponding to
the Hurricane IIB, was intended for R.A.F. service
but few were delivered. The Hurricane XI was identical to the Mark X apart from R.C.A.F. equipment,
and the Hurricane XII and XIIA were also produced
for the R.C.A.F., with the Packard Merlin 29 engine
and twelve and eight machine-guns respectively. A
navalized version of the Mark XIIA was also produced
as the Sea Hurricane XIIA. A project to instal
Packard Merlin engines in British-built air-frames,
the result tentatively being designated Hurricane III,
did not materialize. A few of the Hurricanes built for

the R.C.A.F. equipped squadrons of
that service operating in Europe, but
most remained in Canada. For Canadian operation, Hawker Aircraft developed a ski-equipped Hurricane in
1939, and some machines fitted with
skis were used in Canada.

The experience gained with ski-
equipped Hurricanes came in useful in
Russia, where the Hurricane also saw
service. Nos. 81 and 134 Squadrons
took their Hurricanes to Russia in the
autumn of 1941 as part of the British
aid programme to the Soviet Air
Force. In Russia a two-seat training
variant with tandem open cockpits was developed.

Many variants of the Hurricane were planned in
the period 1939-44. Among those not proceeded with
were Hurricanes with Napier Dagger, Rolls-Royce
Griffon and Bristol Hercules engines, a Hurricane
with a blister hood, another with a direct-vision
windscreen, and one with an A.I. installation. In
conjunction with Short Brothers and Harland, Hawker
Aircraft also investigated the possibility of a Hurricane being carried by a Liberator bomber in a composite arrangement, the scheme being proposed as a
means of providing fighter protection for convoys far
out of fighter range. As part of the investigation conducted by F. Hills and Son into the use of "slip"
wings to facilitate the take-off of heavily laden aircraft, a Canadian-built Hurricane (R.C.A.F. Serial
No. 321) was modified in Britian to have the so-called
slip-wing. This second wing, mounted on struts
above the cockpit, was of similar planform to the
standard wing and was jettisoned after take-off.

In September 1944 Hawker Aircraft delivered the
last Hurricane (PZ865) to the R.A.F., over 14,000
examples of this type having been built, including
2,750 machines built by Gloster Aircraft. The versatility of the Hurricane is unlikely ever to be surpassed
by any other combat aircraft. No matter what role it
was called upon to undertake it fulfilled its task with
distinction. The Hurricane strongly deserved the
place it found among the outstanding combat aircraft
in the history of aviation.

Hawker Hurricane IIB

Dimensions :	Span, 40 ft. 0 in. ; length, 32 ft. 3 in. ; height, 8 ft. 9 in. ; wing area, 257.5 sq. ft.
Armament :	Twelve 0.303-in. Browning machine-guns and two 250-lb. or 500-lb. bombs or eight rocket projectiles.
Power Plant :	One Rolls-Royce Merlin XX twelve-cylinder 60° Vee liquid-cooled engine rated at 1,280 h.p. for take-off and 1,850 h.p. at 21,000 ft.
Weights :	Loaded (with two 500-lb. bombs), 8,470 lb. wing loading, 32.9 lb./sq. ft.
Performance :	Maximum speed (clean), 340 m.p.h. at 21,000 ft., (with two 250-lb. bombs) 320 m.p.h. at 19,700 ft., (with two 500-lb. bombs) 307 m.p.h. at 19,500 ft. ; maximum climb rate, 2,950 ft./min., (with two 250-lb. bombs) 2,530 ft./min., (with two 500-lb. bombs) 2,280 ft./min. ; time to 20,000 ft. (clean), 7.5 min. ; service ceiling (clean), 40,000 ft., (with 500-lb. bomb load) 33,000 ft.